This book is dedicated to the memory of my Charlton Athletic supporting friends who have been taken from us and whose company is sadly missed.

Gordon Ducker, Jean King, Jim Parsons, Terry Phippen, Alice Redden, Derek Redden and Chris Thomas.

Many miles have we travelled, many games have we seen......

Back cover quiz

The answers are (in no particular order) Eamonn Dunphy, Jim Fryatt, Ted Croker, Chris Duffy and Abraham 'Kosha' Goodman. You will have to read the book to find which was which.

Front cover photos

Sam Bartram, Derek Hales, Lee Bowyer, Alan Curbishley and 2021 Player of the Year Jake Forster-Caskey.

THE VALIANT 1000

VOLUME 1

IAN WALLIS

Published by Dixie Fried Publishing, 2022
info@dixiefriedpublishing.co.uk
www.dixiefriedpublishing.co.uk

A CIP catalogue record for this title is available from the British Library
ISBN 978-1-7396856-0-7

Design, Production and IT by Carol Andrews

CONTENTS

ABOUT THE AUTHOR

Ian was brought up in the Maidstone area in a non-sporting family. Eager to watch a Football League match and knowing that the Maidstone to London train stopped at Charlton station, he visited the Valley for the first time in April 1962 and watched Stuart Leary score twice as Bristol Rovers were defeated 2-1, He was literally hooked for life. After leaving school in 1965, he treated himself to a season ticket and has continued to renew it through thick and (a lot of) thin for the last 56 seasons.

During the exile years in the eighties, he was one of the founders of the West Wickham & Hayes Supporters group, which later merged with the newly-formed Bromley Supporters. They are now known as the Bromley Addicks and he has been their chairman for 23 years.

In 2010, the club launched the Fans Forum and Ian has been the representative of Bromley Addicks continually since that time. He is most proud that it was his suggestion which resulted in the introduction of the photographic murals which now adorn the outside of the stadium.

Since 2011 he has arranged the Player of the Year vote and co-organised the end of season Dinner. He is a founding Trustee of the Charlton Athletic Museum and organiser of the Hall of Fame. In recent times he has also sat on the Valley Centenary Committee and is a member of the Commemoration Group.

Away from Charlton, Ian was a blundering centre forward for Addington Manor, a Sunday League team which he ran for some 25 years. He was chairman and general secretary of the London & Kent Border League for a similar period, during the time when they organised football every season for 120 teams and over 2,000 players.

Ian is currently vice-chairman of the London Football Association and has served on their Council since 2002 and on the Board of Directors for 10 years. He is also Chairman of the London FA Cup Committee, which administer 30 different cup competitions in the London area, including the Senior Cup. He was pleased to have received an entry from the Charlton Athletic U23 team in the last couple of seasons.

This is Ian's fourth book, but his first about football. Volumes two and three will be following and hopefully by then Charlton will be clawing their way up the leagues again.

ACKNOWLEDGEMENTS

The inspiration for this project was Colin Cameron's 1991 book, 'The Valiant 500'. This was a groundbreaking work which has more than stood the test of time, although more than 30 years later is long overdue an update. When Colin passed away, much of his archive of Charlton documents and statistics passed to the Charlton Athletic Museum and one evening after a couple of pints of London Pride, it seemed like a good idea to take on the task myself.

With no wish to be compared to Colin, the master statistician, I have approached the task differently and while retaining the statistics section, have expanded each entry to also include full biographies of each player. This and the ever-increasing number of new names has swelled the total from 514 in 1991 to something approaching 1,000 in 2022. Hence, the title of the book. Volume 1 covers alphabetically every player (A to H) who has made a first team appearance for Charlton since they joined the Football League in 1921.

So many people have offered encouragement and assistance and all have been greatly appreciated. My thanks to the following:-

My fellow Museum Trustees, Ben Hayes, Paul Baker, Nick Tondeur, Mick Everett, Clive Harris and Stuart Binns and Museum volunteer Colin Finch.

Charlton players past and present, Paul Elliott, Ritchie Bowman, Mason Burstow, Charlie Barker, Deji Elerewe, Kasim Aidoo, Richard Chin, Charles Clayden, Tyreece Campbell, Nazir Bakrim and 1960s Charlton youth team player, David Burke.

Charlton staff and management, Olly Groome, Tracey Leaburn and Anthony Hayes.

Our gang, Richard & Jean Huelin, Alan Dryland, Marilyn Toft, Oli Bartle, Matthias Gerdes and Marc Stellmacher of the German Addicks, John Robilliard, Laura, Will & Pippa Edwards, Elly Spilberg and my daughter Joanna Mayers.

My colleagues at the London FA, Michael Burke, Lester Newham and Graham Etchell.

Plus in no particular order and with profound apologies to those whose names I cannot instantly bring to mind, Michael Joyce (ENFA), Brian Spurrell (Erith & Belvedere), Douglas Gorman, Heather McKinlay, Neil Fissler, Steve Dixon, Simon Howe (Bath City), Phil Brown (Wycombe Wanderers), Dan Couldridge (Tonbridge), Martin Powell (Bath City), Kevan Cox (son of Keith Cox), Leander Bond (daughter of Peter Firmani), Trish Muir (daughter of Bob Burlison). Gabrielle Bicknell (daughter of Roy Bicknell). Kenneth Breakey and Mike Gibson.

Finally and most importantly, my partner, Carol Andrews, who has lived with this book for so long and has now acquired an unhealthy knowledge of obscure Charlton players from the 1920s. Without her computer programming skills and design flair, I would still be scribbling away in crayon.

FORMAT

This is the first of three volumes and contains 333 biographies, covering all Charlton Athletic players who have made first team appearances in cup or league matches since season 1921-22. It is alphabetical and therefore covers everyone from Pawel ABBOTT to Geoff HAMMOND.   All are included who made their debuts up to March 2022. Appearances for Charlton are shown year by year and are complete up to and including season 2020-21. Wartime games are not included in the totals, but are referred to in the text. International appearances are complete up to February 2022.

Under the Honours section are first listed any individual awards such as international caps, district, county or schools representation etc. Then honours gained while appearing for Charlton at both first team, reserve or youth team levels are listed. Finally, you will find all known honours received when playing for other clubs. For cups, I have shown finalists, including substitute appearances (but not unused subs). League Honours are more difficult to evaluate, but I have included all players who appeared in 25% of any competition's matches.

The UK league career totals shown are for all matches and goals in the Premier League, Football League, Scottish Premier and Scottish League. The V-number symbolizes the numerical order in which any player fits into the Charlton Athletic story. For example, Jock Campbell was V309, or in other words, the 309th to appear for the club. Reports of transfer fees are notoriously unreliable and the modern trend towards 'undisclosed fee' further exacerbates the situation. The figures shown are as accurate as possible, but on occasions are an educated guess.

I have tried to avoid using abbreviations as much as possible, but to make best use of the space, you will find the recent youth successes in the Professional Development League 2 South referred to as PD League 2 South and Under 21 or Under 18 as U21 and U18 etc.

Sponsors' names have not been used as they just cause confusion, so instead of Pizza and Paint, you will find the cups referred to as the Football League Cup or the Football League Trophy. I know that they have re-invented themselves as the EFL, but let's keep things simple.

I have endeavoured to make the biography section as interesting as possible and the relative length of each entry reflects both the amount of available data and the importance of each player. Sam Bartram may have played for 22 years and 722 matches (including wartime appearances) whereas Matt Carter only appeared for two minutes (plus stoppage time), but I have tried to tell each and every story with as much detail as possible and in a way that will interest and entertain the reader.

Researching this book has introduced me to a host of new heroes who preceded my time as a Charlton supporter. John Evans, Bill (alias Georges) Berry and the great Harold Halse may be new names to you as they were to me, but they and all the other 330 players featured here have played their part in the story of this very special football club, Charlton Athletic.

ABBREVIATIONS

Chart of Appearances

A	Appearances	FL Cup	Football League Cup
G	Goals	FM Cup	Full Members Cup
R	Relegation season	FL Trophy	Football League Trophy
P	Promotion season	D3 Cup	Division 3 Cup
		AI Cup	Anglo Italian Cup

Additional appearances as substitute are shown in brackets

'Debut' and 'Finale' refer to the first and last matches played

(H) and (A) denote whether home or away

V   The order in which the player made his first appearance for Charlton

PD   Professional Development

ABBOTT Pawel Tadeusz Howard   2010 - 11

Pawel was born in Yorkshire to a Polish mother and an English father. He lived in Poland as a teenager, but was brought back to the UK by Preston North End, where he was managed by David Moyes. An old-fashioned centre forward, he was reasonably successful in the lower divisions of the Football League and recorded a respectable strike rate of about a goal every three games throughout his career.

Striker   14st 0lbs   6' 1"
Born: 05-05-1982 - York, North Yorkshire

HONOURS

Poland U21 & U18 International
Huddersfield Town 2003-04 Promoted Play Offs Division 3

Zawisza Bydgoszcz 2012-13 Winners 1 Liga, Poland
Arka Gdynia 2015-16 Winners 1 Liga, Poland

CLUBS

LKS Lodz, Poland 07.99 ••Preston North End 16.02.01 (£125,000) ••Bury 09.08.02 (loan) 18.03.03 (loan) ••Huddersfield Town 16.02.04 (loan) 15.03.04 (£125,000) ••Swansea City 22.01.07 (£150,000) ••Darlington 12.07.07 ••Oldham Athletic 02.07.09 ••Charlton Athletic 30.07.10 (£23,000) ••Ruch Chorzow, Poland 28.02.11 ••Zawisza Bydgoszcz, Poland 25.07.12 ••Arka Gdynia, Poland 01.07.14 ••Stomil Olsztyn, Poland 20.07.17

Pawel's most prolific season was 2004-05, when he accumulated 26 league goals for Huddersfield Town, including a second half hat-trick in the 3-0 away win against Port Vale on 11th September 2004. At first, it looked as if the next season was going to go as well, because he scored in each of the first six matches, but the goals gradually dried up and Huddersfield fell short of promotion from League One, losing out against Barnsley in the play-offs. Pawel never again managed the same ratio of goals to games. Any striker joining a new club hopes to get on the scoresheet as quickly as possible to boost his confidence and to get the supporters on his side and Pawel managed two goals in only his second competitive game in a Charlton shirt. He scored twice in the first half hour at Shrewsbury in the League Cup, but the side managed to squander a three goal lead and exit the Cup 4-3 with a pretty dire performance and his early goals were largely forgotten by

the end. From then on, Pawel struggled to make any impact in the side and was unable to record his firs and only league goal until January. He looked far from the player who had scored all those goals for Huddersfield just six years earlier. Prior to joining Charlton, he had played nearly all his football in the north of England and it was expected that he would return there, but instead he moved back to Poland in February 2011, where he successfully managed to get his career back on track with Zawisza Bydgoszcz (a popular club with Scrabble enthusiasts). He scored 15 goals in 27 matches as they won 1 Liga, the second division of Polish football, in 2012-13 and repeated the feat with Arka Gdynia three years later. In between he was hampered by a succession of injuries which side-lined him for long periods. Pawel announced his retirement following a short spell with Stomil Olsztyn, another club in Poland's 1 Liga.

Season	Division	League		FA Cup		FL Cup		FL Trophy		Total	
		A	G	A	G	A	G	A	G	A	G
2010-11	League One	10 (7)	1	1 (2)	0	1	2	3 (1)	1	15 (10)	4
Total		10 (7)	1	1 (2)	0	1	2	3 (1)	1	15 (10)	4

UK LEAGUE CAREER 269 games 92 goals

CHARLTON CAREER
Managers: P Parkinson, C Powell
Debut: AFC Bournemouth (H) 07-08-2010
V706
Finale: Exeter City (H) moved 19-02-2011

ABRAHAMS Lawrence Adam Michael   1977 - 78

Forward   11st 4lbs   5′ 11″
Born: 03-04-1953 - Stepney, London

Charlton had plucked Colin Powell out of non-league football in 1973 and were obviously eager to repeat this winning formula when four years later they signed 24-year-old Lawrie Abrahams from Isthmian League club, Barking. He worked in a tailor's shop and had stated on several occasions that he did not fancy being a professional footballer and if in the end his career in English football fell a long way short of Powell, he nevertheless went on to become one of the most successful imports into the North American Soccer League. When asked about his success in the US, he explained that, 'It was easier to score goals in San Diego in the summer, than at Hull in winter'.

HONOURS

Surrey Schools U15
FA Amateur XI & Isthmian League 1976-77
New England Teamen 1978 Winners NASL Eastern Division

California Surf 1980-81 Winners NASL Southern Division (indoor)
Tulsa Roughnecks 1983 Winners NASL Southern Division
Tulsa Roughnecks 1983 Winners NASL Soccer Bowl

CLUBS

Alfold Minors 1967 (youth) ••Aveley 1976 ••Barking 1976 (semi-pro) ••Charlton Athletic 30.05.77 (£3,000) ••New England Tea Men, USA 04.78 ••Barking 28.10.78 ••Tulsa Roughnecks, USA 1979 ••California Surf, USA 1979 ••Tulsa Roughnecks, USA 06.10.81 ••San Diego Sockers, USA 05.84 (player exchange) ••New York Cosmos, USA 17.10.84 ($25,000 indoor) ••Kansas City Comets, USA 1985 (indoor) ••Melbourne Knights, Australia 1986 ••Wichita Wings, USA 1986 (indoor)

Lawrie made his Charlton debut at Craven Cottage on the opening day of the 1977-78 season and got off to a fine start. It was his goal that put the visitors ahead shortly after half-time, only for Bob Curtis to concede a penalty 10 minutes later, which Fulham duly scored to force a 1-1 draw. He played fairly regularly through the first half of the season, until a run of five straight defeats over the Christmas and New Year period, following which Andy Nelson left him out completely.

In February Charlton announced a tie-up with the US soccer team, New England Teamen and on 1st April Lawrie travelled to Boston to sign for them, being joined a few days later by Mike Flanagan and Colin Powell. They were only committing to loan deals, but for Abrahams it was a permanent move as he turned his back completely on the English game. He did well at first, but developed a reputation for being both blunt and outspoken and not at all enthusiastic about training. Eventually, he fell out with

the coach and was transferred to the Tulsa Roughnecks, where he would go on to enjoy his greatest success.

In 1983 with a shoestring budget, the Tulsa franchise confounded everyone by first winning the Southern Division of the NASL and then going forward to compete in the playoff final for the 83 Soccer Bowl. Laurie (as his name was now spelt in the US) played in the final at Vancouver on 1st October 1983 as the Roughnecks defeated Toronto Blizzard 2-0 before a crowd of 53,326. The following season he was sold to the San Diego Sockers, allegedly in exchange for a player plus two used footballs, but the NASL was now crumbling and he eventually ended his US career playing in the Major Indoor Soccer League. Lawrie Abrahams retired as a player in 1987 but remained in the US and in 2011 was coaching at Irvine Valley College, California. His career record in the NASL was 167 games, 76 goals and 64 assists.

Season	Division	League		FA Cup		FL Cup		Total	
		A	G	A	G	A	G	A	G
1977-78	Division 2	12 (4)	2	1	0	1	0	14 (4)	2
Total		12 (4)	2	1	0	1	0	14 (4)	2

UK LEAGUE CAREER 16 games 2 goals

CHARLTON CAREER
Managers: *A Nelson*
Debut: *Fulham (A) 20-08-1977*
V404
Finale: *Notts County (H) 07-01-1978*

ACHAMPONG Kenneth   1989 - 90

To supporters of both Fulham and Leyton Orient, Kenny Achampong is remembered as a highly entertaining footballer who both excited and frustrated with his maverick style of play. He could run through defences with the ball seemingly glued to his feet and was affectionately known for his 'circular dribbling' in which he would skillfully beat his man and then run round and beat him again to the obvious annoyance of coaches and managers. Kenny was enormously popular during his time at both clubs, but sandwiched between was a year spent battling relegation with Charlton, where sadly his efforts were less appreciated.

Forward   11st 1lb   5' 9"
Born: 26-06-1966 - Kilburn, London
Education: Tulse Hill School.

CLUBS

Fulham 07.12.82 (youth) 03.07.84 (pro) ••West Ham United 14.01.89 (loan) ••Charlton Athletic 08.89 (free) ••Leyton Orient 23.08.90 (loan) 24.09.90 (£25,000)

Kenny made a spectacular start to his Football League career, when as an 18-year-old he scored three goals in his first two matches for Fulham, including a pair in a 3-2 win against Bob Stokoe's Carlisle United on 23rd February 1985. He was of course unable to sustain anything like this impressive strike rate, but through his cavalier play soon became a firm favourite with the Craven Cottage faithful. After four erratic years, Kenny moved to Charlton in August 1989, but the club was in exile at Selhurst Park and battling against all the odds to retain their place in Division 1, so his flamboyant style was probably not what was required at that time. He never really settled nor held down a regular place and left for Leyton Orient at the end of the season.

At Orient, he again became a favourite of the crowd who were mesmerized by his array of back heels, space-creating flicks, knockdowns and pinpoint crosses, but after three years at Brisbane Road his career in English football came to an end and in 1993 he moved to Ghana.

Kenny is of Ghanaian descent and he had earlier been selected (but not played) for the Ghana national side. He did not stay long and later that same year was reportedly in France where he had trials with Olympique de Marseilles. He subsequently resided in Germany for 18 years before returning to North London around 2012.

Season	Division	League		FA Cup		FL Cup		FM Cup		Total	
		A	G	A	G	A	G	A	G	A	G
1989-90 (R)	Division 1	2 (8)	0	0	0	0 (1)	0	2	0	4 (9)	0
Total		2 (8)	0	0	0	0 (1)	0	2	0	4 (9)	0

UK LEAGUE CAREER 174 games 22 goals

CHARLTON CAREER
Managers: *L Lawrence*
Debut: *Southampton (A) (sub) 24-10-1989*
V505
Finale: *Manchester United (A) (sub) 05-05-1990*

AGBOOLA Reuben Omojola Folasanje   1986

An experienced Sunderland defender, Reuben was signed by manager Lennie Lawrence during Charlton's first full season at Selhurst Park. It was a six-week loan to provide cover for injured full back John Humphrey and the team had just recorded an impressive five straight wins in Division 1, but now had to face Arsenal with Colin Walsh also missing through a knee injury. Reuben and George Shipley were brought into the team, but the Gunners proved too strong and the unbeaten run came to an end with a 2-0 home defeat. Shortly after, Reuben pulled a hamstring in training and was therefore unable to add to his single appearance before returning to Wearside.

Defender   11st 9lbs   5' 10"
Born: 30-05-1962 - St Pancras, London
Education: Cheshunt Grammar School.

HONOURS

Nigeria International 1991-93 9 caps 0 goals   Sunderland 1987-88 Winners Division 3
Southampton 1983-84 Runners Up Division 1   Sunderland 1989-90 Promoted Play Offs Division 2

CLUBS

Cheshunt 1973 (youth) ••Southampton 07.78 (youth) 04.80 (pro) ••Sunderland 10.01.85 (£150,000) ••Charlton Athletic 30.10.86 (loan) ••Port Vale 21.11.90 (loan) ••Swansea City 08.11.91 (free) ••Woking 08.83 (free) ••Gosport Borough 11.94 (free)

Reuben had turned professional in 1980 and within a couple of years was holding down the left back spot in the Southampton team. 1983-84 turned out to be the most successful in their history as they fought their way to an FA Cup semi-final and after winning their last three league matches, secured second place behind Liverpool in Division 1. Part of this unexpected success was achieved because Reuben was deployed as a continental style sweeper, a tactic which gave them stability at the back but which was not in common use at that time in English football.

By October 1984, he had lost his place in the Southampton side and three months later was transferred to Sunderland for £150,000. They had problems of their own however and Reuben found it difficult to establish himself as they were twice relegated and he only made a handful of appearances during his first few years on Wearside. It was during this period that he enjoyed his brief encounter in

SE7 and not until 1987-88 that he finally made the left back spot his own as Sunderland clawed their way back up to Division 1 via two promotions in three years.

He qualified to play international football for Nigeria through his father and made his debut against Ghana on 13th April 1991. They qualified for the 1992 Africa Cup Of Nations and advanced to the semi-final stage, eventually defeating Cameroon to secure a third place finish. All of his international appearances came in competitive matches. Reuben finished his Football League career at Swansea City and after a handful of games in the Football Conference for Woking, he took over as licensee of the Pub in the Park, (later known as the Sporting View) in Southampton. Since 2005 he has been working in the motor trade in Southampton and is currently a motor assessor for the Parkway Group.

Season	Division	League		FA Cup		FL Cup		Play Offs		FM Cup		Total	
		A	G	A	G	A	G	A	G	A	G	A	G
1986-87	Division 1	1	0	0	0	0	0	0	0	0	0	1	0
Total		1	0	0	0	0	0	0	0	0	0	1	0

CHARLTON CAREER
Managers: *L Lawrence*
Debut: *Arsenal (H) 01-11-1986*
V483

UK LEAGUE CAREER 268 games 0 goals

AHEARNE-GRANT Karlan Laughton   2014 - 19

Forward   5' 10"
Born: 18-09-1997 - Greenwich, London

Karlan joined Charlton's youth academy at the age of 12 and was soon identified as one to watch. He had speed, skill and an eye for goal and signed professional terms just four days on from his 17th birthday. His first team debut came shortly after on 30th September 2014, a late substitution for Frederic Bulot, as Charlton hung on for a hard-fought 1-0 win at Norwich. A year later on 7th September 2015, he played for England U19 in a 1-1 draw against Croatia in Zagreb having already represented his country at U18 and U17 level.

HONOURS

England U19 International 2015 1 cap 0 goals   Charlton Athletic U18 2015-16 Winners PD National League 2
England U18 International 2014-15 4 caps 0 goals   Charlton Athletic U21 2015-16 Winners U21 PD League 2 South
England U17 International 2014 3 caps 0 goals   Charlton Athletic U21 2015-16 Finalists Kent Senior Cup
Charlton Athletic U18 2012-13 & 2013-14 Winners PD League 2 South   Charlton Athletic U23 2016-17 Winners U23 PD League 2 South
Charlton Athletic U21 2014-15 Winners Kent Senior Cup   Charlton Athletic 2018-19 Promoted Play Offs League One

CLUBS

Charlton Athletic 2009 (youth) 23.09.14 (pro) ••Cambridge United 15.01.16 (loan) ••Crawley Town 30.01.18 (loan) ••Huddersfield Town 30.01.19 (£1.5 million) ••West Bromwich Albion 15.10.20 (£15 million)

With hindsight, Karlan was probably overused at first team level during his formative years and his early promise gradually evaporated. Charlton were going through a turbulent period and a succession of managers seemed happy to use him as a squad player, but did not see enough to give him a lengthy run in the side. It was a three-month loan spell at Crawley Town which turned things around and after nine goals in 15 games in the latter part of the 2017-18 season, he returned to the Valley an altogether more confident and positive person.

Off the field however there were different problems and in June 2018 both Karlan and fellow striker Reeco Hackett-Fairchild were arrested during a holiday in Ibiza, over an alleged sexual assault of a 19-year-old woman. He was quickly released and allowed to return home and no charges were ever brought against either man, but the sordid event was given a good airing in the press, which was not the sort of publicity that Charlton needed at a time when the Belgian owner was seeking a buyer for the club.

Karlan started season 2018-19 by dropping the first part of his surname and becoming simply Karlan Grant. At last, he got a decent run in the side and developed an on field partnership with Lyle Taylor which by January 2019 had delivered 29 goals as Charlton chased promotion from League One. He was in the last year of his contract and both Brentford and Rangers were reported to be interested in signing him, but it was Huddersfield Town who on 30th January 2019 paid a reported £1.5 million plus add-ons for him to savour life in the Premier League. It proved a short-lived experience and Karlan has now twice experienced relegation from the top division, first with Huddersfield and then in 2020-21 with West Bromwich Albion. The jury has yet to decide whether he can sustain a career at the very top of the game.

Season	Division	League		FA Cup		FL Cup		FL Trophy		Play Offs		Total	
		A	G	A	G	A	G	A	G	A	G	A	G
2014-15	Championship	2 (3)	0	0 (1)	0	0	0					2 (4)	0
2015-16 (R)	Championship	7 (10)	1	0	0	3	2					10 (10)	3
2016-17	League One	1 (7)	0	0	0	0 (1)	0	1 (2)	0			2 (10)	0
2017-18	League One	4 (18)	1	1 (1)	1	2	0	5	2	0	0	12 (19)	4
2018-19	League One	25 (3)	14	1	0	0	0	0	0			26 (3)	14
Total		39 (41)	16	2 (2)	1	5 (1)	2	6 (2)	2	0	0	52 (46)	21

UK LEAGUE CAREER 175 games 48 goals

CHARLTON CAREER
Managers: *B Peeters, G Luzon, K Fraeye, J Riga, R Slade, K Robinson, L Bowyer*
Debut: *Norwich City (A) (sub) 30-09-2014*
V787
Finale: *Peterborough United (A) 26-01-2019*

AIDOO Kasim Ishmael Amu-Kadar   2020

Manager Lee Bowyer made it clear on a number of occasions that the Football League Trophy was a competition that he had little time for. He viewed it as an unwelcome addition to the already crowded fixture list, but for several members of the U23 squad, including left back Kasim Aidoo, the match against Leyton Orient on 10th November 2020 provided a first team debut and an evening to remember, wherever his football career may lead him in the future.

Defender   11st 3lbs   5' 11"
Born: 03-11-2001 - Beckton, London
Education: St Edward's Primary School, Upton Park & St Bonaventure's School, Forest Gate

HONOURS

Newham District

CLUBS

Prostar Youth 2015 (youth) ••Charlton Athletic 09.17 (youth) 2019 (pro) ••Eastbourne Borough 28.08.21 (free) ••Cray Wanderers 25.09.21 (free)

Kasim is an East London boy from a Ghanaian family and he joined Charlton after a six-week trial in 2017, having previously represented Newham District. He had progressed through the ranks from U18 to U23 and the Leyton Orient game was his first chance to compete on the big stage.

However, it is hard to imagine a less important match in Charlton's whole history than the one that took place on a dreary Tuesday evening at a deserted Valley, completely devoid of supporters as a result of the Covid lockdown. The Papa John's Trophy, to give it the sponsor's name, was set up initially on a group basis and this was the only outstanding fixture in Group G. Charlton had already been eliminated and Orient were through to the Second Round, making the result of the encounter of absolutely no relevance except for completists who like to see a tidy and fully accurate league table.

The Charlton side also gave debuts to Wassim Aouachria, Hady Ghandour, Dylan Gavin and Johl Powell, all stalwarts of the academy and for them at least, the encounter was significant. Kasim played the full 90 minutes of a surprisingly entertaining game, despite picking up a yellow card after a quarter of an hour. Charlton triumphed 3-1 playing some neat football, but it was of course Orient who progressed to the next stage where they lost at home to Bristol Rovers.

After this brief taste of first team football, Kasim was left hoping that another opportunity would arise before too long, but on 18th May 2021 it was announced that he would not be offered any extension to his contract, so he moved on, initially to Eastbourne Borough and then to Isthmian League club Cray Wanderers.

Season	Division	League		FA Cup		FL Cup		FL Trophy		Total	
		A	G	A	G	A	G	A	G	A	G
2020-21	League One	0	0	0	0	0	0	1	0	1	0
Total		0	0	0	0	0	0	1	0	1	0

UK LEAGUE CAREER 0 games 0 goals

CHARLTON CAREER
Managers: *L Bowyer, N Adkins*
Debut: *Leyton Orient (H) 10-11-2020*
V914

AIZLEWOOD Mark   1982 - 87

Midfield, Defender   12st 8lbs   6' 0"
Born: 01-10-1959 - Newport, Monmouthshire
Education: Hartridge High School, Newport.

Aged only 16 and still at school when he made his debut for Newport County in March 1976, Mark had turned down Arsenal to play for his local club and gained Welsh honours at schoolboy, youth and U23 level before playing his first full international against Saudi Arabia on 15th February 1986. He went on to earn 39 caps, the first four of which came during his time at Charlton. His older brother Steve Aizlewood played for Newport, Swindon and Portsmouth during the seventies.

HONOURS
Wales International 1986-94 39 caps 0 goals
Wales U23 International 1979-80 2 caps 0 goals
Wales Youth & Schoolboy International
Charlton Athletic 1985 & 1986 Player Of The Year

Charlton Athletic 1985-86 Runners Up Division 2
Luton Town 1981-82 Winners Division 2
Cardiff City 1993-94 Finalists Welsh FA Cup

HONOURS AS MANAGER
Carmarthen Town 2012-13 & 2013-14 Winners Welsh League Cup

CLUBS
Cromwell (youth) ••Newport County 1975 (youth) 10.77 (pro) ••Luton Town 12. 04.78 (£50,000) ••Charlton Athletic 04.11.82 (£50,000) ••Leeds United 05.02.87 (£200,000) ••Bradford City 16.08.89 (£200,000) ••Bristol City 08.08.90 (£125,000) ••Cardiff City 15.10.93 (free) 1994 (player coach) ••Merthyr Tydfil 1995 (player coach) ••Barry Town 1995 (free) ••Newport AFC 1996 (free) ••Aberystwyth Town 10.96 (free) ••Cwmbran Town 1997 (free) ••Carmarthen Town 1997 (player coach) 2003 (coach) ••Chester City 09.04 (ass. manager) ••Carmarthen Town 2005 (ass. manager) 07.01.12 (manager) 24.07.21 (coach)

Mark had already gained promotion to Division 1 with Luton Town in 1982, so had the experience as well as the

leadership qualities to make him an attractive signing when he joined Charlton during the final days of the short but eventful managerial tenure of Ken Craggs. Used initially at full back, he took time to be accepted by the supporters, but after being transformed into a combative midfielder and inspirational captain, he led the team to an unlikely promotion to Division 1 while at the same time being voted Player of the Year in both 1985 and 1986.

After switching to Leeds United in February 1987, he initially did well and was handed the captaincy, but was unable to lead the Yorkshire club to his third promotion. After scoring the winning goal against Walsall on 1st May 1989, he celebrated by making an obscene gesture at a section of the Leeds crowd who had been barracking him and was rewarded with a club suspension and a hastily organised transfer to Bradford City.

Mark probably needed an extra yard of pace if he was to have been successful at the highest level and he spent most of his career in Division 2, but his leadership qualities were such that his services were always in demand. After spells with Bristol City and Cardiff, he moved into coaching with Welsh Premier League side, Carmarthen Town, retiring as a player in 2002. Mark eventually spent six years as the Carmarthen manager up to February 2018.

He worked as a pundit for BBC Wales and became Technical Director for the FA of Wales Trust, but was sacked following an altercation with a camera crew during the filming of the BBC programme 'X-Ray' and in 2004 was convicted and fined for assaulting TV reporter Jane Harvey during the same incident. His Welsh language autobiography, 'Amddiffyn Fy Hun' (Defending Myself) was published in 2009 and revealed that he had fought a 27-year battle with alcoholism and gambling. So bad had it become that he had been close to suicide during a trip to Rome in 2003. His ex-wife, also an addict, did finally commit suicide in 2016.

During 2012 Mark was named by several newspapers as being one of six men involved in a major fraud involving some £5 million. It was alleged that they were running a football based apprenticeship scheme but were falsifying the figures and obtaining government grants for students who did not exist. They were eventually charged following an investigation by the Serious Fraud Office and the case was heard at Southwark Crown Court in 2018. Mark was found guilty of conspiracy to commit fraud by false representation and received a six-year jail sentence. He served half of his allotted time, first in Wandsworth and then at Prescoed open prison and was released in 2021, following which he returned to football as coach of Carmarthen Town.

Season	Division	League		FA Cup		FL Cup		FM Cup		Total	
		A	G	A	G	A	G	A	G	A	G
1982-83	Division 2	22	1	1	0	0	0			23	1
1983-84	Division 2	31	1	2	0	2	0			35	1
1984-85	Division 2	38	3	1	1	2	0			41	4
1985-86 (P)	Division 2	35	3	1	0	2	0	1	0	39	3
1986-87	Division 1	26	1	1	0	4	0	1	0	32	1
Total		152	9	6	1	10	0	2	0	170	10

UK LEAGUE CAREER 537 games 23 goals

CHARLTON CAREER
Managers: *K Craggs, L Lawrence*
Debut: *Leeds United (A) 06-11-1982*
V441
Finale: *Nottingham Forest (H) 31-01-1987*

AJDAREVIC Astrit Agim   2014

Astrit was born into an Albanian family in the Republic of Kosovo. They were taking a holiday in Sweden in 1992 when war broke out in Yugoslavia and as a result they remained and made Sweden their home. Astrit's father was a professional footballer and that also became his son's ambition from a very early age. He showed great promise and joined the Liverpool youth set up at the age of 16 and was capped by Sweden from U17 up to U23 level. In 2017, he elected to switch his allegiance to Albania and on 13th November made his full international debut for them as a substitute in the 3-2 win over Turkey. His brothers Arben and Alfred played professional football in Sweden.

Midfield   12st 2lbs   6' 1"
Born: 17-04-1990 - Pristina, Kosovo

HONOURS

Albania International 2017 1 cap 0 goals
Sweden U23 International 2016 4 caps 1 goal

Sweden U21 International 2011-12 14 caps 2 goals
Sweden U19 International 2008-10 18 caps 2 goals

Sweden U17 International 2005-07 20 caps 7 goals   AEK Athens 2017-18 Winners Superleague Greece
Liverpool U18 2006-07 Winners FA Youth Cup

CLUBS

Rinia IF, Sweden 1996 (youth) ••Falkenbergs FF, Sweden 2001 (youth) ••Liverpool 01.07 (youth) 03.05.07 (pro) ••Leicester City 26.03.09 (loan) 30.06.09 (free) ••Hereford United 25.03.10 (loan) ••Orebro SK, Sweden 31.07.10 (free) ••IFK Norrkoping, Sweden 01.04.11 (free) ••Standard Liege, Belgium 03.07.12 (euro 1.5 million) ••Charlton Athletic 03.01.14 (loan) ••Helsingborgs IF, Sweden 19.02.15 (loan) ••Orebro SK, Sweden 11.08.15 (free) ••AEK Athens, Greece 13.12.16 (free) ••Djurgardens, IF, Sweden 09.02.19 (free) ••Akropolis IF, Sweden 17.02.21 (free)

Whilst with Liverpool, Astrit received an FA Youth Cup medal for appearing as a late substitute in the second leg of the 2007 Final in which they narrowly defeated Manchester United in a penalty shoot-out, but he never reached the first team and in 2009 moved on to Leicester City. Here he did at least make a handful of substitute appearances at the tail end of their promotion season from League One, but after failing to establish himself in England, returned to Sweden and signed for Örebro SK in the Allsvenskan, the top league in Swedish football.

The one big money transfer of his career came in July 2012 when Astrit joined Standard Liege for a fee reported to be 1.5 million euros. He played fairly regularly for them during the 2012-13 season, but fell out of favour after Guy Luzon took over as their manager in May 2013. Standard's owner, Roland Duchatelet, added Charlton to his roster of football clubs on 3rd January 2014 and on that very day Astrit became the first of the exodus of foreign players to be sent to SE7, when he arrived on loan for the remainder of the season.

The new owner's highly controversial methods soon led to confusion and unrest among supporters and one immediate area of discontent related to the quality of the players being shipped over to the Valley, some of whom were obviously not up to the standard required to perform in the Championship. This complaint did not however apply to Astrit, who proved to be a very skilful midfield player and a definite asset to the team. Unfortunately he appeared to have problems with his stamina and though he featured in 15 matches, only twice did he complete the full 90 minutes. Nevertheless, at the end of the season and with relegation narrowly averted, many supporters hoped that Astrit could be retained, but it was not to be and he returned to Belgium instead.

His career took him back to Sweden and he enjoyed a further spell with Örebro SK, during which he was converted to a centre forward for a time and in December 2016 signed a two and a half year contract to play for AEK Athens. He was a semiregular in the team when they won the Greek Superleague in 2017-18 but did not feature in either of their two appearances in the Greek Cup Final during that period.

On 9th February 2019 he signed for Swedish club Djurgardens IF where he played alongside another former Charlton player, Fredrik Ulvestad. He is currently playing for Akropolis IF in the Swedish Second Division.

Season	Division	League		FA Cup		FL Cup		Total	
		A	G	A	G	A	G	A	G
2014-15	Championship	13 (6)	2	2 (1)	0	0	0	15 (7)	2
Total		13 (6)	2	2 (1)	0	0	0	15 (7)	2

UK LEAGUE CAREER 25 games 2 goals

CHARLTON CAREER
Managers: C Powell, J Riga
Debut: *Middlesbrough (A) (sub) 18-01-2014*
V768
Finale: *Blackpool (A) 03-05-2014*

AJOSE Nicholas Olushola   2016 - 18

Forward   12st 4lbs   5' 6"
Born: 07-10-1991 - Bury, Lancashire
Education: St Gabriel's Roman Catholic High School, Bury.

A talented youngster who spent more than a decade at Manchester United, Nicky proved unable to break into the first team and since leaving Old Trafford has failed to settle elsewhere, his career becoming a series of loan deals that have sent him the length and breadth of the country, rarely staying long enough in one place to make a positive impact.

HONOURS

England U17 International 2007 I cap 0 goals   Bury 2010-11 Runners Up League Two
England U16 International 2006-07 4 caps 0 goals

CLUBS

Manchester United 1999 (youth) 07.09 (pro) ••Bury 24.09.10 (loan) •Peterborough United 05.07.11 (£300,000) ••Scunthorpe United 22.09.11 (loan) ••Chesterfield 31.01.12 (loan) ••Crawley Town 17.08.12 (loan) ••Bury 23.01.13 (loan) ••Swindon Town 30.08.13 (loan) ••Leeds United 05.08.14 (£150,000) ••Crewe Alexandra 26.11.14 (loan) ••Swindon Town 02.09.15 (free) ••Charlton Athletic 27.06.16 (£800,000) ••Swindon Town 31.01.17 (loan) ••Bury 14.07.17 (loan) ••Mansfield Town 14.01.19 (loan) ••Exeter City 03.07.19 (free) 23.09.21 (coach)

Nicky's first loan move took him to his hometown club Bury and he chipped in with 13 goals in season 2010-11 as they gained promotion from League Two. One goal came in a 2-0 victory over struggling Barnet on 16th April, when he outgunned two other forwards with Charlton connections, Izale McLeod and Mark Marshall, both of whom were playing for the North London side.

This early success resulted in a move to Peterborough United in Summer 2011 for a fee believed to have been in the region of £300,000 and it was from this point that Nicky's nomadic career really kicked in, Unable to hold down a regular spot with the Posh despite a hat-trick against Notts County, he had loan spells with five different clubs and with varying degrees of success, before signing a three-year contract with Leeds United in August 2014. Leeds were very secretive as to the transfer fee involved, but sources indicate that £150,000 is not far off the mark, but whatever the outlay, it proved a disappointing interlude for all concerned. He featured in only three league matches for them without once playing the full 90 minutes and then spent the remainder of the campaign on loan at Crewe Alexandra. After being left out of Leeds' pre-season tour to Austria and Norway, it was agreed on 2nd September 2015 that the remaining two years of his contract would be cancelled by mutual consent and later that same day Nicky signed for Swindon Town.

Season 2015-16 was the most successful of his career with 24 league goals in 38 matches. Six were scored in February alone, including a hat-trick against Blackpool, but even this sudden burst of activity with Swindon did not provide stability and on 27th June 2016 he joined Charlton as one of new manager Russell Slade's first signings as he re-shaped the squad ready for a tilt at promotion. Nicky's goals for Swindon added to the weight of expectation, but he was unable to deliver in anything like the same degree in SE7 and was soon out on loan again, making return trips to both Swindon and Bury.

He rather surprisingly returned to the squad during the later stages of season 2017-18 and although he only found the net on one occasion, his goal was the winner at Portsmouth on 21st April which kept promotion hopes alive for Charlton and was one of the high points of that season for all the travelling fans who that day gave their team unbelievable vocal support. If Nicky Ajose flattered to deceive during much of his time at Charlton, he will nevertheless be remembered with affection for that one goal. After an injury interrupted loan deal with Mansfield Town, he left Charlton in May 2019 and signed for Exeter City. He has recently moved on to their coaching staff.

Season	Division	League		FA Cup		FL Cup		FL Trophy		Play Offs		Total	
		A	G	A	G	A	G	A	G	A	G	A	G
2016-17	League One	17 (4)	6	2 (1)	0	1	0	3	1			23 (5)	7
2017-18	League One	7 (5)	1	0	0	0	0	0	0	2	0	9 (5)	1
2018-19 (P)	League One	6 (3)	1	3	1	1	0	2 (1)	1	0	0	12 (4)	3
Total		30 (12)	8	5 (1)	1	2	0	5 (1)	2	2	0	44 (14)	11

UK LEAGUE CAREER 286 games 82 goals

CHARLTON CAREER
Managers: *R Slade, K Robinson, L Bowyer*
Debut: *Bury (A) 06-08-2016*
V822
Finale: *Coventry City (A) 26-12-2018*

ALLEN Bradley James   1996 - 98

Forward   11st 0lbs   5' 8"
Born: 13-09-1971 - Harold Wood, Essex
Education: Nelmes Primary School & Emerson Park Secondary School,
Hornchurch.

Bradley Allen is part of a modern footballing dynasty. His father Les, cousins Martin and Paul and brother Clive have all played League football while his uncle was the former Charlton player, Dennis Allen. His nephew Oliver and other members of the next generation have continued the tradition and there may well be members of the Allen family at the forefront of English football for some time to come.

Bradley was around the first team at Queens Park Rangers for the best part of seven seasons without ever quite establishing himself in the side, despite eight caps and two goals for England U21's. A hat trick at Goodison Park which led to the 3-0 defeat of Everton in November 1993 was probably the high point of his career.

HONOURS

England U21 International 1992-93 8 caps 2 goals
England Youth International 1988-91 8 caps 2 goals
Essex Schools & London Schools

Charlton Athletic 1997-98 Promoted Play Offs Division 1
Charlton Athletic Reserves 1997-98 Winners Football Combination

CLUBS

Queens Park Rangers 11.03.87 (youth) 30.09.88 (pro) ••Charlton Athletic 27.03.96 (£350,000) ••Colchester United 24.02.99 (loan) ••Grimsby Town 12.07.99 (free) ••Peterborough United 31.08.02 (free) ••Bristol Rovers 28.11.02 (free) ••Hornchurch 09.03 (free) ••Redbridge 2004 (free) ••Tottenham Hotspur (coach)

Bradley joined Charlton in March 1996 when the club was building towards promotion into the Premier League and he opened his account with the winning goal at Norwich on his debut. Unfortunately only two more goals were forthcoming that season and he was unable to add the momentum needed to keep the promotion challenge on track. 1996-97 was his first full season with the club and a combination of injuries and lack of form restricted him to 13 starts in the League which produced only four goals. Clive Mendonca was signed in May 1997 and as the promotion side finally came together, Bradley was obliged to play a supporting role and was no longer among the first names on the team sheet.

He moved on to Grimsby Town where he enjoyed a measure of success but more injuries affected his progress and he finally hung up his boots in 2004. Since retiring he has worked as a PE teacher and enjoyed media work as a commentator for Sky TV and with Radio Humberside. In 2018, he was working as an academy coach for Tottenham Hotspur and as a summariser for Radio London.

Season	Division	League		FA Cup		FL Cup		Play Offs		Total	
		A	G	A	G	A	G	A	G	A	G
1995-96	Division 1	10	3	0	0	0	0	1 (1)	0	11 (1)	3
1996-97	Division 1	13 (5)	4	0	0	3	2			16 (5)	6
1997-98 (P)	Division 1	7 (5)	2	0 (2)	0	0	0	0	0	7 (7)	2
1998-99 (R)	Premier	0	0	0	0	0 (1)	0			0 (1)	0
Total		30 (10)	9	0 (2)	0	3 (1)	2	1 (1)	0	34 (14)	11

UK LEAGUE CAREER 224 games 56 goals

CHARLTON CAREER
Managers: *A Curbishley*
Debut: *Norwich City (A) 30-03-1996*
V556
Finale: *Queens Park Rangers (H) (sub) 22-09-1998*

ALLEN Dennis James　　　　　　　　　　　1957 - 60

Dennis was from the first generation of the footballing Allen family. His brother Les was in the Spurs team that won the FA Cup and League double in 1961 while his son Martin played for both QPR and West Ham.

Forward, Midfield　10st 3lbs　5' 10"
Born: 02-03-1939 - Dagenham, Essex
Died: 09-07-1995 - Reading, Berkshire

Nephews Paul and Clive performed extensively at the top level, as did another nephew Bradley Allen who played for Charlton in the nineties as well as for five other Football League clubs. His grandson Charlie and great nephew Oliver continued the family tradition and have appeared in the Football League since the new millennium.

HONOURS

Essex Youth 1954-55

Malaya Representative XI V Peru & Mexico 1959-60

Charlton Athletic Youth 1956-57 Finalists South East Counties League Cup

Charlton Athletic A 1957-58 Winners London Mid-Week League

Bournemouth & Boscombe Ath. 1970-71 Runners Up Division 4

HONOURS AS MANAGER

Cheltenham Town 1976-77 Runners Up Southern League Division 1 North

CLUBS

South Park Boys (youth) ••Romford Minor (youth) ••Charlton Athletic 06.08.55 (amateur) 15.08.56 (pro) ••Reading 09.06.61 (£900) ••Bournemouth & Boscombe Athletic 06.08.70 (£6,500) ••ASV Oostende, Belgium 1971 (player coach) ••Cheltenham Town 07.74 (player manager)

After joining the ground staff in September 1954, Dennis signed for Charlton as an amateur almost a year later and on professional terms in August 1956. His first team debut came when he lined up at inside right against Cardiff City on 21st September 1957 as deputy for Bobby Ayre. Charlton secured a satisfactory 3-0 away win and Dennis scored the second goal with Billy Kiernan and Stuart Leary claiming the others. His second chance came three weeks later when Leary was missing with flu, but otherwise he was confined to reserve team football.

National Service intervened in August 1958 and Dennis served with the 3rd East Anglian Regiment. He captained their football side against a Combined Services XI in Kuala Lumpur and also played twice for a Malayan Representative XI.

Back at Charlton he still found no clear path to the first team, despite being something of a utility player. He had even replaced an injured Willie Duff in goal on one occasion in a Southern Floodlit Cup game at Portsmouth, but when he was finally recalled for three league matches in November 1960, it was at inside left in place of Eddie Werge. A win at Rotherham was followed by defeats against Liverpool and Bristol Rovers and that concluded Dennis's involvement with the first team. He asked to go on the transfer list in February 1961 and was allowed to leave for Reading in June.

The change of club was a great success and Dennis, playing

either at centre forward or on the left wing, finished leading goalscorer in each of his first two seasons and bagged a hat-trick against Chester in the League Cup. He was highly regarded and very popular at Reading and ended up playing more than 350 league matches for them during a nine-year stay, eventually finishing up at centre half. Over 12,000 turned out for his Testimonial match against an All Stars XI in 1970.

Despite his loyalty, there were no league or cup honours during his time at Reading, but after Dennis switched to Bournemouth he walked straight into their promotion team of 1970-71 and appeared on the right wing for the first half of the campaign alongside full back David Stocks. He lost his place by December but had still played his part in their eventual promotion as runners-up in Division 4. After a spell in Belgium, he joined Cheltenham Town, initially as player manager, but after finally hanging up his boots, stayed on as manager and guided them to promotion from the Southern League Div 1 North in 1976-77, remaining in charge at Whaddon Road until 1979. In later years Dennis worked a spell on the administration staff for Exeter City and scouted for several clubs. He had been working as a scout with the England set up under Terry Venables shortly before his untimely death from cancer in 1995 at the age of 56.

Season	Division	League		FA Cup		Total	
		A	G	A	G	A	G
1957-58	Division 2	2	1	0	0	2	1
1960-61	Division 2	3	0	0	0	3	0
Total		5	1	0	0	5	1

UK LEAGUE CAREER 358 games 89 goals

CHARLTON CAREER
Managers: *J Seed, J Trotter*
Debut: *Cardiff City (A) 21-09-1957*
V278
Finale: *Bristol Rovers (A) 26-11-1960*

ALLEN Henry Albert   1924 - 25

Forward   5' 6"
Born: 28-06-1898 - Hackney, Middlesex
Died: 09-1976 - Tonbridge, Kent

Right-winger Henry Allen was a semiregular in the Charlton side for two seasons, although he rarely hit the headlines, but the one goal of his professional career came at the Valley on 18th April 1925 when Charlton, smarting from a defeat at Millwall five days earlier, produced the best result of an otherwise unremarkable season. Their opponents were Aberdare Athletic and his goal added to an opener from leading scorer Edwin Rees. Two from centre forward Tom Wilson and one from the other winger Bill Cox clinched a 5-1 scoreline.

HONOURS
Essex County FA

CLUBS
Gnome Athletic 1919 ••West Ham United (amateur) •Arsenal (amateur) ••Southend United 01.21 ••Gillingham 05.08.23 ••Charlton Athletic 07.06.24 ••Grays Thurrock United 07.07.26

Henry had worked as a clerk after leaving school and in World War 1 served in the Navy on HMS President. In 1919 and with his military service behind him, he played football for the quaintly named Gnome Athletic. They had started life as the works team for Peter Hooker Ltd, a Walthamstow based engine manufacturers and played in the London League. This led on to brief spells as an amateur with both West Ham and Arsenal, but no appearances at first team level, although he did receive county recognition and was capped by Essex.
He signed for Southend United in January 1921, but not without difficulty. He was still an Arsenal player at the time and they initially objected to the transfer, causing both a delay and a fine for the Essex club, who were found to have breached the rules. Henry eventually made his Football league debut against Southampton on 26th February 1921, lining up on the right wing in a side that included future Charlton captain Arthur Whalley at centre half. He went on to play 23 league games for them before switching to Gillingham in August 1923.
There were not many first team opportunities for Henry during his time with the Gills but he did get to play twice against Charlton, The first game at the Priestfield Stadium

on 29th December 1923 was a 1-0 victory for the Addicks thanks to a last minute goal from right-winger Charlie Hannaford, while the second held at the Mount seven days later ended 0-0. Two months later Hannaford was transferred from Charlton to Clapton Orient and at the end of the season Henry Allen was brought in as his replacement.
The two years that he spent at Charlton were notable only for the club's continuing struggles on and off the field. 1925-26 was Charlton's least successful campaign as a Football League club and the only occasion when they were obliged to seek re-election. Henry played regularly up to the December when they were poised in mid-table, but lost his place after a 1-1 FA Cup draw at Queens Park Rangers, so was missing when the team sunk down to a miserable 21st place in Division 3 (South).
He left in the close season and joined Grays Thurrock United, newly accepted into the Southern League and where his team mates included former Charlton players Freddy Wood and Frank Burton.
Henry died at the age of 78 in Tonbridge and is buried at St Mary's Churchyard at Ticehurst, East Sussex.

Season	Division	League		FA Cup		Total	
		A	G	A	G	A	G
1924-25	Divison 3 (S)	23	1	3	0	26	1
1925-26	Divison 3 (S)	15	0	2	0	17	0
Total		38	1	5	0	43	1

UK LEAGUE CAREER 67 games 1 goal

CHARLTON CAREER
Managers: *W Rayner, A MacFarlane*
Debut: *Northampton Town (A) 08-09-1924*
V061
Finale: *Queens Park Rangers (A) 12-12-1925*

ALLEN Ralph Slack Littlewood   1934 - 36

Ralph Allen was a goal machine and during the first season that he spent at Charlton, he created a scoring record that stands to this day. He signed from Brentford at the end of October 1934 and in just 28 league matches, scored 32 goals, including four on 15th December in an exciting 6-3 win at Gillingham. No other Charlton footballer has ever reached the 30 mark in league games and the following season, with the club now promoted to Division 2, he contributed a further 15 goals as a second consecutive promotion took them into Division 1 for the very first time.

Forward   12st 7lbs   5' 11"
Born: 30-06-1906 - Newburn, Northumberland
Died: 09-05-1981 - Blyth, Northumberland

HONOURS
Charlton Athletic 1934-35 Winners Division 3 (S)   Brentford Reserves 1931-32 & 1932-33 Winners Football Combination
Charlton Athletic 1935-36 Runners Up Division 2

CLUBS
Walbottle 1924 ••Elswick 1925 ••Wombwell 1926 ••Dipton United 1927 ••Fulham 05.28 ••Brentford 13.03.31 (£275) ••Charlton Athletic 26.10 34 (£650) ••Reading 18.06.36 (£828) ••Northampton Town 23.10.36 ••Torquay United 11.11.38 (player exchange) ••Annfield Plain 08.39

There had been unsuccessful trials with The Wednesday and Hartlepools United before Ralph landed a contract with Fulham in 1928. He had limitations as a footballer, but as a natural goalscorer there would always be a demand for his services. After switching to Brentford the goals really started to flow and in three seasons he scored in excess of 100 times for their reserves and captained them to two consecutive Football Combination titles.

Charlton's leading goalscorer Cyril Pearce broke his leg and did not play again for over a year, which left Jimmy Seed in urgent need of a replacement. He could not have made a more inspired choice than Ralph, who bagged both goals on his debut as Clapton Orient were beaten 2-1 on 27th October 1934 and continued to punish defences for the remainder of that memorable campaign. At one stage he scored in seven consecutive league matches which created a club record that remained unchallenged until it was eventually equalled by Derek Hales in October 1976. After Charlton had secured promotion to Division 2, they

were criticised in the media for failing to strengthen the team for the fresh challenge ahead, but Seed's unchanged squad confounded his critics with a second promotion, finishing runners-up behind Manchester United. Ralph's 15 league goals included a hat-trick as Burnley were overrun 4-0 on 31st August 1935, but he was judged unlikely to prosper in Division 1 and was transferred to Reading at the end of that second season. Charlton's record goalscorer departed having netted 48 times in just 54 matches.

The goals continued and at Northampton Town in particular he helped himself to 41 in 52 league games, including hat-tricks against Bristol City and Walsall. It was the outbreak of war which finally forced Ralph into retirement and he eventually moved back to Northumberland and became postmaster in Blyth, where he passed away at the age of 74. His goal scoring feats for Charlton remain unequalled more than 80 years later. His brother Jack Allen was also a fine striker and got both goals in the 1932 FA Cup final for Newcastle United.

Season	Division	League		FA Cup		D3 Cup		Total	
		A	G	A	G	A	G	A	G
1934-35 (P)	Divison 3 (S)	28	32	2	1	0	0	30	33
1935-36 (P)	Division 2	24	15	0	0			24	15
Total		52	47	2	1	0	0	54	48

UK LEAGUE CAREER 171 games 122 goals

CHARLTON CAREER
Managers: *J Seed*
Debut: *Clapton Orient (H) 27-10-1934*
V182
Finale: *Tottenham Hotspur (A) 10-04-1936*

ALLISON Malcolm Alexander   1949

Defender   12st 0lbs   6' 0"
Born: 05-09-1927 - Dartford, Kent
Died: 14-10-2010 - Trafford, Cheshire
Education: Bexleyheath Central School.

The sight of Malcolm Allison dressed in a slick suit, a fedora on his head and an enormous cigar in his mouth, is very much an image of football in the seventies. This egotistical, arrogant but charismatic man was regularly cited as the best, most forward-thinking coach in the UK. In the early fifties he had been astute enough to study the European coaching methods which were light years ahead of the old-fashioned techniques still adopted in the Football League and he proved himself during the period 1965-71 when he was able to put his ideas into practice at Manchester City while working under manager Joe Mercer. However once he had dislodged Mercer and taken over himself, it was a different story. Big Mal had minimal success as a manager and it was undoubtedly as a coach that he really excelled. Earlier his playing career, which commenced at Charlton in the immediate post-war period, had been cut short by serious illness.

HONOURS
London FA 1953 1 cap 0 goals
British Services Combined X1 2 caps

Charlton Athletic Reserves 1949-50 Winners Football Combination
Charlton Athletic Reserves 1950-51 Winners London FA Challenge Cup

HONOURS AS MANAGER
Manchester City 1972 Winners FA Charity Shield
Sporting CP 1981-82 Winners Primeira Divisao

Sporting CP 1981-82 Winners Taca De Portugal

CLUBS
St John's Boys Club (youth) ••Welling Civic (youth) ••Danson Boys Club (youth) ••Erith & Belvedere c1945 (amateur) ••Bromley (amateur) ••Charlton Rovers (amateur) ••Charlton Athletic 30.03.45 (amateur) 04.12.45 (pro) ••West Ham United 22.02.51 (£7,000) ••Sutton United 18.11.58 (coach) ••Romford 08.60 (free) ••Wembley 1962 (coach) ••Cambridge University 1963 (coach) ••Bath City 01.04.63 (player coach) ••Toronto City, Canada 1964 (coach) ••Plymouth Argyle 14.05.64 (manager) ••Manchester City 08.65 (coach) 07.10.71 (manager) ••Cape Town City, South Africa 1972 (coach) ••Crystal Palace 30.03.73 (manager) ••Galatasaray, Turkey 05.76 (coach) ••Memphis Rogues, USA 11.77 (manager) ••Plymouth Argyle 16.03.78 (manager) ••Manchester City 06.01.79 (coach) 16.07.79 (manager) ••Crystal Palace 30.11.80 (manager) ••Yeovil Town 01.81 (consultant) ••Sporting CP, Portugal 1981 (manager) ••Middlesbrough 23.10.82 (manager) ••Willington 1984 (manager) ••Kuwait 1985 (manager) ••Vitoria Setubal, Portugal 02.88 (manager) ••SC Farense, Portugal 01.89 (manager) ••Fisher Athletic 06.89 (manager) ••Bristol Rovers 10.11.92 (manager)

Malcolm's first appearance for Charlton was in a reserve team friendly against Catford Wanderers in March 1945. He was playing centre forward and scored twice in a 3-2 win. After working briefly as a messenger for a Fleet Street photographic agency, he signed a professional contract aged 18 and was converted into a central defender. However, before his football career could really progress, he was called up for two years National Service which was spent with the Army in Austria. He returned, ambitious to succeed at his chosen profession and full of ideas that he had gained from watching training sessions at the Praterstadion in Vienna.

Always outspoken and opinionated, Malcolm did not have an easy relationship with Jimmy Seed, whom he described in his 1975 autobiography, 'The Colours Of My Life,' as 'a distant uninvolved figure' and he was most certainly not impressed with the training methods of Charlton's coach and physiotherapist Jimmy Trotter. 'We were asked to jog aimlessly around the training ground', he recalled. The biggest barrier to his progress was however the formidable presence of Harold Phipps, who was in possession of the number five shirt throughout his time at the club. Malcolm did finally get his chance in the first team on Christmas Eve

1949, when Phipps was injured and both he and inside forward Riley Cullum made their debuts up at Maine Road. It was not a great day for Charlton though. Peter Croker broke his nose and Manchester City won 2-0, with their second goal, a penalty, having been conceded by Allison. Unusually he captained the team in both his first team appearances. In February 1951 he was transferred to West Ham for a fee of £7,000.

To his surprise, Malcolm found the Hammers' training methods were even less satisfactory than at Charlton. The only difference was that they allowed him to organise his own schedules and encouraged him to introduce new methods. On 27th March 1957 he represented the London FA in an Inter Cities Fairs Cup tie in Germany. Stuart Leary and Billy Kiernan were also in the side which lost 1-0 to Frankfurt.

Malcolm held down a first team place for more than six years as West Ham battled in vain to gain promotion to Division 1, but when in 1957-58 they finally did achieve their goal, he had been laid low with a mystery illness that was at first diagnosed as a form of Asian Flu. Eventually it was found to be a severe bout of tuberculosis, as a result of which he had a lung removed in the London Hospital. Despite nine months in a sanatorium, he never recovered sufficiently to return to the West Ham side and in October 1958 announced his retirement as a full time pro. What followed was a period when he consolidated his reputation as a playboy and serial womaniser, while at different times running a West End nightclub, selling cars and operating the racetracks as a professional gambler. He even had a short but steamy affair with Christine Keeler.

By 1962 he had a strong desire to get back into football and after impressing in a coaching role at Cambridge University, took a job with Bath City, spent a Summer with Toronto City and finally in May 1964 was appointed manager of Plymouth Argyle. This gave him the opportunity to fully develop his coaching theories and he became the first British manager to adopt the sweeper system. All went well for a time, but his abrasive and arrogant manner did not go down well with some directors and he was sacked after less than a year.

Previously Malcolm had turned down high profile coaching jobs with both Ajax and Tottenham, but in August 1965 he accepted the role of head coach at Second Division

Manchester City, working alongside the older and more experienced Joe Mercer. They were immediately successful, winning promotion in 1966 and two years later securing the First Division Championship. They landed the FA Cup in 1969 and followed this up with success in both the League Cup and the European Cup Winners Cup in 1970. He became impatient to take sole charge and after a messy interlude Mercer was moved upstairs and Malcolm was promoted to manager in October 1971. His six years coaching at City was unquestionably the high point of his career, but he would never again get even close to that level of accomplishment.

Manchester City soon dropped back into mid-table and after switching to Crystal Palace in 1973, he led them through two consecutive relegations. The most vivid memory of this period is the photo of Allison and porn star Fiona Richmond quaffing champagne in the players' bath, complete with cigar and oversized fedora. The genius coach was becoming a parody and he now moved from club to club with little to show for his efforts. He suffered disastrous second spells at both Plymouth and Manchester City and returned to Crystal Palace in time to see them relegated for the third time. The one exception to this depressing sequence came in 1981-82 when he achieved the cup and league double in Portugal with Sporting Lisbon. Other jobs came and went until his final season as a Football League manager in 1992-93. His Bristol Rovers side locked horns with the rookie management team of Gritt and Curbishley at Twerton Park on 27th January. Two goals from Alan Pardew earned Charlton a useful 2-0 away win and three months later, Bristol Rovers were relegated.

Malcolm was later sacked from his job as a radio summariser for swearing on the air and lived the last years of his life in reduced circumstances suffering from Korsakoff's syndrome, a form of dementia that is exacerbated by alcohol. He passed away in a nursing home at the age of 83 and at his funeral, the coffin was perhaps fittingly adorned with a bottle of Moët et Chandon champagne.

Season	Division	League		FA Cup		Total	
		A	G	A	G	A	G
1949-50	Division 1	2	0	0	0	2	0
Total		2	0	0	0	2	0

UK LEAGUE CAREER 240 games 10 goals

CHARLTON CAREER
Managers: *J Seed*
Debut: *Manchester City (A) 24-12-1949*
V237
Finale: *Portsmouth (H) 26-12-1949*

ALNWICK Benjamin Robert   2013 - 14

Goalkeeper   12st 6lbs   6' 2"
Born: 01-01-1987 - Prudhoe, Northumberland
Education: Prudhoe High School.

The career of Ben Alnwick commenced at Sunderland, for whom he made his Football League debut at the age of 18. He got a run of games during their promotion season of 2006-07 when they won back their place in the Premier League, just as Charlton were heading in the other direction. Ben's form was promising enough for Tottenham Hotspur to pay out £900,000 to secure his services, but like David Button, another future Charlton goalkeeper, he never made the big step-up into the Spurs first team. After more than five years at White Hart Lane, he had only managed one league appearance and that was a 4-2 defeat on 9th May 2010 against a Burnley side that included Chris Eagles and Andre Bikey.

HONOURS

England U21 International 2007 1 cap 0 goals
England U19 International 2005 2 caps 0 goals
England U18 International 2004-05 2 caps 0 goals
England U17 International 2004 5 caps 0 goals

England U16 International 2002-03 9 caps 0 goals
Sunderland 2005-06 Winners Championship
Bolton Wanderers 2016-17 Runners Up League One

CLUBS

Wylam (youth) ••Sunderland (youth) 13.03.04 (pro) ••Tottenham Hotspur 01.01.07 (£900,000) ••Luton Town 28.09.07 (loan) ••Leicester City 07.01.08 (loan) ••Carlisle United 17.10.08 (loan) ••Norwich City 04.08.09 (loan) ••Leeds United 14.10.10 (loan) ••Doncaster Rovers 04.03.11 (loan) ••Leyton Orient 09.09.11 (loan) ••Barnsley 05.07.12 (free) ••Charlton Athletic 04.09.13 (free) ••Leyton Orient 31.01.14 (free) ••Peterborough United 25.07.14 (free) ••Bolton Wanderers 31.08.16 (free)

There were loan deals to keep Ben active while he waited in vain for his chance with Tottenham and these included three months with Luton (cut short after just four weeks), a month each at Carlisle and Doncaster and a three-month stint at Norwich where he played three times while Declan Rudd and their other goalies were injured. In the end however, like every player he needed to play regularly and in July 2012 signed a two-year contract with Barnsley.

His time in South Yorkshire could not have got off to a worse start as he received a red card on his debut at Rochdale, but did play a league match at the Valley on 20th October 2012 from which his Barnsley side escaped with all three points and a 1-0 scoreline. Two weeks later he was dropped following a 4-1 mauling by Nottingham Forest and never got back in the team, his contract being terminated by mutual consent in September 2013.

Two days later Ben signed for Charlton on a one-year deal, but times were financially difficult in SE7 and Chris Powell's team were struggling to keep away from the

bottom of the Championship. Ben Hamer was first choice 'keeper, but managed to injure himself in the warm-up for the home game with Doncaster Rovers on 26th November 2013, so the new goalkeeper was given an early chance to show what he had to offer. He performed well and goals from Dale Stephens and Simon Church clinched a 2-0 win for the Addicks.

With Hamer still absent, Ben remained in the first team through into January 2014 and made a favourable impression with some quality displays. However, during this period, Belgian businessman Roland Duchatelet had purchased the club and was already trying to influence team selection. A French goalkeeper, Yohann Thuram-Ulien, was brought in on loan against the wishes of the manager and seeing no future for himself at Charlton, Ben was allowed to leave and sign for Russell Slade's Leyton Orient on 31st January, the final day of the transfer window.

After just a single appearance for Orient, Ben was freed from his contract because of personal problems and his football career did not re-commence until July when he signed for Peterborough United. Over the next two seasons he was a fixture between the posts for the Posh and appeared in 80 league matches. One evening that he may wish to forget was 25th August 2015 when a less than full strength Charlton side visited London Road for a League Cup tie. Not only were the home team, which included Conor Washington and Marcus Maddison, defeated 4-1, but the Addicks third goal was scored by Ahmed Kashi from the halfway line.

Early in season 2016-17 Ben moved to Bolton Wanderers and featured in their League One promotion team along with Lawrie Wilson, Darren Pratley and Dorian Dervite. He was a semi-regular in the Bolton side for three years, during which the club became increasingly pre-occupied by a worsening financial situation. Ben made his final appearance for them in April 2019, but remained at the club until his contract was cancelled by mutual agreement in December. It was rumoured that he might re-sign for Phil Parkinson's Sunderland in January 2000 but nothing happened and his career appears to be fading away as he has now been without a club for more than two years.

Season	Division	League		FA Cup		FL Cup		Total	
		A	G	A	G	A	G	A	G
2013-14	Championship	10	0	2	0	0	0	12	0
Total		10	0	2	0	0	0	12	0

UK LEAGUE CAREER 239 games 0 goals

CHARLTON CAREER
Managers: *C Powell*
Debut: *Doncaster Rovers (H) 26-11-2013*
V766
Finale: *Doncaster Rovers (A) 28-01-2014*

ALONSO OLANO Mikel   2011

Mikel is the oldest son of Periko Alonso, a Spanish International, while his brother is Xabi Alonso, who enjoyed a glittering career with Liverpool, Real Madrid and Bayern Munich. The family come from the Basque area of Northern Spain and all three came to prominence while playing for Real Sociedad. On five occasions Mikel represented the Basque Country in unofficial friendly matches, the Basque Football Federation not being recognised by FIFA.

Midfield 5' 11"
Born: 17-05-1980 - Tolosa, Spain

HONOURS
Basque Country 2004-07 5 caps
CD Numancia 203-04 Promoted Segunda Division

CD Tenerife 2008-09 Promoted Segunda Division
Real Union 2014-15 Winners Copa Federacion De Espana

CLUBS
Antiguoko, Spain 1994 (youth) ••Athletic Bilbao, Spain 1997 (youth) ••Real Sociedad, Spain 1998 (youth) 1999 (pro) ••CD Numancia, Spain 2003 (loan) ••Bolton Wanderers 06.07.07 (loan) ••CD Tenerife, Canary Islands 01.09 ••Charlton Athletic 21.06.11 (free) ••Real Union, Spain 14.07.14 (free)

Mikel came to England in July 2007. He joined Bolton Wanderers on a loan deal, with an option to sign permanently at the end of the season, but first an injury and then a change of manager left him out in the cold. His final game for Bolton was the 2-2 draw at Bayern Munich in the UEFA Cup in November, after which the loan was terminated.

A trial with Olympiacos came to nothing so Mikel trained with Swansea City before eventually signing for Tenerife in January 2009, where he had a rollercoaster ride as they first gained promotion to La Liega and followed this with two consecutive relegations,

Chris Powell signed Mikel on 21st June 2011 but to say that his time at Charlton was unsuccessful would be something of an understatement. His sole appearance for the first team came in an ignominious 3-0 defeat against Brentford in the League Trophy. Charlton were never in the game and Mikel's contribution was clearly considered unsatisfactory as he was never again called up for first team duty.

Left without a contract after leaving Charlton, Mikel trained with New York Cosmos before eventually joining the Spanish club Real Union in 2014. They competed in Segunda Division B, the third level of Spanish football, where he remained until retiring from the game in December 2018.

Season	Division	League		FA Cup		FL Cup		FL Trophy		Total	
		A	G	A	G	A	G	A	G	A	G
2011-12 (P)	League One	0	0	0	0	0	0	1	0	1	0
Total		0	0	0	0	0	0	1	0	1	0

CHARLTON CAREER
Managers: *C Powell*
Debut: *Brentford (H) 05-10-2011*
V738

UK LEAGUE CAREER 7 games 0 goals

AMBROSE Anthony Leroy   1979 - 82

Midfield   10st 8lbs   5' 7"
Born: 22-06-1960 - Kingstown, Saint Vincent, WI.

West Indian-born Leroy Ambrose enjoyed a varied football career. He was never quite able to fully establish himself as a first team regular at Charlton, but tried his luck with three different clubs in Denmark, before settling down to a long and successful run in the non-league game. He was a part of the exodus of Charlton players who, in the late eighties, managed to bring Fisher Athletic within sight of a place in the Football League. Although this was never attained, they nevertheless achieved during this period, the highest league placing in that club's somewhat chequered history

HONOURS

London FA 1997-99 5 caps
Charlton Athletic Reserves 1979-80 Runners Up Mid-Week League
Charlton Athletic Reserves 1981-82 Winners Mid-Week League

Fisher Athletic 1986-87 Winners Southern League Premier Division
Fisher Athletic 1987-88 & 1988-89 Winners London Senior Cup
Sittingbourne 1992-93 Winners Southern League South Division

CLUBS

Croydon (youth) ••Orient (amateur) ••Charlton Athletic 15.12.78 (pro) ••Hvidovre IF, Denmark 01.07.80 (loan) 1982 (free) ••Kolding IF, Denmark 1983 ••Esbjerg FB, Denmark 1984 ••Fisher Athletic 1985 (free) ••Dover Athletic 03.90 ••Sittingbourne 27.08.92 ••Cray Wanderers 1994 ••AFC Blackheath 1996 ••Tooting & Mitcham 1998 ••Cray Valley (PM) c2004 ••Goldsmiths c2005 ••Metrogas Veterans c2013

The three seasons during which Leroy was contesting a place in the Charlton team were unusually volatile even by their standards. He served under three different managers and the club were first relegated and then promoted back to Division 2. He made his debut in a League Cup match at Peterborough and had an extended run in the side during the early part of the 1979-80 season. Results were worrying right from the start however and he only featured on one winning team, that being against Shrewsbury Town on 22nd September 1979, which finished 2-1 thanks to goals from Colin Powell and Martin Robinson. By early October it was clear that there was a relegation battle coming up and he was removed from the front-line and had to wait until February for his next opportunity. He managed two further appearances that season but both games were lost as the club slipped back into Division 3.

A managerial change at the Valley had seen Andy Nelson replaced by Mike Bailey and with Leroy seemingly excess to requirements, he started 1980-81 with a four-month loan spell in Copenhagen at Hvidovre IF, the then current

Danish FA Cup holders. In his absence, Charlton were mounting a successful promotion campaign, but although he was back in London before Christmas, Leroy only featured in two league matches, one of which was at Gillingham, where a Derek Hales goal just before half-time, clinched a 1-0 win.

His third season saw Alan Mullery at the helm and he finally got a good run in the side, featuring in just over half of the league programme. He even managed to score what proved to be his only goal in the Football League on 24th November 1981 against Chelsea. The match was certainly exciting but Charlton were eventually beaten 4-3 with two of the Chelsea goals courtesy of John Bumstead. At the end of that season Leroy left the Valley and re-joined Hvidovre, before moving in turn to Kolding and then Esbjerg as he sampled the full range of Danish football.

He signed for Fisher Athletic upon his return to the UK and was only one of several players with Charlton connections to be attracted by the competitive wages being paid by the Fish during that heady period when they were being managed by the Cypriot gangster, Dogan Arif. Leroy played in more than 100 league and cup matches and was part of the 1986-87 team that became champions of the Southern League, Premier Division.

In 1988-89 Fisher enjoyed a long run in the FA Cup, playing six matches and eventually meeting Bristol Rovers on 20th November. Their team that day included Leroy plus Tony Towner, Dave Mehmet and Barry Little but their opponents proved too strong and they went down 3-0. The following year Malcolm Allison took over as manager but did not stay long although the Charlton connection was maintained when he was replaced in November 1989 by

Mike Bailey. Leroy departed four months later and joined Dover Athletic.

From then on he moved around within the non-league game, appearing among others for Sittingbourne, who won the Southern League, South Division during his first season, Cray Wanderers and Kent County League side, AFC Blackheath. He kept playing beyond his 50th birthday, eventually switching to veterans football with Metrogas, a side that also contained Colin Powell and Steve Gritt, while also occasionally turning out for Charlton's vets team.

Season	Division	League		FA Cup		FL Cup		Total	
		A	G	A	G	A	G	A	G
1979-80 (R)	Division 2	8 (1)	0	0	0	1	0	9 (1)	0
1980-81 (P)	Division 3	2	0	0	0	0	0	2	0
1981-82	Division 2	18 (4)	1	0	0	0	0	18 (4)	1
Total		28 (5)	1	0	0	1	0	29 (5)	1

UK LEAGUE CAREER 33 games 1 goal

CHARLTON CAREER
Managers: *A Nelson, M Bailey, A Mullery*
Debut: *Peterborough United (A) 11-08-1979*
V415
Finale: *Oldham Athletic (A) 04-05-1982*

AMBROSE Darren Paul Francis   2005 - 09

Darren was an unlucky player. Early on, Newcastle manager Bobby Robson identified him as a possible England player of the future, yet in the end his career largely comprised a series

Midfield   12st 4lbs   6' 0"
Born: 29-02-1984 - Harlow, Essex

of relegation battles for unstable clubs with serious financial problems. Both Ipswich and Crystal Palace were placed in administration during his time with them and his four seasons at Charlton coincided with the crash from the Premier League into League One. Even his final campaign with Colchester resulted in relegation to League Two.

HONOURS
England U21 International 2003-06 10 caps 2 goals   England U20 International 2005 4 caps 1 goal

CLUBS
Ipswich Town 1995 (youth) 03.07.01 (pro) ••Newcastle United 25.03.03 (£1 million) ••Charlton Athletic 11.07.05 (£1.5 million) ••Ipswich Town 11.11.08 (loan) ••Crystal Palace 02.07.09 (free) ••Birmingham City 13.07.12 (£250,000) ••Apollon Smyrnis, Greece 14.01.14 (loan) ••Ipswich Town 11.09.14 (free) ••Colchester United 06.08.15 (free)

Darren's debut for Ipswich came as a late substitute against Arsenal on 21st April 2002. He appeared alongside Herman Hreidarsson, Matt Holland and Marcus Bent but the resultant 2-0 defeat just moved them closer to relegation from the Premier League. By the time of his next match in August 2002, they were playing in the second tier and the financial crisis was accelerating. He performed well enough and scored an impressive 11 times during his first full season in the Football League, but in March 2003 the club were placed in administration and that same month he was transferred to Newcastle United for a very welcome fee of

£1 million.

In his two seasons with Newcastle, Darren was in and out of the side, but at age 20 was attracting attention as a possible star of the future. He played alongside Lee Bowyer in the semi-final of the UEFA Cup against Olympique Marseille on 6th May 2004, but the Geordies having already drawn 0-0 at home, were beaten 2-0 in the away leg. He got less game time in his second season and his career seemed to be losing momentum until in the summer of 2005 he got the opportunity to move to London SE7. When Darren signed for Charlton they were an established

Premier League club and he was able to enjoy the final season of Alan Curbishley's tenure as manager before the wheels came off and the downward spiral began. His debut was not without incident. He received a red card after 55 minutes in a Charlton shirt, as the team recorded an impressive 3-1 win at Sunderland. As time went on it became clear that he was a very skilful player with a powerful shot and the ability to score spectacular goals, but he lacked consistency and seemed to save his most impressive moments for away matches.

His stay at the Valley lasted four years but he was used only sparingly in the later stages, so it was no surprise when he joined Crystal Palace on a free transfer in 2009. The move revitalised his career and in the following season he claimed 15 league goals in yet another relegation battle. He hardly played at all after moving, first to Birmingham City and then back again to Ipswich.

Darren's playing career ended in 2016 with relegation at Colchester and in August of that year he opened a hairdressing business, Mr Barbers, in Ipswich.

Season	Division	League		FA Cup		FL Cup		Total	
		A	G	A	G	A	G	A	G
2005-06	Premier	19 (9)	3	1 (2)	0	2	1	22 (11)	4
2006-07 (R)	Premier	21 (5)	3	1	0	1 (2)	0	23 (7)	3
2007-08	Championship	29 (8)	7	2	1	2 (1)	1	33 (9)	9
2008-09 (R)	Championship	9 (12)	0	2	1	0	0	11 (12)	1
Total		78 (34)	13	6 (2)	2	5 (3)	2	89 (39)	17

UK LEAGUE CAREER 336 games 59 goals

CHARLTON CAREER

Managers: *A Curbishley, I Dowie, L Reed, A Pardew, P Parkinson*

Debut: *Sunderland (A) 13-08-2005*

V626

Finale: *Coventry City (A) (sub) 13-04-2009*

AMMANN Michael Anton   1994 - 96

Goalkeeper   14st 4lbs   6' 3"
Born: 08-02-1971 - Orange, California USA
Education: Mater Dei High School, Santa Ana, USA. California State University, Fullerton, USA.

Mike was a promising high school kicker for the Monarchs football team, but soccer was his number one sport and he was reckoned to be one of the best goalkeepers to come out of Orange County, California. He went to University in 1990 and for four years played on the men's soccer team for the Titans, who represented the California State University in Fullerton. In 1993, they progressed to the Final Four of the NCAA, an American national intercollegiate soccer tournament. He was spotted by Charlton director, Mike Stevens and invited to travel to London for a trial and signed for the club on 20th July 1994. His older brother, Bob Ammann was also a talented goalkeeper but both Brighton and Watford failed in their attempts to secure a work permit for him.

HONOURS

Kansas City Wizards 1996 Runners Up MSL Western Conference   MetroStars 2000 Winners MSL Eastern Conference
Kansas City Wizards 1997 Winners MSL Western Conference

CLUBS

Los Angeles Heat, USA 1989 ••Cal State Fullerton Titans, USA 1990 ••East Los Angeles Cobras, USA 1993 ••Charlton Athletic 20.07.94 (free) ••Kansas City Wizards, USA 06.96 ••MetroStars, USA 02.99 ••D C United, USA 2001

Mike was thrown in at the deep end at Charlton, making his debut only a month after signing, when he took over from the injured Mike Salmon against Barnsley during the opening home game of 1994-95. He managed to record 19 league appearances that season, despite fierce competition for the goalkeeping jersey from not only Salmon but also Andy Petterson, who had joined from Luton five days

before Mike and the same situation continued the following season when all three men again appeared in the first team.

He returned to the US in the summer of 1996 and performed credibly in Major League Soccer for several years. In 2000, whilst playing for the New York team MetroStars, he suffered three broken ribs, a punctured lung and concussion following a collision with a Tampa Bay Mutiny player, but recovered in time to take part in the play offs five weeks later against Chicago Fire and keep a clean sheet. His performances in his two seasons with MetroStars saw him voted MSL Defensive Player of the Year both times.

Further injuries forced his retirement in 2002 and as a result of botched medical treatment he was left with a permanent disability to both arms. The doctor who operated on him was later found guilty of medical malpractice by a jury in Washington. In 2003, Mike started work as a data storage salesman in California but was eventually drawn back to soccer and in 2010 opened a goalkeeping academy in Virginia and has since worked alongside John Robinson, both men engineering programmes to develop young footballers and help them to fulfil their potential.

Season	Division	League		FA Cup		FL Cup		Total	
		A	G	A	G	A	G	A	G
1994-95	Division 1	18 (1)	0	0	0	0	0	18 (1)	0
1995-96	Division 1	10 (1)	0	0	0	1	0	11 (1)	0
Total		28 (2)	0	0	0	1	0	29 (2)	0

UK LEAGUE CAREER 30 games 0 goals

CHARLTON CAREER
Managers: *A Curbishley/S Gritt, A Curbishley*
Debut: *Barnsley (H) (sub) 20-08-1994*
V545
Finale: *Norwich City (A) 30-05-1996*

AMOS Benjamin Paul   2017 - 21

Ben entered the record books in 2017-18 as the first and so far the only loan player to appear through a complete league season for Charlton without missing a game. He was on a sabbatical from Bolton Wanderers and his consistency during 46 league and two play off matches made him an important part of the side which only just fell short of achieving promotion back to the Championship.

Goalkeeper   11st 0lbs   6' 3"
Born: 10-04-1990 - Macclesfield, Cheshire
Education: Fallibroome High School, Macclesfield.

HONOURS

England U21 International 2011-12 3 caps 0 goals
England U20 International 2009 1 cap 0 goals
England U19 International 2008 2 caps 0 goals
England U18 International 2008 3 caps 0 goals

England U17 International 2005-07 7 caps 0 goals
England U16 International 2004-05 3 caps 0 goals
Hull City 2012-13 Runners Up Championship.

CLUBS

Crewe Alexandra (youth) ••Manchester United 2001 (youth) 05.01.08 (pro) ••Peterborough United 29.10.09 (loan) ••Molde FK, Norway 02.10 (loan) ••Oldham Athletic 07.01.11 (loan) ••Hull City 31.07.12 (loan) ••Carlisle United 15.11.13 (loan) ••Bolton Wanderers 30.01.15 (loan) 01.07.15 (free) ••Cardiff City 26.08.16 (loan) ••Charlton Athletic 29.07.17 (loan) ••Millwall 13.07.18 (loan) ••Charlton Athletic 15.07.19 (free) ••Wigan Athletic 28.06.21 (free)

No player spends more than a decade at Manchester United unless he shows exceptional talent and Ben, a local boy from Macclesfield, advanced all the way through the youth system and made his debut in goal against Middlesbrough in a League Cup match on 23rd September 2008 at the age of 18. First team opportunities were few and far between however, although he did keep a clean sheet in his one Premier League appearance against Stoke more than three years later.

There were loan spells with a variety of lower division clubs and three months playing for Molde FK in the Tippeligaen, the top division in Norwegian football, but Ben was unable to force his way into the Manchester United first team and eventually moved on to Bolton Wanderers in 2015. This was probably not an inspired choice as they were struggling on the field and although he played regularly in 2015-16, the club finished bottom of the Championship, 19 points from safety and were relegated along with Charlton, who had fared only slightly better.

Ex-Charlton 'keeper Ben Alnwick was signed by Bolton in August 2016 and this heralded the end of Amos's time in the first team. With three years remaining on his contract, he spent 2016-17 with Cardiff City and the following campaign on loan at the Valley. After taking a little time to settle, his form with Charlton dramatically improved over the season and in the last 12 league games, he only conceded six goals as the team made a late run into the play offs.

His loan was not renewed for 2018-19, so Ben missed out on Charlton's promotion from League One and spent a less rewarding time battling against relegation with Millwall. When his contract with Bolton finally expired in the summer of 2019, he re-joined Charlton but spent a

whole season on the bench as back-up for Dillon Phillips. In 2020-21 he regained his place in the team and was again ever present when the Addicks narrowly failed to reach the League One play offs. In June 2021 Ben declined a new contract and preferring to return north, signed for Wigan Athletic.

Season	Division	League		FA Cup		FL Cup		FL Trophy		Play Offs		Total	
		A	G	A	G	A	G	A	G	A	G	A	G
2017-18	League One	46	0	2	0	0	0	0		0	2	0	50	0
2019-20 (R)	Championship	0	0	0	0	1	0					1	0
2020-21	League One	46	0	0	0	2	0	0	0			48	0
Total		92	0	2	0	3	0	0	0	2	0	99	0

UK LEAGUE CAREER 213 games 0 goals

CHARLTON CAREER
Managers: *K Robinson, L Bowyer, N Adkins*
Debut: *Bristol Rovers (H) 05-08-2017*
V842
Finale: *Hull City (H) 09-05-2021*

ANDERSEN Stephan Maigaard   2005 - 06

Goalkeeper   13st 0lbs   6' 3"
Born: 26-11-1981 - Copenhagen, Denmark

Stephan was a very fine goalkeeper who spent a couple of years at Charlton during the later stages of the Alan Curbishley regime. He was already a full Danish international before he arrived in the UK, having played alongside Claus Jensen in a 2-0 defeat by Spain on 31st March 2004. He was selected for the Danish squad at UEFA Euro 2004, but did not in fact get called upon to play for his country again until 2008, long after his time in the UK was over. However, he eventually earned 30 caps, including an excellent performance against the Netherlands in UEFA Euro 2012, in which he kept a clean sheet as the Danish side, which then also included Dennis Rommedahl, won 1-0.

HONOURS
Denmark International 2004-15 30 caps 0 goals
Denmark U21 International 2001-03 21 caps 0 goals
Denmark U20 International 2002 5 caps 0 goals
Charlton Athletic Reserves 2004-05 Winners Premier Reserve League (South)
Brondby IF 2006-07 Winners Royal League

Brondby IF 2007-08 Winners Danish Cup
FC Copenhagen 2014-15 Runners Up Danish Superliga
FC Copenhagen 2014-15 & 2016-17 Winners Danish Cup
FC Copenhagen 2015-16 Winners Danish Superliga

CLUBS
Hvidovre, Denmark (youth) ••Brondby IF, Denmark (youth) ••Hvidovre, Denmark 1999 (pro) ••AB Copenhagen, Denmark 08.02 (free) ••Charlton Athletic 24.05.04 (£721,000) ••Brondby IF, Denmark 29.11.06 (£300,000) ••Evian TG, France 16.08.11 (£150,000) ••Real Betis, Spain 10.06.13 (free) ••Go Ahead Eagles, Netherlands 30.01.14 (loan) ••FC Copenhagen, Denmark 19.05.14 (free)

Season 2003-04 was a disastrous one for AB Copenhagen who finished bottom of the Danish Superliga, but even in a relegation side, the form of young goalkeeper Stephan Andersen caught the eye and in June 2004 he signed for Charlton for a transfer fee that was reported at DKK 8 million, the sterling equivalent of which was £721,000. He joined a team now established in the Premier League and with Dean Kiely playing consistently well in goal, opportunities were always going to be limited. In fact Stephan had to wait until the end of his first season before his chance came and this proved to be a baptism of fire as

Charlton were comprehensively outplayed and went down 4-0 against Manchester United on 1st May 2005.
With Kiely injured, he commenced 2005-06 in the side and they got off to an amazing start, winning all the first four Premier League matches, including a 3-0 victory at Middlesbrough, while only conceding one goal. This was never going to be maintained however and by the end of October they had dropped away into mid-table, but not before an unexpected League Cup win at Stamford Bridge on 26th October. Charlton held a 1-1 scoreline through extra time and then won the penalty shoot out 5-4, only for

Chelsea's manager Jose Mourinho to disregard the result, claiming that the penalties did not really count and in his opinion their unbeaten home record was still intact.
A series of defeats in November and the return of Dean Kiely heralded the end of Stephan's run in the Charlton side. His final match was a replay of his debut. On 7th May 2006 and in front of an Old Trafford crowd of 73,006, Manchester United overwhelmed them and the result was another 4-0 score. Although he remained at the Valley for a further six months, there was no more first team action and a proposed loan move to Leeds United in August was cancelled when Charlton insisted on a recall clause.

He eventually departed back to Denmark and joined Brondby IF, with whom he won the Danish Cup in 2007 and subsequent moves found him plying his trade in France and Spain, before controversially signing for Brondby's arch rivals FC Copenhagen in May 2014. He was cruelly barracked and coins were thrown at him when the two teams met, but got his revenge on 25th May 2017 when at the age of 35 he played in the FC Copenhagen side that defeated Brondby 3-1 in the Danish Cup Final. No longer first choice 'keeper he remained part of the first team squad in 2021.

Season	Division	League		FA Cup		FL Cup		Total	
		A	G	A	G	A	G	A	G
2004-05	Premier	2	0	0	0	0	0	2	0
2005-06	Premier	15	0	0	0	1	0	16	0
Total		17	0	0	0	1	0	18	0

UK LEAGUE CAREER 17 games 0 goals

CHARLTON CAREER
Managers: *A Curbishley*
Debut: *Manchester United (H) 01-05-2005*
V623
Finale: *Manchester United (A) 07-05-2006*

ANDERSON Darren Irwin   1984 - 85

A big strong centre half, Darren made an impressive start, representing his country in 1983 at U16 level and playing alongside Tony Adams at the heart of the England defence. They made third

Defender   13 st 5 lbs   6' 1"
Born: 06-09-1966 - Wimbledon, London
Education: Pelham High School, Wimbledon.

place in the 1984 U16 European Championships in West Germany. Later he progressed to U17 and was also capped twice at youth (U18) level. He signed professional terms for Charlton at the age of 17 and did not have long to wait for his first team debut, being thrown in the deep end for the final game of 1983-84, which was a 1-0 defeat up at Leeds,

HONOURS
England Youth International 1984 2 caps 0 goals
England U17 International 1984 4 caps 1 goal

England U16 International 1983-84 7 caps 2 goals
Aldershot 1986-87 Promoted Play Offs Division 4

CLUBS
Queens Park Rangers 17.08.82 (youth) ••Coventry City 1983 (youth) ••Charlton Athletic 28.02.84 (non contract) 10.03.84 (pro) ••Crewe Alexandra 10.85 (loan) ••Aldershot 04.86 (free) ••Slough Town 08.90 (free) ••Sutton United 01.10.93 (free) ••Staines Town 1996 (free)

Darren got a run of nine games in the Charlton side during the 1984-85 season and even netted a late equaliser at Shrewsbury in a 1-1 draw on 9th March, but obviously did not impress manager Lennie Lawrence sufficiently to be included in his plans for the future. He was not involved with the squad that would ultimately gain promotion back to Division 1 and instead was packed off for a short loan spell at Crewe Alexandra in October 1985.
He never got another chance with Charlton after Steve Thompson and John Pender became fixtures in the centre

of defence and moved on to Aldershot the following summer, where he spent a reasonably productive four years, including 1986-87 in which he and his former Charlton colleague Paul Friar helped them to promotion from Division 4 in the first season of the play offs.
Since retiring from football, Darren has worked for several years as an enforcement officer and bailiff. In 2018, he additionally set up Direct Approach Property Services, relocation specialists, based in Worcester Park, Surrey.

Season	Division	League		FA Cup		FL Cup		Total	
		A	G	A	G	A	G	A	G
1983-84	Division 2	1	0	0	0	0	0	1	0
1984-85	Division 2	9	1	0	0	0	0	9	1
Total		10	1	0	0	0	0	10	1

UK LEAGUE CAREER 113 games 5 goals

CHARLTON CAREER
Managers: *L Lawrence*
Debut: *Leeds United (A) 12-05-1984*
V455
Finale: *Huddersfield Town (A) 30-03-1985*

ANDERSON Terrique Dominic Hall   2018

Forward   5' 6"
Born: 11-11-1998 - Lambeth, London

Terrique's only first team appearance for Charlton came at the Valley on 13th November 2018. He entered the field as substitute for Brendan Sarpong-Wiredu after 74 minutes of the League Trophy match against Swansea City U21's in front of a pitiful crowd of only 740. The Trophy, at that time sponsored by Checkatrade, was notoriously unpopular with supporters and there was considerable speculation that this match would see Charlton's lowest ever home crowd. Several people attended the game just so they could be participants in creating this unwelcome record and this threatened to be self defeating, but in the end the previous figure of 793 for the Trophy match earlier in the season against Stevenage was never reached and a new record set.

HONOURS
Charlton Athletic U18 2015-16 Runners Up PD League 2 South   Charlton Athletic U23 2017-18 Runners Up PD League 2 South
Charlton Athletic U18 2015-16 Winners PD National League 2

CLUBS
Junior Elite (youth) ••Charlton Athletic 2015 (youth) 09.05.17 (pro) ••East Grinstead 21.01.20 (free) ••South Park 11.09.21 (free)

A speedy and agile forward, Terrique joined Charlton at the age of 16 and played regularly in the U18 team during season 2015-16. The following campaign was largely lost to him through injury, but he had made sufficient impact to earn himself a two-year professional contract in May 2017 and then continued to progress with regular games at U23 level.

The day after his cameo appearance for the first team, Terrique played against Bromley and scored twice in a Kent Senior Cup tie, but no further opportunities came his way and shortly after promotion from League One was spectacularly won via the Wembley final in May 2019, his name appeared on the list of players to be released as Charlton prepared for life back in the Championship. He is currently playing for the Reigate based club, South Park, in the Isthmian League.

Season	Division	League		FA Cup		FL Cup		FL Trophy		Play Offs		Total	
		A	G	A	G	A	G	A	G	A	G	A	G
2018-19 (P)	League One	0	0	0	0	0	0	0 (1)	0	0	0	0 (1)	0
Total		0	0	0	0	0	0	0 (1)	0	0	0	0 (1)	0

UK LEAGUE CAREER 0 games 0 goals

CHARLTON CAREER
Managers: *L Bowyer*
Debut: *Swansea City U21 (H) (sub) 19-11-2018*
V870

ANEKE Chukwuemeka Ademola Amachi   2019 -

Big Chuks signed for Charlton during Summer 2019, having finished the previous season among the leading goalscorers in League Two. His tally of 17 had helped Milton Keynes Dons to promotion via the play offs and it was hoped that he would cope with the higher standard of the Championship and achieve similar results for his new club. Regrettably he never got properly match fit nor was able to show more than glimpses of his best form. It was not until his second season that he got a run of games (although usually starting from the bench) but then the goals did start to flow.

Forward, Midfield   13st 1lb   6' 3"
Born: 03-07-1993 - Canning Town, London
Education: St Bonaventure's School, Forest Gate.

HONOURS

England U19 International 2011 1 cap 0 goals
England U18 International 2010 1 cap 0 goals
England U17 International 2009-10 7 caps 3 goals

England U16 International 2008 5 caps 0 goals
Crewe Alexandra 2012-13 Winners Football League Trophy
Milton Keynes Dons 2018-19 Promoted Play Offs League Two

CLUBS

Arsenal 2001 (youth) 07.10 (pro) ••Stevenage 23.11.11 (loan) ••Preston North End 22.03.12 (loan) ••Crewe Alexandra 08.09.12 (loan) 02.08.13 (loan) ••SV Zulte Waregem, Belgium 21.06.14 (free) ••Milton Keynes Dons 02.08.16 (undisclosed) ••Charlton Athletic 28.06.19 (free) ••Birmingham City 25.06.21 (free) ••Charlton Athletic 14.01.22 (£300,000)

An East London boy from a Nigerian family, Chuks spent 13 years with Arsenal and progressed all the way through their youth academy, but like so many other young footballers, he was never given a real chance in the first team. All he had to show for his efforts was a stoppage time cameo appearance in a League Cup tie against Shrewsbury Town. He was recognised on the international stage however and represented England at the various age groups up to and including the Under 19's for whom he played on 1st September 2011 in a 0-0 draw with the Netherlands. It took loans at Stevenage, Preston and Crewe to kick-start his club career, but when he did eventually break free from Arsenal in June 2014, he rather surprisingly signed for the Belgian club Zulte Waregem.

It was surprising because he had no language skills and it was a cultural shock moving to a foreign country where at the age of 21 he was unable to express himself and admits to having struggled just to order his own breakfast. Despite injury problems he stuck it out for two years of his three-year contract and even scored in the UEFA Europa League

as the Polish side Zawisza Bydgoszcz were beaten over two legs.

Until he signed for Milton Keynes Dons, Chuks had not always played as an out and out striker, but since his goal success in 2018-19, he had been viewed more as a target man. He lacks pace but has considerable skill to go with his undoubted strength and size. He eventually delivered 15 goals for Charlton in 2020-21, despite ongoing fitness concerns that restricted him to a good deal less than 90 minutes on the field in the majority of his games. With his contract at an end he turned down a new deal in the summer of 2021 and instead followed his old boss, Lee Bowyer, to Birmingham City.

The grass is not always greener and only seven months later he was back in SE7, a transfer fee believed to be in the region of £300,000 had changed hands and he had re-joined Charlton until 2025. On 15th January 2022 he capped his second Charlton debut with a last second equaliser to ensure a 1-1 draw at Cheltenham Town.

Season	Division	League		FA Cup		FL Cup		FL Trophy		Total	
		A	G	A	G	A	G	A	G	A	G
2019-20 (R)	Championship	2 (18)	1	0	0	1	0			3 (18)	1
2020-21	League One	11 (27)	15	1	0	0 (2)	0	0	0	12 (29)	15
Total		13 (45)	16	1	0	1 (2)	0	0	0	15 (47)	16

UK LEAGUE CAREER 225 games 67 goals

CHARLTON CAREER
Managers: L Bowyer, N Adkins, J Jackson
Debut: *Stoke City (H) (sub) 10-08-2019*
V878

ANYINSAH Joseph Greene   2010 - 11

Forward   12st 8lbs   5' 8"
Born: 08-10-1984 - Bristol
Education: Clifton College, Bristol (sports science)

Joe had considerable ability but never really settled long enough with any club to fully express himself. He joined the Bristol City academy at age nine and developed into a skilful and pacey forward, eventually moving around eight League clubs. He should have achieved more in his career, but when fit was always a potential match winner.

HONOURS
Carlisle United 2009-10 Finalists Football League Trophy

CLUBS
Bristol City c1994 (youth) 24.10.01 (pro) ••Hereford United 01.05 (loan) ••Preston North End 13.07.05 (free) ••Bury 09.02.06 (loan) ••Carlisle United 20.09.07 (loan) ••Crewe Alexandra 07.03.08 (loan) ••Brighton & Hove Albion 11.09.08 (loan) ••Carlisle United 09.01.09 (free) ••Charlton Athletic 31.08.10 (free) ••Bristol Rovers 06.07.11 (free) ••Wrexham 01.08.13 (free) ••Hayes & Yeading 06.08.14 (free)

It was probably inconsistency that hampered Joe's career as he certainly had the raw talent, but until his second spell at Carlisle United, he never got a decent run of matches. In 2009-10 he did at last get to compete in the majority of games and found the net on 11 occasions, including the winner, when Carlisle unexpectedly beat Leeds United 2-1 at Elland Road in the Northern final of the Football League Trophy. At that time it was sponsored by Johnstone's Paint and despite the reported apathy towards the competition, a crowd of 73,476 turned up at Wembley for the National final. Joe made an appearance from the sub's bench, but Southampton proved too strong on the day and were worthy winners 4-1. Five months later he came south and signed for Charlton.

Joe made an immediate impact at the Valley, entering the field as a substitute and scoring the winning goal on his debut against Notts County. In September, he featured in an exciting 4-3 win up at Carlisle. He scored during the first half and shortly after the interval Charlton were in a 3-0 lead, only to concede three goals, before Paul Benson grabbed a stoppage time winner. As the season went on however, Joe's performances lacked consistency, although he was always an attacking threat and difficult to knock off the ball. A series of injuries and the arrival of Bradley Wright-Phillips reduced his first team opportunities and he was not offered a further contract at the end of the 2010-11 season. He then spent two years with Bristol Rovers, before dropping into non-league.

By 2015, Joe was working as a prison officer and has since become a re-settlement caseworker, helping and mentoring young offenders. He is also a director of LSM, an FA licensed football intermediary.

Season	Division	League		FA Cup		FL Cup		FL Trophy		Total	
		A	G	A	G	A	G	A	G	A	G
2010-11	League One	14 (5)	3	4	2	0	0	0 (1)	0	18 (6)	5
Total		14 (5)	3	4	2	0	0	0 (1)	0	18 (6)	5

UK LEAGUE CAREER 175 games 27 goals

CHARLTON CAREER
Managers: *P Parkinson, C Powell*
Debut: *Notts County (H) (sub) 11-09-2010*
V713
Finale: *Rochdale (A) 29-03-2011*

AOUACHRIA Wassim   2020 -

It was a significant personal triumph for Wassim, when the young French Algerian made his Charlton debut at the Valley on 10th November 2020 in the Football League Trophy match against Leyton Orient. He had missed almost all the previous season following a torn anterior cruciate ligament incurred while training and celebrated his big chance by scoring the opening goal in a 3-1 win. Although he was replaced after 72 minutes by another young forward, Dylan Gavin, his performance was encouraging and confirmed that he has a promising future if he can steer clear of further injuries.

Forward
Born: 12-03-2000 - Roubaix, France

HONOURS
Algeria U18 International 2018 3 caps 0 goals

CLUBS
Aubagne, France 2006 (youth) ••Olympique Marseille, France 2013 (youth) ••Charlton Athletic 08.01.19 (pro) ••Aldershot Town 31.08.21 (loan) ••Braintree Town 11.12.21 (loan) ••Hampton & Richmond Borough 18.03.22 (loan)

Wassim joined Marseille at the age of 13 and made rapid progress. In June 2018 he represented Algeria at U18 level in the Mediterranean Games in Spain and seven months later signed a short term contract with Charlton. He had already found the net five times in nine matches for the U23's before his injury and his contract was later twice renewed to take him up to the end of season 2021-22. This bought him the time to progress his career and try to find a place in the first team squad. Since August 2021 he has enjoyed loan spells with National League teams, Aldershot Town and Braintree.

Season	Division	League		FA Cup		FL Cup		FL Trophy		Total	
		A	G	A	G	A	G	A	G	A	G
2020-21	League One	0	0	0	0	0	0	1	1	1	1
Total		0	0	0	0	0	0	1	1	1	1

UK LEAGUE CAREER 0 games 0 goals

CHARLTON CAREER
Managers: *L Bowyer, N Adkins, J Jackson*
Debut: *Leyton Orient (H) 10-11-2020*
V912

APPLETON Colin Harry   1966 - 67

Colin was selected in the 18-man squad for the England FA's grandly named 'World Tour' in May and June 1961. 11 matches were

Midfield   11st 10lbs   5' 9"
Born: 07-03-1936 - Scarborough, North Yorkshire
Died: 31-05-2021 - Scarborough, North Yorkshire
Education: Northstead Primary School and Scarborough Secondary Modern School.

played and won in five different countries and he appeared in most of them, including those against Malaya (4-2), Singapore (9-0), Hong Kong (4-2) and New Zealand (6-1). They also travelled to the USA and the final match took place in San Francisco. In addition, he represented the Football League against the Irish League at Norwich on 31st October 1962, winning 3-1, thanks to a hat trick from future Charlton striker Ray Crawford.

HONOURS
FA World Tour 1961
Football League XI 1962 1 cap
North Riding Youth XI 1953
Leicester City 1956-57 Winners Division 2

Leicester City 1960-61 & 1962-63 Runners Up FA Cup
Leicester City 1963-64 Winners League Cup
Leicester City 1964-65 Runners Up League Cup
Scarborough 1972-73 Winners FA Trophy

HONOURS AS MANAGER

Scarborough 1975-76 & 1976-77 Winners FA Trophy   Hull City 1982-83 Runners Up Division 4
Scarborough 1976-77 Winners Northern Premier League Cup

CLUBS

Scarborough 1951 (youth) 1953 (amateur) ••Leicester City 19.03.54 (pro) ••Charlton Athletic 26.05.66 (£7,500) ••Barrow 03.08.67 (player manager £4,000) ••Scarborough 18.06.69 (player manager) 05.73 (manager) ••Grimsby Town 01.11.73 (coach) ••Scarborough 06.75 (manager) ••Hull City 08.06.82 (manager) ••Swansea City 16.05.84 (manager) ••Exeter City 04.06.85 (manager) ••Bridlington Town 1988 (manager) ••Hull City 22.05.89 (manager)

The lion's share of Colin's career was spent with Leicester City for whom he made more than 300 appearances, captaining them to four cup finals during his 12 years with the club. The FA Cup campaigns of 1961 and 1963 both ended in disappointment, but in season 1963-64, both Colin and Ian King helped bring Leicester their first major honour as they triumphed over Stoke City in a two legged final of the Football League Cup. They nearly repeated the feat the following season, but were narrowly beaten by Chelsea over the two games.

He was transferred to Charlton in May 1966, joining his Leicester teammate Ian King who had arrived a couple of months earlier. It was reasonable to assume that two such experienced players would prove real assets, but in truth neither man enhanced his reputation and the form of Appleton in particular was a disappointment. His stay in SE 7 was limited to just one season before he moved back

up North and joined Barrow as player manager.

By 1973, Colin was still occupying the dual roles of player manager, but back with his hometown club, Scarborough. He led them all the way to Wembley in the FA Trophy, neatly rounding off his playing career on 28th April with victory over Wigan Athletic, 2-1 after extra time. Later he returned to Wembley twice more as Scarborough's manager, making it a hat trick of FA Trophy successes. He returned to the Football League as manager of Hull City, guided them to promotion from Division 4 in 1982-83 and continued on the managerial merry go round until 1989 when a second spell at Hull ended badly. This brought to a close Colin's 46-year career in football and he retired back to live near Scarborough until his death in 2021 at the age of 85. In 2014 a book, 'The Colin Appleton Story' was published by McRay Press.

Season	Division	League		FA Cup		FL Cup		Total	
		A	G	A	G	A	G	A	G
1966-67	Division 2	28	1	1	0	0	0	29	1
Total		28	1	1	0	0	0	29	1

UK LEAGUE CAREER 348 games 21 goals

CHARLTON CAREER
Managers: *R Stokoe*
Debut: *Cardiff City (H) 24-09-1966*
V325
Finale: *Birmingham City (H) 12-05-1967*

ARIBO Joseph Oluwaseyi Ternitope Ayodele   2016 - 19

Midfield   11st 13lbs   6' 0"
Born: 21-07-1996 - Camberwell, London

In his near four-year spell at Charlton, Joe matured from a raw teenager with a strong work ethic and an abundance of natural talent, into a top class midfield player and his performances during season 2018-19 attracted the attention of several other clubs both at home and abroad. His form during the later stages of that promotion campaign was sometimes devastating and his goal at Doncaster on 12th May in the first leg of the play off semi-final proved vital as the team battled towards a never to be forgotten Wembley final.

HONOURS

Nigeria International 2019-22 14 caps 2 goals   Charlton Athletic 2018-19 Promoted Play Offs League One
Charlton Athletic 2018 Young Player Of The Year   Rangers 2019-20 Runners Up Scottish Premier League
Charlton Athletic U21 2015-16 Winners PD League 2 South   Rangers 2019-20 Finalists Scottish League Cup
Charlton Athletic U21 2015-16 Finalists Kent Senior Cup   Rangers 2020-21 Winners Scottish Premier League
Charlton Athletic U23 2016-17 Winners U23 PD League 2 South

CLUBS

Kinetic Academy 2012 (youth) ••Staines Town 2014 (pro) ••Charlton Athletic 01.09.15 (free) ••Rangers, Scotland 27.06.19 (free)

Joe was a comparative latecomer into the professional game, only breaking into the first team at Staines Town during 2014-15. Although they finished the season bottom of the Football Conference South, his personal contribution was such that he was recommended to Jason Euell at Charlton and after a two-month trial became a key member of the U21 side which finished champions of the Professional Development League 2 South in 2015-16.

Only a year later he was part of the first team squad and by 2017-18 was a regular in the centre of midfield as the club chased promotion from League One, while his increasing maturity on the field was acknowledged when he was voted the Young Player of the Year for 2018. It was in the promotion season when he really came into his own under the watchful eye of manager Lee Bowyer, with his

performances underlining the fact that he had outgrown the third tier of English football. The earlier decision by the club not to place him on a longer contract proved costly when in June 2019 he became a free agent and chose to sign for Rangers rather than stay and help Charlton consolidate their place in the Championship.

Since moving to Scotland, Joe has become a fixture in the Rangers side and in 2020-21 helped them to overcome a nine-year period of dominance by Celtic and regain the Scottish Premier League title by an incredible 25 point margin. He has also become a Nigerian international and participated in the 2022 African Cup of Nations. Most recently he has acquired a hyphen and possibly in recognition of his Nigerian parentage is now being referred to as Joe Ayodele-Aribo.

Season	Division	League		FA Cup		FL Cup		FL Trophy		Play Offs		Total	
		A	G	A	G	A	G	A	G	A	G	A	G
2016-17	League One	13 (6)	0	1	0	0	0	1 (1)	0			15 (7)	0
2017-18	League One	19 (7)	5	1	0	2	0	5	1	1 (1)	0	28 (8)	6
2018-19 (P)	League One	35 (1)	9	0	0	0	0	0	0	3	1	38 (1)	10
Total		67 (14)	14	2	0	2	0	6 (1)	1	4 (1)	1	81 (16)	16

UK LEAGUE CAREER 139 games 24 goals

CHARLTON CAREER
Managers: *G Luzon, K Fraeye, J Riga, R Slade, K Robinson, L Bowyer*
Debut: *Crawley Town (H) (sub) 04-10-2016*
V833
Finale: *Sunderland (N) 26-05-2019*

ARMITAGE George Henry 'Tishy'   1924 - 30

George "Tishy" Armitage was one of the leading amateur footballers of the 1920s and became Charlton's third full England International when on 24th October 1925 (not 1926, as has been widely reported), he appeared in the 0-0 draw

Defender, Forward   11st 9lbs   5' 10"
Born: 17-01-1898 - Stoke Newington, London
Died: 28-08-1936 - Aylesford, Kent
Education: Wordsworth Road School, Hackney.

against Ireland at Windsor Park. He also earned five Amateur International caps, the last two against Wales and Ireland, also in 1925 whilst at Charlton. During the 1920s it was usual for the FA Charity Shield to be contested between representative teams of Amateurs and Professionals and on two occasions George participated in these matches. The Amateurs went down 2-0 in 1923, when he was a Wimbledon player, but ran out 6-1 winners at White Hart Lane in 1925.

HONOURS

England International 1925 1 cap 0 goals
England Amateur International 1923-25 5 caps
Charlton Athletic 1928-29 Winners Division 3 (S)
Wimbledon 1920-21 Runners Up Athenian League
London FA 1921-23 6 caps

Surrey FA
Amateurs XI 1923 Runners Up FA Charity Shield
Amateurs XI 1925 Winners FA Charity Shield
London Amateurs XI 1926 Lord KInnaird Memorial Match

CLUBS

St Saviours (Chelsea) ••Wimbledon 23.08.19 ••Charlton Athletic 12.03.24 (amateur) ••Leyton 01.31

George's life started and finished in tragic circumstances. In 1910 his father, a milk carrier, who was violent when drunk, committed suicide by taking poison after having spent time in prison for watering down the milk. His mother passed away three years later leaving young George to be brought up in Isleworth by his sister.

He showed outstanding promise as a footballer from an early age and represented Hackney Schools in 1912-13. He volunteered for the Army in November 1914, claiming his age to be 18 and not 16 and served throughout the First World War, spending time in France and as part of the Anglo French force who went to Greece in 1916 to assist the Serbs. Later he was promoted to the rank of corporal, but was eventually invalided out of the Army on 21st April 1919 suffering with tuberculosis.

When his health recovered, George returned to football and joined Wimbledon where he played initially as a centre forward, while at the same time working as a railway audit clerk. He scored a hat trick against Pearl Assurance in the FA Cup and claimed some 20 goals during 1919-20 before converting to centre half and the following season helped Wimbledon to the runners-up position in the Athenian League at a time when the standard of amateur football was extremely high. He was capped by Surrey FA and appeared six times for London FA, including three representative matches out in Sweden in July 1923.

George signed for Charlton in March 1924 and went straight into the first team for the remainder of that traumatic season, playing against Bournemouth on 3rd May in the final match at the Mount, prior to the return to the Valley for 1924-25. He was a fixture in the Charlton team for the next five seasons as the fortunes of the club slowly improved and captained them to their first Football League promotion in 1929 as champions of Division 3 South, eventually transferring to Leyton in January 1931, where he became the club captain and later, a member of their committee.

By 1936 George and his wife Elsie were living in The Drive, Beckenham, but his health had deteriorated through a recurrence of the wartime tuberculosis and he was admitted to the Preston Hall Sanatorium at Barming, near Maidstone. He became depressed by the illness and discharged himself against medical advice. The following day on 28th August he ran out in front of the 13.08 Maidstone East train at Allington and was killed instantly. The inquest concluded suicide whilst of unsound mind.

In October 2017, George's great nephew Phil Taylor, presented to the Charlton Museum one of his England caps, which is now proudly displayed as a tribute to one of the club's first great heroes.

Season	Division	League		FA Cup		Total	
		A	G	A	G	A	G
1923-24	Divison 3 (S)	8	0	0	0	8	0
1924-25	Divison 3 (S)	32	1	3	0	35	1
1925-26	Divison 3 (S)	31	1	4	0	35	1
1926-27	Divison 3 (S)	28	1	2	0	30	1
1927-28	Divison 3 (S)	27	1	2	0	29	1
1928-29 (P)	Divison 3 (S)	30	0	2	0	32	0
1929-30	Division 2	9	0	4	0	13	0
Total		165	4	17	0	182	4

UK LEAGUE CAREER 165 games 4 goals

CHARLTON CAREER
Managers: *W Rayner, A MacFarlane, A Lindon, A MacFarlane*
Debut: *Brighton & Hove Albion (A) 15-03-1924*
V057
Finale: *Swansea Town (H) 18-04-1930*

ARNOLD John Walter Leonard   1973

Charlton were stuck mid-table in Division 3 as the 1972-73 season moved towards a close. One of the few highlights of this

Forward   11st 4lbs   5' 10''
Born: 06-12-1954 - Deptford, London
Education: Beaufoy School, Kennington & South East London College of Education.

mediocre campaign had been the signing of winger Colin Powell from non-league Barnet in January. His form promised much for the future but he was absent for the Good Friday fixture at Vicarage Road on 20th April 1973 and his number seven shirt was passed instead to 18-year-old John Arnold who made his debut in the 1-1 draw against a Watford side that included Powell's predecessor on the Charlton wing, Mike Kenning. An early goal from Arthur Horsfield raised the expectation levels of the away supporters, but a second half Watford goal decreed that the points would be shared.

CLUBS

Charterhouse Boys (youth) ••Charlton Athletic 27.06.68 (youth) 07.03.73 (pro) ••Dover 01.74 (loan) 02.74 (£2,000) ••Wealdstone 07.76 ••Romford 02.77 ••Wealdstone 08.78 ••Aylesbury United 07.79 ••Erith & Belvedere 08.81 •Clapton 1992 (manager) ••Tring Town 1996 (manager)

John had only signed a professional contract the month before the Watford match and although he gave an adequate performance, Powell returned to the side for the next game which came just 24 hours later. It was not until September 1973 that he was called into action again and then only from the substitute's bench. He featured four times, the most memorable being against Blackburn Rovers at the Valley. That was an evening match in front of a paltry crowd of 4,785 during which Bob Curtis injured his ankle. John was brought on before half time as the match ebbed and flowed, Charlton twice falling behind despite goals from Dave Shipperley and Derek Hales. They rallied however and further strikes from Arthur Horsfield and

Mike Flanagan secured an unlikely 4-3 home win.
He made one final appearance, again as substitute, on 24th November in an FA Cup tie at Bournemouth before departing to Southern League club Dover in January 1974. The deal was originally set up as a loan but was quickly converted to a permanent transfer. John later turned out for Wealdstone and Romford. He had a trial with Dartford in August 1978 but re-joined Wealdstone instead. His last known club was Erith & Belvedere, but he re-appeared as manager of Clapton in the early nineties and with Tring Town in 1996.

Season	Division	League		FA Cup		FL Cup		Total	
		A	G	A	G	A	G	A	G
1972-73	Division 3	1	0	0	0	0	0	1	0
1973-74	Division 3	0 (4)	0	0 (1)	0	0	0	0 (5)	0
Total		1 (4)	0	0 (1)	0	0	0	1 (5)	0

UK LEAGUE CAREER 5 games 0 goals

CHARLTON CAREER
Managers: *T Foley*
Debut: *Watford (A) 20-04-1973*
V381
Finale: *AFC Bournemouth (A) (sub) 24-11-1973*

ARTER Harry Nicholas   2007 - 21

Midfield   11st 0lbs   5' 10"
Born: 28-12-1989 - Sidcup, Kent
Education: St Simon Stock Catholic School, Maidstone.

Every club can point to players that they have released at a young age and who have then gone on to be successful elsewhere. Harry Arter is a classic case and very much one that got away. For more than a decade he progressed through the Charlton youth academy, but in the end failed to impress manager Phil Parkinson sufficiently to earn a first team spot. His career blossomed after signing for AFC Bournemouth in 2010 and he went on to make nearly 100 appearances in the Premier League as well as earning several full international caps for the Republic of Ireland. His brother in law is Scott Parker who is married to Harry's sister, Carly.

HONOURS

Republic of Ireland International 2015-21 19 caps 0 goals
Republic of Ireland U19 International 2006-07 7 caps 0 goals
Republic of Ireland U17 International 2006 4 caps 0 goals
Republic of Ireland U15 International c2004
Charlton Athletic Reserves 2007-08 Runners Up Premier Reserve League

(South)
AFC Bournemouth 2012-13 Runners Up League One
AFC Bournemouth 2014-15 Winners Championship
Fulham 2019-20 Promoted Play Offs Championship

CLUBS

Charlton Athletic 1997 (youth) 07.07 (pro) ••Staines Town 11.08 (loan) ••Welling United 03.09 (loan) ••Woking 02.06.09 (free) ••AFC Bournemouth 07.06.10 (£4.000) ••Carlisle United 04.03.11 (loan) ••Cardiff City 09.08.18 (loan) ••Fulham 06.08.19 (loan) ••Nottingham Forest 22.09.20 (undisclosed) ••Charlton Athletic 31.08.21 (loan) ••Notts County 16.03.22 (loan)

A hard-working and combative midfield player, Harry's only initial appearance for Charlton first team came in an uninspiring League Cup encounter at Luton, in which he was a second half substitute for Svetoslav Todorov. They were outplayed by the home side, which included both Chris Perry and Matt Spring and did not deserve more than the resultant 3-1 cup exit. No further chances came his way and after almost a year out with chronic tendonitis, he had slipped back in the pecking order and was eventually freed at the end of season 2008-09.

Harry spent a year in non-league with Woking, where his footballing pedigree was soon apparent. They only narrowly missed promotion from the Conference South before he returned to the Football League in June 2010, having impressed AFC Bournemouth's assistant manager Jason Tindall, himself a former Charlton youth player. He joined a club on the ascendancy and participated in the journey that took them from League One into the Premiership in just three years, the second promotion being wrapped up at the Valley on 2nd May 2015 when a rampant Bournemouth side that also included Simon Francis and Yann Kermorgant, won comfortably by 3-0, the

second being scored by Harry himself. During the month of December 2014 he had scored in each of their five league matches and his powerhouse displays throughout that campaign greatly contributed to the eventual promotion. Because his grandparents came from Sligo, Harry was eligible to play international football for the Republic of Ireland and he made his full debut on 7th June 2015 in a 0-0 draw against England. To date he has clocked up 19 caps, but has not always given the impression of being fully committed to the Irish cause having declared himself unavailable for selection on several occasions.

He lost his place in the Bournemouth team in January 2018 and subsequently had spells on loan with Cardiff City and Fulham, participating in an unexpected 2019-20 promotion to the Premier League with the latter. In September 2020 he transferred to Nottingham Forest, but the biggest surprise of all came one year later when he re-signed for Charlton on a season's loan. He featured in just six matches during the first half of 2021-22 and with the considerable competition for places in midfield restricting his game time, exercised his option to discontinue the loan. On 4th January he returned to Forest.

Season	Division	League		FA Cup		FL Cup		Total	
		A	G	A	G	A	G	A	G
2007-08	Championship	0	0	0	0	0 (1)	0	0 (1)	0
Total		0	0	0	0	0 (1)	0	0 (1)	0

UK LEAGUE CAREER 303 games 31 goals

CHARLTON CAREER
Managers: *A Pardew, P Parkinson, N Adkins, J Jackson*
Debut: *Luton Town (A) (sub) 25-09-2007*
V658
Finale: *Aston Villa U21 (H) 30-11-2021*

ASHTON Nathan Wesley   2006

Nathan was an outstanding player at youth level, being capped by England on 19 occasions from Under 16 to Under 19, but failed to fulfil his potential. Instead, he allowed himself to develop a harmful and excessive gambling habit which led him to make a series of wrong decisions that left him to serve an extremely long prison sentence. His story is very much a cautionary tale of how not to behave.

Midfield, Utility.   5' 9"
Born: 30-01-1987 - Beckton, London

HONOURS

England U19 International 2005-06 3 caps 0 goals
England U18 International 2004 1 cap 0 goals
England U17 International 2004 10 caps 0 goals
England U16 International 2002-03 5 caps 0 goals
Charlton Athletic Reserves 2003-04 & 2004-05 Winners Premier Reserve

League (South)
Charlton Athletic U19 2003-04 Runners Up FA Premier Academy League
Charlton Athletic U18 2004-05 Runners Up FA Premier Academy League
Wycombe Wanderers 2008-09 Promoted League 2

CLUBS

Charlton Athletic c2002 (youth) 26.05.05 (pro) ••Fulham 23.08.07 (free) ••Crystal Palace 27.03.08 (loan) ••Wycombe Wanderers 30.07.08 (free) ••AFC Wimbledon 29.10.09 ••Aveley 11.10 ••Cray Wanderers 12.10 ••Marlow 25.01.11 ••Dover Athletic 18.03.11 ••Thurrock 12.11 ••Marlow 2012 ••Billericay Town 03.13 ••Tilbury 2013 ••Marlow 2014 (player coach) 2015 (ass. manager)

Nathan was a graduate of the Charlton youth academy and had every prospect of a worthwhile career as a professional footballer when on 19th September 2006, he made his first team debut at left back in the League Cup match with Carlisle United at the Valley. He played the full 90 minutes, Darren Bent scoring the only goal to put the Addicks through to Round 3. This however proved to be his only chance with the first team and he soon moved on first to Fulham and then to Wycombe Wanderers, where he did at least get to play a part in their 2009 promotion from League Two.

After that Nathan dropped into non-league football and during 2010 had to endure a high profile court case after being charged with the statutory rape of a 12-year-old girl. His former Charlton manager, Iain Dowie, was a character witness for him during the proceedings at Aylesbury Crown Court and he was unanimously acquitted by the jury.

In January 2011 he had a trial with the Czech team, Slovan Bratislava, but when it came to nothing he continued to drift from club to club, his career going backwards, until eventually settling with Southern League side Marlow, where he featured both as a player, coach and eventually assistant manager.

Nathan had become a heavy gambler and by 2015 had debts estimated at £100,000. He was also serving a three-month suspended sentence for stalking an ex-girl friend when the big story broke in November 2015 and he was additionally charged with a series of armed robberies. As it was later explained at Kingston Crown Court, a friend had suggested that robbing betting shops was an easy way to raise cash and presumably solve his gambling problem. He pleaded guilty to ten separate robberies and in July 2016 was sentenced to 15 years imprisonment.

It will be some time yet before he can continue his football career.

Season	Division	League		FA Cup		FL Cup		Total	
		A	G	A	G	A	G	A	G
2006-07 (R)	Championship	0	0	0	0	1	0	1	0
Total		0	0	0	0	1	0	1	0

CHARLTON CAREER
Managers: *A Curbishley, I Dowie, L Reed, A Pardew*
Debut: *Carlisle United (H) 19-09-2006*
V640

UK LEAGUE CAREER 13 games 0 goals

ASTLEY David John 'Dai'   1928 - 31

Forward   11st 11lbs   5' 11"
Born: 11-10-1909 - Dowlais, Mid Glamorgan
Died: 07-11-1989 - Birchington, Kent
Education: Central School, Dowlais.

Dai Astley had the impressive record of scoring 12 goals in his 13 appearances for Wales and was a part of the most successful Welsh team of all time and winners of back to back Home International Championships in the period 1932-34. It was his two goals in the final match against Ireland which clinched the 1933 title. He also played in four further Wartime internationals which do not feature in the record books as official appearances. Only his first Welsh cap was earned while Dai was a Charlton player, this being on 22nd April 1931 in a 3-2 win over Ireland.

HONOURS

Wales International 1931-38 13 caps 12 goals
Wales Schoolboy International 1923
Wales-Ireland Combined XI 1935

Charlton Athletic 1928-29 Winners Division 3 (S)
Aston Villa 1932-33 Runners Up Division 1

HONOURS AS MANAGER

Internazionale 1948-49 Runners Up Serie A
Djurgardens IF 1950-51 Runners Up Svenska Cupen

Sandvikens 1954-55 Winners Svenska Division 2

CLUBS

New Road Amateurs (youth) ••Dowlais Welfare 1926 ••Merthyr Town 1927 •Charlton Athletic 30.01.28 (£100) ••Aston Villa 06.06.31 (£2,750) ••Derby County 12.11.36 (£5,250) ••Blackpool 20.01.39 (free) ••Metz, France 1946 (free) ••Internazionale, Italy 1948 (manager) ••Genoa, Italy 1949 (manager) ••Djurgardens IF, Sweden 1950 (manager) ••Sandvikens, Sweden 1954 (manager)

After working at Pen-y-Darren pit in Cwm Bargoed as a youngster, Dai signed for Merthyr Town in 1927 and in only his second match played at the Valley in an FA Cup replay which Charlton won 2-1 thanks to goals from David Sherlaw and Jackie Horton. He must have played well that day as two months later Charlton paid a fee of £100 to bring him to South London, but not before the teenager had destroyed a Brentford side (including Ernie Watkins and Bill Berry) with a hat-trick on 10th December 1927. Still it is hard to imagine a less auspicious debut than the 5-0 thrashing by Millwall that greeted him when he joined Charlton, but happily things improved considerably during his second season. He was part of the promotion winning side of 1928-29 and then remained with the club a further two years as they became established for the first time in Division 2. Clearly this was a young player with a lot more to offer, but as has so often been the case at Charlton, financial pressure forced them to sell him to Aston Villa in June 1931, just weeks after playing his first

game for Wales. The directors had hoped for a fee of £4,000, but with Summer wages to be paid, were obliged to accept just £2.750

Dai enjoyed his greatest playing success with Villa who became runners-up in Division 1 in 1932-33 and he went on to be their leading goalscorer for each of the next three seasons. On 27th January 1934 he helped himself to four goals in an FA Cup match against Sunderland which finished 7-2 and even during Villa's relegation season of 1935-36 he hit the net on 21 occasions.

After switching to Derby County, he recorded a very acceptable 45 First Division goals in 93 games, including a golden spell which included two hat-tricks in four days against Brentford and Arsenal in 1937. His career then took him to Blackpool, but was cut short by the outbreak of war. He guested back at Charlton in four wartime matches in 1939 and also turned out similarly for Clapton Orient in 23 games. When peace was restored he managed one final season playing for Metz in the French Ligue 1 in 1946-47,

scoring against Montpellier in his farewell game.
Dai then turned his hand to management with spells in Italy at Inter Milan and Genoa. After moving to Sweden, he took over the reins at Djurgardens in Stockholm where one of his players was the Swedish International striker Hans Jeppson and he no doubt influenced him to sign amateur terms with Charlton during a three-month business visit to London in January 1951.
Dai steered Djurgardens to the final of the Svenska Cupen which took place on 22nd July 1951 against Malmo. They went down 2-1 but the Swedish crowd had the probably

unique experience of watching the teams led out by two ex-Charlton players, Malmo's manager being Bert Turner. Equally, unique was the fact that the two men were brothers in law.
After returning to the UK in 1957 he took over as landlord of the White Horse at Ramsgate and was again in competition with Bert Turner who was running the Jolly Farmers up the road in Manston. Both men were resident in Birchington and it was there that Dai passed away on 7th November 1989 at the age of 80.

Season	Division	League		FA Cup		Total	
		A	G	A	G	A	G
1927-28	Divison 3 (S)	1	0	0	0	1	0
1928-29 (P)	Divison 3 (S)	22	10	2	2	24	12
1929-30	Division 2	39	6	4	2	43	8
1930-31	Division 2	34	11	3	1	37	12
Total		96	27	9	5	105	32

UK LEAGUE CAREER 377 games 173 goals

CHARLTON CAREER
Managers: *A Lindon, A MacFarlane*
Debut: *Millwall (A) 18-02-1928*
V115
Finale: *West Bromwich Albion (A) 02-05-1931*

AYRE Robert William   1953 - 58

Injury blighted the career of Bobby Ayre, a pint sized striker who at one stage looked likely to go to the very top. As a youngster he had represented the Great Britain Army Cadets, but came to

Forward   10st 0lbs   5' 6"
Born: 26-03-1932 - Berwick-Upon-Tweed, Northumberland
Died: 31-07-2018 - Leeds, West Yorkshire
Education: Bell Tower School, Berwick.

Charlton's attention whilst turning out for Chippenham Town during his period of National Service in the RAF. He was sold to Reading against his wishes at the end of the 1957-58 season because Charlton needed an urgent injection of cash to balance the books.

HONOURS
England U23 International 1955 2 caps 1 goal
FA Tour of South Africa 1956

Charlton Athletic Reserves 1952-53 Runners Up Football Combination Cup

CLUBS
Highfield Juniors 1949 (youth) ••Newcastle United 1949 (amateur) ••Bath City c1950 ••Chippenham Town 1951 ••Charlton Athletic 13.08.51 (amateur) 10.07.52 (pro) ••Reading 21.05.58 (£7,000) ••Weymouth 07.60 (free)

Bobby had got off to a good start at Charlton, scoring the winner against Wolves in only his second match, but it was season 1954-55 when he enjoyed his greatest success, claiming 19 league and cup goals, including a second half hat trick in one 17 minute spell which dispatched West Bromwich Albion from the FA Cup in January.
That same month he was called up for the newly formed England Under 23 team, appearing in only their second fixture, a 5-1 win against Italy in which he scored the opening England goal. He retained his place and on 8th

February 1955 helped thrash Scotland 6-0 in Glasgow but was obliged to leave the field after a bone crunching tackle. Bobby was also picked for the Football League to play the Scottish League in 1955 although he was forced to withdraw with an arm injury.
He was selected for the FA tour of South Africa and Rhodesia that commenced in Johannesburg on 12th May 1956 and which also included former Charlton player Fred Ford as trainer. The tour lasted for more than two months and they remained unbeaten in all 18 matches. Bobby's

contribution was four goals in nine games.

Despite his lack of height, Bobby was a very effective goalscorer and when he eventually departed from Charlton in May 1958 he had managed an impressive 54 in only 115 competitive matches. He continued in a similar vein at Reading, but became increasingly injury prone and after dropping into the Southern League with Weymouth, was forced into early retirement in January 1961. At least some of his long-term injury problems were self-imposed as

throughout his career he forced his feet into tiny size 5 1/2 boots which were too small and as a result of which he developed osteoarthritis in both of his big toes.

He remained resident in the Reading area and later worked for more than 30 years as a representative for a sports goods company. Bobby Ayre passed away on 31st July 2018 at the age of 86. His son-in-law Shaun Smith played over 400 matches for Crewe Alexandra.

Season	Division	League		FA Cup		Total	
		A	G	A	G	A	G
1952-53	Division 1	2	1	0	0	2	1
1953-54	Division 1	21	5	2	2	23	7
1954-55	Division 1	29	16	1	3	30	19
1955-56	Division 1	22	7	2	1	24	8
1956-57 (R)	Division 1	15	8	0	0	15	8
1957-58	Division 2	20	11	1	0	21	11
Total		109	48	6	6	115	54

UK LEAGUE CAREER 166 games 72 goals

CHARLTON CAREER
Managers: *J Seed, J Trotter*
Debut: *Bolton Wanderers (A) 01-01-1953*
V252
Finale: *Bristol Rovers (H) 29-03-1958*

AYRES George Alexander   1922 - 24

Forward, Utility.   11st 0lbs   5' 8"
Born: 05-09-1901 - Islington, London
Died: 17-01-1983 - Seaford, East Sussex

For most of his time at Charlton, George played as an amateur, only turning professional in the middle of his second season. He was a good all round sportsman and also excelled at cricket. He was on the staff of Surrey CCC for a time although he did not make any first class appearances.

HONOURS
Charlton Athletic 1923-24 Finalists London Challenge Cup

CLUBS
RAF (Cranwell) 1921 (amateur) ••Charlton Athletic 26.08.22 (amateur) 18.02.24 (pro) ••The Wednesday 02.05.24 ••Blackpool 18.05.26 (£350)

George came to Charlton during the club's second season as a Football League club. They were competing in Division 3 South and he was called up on seven occasions, always at centre forward, but only managed one goal, the third in the home fixture against Swindon Town on 3rd May 1923, which added to strikes by Harold Miller and Sid Castle in a 3-1 win. He must have impressed manager Walter Rayner however, as in the following campaign he figured a good deal more regularly, including the first match after the club moved to The Mount in December.

He managed four goals in 1923-24, which was still a modest return for a striker, but clearly there were other attributes to his game because he was transferred to The Wednesday,

(as the Sheffield club were known in those far off times), just one day before the end of the season and ironically enough celebrated his Division 2 debut for them with a goal in the 2-0 win against Manchester United, before he had even had time to properly unpack.

His first full season with Wednesday went reasonably well and he scored a hat-trick against Stockport County on 20th September, but the team were showing indifferent form. This situation changed in 1925-26 when they stormed to the Division 2 title, but George only featured briefly despite contributing four goals in just five games and his final season in the Football League was for Blackpool, where he started off at inside forward, was moved to wing half in

December and finished with a run of games at centre half. He was still a young man and this apparent versatility might have opened up all sorts of possibilities had not injury brought his playing days to an abrupt end.

By 1929 George was working as the football and cricket coach at Stamford School in Surrey and he passed away in Seaford at the age of 81.

Season	Division	League		FA Cup		Total	
		A	G	A	G	A	G
1922-23	Divison 3 (S)	7	1	0	0	7	1
1923-24	Divison 3 (S)	26	4	3	0	29	4
Total		33	5	3	0	36	5

CHARLTON CAREER
Managers: *W Rayner*
Debut: *Southend United (H) 23-12-1922*
V044
Finale: *Bournemouth (A) 26-04-1924*

UK LEAGUE CAREER 99 games 20 goals

AZEEZ Adebayo Linford Karim   2013

Ade was a graduate of Charlton's highly successful youth academy and featured regularly in the Under 21 side which in season 2012-13 won the Professional Development League 2 South. In 2012, he was capped three times for the England Under 19's which included two matches that were played in Tallin, the capital of Estonia, as part of the qualifying competition for the UEFA U19 Championships.

Forward   12st 8lbs   6' 0"
Born: 08-01-1994 - Orpington, Kent
Education: Coopers Technology College, Chislehurst.

HONOURS

England U19 International 2012 3 caps 0 goals
Charlton Athletic U21 2012-13 Winners PD League 2 South
Charlton Athletic U21 2012-13 Winners Kent Senior Cup

Charlton Athletic U21 2012-13 Winners PD National League 2
AFC Wimbledon 2015-16 Promoted Play Offs League Two

CLUBS

Rivercray (youth) ••Charlton Athletic 2008 (youth) 07.11 (pro) ••Wycombe Wanderers 22.11.12 (loan) •Leyton Orient 18.01.13 (loan) ••Torquay United 26.09.13 (loan) ••Dagenham & Redbridge 08.02.14 (loan) ••AFC Wimbledon 26.06.14 (free) ••Partick Thistle, Scotland 15.06.16 (free) ••Cambridge United 05.07.17 ••Dover Athletic 23.02.18 (loan) ••Newport County 31.01.19 (free) ••Torquay United 11.02.20 (loan) ••Dover Athletic 03.10.20 (free) ••Dartford 16.06.21 (free)

Things did not go well for Charlton on 5th January 2013. A crowd of 6,657 had gathered at the Valley for the FA Cup match against Huddersfield Town, only for the visitors to take an early lead. To make matters worse, Dorian Dervite was sent off in the second half, so with just 12 minutes (plus stoppage) remaining, manager Chris Powell withdrew Bradley Wright-Phillips and introduced Ade Azeez in a final attempt to force an equaliser. The gamble did not pay off. The score remained at 0-1 and this brief cameo proved to be his only appearance at first team level.

Ade did better after he moved to AFC Wimbledon in

Summer 2014 and his pacey, direct style ensured that he was a fairly regular member of their promotion side in 2015-16, although often as substitute. He was on the bench for their Wembley play off final against Plymouth on 30th May 2016 when they clinched promotion from League Two and came on as a substitute for Lyle Taylor in the 97th minute of the match. 2016-17 was spent in Scotland for Partick Thistle, after which he served time with Cambridge United and Newport County before dropping into non-league. Currently, Ade is with Dartford and is chasing promotion from the National League South.

Season	Division	League		FA Cup		FL Cup		Total	
		A	G	A	G	A	G	A	G
2012-13	Championship	0	0	0 (1)	0	0	0	0 (1)	0
Total		0	0	0 (1)	0	0	0	0 (1)	0

CHARLTON CAREER
Managers: *C Powell, J Riga, B Peeters*
Debut: *Huddersfield Town (H) (sub) 05-01-2013*
V756

UK LEAGUE CAREER 203 games 21 goals

BA El Hadji   2015 - 16

A French midfield player of Senegalese descent, El Hadji Ba played one season at Charlton, but although he showed some early promise, did not seem physically equipped for the rigours of a relegation battle in the English Football League. He was never more than a squad player and spent much of the campaign as a substitute. He had joined on a two-year deal, but after relegation in 2016 did not appear again, his contract being terminated at the end of January 2017.

Midfield   11st 7lbs   6' 0''
Born: 05-03-1993 - Paris, France

HONOURS

France U20 International 2012-13 5 caps 0 goals   France U18 International 2010-11 6 caps 0 goals
France U19 International 2012 8 caps 0 goals

CLUBS

Esperance Aulnay, France c1999 (youth) ••Le Havre, France 2007 (youth) 2011 (pro) ••Sunderland 10.07.13 (free) ••SC Bastia, Corsica 07.08.14 (loan) ••Charlton Athletic 30.06.15 (undisclosed) ••Stabaek, Norway 06.03.17 (free) ••Sochaux, France 06.07.17 ••RC Lens, France 20.07.18 (free) ••EA Guingamp, France 20.08.19

After growing up in Aulnay-sous- Bois, a suburb of Paris, El Hadji Ba made his name as a young footballer with Le Havre, for whom he made his professional debut at the age of 18. He also received international recognition and was capped by France at different age groups including five appearances for the U20's. There was talk of a transfer to England and at first it looked as if Tottenham Hotspur would be his destination, but in July 2013 he instead joined Sunderland whose manager at the time was Paolo Di Canio.

Unfortunately the erratic Mr Di Canio did not stay long in the job and neither of his successors shared his enthusiasm

for the young Frenchman, so after two seasons of inactivity Ba made the move to Charlton. Although he certainly got more game time in London, in league games he only played the full 90 minutes on one occasion and that was a disappointing home defeat against Wolverhampton Wanderers on 28th December 2015 in which he failed to impose himself in midfield. By July 2017 he was back in France, via a short spell in the Norwegian League with Stabaek.

Since the 2019-20 season he has been plying his trade in the French Ligue 2 with EA Guingamp.

Season	Division	League		FA Cup		FL Cup		Total	
		A	G	A	G	A	G	A	G
2015-16 (R)	Championship	13 (12)	0	0	0	3	0	16 (12)	0
Total		13 (12)	0	0	0	3	0	16 (12)	0

UK LEAGUE CAREER 26 games 0 goals

CHARLTON CAREER
Managers: *G Luzon, K Fraeye, J Riga, R Slade, K Robinson*
Debut: *Queens Park Rangers (H) 08-08-2015*
V800
Finale: *Burnley (H) (sub) 07-05-2016*

BACON Ernest Frederick   1921 - 23

There were not many high points for Ernie during his 21 months as a Charlton player. His first team opportunities were few and far between and of the five matches played, only one was a home game. This was on 12th November 1921 when he filled in at left back against Watford for the absent Kosha Goodman. It was also his only time on a winning side thanks to the goal from inside right Harold Halse. He retained his place, but seven days later the side crashed to a 6-0 defeat at Southampton, after which he was quietly removed from the firing line.

Defender, Midfield
Born: 19-02-1896 - Leicester, Leicestershire
Died: 09-01-1972 - Aylestone, Leicestershire

HONOURS

England Schoolboy International   Leicester Schools

CLUBS

Oxford Street 1913 (youth) ••St Andrews (Leicester) 1914 (youth) ••Leicester City 08.19 (pro) ••Watford 05.20 (free) ••Charlton Athletic 22.08.21 (free) ••Nuneaton Town 05.23 ••Kettering 1924 ••Barwell United 1924 ••Rothwell Town 1927 ••Erith & Belvedere 1928 ••Callenders Athletic 1929

Born in the Belgrove district of Leicester, Ernie attained international standard as a young footballer and represented England Schoolboys, but by the age of 15 had finished his education and was working as an apprentice shoemaker. In the Great War he attained the rank of sergeant and served in the Royal Garrison Artillery out in Salonika, but did turn out for Coventry City as a wartime guest player. By 1919 he was back home in Leicester where he signed on as a professional footballer.

The old club, Leicester Fosse, had severe financial difficulties and was placed into liquidation in July 1919 with the newly branded Leicester City being launched the following month. Ernie was one of the very first signings and made his Football League debut on 13th September in a home match against Fulham. They won 3-2 but he did not keep his place and only managed four appearances before transferring to Watford at the end of the season.

They were newly elected to the Football League and he played in their debut match, a 2-1 win at Queens Park Rangers on 28th August 1920 and in a resounding 7-1 victory over Northampton Town the following month. Otherwise, he still remained mainly on the sidelines and was never given a decent run in the side. Up until now he had been operating as a wing half but after moving to Charlton in August 1921, he converted to full back. In fact, he even turned out as a makeshift goalkeeper on several occasions in reserve games during February and March 1922. Ernie added two further appearances to his first team tally during his second season in SE7 but then dropped into non-league for the remainder of his career.

In 1939, he was back in Leicester again and working in the timber business. He died at the age of 75 in the Leicester suburb of Aylestone.

Season	Division	League		FA Cup		Total	
		A	G	A	G	A	G
1921-22	Divison 3 (S)	3	0			3	0
1922-23	Divison 3 (S)	2	0	0	0	2	0
Total		5	0	0	0	5	0

UK LEAGUE CAREER 21 games 0 goals

CHARLTON CAREER
Managers: *W Rayner*
Debut: *Bristol Rovers (A) 10-09-1921*
V022
Finale: *Northampton Town (A) 03-04-1923*

BACON Paul Darren   1989 - 93

Midfield, Defender   11st 3lbs   5' 9"
Born: 20-12-1970 - Forest Gate, London
Education: Thames View Primary School and Eastbury Secondary School, Barking.

Since 1952 the FA Youth Cup has been the UK's premier competition for footballers under the age of 18 and currently attracts an annual entry of nearly 500 clubs. Charlton are rightly proud of the number of top players that they have produced over the years, yet only once have they reached the final of this prestigious competition. In season 1986-87 the team included Scott Minto, Mickey Bennett, Carl Leaburn, Ronnie Mauge and Darren Pitcher, plus at right back, a fair haired lad from East London named Paul Bacon. They fought through to the final and on 28th April 1987 held Coventry City to a 1-1 draw in the home leg. The second match took place at Highfield Road on 13th May and after 90 minutes the score was 0-0, only for Coventry to score during extra time and win the cup with an aggregate score of 2-1.

HONOURS

Barking & Dagenham Schools   Charlton Athletic U18 1986-87 Finalists FA Youth Cup

CLUBS

Charlton Athletic 15.11.85 (youth) 02.02.89 (pro) ••Dagenham & Redbridge 07.93 (free)

Football is littered with the names of countless players who have been outstanding youth prospects but in the end have failed to turn that early promise into a long term career in the professional game. Regrettably Paul must be included in that category, even though he featured in 42 competitive matches strung over four different seasons in the early nineties. His potential had been noted while still a pupil at Thames View Primary School in Barking and he represented Barking and Dagenham Schools in both seasons 1980-81 and 1981-82 before going on to join Charlton as an associated schoolboy in 1985. At one stage he was placed on stand-by for the England U17 squad. Despite making his first team debut in a low-key Full Members Cup match against Crystal Palace, it was not until 21st August 1991 that Paul got to play a full 90 minutes. The occasion was a Football League Cup tie against Fulham and interestingly, more than four years on from that FA Youth Cup final, the Charlton side included not only Paul, but also Minto, Pitcher and Leaburn. Both Carl and Scott were amongst the scorers as Fulham were dispatched 4-2. He was given plenty of opportunities in 1991-92, mainly in midfield and one league match that he started was against Millwall on 7th March 1992 at the Boleyn Ground. However, after 74 minutes Paul was substituted in favour of loanee John Hendry, who scored ten minutes later, thereby clinching a rare 1-0 victory over the Lions.

He continued as a squad member in 1992-93 but was never able to fully establish himself in the team. His final match came against Birmingham City at St Andrews and he was taken off after 70 minutes as Charlton chased the game. Carl Leaburn was added to the attack in his place, but the home side held on for a 1-0 win. Freed at the end of the season, Paul joined Dagenham & Redbridge in July 1993. This was just a year after the merger of Dagenham and Redbridge Forest and the newly re-shaped club was competing in the Football Conference. He stayed with them for one season after which his football career appears to have reached a premature end.

Paul moved into the building trade and has been a director of PPS Building Services Ltd and as a flooring contractor was also a director of the Essex based company Sunshine Building & Flooring Services Ltd.

Season	Division	League		FA Cup		FL Cup		FM Cup		AI Cup		Total	
		A	G	A	G	A	G	A	G	A	G	A	G
1989-90 (R)	Division 1	0	0	0	0	0	0	1	0			1	0
1990-91	Division 2	0 (1)	0	0	0	0	0	0	0			0 (1)	0
1991-92	Division 2	11 (3)	0	1	0	4	0	1	0			17 (3)	0
1992-93	Division 1	14 (4)	0	0	0	1	0			1	0	16 (4)	0
Total		25 (8)	0	1	0	5	0	2	0	1	0	34 (8)	0

CHARLTON CAREER

Managers: *L Lawrence, A Curbishley/S Gritt*

Debut: *Crystal Palace (A) 19-12-1989*

V508

Finale: *Birmingham City (A) 08-05-1993*

UK LEAGUE CAREER 33 games 0 goals

BAGHERI KARVIGH Karim   2000

2nd June 1997 was a memorable day for Iranian midfielder Karim Bagheri. He played in a FIFA World Cup qualifier against the Maldives at the Al Abbasiyyin Stadium in Damascus in front of a modest crowd of 5,000 and scored a hat-trick in the first 16 minutes. He added a second hat-trick during a six-minute spell in the second half and then grabbed his seventh goal of the day five minutes from the end to equal the record for the most goals scored in a World Cup match. The final score was a fairly conclusive 17-0.

Midfield   12st 4lbs   6' 1"
Born: 20-02-1974 - Tabriz, Iran

HONOURS

Iran International 1993-10 87 caps 50 goals

Iran 1998 Winners Asian Games

Persepolis 1996-97 Winners Azadegan League

Arminia Bielefeld 1998-99 Winners Bundesliga Division 2

Persepolis 2005-06 Finalists Hazfi Cup

Persepolis 2007-08 Winners Persian Gulf Cup

CLUBS

Tractor Sazi, Iran 1992 ••Keshavarz, Iran 1994 ••Persepolis, Iran 08.96 (free) •Arminia Bielefeld, Germany 08.97 ••Persepolis, Iran 2000 ••Al-Nasr, UAE 2000 (loan) ••Charlton Athletic 14.08.00 (£400,000) ••Al- Sadd, Qatar 2001 (free) ••Persepolis, Iran 2002 (free) 2012 (coach) ••Iran 04.03.20 (coach)

Karim was already a full international before he signed for the Tehran club Persepolis in August 1996. They were the reigning champions of Iran and in his first season they retained their title, winning the Azadegan League by six points. It has since been claimed that the Persepolis team of 1996-97 was perhaps the greatest ever Iranian club side. Karim's performances earned him a move to Europe and a contract with the German club Arminia Bielefeld, the first two years of which were eventful and involved both relegation from and promotion back to the Bundesliga. By his third year however he became discontented and eventually bought back his contract and returned to Iran. After a short loan spell in Dubai, Karim signed for Charlton for a fee of £400,000 which could potentially have increased to £1.1 million dependent upon appearances. Alan Curbishley was seeking cover for skipper Mark Kinsella and the Iranian captain looked to be the perfect candidate. Unfortunately the reality proved somewhat different and he never got going at all. A combination of international call-ups, a variety of niggling injuries and a lengthy absence following the death of his father, kept him away from the club, although he trained well enough and looked good when he was available for the Reserves. His one first team outing came against an Ipswich side that included both Matt Holland and Herman Hreidarsson. Karim replaced Matt Svensson after 72 minutes with the score 0-0, but Holland scored eight minutes later and Charlton slipped to a 2-0 defeat. Although he made no impact in London SE7, Karim's international career continued to flourish during his time in England. He played six matches for Iran and scored eight times, including a six goal haul against Guam on 24th November 2000. By the time he finally retired from international football, Karim has amassed 50 goals in 87 appearances and had represented his country at the 1998 World Cup finals in France and a year earlier scored against Kuwait in the final of the Asian Games.

Following his year in England, he spent a season playing in Qatar before returning once again to Persepolis where he remained until eventually retiring as a player in December 2010. He later moved into coaching with Persepolis and on 4th March 2020 was appointed assistant coach of the Iran national team.

Season	Division	League		FA Cup		FL Cup		Total	
		A	G	A	G	A	G	A	G
2000-01	Premier	0 (1)	0	0	0	0	0	0 (1)	0
Total		0 (1)	0	0	0	0	0	0 (1)	0

UK LEAGUE CAREER 1 game 0 goals

CHARLTON CAREER
Managers: *A Curbishley*
Debut: *Ipswich Town (A) (sub) 11-11-2000*
V596

BAILEY Daniel   1921 - 22

Forward
Born: 26-06-1893 - East Ham, Essex
Died: 03-04-1967 - Norwich, Norfolk
Education: Napier Road School, East Ham.

Dan had the distinction of being Charlton's leading goalscorer in 1921-22 which was the club's first season in the Football League. He netted eight in 33 games including a vital penalty against Millwall on 14th January 1922 and this added to an earlier effort by Harold Halse ensured a 2-1 scoreline for the Addicks. A fortnight earlier Dan had been in the Charlton side which won 1-0 at the Den before an excitable 25,000 crowd, so this meant a league double against their South London neighbours and the jubilant Charlton supporters no doubt travelled home confident that they had secured the upper hand in the local derby for evermore.

CLUBS

East Ham Park Rangers ••South Weald ••Tottenham Hotspur (amateur) ••Custom House 1911 ••West Ham United 1912 ••Charlton Athletic 18.05.21 ••Clapton Orient 06.22 ••Margate 1925

Always a promising young footballer, Dan represented both East Ham Schools and London Schools. He was working as a builder's labourer when he first joined West Ham in 1912 and appeared for them in the Southern League scoring 13 goals in 49 games until the War temporarily curtailed his progress. He served as a Private in the Machine Gun Corps out in Egypt and Salonika during the hostilities but returned to football in time to re-join the Hammers as they made their entry into the Football League in season 1919-20.

His debut came two months into the season against Leicester City in a West Ham side that also contained Frank 'Bronco' Burton and Harry Lane. However, it finished 0-0 and Dan had to wait until his fifth match which was against Coventry City on 13th December 1919 before registering his first goal in the Football League. He finished the season with eight league and one cup goal, but was unable to maintain this standard and lost his place during the following campaign when the goals dried up completely. After transferring to Charlton in May 1921, Dan was one of those tasked with providing the fire-power during the first season in the Football League. Goals proved hard to

come by and the team only managed 43 in their 42 games. Billy Cox scored seven, while veteran Harry Halse contributed five, but Dan topped the chart with eight. Leading goalscorer he may have become, but earlier in the season there had been serious problems between Dan and manager Walter Rayner. As early as 29th September Rayner complained to the directors that he wanted him transfer listed as 'the service being rendered was far from satisfactory'. They agreed but suggested a fee of £1,000 and it is now unclear whether they subsequently had second thoughts or there were just no takers, but Dan opened his account on 15th October with a goal against Aberdare Athletic and remained in the team for the rest of the season. He joined Clapton Orient in June 1922 but despite a good run in the side, found goals hard to come by. He did not feature at all in his second season through injury and announced his retirement in May 1924, although he did attempt a brief comeback with Margate a year later.

By 1939 Dan and his wife Elsie were residing in Hornchurch and he was working as a painter and decorator. He passed away in Norwich at the age of 73.

Season	Division	League		Total	
		A	G	A	G
1921-22	Divison 3 (S)	33	8	33	8
Total		33	8	33	8

UK LEAGUE CAREER 86 games 21 goals

CHARLTON CAREER
Managers: *W Rayner*
Debut: *Exeter City (A) 27-08-1921*
V008
Finale: *Luton Town (H) 22-04-1922*

BAILEY Dennis Lincoln   1993

There must have been Saturdays when Dennis awoke and had to think hard to recall which club he was playing for that week. A journeyman striker who moved around with alarming regularity, he nevertheless grabbed centre stage on one memorable occasion whilst with Queens Park Rangers. On New Year's Day 1992, he scored a hat trick in the 4-1 defeat of Manchester United and for nearly thirty years remained the last player to perform this feat in a league game at Old Trafford. It was not until October 2021 that Mo Salah equalled his record when United crashed 5-0 at home to Liverpool.

Forward   11st 6lbs   5' 10"
Born: 13-12-1965 - Lambeth, London
Education: Tulse Hill Comprehensive School

HONOURS

Birmingham City 1990-91 Winners Football League Trophy   Halesowen Town 2001-02 Winners Southern League Western Division
Gillingham 1995-96 Runners Up Division 3

CLUBS

Watford 1982 (youth) 08.03.83 (non contract) ••Barking 1985 ••Fulham 08.11.86 (non contract) ••Farnborough Town 02.87 ••Crystal Palace 02.12.87 (£10,000) ••Bristol Rovers 27.02.89 (loan) ••Birmingham City 03.08.89 (£80,000) ••Bristol Rovers 28.03.91 (loan) ••Queens Park Rangers 02.07.91 (£175,000) ••Charlton Athletic 29.10.93 (loan) ••Watford 24.03.94 (loan) ••Brentford 26.01.95 (loan) ••Gillingham 15.08.95 (£50,000) ••Lincoln City 26.03.98 (non contract) ••Farnborough Town 08.98 ••Cheltenham Town 17.03.99 ••Forest Green Rovers 03.08.99 (£15,000) ••Aberystwyth Town 24.01.01 ••Tamworth 08.01 ••Halesowen Town 04.01.02 ••Stafford Rangers 08.02 ••Moor Green 12.03 ••Stratford Town 12.04 ••Heanor ••Renewal Solihull c2010 (player coach)

Sadly there were more near misses than solid achievements throughout Dennis's career. Crystal Palace paid a fee to bring him to South London in 1987 but never used him other than as a substitute. At Bristol Rovers they looked as if promotion was a strong possibility but missed out in the 1989 play-offs. The best season of his career came in 1989-90 while he was with Birmingham City. They also missed out on promotion and finished seventh in Division 3, but his personal contribution was an impressive 20 league and cup goals, including five in the first seven games. Dennis joined Charlton on a short term loan in October 1993 and at first sight his contribution appears marginal, his four league appearances all being made from the substitute's bench. Interestingly he did however also get to play in two of that season's games in the short-lived Anglo Italian Cup, including the away match against Ancona, in which Carl Leaburn scored the equaliser in a 1-1 draw.

He had made a substitute appearance for Birmingham City in the final of the Football League Trophy at Wembley in 1991, but otherwise it was not until he joined Gillingham, his ninth Football League club, that Dennis got among the honours, and was almost ever present in season 1995-96 as the Gills clinched promotion to Division 2.

His nomadic career finally came to an end when he announced his retirement from playing in November 2006 shortly before his 41st birthday. A devout Christian, he now spends much of his time giving motivational talks and coaching in schools and youth clubs, but as recently as 2011 would still occasionally lace up his boots and turn out for Renewal Solihull in Division 2 of the West Midlands Christian League.

Season	Division	League		FA Cup		FL Cup		AI Cup		Total	
		A	G	A	G	A	G	A	G	A	G
1993-94	Division 1	0 (4)	0	0	0	0	0	2	0	2 (4)	0
Total		0 (4)	0	0	0	0	0	2	0	2 (4)	0

UK LEAGUE CAREER 253 games 63 goals

CHARLTON CAREER
Managers: *A Curbishley/S Gritt*
Debut: *Oxford United (H) (sub) 30-10-1993*
V542
Finale: *Ascoli (H) 16-11-1993*

BAILEY John Hunter 1926

Goalkeeper   11st 0lbs   6' 0"
Born: 22-03-1901 - Norwood, Surrey
Died: 27-08-1967 - Sittingbourne, Kent

The entire Football League career of Jack Bailey was packed into a highly eventful five-day period over Easter 1926, Regular goalkeeper Charlie 'Spider' Preedy was missing, presumably through injury, so Jack was called up for no less than four matches commencing on Good Friday and continuing through the Saturday, Monday and Tuesday and with only Easter Sunday off. It is not hard to imagine the reaction of a 21st century football manager if such a programme of fixtures was presented today.

CLUBS

Bostall Heath 1923 ••Tilbury 1924 ••Charlton Athletic 25.06.25 (amateur) 12.12.25 (pro) ••Sittingbourne 06.26 ••Dartford 06.30 ••Sittingbourne 1932

Jack was born into a sporting family. His father Alf Bailey was a professional cricketer who played for Somerset until 1911, following which he ran a tobacconist shop in Sangley Road, Catford. After leaving school, young Jack found work as a clerk, but in August 1923 sailed to Quebec, Canada and then on to Seattle, Washington and Vancouver before ending his adventure and returning to the UK in the December. By now the family was resident at 45 Priolo

Road, Charlton, which places him just a few minutes walk from the Valley at the very time the club was re-locating to Catford.

It soon became clear that the Catford move was a mistake and Charlton were back home at the Valley by the time Jack signed amateur forms in June 1925. His progress was rewarded with a professional contract six months later, but he was still very inexperienced when his big chance arrived in April 1926. His run of games commenced with a trip to Luton and a home game against Brentford on consecutive days and both ended in defeat. After a day to rest and lick his wounds, Jack lined up for the return fixture with Luton and enjoyed the taste of a 2-1 victory thanks to a Baden

Herod penalty and the winner from Reg Tricker. There was little time to celebrate the win however as the team had to travel to Bristol the next day and they suffered another defeat when Rovers hit four past him with only a consolation goal from Ford Currie in reply. So ended Jack's time in the Charlton Athletic first team.

He left the club at the end of the season but carried on playing non-league football, including two spells with Sittingbourne. He married a local girl in 1932, settled permanently in the area and worked as a labourer in a brickworks. He passed away in the Memorial Hospital, Sittingbourne at the age of 66.

Season	Division	League		FA Cup		Total	
		A	G	A	G	A	G
1925-26	Divison 3 (S)	4	0	0	0	4	0
Total		4	0	0	0	4	0

UK LEAGUE CAREER 4 games 0 goals

CHARLTON CAREER
Managers: *A MacFarlane*
Debut: *Luton Town (A) 02-04-1926*
V086
Finale: *Bristol Rovers (A) 06-04-1926*

BAILEY Michael Alfred   1960 - 66

Any listing of the greatest post-war Charlton captains would include not only Don Welsh, Benny Fenton and Mark Kinsella but also Mike Bailey

Midfield   11st 1lb   5' 8"
Born: 27-02-1942 - Wisbech, Cambridgeshire
Education: Edward Worlledge School, Great Yarmouth & Alderman Leach School, Gorleston.

who led the team from March 1962 until he departed for Wolverhampton Wanderers almost four years later. An inspiring wing half, once described by Cliff Durandt as having a bone shuddering solidity in the tackle, he played twice for England and five times at U23 level during his time at the Valley and during his later career skippered the Wolves to cup and league honours. He returned to Charlton in 1979 in a coaching capacity and after taking over from Andy Nelson as manager guided the team to promotion from Division 3 in season 1980-81.

HONOURS

England International 1964 2 caps 0 goals
England U23 International 1964 5 caps 0 goals
England U23 v England 1964
Norfolk Schools 1955
Kent Youth 1958 1 cap 0 goals
Football league X1 1967-69 3 caps 1 goal
Charlton Athletic A !958-59 & 1959-60 Winners London Mid-Week League

Charlton Athletic A 1959-60 Winners Aetolian League Cup
Charlton Athletic 2019 Hall Of Fame
Wolverhampton Wanderers 1966-67 Runners Up Division 2
Wolverhampton Wanderers 1970-71 Winners Texaco Cup
Wolverhampton Wanderers 1971-72 Finalists UEFA Cup
Wolverhampton Wanderers 1973-74 Winners Football League Cup
Minnesota Kicks 1977 Winners NASL Western Division

HONOURS AS MANAGER

Charlton Athletic 1980-81 Promoted Division 3

CLUBS

Precasters (youth) ••Gorleston 1957 (youth) ••Charlton Athletic 28.05.57 (youth) 24.03.59 (pro) ••Wolverhampton Wanderers 28.02.66 (£35,000) ••Minnesota Kicks, USA 1977 (£15,000 player coach) ••Hereford United 06.78 (player manager) ••Charlton Athletic 10.79 (coach) 28.03.80 (manager) ••Brighton & Hove Albion 30.06.81 (manager) ••Bexley 1985 (player manager) ••Fisher Athletic 27.11.89 (manager) ••Portsmouth 02.07.91 (coach) ••Charlton Athletic 1994 (scout) ••Leatherhead 1995 (general manager)

Mike's football education commenced in the Norfolk town of Gorleston, which was very good news for Charlton, because in the fifties they were managed first by Sailor Brown and then Joe Jobling. They competed in the Eastern Counties League and young Mike was good enough to play in their first team at the age of 15. Jobling got him a trial with Charlton and he turned out for the colts in 1957-58. Initially he was playing at centre half but was soon converted into a wing half and right from the word go stood out as a young player who had the ability, attitude and leadership qualities to succeed.

He signed his first professional contract in March 1959 and made his league debut on 27th December 1960. The side had recorded a 6-4 win at the Valley over Plymouth Argyle on Boxing Day and 24 hours later played the return fixture, but this time with Mike replacing Fred Lucas at left half. Amazingly the game produced another 6-4 scoreline, but this time with Argyle the winners. Mike found it difficult to adapt to the pace of the game but did well enough to be picked for a further three matches that season.

It was shortly after his 20th birthday that he took over as Charlton's captain and on the field he led very much by example. Always described in the press as 'barrel chested', Mike was a non-stop worker, with great reserves of energy and fierce in the tackle. Because he never shirked a challenge, he was probably more susceptible to injuries than most and he dislocated a shoulder against Scunthorpe in September 1962 which resulted in a pin being inserted at Greenwich Hospital and seven weeks out of the game. At this stage Mike was sharing digs with Peter Godfrey in Merriman Road, Blackheath and it was through Peter that he met his wife, Barbara.

One memorable match was at the Valley on 16th March 1963 and the opponents were again Plymouth Argyle. It was another high scoring affair and finished 6-3. Mike scored twice that day while the other Charlton goals came courtesy of Keith Peacock, Mike Kenning, Fred Lucas and Jim Ryan. Three weeks later however he broke a bone in his left foot at Cardiff, but played on as a makeshift winger. (No substitutes in those days). They hung on for a 2-1 win, the Charlton scorers being Cliff Durandt and Mike himself, before his injury.

On 5th February 1964, Mike made his England U23 debut in a 3-2 win against Scotland at St James's Park. This was the first of five such caps, although he also played in an unofficial international three months later between the U23's and a full England side which was won by the latter 3-0. His international career was curiously condensed into a very short time period and only a week after his final game

for the U23's out in Istanbul, Mike made his full England debut in New York, thereby on 27th May 1964 becoming the first Charlton player to earn an England cap since Derek Ufton in 1953. However, there was little opportunity to stand out in the match as the USA team was woefully weak and went down 10-0. His second and final cap was against Wales and was played at Wembley on 18th November 1964. England won 2-1.

Charlton were playing at Middlesbrough on 1st February 1965. It was an FA Cup replay and in the 10th minute a late tackle in the goalmouth left Mike with a double fracture of his left leg which kept him out of football for four months. He had just been called up for an England training camp at Lilleshall, but this injury blew away his England aspirations as he was never selected for his country again. He became restless at Charlton where the team were locked into a seemingly endless struggle in the nether regions of Division 2 and in February 1966 was transferred to Wolverhampton Wanderers for a fee of £35,000 which equalled the amount received when Eddie Firmani was sold to Italy in 1955.

Without question Wolves got themselves a bargain when they signed Bailey. He soon took over as captain and eventually played more than 400 matches for them in a stay of more than a decade. They gained promotion back to Division 1 during his first full season, triumphed in the Texaco Cup in 1971, (beating Heart Of Midlothian in a two legged final) and the following year progressed to the UEFA Cup final. This was another two legged affair with Tottenham the opponents and Mike missed the first match with a groin injury, but came off the bench in the second leg, although he was unable to prevent a 3-2 aggregate defeat. In March 1974 he lifted the Football League Cup for Wolves at Wembley, after defeating Ron Saunders' Manchester City 2-1. He was a massive presence throughout this period and a great favourite with the supporters. On three occasions he represented the Football League and scored in the 3-0 defeat of the League Of Ireland in 1969. For a while he was even joint owner of a popular Birmingham restaurant, the' Savoury Duck'. Mike's time with Wolves came to an end in 1977. He had been suffering for some time with a persistent Achilles tendon problem and he moved to Minneapolis for two years as a player coach with Minnesota Kicks. His first managerial post came with Hereford United and he spent an educational 15 months keeping them afloat in Division 4 before returning to the Valley in October 1979. After meeting with the chairman, Michael Gliksten, he accepted what he understood was to be the manager's job at

Charlton, only to find that he was being installed as chief coach and that Andy Nelson was continuing in the manager's chair for the foreseeable future. This caused both confusion and embarrassment as Mike explained in his 2015 autobiography, 'The Valley Wanderer'. Results on the field were not good enough either and Nelson was finally sacked in March 1980 with the team firmly planted at the foot of Division 2. Bailey took over with nine league matches remaining but could do nothing to avoid the inevitable relegation.

Gliksten made no funds available for team building so Mike approached 1980-81 with much the same squad as before. The season could not have been more different, however. A strike force that included Derek Hales, Martin Robinson and Paul Walsh always promised goals and the defence which was built around Les Berry and Peter Shaw was more than a match for most Third Division sides. Promotion was secured at the first attempt and the team won a then club record of 11 away matches in the process. Sadly Mike's time at the helm was destined to be short and sweet. He was not getting on with Michael Gliksten and after the chairman would not reward him with an extended contract, he moved on to Brighton & Hove Albion while their manager, Alan Mullery, replaced him at the Valley.

Brighton were embarking upon only their third season in the top tier when Mike took over and the team performed well, making 1981-82 their most successful ever, thanks to a final league placing of 13th in Division 1. Again this proved to be a short lived appointment, because after 18 months he left by mutual consent following criticism of Brighton's playing style and this effectively closed the door on Mike's managerial career, although he did spend six months coaching in Crete and a brief period in charge at Fisher Athletic. He was interviewed unsuccessfully for the job of Wolves manager in June 1984, but by then was publican at the 'White Horse' on the Woolwich Road and a year later took over the running of Charlton's 'Valley Club'. He also coached at Portsmouth, spent a year as general manager of Leatherhead and worked as a scout for Charlton and elsewhere.

In October 2019, Mike returned along with several of his playing contemporaries as part of the celebrations for the Valley Centenary. He looked in excellent shape but sadly it was revealed that he has ongoing health problems. Now resident in Oxted, Surrey, Mike was elected into the Charlton Athletic Hall of Fame in 2019.

Season	Division	League		FA Cup		FL Cup		Total	
		A	G	A	G	A	G	A	G
1960-61	Division 2	4	0	0	0	0	0	4	0
1961-62	Division 2	30	7	3	0	1	0	34	7
1962-63	Division 2	23	4	2	0	1	0	26	4
1963-64	Division 2	41	3	1	0	1	0	43	3
1964-65	Division 2	26	2	3	1	3	1	32	4
1965-66	Division 2	27	4	1	0	2	0	30	4
Total		151	20	10	1	8	1	169	22

UK LEAGUE CAREER 528 games 40 goals

CHARLTON CAREER
Managers: *J Trotter, F Hill, R Stokoe*
Debut: *Plymouth Argyle (A) 27-12-1960*
V287
Finale: *Leyton Orient (A) 26-02-1966*

BAILEY Nicholas Francis   2008 - 10

In his two-year stay at Charlton, Nicky was an inspirational captain and a powerhouse in midfield, who never shirked a tackle nor allowed his head to drop when things went

Midfield   12st 5lbs   5' 10"
Born: 10-06-1984 - Putney, London

wrong. Sadly and most unfairly his reputation has been tarnished through one misplaced penalty against Swindon Town at the Valley on 17th May 2010. Victory would have placed Charlton in the League One play off final at Wembley, but his shot went high and wide and the chance was gone. Nicky left the field in tears and never kicked another ball for Charlton. He was transferred to Middlesbrough shortly thereafter.

HONOURS

England C International (semi pro) 2005 4 caps 0 goals
Charlton Athletic 2009 Player Of The Year

Sutton United 2003-04 Runners Up Isthmian League Premier Division
Barnet 2004-05 Winners Football Conference National Division

Sutton United 2015-16 Winners National League South

CLUBS

Fulham (youth) ••Sutton United 2000 (youth) 2001 (pro) ••Barnet 02.07.04 (£10,000) ••Southend United 03.07.07 (£175,000) ••Charlton Athletic 15.08.08 (£75,000) ••Middlesbrough 08.07.10 (£1,400,000) ••Millwall 19.07.13 (free) ••Barnet 23.10.15 (free) ••Sutton United 26.01.16 (free) ••Havant & Waterlooville 04.06.19 (free) ••Gosport Borough 19.09.20 (free) •Cray Wanderers 03.09.21 (free)

Nicky made his name at Barnet where he was a key member of the 2004-05 promotion side which regained a place in the Football League. He also earned four caps for the England C team which is selected from within the non-league game. A year was spent with Southend United and he then joined Charlton in August 2008.

He arrived when the club were locked into a downward spiral and struggling in vain to retain a place in the Championship. He had an outstanding first season, playing in central midfield and finishing as leading goalscorer with an impressive 13 league goals. He was also voted Player of the Year. The following season was no less of a struggle, as financial considerations were paramount and the team was being asset stripped at every opportunity. Working in such trying circumstances, manager Phil Parkinson did an admirable job in guiding them into the play offs, only for the missed penalty to scupper any hopes of an unlikely promotion. Overall though Nicky had been a great success with Charlton and 25 league goals from midfield in 87 games is an outstanding return by any standards.

He went on to play well at Middlesbrough, but never again approached the same level of goal scoring as in his two years at the Valley. Homesick for London, he left the North East and signed for Millwall in 2013 but a series of calf injuries restricted his appearances for the Lions.

His career now seemed to go into reverse and he returned first to Barnet and then to his original club, Sutton United, who in 2016-17 had a spectacular FA Cup run. On 29th January, Nicky and goalkeeper Ross Worner were in the Sutton side which defeated Leeds United 1-0 in Round 4. This was a headlining grabbing feat of giant killing and earned them a tie with Arsenal, but the fairy tale came to an end when they went down 2-0 after a brave fight.

At a time of strict dietary control for professional sportsmen, Nicky's own pre-match arrangements were revealed around the time of the Leeds match. Despite his parents having run a fruit and veg stall, he claimed to have never eaten a salad or vegetable in his life, preferring his regular fare of nine tasty chicken nuggets from McDonald's before every game.

Season	Division	League		FA Cup		FL Cup		FL Trophy		Play Offs		Total	
		A	G	A	G	A	G	A	G	A	G	A	G
2008-09 (R)	Championship	43	13	3	0	0	0					46	13
2009-10	League One	43 (1)	12	1	0	0 (1)	0	1	1	2	0	47 (2)	13
Total		86 (1)	25	4	0	0 (1)	0	1	1	2	0	93 (2)	26

CHARLTON CAREER
Managers: *A Pardew, P Parkinson*
Debut: *Watford (A) 16-08-2008*
V671
Finale: *Swindon Town (H) 17-05-2010*

UK LEAGUE CAREER 358 games 51 goals

BAKER James Edward   1931 - 34

Defender, Forward.   12st 2lbs   5' 11"
Born: 03-08-1911 - Wolverhampton, Staffordshire
Died: 22-02-1974 - Pennington, Cumbria

A well built defender with pace and a powerful kick, Jim came to SE7 after spending a season with his home town club Wolverhampton Wanderers. He had no first team experience however and curiously his Football League debut for Charlton took place at Molineux where a 3-1 defeat by Wolves left the Addicks one from bottom of Division 2 as they moved into the second half of the 1931-32 campaign. He held down the right back spot for the remainder of that season and his defensive partnership with another Midlander Frank Searle, at left back, had a lot to do with Charlton's improved form and eventual mid-table league placing.

CLUBS

Darlaston 1926 ••Chillington Athletic 1927 ••Shrewsbury Town 1928 ••Sedgley Rovers 1929 ••Cradley Heath 1930 ••Wolverhampton Wanderers 10.30 ••Charlton Athletic 19.05.31 (free) ••Port Vale 06.34 (free) ••Barrow 06.36 (free)

Everything went wrong for both club and player in 1932-33. Jim played in the opening four matches, none of which were won, after which he was dropped and the right back position was passed to Norman Smith and later Teddy Ivill. Things went from bad to worse and after conceding 91 league goals, Charlton finished the season rock bottom. Jim never got another chance in the league team but remained with the club for another two years.

In reserve team matches Jim was able to show off his versatility making occasional appearances in attack and on 4th November 1933 gave an impressive showing at outside right scoring twice against Bournemouth Reserves. He even gave a good account of himself as a stand in goalkeeper on more than one occasion but could not persuade new manager Jimmy Seed to try him again in the league side. He did however have one final outing on 14th February 1934 when Charlton made one of only two appearances in the short lived Third Division Southern Section Cup. This competition was probably no more popular than the

modern day Football League Trophy and involved a game with a Torquay United side that included a young Don Welsh. Jim played left back, but the game was lost 2-1, Charlton's goal coming courtesy of Stan Prior. This really was the finale for Jim and by the end of the season he was laid up and receiving treatment for a fractured fibula. Freed by Charlton, he signed for Port Vale and soon re-invented himself as a centre forward, making his first appearance in that role up at Newcastle on 9th March 1935, where he scored both goals in a 2-1 win which ended Vale's run of 24 away games without a victory. Playing alongside him that day were former Charlton colleagues Jack Vickers and Jack Blackwell.

His final league club was Barrow and he spent two seasons with them mainly playing at right back, but results got steadily worse until his career came to an abrupt halt at the end of season 1937-38 with Barrow in 21st place in Division 3 North and seeking re-election. Jim remained in the Lake District where he passed away at the age of 62.

Season	Division	League		FA Cup		D3 Cup		Total	
		A	G	A	G	A	G	A	G
1931-32	Division 2	21	0	1	0			22	0
1932-33 (R)	Division 2	4	0	0	0			4	0
1933-34	Divison 3 (S)	0	0	0	0	1	0	1	0
Total		25	0	1	0	1	0	27	0

UK LEAGUE CAREER 95 games 11 goals

CHARLTON CAREER

Managers: *A MacFarlane, A Lindon, J Seed*

Debut: *Wolverhampton Wanderers (A) 28-12-1931*

V151

Finale: *Torquay United (A) 14-02-1934*

BAKRIN Nazir Oladayo   2021 -

There was an encouraging array of talent emerging via Charlton's U18 team in season 2020-21. They finished as champions of the Professional Development League 2 South and an important part of this success was the central defensive partnership of Deji Elerewe and Nazir Bakrin. Both young men have now had a taste of first team football and look to be destined for worthwhile careers.

Defender   11st 4lbs   6' 3"
Born: 23-10-2002 - Croydon, Surrey
Education: Shirley High School, Croydon.

HONOURS

Surrey Schools

Charlton Athletic U18 2020-21 Winners PD League 2 South

Charlton Athletic U18 2020-21 Runners Up PD National League 2

CLUBS

Junior Elite 2012 (youth) ••Fulham 2015 (youth) ••Charlton Athletic 2019 (youth) 2021 (pro)

From a Nigerian family but born in Croydon, Nazir spent   four years in the Fulham academy before switching to

Charlton in 2019 at the age of 16. Since then, he has made excellent progress, displaying composure and calmness on the ball and fine positional sense. Already he has

comfortably made the transition from U18 to U23 football and with two first team appearances under his belt is very much one to watch.

UK LEAGUE CAREER 0 games 0 goals

CHARLTON CAREER
Managers: *N Adkins, J Jackson*
Debut: *Leyton Orient (A) 09-11-2021*
V936

BALMER Stuart Murray   1990 - 98

Defender   12st 6lbs   6' 1"
Born: 24-09-1969 - Falkirk, Stirlingshire
Education: Bainsford Primary School & Falkirk High School.

Affectionately known by supporters as Sweaty Balmer, Stuart was an important and popular member of the Charlton defence through most of the nineties. He was signed by Lennie Lawrence during the final season at Selhurst Park, played at the Boleyn Ground and in the first match back at the Valley in 1992, then remained at the club long enough to be part of Alan Curbishley's side which won promotion into the Premier League in 1998. He was very much one of the unsung heroes during that difficult period when the club was re-building after the negligence and near suicidal ground-sharing catastrophe of the previous decade.

HONOURS

Scotland Youth International 11 caps
Scottish Schools & Central Scottish Schools
Scottish Schoolboy Of The Year 1986
Charlton Athletic 1993 Player Of The Year

Charlton Athletic 1997-98 Promoted Play Offs Division 1
Charlton Athletic Reserves 1997-98 Winners Football Combination
Wigan Athletic 1998-99 Winners Football League Trophy

CLUBS

Grahamston, Scotland 1978 (youth) ••Celtic Boys, Scotland 1984 (youth) ••Celtic, Scotland 06.85 (youth) 01.07.87 (pro) ••Charlton Athletic 24.08.90 (£100,000) ••Wigan Athletic 18.09.98 (£200,000) ••Oldham Athletic 20.07.01 (free) ••Scunthorpe United 10.10.02 (loan) ••Boston United 13.12.02 (loan) 02.03 (free) 2003 (player coach) ••Clyde, Scotland 09.07.04 (player ass. manager) ••Hamilton Academicals, Scotland 06.05 (player ass, manager) ••St Mirren,, Scotland 06.06 (coach) ••Ross County, Scotland 01.11 (ass. manager) ••Airdrieonians, Scotland 01.11.13 (ass. manager) ••Forfar Athletic, Scotland 12.15 (ass. manager) ••Queens Park, Scotland 01.18 (ass. manager) ••Stenhousemuir, Scotland 15.12.18 (ass. manager)

Stuart was identified as a promising footballer from a very young age. He represented Scottish Schools on five separate occasions and in 1986 was named as the Scottish Schoolboy of the Year. He earned 11 Scottish Youth International caps and signed professional terms with Celtic in July 1987 at the age of 18. One of the reasons that he was unable to progress further was the presence of Paul Elliott who at that time was playing extremely well at centre half. Although he never appeared at first team level, he did captain their reserves and was talked about in the Scottish media as a name to watch for the future. Instead, he opted to sign for Charlton in August 1990 at a cost to the financially strapped club, of £100,000.
The club had just been relegated and was facing life in Division 2 when Stuart signed. John Humphrey had reluctantly been sold to Crystal Palace to clear the back rent

that had built up during the ground share and this provided the cash to fund his transfer. With smaller and smaller crowds anticipated in the immediate future, there was little room for optimism, however. They made a terrible start to season 1990-91 and only managed one win in the first 11 league matches, while Stuart was unfortunate enough to score an own goal on his home debut, a 2-1 defeat against Leicester City on 13th October. Gradually the results improved and the crowd warmed to his wholehearted displays at the centre of the defence and in the circumstances, the final league placing of 16th was just about acceptable.
During Stuart's eight years at Charlton, the club gradually recovered from the errors of the past and started to move forward again. His best season was probably 1992-93 in which he was almost ever present. This was the joyous

period during which the club returned to the Valley and although they lacked the finances to do more than occupy a mid-table place in Division 2, the reliable pairing of Stuart and Simon Webster was invaluable at the heart of the defence.

Through the years he remained an important member of the Charlton squad until eventually he was eased out of the side by first the emergence of Richard Rufus and then the signing of Eddie Youds from Bradford City. His final start for Charlton was at Crewe on 21st March 1998 and the following week Youds made his debut against Nottingham Forest. This signalled the end of Stuart's Charlton career and in September he was sold to Wigan for £200,000, which even after eight years provided the club with a 100% profit on their original outlay.

He may have missed out on a Wembley appearance for Charlton in 1998 but Stuart did play in the Wigan team which captured the Football League Trophy (Auto Windscreens Shield) at that same venue on 18th April 1999 by defeating a Millwall side (which contained Jamie Stuart

and Ben Roberts), by 1-0. A year later he was back at Wembley when Wigan reached the Division 2 Play Off final, but were beaten 3-2 by Gillingham. He moved on to Oldham Athletic in 2001 and a year later switched to Boston United. 2002-03 was their first season in the Football League and playing alongside Neil Redfearn, he captained them to a safe mid-table finish.

His playing days came to an end back in Scotland via short stays with Clyde and Hamilton Academicals, where he also held the position of assistant manager and since 2006 he has held similar posts with a procession of different Scottish League clubs, most recently Forfar Athletic, Queens Park and Stenhousemuir. Football at this level being semi-professional, Stuart has since 2013 also worked as a fork lift operator for Diageo, Scotland's largest exporters of Scotch whiskey.

Season	Division	League		FA Cup		FL Cup		FM Cup		AI Cup		Play Offs		Total	
		A	G	A	G	A	G	A	G	A	G	A	G	A	G
1990-91	Division 2	19 (5)	0	0	0	0	0	1	0					20 (5)	0
1991-92	Division 2	16 (2)	0	0	0	0	0	0	0					16 (2)	0
1992-93	Division 1	42 (3)	2	2	0	2	0			2	0			48 (3)	2
1993-94	Division 1	25 (6)	1	4	0	2	0			6	1			37 (6)	2
1994-95	Division 1	28 (1)	2	0	0	2	0							30 (1)	2
1995-96	Division 1	30 (2)	1	3	0	4	0					2	0	39 (2)	1
1996-97	Division 1	28 (4)	2	0	0	3	0							31 (4)	2
1997-98 (P)	Division 1	13 (3)	0	0 (1)	0	2	0					0	0	15 (4)	0
Total		201 (26)	8	9 (1)	0	15	0	1	0	8	1	2	0	236 (27)	9

UK LEAGUE CAREER 445 games 22 goals

CHARLTON CAREER
Managers: *L Lawrence, A Curbishley/S Gritt, A Curbishley*
Debut: *Brighton & Hove Albion (A) (sub) 15-09-1990*
V511
Finale: *Tranmere Rovers (H) (sub) 25-04-1998*

BARKER Charlie Mel   2020 -

Charlie emerged from the wreckage of Charlton's Covid induced relegation and the chaos of the ownership struggle that at one stage had threatened to completely engulf the club. The son of former assistant manager Ritchie Barker, he was unexpectedly named for the opening fixture in 2020-21, an EFL Trophy match against AFC Wimbledon. The club were forced to operate under a transfer embargo and with captain Jason Pearce injured, there was a distinct lack of central defenders in the building. He grabbed his chance with both hands and at the age of 17, showed an extraordinary degree of maturity and confidence, so much so that he kept his place for the first seven games of the season.

Defender
Born: 12-02-2003 - Rotherham, South Yorkshire

HONOURS
Sussex Schools & Brighton & Hove Schools

CLUBS

Wickersley Youth 2011 (youth) ••Hove Park Colts 2015 ••Charlton Athletic 04.17 (youth) 02.10.20 (pro) ••Wealdstone 24.09.21 (loan)

A month after his first team debut, Charlie signed his first professional contract with Charlton. He had made a very good impression during his spell in the first team and it is hoped that this will be the start of a worthwhile career. It is players like Charlie, emerging through the academy, that represent the future of the club.

Season	Division	League		FA Cup		FL Cup		FL Trophy		Total	
		A	G	A	G	A	G	A	G	A	G
2020-21	League One	3	0	1	0	2	1	3	0	9	1
Total		3	0	1	0	2	1	3	0	9	1

UK LEAGUE CAREER 3 games 0 goals

CHARLTON CAREER
Managers: L Bowyer, N Adkins, J Jackson
Debut: *AFC Wimbledon (A) 01-09-2020*
V896

BARNARD Christopher Leslie 1972

Forward, Midfield   10st 10lbs   5' 8"
Born: 01-08-1947 - Cardiff, Glamorgan

Midfielder Chris Barnard was signed by Charlton on a two-month trial at a time when the club was hovering dangerously close to the foot of Division 2. His single appearance came at Ashton Gate when he replaced Ray Treacy in the 64th minute of a 2-0 defeat against Bristol City and when his trial period expired, manager Theo Foley chose not to further extend his time in SE7

CLUBS

Southend United (youth) 02.08.65 (pro) ••Ipswich Town 05.07.66 (free) ••Torquay United 29.10.70 (£8,000) ••Charlton Athletic 26.01.72 (free) ••Chelmsford City 07.72 (free) ••Cambridge City 07.73 (free) ••Chelmsford City 07.74 (free) ••Tilbury ••Walthamstow Avenue

Chris got off to a spectacular start to his footballing career. On his debut for Southend United on 1st September 1965, he scored both goals in a 2-2 draw against Newport County in a League Cup match where he lined up alongside Derek Woodley and Eddie Firmani. In the replay he scored again, as did Firmani, but whereas Eddie was regularly among the goals, it would be more than five years before Chris managed another one.

His early promise did however earn him a move to Ipswich Town where he stayed for four years. His first game for the Tractor Boys was at the Valley on 20th December 1966, but Mike Kenning spoiled the occasion for him and scored in each half to give Charlton a 2-1 win. This proved to be a rare first team outing for Chris who was fundamentally a reserve throughout his time at Ipswich. Surprisingly he earned a call-up for the Wales U23 squad against Northern Ireland that was scheduled for 4th March 1970, but in the end the fixture had to be cancelled because of snow.

In October 1970 he transferred to Torquay United for a reported fee of £8,000 and at last got a run of first team matches, mainly at inside right. His best day came on 2nd January 1971 when he scored the final two goals to earn the Gulls a 4-3 FA Cup win against Lincoln City, but sadly in his second season the club was nose-diving towards relegation and all of his last eight games ended in defeat. It was against this depressing backdrop that Chris arrived at the Valley for his two-month trial and his subsequent cameo at Bristol did nothing to improve his fortunes.

After leaving Charlton, he joined Southern League side Chelmsford City and fate determined that the two clubs be drawn together in the FA Cup. Most supporters had never seen Chris in a Charlton shirt, but they did get one final chance to at least see him play on 23rd November 1974 when a sizeable crowd packed into the New Writtle Street Stadium. There was fighting on the terraces and a real cup tie atmosphere, but a goal from Arthur Horsfield settled the affair in Charlton's favour. Chris was left as just a footnote in the club's history.

Season	Division	League		FA Cup		FL Cup		Total	
		A	G	A	G	A	G	A	G
1971-72 (R)	Division 2	0 (1)	0	0	0	0	0	0 (1)	0
Total		0 (1)	0	0	0	0	0	0 (1)	0

UK LEAGUE CAREER 62 games 3 goals

CHARLTON CAREER

Managers: *T Foley*

Debut: *Bristol City (A) 19-02-1972*

V369

BARNES Aaron Christopher   2017

Aaron was spotted by Arsenal scouts while competing in a youth tournament in Denmark in July 2006 and spent

Defender   12st 0lbs   6' 1"
Born: 14-10-1996 - Croydon, Surrey
Education: Shernold Preparatory School, Maidstone & Oakwood Park Grammar School, Maidstone.

nearly seven years with the North London club, where he played alongside Regan Charles-Cook. Both players switched to SE7 in 2013 and continued to progress through the Charlton academy until they were eventually rewarded with first team opportunities.

HONOURS

Charlton Athletic U18 2013-14 & 2014-15 Winners PD League 2 South
Charlton Athletic U18 2014-15 Winners PD National League 2
Charlton Athletic U21 2014-15 Winners Kent Senior Cup
Charlton Athletic U21 2015-16 Winners PD League 2 South

Charlton Athletic U21 2015-16 Finalists Kent Senior Cup
Charlton Athletic U23 2016-17 Winners PD League 2 South
Charlton Athletic U23 2017-18 Runners Up PD League 2 South

CLUBS

Arsenal 11.07 (youth) ••Charlton Athletic 03.13 (youth) 12.12.14 (pro) ••Torquay United 12.01.18 (loan) ••Colchester United 31.01.18 (free) ••Torquay United 01.02.18 (loan) ••Dulwich Hamlet 30.07.19 (free) ••Welling United 03.07.21 (free)

For Aaron, his only league appearance for Charlton came at the Valley in the dying minutes of a 3-0 win against Swindon Town as replacement for Chris Solly at right back. In 2017-18 he also featured in three matches in the Football League Trophy but despite winning each game, his personal contribution was not sufficient to persuade manager Karl Robinson to use him further and in January 2018 he departed on loan to Torquay United.

That same month he signed a permanent transfer to Colchester United who immediately loaned him back to Torquay for the remainder of the season. He scored his first senior goal on 10th February 2018 in a 2-1 win at Maidenhead and has since moved on, first to Dulwich Hamlet and then to Welling United, where he played against Charlton in the annual friendly on 13th July 2021. Since 2019 Aaron has been a part-time coach with the Pro Soccer Academy and in September 2021 it was reported that he was also working with Charlton's analytics team, helping to analyse the data obtained from an algorithm created to highlight players who match the club's intended playing style.

Season	Division	League		FA Cup		FL Cup		FL Trophy		Play Offs		Total	
		A	G	A	G	A	G	A	G	A	G	A	G
2016-17	League One	0 (1)	0	0	0	0	0	0	0			0 (1)	0
2017-18	League One	0	0	0	0	0	0	3	0	0	0	3	0
Total		0 (1)	0	0	0	0	0	3	0	0	0	3 (1)	0

UK LEAGUE CAREER 1 game 0 goals

CHARLTON CAREER

Managers: *B Peeters, G Luzon, K Fraeye, J Riga, R Slade, K Robinson*

Debut: *Swindon Town (H) (sub) 30-04-2017*

V839

Finale: *Swansea City U21 (A) 05-12-2017*

BARNES Edward   1921 - 22

Goalkeeper
Born: 21-07-1898 - Royston, Hertfordshire
Died: 1975 -

Ted joined Watford after the First World War. They were already a professional club by that stage, but would not be elected to the Football League until 1920 by which time he had moved on to Southend United. He did manage one League Division 3 (South) appearance for them namely a 2-1 home win against Plymouth Argyle in December 1920. It took place at the old Kursaal ground and he played behind his future teammate Arthur Whalley. Later that same month he dropped down to play Southern League football with Charlton.

HONOURS
St Albans City 1923-24 Winners Isthmian League

CLUBS
Watford 1919 ••St Albans City 1920 ••Southend United 1920 ••Charlton Athletic 12.20 ••Queens Park Rangers 1922 ••St Albans City 12.22

Ted Barnes went straight into the Charlton team, making his Southern League debut in goal against Millwall on Boxing Day 1920 in front of a Valley crowd of 4000. He was first choice goalie for the remainder of the campaign, but lost his place to new signing Joe Hughes when Charlton commenced their opening season in the Football League. He was recalled at Christmas 1921 and held his place for the rest of the season, but letting in five goals at home in the final match did not help him consolidate his position.

The club decided to look elsewhere for a goalkeeper, signing Freddy Wood from Millwall and both Barnes and Hughes were moved on. Ted joined Queens Park Rangers but made no further appearances in the Football League. He did however play in the St Albans team which won the Isthmian League in 1923-24, despite conceding nine goals in one afternoon against Wycombe Wanderers during September.

Season	Division	League		Total	
		A	G	A	G
1921-22	Divison 3 (S)	21	0	21	0
Total		21	0	21	0

UK LEAGUE CAREER 22 games 0 goals

CHARLTON CAREER
Managers: *W Rayner*
Debut: *Southern League Millwall (H) 25-12-1920 Football League Norwich City (H) 26-12-1921*
V027
Finale: *Swindon Town (H) 06-05-1922*

BARNES John Charles Bryan   1999 - 95

Forward, Midfield   12st 7lbs   5' 11"
Born: 07-11-1963 - KIngston, Jamaica
Education: St George's College, Kingston, St Marylebone Grammar School and Havelock Comprehensive, Chalk Farm.

John was one of the leading footballers of his generation. He was a fast, skilful winger and on his day was almost unplayable, After being a key member of the Watford side who finished runners-up in Division 1 in season 1982-83, he went on to enjoy a glittering career with Liverpool and England and spent three months with Charlton in 1999 just as his playing days were nearing their end. Unfortunately he was unable to prevent Alan Curbishley's team from being relegated after just one season in the Premier League. John had earlier been awarded the MBE in June 1998.

HONOURS
England International 1983-95 79 caps 11 goals
England U21 International 1982-83 3 caps 1 goal
PFA Player's Player Of The Year 1987-88

FWA Footballer Of The Year 1987-88 & 1989-90
Watford 1981-82 Runners Up Division 2
Watford 1982-83 Runners Up Division 1

Watford 1983-84 Finalists FA Cup
Liverpool 1987-88 & 1989-90 Winners Division 1
Liverpool 1987-88 & 1995-96 Finalists FA Cup
Liverpool 1988 & 1989 Winners FA Charity Shield
Liverpool 1988-89 Winners FA Cup

Liverpool 1988-89 & 1990-91 Runners Up Division 1
Liverpool 1990 Shared FA Charity Shield
Liverpool 1994-95 Winners Football League Cup
Newcastle United 1997-98 Finalists FA Cup

HONOURS AS MANAGER

Celtic 1999-00 Runners Up Scottish Premier League   Jamaica 2008 Winners Caribbean Cup

CLUBS

Bartex, Jamaica (youth) ••Stowe Boys Club 1977 (youth) ••Sudbury Court 09.80 (youth) ••Watford 23.04.81 (youth) 14.07.81 (pro) ••Liverpool 19.06.87 (£900,000) ••Newcastle United 14.08.97 (free) ••Charlton Athletic 10.02.99 (free) ••Celtic, Scotland 10.06.99 (manager) ••Jamaica 16.09.08 (manager) ••Tranmere Rovers 15.06.09 (manager)

After moving with his family from Kingston, Jamaica to the UK at the age of 12, John joined Watford in 1981 and burst into their first team as a 17-year-old, making his full league debut in a 3-1 away win at Chelsea on 12th September 1981. It was immediately apparent that he was an outstanding talent and he played a major role as Watford secured promotion from Division 2 and then the following year finished as runners-up in the First Division. All this was achieved while he was still a teenager. He played in the 1984 FA Cup Final when Watford lost 2-0 to Everton and went on to make 233 league appearances and score 65 goals for the Hornets, before transferring to Liverpool in June 1987.

English football was dominated by Liverpool throughout the 1980s and John joined them while they were at their peak. Indeed, they only narrowly missed achieving the FA Cup and League double in each of his first three seasons. He spent ten years on Merseyside, eventually amassing two First Division championship medals as well as playing in three FA Cup finals, two of which ended in defeat. He missed the 1992 final through injury, but was in the side that defeated Everton 3-2 on 20th May 1989. He completed his full set of domestic medals when Liverpool beat Bolton Wanderers 2-1 to claim the League Cup on 2nd April 1995. Space precludes more detailed mention of Liverpool's many achievements during this period, but one match which cannot be forgotten was on 12th September 1989 when they demolished a Crystal Palace team, which included Mark Bright and Alan Pardew, by 9-0. John scored goal number seven. On two occasions he was voted the Football Writers' Player of the Year.

His international career lasted for 12 years, from May 1983 until September 1995 and covered 79 matches. High points included his second half performance against Argentina in the 1986 FIFA World Cup finals, but generally he was perceived to have under-performed in an England shirt. He was picked on by the crowds and suffered racial abuse on several occasions. When the team were playing badly, it was John who invariably became the target of the boo boys. Despite everything, his own behaviour was impeccable and without question he will be best remembered for his amazing solo goal against Brazil on 10th June 1984, which is considered among the finest scored by an England player. Liverpool gave John a free transfer in 1997 after 384 league appearances and 84 goals and he signed for Newcastle United. He finished 1997-98 as their leading goalscorer and with Robert Lee alongside him, they contested the 1998 FA Cup final at Wembley, although Arsenal proved too strong and won 2-0. By February 1999 a managerial change at Newcastle had left him out in the cold and he joined Charlton, who were already involved in a battle to preserve their newly acquired Premier League status. John may have lost much of his pace, but was still a very skilful and intelligent player. His debut came as a second half substitute for Neil Redfearn on 13th February 1999, ironically enough against Liverpool. Four minutes later Keith Jones scored the only goal of the match to give the Addicks an unexpected three points. From then on John was utilised mainly as a substitute, but although it went to the final game, relegation could not be avoided and he announced his retirement as a player soon after.

With no significant coaching experience behind him, it was something of a shock when John was fast-tracked into the manager's chair at Celtic the following month. He had no option but to learn on the job and quickly found that finishing second to Rangers was not going to prove acceptable. With the league form uninspiring, a home defeat against Inverness Caledonian Thistle in the Scottish League Cup proved to be his undoing and he was sacked in February 2000 after just eight months in charge.

In September 2008 John was appointed manager of Jamaica and he guided them to the final of the Caribbean Cup, where they defeated Grenada 2-0 on 14th December 2008 in Kingston, the city of his birth. He left six months later and accepted the manager's job at Tranmere Rovers, but they only scraped two league wins during the eleven matches of his reign. This included a 4-0 drubbing against Charlton at Prenton Park on 29th August 2009, courtesy of goals from Lloyd Sam (2). Jose Semedo and Nicky Bailey. By October, they were 22nd in League Two and John's managerial career was abruptly terminated.

Over the years John has been a familiar face on British television and has appeared in 'Blankety Blank', 'Strictly Come Dancing', 'Question Time', 'Waterloo Road' and 'Celebrity Big Brother' among others. In 2001, he was the subject of 'This Is Your Life'. He recorded several rap records, including his version of the 1990 World Cup song, 'World In Motion' and has featured in adverts for Lucozade. He has worked extensively for charity and is an ambassador for 'Save The Children'. His life story, 'John Barnes The Autobiography' was published in 1999 and a second book, 'The Uncomfortable Truth About Racism' followed in 2021. He remains active as a television commentator and pundit.

Season	Division	League		FA Cup		FL Cup		Total	
		A	G	A	G	A	G	A	G
1998-99 (R)	Premier	2 (10)	0	0	0	0	0	2 (10)	0
Total		2 (10)	0	0	0	0	0	2 (10)	0

UK LEAGUE CAREER 586 games 155 goals

CHARLTON CAREER
Managers: *A Curbishley*
Debut: *Liverpool (H) (sub) 13-02-1999*
V581
Finale: *Sheffield Wednesday (H) (sub) 16-05-1995*

BARNESS Anthony 'Barney'   1991 - 00

Defender   11st 4lbs   5' 10"
Born: 25-02-1973 - Lewisham, London
Education: Our Lady of Lourdes Primary School, Lewisham & St Joseph's Academy, Blackheath.

A solid, no frills, defender, Barney had two spells at Charlton, either side of a slightly disappointing sojourn with Chelsea for whom he played only 14 Premier League games in four years. He had been an outstanding prospect as a teenager and captained Charlton's youth team in the South East Counties League during 1990-91, before making his first team debut in September 1991. The following year he was named as Young Player of the Year.

HONOURS
Blackheath Schools & London Schools
Charlton Athletic 1992 Young Player Of The Year
Charlton Athletic 1997-98 Promoted Play Offs Division 1
Charlton Athletic Reserves 1997-98 & 1998-99 Winners Football Combination
Charlton Athletic 1999-00 Winners Division 1

Charlton Athletic Reserves 1999-00 Runners Up FA Premier Reserve League South
Bolton Wanderers 2000-01 Promoted Play Offs Division 1
Lewes 2007-08 Winners Conference South

CLUBS
Charlton Athletic 27.01.88 (youth) 06.03.91 (pro) ••Chelsea 08.09.92 (£350,000) ••Middlesbrough 12.08.93 (loan) ••Southend United 02.02.96 (loan) ••Charlton Athletic 08.08.96 (£165,000) ••Bolton Wanderers 06.07.00 (free) ••West Ham United 15.01.04 (loan) ••Plymouth Argyle 04.07.05 (free) ••Grays Athletic 09.03.07 (loan) ••Lewes 17.08.07 (free)

In the early nineties Charlton were fortunate to have two outstanding prospects for the position of left back. Scott Minto was 18 months older than Barney and by September 1992 it was he who was first choice for the team. The club was seriously strapped for cash after seven years in exile and with only a few months remaining before the long awaited return to the Valley, nobody was surprised when Chelsea came calling, but there was considerable astonishment when it was Barness and not Minto who headed off to West London.

The move probably came too soon for Barney who was not yet the finished article and an early change of manager at Chelsea did not help his cause, leaving him to languish for long periods on the sidelines. There were loan transfers to both Lennie Lawrence's Middlesbrough and to Southend where he played alongside Simon Royce, but his career did not really come back on track until he re-signed for Charlton in August 1996. Ironically enough, Minto had by then himself departed for Chelsea, so he was able to regain the left back spot for 1996-97, which turned out to be his most successful season. He only missed one league game and played consistently well throughout. Barney never quite reached the same standard again and although he played regularly during the promotion campaign of 1997-98, he eventually lost his place to Mark Bowen and consequently missed out on an appearance in the play off final at Wembley.

He left for Bolton Wanderers in the Summer of 2000 and stepped straight into another promotion campaign which took him to the Millennium Stadium in Cardiff on 28th May 2001. This was the play off final in which they defeated Preston North End 3-0 and followed Charlton into the Premier League where Barney remained a semi-regular over the next three seasons. Bolton were generally

quite successful against Charlton during that period, but Barney was playing on 24th August 2002 when the Addicks snatched a 2-1 victory at the Reebok Stadium, courtesy of Jason Euell and a Chris Bart-Williams penalty. A loan transfer to West Ham in January 2004 was aborted after just one day when he was recalled to the Bolton team because of a sudden injury crisis and he was an unused substitute in the League Cup final in February.

A move to Plymouth Argyle came in 2005, but after little more than a year his Football League career was at an end. Following an unsuccessful trial with Yeovil Town, Barney joined Lewes and helped steer them to promotion from the Conference South in 2007-08. Since hanging up his boots, he has run a ceramic tiling business in Brighton and is an enthusiastic snooker player and an accomplished cook.

Season	Division	League		FA Cup		FL Cup		FM Cup		AI Cup		Play Offs			
		A	G	Total	G	A	G	A	G	A	G	A	G	A	G
1991-92	Division 2	16 (6)	1	3	0	2	0	1	0					22 (6)	1
1992-93	Division 1	5	0	0	0	0	0			0 (1)	1			5 (1)	1
1996-97	Division 1	45	2	2	0	4	0							51	2
1997-98 (P)	Division 1	21 (8)	1	0 (1)	0	2 (1)	0					0	0	23 (10)	1
1998-99	Premier	0 (3)	0	0	0	0	0							0 (3)	0
1999-00 (P)	Division 1	17 (2)	0	1	0	0	0							18 (2)	0
Total		104 (19)	4	6 (1)	0	8 (1)	0	1	0	0 (1)	1	0	0	119 (22)	5

CHARLTON CAREER
Managers: L Lawrence, A Curbishley/S Gritt, A Curbishley
Debut: *Sunderland (H) (sub) 17-09-1991*
V522
Finale: *West Bromwich Albion (A) 07-05-2000*

UK LEAGUE CAREER 272 games 4 goals

BARRON William   1938

Bill was a fine all round sportsman and played both football and cricket to a good standard. As a cricketer he played for Durham in the thirties, then after wartime service with the RAF, made his first class debut for Lancashire in 1945. A year later he switched to Northants and appeared for them in 118 first class matches, scoring nearly 5,000 runs. He was a left handed batsman and occasional leg break bowler. His highest first class score of 161 was made against Cambridge University in 1948.

Defender, Forward   10st 8lbs   5' 8"
Born: 26-10-1917 - Herrington, Durham
Died: 02-01-2006 - Northampton, Northamptonshire

HONOURS
Northampton Town 1949-50 Runners Up Division 3 (S)

CLUBS
Hetton Juniors 1934 (youth) ••Bishop Auckland 1935 (Youth) ••Annfield Plain 1936 ••Hartlepools United 08.09.36 (amateur) ••Wolverhampton Wanderers 02.11.36 ••Annfield Plain 1937 ••Charlton Athletic 04.11.37 (£350) ••Northampton Town 05.38 (free) ••Kettering Town 1951

Bill was only 19 when he signed for Charlton in October 1937, but had already spent brief periods with two Football League clubs. His stay had lasted only seven months when he was unexpectedly called up for first team duty, after Harold Hobbis broke his leg in an FA Cup match at

Highbury. His debut came against Brentford on 26th February, before a Valley crowd of 35,572. Bill played outside left in a closely contested match and scored the winning goal three minutes from time for a 1-0 scoreline. He retained his place for two further games and scored again when Charlton played Stoke a few days later, but was rather surprisingly discarded following defeat at Bolton. Jimmy Seed shuffled the side, recalling George Tadman at centre forward and moving Sailor Brown on to the left wing and that marked the end of Bill's brief but eventful time as a Charlton player.

At the end of that season, he moved to Northampton

Town where he remained for 13 years, playing mainly at left back. During the war he also guested for both Luton Town and Leicester City. Bill had a fine singing voice and would often entertain his teammates on long coach journeys. He died at the age of 88. His son, Roger Barron, played in goal for Northampton Town in the sixties.

Season	Division	League		FA Cup		Total	
		A	G	A	G	A	G
1937-38	Division 1	3	2	0	0	3	2
Total		3	2	0	0	3	2

UK LEAGUE CAREER 169 games 6 goals

CHARLTON CAREER
Managers: *J Seed*
Debut: *Brentford (H) 26-02-1938*
V200
Finale: *Bolton Wanderers (A) 05-03-1938*

BARRY Kevin Anthony   1953

Forward   10st 0lbs   5' 8"
Born: 13-09-1930 - Woolwich, London
Died: 07-2016 -
Education: St Patrick's School, Plumstead, & Woolwich Polytechnic.

Kevin was a left winger who spent more than seven years at Charlton. Although he performed consistently well in the Reserves, his passage into the first team was blocked by the excellence of Billy Kiernan. He did however step into the limelight for a brief spell during season 1952-53 when Kiernan was absent through injury. He had earlier represented London Boys against Glasgow Boys up at Hampden Park in 1947.

HONOURS

London Boys X1 1947 1 cap 0 goals
Charlton Athletic A 1950-51 Winners London Mid-Week League
Charlton Athletic Reserves 1951-52 Finalists London FA Challenge Cup

Charlton Athletic Reserves 1952-53 Runners Up Football Combination Cup
Cambridge United 1957-58 Runners Up Eastern Counties League

CLUBS

Woolwich Polytechnic (youth) ••Gorman Rovers (youth) ••London Telecoms (amateur) ••Charlton Athletic 16.06.47 (amateur) 09.12.47 (pro) ••Sittingbourne 1955 (free) ••Cambridge United 06.56 (free) ••Wisbech Town 1959 (free) ••Argyle Sports 1959 ••Chatham Town 1960 ••Beckenham Town 1960 ••Woolwich Town 1961

It was whilst working as an apprentice telephone engineer that Kevin attracted the attention of Charlton and he signed amateur forms in June 1947, before taking the plunge as a professional six months later. After National Service in the RAF, he settled down as a regular in the Reserves and in season 1951-52 scored a very impressive 25 competitive goals.

His first team debut came in January 1953 in a disappointing FA Cup defeat at Hull, but he did enough to keep his place the following week when Sheffield Wednesday were comprehensively beaten 3-0 at the Valley thanks to two strikes from Stuart Leary, either side of a goal by Syd O'Linn. Undoubtedly the highlight of Kevin's time with the first team came in his third match, however. Before a Highbury crowd of 66,555, Charlton twice came from

behind to secure a 2-2 draw against Arsenal, largely thanks to Gordon Hurst who scored both goals, the second coming late in the match. This ended Kevin's brief run in the side, although he managed one further appearance in April when Kiernan was again absent. A long spell in the treatment room following a cartilage operation in 1954 hastened his Valley exit.

After being freed by Charlton in 1955, he had a spell with Sittingbourne before joining Cambridge United, then competing in the lowly Eastern Counties League. During this period his teammates included the legendary Wilf Mannion, then in the final stages of his career. Kevin got to play in a Benefit match for Mannion in 1958 alongside many of the top players of the time, including another Cambridge colleague and former Charlton player, Frank

Lock.

Kevin was a fine cricketer and had a trial with Kent. He also boxed and for a time was secretary of the St Peter's Amateur Boxing Club in Woolwich. After marrying in 1960 he lived for many years in Eastview Avenue, Plumstead, but in 1993 was obliged to retire from his work at the Clockhouse Community Centre suffering with glaucoma. He passed away at the age of 85.

Back in 1955 Kevin appeared in the film 'The Love Match' starring Arthur Askey. Part of the action was shot at the Valley and he played the part of a linesman.

Season	Division	League		FA Cup		Total	
		A	G	A	G	A	G
1952-53	Division 1	3	0	1	0	4	0
Total		3	0	1	0	4	0

UK LEAGUE CAREER 3 games 0 goals

CHARLTON CAREER
Managers: *J Seed*
Debut: *Hull City (A) 10-01-1953*
V253
Finale: *Stoke City (A) 11-04-1953*

BART-WILLIAMS Christopher Gerald   2001 - 03

Born in Sierra Leone, Chris and his mother came to England when he was aged four. His start in football came early and when he made his debut for Leyton Orient at age 16, he was one of the youngest players ever to represent them. (Their record is still held by Paul Went, who was only 15). He scored on his home debut against Tranmere Rovers on 2nd February 1991 and soon attracted attention from other clubs placed further up the food chain. Sheffield Wednesday paid £500,000 for his signature in November 1991, plus goalkeeper Chris Turner, valued at £75,000.

Midfield, Defender   11st 6lbs   5' 11"
Born: 16-06-1974 - Freetown, Sierra Leone

HONOURS

England B International 1994 1 cap 0 goals
England U21 International 1992-95 16 caps 2 goals
England U19 International 1993 7 caps 1 goal

England U18 International 1991-92 7 caps 3 goals
Sheffield Wednesday 1992-93 Finalists FA Cup Final
Nottingham Forest 1997-98 Winners Division 1

CLUBS

Grasshoppers (New Southgate) 1985 (youth) ••Arvensdale c1989 (youth) ••Leyton Orient 24.08.89 (youth) 18.07.91 (pro) ••Sheffield Wednesday 21.11.91 (£500,000 + player) ••Nottingham Forest 01.07.95 (£2.5 million) ••Charlton Athletic 03.12.01 (loan) 28.01.02 (free) ••Ipswich Town 12.09.03 (loan) 12.12.03 (free) ••APOEL, Cyprus 29.09.04 (free) ••Marsaxlokk, Malta 06.08.05 (free)

Chris featured in the 1993 FA Cup final for Sheffield Wednesday as a substitute, in both the drawn match and the replay in which Arsenal won 2-1. The same year, he also played at the FIFA World Youth Championships in Australia where England gained third place. In fact, it was a busy year for him as he played in international matches for England at both U19 and U21 level.

In 1995, he followed his old Orient boss, Frank Clark, to Nottingham Forest where he enjoyed probably the best period of his career. The 'Bartman' was made club captain and he led them to the Division 1 title in 1997-98 and went on to play almost 250 competitive matches before he was forced out of the club in rather unpleasant circumstances. Forest were in a financial mess and became desperate to get Chris off the wage roll, eventually refusing to play him and forcing him to train away from the first team. At this point

Charlton came into the picture and signed him, initially on loan but later on a permanent basis.

Skipper Mark Kinsella had been ruled out of the Charlton side with a nasty knee injury which brought about the need for Chris to bolster the midfield and he played fairly regularly until Mark returned, even scoring the winner in the 1-0 defeat of Derby County at the Valley on 29th January 2002. In his second season, first team opportunities were less frequent and he eventually moved on to Ipswich Town.

His playing career came to a close after brief spells in both Cyprus and Malta and he then moved to the USA, where he coached Boston Breakers, a team in the Women's Professional Soccer League. By 2013 he was coaching at Quinnipiac University in Connecticut and went on to run his own soccer training and college recruitment service,

CBW Soccer Elite.

Season	Division	League		FA Cup		FL Cup		Total	
		A	G	A	G	A	G	A	G
2001-02	Premier	10 (6)	1	2	0	0	0	12 (6)	1
2002-03	Premier	7 (6)	1	1 (1)	0	0	0	8 (7)	1
Total		17 (12)	2	3 (1)	0	0	0	20 (13)	2

UK LEAGUE CAREER 422 games 52 goals

CHARLTON CAREER
Managers: *A Curbishley*
Debut: *Tottenham Hotspur (H) (sub) 08-10-2001*
V604
Finale: *Manchester United (A) (sub) 03-05-2003*

BARTLETT Thurston Shaun　　　　　　　　　2000 - 06

Forward　12st 4lbs　6' 1"
Born: 31-10-1972 - Cape Town, South Africa

For ten years Shaun was a vital part of the South Africa team and his total of 74 caps ranks him sixth in their all-time appearance listing, while his 28 goals have only once been exceeded. During his time as a Charlton player he scored nine of his international goals in 25 matches. Along with Mark Fish, he was part of the South African team which triumphed in the final of the 1996 Africa Cup of Nations, beating Tunisia 2-0 in front of an 80,000 crowd. Shaun also played in the 1998 World Cup Finals in France and scored both goals in a 2-2 draw against Saudi Arabia. He was the complete centre forward, strong physically, well able to shield and hold the ball as well as possessing a powerful shot and was an important part of the Charlton team during the final six years of the Curbishley era.

HONOURS

South Africa International 1995-05 74 caps 28 goals
Cape Town Spurs 1994 Runners Up NSL First Division
Cape Town Spurs 1995 Winners NSL First Division
Cape Town Spurs 1995 Winners Bob Save Super Bowl (FA Cup)
FC Zurich 1999-00 Winners Swiss FA Cup

CLUBS

Norway Parks, South Africa (youth) ••Vasco Da Gama, South Africa (youth) •Cape Town Spurs, South Africa 06.92 (pro) ••Colorado Rapids, USA 1996 (free) ••AmaZulu, South Africa 1996 (free) ••New York/New Jersey MetroStars, USA 1997 (free) ••Cape Town Spurs, South Africa 1997 (loan) ••FC Zurich, Switzerland 1998 (free) ••Charlton Athletic 01.12.00 (loan) 22.05.01 (£2 million) ••Kaizer Chiefs, South Africa 2006 (free) ••Bloemfontein Celtic, South Africa 2008 (free) ••Lamontville Golden Arrows, South Africa 26.04.12 (coach) ••AmaTuks, South Africa 28.01.16 (coach) ••South African FA 09.18 (coach) ••Kaizer Chiefs, South Africa 10.12.18 (ass. coach) ••TS Galaxy, South Africa 17. 01.21 (ass. coach) ••Cape Town Spurs 25.10.21 (coach)

Shaun's professional career commenced with Cape Town Spurs and in 1995, with him in the side, they won the NSL First Division for the first and only time in their history. They completed the double that same year by also securing the South African FA Cup (then branded as the Bob Save Super Bowl). Pretoria City were beaten 3-2 in the final and Shaun netted the winner in the 89th minute. Other opportunities now presented themselves and he had two short spells playing in the USA, the second of which was for New York/New Jersey MetroStars, who had not long since been managed by Eddie Firmani.
In 1998, he made the move to Europe, signing for FC Zurich and helped them to win the Swiss FA Cup for the first time in over 20 years. The final against Lausanne took place on 28th May 2000 and was all square after 90 minutes. Shaun himself scored during extra time, but it

took kicks from the penalty spot before Zurich finally emerged as winners.
He arrived in London SE7 in December 2000 under a loan arrangement which was later converted into a full transfer, via a fee of £2 million and he made his Charlton debut one day after his registration was cleared. The opposition were Liverpool and the Anfield crowd was at full throttle when he replaced Martin Pringle as a second half substitute. His presence could not stem the tide though and the Addicks were well beaten 3-0. A week later on 9th December the Valley faithful got a first look at their new South African signing. This time they faced Manchester United, but made a promising start when Shaun scored after 10 minutes. However by the middle of the second half United had gone into a 3-1 lead and the position was looking grim. Then on 79 minutes Shaun got a second and amazingly

John Robinson added a late third for an unexpected but highly deserved 3-3 draw.

If that Manchester United match introduced Shaun to South London, then it was another very special goal later that same season for which he will always be remembered. Leicester City were the visitors on 1st April and Charlton were defending a 1-0 first half lead courtesy of an Andy Todd penalty. With eight minutes remaining, Graham Stuart brought the ball over the halfway line and hit an inch perfect pass, which Shaun volleyed across the goalkeeper and into the net for a 2-0 scoreline. It was voted the Goal of the Season by the ITV television viewers, (BBC had temporarily lost the broadcasting rights) and is the only occasion when a Charlton goal has been honoured in this way.

Unfortunately Shaun picked up more than his share of injuries whilst at Charlton and this combined with additional absences through international commitments restricted his appearances. A damaged Achilles tendon kept him sidelined during the second half of season 2001-02 and cost him his place in the World Cup finals, while a knee injury sustained at Portsmouth in April 2005 meant his absence at a critical time in that season. He did not feature much during 2005-06 and his final goal in English football came at the Valley against West Ham on 31st December 2005. Darren Bent scored a second for a 2-0 win against a Hammers line-up which included Paul Konchesky, Christian Dailly and Shaun Newton. The club gave Shaun a free transfer in May 2006 and he returned to South Africa.

The next two years were spent with the Johannesburg club, Kaiser Chiefs, competing in the Premier League of South African football after which he announced his retirement, only to be persuaded to carry on for a further year with Bloemfontein Celtic. He finally called it a day in 2009 and since then has remained active as a coach within South Africa. Shaun has worked for a variety of different clubs, but in October 2021 he accepted not just a coaching job but was appointed manager of Cape Town Spurs, his hometown club and with whom he commenced his football career nearly 30 years earlier.

Season	Division	League		FA Cup		FL Cup		Total	
		A	G	A	G	A	G	A	G
2000-01	Premier	16 (2)	7	2	0	0	0	18 (2)	7
2001-02	Premier	10 (4)	1	0 (1)	0	2	0	12 (5)	1
2002-03	Premier	25 (6)	4	2	0	1	0	28 (6)	4
2003-04	Premier	13 (6)	5	0	0	0	0	13 (6)	5
2004-05	Premier	25	6	2	2	0	0	27	8
2005-06	Premier	6 (10)	1	4 (1)	0	1	0	11 (11)	1
Total		95 (28)	24	10 (2)	2	4	0	109 (30)	26

UK LEAGUE CAREER 123 games 24 goals

CHARLTON CAREER
Managers: *A Curbishley*
Debut: *Liverpool (A) (sub) 02-12-2000*
V597
Finale: *Manchester United (A) 07-05-2006*

BARTRAM Samuel   1934 - 56

Charlton have spent a hundred years in the Football League, yet the contribution of only one man has been deemed important enough to warrant a permanent monument. The impressive statue of Samuel Bartram stands proudly alongside the main entrance at the Valley, the stadium which he graced with such distinction for 22 years. He was the goalkeeper in 1937 when the club finished runners up in Division 1 and ten years later for the FA Cup final victory against Burnley.. His total of 579 league and 44 cup appearances is an all-time club record and does not include a further 109 matches during World War 2. In addition to the statue, he is further honoured at the Lansdowne Mews entrance to the ground where the Sam Bartram Gate is to be found and at the back of the West Stand, where Bartrams is the name of the club bar. In 1976 a newly constructed road near to the Valley was named Sam Bartram Close and not surprisingly he was one of the first three players inducted into the Hall of Fame when it was introduced in 2012.

Goalkeeper   13st 0lbs   6' 0"
Born: 22-01-1914 - Simonside, South Shields
Died: 17-07-1981 - Harpenden, Hertfordshire
Education: Boldon Colliery School.

HONOURS

England Wartime International 1940-41 3 games 0 goals
Sunderland Schools & Durham County Schools 1927-28
FA Tour of South Africa 1939
FA Xl 1939 in aid of the Red Cross
FA Tour of Australia 1951
London FA 1953 3 caps 0 goals
England Over 30 Xl 1954 v Young England
Charlton Athletic 1934-35 Winners Division 3 (South)
Charlton Athletic 1935-36 Runners Up Division 2

Charlton Athletic 1936-37 Runners Up Division 1
Charlton Athletic 1943-44 Winners FL South Cup
Charlton Athletic 1943-44 Winners Alexander Cup
Charlton Athletic 1945-46 Finalists FA Cup
Charlton Athletic 1946-47 Winners FA Cup
Charlton Athletic 2012 Hall Of Fame
Boldon Villa 1933-34 Winners Tyne Alliance League Cup
Millwall (guest) 1944-45 Finalists FL South Cup

HONOURS AS MANAGER

York City 1958-59 Promoted Division 4

CLUBS

Boldon Villa ••North Shields ••Boldon Villa ••Jarrow ••Boldon Villa ••Reading 1931 (trial) ••Boldon Villa ••Easington Colliery ••Boldon Villa ••North Shields 07.34 ••Boldon Villa 1934 ••Charlton Athletic 15.09.34 (pro) ••York City 11.03.56 (manager) ••Luton Town 20.07.60 (manager)

Sam was born in Simonside, three miles from South Shields. His father was a coal miner who passed away when his son was only nine years old, but by then the family were living in Boldon Colliery, a small mining village nearby. He was already playing football at every opportunity and received encouragement at school where he captained the side from left half, although when kicking about with his friends, he usually ended up playing in goal. Boldon is four miles from Sunderland and at weekends Sam and his pals would walk to Roker Park to watch their heroes play. Money was extremely tight and would not stretch to bus fares.

During season 1927-28 he represented Sunderland Boys in the England Schools Shield and skippered County Durham against Northumberland, even scoring in a 1-0 win, while as further evidence of his progress, he received a call-up for England Schoolboys. Sadly he had to decline as he had started work as a miner at Boldon Colliery and was playing for the local village team, Boldon Villa. His dream was to play professional football and he tried out with bigger clubs, North Shields (as a centre forward) and Jarrow (left half) in an attempt to get himself noticed, but on each occasion soon returned to Boldon Villa where increasingly scouts were following the progress of this exciting young prospect.

He made his first trip south in 1931 for a month's trial with Reading and played four times for their reserves in the London Combination at left half, but was not kept on and was soon back at the Villa where he was now being asked to play at centre forward. There were further moves to Easington Colliery and North Shields (again), but no real progress and as always Sam returned to Boldon Villa where on Good Friday 1934, they contested the final of the Tyne Alliance Challenge Cup and this was the day when his

extraordinary career really got going. The Boldon Villa goalkeeper was injured and Sam persuaded the club to let him deputise. He had always liked to perform in goal during training sessions and after keeping a clean sheet, began to be selected as a goalkeeper rather than a centre forward.

Jimmy Seed's brother Angus had watched Sam play several times, both on the field and in goal. He had recommended him to the club even before the tragedy which hit Charlton following a 2-1 win over Torquay United on 5th September 1934. The players had gone to the beach and first team 'keeper Alex Wright broke his neck whilst diving from a raft into the sea. He died in Torbay Hospital two days later. A replacement was urgently required and at the Charlton Director's Meeting on 14th September, inevitably the main business of the day covered the arrangements for the forthcoming funeral, but it was also reported, almost as a footnote, that Sam Bartram goalkeeper, had been signed on a one-month trial at £5 per week. Sam had previously been earning 17/6 (about 88p) a week after six years of working as a coal miner.

The reserve goalkeeper at Charlton was Harry Wright (no relation to Alex) and initially he took over the first team spot while Sam was being tried out in the reserves. Bartram was not an instant success and was only granted a second monthly trial on the understanding that he must do better, but happily an outstanding showing against Chelsea Reserves in November 1934 convinced Seed to upgrade his new signing on to a permanent contract. The first team had made an impressive start to the 1934-35 season and was already in pole position in Division 3 (South) when Sam made his debut at Watford on 1st December. The game was lost 2-0, but a week later, Newport County were crushed 6-0. Harry Wright then returned from injury and re-claimed his place for the next five matches, but after Sam was recalled against Brighton on 5th January 1935, Charlton went on to win Division 3 (South) at a canter. He made 18 league appearances that first season, was now first choice goalie and would never again be dropped, right up to his retirement in March 1956.

Jimmy Seed ignored his critics and kept a largely unchanged squad in 1935-36 and with Sam missing only three matches, Charlton finished runners-up, just a point behind Manchester United. They earned promotion to Division 1 for the first time, but surely nobody expected a third season of success. This was probably the greatest Charlton side of all, and they went on to lead the First Division table in 1936-37 with 10 matches remaining. It took a pair of defeats at Derby and Chelsea in March to eventually peg them back and they finished in second place behind Manchester City. Sam was the only player who appeared in every game and the home form, which saw only 13 goals conceded in 21 matches, was the key to the team's achievement.

Football in the thirties was a very much more physical pursuit than in modern times. In those early days, Sam was criticised for being too flamboyant and also for the sometimes reckless way he would dive at the feet of opposing forwards. Against Newcastle in October 1935 he went in at half-time with blood spurting from the back of his leg and had to have seven stitches in his calf before the start of the second half. Fortunately, he never suffered a serious injury throughout his career and was of the opinion that it was hesitation which caused a goalkeeper to be injured. Charlton remained a leading club right up to the war and Sam figured in all the big games, especially the epic battles with Arsenal. He got married on 25th September 1937, but was obliged to leave the reception in time for the home match with Middlesbrough, a 1-0 win. On Christmas Day 1937 thick fog descended on Stamford Bridge during the fixture with Chelsea. The referee abandoned the match and the players returned to the dressing room. It was some time before a policeman spotted Sam, still patrolling his goalmouth and unaware that the game was over. Football violence was alive and well pre-war. Sam was hit on the back of the head by a half brick after saving a penalty at Portsmouth and the same crowd managed to set fire to his goal netting.

World War 2 did not quite bring football to a halt. The Football League organised regional competitions and Sam played whenever he was available. Initially he signed up for the War Reserve Police, but later enlisted in the RAF, where he was taught to be a physical training instructor. As well as more than 100 wartime matches for Charlton, he also made guest appearances for Notts County, Bournemouth, Liverpool, Brentford, Crewe Alexandra, West Ham, Bradford City, Crystal Palace, Millwall, Birmingham and York City. With the latter, he took and scored two penalties in one match.

On 15th April 1944 Charlton played Chelsea at Wembley in the final of the wartime Football League (South) Cup in front of a crowd of 85,000. Goals from Charlie Revell (2) and Don Welsh ensured a 3-1 victory for the Addicks. Sam played in this match plus the decider between the North and South winners, which took place at Stamford Bridge five weeks later. This was played for the Alexander Cup and Aston Villa were the opponents. Revell scored again, but Aston Villa earned a 1-1 draw and the cup was shared. Guest players were permitted during the war and twelve months later both Sam and Sailor Brown were back at Wembley, but this time guesting for Millwall. They had four guests in their team and their opponents, Chelsea, no less than eight for the 1944-45 Football League (South) final, which became sarcastically known as the 'lease-lend final'. Chelsea won 2-0.

It was extraordinary that Sam never played in a full England international. He did however play in three wartime games, including a 3-2 win against Wales in Cardiff on 7th June 1941. Furthermore, he was picked on two further occasions, but his RAF commitments prevented him from playing. He toured South Africa in 1939 with an England XI and he was in the team which beat a South African XI 3-0 in Johannesburg. Sam took part in a lengthy England tour of Australia commencing in May 1951. The England party, which included Gordon Hurst and Frank Lock, played and won 21 games, five of which were described as 'Test Matches'. He played in four of them, but the opposition was chronically weak and one match was won 17-0. He also represented England Over 30s against Young England in 1954.

Charlton fought through to the final of the first post-war FA Cup on 27th April 1946, but Sam had to accept the disappointment of losing 4-1 in extra time against Derby County. Against all the odds they returned to Wembley again a year later and he was this time able to keep a clean sheet as Burnley were defeated 1-0 and the FA Cup came to SE7 for the only occasion to date. Including his guest appearance for Millwall, this now meant that Sam had played in a record four consecutive Wembley Cup Finals. In fact, when weighed alongside the 1930s league successes, it can be seen that all of Charlton's greatest cup and league achievements occurred when Sam was between the posts.

One extraordinary match took place on 7th February 1948 at Huddersfield. It was an FA Cup Round 5 tie against Manchester United and Charlton, with a sightly weakened side, were up against it from the start. United were rampant and shot after shot was fired at the Charlton goal, only to find Sam in the form of his life. Shots came at him from all angles and eventually he was beaten twice for a scoreline of 2-0. At the final whistle, however, Sam received congratulations from the players of both teams and from the referee. He was chaired off the field by his teammates and warmly applauded by all the crowd. By the early fifties the rest of the pre-war players had dropped away but Sam remained, as consistent as ever and very much the face of Charlton Athletic. He and his wife Helen opened a sports shop in Floyd Road and he was always happy to meet supporters, sign autographs or just chat about football.

On 13th March 1952 Sam played at Highbury when a Charlie Vaughan goal proved insufficient to see off a strong Arsenal team who were victorious 2-1. The significance of this match was that it was Sam's 418th league game for Charlton and moved him ahead of Norman Smith in the club appearance records. He has remained at the top of the list ever since. His 500th league match was against Portsmouth at the Valley on 6th March 1954.(It was actually match 701 if you count wartime games, cups and friendlies). The club produced a cake to mark the occasion and after the candles had been extinguished, Portsmouth were blown away 3-1, thanks to goals from Stuart Leary and Eddie Firmani (2). Sam's mother travelled down to be present for this special occasion.

By this point in his career, Sam had agreed with Jimmy Seed that he would never be dropped. The two men had been together for over 20 years and there was a good deal of mutual respect. Sam asked that he be told if his goalkeeping ever fell below the required standard and he would then retire gracefully. In the event, that day was never reached because in March 1956 he accepted an offer to become manager of York City. It all came about very rapidly and on 10th March 1956 at the age of 42, Sam played the final match of his extraordinary career. Fittingly, Arsenal were the opponents and a Valley crowd of 40,553 saw him check out with a clean sheet and a 2-0 win, courtesy of two goals from Jimmy Gauld.

Sam had played over 100 wartime matches for York while stationed with the RAF in Harrogate, so was already comfortable with his surroundings. He took over a team in mid-table in Division 3 (North) and remained in charge for over four years. During this time, the Football League removed the regionalization and created Divisions 3 and 4. York were founder members of the new Division 4 and Sam steered them to promotion at the first attempt. He moved on to Luton Town in 1960 and managed them for two seasons in Division 2 which put him in opposition with Charlton. He returned to the Valley with his Luton side on 17th September 1960 but received a 4-1 battering thanks to goals from Sam Lawrie, Johnny Summers and Dennis Edwards (2). Sam did better on his second visit, edging a 1-0 win in September 1961, but resigned in June 1962 largely because lack of funding was preventing him from pushing for promotion.

A weekly column in The People kept Sam in the public eye and he returned to SE7 in 1975 for the topping out ceremony and the opening of Sam Bartram Close. He died unexpectedly in 1981 after collapsing at his home in Harpenden. He was aged 67. Sadly, he did not live to see the unveiling of his statue in June 2005, but his daughter Moira flew over from her home in Canada and performed the honours on his behalf. Sam's autobiography, 'Sam Bartram', was published in 1956 and other books about him have appeared in the years since. The most comprehensive is 'Sam Bartram – The Story Of A Goalkeeping Legend' by Mike Blake.

It is not only at the Valley where Sam's name is revered. His original club Boldon Villa are still playing and have a photo montage in their clubhouse dedicated to him and to Jack Shreeve. That this small club produced two of Charlton's FA Cup winning team is quite extraordinary and they have recently forged a friendly alliance with Charlton Athletic Museum. It is hoped that one day Charlton will send a team up to Boldon and play a match in Sam's backyard.

Season	Division	League		FA Cup		Total	
		A	G	A	G	A	G
1934-35 (P)	Divison 3 (S)	18	0	0	0	18	0
1935-36	Division 2	39	0	1	0	40	0
1936-37	Division 1	42	0	1	0	43	0
1937-38	Division 1	41	0	5	0	46	0
1938-39	Division 1	42	0	1	0	43	0
1945-46	Division 1			10	0	10	0
1946-47	Division 1	41	0	6	0	47	0
1947-48	Division 1	42	0	3	0	45	0
1948-49	Division 1	41	0	1	0	42	0
1949-50	Division 1	42	0	4	0	46	0
1950-51	Division 1	37	0	2	0	39	0
1951-52	Division 1	41	0	1	0	42	0
1952-53	Division 1	38	0	1	0	39	0
1953-54	Division 1	40	0	2	0	42	0
1954-55	Division 1	42	0	3	0	45	0
1955-56	Division 1	33	0	3	0	36	0
Total		579	0	44	0	623	0

UK LEAGUE CAREER 579 games 0 goals

CHARLTON CAREER

Managers: *J Seed*

Debut: *Watford (A) 01-12-1934*

V184

Finale: *Arsenal (H) 10-03-1956*

BASEY Grant William   2007 - 10

Grant was a product of Charlton's youth academy and spent 11 years with the club from the age of nine. The high point of his

Defender   14st 5lbs   6' 0''
Born: 30-11-1988 - Farnborough, Kent
Education: Red Hill Primary School, Chislehurst. Coopers Technical College, Chislehurst. Orpington College.

injury shortened career came on 27th March 2009 when he was capped by Wales U21's in a qualifying match for the UEFA European U21 Championships. He was eligible because of his Cardiff born grandfather and featured at left back against Luxembourg in a 0-0 draw, the Welsh forward line being led by Simon Church.

HONOURS

Wales U21 International 2009 1 cap 0 goals

Wales U19 & U17 International

Charlton Athletic Reserves 2007-08 Runners Up Premier Reserve League (South)

CLUBS

Charlton Athletic 1998 (youth) 03.07 (pro) ••Brentford 17.07.07 (loan) ••Barnet 27.09.10 (free) ••Peterborough United 21.01.11 (free) ••Wycombe Wanderers 06.10.11 (loan) 01.01.12 (free) ••Ebbsfleet United 01.10.13 (free) ••VCD Athletic 2014 (free) ••Cray Wanderers 07.15 (free) ••Charlton Athletic 2017 (youth coach) 02.18 (kit manager) 16.09.19 (coach) ••Cray Wanderers 31.12.21 (manager)

After a series of impressive performances in the Charlton youth teams, the breakthrough for Grant came in 2007 when a successful loan period with Brentford was followed by a shock call up for first team duty on 27th October. A catalogue of injuries within the squad gave him his chance and although the game was lost 1-0 to Queens Park Rangers, he was praised for the quality of his display. The next four league games were all won without a goal being conceded and at that point the future for Grant Basey looked extremely rosy.

Injuries and a worrying lack of pace did however affect his progress and he was out of the side for much of the relegation season of 2008-09. He regained his place the following term until a horrendous tackle after only 15 seconds at Bristol Rovers left him in hospital overnight with very serious ankle ligament damage. He did recover but never played for Charlton first team again and left the club in the Summer of 2010 when a promised new contract did not materialise and a move to Aberdeen fell through. He eventually signed for Barnet and played twice against

Charlton in FA Cup ties during November 2010 and his mature performance in the centre of midfield, especially in the first match at Underhill, indicated that this was potentially his best position. The game finished 0-0, despite both Mark Marshall and Ricky Holmes lining up in the home side.

After only four months at Barnet, Grant moved on first to Peterborough and then Wycombe Wanderers, but injuries persisted and after rupturing an anterior cruciate ligament in training, his Football League career came to an end in May 2013. He carried on for a time in the non-league game,

but despite one bright spell with Cray Wanderers, retired completely in February 2017 at the age of 28.

Grant is a good golfer and cricketer and has played for Bromley CC. He ran the London Marathon on two occasions and in 2017 returned to Charlton as an academy coach, obtaining his UEFA A licence on the same course as Johnnie Jackson. In February 2018 it was announced that he had become the first team Kit Manager and on 16th September 2019 was transferred back to coaching duties. On 31st December 2021 he was appointed interim manager of Cray Wanderers.

Season	Division	League		FA Cup		FL Cup		FL Trophy		Play Offs		Total	
		A	G	A	G	A	G	A	G	A	G	A	G
2007-08	Championship	8	1	0(1)	0	0	0					8(1)	1
2008-09 (R)	Championship	10(9)	0	2	0	1	0					13(9)	0
2009-10	League One	14(5)	0	0	0	1	0	2	0	0	0	17(5)	0
Total		32(14)	1	2(1)	0	2	0	2	0	0	0	38(15)	1

UK LEAGUE CAREER 110 games 5 goals

CHARLTON CAREER
Managers: *A Curbishley, I Dowie, L Reed, A Pardew, P Parkinson*
Debut: *Queens Park Rangers (H) 27-10-2007*
V659
Finale: *Bristol Rovers (A) 15-02-2010*

BAUER Patrick   2015 - 19

Defender   6' 4"
Born: 28-10-1992 - Backnang, Germany

Those Charlton supporters fortunate enough to have been present at Wembley for the Play Off final against Sunderland in 1998 were rewarded with high drama and wonderful memories that will stay with them forever. Surely nobody among the crowd of 76,155 who walked down Empire Way on 26th May 2019 could have dreamed that this repeat fixture with Sunderland was about to serve up something at least comparable if not quite equalling Clive Mendonca's finest hour some 21 years earlier. The occasion was the League One Play Off final and Charlton got off to the worst possible start with a Keystone Cops inspired own goal after just five minutes. Happily they equalised before half-time, but with no further goals forthcoming and the game eating into stoppage time, Patrick chose precisely the right moment to score his first goal of the season. Manager Lee Bowyer checked with the assistant referee and was assured that only five seconds remained on the clock when the big German bundled the ball into the Sunderland net and clinched promotion for the Addicks.

HONOURS
Germany U20 International 2011 2 caps 1 goal
Germany U18 International 2009 5 caps 1 goal
Germany U17 International 2009 3 caps 0 goals
Charlton Athletic 2018-19 Promoted Play Offs League One

CLUBS
TSG Backnang, Germany (youth) ••VFB Stuttgart, Germany 2005 (youth) 2010 (pro) ••CS Maritimo, Madeira 17.08.12 (loan) 25.07.13 (£135,000) ••Charlton Athletic 22.06.15 (£1.35 million) ••Preston North End 19.06.19 (free)

The BFG, as this amiable German giant was affectionately nicknamed by Charlton supporters, was born in Backnang, a small town 30 km north east of Stuttgart. His early life was scarred by the tragic death of his father in 2002. Hans Bauer had been both a coach and player with TSG Backnang and Pat was in the crowd when he collapsed and died of a heart attack during a charity match.

Unsurprisingly it took a long time for him to come to terms with his loss and the memory of his father became the inspiration for him to succeed in his chosen profession. He developed within the youth academy at VFB Stuttgart but after turning professional, found that first team opportunities were limited, so in 2012 agreed to go out on loan to CS Maritimo, a club based on the island of Madeira, but who competed in the Portuguese League. Initially Pat appeared for the Maritimo B side, but after the loan was converted into a permanent transfer in July 2013 he played 45 matches for their first team in the Primeira Liga, the top division in Portugal, before switching to Charlton at the end of the 2014-15 season.

The transfer fee paid by Charlton went undisclosed by the club, but was rumoured to be in the region of £1.35 million and what they got for their money was a solid and reliable central defender well able to deal with the physical requirements of English football and as it turned out, of the standard required to compete in the Championship. The hopeless transfer policy adopted by the Belgian owner left much to be desired, but Patrick Bauer was one signing that they got right. His debut came in August 2015 at home to a Queens Park Rangers side which included Paul Konchesky and the Addicks triumphed 2-0, thanks to goals from Tony Watt and Morgan Fox. Pat settled in immediately and remained first choice centre half for the whole of his four-year stay in SE7, only missing out through injury and the consequences of four red cards which he accumulated along the way.

His contract was coming to an end as Charlton approached the League One play offs in May 2019. There were several clubs expressing an interest in signing Pat and prepared to offer more favourable terms than the Belgian owner who was trying desperately to dispose of the club and prioritised the reduction in spending over any ambition to strengthen the playing squad. Even as that last gasp shot was entering the Sunderland net, it was clear for all to see that the short-term future of the club remained very uncertain. Pat duly signed for Preston North End three weeks after the Wembley experience while Charlton received no financial recompense, having negligently allowed his contract to run down.

Pat etched his name into Charlton history with his Wembley goal, but for him the second half of May 2019 contains more than the one happy memory. On 17th May his daughter, Kayleen, was born and this was the same day as he and his teammates secured the trip to Wembley by defeating Doncaster Rovers at the Valley. If the excitement of the new baby meant a lack of sleep, he did not seem to have suffered unduly as he was still alert enough to stretch for that last gasp goal just nine days later.

As expected, Pat proved a success after his move to Preston and has become a favourite with the supporters of his new club. He did pick up an Achilles tendon injury against AFC Bournemouth on 1st December 2020 which kept him on the sidelines for the remainder of that season, but has since returned to top form and in January 2022 he agreed a new three-year contract with Preston.

Courtesy of Charlton Athletic announcer Brian Cole, Pat's shirt from the Wembley final is now displayed in the Charlton Museum, where it shares cabinet space with Clive Mendonca's shirt from 1998.

Season	Division	League		FA Cup		FL Cup		FL Trophy		Play Offs		Total	
		A	G	A	G	A	G	A	G	A	G	A	G
2015-16 (R)	Championship	19	1	0	0	2	0					21	1
2016-17	League One	34 (2)	4	2	0	0	0	0	0			36 (2)	4
2017-18	League One	33 (1)	3	0	0	0	0	1	0	2	0	36 (1)	3
2018-19 (P)	League One	35	0	1	0	0	0	0	0	3	1	39	1
Total		121 (3)	8	3	0	2	0	1	0	5	1	132 (3)	9

UK LEAGUE CAREER 177 games 12 goals

CHARLTON CAREER
Managers: *G Luzon, K Fraeye, J Riga, R Slade, K Robinson, L Bowyer*
Debut: *Queens Park Rangers (H)*
08-08-2015
V798
Finale: *Sunderland (A) 26-05-2019*

BEACH Henry Cyril   1929 - 32

A former clerk who started out playing as an amateur with Hounslow Town, Cyril was a skilful footballer who played at either wing half or inside forward. He spent four years at Charlton but despite several opportunities in the first team, never quite managed to hold down a regular place

Forward, Midfield   11st 6lbs   5' 9"
Born: 23-06-1908 - Hounslow, Middlesex
Died: 14-01-1994 - Brigg, South Humberside

HONOURS

Sunderland 1932-33 Winners Durham FA Senior Professional Cup

CLUBS

Hounslow Town 1927 (amateur) ••Charlton Athletic 30.08.28 (amateur) 09.03.29 (pro) ••Sunderland 14.09.32 ••Hayesco Sports 1933 ••Peterborough United 09.35

Cyril's debut came in the Division 3 promotion season of 1928-29 when he replaced injured skipper George Armitage in the Charlton side for the trip to Newport County, but he had to wait more than a year before his next two appearances and all these three matches ended in defeat. He got a longer run in the team the following season and scored the equaliser at Turf Moor on 29th November 1930 in a 1-1 draw with Burnley and also featured in two of the three epic FA Cup matches against West Bromwich Albion in January 1931. He added to Tommy Wyper's goal to earn Charlton a 2-0 lead in the game at the Hawthorns, only for Albion to pull back to 2-2. Four days later the replay at the Valley ended 1-1, but Cyril did not play in the third match at Villa Park which saw the Londoners exit from the Cup 3-1.

Unfortunately Cyril did not fare at all well during his final term in SE7. The team were under the cosh during the first half of 1931-32 and he only played once on a winning side in 11 appearances up to 14th November. On that afternoon he netted his only goal of the campaign in a 2-2 draw at Notts County but was not picked again until March. Despite his undoubted ability, Cyril frustratingly seemed to reserve his best performances for away games and was therefore not fully appreciated by the Charlton supporters, away travel being much less common in those days.

He refused the offer of a new contract at the end of the season and when Charlton would not place him on the transfer list, but wanted to retain his registration, he effectively took strike action and went without his summer wages. There was interest from several clubs and eventually the board relented and he moved on to Sunderland in September 1933. He appeared three times for them in the First Division the following month, but this was only a brief encounter and before the end of the year he was back in London, his professional career at an end and playing as a permit player for a Middlesex works team, Hayesco Sports. Cyril married Violet Schroder in January 1939, but hit a spot of bother that same year when it was reported in the 'Middlesex Chronicle' that a young lady called Joyce Hardy was pursuing a paternity order against him in respect of a recently born male baby. Cyril's post-football career was in the film industry where he worked as an electrician. He passed away in Brigg, South Humberside aged 85.

Season	Division	League		FA Cup		Total	
		A	G	A	G	A	G
1928-29 (P)	Divison 3 (S)	1	0	0	0	1	0
1929-30	Division 2	2	0	0	0	2	0
1930-31	Division 2	11	3	2	1	13	4
1931-32	Division 2	15	1	0	0	15	1
Total		29	4	2	1	31	5

UK LEAGUE CAREER 32 games 4 goals

CHARLTON CAREER

Managers: *A MacFarlane*

Debut: *Newport County (A) 05-01-1929*

V122

Finale: *Oldham Athletic (A) 16-04-1932*

BEGGS William   1986

Midfield, Forward
Born: 27-08-1967 - Ballymena, Northern Ireland
Died: 19-03-2012 - Randalstown, Northern Ireland

loanee Alan McDonald.

Billy was an outstanding young player who played regularly in the youth teams at Queens Park Rangers. He was a real character and for a time shared a house with future Charlton

HONOURS

Northern Ireland Youth International

CLUBS

Wakehurst, N. Ireland (youth) ••Queens Park Rangers 08.08.83 (youth) 10.08.85 (pro) ••Charlton Athletic 23.08.86 (free) ••Aldershot 02.11.89 (free) ••Coleraine, N. Ireland (free) ••Randalstown Athletic, N. Ireland (manager)

Billy's time at Charlton was restricted to one season as he was not re-engaged at the end of the 1986-87 campaign. His brief stay was limited to just a single first team appearance in the generally unappreciated Full Members Cup, but with hindsight perhaps his contribution was more significant than he was given credit. He notched Charlton's second goal against Birmingham City at Selhurst Park before a depressingly small crowd of 821 and they ran out winners 3-2. But for Billy's goal, the cup run may not have happened and Charlton supporters would have been deprived of an all too rare trip to Wembley for the Full Members Cup final the following March, by which time the crowd had swelled to 43,789.

Beggs was unable to build on his early promise as a young footballer and was soon back in Northern Ireland where he worked at a number of delivery jobs and at O'Kane's pub in Ballymena. He was known as a devoted family man and as well as football was involved with both Randalstown Rugby Club and Old Bleach Bowling Club. He passed away at the age of 44.

Season	Division	League		FA Cup		FL Cup		FM Cup		Total	
		A	G	A	G	A	G	A	G	A	G
1986-87	Division 1	0	0	0	0	0	0	1	1	1	1
Total		0	0	0	0	0	0	1	1	1	1

UK LEAGUE CAREER 0 games 0 goals

CHARLTON CAREER

Managers: *L Lawrence*

Debut: *Birmingham City (H) 04-11-1986*

V484

BELLOTTI Derek Christopher   1970 - 71

Derek was a promising schoolboy goalkeeper, who along with another future Charlton player, Dennis Bond, represented the Walthamstow U16's when in 1962 they came close to winning the England Schools Trophy. He went on to play for London Schools and signed for Queens Park Rangers the following year, but never reached the first team, instead spending two seasons on loan with non-league Bedford Town.

Goalkeeper   13st 0lb   6' 1"
Born: 25-12-1946 - East Ham, London

HONOURS

London Schools 1962   Southend United 1971-72 Winners Division 4

CLUBS

Queens Park Rangers 09.63 (youth) 1964 (pro) ••Bedford Town 1964 (loan) ••Gillingham 11. 07.66 (free) ••Southend United 14.10.70 (loan) ••Charlton Athletic 28.10.70 (£5000) ••Fulham 22.10.71 (loan) ••Southend United 15.12.71 (loan) 28.01.72 (free)) ••Swansea City 15.05.74 (£3,000) ••Maidstone United 1975 ••Margate 01.78 (loan) ••St Blazey 1978 ••Torquay United 25.10.79 (free) ••Falmouth Town 1982 ••Bideford 1983 ••Saltash United 1984 ••Newquay c1986 ••Torrington 1988 ••Ilfracombe Town 12.97

Derek made his Football League debut with Gillingham on 3rd September 1966 in a 0-0 draw against Walsall. Six days later he kept another clean sheet as the Gills grabbed a handy 1-0 away victory against an Orient side that contained Brian Whitehouse, Cliff Holton, Mick Jones and a 16-year-old Paul Went, but despite this impressive start he spent most of his four-year stay in the Medway town as no more than second choice 'keeper.

Much the same situation persisted when Derek joined Charlton in October 1970 and his first season was spent as understudy for the popular Charlie Wright, but when Charlie moved on to Bolton Wanderers he was given the goalkeepers jersey for the first ten games of the 1971-72 season. This was an opportunity to cement a firm place for himself in the team, but he was unable to do so and instead it was new signing John Dunn who became first choice between the sticks.

Derek was transferred to Southend two months later, initially on loan, but in January 1972 the deal was made permanent. He probably enjoyed the best spell of his career with the Shrimpers, for whom the runners-up spot in Division 4 was achieved that same year, although a broken arm stopped him participating in the final promotion clincher.

After a short time with Swansea City, he dropped down into non-league football and in 1978 moved to the West Country and continued playing for an array of different teams into his forties. He even turned out as an emergency goalkeeper for Ilfracombe Town in December 1997 at the age of 50. Derek got interested in print during his time with Maidstone United and later started his own Kingfisher Print & Design which has grown into a sizeable business and is now run by his son Ross Bellotti, himself a former player with Exeter City, although Derek remains a director.

Season	Division	League		FA Cup		FL Cup		Total	
		A	G	A	G	A	G	A	G
1970-71	Division 2	4	0	0	0	0	0	4	0
1971-72 (R)	Division 2	10	0	0	0	2	0	12	0
Total		14	0	0	0	2	0	16	0

UK LEAGUE CAREER 145 games 0 goals

CHARLTON CAREER
Managers: *T Foley*
Debut: *Cardiff City (H) 21-11-1970*
V359
Finale: *Orient (A) 02-10-1971*

BEN HAIM Tal   2014 - 15

Defender   11st 9lbs   6' 0"
Born: 31-03-1982 - Rishon LeZion, Israel

Tal took part in 95 full internationals over a period of nearly 16 years, which is highly impressive by any standards. He was an accomplished and classy central defender, but unfortunate that during this period Israel were never strong enough to qualify for the finals of a major tournament. He played in six matches, all qualifiers for UEFA Euro 2016, during his time at Charlton, but they could only finish fourth in their group and did not therefore reach the finals in France.

HONOURS

Israel International 2002-17 95 caps 2 goals
Israel U23 International 2001-02 6 caps 0 goals
Maccabi Tel Aviv 2001-02 Winners Israel State Cup
Maccabi Tel Aviv 2002-03 Winners Israel Premier League
Maccabi Tel Aviv 2003-04, 2015-16 & 2016-17 Runners Up Israel Premier

League
Chelsea 2007-08 Runners Up Premier League
Standard Liege 2013-14 Runners Up Belgian League
Maccabi Tel Aviv 2016-17 Finalists Israel State Cup
Maccabi Tel Aviv 2017-18 Winners Israel Toto Cup Al

CLUBS

Maccabi Tel Aviv, Israel 1998 (youth) 2001 (pro) ••Bolton Wanderers 30.07.04 (£150,000) ••Chelsea 14.06.07 (free) ••Manchester City 30.07.08 (£5 million) ••Sunderland 01.02.09 (loan) ••Portsmouth 01.09.09 ••West Ham United 03.08.10 (loan) ••Queens Park Rangers 04.01.13 ••Toronto, Canada 09.05.13 (loan) ••Standard Liege, Belgium 24.07.13 ••Charlton Athletic 11.07.14 ••Maccabi Tel Aviv, Israel 03.06.15 ••Beitar Jerusalem, Israel 13.08.18

Tal was already an established international when Sam Allardyce brought him to Bolton in the Summer of 2004. The transfer was later the subject of an enquiry by the Israeli FA over the involvement of an unlicensed agent, but for the player it was the start of a rollercoaster 11 year spell in English football, much of which was played in the Premier League.

He spent three seasons with Bolton before signing for Chelsea on a Bosman transfer, but a change of manager shortly after his arrival led to an unhappy season spent

largely on the sidelines. Manchester City had seen enough to splash out a £5 million transfer fee to take him back up north, but again he played only infrequently and a year later was on the move again, this time on a three-year contract to Portsmouth where injury prevented him from playing in the 2010 FA Cup Final.

Tal may have missed out on the FA Cup glory, but he hung around long enough at Pompey to experience two consecutive seasons of relegation as the proud old club was torn apart through a series of financial crises. In 2011-12 he did at least get to play regularly as they crashed out of the Championship, but with the club now in financial administration and his weekly wage, (reported in the media at £36,000), a real problem for the cash-strapped club, he refused a pay cut, allegedly suggesting that the administrator take one instead. He did not play for Portsmouth again, eventually moving out to Belgium, where he enjoyed a successful season with Standard Liege. In Summer 2014 Tal joined the exodus of foreign players being shipped into Charlton by Belgian owner Roland Duchatelet and perhaps after his torrid time at Portsmouth he felt at home amidst the upheaval and protests that awaited him. He performed well throughout 2014-15 and his solid displays in the centre of the defence had much to do with the club attaining a comfortable mid-table position in the Championship.

Many hoped that he would stay longer in London SE7, but

after just the one season he returned to Israel and re-joined his hometown club, Maccabi Tel Aviv, where over the next three years they did well in both cup and league competitions. However, the bad luck which seemed to haunt Tal throughout much of his career re-surfaced in Jerusalem on 25th May 2017, in the final of the Israel State Cup against rivals Blenei Yehuda Tel Aviv. The game was goalless and after extra time it was he who missed the crucial penalty to hand victory to their opponents.

There was a familiar face to welcome Tal when he signed for Beitar Jerusalem in August 2018. His manager was Guy Luzon, but the two men had only nine days to get re-acquainted before another spin of the managerial merry go round sent Luzon on his way again. Tal spent three seasons with Beltar, but left the club after the 2020-21 season and at the age of 40 is finally reaching the end of his playing career.

Season	Division	League		FA Cup		FL Cup		Total	
		A	G	A	G	A	G	A	G
2014-15	Championship	37	0	1	0	0	0	38	0
Total		37	0	1	0	0	0	38	0

UK LEAGUE CAREER 218 games 1 goal

CHARLTON CAREER
Managers: B Peeters, G Luzon
Debut: *Brentford (A) 09-08-2014*
V778
Finale: *AFC Bournemouth (H) 02-05-2015*

BENNETT Michael Richard   1986 - 95

Unusually Mickey Bennett played for five London Football League clubs. He was an outstanding young player who, along with Carl Leaburn, toured Brazil with the England U20 squad in June 1988. Two matches were played against club sides and he featured in the 1-1 draw against Londrina. He was also a member of the Charlton team that was beaten by Coventry City in the final of the FA Youth Cup in 1987. He became extremely popular with Charlton supporters and but for injury may well have enjoyed a more fruitful career.

Forward   12st 4lbs   5' 10"
Born: 27-07-1969 - Camberwell, London

HONOURS
England U20 1988 Tour of Brazil
Charlton Athletic 1987 Young Player Of The Year

Charlton Athletic U18 1986-87 Finalists FA Youth Cup

CLUBS
Charlton Athletic 08.85 (youth) 27.04.87 (pro) ••Wimbledon 09.01.1990 (£250,000) ••Brentford 14.07.92 (loan) 10.08.92 (£60,000) ••Charlton Athletic 24.03.94 (free) ••Millwall 16.05.95 (free) ••Cardiff City 14.08.96 (non contract) ••Cambridge City 12.96 (free) ••Leyton Orient 08.12.97 (free) ••Brighton & Hove Albion 03.08.98 (free) ••Canvey Island 08.99 (free)

The career of Mickey Bennett was ultimately defined by one unfortunate injury. He had burst into the Charlton side during the dark days at Selhurst Park and shown exceptional skill and ability as the team somehow managed to compete against the very top sides in English football, despite limited resources and in front of tiny crowds. This

was Lennie Lawrence's miracle and one that seems all the more unbelievable as time goes by. The sight of Mickey, Paul Williams and the young Paul Mortimer continually turning defence into attack with their great pace as the three men raced the length of the pitch, is one of the few positive memories of 1988, but even that was to be a short lived pleasure.

Mickey sustained a serious knee injury during the home match against Queens Park Rangers on 10th December. He ruptured his anterior cruciate ligament and crushed the cartilage in his knee and did not play again for 11 months. In January 1990 he was sold to Wimbledon, where on his debut, he scored a last minute winning goal against Arsenal. In April, he was back at Selhurst when they plundered a 2-1 win against Charlton, but although he remained with the Dons for two and a half years, he only started in 12 league matches. He got more game time after moving to Brentford in 1992 but only as they sunk to relegation from Division 1. A training ground incident on 16th November 1993 left a teammate with a fractured jaw, following which his contract was cancelled and then reinstated after an FA

Appeals Commission. However, he never played for their first team again.

His career carried on for several years, including a second spell with Charlton, now back at the Valley, but he never fully regained the joyous and exciting form of those early games. His final League club was Brighton & Hove Albion where he did at least play a full season in 1998-99. Mickey retired from full time football at the age of 29.

He then went on to coach in local schools and in 2004 qualified as a counsellor and set up a company, Unique Sports Counselling to work with sportsmen suffering mental health issues. He has since joined the PFA as Head of Player Welfare as well as sitting on the panel of Kick It Out, the mentoring programme for football's equality and inclusion campaign.

Season	Division	League		FA Cup		FL Cup		Play Offs		FM Cup		AI Cup		Total	
		A	G	A	G	A	G	A	G	A	G	A	G	A	G
1986-87	Division 1	2	0	0	0	0	0	0	0	1 (1)	0			3 (1)	0
1987-88	Division 1	9 (7)	1	1	0	1	0			2	0			13 (7)	1
1988-89	Division 1	11	0	0	0	3	0			1	0			15	0
1989-90 (R)	Division 1	2 (4)	1	0	0	0	0			2	0			4 (4)	1
1993-94	Division 1	10	1	0	0	0	0					0	0	10	1
1994-95	Division 1	9 (5)	0	1	0	0	0							10 (5)	0
Total		43 (16)	3	2	0	4	0	0	0	6 (1)	0	0	0	55 (17)	3

CHARLTON CAREER
Managers: *L Lawrence, A Curbishley/S Gritt*
Debut: *Birmingham City (H) (sub) 04-11-1986*
V485
Finale: *Reading (A) 07-05-1995*

UK LEAGUE CAREER 179 games 10 goals

BENSON Paul Andrew   2010 - 11

Forward   11st 3lbs   6' 2"
Born: 12 10 1979 - Southend-on-Sea, Essex
Education: Cecil Jones High School, Southend.

Paul made his name in non-league football and was almost 28 by the time he made his Football League debut. Rejected by his home town club Southend United, he trained to be an accountant while playing for White Ensign in the Essex Olympian League, where he scored a staggering 96 goals in 59 league appearances. This attracted further attention from Southend and after they invited him back, he notched four goals in three appearances for their Reserves, but was still not offered a contract.

HONOURS

England C International (semi pro) 2007 1 cap 1 goal
White Ensign 2003-04 & 2004-05 Winners Essex Olympian League
Dagenham & Redbridge 2006-07 Winners Football Conference
Dagenham & Redbridge 2009-10 Promoted Play Offs League Two

Swindon Town 2011-12 Finalists Football League Trophy
Swindon Town 2011-12 Winners League Two
Luton Town 2013-14 Winners Football Conference

CLUBS

Southend United 1997 (youth) ••White Ensign 2003 (semi pro) ••Southend United 2005 (non contract) ••Dagenham & Redbridge 26.05.05 (pro) ••Charlton Athletic 30.08.10 (£270,000) ••Swindon Town 01.01.12 (player exchange) ••Portsmouth 15.11.12 (loan) ••Cheltenham Town 29.01.13 (loan) ••Luton Town 07.13 (loan) 22.07.14 (free) ••Dagenham & Redbridge 01.08.16 (free) ••Boreham Wood 01.07.17 (free) ••Bedford Town 26.01.18 (loan) 26.06.18 (player coach) ••Luton Town 24.06.19 (youth coach)

It was Dagenham & Redbridge who finally gave Paul the opportunity to test himself in a higher standard of football

and he signed for them in May 2005, although his first season was wrecked by a broken leg which sidelined him for over three months. In 2006-07 however, he weighed in with 28 league goals and finished as the leading scorer in the Football Conference, as the Daggers were crowned champions and gained entry into the Football League for the first time. This led to international recognition and on 13th February 2007 he scored as England C went down 3-1 against Northern Ireland.

Paul remained a key member of the Dagenham team as they established themselves as a League club and on 30th May 2010 played at Wembley in the League Two play off final against Rotherham United. They won 3-2 and two of the Dagenham goals came from Paul Benson and Danny Green.

He switched to Charlton for an 'undisclosed' fee, believed to be in the region of £270,000 and appeared regularly through 2010-11 contributing 10 league goals, despite picking up red cards at both Colchester and MK Dons. Paul became surplus to requirements the following season however, as manager Chris Powell's newly shaped team

swept to promotion with Bradley Wright-Phillips, Paul Hayes and Yann Kermorgant supplying the fire power and he moved on to Swindon Town in January 2012 in exchange for another striker, Leon Clarke.

His first nine league games for Swindon were all won and they ended the season as champions of League Two under manager Paolo Di Canio. There was another trip to Wembley on 25th March 2012 for the final of the Football League Trophy, but the Swindon team which included Paul, Jay McEveley and Alan McCormick went down 2-0 to Chesterfield.

He spent season 2013-14 on loan at Luton Town and his 17 goals in 36 league matches helped them to regain their Football League status, winning the Football Conference by an emphatic 19 points. In 2016, he returned to Dagenham and as his playing career started to wind down, he moved into coaching. On 26th June 2018 Paul was appointed a player coach at Bedford Town but he is now back at Luton coaching in their academy.

Season	Division	League		FA Cup		FL Cup		FL Trophy		Total	
		A	G	A	G	A	G	A	G	A	G
2010-11	League One	28 (4)	10	3 (1)	0	0	0	1 (2)	0	32 (7)	10
2011-12	Championship	0 (1)	0	0	0	2	0	0	0	2 (1)	0
Total		28 (5)	10	3 (1)	0	2	0	1 (2)	0	34 (8)	10

UK LEAGUE CAREER 231 games 73 goals

CHARLTON CAREER
Managers: *P Parkinson, C Powell*
Debut: *Dagenham & Redbridge (H) 31-08-2010*
V712
Finale: *Preston North End (H) 13-09-2011*

BENT Darren Ashley   2005 - 07

The transfer fee of £16.5 million that Charlton received when Darren Bent was sold to Tottenham Hotspur in June 2007, was the highest in the history of the club and remains

Forward   11st 7 lbs   5' 11"
Born: 06-02-1984 - Tooting, London
Education: Hinchingbrooke School, Huntingdon.

so to this day. The sale had become necessary as a direct result of relegation from the Premier League and at a time when desperate measures were required because of the massive reduction in television revenue. Even the parachute payments provided for newly relegated clubs were insufficient to cover the vast reduction in turnover. Darren had been a great success during his two seasons at the Valley and had been the club's leading goalscorer both times. Several reasons can be put forward to explain Charlton's decline after seven years in the Premier League, but no blame can be attached to Darren who was a class act and perhaps the best forward so far to play for Charlton in the new millennium.

HONOURS
England International 2006-11 13 caps 4 goals
England U21 International 2003-05 14 caps 9 goals
England U19 International 2002 3 caps 3 goals
England U16 International 2000-01 11 caps 3 goals

England U15 International 1999-00 8 caps 7 goals
Charlton Athletic 2006 Player Of The Year
Tottenham Hotspur 2008-09 Finalists Football League Cup

CLUBS

Godmanchester Rovers (youth) ••Ipswich Town 1998 (youth) 02.07.01 (pro) ••Charlton Athletic 03.06.05 (£2.5 million) ••Tottenham Hotspur 29.06.07 (£16.5 million) ••Sunderland 05.08.09 (£16.5 million) •Aston Villa 18.01.11 (£18 million) ••Fulham 16.08.13 (loan) ••Brighton & Hove Albion 26.11.14 (loan) ••Derby County 03.01.15 (loan) 01.07.15 (free) ••Burton Albion 26.01.18 (loan)

A graduate of the Ipswich Town youth academy, Darren broke into their first team in season 2001-02 and played a handful of games alongside Matt Holland, Marcus Bent (no relation) and Herman Hreidarsson. It was not a happy time for the Tractor Boys who were sinking to relegation from the Premier League, but the teenager showed great promise and his two league goals in that first campaign included the winner against Middlesbrough on 24th April. The following season he became a regular starter for Ipswich and as time went on, evolved into their main striker. By 2004-05 he was the finished article and contributed 20 league goals as they narrowly failed to gain promotion back to the top division.

In June 2005, Darren was transferred to Charlton for £2.5 million and the following month was joined by a former Ipswich teammate, Darren Ambrose. The attitude of these two new signings was commented on by manager Alan Curbishley, who was impressed by the exceptional enthusiasm of both men. They would regularly stay on after training and had seemingly unlimited energy and determination to succeed. When the season started, Darren Bent scored after just 11 minutes on his debut up at the Stadium of Light. He added a second late in the game and with Danny Murphy also finding the net, this resulted in a very pleasing 3-1 opening day win at Sunderland on 13th August 2005. Even more so, because Ambrose had been sent off and Charlton were obliged to play the last 35 minutes with 10 men.

The goals kept coming for Darren and he eventually netted 22 in cup and league during his first season as a Charlton player. He was most effective when receiving a pass to run on to and his exceptional pace and predatory finishing made him a tremendous asset to the club. Few players in a Charlton shirt have been more effective in a one on one situation with a goalkeeper. He seemed to score every time. He was no less effective in his second season, but after scoring in a 2-1 win against Aston Villa in December 2006, he picked up a knee injury which kept him sidelined for nearly two months. With the team in desperate trouble, he was probably rushed back too quickly, but still finished as the leading scorer with 15 cup and league goals.

As the horrendous effects of relegation started to bite, Darren's sale to Tottenham for such a large fee was a financial godsend to Charlton. He turned down a move to

West Ham, but if Spurs were his preference, he never really seemed to be theirs. They did not appear willing to adapt their style of play to get the best out of their new signing and he spent far too long warming the sub's bench. His best return as a Spurs player came on 6th November 2008 against Dinamo Zagreb in the UEFA Cup. Playing in the same side as Chris Gunter, he scored three times in a resounding 4-0 victory. He did get to play in a Wembley final when they were beaten by Manchester United in the 2008-09 League Cup, but it did not come as a big surprise when he moved on to Sunderland after another £16.5 million changed hands in August 2009.

The run of goals continued after the move to Wearside and he notched 32 in 58 league appearances before submitting a transfer request in January 2011. Within days, he was an Aston Villa player and they had smashed their transfer record by paying out a fee of £18 million. All along he had kept scoring and Darren's time with Villa commenced the same way. He netted the winner against Manchester City on his debut and got both goals in a memorable 2-1 win at Arsenal on 15th May. His problems started in a match at Wigan in February 2012 during which he was stretchered off the pitch and following which a scan revealed that he had ruptured his ankle ligament. He did regain his place in the Villa side after a six month lay-off, but by season 2013-14 was no longer an automatic choice and for the remainder of his contract was shipped out on loan to Fulham, Brighton and finally to Derby County. He came up against Charlton again in a match at Pride Park on 24th February 2015, but was not the same player who had left the Valley nearly eight years earlier. Injuries had taken their toll but he kept going and still found the net on an acceptable number of occasions for Derby, if normally from the bench.

Sunderland's supporters had given Darren a hard time when he left them for Aston Villa, so it was ironic that the final goal of his Football League career came at the Stadium of Light in January 2018 while he was on loan at Burton Albion and this goal contributed to an unexpected 2-1 away win for the Brewers. Without question, Darren was not a lucky player and despite his big money transfers, which totalled in excess of £50 million in aggregate and his immense goal scoring talent, he never found real success at club level at any point in his career.

He was equally unlucky on the international stage. Already an U21 international when he joined Charlton, he earned his last two caps whilst at the Valley and scored against France in a UEFA U21 qualifying match on 15th November 2015. The first two of his 13 full caps came before his departure to Tottenham., but he was controversially left out of the England World Cup squads in both 2006 and 2010. One place where Darren was fully appreciated however was in London SE7 and he was voted

Charlton's Player of the Year in 2006.

Since retiring as a player, he has worked as a commentator and pundit for Sky TV and even appeared on Celebrity Mastermind in March 2020 but with very limited success. Scoring goals came easier to him than sitting in the 'hot seat'.

Season	Division	League		FA Cup		FL Cup		Total	
		A	G	A	G	A	G	A	G
2005-06	Premier	36	18	5	2	2 (1)	2	43 (1)	22
2006-07 (R)	Premier	32	13	0	0	2 (1)	2	34 (1)	15
Total		68	31	5	2	4 (2)	4	77 (2)	37

UK LEAGUE CAREER 486 games 180 goals

CHARLTON CAREER
Managers: *A Curbishley, I Dowie, L Reed, A Pardew*
Debut: *Sunderland (A) 13-08-2005*
V627
Finale: *Liverpool (A) 13-05-2007*

BENT Marcus Nathan   2006 - 07

Including Charlton, no less than eight Premier League clubs enjoyed the services of Marcus during his long career, although four of them suffered

Forward   12st 4lbs   6' 2"
Born: 19-05-1978 - Hammersmith, London

relegation from the top division of English football whilst he was on the payroll. A big strong target man, he was not a natural goal scorer and despite a series of sizeable transfer fees which totalled in excess of £10 million, he never remained with any team for more than a couple of years after leaving Brentford for Crystal Palace as a highly promising teenager. Since retiring as a player he has featured regularly in the tabloids which have printed a succession of lurid stories about his somewhat dysfunctional private life.

HONOURS
England U21 International 1998 2 caps 0 goals
Blackburn Rovers 2000-01 Runners Up Division 1

Birmingham City 2008-09 Runners Up Championship

CLUBS
Brentford 1988 (youth) 21.07.95 (pro) ••Crystal Palace 08.01.98 (£300,000) ••Port Vale 15.01.99 (£375,000) ••Sheffield United 28.10.99 (£300,000) ••Blackburn Rovers 24.11.00 (£2.1 million) ••Ipswich Town 23.11.01 (£3 million) ••Leicester City 01.09.03 (loan) ••Everton 08.07.04 (£450,000) ••Charlton Athletic 17.01.06 (£2.5 million) ••Wigan Athletic 31.08.07 (loan) ••Birmingham City 18.07.08 (£1 million) ••Middlesbrough 30.10.09 (loan) ••Queens Park Rangers 01.02.10 (loan) ••Wolverhampton Wanderers 31.08.10 (loan) ••Sheffield United 18.01.11 (loan) ••Mitra Kukar, Indonesia 03.11.11 (free) ••Wick 13.09.17 (free) ••Cornard United 03.01.20 (free)

Marcus rose through the youth ranks at Brentford and made his Football league debut against Shrewsbury Town on 4th November 1995 at the age of 17. Two years later and with 70 appearances under his belt he secured his transfer to Crystal Palace, arriving in time to join a Premier League relegation battle that, despite his efforts, was eventually lost. He did receive international recognition around this time however, appearing twice for England U21's, including a 2-0 defeat against Argentina on 13th May 1998 where his team-mates included Jason Euell. Things got worse at Palace the following season. The club hit a financial crisis

and with administration looming, Marcus was offloaded to Port Vale, but stayed only nine months before another move took him to Sheffield United.
Things went better at Bramall Lane. He got among the goals and grabbed a hat-trick in a 6-0 win over West Bromwich Albion on 19th February 2000, but was less successful seven days later at the Valley when a John Robinson goal gave Charlton a narrow 1-0 victory on their way to the Division 1 title. Blackburn paid big bucks to sign Marcus in November and were rewarded with promotion to the Premier League but after just 12 months

in Lancashire he was on the move again and a transfer fee of £3.5 million took him to Ipswich Town and another unsuccessful relegation battle. Matt Holland and Herman Hreidarsson were with him at the Valley as he scored twice against Charlton on 1st January 2002, only for goals from Robinson, Parker and Euell to ensure a 3-2 win for the Addicks.

By now Ipswich were having their own financial problems and Marcus was loaned out to Leicester City, but they managed only two wins in the last 24 league games of 2003-04 making another relegation inevitable. A cut price transfer to Everton followed in July 2004 and led to a successful first season at Goodison Park, despite losing twice in the league to Charlton., who in January 2006 laid out a reported £2.5 million to bring him back to South London.

There could not have been a better start for Marcus who made his Charlton debut at Stamford Bridge as a substitute and after replacing Dennis Rommedahl, scored to force a 1-1 draw against a strong Chelsea side, but subsequent goals were few and far between. Just one in the league during the whole of the 2006-07 season was not good enough to prevent Charlton's seven-year stay in the Premier League from coming to an end. He was loaned out to Wigan Athletic and eventually sold to Birmingham City

in the Summer of 2008. They did at least manage a promotion in 2008-09 but for Marcus the goals had now dried up completely and he bounced around a further four clubs without managing a single strike. He rounded off his career with a short stint for the Indonesian club Mitra Kukar before announcing his retirement in April 2012. His mental health issues and complex love life have kept the tabloids on high alert. In September 2015 he was charged with possession of a Class A drug and with affray after a drug induced incident at his Surrey home led to him being tasered. He had called for assistance and when the police arrived challenged them whilst armed with a knife and a meat cleaver. He received a suspended prison sentence and 200 hours of community service. Then in June 2016 he was fined £350 for possession of cocaine at the Chessington World of Adventures theme park. In January 2019 he was declared bankrupt with huge debts owed to HMRC and was back in the news during March 2022 when he received a 32-month drink driving ban at Wimbledon Magistrate's Court.

Depression and mental illness are finally being recognised as a potential problem for those who live in the goldfish bowl world of professional sport and Marcus is now obtaining the help that he needs to get his life back on track. He is also starting a new job building summerhouses.

Season	Division	League		FA Cup		FL Cup		Total	
		A	G	A	G	A	G	A	G
2005-06	Premier	12 (1)	2	0	0	0	0	12 (1)	2
2006-07 (R)	Premier	17 (13)	1	1	0	4	1	22 (13)	2
2007-08	Championship	3	1	0	0	1	0	4	1
Total		32 (14)	4	1	0	5	1	38 (14)	5

UK LEAGUE CAREER 489 games 93 goals

CHARLTON CAREER
Managers: *A Curbishley, I Dowie, L Reed, A Pardew*
Debut: *Chelsea (A) (sub) 22-01-2006*
V632
Finale: *Sheffield Wednesday (H) 25-08-2007*

BERGDICH Zakarya   2015 - 16

Defender, Utility   10st 12lbs   5' 10"
Born: 07-01-1989 - Compiegne, France

Although French-born, Zak also qualified to play international football for Morocco and made his debut for their U23's in 2011 while playing for Lens. He was called up for his first full cap the following year, in time to participate in the 2012 Olympic Games in the UK. He retained his place for the finals of the Africa Cup of Nations in South Africa in 2013, but the Moroccan team failed to win a single match and were eliminated at the group stage.

HONOURS

Morocco International 2012-13 11 caps   Morocco U23 International

CLUBS

RC Strasbourg Alsace, France 2004 (youth) ••US Creteil, France 2007 (youth) ••UJA Alfortville, France 2009 (pro) ••RC Lens, France 30.06.10 (free) ••Real Valladolid, Spain 30.06.13 (£675,000) ••Genoa, Italy 01.02.15 (loan) ••Charlton Athletic 23.07.15 (£225,000) ••Cordoba CF, Spain 28.08.16 (free) ••Sochaux, France 19.07.17 (free) ••Belenenses, Portugal 04.07.18 (free) ••Denizlispor, Turkey 29.07.19 (undisclosed) ••BB Erzurumspor, Turkey 01.02.21 (undisclosed)

Zak came to prominence during season 2012-13 while playing in the French Ligue 2 for RC Lens. Primarily a left back, he was transferred to Spanish club, Real Valladolid and appeared consistently for them the following season when they finished second from bottom of La Liga and were relegated to the second level of Spanish football. He spent the early part of 2015 on loan at Genoa and featured in their first team in the Italian Serie A, holding his own against some very strong opposition.

In the summer of 2015, Zak was brought to England by Charlton manager Guy Luzon and he spent a torrid year as the club tore itself apart and engineered a quite needless relegation from the Championship. The season started well enough, but a disastrous run in which they failed to win a league match between 22nd August and 7th November left them at the wrong end of the table. By now Luzon had been replaced by the hapless interim manager, Karel Fraeye

and there was a high level of supporter unrest and demonstrations about the way in which the club was being run. Morgan Fox was generally preferred in the left back position so Zak was mainly used as either left midfield or as substitute and it was very difficult for him to make a positive impact. There was no happy ending to this sad tale and Charlton were duly relegated to League One.

Zak moved back to Spain following his unhappy year in English football and joined Cordoba, with whom he enjoyed a more peaceful season finishing mid-table in the Segunda Division. He then returned to France and in 2017-18 was competing in Ligue 2 for Sochaux alongside his former Charlton teammate El-Hadji Ba.

In July 2018 he was on the move again and signed a two-year contract with Portuguese club, Belenenses, but before long he had re-located to Turkey where he is currently without a club.

Season	Division	League		FA Cup		FL Cup		Total	
		A	G	A	G	A	G	A	G
2015-16 (R)	Championship	11 (12)	0	0	0	3	1	14 (12)	1
Total		11 (12)	0	0	0	3	1	14 (12)	1

UK LEAGUE CAREER 23 games 0 goals

CHARLTON CAREER
Managers: *G Luzon, K Fraeye, J Riga*
Debut: *Queens Park Rangers (H) (sub) 08-08-2015*
V802
Finale: *Bolton Wanderers (A) (sub) 19-04-2016*

BERRY Leslie Dennis   1975 - 86

Big Les was the cornerstone of Charlton's defence for a decade, during which he made almost 400 appearances for the club. He played all but one season in the second tier of English football and was very much an old-fashioned defender. He may have lacked some of the finer skills and been a long way from the ball-playing centre halves of the 21st century, but was an effective and popular stopper in an era when the sport was a good deal more physical than today. He was ever present in the campaigns of 1979-80 and 1983-84 and in the promotion season of 1980-81 played a bruising 54 competitive matches.

Defender   12st 6lbs   6' 1"
Born: 04-05-1956 - Plumstead, London
Education: Hawes Down School, West Wickham.

HONOURS

Bromley & District Schools
Charlton Athletic 1980 Player Of The Year
Charlton Athletic 1980-81 Promoted Division 3

Charlton Athletic Reserves 1981-82 Winners Mid-Week League
Maidstone United 1988-89 Winners Football Conference

CLUBS

Welling United (youth) ••Plumstead Maybloom (youth) ••Charlton Athletic 03.72 (youth) 01.03.74 (pro) ••Brighton & Hove Albion 08.86 (free) ••Gillingham 03.87 (loan) 1987 (free) ••Maidstone United 08.88 (free) ••Margate 03.91 (free) ••Welling United 03.81 (free)

Les trained at Charlton from the age of 11 and first appeared for the colts as an amateur in 1972. He signed his first professional contract in March 1974, so by the time he made his debut against Oxford United on 29th September 1975, he had already been around the club for some eight years. The occasion was a second replay in the Football League Cup and it had been squeezed into the schedule on a Monday evening. Les was substitute, (only one was allowed in those days) and entered the fray at the start of extra time with the score 2-2. He replaced young winger John Harrison, who himself was making only his third appearance for the club. It was a strange decision by manager Andy Nelson as he did not deploy Les as an extra defender, but instead left him to operate on the right wing where he looked far from comfortable racing backwards and forwards with great enthusiasm, but little effect. Fortunately, Derek Hales broke the deadlock and scored his second of the match to secure a 3-2 victory for the Addicks.

That was the only occasion when Les was played as a winger, but by the end of February 1976 he had settled into the Charlton defence and soon became one of the first names on the team sheet. Despite his height and heading ability, Les did not score many goals, but he did manage an important strike on 27th October 1979 against a Cardiff City side which included Alan Campbell and Graham Moore. In a very close contest, Charlton scraped home 3-2 with the other two goals coming from Steve Gritt.

After being voted Player of the Year in the disappointing relegation season of 1979-80, Les maintained his own good form and was one of the mainstays of Mike Bailey's team which regained a place in Division 2 only 12 months later. Charlton also had a run in the FA Cup that year and in Round 4 it was Les and Peter Shaw who kept the Fulham forwards at bay, enabling goals from Shaw and Derek Hales to earn an unexpected 2-1 win at Craven Cottage. It was his consistency that made Les such an influential member of the side and his loyalty was rewarded with a Testimonial match against Arsenal in 1984. He finally lost his place after the move to Selhurst Park and departed for Brighton & Hove Albion in August 1986.

He spent less than a year on the Sussex coast before switching to Gillingham where manager Keith Peacock was chasing promotion from Division 3 in 1986-87. A two legged play off final against Swindon Town finished all square and both Les and Martin Robinson played for the Gills in the decider which was held at Selhurst Park on 29th May 1987. It was however Steve White, another ex-Charlton player, who scored the goals that resulted in a 2-0 win for Swindon. After transferring to Maidstone United in August 1988, Les was in the side which won the Football Conference by eight points and gained promotion to the Football League for the first time in 1988-89 and he retained his place for two further seasons in Division 4. Keith Peacock was again his manager and his teammates at Maidstone included Dave Madden and Nicky Johns. After his playing days, Les went into the family business of electrical wholesalers. His father Dennis Berry was a former director of Gillingham and Maidstone United.

Season	Division	League		FA Cup		FL Cup		FM Cup		Total	
		A	G	A	G	A	G	A	G	A	G
1975-76	Division 2	14 (1)	1	0	0	0 (1)	0			14 (2)	1
1976-77	Division 2	39	2	1	0	1	0			41	2
1977-78	Division 2	40 (1)	2	1	0	1	0			42 (1)	2
1978-79	Division 2	36 (2)	1	3	0	3	0			42 (2)	1
1979-80 (R)	Division 2	42	2	1	0	2	0			45	2
1980-81 (P)	Division 3	44	2	5	0	5	0			54	2
1981-82	Division 2	24 (1)	0	1	0	0	0			25 (1)	0
1982-83	Division 2	39	1	1	0	2	0			42	1
1983-84	Division 2	42	0	2	0	2	0			46	0
1984-85	Division 2	25 (1)	0	2	0	2	0			29 (1)	0
1985-86 (P)	Division 2	7	0	0	0	1	0	1	0	9	0
Total		352 (6)	11	17	0	19 (1)	0	1	0	389 (7)	11

CHARLTON CAREER
Managers: *T Foley, A Nelson, M Bailey, A Mullery, K Craggs, L Lawrence*
Debut: *Oxford United (A) (sub) 29-09-1975*
V395
Finale: *Millwall (H) 15-04-1986*

UK LEAGUE CAREER 475 games 13 goals

BERRY William George   1923

The story of how Bill Berry, journeyman left winger from Hackney, transformed during a 40-year career into Georges Berry, much respected European football manager, is one that almost justifies a movie and perhaps Hollywood may yet be interested as the story defies belief.

Forward
Born: 18-08-1904 - Hackney, London
Died: 15-09-1972 - Manor Park, London

HONOURS AS MANAGER

SC Fives 1940-41 Runners Up Coupe de France
Lille OSC 1944-45 Runners Up Coupe de France
Lille OSC 1945-46 Winners Ligue 1 France
Lille OSC 1945-46 Winners Coupe de France
Lierse SK 1952-53 Runners Up Belgian Second Division
OGC Nice 1953-54 Winners Coupe de France
CS Hammam-Lif 1955-56 Winners Tunisian League

Etoile du Sahel 1956-57 & 1957-58 Runners Up Tunisian Cup
Etoile du Sahel 1957-58 Winners Tunisian League
Jeunesse Esch 1958-59 & 1959-60 Winners Luxembourg League
Union Sportive 1961-62 Winners Luxembourg League
Union Sportive 1961-62 Runners Up Luxembourg Cup
Union Sportive 1962-63 Winners Luxembourg Cup

CLUBS

Royal Naval Depot (Chatham) c1922 ••Charlton Athletic 15.08.23 (amateur) ••Gillingham 01.02.24 (loan) 1924 (pro) ••Brentford 05.26 ••Crystal Palace 10.11.32 (player exchange) ••Bournemouth & Boscombe Albion 06.33 ••Sporting Club Fives, France 1934 (free) 1936 (manager) ••Lille Olympique Sporting Club, France 1944 (manager) ••Lierse SK, Belgium 1946 (manager) ••Olympique Gymnaste Club Nice, France 1953 (manager) ••CS Hammam-Lif, Tunisia 01.07.55 (manager) ••Etoile Sportive Du Sahel, Tunisia 1956 (manager) ••Jeunesse Esch, Luxembourg 01.07.58 (manager) ••Union Sportive Luxembourg 1961 (manager)

Bill signed for Charlton in August 1923 and during the first half of that most difficult of seasons, was at least a contender for the outside left position. He did enjoy a reasonable run in the team during October and November but the club were in a financial mess and by December had made the foolish decision to leave the Valley and ground share at the Mount in Catford. Bill played in the final home game at the Valley on 8th December but was never selected again and joined Gillingham shortly thereafter. He went on to make more than 250 Football League appearances over the next decade, mainly for Gillingham and Brentford, but never rose above Division 3 standard. He came up against Charlton several times with mixed results, but on 17th December 1927 and when playing for Brentford in a team that also contained Ernie Watkins, he scored the equaliser to clinch a 1-1 draw at Griffin Park. Winger Charlie McKinley had opened the scoring for the Addicks. Bill's best season was without doubt 1930-31 when he managed 18 league goals in 32 matches and Brentford only just missed out on promotion. When Bournemouth failed to win more than one of the 14 matches in which he participated in season 1933-34, the

end of the road had been reached. His football career in England now a memory, he moved out to France and played two seasons with SC Fives, becoming first trainer and then in 1936 their manager.

Clearly this was where his real talent lay and he went on to enjoy success at every club he managed, moving between France and Belgium and on to Tunisia and Luxembourg. Career highlights include winning the French Ligue I with Lille in the first post war season and twice winning the Coupe de France. On the second occasion his Nice side, which included the legendary Just Fontaine, triumphed 2-1 against Marseilles on 23rd May 1954 in a classic final in front of a crowd of 56,803. Georges Berry, as he had now become, also achieved the unlikely feat of taking a team from tiny Luxembourg into the second round of the European Cup. This happened in 1959-60 when Jeunesse defeated the Polish champions and then went on to give a good account of themselves against Real Madrid.

Few people in England were aware of Georges Berry's achievements and his passing in 1972, back home in East London, sadly went unnoticed in the football world.

Season	Division	League		FA Cup		Total	
		A	G	A	G	A	G
1923-24	Divison 3 (S)	11	2	0	0	11	2
Total		11	2	0	0	11	2

UK LEAGUE CAREER 253 games 57 goals

CHARLTON CAREER
Managers: *W Rayner*
Debut: *Millwall (A) 29-09-1923*
V050
Finale: *Swansea Town (H) 08-12-1923*

BESSONE LUNA Federico   2011

Defender   11st 6lbs   5' 10"
Born: 23-01-1984 - Cordoba, Argentine

Although born in Argentina, Fede moved to LLeida in the Catalonia region of Spain as a youngster and entered Barcelona's La Masia Academy where he learned his football alongside the young Lionel Messi. He did not reach the Barcelona first team, but after spells with two other Catalonian clubs, Español and Nastic, attracted the attention of Swansea City, who brought him to the UK in June 2008.

HONOURS
FC Andorra 2018-19 Winners Primera Catalana (Spanish Regional League)

CLUBS
Barcelona, Spain 2001 (youth) 2002 (pro) ••RCD Espanyol, Spain 2005 (free) ••Gimnastic de Tarragona, Spain 2007 (loan) ••Swansea City 25.06.08 (free) ••Leeds United 16.06.10 (free) ••Charlton Athletic 31.01.11 (loan) ••Swansea City 31.08.11 (free) ••Swindon Town 31.08.12 (free) ••Oldham Athletic 28.03.13 (free) ••Sporting Kansas City, USA 09.09.13 (free) ••Millwall 18.02.14 (free) ••AE Prat, Spain 16.07.15 (free) ••FC Andorra, Spain 12.18 (free) ••Inter Club d'Escaldes, Andorra 01.07.20 (free)

Fede was plagued by injuries during his time at Swansea, but he did feature in half of their league matches during his second season and scored what proved to be his only goal in the Football League against Derby County on 20th November 2009 in a 1-0 victory at the Liberty Stadium. He was offered a new contact in the summer of 2010, but turned it down in favour of a move to Leeds United.
He never really got going at Leeds and lost his place in the first team by mid-September, later admitting in a newspaper interview that he had failed to reach his best form. He joined Charlton on loan shortly after Chris Powell took over as manager in January 2011 and held down the left back spot for the remainder of that season. There was vague talk about a permanent move to the Valley but nothing came of it and he left Leeds by mutual consent in August.
A return to Swansea did not work out and was followed by a short stay with Swindon Town during the managerial tenure of Paolo Di Canio and then an even briefer spell at

Oldham Athletic where he failed to play a single match because of a calf injury. With his career in England fading fast, Fede tried his luck in the USA with Sporting Kansas City where he learned the true meaning of 'warming the bench', being an unused substitute during the Major League Soccer final at Sporting Park, Kansas on 7th December 2013 that was played in a temperature of 20 degrees Fahrenheit.
After a short term contract with Millwall, Fede returned to Spain and hooked up with the Catalonian club, AE Prat. He continued to play as a part time professional while in 2016 setting up with his brother Fran, the Learning Soccer Academy, which promotes football training activities for young people as well as teaching the English language.
At the end of December 2018, he signed for FC Andorra along with Ruben Bover and both men were part of the team which in 2018-19 ended champions of the Primera Catalana, the fifth tier of the Spanish league system.

Season	Division	League		FA Cup		FL Cup		FL Trophy		Total	
		A	G	A	G	A	G		G	A	G
2010-11	League One	13	0	0	0	0	0	0	0	13	0
Total		13	0	0	0	0	0	0	0	13	0

UK LEAGUE CAREER 63 games 1 goal

CHARLTON CAREER
Managers: *C Powell*
Debut: *Colchester United (H) 01-02-2011*
V716
Finale: *Hartlepool United (H) 07-05-2011*

BEST Leon Julian Brendan   2017 - 18

There were high points in the career of Leon Best. He was capped seven times for Ireland, was the subject of a £3 million transfer to Blackburn Rovers and scored a memorable hat trick for Newcastle on 5th January 2011 as a West Ham side containing Tal Ben Haim, Scott Parker and Carlton Cole was dispatched 5-0 in a Premier League game. However, there were a greater number of low points and when Leon signed for Charlton on a short term contract in November 2017 he had not scored a goal in 19 months and was still not fully recovered from a groin operation that had put him in intensive care for four days

Forward   11st 9lbs   6' 1"
Born: 19-09-1986 - Nottingham, Notts

HONOURS

Ireland International 2009-10 7 caps 0 goals
Ireland U21 International 2008 1 cap 0 goals
Ireland U19 & U17 International

Southampton 2004-05 Finalists FA Youth Cup
Newcastle United 2009-10 Winners Championship

CLUBS

Notts County 2002 (youth) ••Southampton 21.09.04 (pro) ••Queens Park Rangers 17.12.04 (loan) ••Sheffield Wednesday 04.08.05 (loan) 31.01.06 (loan) ••AFC Bournemouth 04.08.06 (loan) ••Yeovil Town 23.11.06 (loan) ••Coventry City 12.07.07 (£650,000) ••Newcastle United 01.02.10 (£1.5 million) ••Blackburn Rovers 02.07.12 (£3 million) ••Sheffield Wednesday 14.02.14 (loan) ••Derby County 04.08.14 (loan) ••Brighton & Hove Albion 20.01.15 (loan) ••Rotherham United 16.11.15 (free) ••Ipswich Town 30.08.16 (free) ••Charlton Athletic 29.11.17 (free)

Leon made his debut for Southampton on his 18th birthday, just two days before signing professional terms. He played for them in the FA Youth Cup Final of 2005, but they were beaten over two legs by an Ipswich side that included Danny Haynes. By then however the pattern for his whole career had started to take shape and he was loaned out no less than five times by Southampton before eventually joining Coventry in the Summer of 2007. Although they struggled in the Championship throughout the three seasons that he spent with them, this probably represented the most successful spell of Leon's career. He was a skilful player, although not a natural goalscorer, but while with Coventry played regularly despite a cheekbone fracture which resulted in him wearing a protective mask and earning the nickname, Zorro. He qualified to play for Ireland through his Dublin born mother and made his full international debut on 29th May 2009, alongside Kevin Foley. It was a 1-1 draw and Leon was in direct opposition to Nigeria's centre half, Sam Sodje.
A big money transfer took him to Newcastle United but he never really established himself in their team. Competition for places and a cruciate injury in 2010 left him sidelined

for long periods. An even bigger transfer fee took him to Blackburn where he played even less and was out injured for the first nine months of his contract. He was shipped out on loan three more times and during what was his third loan spell with Sheffield Wednesday, played and scored against Charlton in Round 5 of the FA Cup on 24th February 2014. However, goals by Callum Harriott and Simon Church saw the Addicks victorious.
Best himself admitted in an interview that he had acquired a reputation as a troublemaker, although it is more likely the disruptive series of injuries that had plagued him and the long dry spells without scoring which caused his career to misfire.
He had been released by Ipswich when Karl Robinson signed him in November 2017 in what must be viewed as a desperate measure. He was far from match fit and never completed 90 minutes in any of his seven matches. He only found the net once and that was an own goal, scored at Blackburn just three minutes after replacing the injured Billy Clarke. A further serious knee injury acquired against Gillingham on 1st January 2018 brought his time at Charlton and his football career to a premature end.

Season	Division	League		FA Cup		FL Cup		FL Trophy		Play Offs		Total	
		A	G	A	G	A	G	A	G	A	G	A	G
2017-18	League One	2 (3)	0	0 (1)	0	0	0	1	0	0	0	3 (4)	0
Total		2 (3)	0	0 (1)	0	0	0	1	0	0	0	3 (4)	0

UK LEAGUE CAREER 286 games 59 goals

CHARLTON CAREER
Managers: *K Robinson*
Debut: *Peterborough United (H) 28-11-2017*
V852
Finale: *Gillingham (H) (sub) 01-01-2018*

BETHELL Roy   1928 - 29

Forward   11st 4lbs   5' 11"
Born: 09-08-1906 - Watford, Hertfordshire
Died: 05-11-1976 - Watford, Hertfordshire

Roy made his name with St Albans City during the most successful period in that club's long history. They were one of the leading amateur teams in the 1920s and he scored at more than a goal a game as they won the Isthmian League two years running. He also represented Hertfordshire FA when they won the Southern Counties Amateur Championship, scoring four goals in the final against Norfolk FA.

HONOURS

Hertfordshire FA 1926-27 Winners Southern Counties Amateur Championship

St Albans City 1926-27 & 1927-28 Winners Isthmian League

CLUBS

Watford St Marys 08.25 (amateur) ••St Albans City 04.26 (amateur) ••Charlton Athletic 25.11.27 (amateur) 01.03.28 (pro) ••Gillingham 24.05.29

Roy had few opportunities at first team level during his time at Charlton and was unable to force himself into the promotion winning side of 1928-29 until late in the season when he featured in the vital 1-0 home win against Brentford. It was no surprise when he was transferred to Gillingham a month later and he enjoyed a great deal more success with the Kent club chalking up 165 appearances in

Division 3 South during his six-year stay. His most productive season was 1930-31 when he contributed 14 goals in 40 league games, including two on 27th September 1930 when Crystal Palace were spanked 6-2.
In later years Roy worked as a fruiterer and greengrocer in Watford and was resident in Hempstead Road at the time of his death from pneumonia at the age of 70.

Season	Division	League		FA Cup		Total	
		A	G	A	G	A	G
1927-28	Divison 3 (S)	2	0	0	0	2	0
1928-29 (P)	Divison 3 (S)	1	0	0	0	1	0
Total		3	0	0	0	3	0

UK LEAGUE CAREER 168 games 32 goals

CHARLTON CAREER
Managers: *A Lindon, A MacFarlane*
Debut: *Exeter City (A) 10-03-1928*
V116
Finale: *Brentford (H) 22-04-1929*

BICKNELL Roy   1947 - 48

Although he had made wartime guest appearances for Notts County and Swindon Town, Roy's peace time debut and his only first team outing for Wolverhampton Wanderers came on 30th January 1946 in the FA Cup Round 4. In this first post war season the games were played over two legs and their opponents Charlton had built a solid 5-2 lead at the Valley only four days earlier. Roy was selected at centre half and handed the task of marking Arthur Turner, a formidable opponent who went on to notch seven goals in nine FA Cup games that season. He did not score that day however and the game finished 1-1. Roy's efforts must have been noted by the ever vigilant Jimmy Seed, because on 6th August 1947, a £600 transfer fee was paid to bring him to Charlton.

Defender   11st 10lbs.   5' 10"
Born: 19-02-1926 - Edlington, South Yorkshire
Died: 31-01-2005 - Colchester, Essex

HONOURS
London FA 1948 1 cap

HONOURS AS MANAGER
Clacton Town 1959-60 Winners Southern League Div 1

CLUBS
Doncaster Rovers (youth) ••Wolverhampton Wanderers 09.43 (youth) 1945 (pro) ••Charlton Athletic 06.08.47 (£600) ••Bristol City 13.06.49 (£2,000) ••Gravesend & Northfleet 03.08.51 (free) ••Colchester United 21.06.52 (free) ••Clacton Town 1954 (free) 04.58 (manager) ••Brantham Athletic c1961 (manager)

Roy spent almost two years at Charlton during which he was only called up for first team duty on those rare occasions when Harold Phipps was absent. One game in which he played might have ended in total disaster and that was the FA Cup Round 5 tie played against Manchester United on 7th February 1948. With Phipps injured, Roy lined up at centre half against very strong opposition, but the Charlton team was over run and it was only the brilliance of Sam Bartram that kept the score to a respectable 0-2. So well had Sam played that he was chaired off the pitch by his teammates after the final whistle. With his opportunities limited in London SE7, Roy was transferred to Bristol City in the summer of 1949 and he was a semi-regular for them over the next year or so, before dropping into non-league with Gravesend & Northfleet. He reappeared with Colchester United in 1952 but they struggled to keep away from the foot of Division 3 (South) and only narrowly avoided seeking re-election during his

time with them.
His playing career ended at Clacton Town when injury forced him into retirement in 1955, but after taking over as manager and with Frank Lock marshalling their defence, he guided them to the Southern League, Division 1 championship in 1959-60, the highest honour in the Essex club's history.
Roy, who married three times, became a bookmaker for a short while, co-owned a popular transport cafe in Colchester called Hythe Coffee House and later worked for Colchester County Court until his retirement in 1987. He passed away at the age of 78 from a pulmonary embolism, during a battle with Alzheimer's. His funeral was held at Colchester Crematorium on 9th February 2005. His father Ernie Bicknell was a professional boxer who fought for the British Featherweight title, while his cousin, Charlie Bicknell was captain of West Ham in the thirties,

Season	Division	League		FA Cup		Total	
		A	G	A	G	A	G
1947-48	Division 1	7	0	1	0	8	0
Total		7	0	1	0	8	0

UK LEAGUE CAREER 53 games 0 goals

CHARLTON CAREER
Managers: J Seed
Debut: Bolton Wanderers (H) 04-10-1947
V226
Finale: Grimsby Town (A) 24-04-1948

BIELIK Krystian   2018 - 19

Midfield, Defender   6' 2"
Born: 04-01-1998 - Konin, Poland

A key member of the 2018-19 promotion team, Krystian only spent one season on loan at Charlton, but scored the vital opening goal in the home leg of the play off semi-final against Doncaster Rovers and was arguably man of the match as Sunderland were defeated in that unforgettable Wembley final on 26th May 2019. He arrived from Arsenal as a raw but highly talented young player and returned nine months later as the finished article, but sadly there was never any real prospect of him remaining permanently in SE7 as Charlton's then transfer budget made such a move impossible. He was sold to Derby County in August 2019 for a fee which was reportedly structured to rise to £10 million should he prove a success., while Charlton continued to shop for bargain basement signings and loan players.

HONOURS

Poland International 2019 3 caps 0 goals
Poland U21 International 2017-19 6 caps 3 goals
Poland U19 International 2017 2 caps 0 goals
Poland U18 International 2015 3 caps 0 goals

Poland U17 International 2014-15 8 caps 3 goals
Poland U16 International 2013-14 3 caps 0 goals
Charlton Athletic 2018-19 Promoted League One Play Offs
Lech Poznan 2013-14 Winners Poland U17 FA Cup

CLUBS

Gornik Konin, Poland c 2007 (youth) ••Lech Poznan, Poland 2012 (youth) ••Legis Warsaw, Poland 07.14 (£9,000) ••Arsenal 21.01.15 (£2.4 million) ••Birmingham City 31.01.17 (loan) ••Walsall 31.01.18 (loan) ••Charlton Athletic 16.08.18 (loan) ••Derby County 02.08.19 (£7.5 million & add ons)

Both of Krystian's parents were physical education teachers in his hometown of Konin in Poland and from an early age his potential as a footballer was given every opportunity to develop. By his second year in elementary school he was training with Gornik Konin and playing against boys two years older than himself. After switching to Lech Poznan he received international recognition for Poland at U16 level and was transferred to Legia Warsaw in July 2014 for a fee of 50,000 zloty (about £9,000). His debut in the Ekstraklasa, the Polish Premier League, came against Korona Kielev on 24th August 2014, while still aged just 16.

Arsenal paid £2.4 million to bring Krystian to England the following January, but although highly rated, he was unable to force his way into their first team. He spent time out on loan with Birmingham City where he deputised for the injured Michael Morrison, but his career stalled when he failed to make a single appearance for Walsall during a second loan, thanks to successive knee, shoulder and hamstring injuries.

Krystian finally got a run of games and noticeably matured as a footballer during his time at Charlton, where he received valuable guidance from manager Lee Bowyer. He made appearances in the centre of defence but was most effective playing in a deep midfield role just in front of the back four.

He was capped by Poland U21's during his time at Charlton and scored in the 3-1 defeat of Portugal U21's on 20th November 2018 in a Euro U21 Championship qualifier before going on to compete in the finals in June 2019. He made his full international debut as a substitute against Slovenia on 6th September 2019.

Since the move to Derby County, Krystian has been most unfortunate with injuries. After being sent off against Charlton on 30th December 2019, he did not then play again for almost 11 months because of anterior cruciate ligament damage Then after just 13 further appearances and when he was getting back to top form, he received a similar injury during the first half of the match against Bristol City on 30th January 2021. While he was laid up for the second time Derby entered administration and the extent of their horrendous debts gradually became public knowledge, including an estimated £8 million still owed to Arsenal from Krystian's transfer two years earlier.

Season	Division	League		FA Cup		FL Cup		FL Trophy		Play Offs		Total	
		A	G	A	G	A	G	A	G	A	G	A	G
2018-19 (P)	League One	30 (1)	3	0	0	0	0	0	0	3	1	33 (1)	4
Total		30 (1)	3	0	0	0	0	0	0	3	1	33 (1)	4

UK LEAGUE CAREER 74 games 5 goals

CHARLTON CAREER
Managers: *L Bowyer*
Debut: *Accrington Stanley (A) 18-08-2018*
V864
Finale: *Sunderland (A) 26-05-2019*

BIKEY-AMOUGOU Andre Stephane   2014 - 15

The much travelled Andre Bikey was once described by the Middlesbrough Gazette as 'an absolute monster with a massive turning circle, who did a solid if erratic job, but was always worth one heart-stopping moment of madness per game'. During his time playing in Russia, he was a victim of racial abuse to such an extent that he was forced to carry a gun while in Moscow to protect himself from racist gangs. In 2008, he represented Cameroon in the Africa Cup of Nations in which they finished as runners-up. Andre was suspended and missed the final however, having been sent off in the previous round for pushing over a Ghanaian stretcher bearer.

Defender   15st 10lbs   6' 1"
Born: 08-01-1985 - Douala, Cameroon

HONOURS
Cameroon International 2006-10 25 caps 1 goal   Cameroon U23 International 2008 4 caps 0 goals

CLUBS
RCD Espanyol, Spain 2001 (youth) ••Futebol Clube do Marco, Portugal 07.02 ••Pacos de Ferreira, Portugal 07.03 ••CD Aves, Portugal 01.04 ••Uniao de Leiria, Portugal , 2004 ••Shinnik Yaroslav, Russia 01.05 ••Lokomotiv Moscow, Russia 21.06.05 ••Reading 08.06 (loan) 07.07 (£1 million) ••Burnley 18.08.09 (£2.8 million) ••Bristol City 22.03.12 (loan) ••Middlesbrough 11.09.12 (free) ••Panetolikos, Greece 16.09.13 (free) ••Charlton Athletic 09.07.14 (free) ••NorthEast United, India 20.10.15 (free) ••Pune City, India 26.07.16 (Injured did not play) 08.02.17 (re-signed) ••Port Vale 17.03.17 (free) ••Jamshedpur, India 29.08.17 (free) ••ATK, India 18.08.18 (free) ••UD Almeira, Spain 27.07.20 (coach)

Rightly or wrongly the often maligned Andre Bikey-Amougou acquired a reputation as a player who made an instant impact each time he joined a new club but never seemed able to sustain his good start and would soon move on to pastures new. He arrived in the UK during 2006 and was twice relegated from the Premier League, the first time being with Reading in 2007-08. However, he had his most productive campaign for them in the following year when they finished 4th in the Championship. Unfortunately he was sent off during the first leg of the play off semi-final at home to Burnley, having already conceded the penalty which gave the visitors a 1-0 victory. He caused a scene when shown the red card and never played for Reading again. Instead, he moved to Burnley for a sizeable fee and was relegated with them the following season.
Andre was signed to Charlton by manager Bob Peeters

ahead of the 2014-15 season after a spell in Greece with Panetolikos and went straight into the team as replacement for the popular and dependable Michael Morrison. Most supporters considered this a strange decision, but he started well enough and his tremendous physical presence helped enormously. Gradually however his lack of pace started to cause problems while at the same time bizarre errors were creeping into his game and well before the end of the season he was sidelined, thereby confirming the prophecy of doom.
He continued his travels after leaving Charlton, trying his luck with a succession of different clubs in India but after ending his playing career with the Bengali club, ATK, was in 2020 appointed assistant manager of UD Almeira, a Spanish Second division side.

Season	Division	League		FA Cup		FL Cup		Total	
		A	G	A	G	A	G	A	G
2014-15	Championship	29 (2)	1	1	0	2	0	32 (2)	1
Total		29 (2)	1	1	0	2	0	32 (2)	1

UK LEAGUE CAREER 210 games 11 goals

CHARLTON CAREER
Managers: *B Peeters, G Luzon*
Debut: *Brentford (A) 09-08-2014*
V779
Finale: *Millwall (A) (sub) 03-04-2015*

BISWELL George William   1925 - 34

Forward, Midfield   11st 2lbs   5' 8"
Born: 01-09-1904 - Watford, Hertfordshire
Died: 26-09-1981 - Watford, Hertfordshire

The early career of George Biswell mirrored that of another Watford boy, Charlton's England International, Harold Miller. Both men were inside forwards who started with Villa Juniors before joining St Albans City, a very powerful amateur club during the 1920s. George scored 10 league goals in their Isthmian League championship team of 1923-24 and then, like Miller before him, signed for Charlton.

HONOURS
St Albans City 1923-24 Winners Isthmian League

CLUBS

Villa Juniors (youth) ••Shaftesbury Athletic ••St Albans City 09.23 (amateur) ••Watford 1924 (amateur) ••Charlton Athletic 17.09.24 (amateur) 05.06.25 (pro) ••Chelsea 27.01.28 (£3,500) ••Chester 1930 (loan) ••Ards, N Ireland 1931 (free) ••Charlton Athletic 21.08.31 (free)

George was a success during his initial spell at Charlton and helped to stabilise the struggling team into a safe mid-table position in Division 3 (South) after having to seek re-election to the Football League during his first season. One memorable match came on Christmas Eve 1927 at the Valley when he scored twice against Luton Town which helped secure a 4-3 victory. Charlton's other scorers were John Rankin and David Sherlaw. However, in January 1928 he was sold to Chelsea, just as Harold Miller had been, for a record fee of £3,500.

Unlike Miller though, he did not settle in West London and only featured occasionally in the Chelsea first team. The two men did play together up front on 9th March 1929 at the Dell when George got the winner against Southampton (2-1) and in the end he made a total of 24

appearances for Chelsea for a return of 10 goals, before he moved on, first to non-league Chester and then briefly to Ards in Northern Ireland, before re-joining Charlton, now a Second Division team, in 1931.

Things went less well the second time around and his first team chances were few and far between, although he did get a run of games in season 1932-33, during which the defensive frailties of the side were exposed and they were relegated after conceding 91 league goals. George played on for just one more season, before announcing his retirement. He returned to the Watford area where he worked as a labourer. He was living in Ashfield Avenue, Bushey immediately prior to his death in Watford General Hospital at the age of 77.

Season	Division	League		FA Cup		D3 Cup		Total	
		A	G	A	G	A	G	A	G
1925-26	Divison 3 (S)	13	3	0	0			13	3
1926-27	Divison 3 (S)	28	7	0	0			28	7
1927-28	Divison 3 (S)	22	9	6	4			28	13
1931-32	Division 2	8	2	1	0			9	2
1932-33 (R)	Division 2	19	1	0	0			19	1
1933-34	Divison 3 (S)	1	0	2	0	1	0	4	0
Total		91	22	9	4	1	0	101	26

UK LEAGUE CAREER 115 games 32 goals

CHARLTON CAREER
Managers: *A MacFarlane, A Lindon, J Seed*
Debut: *Bristol Rovers (H) 29-08-1925*
V071
Finale: *Coventry City (H) 24-02-1934*

BLACK James

1931 - 33

Of the many Scottish footballers brought down to the Valley by Charlton's Airdrie born manager Alex 'Sandy' MacFarlane during his two spells in charge, Jim Black looked one of the more likely to succeed. By the time he arrived in South London in the summer of 1931, he had played in total more than 150 league matches for St Johnstone and Cowdenbeath, both clubs at that time competing in the Scottish First Division. At the age of 25 he should have been at his peak and as further evidence of the high level of expectation, Charlton handed over a transfer fee when acquiring his services, a sure sign that great things were expected of him. His elder brother Sammy Black played more than 500 matches for Plymouth Argyle between the wars.

Forward 11st 8lbs 5' 9"
Born: 04-05-1906 - Motherwell, Lanarkshire
Died: Unknown -

CLUBS

Carluke Rovers, Scotland ••St Johnstone, Scotland c1925 ••Cowdenbeath, Scotland 1929 ••Charlton Athletic 06.07.31 (£150) ••Burton Town 1933 (free) ••Aldershot 1934 ••Cheltenham Town 14.08.35 ••Cowdenbeath, Scotland 1935

Season 1931-32 must be considered a successful one for Charlton as their final placing of 10th in Division 2 was their best to date. Jimmy went straight into the team for the opening fixture at inside left but only kept his place for the first three matches. He was back in the side on 28th December however and scored the consolation goal as they went down 3-1 to the league leaders Wolverhampton Wanderers. He continued in the team for the second half of the season as they clawed their way up the table and was among the scorers in the exciting 3-3 draw at the Valley with Swansea Town on 12th March. Ominously for Jimmy, two of the Swansea goals that day were scored by Cyril Pearce who would sign for Charlton three months later. He was never more than a bit part player during his second season and did not score in any of his eight first team appearances in sharp contrast to Pearce who bagged 23 goals. His final game was a disappointing 4-1 home defeat

against Millwall, but although his time in SE7 was at an end he re-appeared in the Football League with Aldershot a year later where his manager was Angus Seed, brother of Charlton's Jimmy Seed.

The brothers came up against each other three times during 1934-35 season with Angus getting the upper hand and Black being one of the scorers when Aldershot triumphed 6-1 in the Third Division Cup in September. In the two league games which took place over Easter, Black and John Oakes (later a Charlton player) both played in the 3-2 home win on Good Friday, but Jimmy was missing three days later when Charlton gained revenge with a 4-0 scoreline at the Valley. His time in English football had run its course and after a brief stop at Cheltenham he returned home to Scotland.

Season	Division	League		FA Cup		Total	
		A	G	A	G	A	G
1931-32	Division 2	23	3	1	0	24	3
1932-33 (R)	Division 2	8	0	0	0	8	0
Total		31	3	1	0	32	3

UK LEAGUE CAREER 220 games 50 goals

CHARLTON CAREER
Managers: *A MacFarlane, A Lindon*
Debut: *Nottingham Forest (H) 29-08-1931*
V145
Finale: *Millwall (H) 25-03-1933*

BLACKETT-TAYLOR Corey Josiah Paul   2021 -

Forward, Midfield   6' 0"
Born: 23-09-1997 - Erdington, West Midlands
Education: Handsworth Grammar School. Birmingham.

Signed on a short-term contract at the beginning of the 2021-22 season, Corey made an impressive start to his time as a Charlton player. He was named in the line-up versus Crawley Town on 31st August for a group match in the Football League Trophy and gave a devastating display of old fashioned dribbling against admittedly weak opposition. He capped his fine performance with a spectacular solo goal as the Red Devils were swept away 6-1. His brother, Daryl Taylor played for Walsall in the early 2000s.

HONOURS
England U17 International 2013 4 caps 2 goals

CLUBS
Aston Villa 2007 (youth) 2016 (pro) ••Walsall 31.01.19 (loan) ••Tranmere Rovers 26.06.16 (free) ••Charlton Athletic 20.08.21 (free)

Corey spent a decade in the youth academy at Aston Villa and was capped by England at Under 17 level. He scored in the final of the Nordic Tournament in Norway in August 2013 as England triumphed against the host nation 4-0, but found it harder to progress at club level. After a loan spell in which he featured in 10 win-less matches for Walsall, he moved to Tranmere Rovers, but they too were struggling on the field and both clubs suffered relegation from League

One during his watch.

Freed by Tranmere, Corey was one of the players on the radar of Charlton's Director of Football, Steve Gallen, in the summer of 2021. Although he had yet to fulfill his potential, his speed and raw talent were worth further investigation and his short term contract was designed for that very purpose. On 18th November he signed an extension which should keep him at the club until 2023.

UK LEAGUE CAREER 55 games 3 goals

CHARLTON CAREER
Managers: *N Adkins, J Jackson*
Debut: *Wigan Athletic (H) (sub) 21-08-2021*
V929

BLACKWELL John   1932 - 34

Forward
Born: 28-10-1909 - Sheffield, Yorkshire
Died: 25-10-2001 -

Jack Blackwell spent 16 months at Charlton, but most of his first team action came during the relegation season of 1932-33, in which the club slid back down to Division 3 (South) after conceding a horrendous 91 league goals during a highly forgettable campaign. He had been signed from Huddersfield Town for the not insignificant fee of £1,500 and was the replacement at inside right for Bobby McKay who departed for Bristol Rovers shortly after his arrival. Jack had only played three league games prior to his move to London which implies something of a gamble by manager Alex MacFarlane, but there is little to suggest that the club got value for money and he was offloaded to Port Vale in February 1934, by which time it was apparent that he did not figure in the plans of new manager, Jimmy Seed.

HONOURS
Ipswich Town 1936-37 Winners Southern League

CLUBS

Chapel-En-Le-Frith (youth) ••Huddersfield Town 10.31 ••Charlton Athletic 28.10.32 (£1,500) ••Port Vale 21.02.34 (£900) ••Boston United 05.35 (free) ••Ipswich Town 02.07.36 ••Bridlington Town

Born in the Sheffield suburb of Eccleshall, Jack joined Huddersfield Town in 1931. They were among the leading clubs of the period and his three Division 1 appearances included a 4-0 win at Newcastle, but after his first season at Charlton his first team opportunities gradually reduced until eventually the club sanctioned his move to the Potteries and accepted the opportunity to re-coup at least some of his transfer fee.

He spent the best part of two seasons with Port Vale and got off to an excellent start, scoring twice on his debut in a 5-1 win against Millwall on 24th February 1934, but only managed one further goal in his next 11 games. He then picked up a serious knee injury in the opening game of the following campaign against Sheffield United which kept

him sidelined for four months. He did eventually regain his place in the side but was released at the end of the season. Jack moved on, first to Boston United and then in 1936 to Ipswich Town, who had just made the decision to become a professional club and been accepted to compete in the Southern League. He played in their very first match on 29th August 1936 and scored in a 3-1 win against Tunbridge Wells Rangers. The Tractor Boys stormed through that first season, finishing Southern League champions by five clear points, Jack's personal contribution being 15 league and cup goals. He later had a spell with Bridlington Town before World War 2 brought organised football to a close and his career to an end.

Season	Division	League		FA Cup		D3 Cup		Total	
		A	G	A	G	A	G	A	G
1932-33 (R)	Division 2	27	5	1	1			28	6
1933-34	Divison 3 (S)	8	2	3	0	1	0	12	2
Total		35	7	4	1	1	0	40	8

UK LEAGUE CAREER 62 games 2 goals

CHARLTON CAREER

Managers: *A MacFarlane, A Lindon, J Seed*

Debut: *Swansea Town (A) 29-10-1932*

V162

Finale: *Torquay United (A) 14-02-1934*

BLOMQVIST Lars Jesper   2002 - 03

Jesper was a highly talented left winger who came to prominence when IFK Gothenburg dominated Swedish football during the mid-nineties. He played in the 1994

Midfield, Forward   5' 9"
Born: 05-02-1974 - Tavelsjo, Sweden

FIFA World Cup, although he was an unused substitute in their final match in which Sweden defeated Bulgaria to claim third place in the tournament. In 1996, he transferred to Serie A champions, AC Milan but they were in a period of transition and he failed to make any great impact. A second season in Italy with Parma went better and in July 1998 Alex Ferguson arrived with his cheque book to bring Jesper to England.

HONOURS

Sweden International 1994-02 30 caps 0 goals
Sweden U23, U18 & U16 International
Sweden 1994 Third Place FIFA World Cup
Umea 1992 Winners Division 2 Norra Norrland

IFK Gothenburg 1994, 1995 & 1996 Winners Allsvenskan (league)
Manchester United 1988-89 Winners UEFA Champions League
Manchester United 1988-89 Winners Premier League

CLUBS

Tavelsjo AIK, Sweden (youth) ••Umea, Sweden 1992 ••IFK Gothenburg, Sweden 11.09.93 ••AC MIlan, Italy 1996 ••Parma, Italy 1997 ••Manchester United 31.07.98 (£4.4 million) ••Everton 10.11.01 (free) ••Charlton Athletic 30.08.02 (free) ••Djurgardens IF, Sweden 2003 (free) ••Enkopings SK, Sweden 2008 (player coach) ••Hammarby IF, Sweden 12.09 (ass. manager)

Jesper's Manchester United debut came at Old Trafford on 9th September 1998 against Charlton who were well beaten, having only a Mark Kinsella consolation goal to ease

the pain of a 1-4 scoreline. United dominated the 1998-99 season winning the Premier League and the FA Cup, although Jesper was an unused substitute in the Final. He was however in the starting line-up for the UEFA Champions League Final against Bayern Munich on 26th May 1999, but had been substituted before the two late goals which stunned the Germans and brought the cup back to Manchester.

At this point things started to unravel for Jesper and a serious knee injury prevented him from playing football for two years. In fact the match with Bayern Munich proved to be his final appearance in a Manchester United shirt. He joined Everton in November 2001 but his injury problems persisted. He did feature for their match at Goodison Park on 29th December, when Charlton plundered an impressive 3-0 win, but was not offered an extension to his contract at the end of that season.

It is always a heavy gamble to take on a player with such a history of injuries, but Alan Curbishley thought the risk worthwhile as a fit Jesper Blomqvist would have been a real asset, so he was signed for the 2002-03 season. Sadly the gamble failed and he only appeared in three Premier League matches, each time as a substitute and all three were lost. His one start came in the FA Cup against Exeter City on 4th January. It was won 3-1, but even then he was unable to complete 90 minutes and was replaced by Kevin Lisbie during the second half.

Jesper returned to Sweden and joined Djurgaarden IF, but further injuries restricted him to a handful of games as they won the Allsvenskan in 2003. He had accumulated 30 International caps, (none during his time at Charlton), but finally called a halt to his injury ravaged career in August 2005. He coached and played a few games for Enkopings SK and had a spell as assistant manager of Hammarby IF, but now seems to have settled for life in the media, becoming a football pundit for Swedish TV4 and in 2017 competing in and winning the Swedish celebrity dance show, 'Let's Dance'.

Season	Division	League		FA Cup		FL Cup		Total	
		A	G	A	G	A	G	A	G
2002-03	Premier	0 (3)	0	1	0	0	0	1 (3)	0
Total		0 (3)	0	1	0	0	0	1 (3)	0

UK LEAGUE CAREER 43 games 2 goals

CHARLTON CAREER
Managers: *A Curbishley*
Debut: *Arsenal (H) (sub) 14-09-2002*
V606
Finale: *Blackburn Rovers (A) (sub) 12-04-2003*

BLOTT Cyril Leslie Coldham　　　　　　　　　　　　1938 - 39

Forward　5' 8"
Born: 10-08-1917 - Southend-on-Sea, Essex
Died: 22-05 1994 - Horsham, West Sussex

Cyril was no 'Blott on the Landscape' and but for the Second World War may well have gone on to make a significant name for himself in the world of football. Instead, he served his country with great distinction in Burma. After hostilities ceased and by then promoted to the rank of Major, he remained in the forces and his potential as a centre forward was never given the opportunity to develop.

CLUBS

Romford 1936 ••Charlton Athletic 30.08.37 (amateur) 13.11.37 (pro)

Romford were champions of the Athenian League by a 10 point margin in 1936-37 which was the season when Cyril joined them and as a teenage striker he must have shown great promise to even make their squad while the team were amassing 102 league goals in a 26 match season. He only played nine times in all for the Essex club before joining Charlton on amateur terms in August 1937 and turning pro three months later.

His debut came up at Everton in April 1938 and he kept his place for the remainder of that season playing at inside right whilst George Tadman was out of action with a knee injury.

Cyril scored against Blackpool at the Valley on Easter Monday, his strike adding to Sailor Brown's hat-trick for a 4-1 scoreline.

Charlton had one of their finest teams during this period so it is all credit to Cyril that he featured in a further 10 games in his second season. This included two wins over Chelsea and a 1-0 victory against Aston Villa at the Valley on 8th April 1939 when he scored the winner. His final appearance came versus Preston at the Valley on 6th May and his goal plus a brace from Don Welsh ensured that the last full season before World War 2 ended on a high note for

Charlton at 3-1.

We will never know how good a player Cyril Blott would have become. He was still only 22 when his football career was ended so suddenly by the war, but all the signs were that Jimmy Seed had found another winner. Cyril was married in the Indian town of Ranchi during July 1946, spent time in Hong Kong and the Far East where he worked as an accountant with Jardine Matheson & Co,

eventually becoming their Company Secretary and later Finance Director. He returned to the UK in 1973 to work in Jardine's London office before taking early retirement through ill health. He rarely talked about his footballing past but had also been an accomplished cricketer and a good tennis player. He passed away at the age of 76 and is buried in St Peter's Churchyard in the village of Parham, West Sussex.

Season	Division	League		FA Cup		Total	
		A	G	A	G	A	G
1937-38	Division 1	6	1	0	0	6	1
1938-39	Division 1	10	3	0	0	10	3
Total		16	4	0	0	16	4

UK LEAGUE CAREER 16 games 4 goals

CHARLTON CAREER
Managers: *J Seed*
Debut: *Everton (A) 16-04-1938*
V201
Finale: *Preston North End (H) 06-05-1939*

BLUMBERG Ryan   2018

Ryan's time with Charlton left only a faint footprint, his first team debut being an early season League Cup encounter at Milton Keynes.

Defender   6' 1"
Born: 12-12-1998 - Sydney, Australia
Education: Moriah War Memorial College, Sydney. Nike Academy, Burton Upon Trent. University of Maryland, USA.

Lee Bowyer chose that occasion to field a side almost entirely selected from the Development squad and not surprisingly they made a very nervy start. The game was effectively lost in the first 16 minutes when they conceded twice, although they did improve as the match progressed and the final score of 3-0 undoubtedly flattered their opponents. He got a second chance at the Valley three months later when again a weakened side was fielded against Swansea City U21 and the club's lowest recorded attendance of 740 watched as Charlton crashed out of the Football League Trophy 1-0.

HONOURS
Charlton Athletic U23 2017-18 Runners Up PD League 2 South

CLUBS
Maccabi Hakoah, Australia 2011 (youth) ••APIA Leichhardt Tigers, Australia 2014 (youth) ••Western Sydney Wanderers, Australia 09.15 (youth) ••Maccabi Hakoah, Australia 03.16 (youth) ••Charlton Athletic 29.06.17 (pro) ••Maryland Terrapins, USA 2019

From a Jewish family, Ryan was identified as an outstanding footballing prospect from an early age. He played in the Eastern Metro representative teams at both U11 and U12 and was captaining Western Sydney Wanderers U20 side at the age of 17. He switched to Maccabi Hakoah and in May 2017 was nominated to represent them in the Nike 'most wanted' trials where he was selected from 600 hopefuls and travelled to France for the Nike Global trials, again coming through from a field of 44 and winning himself a place at the Nike Academy at the St George's Park National Football Centre.

Shortly after it was announced that the Nike Academy was to close at the end of the 2016-17 season, Ryan signed for

Charlton on a one-year contract, the second Academy graduate to do so, Anfernee Dijksteel having followed the same route to SE7. He played regularly at centre half for the Charlton U23 team through 2017-18 when they finished runners-up in the Professional Development League South and was in the team beaten 3-1 in the National play off semi final at Bolton on 1st May 2018. His efforts earned him a new 12-month contract.

In January 2017 Ryan had been offered a place at the University of Maryland and it was announced on 19th December 2018 that he was leaving Charlton and had returned home to Australia but would be taking up his two-year scholarship in the USA later in the year. While at

Uni he played for the Maryland Terrapins in the Big Ten, which is the oldest Division 1 collegiate athletic conference

in the USA.

Season	Division	League		FA Cup		FL Cup		FL Trophy		Total	
		A	G	A	G	A	G	A	G	A	G
2018-19	League One	0	0	0	0	1	0	1	0	2	0
Total		0	0	0	0	1	0	1	0	2	0

UK LEAGUE CAREER 0 games 0 goals

CHARLTON CAREER
Managers: *K Robinson, L Bowyer*
Debut: *Milton Keynes Dons (A) 14-08-2018*
V859
Finale: *Swansea City U21 (H) 13-11-2018*

BOGLE Omar Hanif   2020 - 21

Forward   12st 8lbs   6' 3"
Born: 26-07-1993 - Sandwell, West MIdlands
Education: Menzies High School, West Bromwich.

Omar Bogle is a legend in Grimsby where his name is sometimes spoken of in the same sentence as another of their former strikers, Clive Mendonca. Sadly he made a good deal less impact than Clive during his short stay in London SE7 but for the Mariners he is fondly remembered for the two Wembley goals that he scored on 16th May 2016. The occasion was the National League play off final and the 3-1 defeat of Forest Green Rovers that day brought Grimsby Town back into the Football League after an absence of seven years.

HONOURS

England C International 2014 1 cap 1 goal   Cardiff City 2017-18 Runners Up Championship
Grimsby Town 2015-16 Promoted Play Offs National League

CLUBS

West Bromwich Albion 2007 (youth) ••Birmingham City 2009 (youth) ••Celtic, Scotland 09.11 (youth) ••Hinckley United 03.12 (pro) ••Solihull Moors 07.07.12 (free) ••Grimsby Town 15.06.15 (undisclosed) ••Wigan Athletic 31.01.17 (undisclosed) ••Cardiff City 17.08.17 (£700,000) ••Peterborough United 01.02.18 (loan) ••Birmingham City 07.08.18 (loan) ••Portsmouth 28.01.09 (loan) ••ADO Den Haag, Netherlands 31.01.20 (loan) ••Charlton Athletic 09.10.20 (free) ••Doncaster Rovers 29.01.21 (free) ••Hartlepool United 27.01.22 (free)

An early grounding in the West Bromwich Albion youth academy and time spent with Celtic at U19 level gave Omar a great start to his football career, but he had to drop into the non-league game before he could really progress. He spent three seasons with Solihull Moors playing in the Conference North and was their leading goalscorer on each occasion, eventually netting 62 times in 111 league matches. He was called up for the England C international match against Estonia U23's on 18th November 2014 and scored the opening goal in a 4-2 victory.

His reputation grew even more after switching to Grimsby in June 2015 and following the euphoria of the play off success, he had his most successful spell during the first half of 2016-17, scoring a hat-trick against Stevenage and then seven league goals in just four games during November as Grimsby settled back into life in League 2. By January, he had 19 goals to his name and clubs were lining up to sign him. When the dust settled, he moved to Wigan Athletic for a sizeable but undisclosed fee, although it is fair to say that since leaving Grimsby the goals have largely dried up.

After only six months, a fee of £700,000 took Omar to Cardiff City in August 2017, but they appeared to want him as cover for their existing strikers When he featured at all, it was mainly from the bench and there were no less than four loan spells over the next three years with varying degrees of success. He played for Peterborough alongside Marcus Maddison on 10th March 2018 when Charlton were defeated 4-1, but his most fascinating loan was to the Netherlands in January 2020 where Den Haag were involved in a desperate relegation battle and the new management team of Alan Pardew and Chris Powell had been brought in to steady the ship. Omar managed just one goal in five games before the Covid pandemic brought their season to a premature close.

Charlton spent much of 2020 locked into an ownership battle and subject to a transfer embargo, so when both issues were finally resolved there was a mad scramble to sign players before the transfer window closed. Omar joined on 9th October and made his debut eight days later in a 1-0 win against Wigan Athletic. He replaced Chuks Aneke from the bench and this became the pattern as the two men alternated game by game – one starting the match and the other taking over during the second half. Amazingly all of Omar's first six Charlton appearances were won, but although he showed strength and skill and never lacked application, he was less effective and less of a goal threat than Chuks.

He did not stay long at the Valley and in the next transfer window moved on to Doncaster Rovers where he demonstrated not only his footballing skills but also his unexpected talent as a rapper.

Season	Division	League		FA Cup		FL Cup		FL Trophy		Total	
		A	G	A	G	A	G	A	G	A	G
2020-21	League One	12 (5)	2	0	0	0	0	0	0	12 (5)	2
Total		12 (5)	2	0	0	0	0	0	0	12 (5)	2

UK LEAGUE CAREER 132 games 36 goals

CHARLTON CAREER
Managers: *L Bowyer*
Debut: *Wigan Athletic (H) (sub) 17-10-2020*
V910
Finale: *Peterborough United (A) 19-01-2021*

BOLDER Robert John   1986 - 93

A big man with a massive personality, Bob is considered by Lennie Lawrence to have been one of the five best signings that

Goalkeeper   14st 7lbs   6' 3"
Born: 02-10-1958 - Dover, Kent
Education: St Mary's Catholic Primary School, Deal and St Edmunds School, Dover.

he made during his near 25-year career as a football manager. He was a very important member of Lennie's Charlton side that fought against all the odds during the 1980s and kept the club afloat in the First Division during the exile years. They were relegated after four seasons, but by then the directors had seen the futility of the ground-share at Selhust Park and the long battle for the return to the Valley had commenced. Bob was voted Player of the Year in 1987 and was ever present in league matches in three separate seasons for Charlton.

HONOURS
Charlton Athletic 1986-87 Finalists Full Members Cup   Sheffield Wednesday 1979-80 Promoted Division 3
Charlton Athletic 1987 Player Of The Year

CLUBS
Charlton Athletic 1975 (youth) ••Dover 1975 (semi pro) ••Sheffield Wednesday 03.77 (£1,000) ••Liverpool 08.08.83 (£125,000) ••Sunderland 16.10.85 (£30,000) ••Luton Town 21.02.86 (loan) ••Charlton Athletic 15.08.86 (£20,000) ••Margate 08.07.94 (free) ••Dagenham & Redbridge 09.94 (player coach) ••Cromptons 1995 (non contract)

As a teenager, Bob had trials with Charlton and made his debut for the Colts against Queens Park Rangers on 19th April 1975 at the Unilever Sports Ground, New Eltham. He was not granted a contract however and instead found work as an agricultural labourer while turning out for his home town club, Dover. His performances attracted the attention of Sheffield Wednesday, who signed him in March 1977 at the age of 18 and his Football League career commenced nine months later on 27th December with a satisfactory 1-0 home win over Rotherham United. He quickly became the regular 'keeper for the Owls, who at that time were languishing in Division 3 and featured in their promotion team of 1979-80, the highlight of which

was undoubtedly the 4-0 destruction of Sheffield United on Boxing Day.
Bob first came up against Charlton on 17th October 1981 at the Valley. The Wednesday team that day also included Peter Shirtliff and John Pearson, but was soundly beaten 3-0 courtesy of goals from Paul Walsh (2) and Martin Robinson. Almost two years later in August 1983 he made what seemed a dream move to Liverpool, who at that time were the leading club in the country, but in the end it proved a frustrating period owing to the consistency and brilliance of goalkeeper Bruce Grobbelaar, who never missed a single match during the two years that Bob was a Liverpool player. Consigned to life on the sub's bench, he

did at least receive a European Cup winner's medal in 1984, of which he is understandably proud, although he was still not called upon to play.

A loan spell at Sunderland was converted into a permanent transfer in October 1985 and that same month Bob played against Charlton in what was their first 'home' game following the move to Selhust Park. Goals from Mark Reid and Mark Stuart ensured a 2-1 win for the Addicks in front of a miserable crowd numbering just 5,552, few of whom at that stage believed that the club was capable of gaining promotion. Manager Lennie Lawrence evidently thought otherwise and pulled off a near miracle by achieving a place in Division 1 for 1986-87 and then strengthened his squad by signing Bob to compete with Nicky Johns for the goalkeeping jersey.

This time Bob did not have as long to wait on the bench because Nicky hurt his ankle at Watford on 8th November, so he made his debut the following weekend. Johns returned to the team but was then sent off in his comeback match, after which Bob became first choice, a position that he maintained until eventually losing out to Mike Salmon six long years later. He was a model of consistency throughout the period of exile and remained in the side long enough to wear Charlton's colours at the Valley for the first time on 5th December 1992 when the club finally returned home. Later that season he picked up a serious injury to his knee which despite a series of operations eventually brought his career to a close. He was given a free transfer in May 1994 and was granted a Testimonial match which took place on 24th April 1995 against Sheffield Wednesday.

Returning to Charlton in August 1995, Bob started work for the Community Trust, initially to develop support in East Kent and later in a host of roles, including coaching and fund raising. He visited South Africa to coach under-privileged youngsters and while there played in the Testimonial match for the victims of the Ellis Park Disaster in which 43 fans were crushed to death. Since 1997 he has been a highly visible presence around the club and often works as a match-day host. His extrovert and witty persona make him an ever-popular figure. As recently as July 2021 he announced that he would be cycling from Land's End to John O'Groats, a distance of 874 miles, to raise money on behalf of the Community Trust.

Season	Division	League		FA Cup		FL Cup		Play Offs		FM Cup		AI Cup		Total	
		A	G	A	G	A	G	A	G	A	G	A	G	A	G
1986-87	Division 1	26	0	1	0	1	0	5	0	4	0			37	0
1987-88	Division 1	35	0	1	0	2	0			2	0			40	0
1988-89	Division 1	38	0	3	0	3	0			1	0			45	0
1989-90 (R)	Division 1	38	0	2	0	3	0			2	0			45	0
1990-91	Division 2	39	0	1	0	1	0			1	0			42	0
1991-92	Division 2	46	0	3	0	4	0			1	0			54	0
1992-93	Division 1	27	0	2	0	2	0					2	0	33	0
Total		249	0	13	0	16	0	5	0	11	0	2	0	296	0

UK LEAGUE CAREER 467 games 0 goals

CHARLTON CAREER
Managers: L Lawrence, A Curbishley/S Gritt
Debut: *Manchester City (A) 15-11-1986*
V508
Finale: *Grimsby Town (A) 06-02-1993*

BOLLAND Gordon Edward   1967 - 68

Forward, Midfield   12st 10lbs   6' 0"
Born: 12-08-1943 - Boston, Lincolnshire
Education: Kitwood Secondary Modern School, Boston

A clever and creative inside forward, Gordon played over 100 Division 2 league games for Norwich City and almost 250 for Millwall in a period of 12 years between 1964 and 1975. Squeezed in between was a period of 11 months when he wore the colours of Charlton Athletic, although in truth, he did not wear them very often. Eddie Firmani had only been manager for two months when Gordon was signed from Norwich City for a fee of £20,000, yet he was discarded after only 12 appearances and Millwall became the grateful recipients of this apparent generosity. It does seem strange that he was not used more often, but in that period Charlton had forwards of the calibre of Tees, Treacy and Gregory to choose from and perhaps Gordon had just turned up at the wrong time.

HONOURS

LIncolnshire Schools

Chelsea U18 1959-60 & 1960-61 Winners FA Youth Cup

Charlton Athletic Reserves 1968-69 Runners Up London Mid-Week League

HONOURS AS MANAGER

Boston United 1976-77 Winners Northern Premier League

Boston United 1976-77 Winners Northern Premier League Shield

CLUBS

Boston United 1959 (youth) ••Chelsea 02.59 (amateur) 25.08.60 (pro) ••Leyton Orient 03.03.62 (£8,000) ••Norwich City 14.03.64 (£30,000) ••Charlton Athletic 28.11.67 (£20,000) ••Millwall 29.10.68 (£10,000) ••Boston United 1975 (free) 1976 (player manager)

Although a Lincolnshire boy, Gordon came through the youth set-up at Chelsea and made his name during the FA Youth Cup campaign of 1959-60. He scored 15 goals in the competition, including four in each of the first two matches. They beat Preston North End in the final and he was rewarded with a professional contract shortly after his 17th birthday. The next season they retained the cup by beating Everton 5-3 on aggregate and he contributed a further seven goals in nine matches. First team prospects were limited however and in March 1962 he was transferred to Leyton Orient.

This gave Gordon the first team football that he needed and a visit to the Valley only three weeks later resulted in a 2-1 defeat for Charlton in front of a crowd of nearly 30,000. The large attendance reflected the fact that Orient were poised to clinch promotion to the top division of English football for the only time in their history. Gordon had arrived late in the promotion drive but played fairly regularly the following season while they were being hopelessly outclassed in Division 1. One of their few good results came on 12th September 1962 when Everton were beaten 3-0 and Gordon was among the scorers.

After transferring to Norwich City, he made a spectacular start to the 1964-65 season, scoring 15 goals in his first 16 games. This included a League Cup hat-trick against Chester, as well as a consolation goal against Charlton on 3rd October. The Addicks had a weakened side out that day, but Jim Ryan, deputising for Eddie Firmani, scored twice for a 2-1 win. Gordon could never maintain that same scoring rate during the remainder of his time with Norwich, but was still viewed as a quality forward by the time he signed for Charlton in November 1967.

The club were languishing in the lower reaches of Division 2 and results continued to be disappointing. Gordon only managed two goals and they were both scored against his old club, Norwich. By Christmas Charlton had slipped to 19th place and relegation was looking a strong possibility. After just two months in the team, it was the depressing 3-0 FA Cup defeat at Coventry on 27th January which cost him his place and although relegation was eventually avoided, that effectively concluded Gordon's time as a Charlton first team player.

So often in football, a change of club can mean a change of fortune and that was certainly the case for Gordon after he moved on to Millwall. He spent almost seven years at the Den and was a model of consistency, hardly missing a game for long periods and re-capturing his best scoring form, Perhaps inevitably he grabbed the winner in an exciting 3-2 derby on 1st March 1969 after Paul Went had twice scored and raised Charlton's hopes. Then during 1971-72, when Millwall missed out on promotion to Division 1 on the final day of the season, he was ever present and contributed 14 league goals.

Gordon left London in 1975 and re-joined Boston United from where he had started out as a youngster. The following year he was elevated to the role of joint manager following the departure of future England caretaker manager Howard Wilkinson and guided them to the top of the Northern Premier League in 1976-77 although a persistent hip injury brought his playing days to an end. He became a sales representative and later became first the commercial manager and then during the period 1995-96 a director of Boston United. By 2006 Gordon was running a mini cab firm but is now fully retired.

Season	Division	League		FA Cup		FL Cup		Total	
		A	G	A	G	A	G	A	G
1967-68	Division 2	8 (2)	2	1	0	0	0	9 (2)	2
1968-69	Division 2	1		0	0	0	0	1	0
Total		9 (2)	2	1	0	0	0	10 (2)	2

UK LEAGUE CAREER 425 games 112 goals

CHARLTON CAREER

Managers: *E Firmani*

Debut: *Birmingham City (H) 02-12-1967*

V336

Finale: *Crystal Palace (A) 31-08-1968*

BOND Dennis Joseph Thomas   1970 - 73

Midfield   10st 10lbs   5' 7"
Born: 17-03-1947 - Walthamstow, London

It was Watford who got the best out of Dennis Bond. He had been earmarked early on as a special footballing talent and gained his first England cap at U15 level, going on to play for his club in Division 3 before his 18th birthday. On 21st April 1965 he, (along with Jack Burkett), starred in the England Youth team, scoring in the 5-0 demolition of Hungary as part of the UEFA Youth Tournament and was regularly spoken of as a star of the future. Sadly he proved unable to live up to such high expectations and during his time wearing a Charlton shirt, his level of performance rarely reached the predicted level.

HONOURS

England Youth International 1965 3 caps 2 goals   Walthamstow Schools
England Schoolboy U15 International 1961-62 4 caps

CLUBS

Watford 05.62 (youth) 03.64 (pro) ••Tottenham Hotspur 14.03.67 (£30,000) ••Charlton Athletic 29.10.70 (£25,000) ••Watford 23.02.73 (loan) 11.07.73 (£13,500) ••Dagenham 07.08.78 (free) ••Highfield Sports 1981 (player manager) ••Boreham Wood 1982 ••Waltham Abbey 1982 ••Mount Grace Old Boys 1983

His consistently classy performances for Watford inevitably led to interest from the clubs further up the food chain and in March 1967 Tottenham Hotspur signed Dennis (who was suffering with chicken pox at the time), for £30,000, which was a record transfer fee for the Hornets. It meant however that he was no longer a star turn in the Third Division and had to compete for a place among some of the finest midfield players of that era. This proved hard for him and in his first two years with Spurs he only featured in nine league matches. One of his best performances came in a European game at White Hart Lane against Olympique Lyonnais on 13th December 1967, when his outstanding midfield play contributed to a 4-3 win. He also appeared in the 7-0 thrashing of Burnley on 7th September 1968, but overall his lack of game time proved frustrating, so he welcomed the chance to re-activate his career through a transfer to Charlton in October 1970.

Dennis joined a club struggling desperately at the wrong end of the Second Division and although he got off to a reasonable start, scoring the winner in a 2-1 victory over Cardiff City on 21st November, the team continued to leak goals and ended that season just one place clear of relegation. Season 1971-72 proved even worse and the midfield which included both Dennis and Eamonn Rogers was found wanting on too many occasions. A humiliating

5-0 defeat at Blackpool confirmed that Charlton would return to Division 3 for the first time since 1935.

The following campaign started brightly and Charlton reached second place in the league during October. Dennis was no longer an automatic choice though and by December the team was sliding towards mid-table and he was left out completely after a dreary 0-0 draw with Southend on Boxing Day. It looked like the end of his time in SE7 when he returned on loan to Watford in February, but after playing three matches for them, he was recalled to the Valley and made three further appearances for Charlton who were without Phil Warman and Eamonn Rogers following a car crash. This was only a temporary reprieve however and in July 1973 Dennis re-joined Watford on a permanent transfer and spent five more seasons at Vicarage Road, eventually clocking up a career total of more than 300 matches for them.

After retiring, Dennis lived in Cheshunt and worked as a general builder and shopfitter. During a recent interview he looked back with affection on his early days as a footballer with Watford. On the occasion of his first team debut he had already played a full 90 minutes for the Youth team in the morning, only to be called up for a second match on the same afternoon, a scenario that would surely be impossible today.

Season	Division	League		FA Cup		FL Cup		Total	
		A	G	A	G	A	G	A	G
1970-71	Division 2	22 (1)	2	1	0	0	0	23 (1)	2
1971-72 (R)	Division 2	36 (1)	1	2	0	3	1	41 (1)	2
1972-73	Division 3	12 (3)	0	2	0	3	1	17 (3)	1
Total		70 (5)	3	5	0	6	2	81 (5)	5

UK LEAGUE CAREER 370 games 41 goals

CHARLTON CAREER
Managers: *T Foley*
Debut: *Oxford United (A) 31-10-1970*
V358
Finale: *Halifax Town (A) 21-04-1973*

BONDS William Arthur   1965 - 67

A massively talented player, Billy enjoyed an outstanding career which eventually extended to more than 900 matches over a

Defender, Midfield   13st 7lbs   6' 0"
Born: 17-09-1946 - Woolwich, London
Education: Middle Park Junior School & Eltham Green Comprehensive.

period of 24 seasons. It seems extraordinary that, like Sam Bartram before him, he never played for his country, although he was selected for three England squads and was an unused substitute at Wembley against Italy on 16th November 1967. His greatest successes came for West Ham United, yet it should not be forgotten that his formative years were spent at Charlton for whom he made exactly 100 first team appearances before being transferred to the Hammers. There are two events that adequately sum up the enormity of his achievements. In 1988, he was awarded the MBE for services to football and then in March 2019 the East Stand at West Ham's new London Stadium was re-named the Billy Bonds Stand.

HONOURS

England U23 International 1968 2 caps 0 goals
Woolwich & Kent Schools
Charlton Athletic A 1963-64 Winners Metropolitan League
Charlton Athletic A 1963-64 Finalists Metropolitan League Cup
West Ham United 1974-75 & 1979-80 Winners FA Cup

West Ham United 1975-76 Finalists European Cup Winners Cup
West Ham United 1980 Runners Up FA Charity Shield
West Ham United 1980-81 Winners Division 2
West Ham United 1980-81 Finalists FA League Cup

HONOURS AS MANAGER

West Ham United 1990-91 Runners Up Division 2

West Ham United 1992-93 Runners Up Division 1

CLUBS

Moatbridge (youth) ••Charlton Athletic 07.05.62 (youth) 19.09.64 (pro) ••West Ham United 05.67 (£47,500) 1988 (youth coach) 23.02.90 (manager) ••Havering NALGO 09.94 (non contract) ••Queens Park Rangers 12.12.94 (youth coach) ••Reading 19.02.97 (coach) ••Millwall 08.05.97 (manager)

Born in Woolwich and brought up in Eltham, Billy joined Charlton as an amateur on 7th May 1962. For a couple of months that Summer he worked in the drawing office at a local engineering company but on 10th September signed on at the Valley as an apprentice. After appearing regularly for the colts, he became a full-time professional in September 1964 and was introduced into the first team later that same season, his debut being against Northampton Town (including Theo Foley) on 20th February 1965. Once he had made the transition to first team football, he never lost his place at right back and veteran John Hewie was re-deployed to wing half. One bright spot during Billy's first season was the 5-1 win at Malcolm Allison's Plymouth Argyle on 10th April during which Keith Peacock scored a hat-trick.

Over the next two campaigns, Billy missed just two league games and was ever present in 1966-67. He consistently performed to a very high standard and it soon became obvious that he was destined for more than Second Division football. Charlton were well short of a promotion side and it took wins in the final two games of the season for them to scramble into 19th place. Opposition to the inevitable transfer came loud and clear from Charlton supporters, but as has occurred on so many occasions, the directors went ahead and clinched a deal with West Ham whereby they would receive a fee of £47,500. A further £2,475 would have been paid if he had later played for England and he did captain his country twice in 1968, but only at U23 level, including a 3-1 win over Wales. The balance of the transfer fee never became payable.

Billy moved straight into the West Ham side at right back, replacing Jack Burkett who was destined to make the reverse journey to Charlton one year later, but with considerably less success. The Hammers were secure in the middle of Division 1 and still retained the nucleus of the team which had brought them cup glory in both 1964 and 1965. His swashbuckling style made him a firm favourite with the fans and as the team went through a period of transition, so he became an increasingly important part of their set-up. By the early 70s he had moved into midfield and when they reached the 1975 FA Cup final, he skippered the West Ham team which defeated Fulham 2-0 at Wembley.

They battled through to the final of the 1976 European Cup Winners Cup, only to lose out to Anderlecht by 4-2, but then after five seasons of struggle in the league, were finally relegated in 1978. They were still able to enjoy further FA Cup glory however and as a Second Division club fought their way through to the final again in 1979-80

and beat Arsenal 1-0. Billy remained with the Hammers throughout this period and after three seasons out of the limelight, led them to the Division 2 title in 1980-81 by a massive 13 point margin. The one constant factor for West Ham was always Billy Bonds and his loyalty was rewarded with two separate testimonial matches. He finally retired in May 1988, having played a record 663 league matches for the Hammers.

After a period on the coaching staff, Billy was appointed the West Ham manager on 23rd February 1990. They experienced two promotions and one relegation during his time at the helm, but he eventually resigned in August 1994. His long career in football finally came to an end in May 1998 when he was sacked after a year as Millwall manager. Now in retirement at his Chislehurst home, Billy is rightly viewed as one of the footballing giants. A family man who has always enjoyed the quiet life, his preferences are known to favour country walks, ornithology and the novels of Thomas Hardy.

Season	Division	League		FA Cup		FL Cup		Total	
		A	G	A	G	A	G	A	G
1964-65	Division 2	13	0	0	0	0	0	13	0
1965-66	Division 2	40	0	1	0	2	0	43	0
1966-67	Division 2	42	1	1	0	1	0	44	1
Total		95	1	2	0	3	0	100	1

CHARLTON CAREER
Managers: *F Hill, R Stokoe*
Debut: *Northampton Town (H) 20-02-1965*
V307
Finale: *Birmingham City (H) 13-05-1967*

UK LEAGUE CAREER 758 games 49 goals

BONNE Macauley Miles   2019 - 20

Forward   5' 11"
Born: 26-10-1995 - Ipswich, Suffolk
Education: Chantry High School, Ipswich.

Manager Lee Bowyer made ten new signings during the summer of 2019 following promotion from League One and it is fair to say that Mac was the one who created the least excitement among Charlton supporters. His arrival from non-league football represented a jump of three divisions and although he had finished as leading goalscorer when Leyton Orient re-gained their Football League status by winning the National League, few expected him to make any sort of immediate impact at the Valley.

HONOURS
Zimbabwe International 2017 2 caps 0 goals
Zimbabwe U23 International 2014 1 cap 1 goal
Leyton Orient 2018-19 Winners National League
Leyton Orient 2018-19 Finalists FA Trophy

CLUBS
Ipswich Town 2003 (youth) ••Norwich City 2009 (youth) ••Colchester United 2009 (youth) 20.10.13 (pro) ••Lincoln City 02.09.16 (loan) ••Woking 27.01.17 (loan) ••Leyton Orient 14.07.17 (undisclosed) ••Charlton Athletic 17.06.19 (£200,000) ••Queens Park Rangers 02.10.20 (£2 million) ••Ipswich Town 26.06.21 (loan)

During four years spent as a young professional with Colchester United, Mac played 84 competitive matches for

the Essex club without ever getting a long run in the starting eleven. The highlight of his early career came on

7th November 2015 when he scored four goals at Wealdstone in a 6-2 FA Cup victory. His teammates that day included Callum Harriott, Marvin Sordell and Alex Gilbey, while 41-year-old Scott McLeish appeared for the home side.

The opportunity to gain regular first team football saw him move to Leyton Orient in July 2017. They had just lost their place in the Football League and he proved an instant success scoring 22 league goals in 2017-18 and then 23 the following season when they won the National League to regain their place in League Two. He was their top goalscorer in both seasons.

Although born in Ipswich, both of Mac's parents came from Zimbabwe and on 8th November 2017 he made his full international debut in a 1-0 defeat against Lesotho and then gained a second cap against Namibia three days later. Since then his international ambitions have been somewhat thwarted through a combination of passport and medical problems. He will certainly have to wait a little longer before appearing for Zimbabwe in a home fixture as they have been banned from staging further fixtures since February 2020 because their stadiums are deemed below the required standard.

Macauley confounded all the cynics who had insisted that his signing for Charlton did no more than make up the numbers. On paper the club had an abundance of strikers, but when first choice Lyle Taylor became injured and others were clearly not match fit either, he was drafted into the starting line-up for the home game with eventual champions Leeds United on 28th September 2019 and scored in the 1-0 victory. He retained his place until Taylor returned at the end of December but continued to receive game time as the club limped on with an injury list of almost biblical proportions. Charlton's nightmare season was interrupted by the Covid-19 pandemic in March and when it finally re-started three months later in front of empty stadiums, Mac had to shoulder the responsibility of now being the club's main goalscorer. He finished the season with a tally of 11 league goals against his name and although 2019-20 will be remembered for the seemingly endless list of problems faced by Charlton both on and off the field, no blame attached to Mac for the relegation that was finally confirmed in the dying seconds of the campaign. Nevertheless, it was a surprise when Queens Park Rangers paid a fee believed to be £2 million to acquire Mac's services in October 2020 and clearly he struggled to live up to expectations, only managing three league goals in his first season with them. In June 2021 he moved back home to Ipswich on loan and so far seems to have re-discovered his shooting boots.

Season	Division	League		FA Cup		FL Cup		FL Trophy		Total	
		A	G	A	G	A	G	A	G	A	G
2019-20 (R)	Championship	26 (7)	11	0	0	1	0			27 (7)	11
2020-21	League One	3	0	0	0	2	1	0 (1)	0	5 (1)	1
Total		29 (7)	11	0	0	3	1	0 (1)	0	32 (8)	12

UK LEAGUE CAREER 108 games 18 goals

CHARLTON CAREER
Managers: *L Bowyer*
Debut: *Forest Green Rovers (H) 13-08-2019*
V879
Finale: *Lincoln City (A) 27-09-2020*

BOOTH Anthony John   1979

Tony was a forward who spent three years at Charlton in the late seventies. Although he reached the fringe of the first team, he was never given a run of games and this must have

Forward   10st 3lbs   5' 8"
Born: 20-06-1961 - Biggin Hill, Kent

been frustrating for him, as the club was continually fighting against relegation from Division 2 at the time. The high point of Tony's brief career was probably the 1-1 draw at Turf Moor on 21st August 1979. He lined up at inside left against a strong looking Burnley side and played the full 90 minutes. A late goal from Martin Robinson secured an unexpected 1-1 draw and a useful point, but any optimism derived from this performance was short-lived. Two months later the team had still only managed one league win and was heading for Division 3.

HONOURS
Charlton Athletic Reserves 1979-80 Runners Up Mid-Week League

Charlton Athletic 20.12.76 (youth) 29.03.79 (pro) ••Oxford City 22.01.80 (free) ••Carshalton United c1980 ••Woking 1981 ••Welling United 1982
••Bromley 1983 ••Tonbridge Angels 01.84 ••Gravesend & Northfleet 1988 ••Cray Wanderers 08.91 ••Croydon 1992 ••Tonbridge Angels 1993

Starting out with Charlton's colts team, Tony made steady progress despite being sent off in a South East Counties League game against Crystal Palace in October 1978. His first team chance eventually came at Craven Cottage on 31st March 1979 when he was called on as a substitute to replace Gary Churchouse after 65 minutes of the match. Already a goal down, his intervention did not make any material improvement and it ended 3-1 to Fulham, with only a consolation goal from Derek Hales to show for the afternoon's work. Over the next nine months he was called up on a total of eight occasions but never once played in a winning team, his tally of three draws and five defeats probably reflecting more on the overall strength of the team than on his personal performances

The influence of manager Andy Nelson was waning by October 1979 when Tony made his final appearance. Chief coach Mike Bailey started to take on the role of team manager and presumably was having a considerable say in team selection, his predecessor being re-branded as general manager. This uneasy alliance came to a head the following March when Nelson left by 'mutual consent' and Bailey officially took over as manager. By then Tony had gone, the indications being that he did not figure at all in the new manager's plans.

He joined Isthmian League side Oxford City in January 1980 and embarked upon a lengthy and successful career in the non-league game, moving around among the leading clubs in the Kent and Surrey area. His greatest contribution was for Tonbridge Angels, whom he joined in January 1984 and where the manager was former Charlton defender John Keirs. Tony went on to play 372 competitive matches for Tonbridge. He later spent two seasons with Gravesend & Northfleet and in 1988-89 they finished as runners-up in the Southern League, South Division.

Away from football, Tony worked in the recruitment sector for both Mark Goldberg's MSB and for the Bromley firm Logix Resourcing.

Season	Division	League		FA Cup		FL Cup		Total	
		A	G	A	G	A	G	A	G
1978-79	Division 2	0 (2)	0	0	0	0	0	0 (2)	0
1979-80 (R)	Division 2	2 (4)	0	0	0	0	0	2 (4)	0
Total		2 (6)	0	0	0	0	0	2 (6)	0

UK LEAGUE CAREER 8 games 0 goals

CHARLTON CAREER
Managers: *A Nelson*
Debut: *Fulham (A) (sub) 31-03-1979*
V414
Finale: *Brristol Rovers (A) (sub) 20-10-1979*

BOOTH Dennis　　　　　　　　　　　　　　1967 - 70

Midfield, Utility.　10st 5lbs　5' 7"
Born: 09-04-1949 - Stanley Common, Derbyshire
Education: Smalley Common Primary School & Scargill Secondary Modern School, West Hallam.

Dennis was a tough, uncompromising midfielder who took no prisoners in a long playing career which ran to more than 600 competitive games. He was not generally known for his goal scoring feats however, which made the events of 6th April 1974 all the more amazing. Playing for Lincoln City against Bury in a Division 4 league match, he scored a hat trick of headed goals in one thirteen minute spell. There must have been red faces among the Bury defenders that day as Dennis only stands at 5' 7" tall.

Ilkeston & Heanor Schools
Derbyshire Schools
Charlton Athletic Youth 1965-66 Winners South East Counties League Cup
Charlton Athletic Youth 1965-66 Winners London FA Youth Cup
Charlton Athletic Youth 1966-67 Winners South East Counties League
Charlton Athletic Youth 1966-67 Finalists South East Counties League Cup

Charlton Athletic Reserves 1968-69 Runners Up London Mid-Week League
Southend United 1971-72 Runners Up Division 4
Lincoln City 1975-76 Winners Division 4
Watford 1978-79 Runners Up Division 3
Hull City 1982-83 Runners Up Division 4
Watford 1977-78 Winners Division 4

CLUBS

Charlton Athletic 10.06.64 (youth) 09.04.66 (pro) ••Blackpool 14.07.71 (£7,000) ••Southend United 08.03.72 (£7,000) ••Lincoln City 14.02.74 (loan) 13.08.74 (£9,000) ••Watford 27.10.77 (£10,000) ••Hull City 22.05.80 (£40,000) 06.85 (ass. manager) •Aston Villa 07.89 (coach) ••Stafford Rangers 11.91 (coach) 01.92 (manager) ••Bristol Rovers 03.93 (ass. manager) ••Huddersfield Town 1995 (ass. manager) ••Walsall c1997 (scout) ••Notts County 1998 (scout) ••Port Vale 1999 (chief scout) ••Nottingham Forest 1999 (chief scout) ••Nuneaton Borough c2000 (ass. manager) •England U21 04.02 (scout) ••Carlisle United 16.10.03 (ass. manager) ••Preston North End 06.06 (ass. manager) ••Carlisle United 08.07 (ass. manager) 2011 (director of football)

Dennis initially signed for Charlton as a 15-year-old schoolboy, becoming an apprentice six weeks later and a full professional on his 17th birthday. He had earlier represented Ilkeston & Heanor Schools and Derbyshire Schools where he played alongside Vic Halom and in 1966-67 skippered the Charlton colts team when they took the South East Counties League title for the first time. He was used very much as a utility player when he broke through into the first team and did not get a good run in any fixed position until 1969-70 when he held down the right back spot for three months.

In October 1970 Dennis fractured his left leg in a reserve match and never returned to first team duty, leaving for Blackpool at the end of that season to be reunited with Bob Stokoe, the manager who had first given him his chance at

Charlton. Over the next 15 years he performed consistently around the lower divisions, gaining promotion from Division 4 with Southend United, Lincoln City and Hull City and was with Watford when they secured back to back promotions on their rise to the top during the Elton John era. He was captain of the Watford team that went to Old Trafford on 4th October 1978 and knocked Manchester United out of the League Cup with an unexpected and stunning 2-1 victory.

Since his playing career came to an end in 1986, Dennis has remained involved in football with a whole succession of roles as manager, coach or scout and by the time he left Carlisle United in April 2013, had been active in the game for nearly 50 years.

Season	Division	League		FA Cup		FL Cup		Total	
		A	G	A	G	A	G	A	G
1966-67	Division 2	3	0	0	0	0	0	3	0
1967-68	Division 2	13 (4)	0	1	0	0	0	14 (4)	0
1968-69	Division 2	18 (3)	5	0	0	0	0	18 (3)	5
1969-70	Division 2	27 (3)	0	3	0	0	0	30 (3)	0
1970-71	Division 2	6	0	0	0	1	0	7	0
Total		67 (10)	5	4	0	1	0	72 (10)	5

UK LEAGUE CAREER 552 games 19 goals

CHARLTON CAREER
Managers: F Hill, R Stokoe, E Firmani, T Foley
Debut: *Carlisle United (A) 28-03-1967*
V330
Finale: *Bolton Wanderers (A) 10-10-1970*

BORLAND John Thompson Mathieson   1928

John was a Scottish winger who roamed from club to club during the Twenties, rarely staying for long in one place. He played to a good standard however, as Kilmarnock, Raith Rovers and Hamilton Academicals were all competing in the First Division of the Scottish League during this period and he chalked up 135 games in total between them.

Forward   10st 2lbs   5' 7"
Born: 09-11-1903 - Rutherglen, Scotland
Died: 08-12-1979 - Rutherglen, Scotland

CLUBS

Rutherglen Glencairn, Scotland 1921 ••Raith Rovers, Scotland 03.05.22 ••Kilmarnock, Scotland 1923 ••Cowdenbeath, Scotland 1924 (loan) ••Hamilton Academicals, Scotland 1925 ••Charlton Athletic 23.06.27 ••Merthyr Town 1928 ••Southend United 17.05.29 ••Alloa Athletic, Scotland 1930 ••Stenhousemuir, Scotland 08.32 •Alloa Athletic, Scotland 1933 ••Rutherglen Glencairn, Scotland c 1933

Charlton manager Sandy MacFarlane brought John down to London in June 1927, for his first experience of football outside Scotland and the following season saw a welcome

improvement on the field as the club secured a final placing in the top half of Division 3 South for the first time. Jack Horton occupied the left wing position through the first half of the campaign but was moved across to the right on 7th January to allow John a game in his favoured position. All went well and he scored the first Charlton goal in a 2-1 win against Coventry City at the Valley. Unfortunately for him however, MacFarlane resigned later that same month to take up the manager's job at Dundee and before long John was out of the side again and Horton reinstated at outside left.

He spent a season each with Merthyr Town and Southend United before heading back north once again. A trial with Barrow did not come to anything so he finished his career where it had begun, up in Scotland, passing away at the age of 76 in his hometown of Rutherglen, South Lanarkshire.

Season	Division	League		FA Cup		Total	
		A	G	A	G	A	G
1927-28	Divison 3 (S)	5	1	2	0	7	1
Total		5	1	2	0	7	1

UK LEAGUE CAREER 204 games 23 goals

CHARLTON CAREER
Managers: *A MacFarlane, A Lindon*
Debut: *Coventry City (H) 07-01-1928*
V113
Finale: *Bristol Rovers (A) 25-02-1928*

BORROWDALE Gary Ian   2010

Defender   12st 2lbs   6' 0"
Born: 16-07-1985 - Sutton, Surrey
Education: Greenshaw High School, Sutton.

A tidy, orthodox full back, Gary spent two months at the Valley during the final weeks of 2009-10, during which Charlton were fighting for promotion from League One. Arriving from Queens Park Rangers on a short term emergency loan, he slotted straight into the team at left back and performed solidly for the duration of his stay. He had started out as a youngster with Crystal Palace, but after leaving them while still only 21, his surname of Borrowdale had proved very apt, as it reflected a promising career which frustratingly dissolved into just a series of loan moves.

HONOURS
England U20 International 2004-05 3 caps 0 goals
England U19 International 2004 2 caps 0 goals
England U18 International 2002 1 cap 0 goals

England U17 International 2001-02 14 caps 0 goals
Sutton Schools 1998
Crystal Palace 2003-04 Promoted Play Offs Division 1

CLUBS
Crystal Palace (youth) 06.12.02 (pro) ••Coventry City 05.07.07 (£650,000) ••Colchester United 25.09.08 (loan) ••Queens Park Rangers 27.11.08 (loan) 02.01.09 (free) ••Brighton & Hove Albion 06.03.09 (loan) ••Charlton Athletic 18.03.10 (loan) ••Carlisle United 08.02.11 (loan) ••Barnet 30.09.11 (loan) ••Carrick Rangers. N Ireland 21.02.13 (free) ••Tonbridge Angels 31.07.13 (free) •Margate 08.11.13 (free) ••Gillingham 30.01.14 (free) ••Greenwich Borough 05.08.14 (free) 05.16 (coach)

Gary was outstanding as a junior and represented England on 20 occasions in different age groups. He played for the U17's who won the Nordic Trophy in Denmark during 2001 and the following year came third in the UEFA European U17 Championships. He progressed as far as the U20's and played at the Valley along with Lloyd Sam and Bradley Wright-Phillips on 8th February 2005 when Russia were beaten 2-0. His early club career was equally impressive. Having made his debut for Crystal Palace in 2002, he appeared regularly during the first half of the 2003-04 season, although he was not involved when they clinched promotion to the Premier League via a play off victory over West Ham in May. He had however played

more than 100 competitive matches for Palace by the time that he signed for Coventry City in July 2007.
It is unclear why Gary was never able to build on such a positive start. He joined a club managed by his former Palace manager Iain Dowie, who had briefly held the reins at Charlton the previous year. He was in the Coventry team, (as was Leon Best), which battled to a 1-1 draw against Charlton at the Ricoh Arena on 29th September 2007, but by the end of January he was out of the side and after Dowie departed a few weeks later he never played for them again.
Instead, he started 2008-09 on loan to Colchester United, where his teammates included Johnnie Jackson and from

there had a loan spell with Queens Park Rangers, which was soon turned into a permanent deal. He finished that season with Russell Slade's Brighton team who were competing in the bottom half of League One, before finally getting a run of games with QPR.

By the time Gary had concluded his loan with Charlton, he was only aged 25, yet his Football League career was coming to an end. He played one league match for Carlisle United against Southampton on 12th February 2011 but was sent off before half-time. He did feature in 15 competitive games for a Barnet team which also included Mark Marshall, Izale McLeod and Ricky Holmes but this was another short term loan and in January 2012 he returned to QPR from where he was released at the end of the season.

Gary tried his luck in Northern Ireland with Carrick Rangers before drifting into non-league with Tonbridge Angels and Margate, He admits to having become disillusioned with football but got one final chance to kick-start his career on 30th January 2014 when he signed for Gillingham on the same day that a young Joe Pigott joined them on loan from Charlton. It did not work out as he was unable to reach the required level of fitness and was released at the end of the season without having played a match. After a brief period with Southern Counties East League club Greenwich Borough, Gary has moved into coaching and formed Premier Kickers Coaching Ltd in 2017 from his home in Snodland.

Season	Division	League		FA Cup		FL Cup		Play Offs		Total	
		A	G	A	G	A	G	A	G	A	G
2009-10	League One	10	0	0	0	0	0	2	0	12	0
Total		10	0	0	0	0	0	2	0	12	0

UK LEAGUE CAREER 179 games 0 goals

CHARLTON CAREER
Managers: *P Parkinson*
Debut: *Gillingham (H) 20-03-2010*
V702
Finale: *Swindon Town (H) 17-05-2010*

BOTAKA Jordan Rolly   2016 - 17

Although born in the Congo, Jordan's family lived first in the Netherlands and later in Antwerp, Belgium. He spent just 22 months playing in the UK, including season 2016-17 when he was on loan with Charlton. An old fashioned winger, who was nicknamed 'the Wizard' because of his speed and trickery, he invariably featured as a substitute during his time at the Valley.

Forward, Midfield   11st 7 lbs   6' 0"
Born: 24-06-1993 - Kinshasa, DR Congo

HONOURS
DR Congo International 2015-20 18 caps 4 goals
Netherlands U19 International 2012 3 caps 0 goals

SBV Excelsior 2013-14 Promoted Play Offs Eerste Divisie (Netherlands)

CLUBS
RKVV Westlandia, Netherlands (youth) ••ADO Den Haag, Netherlands (youth) ••RSC Anderlecht, Belgium (youth) ••KSK Beveren, Belgium (youth) ••KSC Lokeren, Belgium (youth) ••Club Brugge, Belgium 23.01.12 (pro) ••Belenenses, Portugal 31.01.13 (loan) ••SBV Excelsior, Netherlands 27.07.13 ••Leeds United 01.09.15 (£1 million) ••Charlton Athletic 11.08.16 (loan) ••Sint-Truiden, Belgium 26.06.17 (free) ••KAA Gent, Belgium 19.05.20 (undisclosed) ••Royal Charleroi, Belgium 23.01.21 (loan) ••Fortuna Sittard, Netherlands 28.01.22 (loan)

Jordan first earned himself a professional contract for Club Brugge where he played for the reserves, before switching to SBV Excelsior in the summer of 2013. He then quickly established himself in the first team and scored 10 league goals from the wing as they clinched promotion to the top level of Dutch football, via the play offs. This did not go unnoticed and on the final day of the August 2015 transfer window, Leeds paid a fee reported to be in the region of £1 million to bring him to England.

Unfortunately Jordan was given little chance to shine after arriving at Elland Road, being mainly used as a substitute and only starting three league games during the whole of 2015-16. It was not until his final appearance on 30th April 2016 that he played the full 90 minutes and this was against Charlton, who recorded a useful 2-1 away win thanks to goals either side of half time from Johann Berg Gudmundsson and Ademola Lookman. Four months later he travelled down to London and joined Charlton on a season's loan.

Since 2015 Jordan had been playing international football for DR Congo and during his time at Charlton earned five caps, including one against the Central African Republic in an African Cup of Nations qualifier in Kinshasa on 4th September, where he was among the goalscorers in a 4-1 win.

For most of his time at Charlton, he was named among the substitutes, much as had been the case at Leeds and he regularly appeared late in a game when his attacking flair and pace were considered an asset against tiring defenders. One of the few occasions when he featured for the whole

game was on 2nd January 2017 against Bristol Rovers at the Valley. It ended in a very satisfactory 4-1 win for the Addicks and included a hat trick by Josh Magennis.

After his season in SE7, Jordan returned to Belgium and signed for Sint-Truiden on 26th June 2017. This move proved positive and he settled down to make over 80 league appearances for them having been converted into a wing back. He was named as captain at the start of season 2019-20 but moved on to KAA Gent in May 2020 on a four-year deal.

Season	Division	League		FA Cup		FL Cup		FL Trophy		Total	
		A	G	A	G	A	G	A	G	A	G
2016-17	League One	8 (18)	2	2 (1)	0	0	0	0	0	10 (19)	2
Total		8 (18)	2	2 (1)	0	0	0	0	0	10 (19)	2

UK LEAGUE CAREER 39 games 2 goals

CHARLTON CAREER
Managers: *R Slade, K Robinson*
Debut: *Northampton Town (H) (sub) 13-08-2016*
V829
Finale: *Chesterfield (A) (sub) 22-04-2017*

BOTHROYD Jay   2005 - 06

Forward   13st 6lbs   6' 3"
Born: 07-05-1982 - Islington, London

During his year as a Charlton player, Jay was described by one of the management team as being 'very high maintenance' and therein may lie the reason why such a gifted and talented footballer so often failed to deliver, especially during the early years of his career. Along with Jerome Thomas, he was part of the Arsenal team that won the FA Youth Cup in 2000 defeating Coventry City in both games of a two legged final. Shortly after he was playing against West Ham in an FA Academy play off match and when substituted, petulantly threw his shirt on to the ground and stormed off, following which he was immediately transfer listed and did not play for Arsenal again. This regrettable incident followed Jay around for many years and was the basis for his reputation as one of football's bad boys.

HONOURS
England International 2010 1 cap 0 goals
England U21 International 2001 1 cap 1 goal
England U20 International 2001-02 2 caps 0 goals
Eng;land U18 International 2000-01 2 caps 0 goals

England U16 International 1999 2 caps 1 goal
Arsenal U18 1999-00 Winners FA Youth Cup
Arsenal U19 1999-00 Runners Up FA Academy U19 League Play Offs
Jubilo Iwata 2015 Runners Up Meiji Yasuda J2 League

CLUBS
Arsenal 03.05.97 (youth) 08.07.99 (pro) ••Coventry City 13.07.00 (£1 million) ••Perugia, Italy 10.07.03 ••Blackburn Rovers 09.09.04 (loan) ••Charlton Athletic 31.08.05 (free) ••Wolverhampton Wanderers 26.07.06 (free) ••Stoke City 14.03.08 (loan) ••Cardiff City 05.08.08 (£350,000) ••Queens Park Rangers 13.07.11 ••Sheffield Wednesday 31.08.12 (loan) ••Muangthong United, Thailand 08.01.14 (free) ••Jubilo Iwata, Japan 02.15 ••Hokkaido Consadole Sapporo, Japan 07.17

Years later Jay looked back on the early part of his career and admitted to having been both arrogant and immature. Although he had the ability to go to the very top, his attitude held him back. After his forced departure from Arsenal he joined Coventry City, but they were a club in decline and lost their place in the Premier League at the end of his first season with them. Eventually he tried his luck

overseas and made a move to the Italian club Perugia, where he played in Serie A for much of season 2003-04. They were a somewhat strange set up and also ended in one of the relegation places. One of his teammates in Italy was the son of the then Libyan dictator, Colonel Gaddafi. When they eventually hit a financial crisis, Jay was freed of his contract and returned home.

He joined Charlton on a free transfer at the end of August 2005 and on his debut scored a blistering goal in a League Cup match against Hartlepool United. He had an extremely powerful shot and considerable skill but seemed to drift in and out of matches. He was mainly used as a substitute and did score Premier League goals against both Manchester City and Newcastle, but never did enough to become a regular in the side. His name hit the headlines in December when 'The Sun' claimed that he had taken drugs prior to a minor car accident at Elstree in which he drove into a wooden post. Both Jay and the club denied the allegations and expressed concern at his sudden and unexplained blackout.

Charlton chose not to retain him after just one season and Jay next moved to Wolverhampton where he soon clashed with the manager Mick McCarthy. Later he was in trouble again for directing a disrespectful gesture at him during a friendly match. It was only when his career took him to Cardiff City in 2008 that he forced himself to work really hard and to achieve the week by week consistency that had been lacking in the past. In 2010-11 he scored 15 goals in a 16 game spell and was rewarded with a full international call up, appearing against France on 13th November 2010 and thereby becoming the first Cardiff City player to ever be capped for England.

In 2014, Jay went abroad again, first to Thailand and then later to Japan where he had a tremendous season with Jubilo Inata as they finished runners-up in the Japanese J2 League in 2015. His personal contribution of 20 goals made him the league's highest scorer. In 2020 and now aged 38 he was still playing for J1 club, Hokkaido, situated in Sapporo on the northernmost of Japan's main islands. He even had his own song, 'Jay Bothroyd, You Are Our Hero', sung of course in Japanese.

Season	Division	League		FA Cup		FL Cup		Total	
		A	G	A	G	A	G	A	G
2005-06	Premier	3 (15)	2	1 (3)	3	0 (3)	1	4 (21)	6
Total		3 (15)	2	1 (3)	3	0 (3)	1	4 (21)	6

UK LEAGUE CAREER 315 games 74 goals

CHARLTON CAREER
Managers: *A Curbishley*
Debut: *Hartlepool United (H) (sub) 20-09-2005*
V631
Finale: *Bolton Wanderers (A) (sub) 22-04-2006*

BOUAZZA Hameur   2008 - 09

Hameur came to Charlton at a very difficult time. By the summer of 2008 the club was twelve months on from Premier League relegation and having failed to regain its place at the first attempt, was coming under intense financial pressure as a result of severely reduced television income. He transferred to SE7 on a season long loan from Fulham, but as results on the field worsened and another relegation loomed, he was able to activate a 'get out' clause in the loan agreement and in January 2009 abruptly departed and joined Birmingham City for the remainder of that season. It is doubtful if a fully motivated Hameur Bouazza would have kept Charlton in the Championship, but the nature and timing of his departure did nothing for squad morale at a time when the club needed everyone pulling in the same direction.

Forward, Midfield
Born: 22-02-1985 - Evry, France

HONOURS
Algeria International 2007-13 21 caps 3 goals
Watford 2005-06 Promoted Play Offs Championship
Birmingham City 2008-09 Runners Up Championship
Blackpool 2009-10 Promoted Play Offs Championship
Red Star 2014-15 Winners Championnat National Ligue
Etoile du Sahel 2016-17 Runners Up Tunisian Ligue 1

CLUBS
AJ Auxerre, France 2000 (youth) ••Evry, France 2001 (youth) ••Watford 2003 (youth) 02.07.04 (pro) ••Swindon Town 07.10.05 (loan) ••Fulham 08.08.07 (£3 million) ••Charlton Athletic 09.08.08 (loan) ••Birmingham City 09.01.09 (loan) ••Sivasspor, Turkey 18.08.09 (free) ••Blackpool 01.09.09 (free) ••Arles-Avignon, France 12.07.10 (free) ••Millwall 28.01.11 (loan) 19.04.11 (£100,000) ••AC Omonia, Cyprus 02.06.12 (free) ••Racing de Santander, Spain 06.09.12 (free) ••ES Setifienne, Algeria 02.10.13 (free) ••Red Star, France 31.08.14 ••Etoile du Sahel, Tunisia 12.01.17 ••Tours, France 01.07.17 ••FC Fleury 91, France 21.12.17 (free)

Born just south of Paris, Hameur was spotted by Watford   and brought to the UK at the age of 17. His club career blossomed very quickly and he scored the opening goal in the 2-0 defeat of Preston North End on his full league debut in February 2004. They gained promotion to the Premier League and he clocked up almost 100 competitive appearances, including a 2-2 draw against Charlton on 3rd March 2007. In this match he scored an early goal as the Hornets raced into a 2-0 lead, only for strikes from Luke Young and Darren Ambrose to earn the Londoners a valuable away point.

After Watford were relegated, Fulham paid a fee reported at £3 million for Hameur, but the move did not really work out. He made 20 league appearances, but only twice finished on a winning side. A red card at Birmingham did not help the situation and in August 2008 he was bundled off to Charlton for what was intended to be a season's loan. The campaign opened with Charlton's loyal supporters still hopeful of a return to Premier status and there were some early victories, including the 4-2 defeat of Reading on 23rd August in which Hameur was among the scorers. It soon turned sour though and his final 16 matches for Charlton failed to include a single victory. Nevertheless, it was a shock when he walked away from an increasingly desperate relegation battle to transfer his energies to the cause of Birmingham City at the other end of the table.

If his departure from Charlton was controversial, it was nothing compared to Hameur's time with the Turkish Super Lig side Sivasspor. He signed for them in August 2009, played in one home defeat and then left by mutual agreement after just five days. Maybe he was not partial to kebabs, but whatever the reason, his next move was to Blackpool, where he spent the remainder of 2009-10, playing spasmodically, while they unexpectedly clinched promotion into the Premier League.

He played international football for Algeria, making his debut against Libya in 2007. Two years later while travelling to a World Cup qualifier in Cairo, their team bus was stoned and three of his teammates were injured from flying glass. He only remained unharmed by lying on the floor of the bus. On a happier note it was Hameur who scored the winning goal against the Ivory Coast in the quarter final of the Africa Cup of Nations in January 2010. The match ended 3-2 and the other Algerian goalscorers included Madjid Bougherra. None of his 22 international caps came during his time at Charlton.

After a few months back in France, Hameur signed for Millwall in January 2011, initially on loan but eventually for a £100,000 fee. He did reasonably well, but after 18 months was on the move again, first to Cyprus and then to Racing de Santander, who were struggling badly in the Spanish Liga 2. Following a run of home defeats, he was followed home by three masked men who confronted him with threats and racial abuse. Although shaken up by this unpleasant incident, he carried on until the end of the 2011-12 season and then concluded his career with spells in Algeria, Tunisia and France. He retired from playing in 2018.

Season	Division	League		FA Cup		FL Cup		Total	
		A	G	A	G	A	G	A	G
2008-09 (R)	Championship	22 (3)	4	1	0	1	0	24 (3)	4
Total		22 (3)	4	1	0	1	0	24 (3)	4

UK LEAGUE CAREER 214 games 21 goals

CHARLTON CAREER
Managers: *A Pardew, P Parkinson*
Debut: *Swansea City (H) (sub) 09-08-2008*
V670
Finale: *Norwich City (H) 03-01-2009*

BOUGHERRA Majid   2006 - 08

Defender   6' 3"
Born: 07-10-1982 - Dijon, France

An Algerian international centre half, Majid enjoyed his greatest success during the three years that he spent in Glasgow. Rangers were completely dominating Scottish football and he came away with three Premier League Championship medals, played in the 1-0 victory against Falkirk which secured the Scottish Cup in May 2009 and contested the Scottish League Cup Final in March 2011. The latter was a close fought affair but Celtic were eventually beaten 2-1, which gave him a full set of Scottish silverware. There was still a year of his four-year contract left to run, but he declined to extend it and was permitted to leave in the Summer of 2011. Twelve months later the club would become embroiled in a massive financial scandal which placed them into administration and a forced relegation to the Scottish League Division 3.

HONOURS

Algeria International 2004-15 70 caps 4 goals

Algeria U23 International 2004 3 caps 0 goals

Rangers 2008-09, 2009-10 & 2010-11 Winners Scottish Premier League

Rangers 2008-09 Winners Scottish FA Cup

Rangers 2010-11 Winners Scottish League Cup

Lekhwiya 2011-12 & 2013-14 Winners Qatar Stars League

Lekhwiya 2012-13 Runners Up Qatar Stars League

Lekhwiya 2012-13 Winners Qatar Crown Prince Cup

CLUBS

AS Quetigny, France 1999 (youth) ••AS Longvic, France 2001 ••FC Gueugnon, France 07.02 ••Crewe Alexandra 31.06.06 (loan) ••Sheffield Wednesday 03.08.06 (£250,000) ••Charlton Athletic 28.01.07 (£2.5 million) ••Rangers, Scotland 31.07.08 (£2.5 million) ••Lekhwiya, Qatar 10.08.11 (£1.7 million) ••Al-Fujairah, UAE 02.08.14 (free) ••Aris Thessaloniki, Greece 09.09.16 (free) ••Al-Duhail, Qatar 2017 (reserves manager) ••Al-Fujairah, UAE 16.06.19 (manager) ••Algeria A 22.06.20 (manager)

Majid started out playing for Gueugnon in Ligue 2, which is the second tier of French football. He was already a full Algerian international by the time he first appeared in the UK as a result of a loan move to Crewe Alexandra in the second half of the 2005-06 season. A quick and skilful defender, there was soon interest from several clubs but it was to Sheffield Wednesday that he transferred in August 2006 and he did well during a five-month stay in which he lined up alongside Deon Burton and after a slow start they had settled mid-table in the Championship by the time he was on the move again in January 2007.

Charlton were in free-fall and on to their third manager of the 2006-07 campaign when Majid arrived at the Valley for the not inconsiderable fee of £2.5 million. Life after Alan Curbishley was proving far worse than had been feared and they were positioned one place off the bottom of the Premier League table when he made his debut at Old Trafford in a 2-0 defeat against Manchester United on 10th February 2007. If Majid was looked upon as the saviour who would tighten up the Addicks defence, then that faint hope was dashed almost immediately as a calf injury kept him in the treatment room and he did not play again for over two months, by which time relegation had become unavoidable.

He contributed much more in his second season when the target was a quick return to Premier status and he was a pivotal figure in the centre of defence, until a foot injury took him out of the firing line for most of February and March. Up to that point the team had settled comfortably in the play off places, but a late season decline scuppered

any promotion hopes and with the financial pressures intensifying, Charlton cashed in yet another of their assets as Majid departed to Rangers at the end of July 2008 for a money-back £2.5 million.

In all, Majid earned 70 international caps over an 11-year period, qualifying through his Algerian grandfather. His debut had been in a World Cup qualifier against Zimbabwe in June 2004 and during his time at Charlton he played nine times and scored once, his goal coming on 2nd June 2007 against Cape Verde. This was a 2-2 draw in a qualifying match for the Africa Cup of Nations. He later captained Algeria in the 2014 World Cup finals in Brazil.

After leaving Rangers in August 2011, he signed for the Qatari club Lekhwiya, with whom he went on to win the Qatar Stars League on two occasions, before taking up a two-year contract in the United Arab Emirates with Al-Fujairah. In 2015, Majid was kidnapped at gunpoint from an Algerian cafe, blindfolded and driven out into the desert by terrorists. Poised to apparently execute him, they revealed themselves at the last moment to be actors from the TV show 'Camera Cache', a sort of 'Game For A Laugh' type programme. The Asian sense of humour appears a little different to ours.

After a few months playing in Greece for Aris Thessaloniki, injury forced him to retire on 22nd December 2016., since when Majid has moved into management and on 22nd June 2020 he took over as manager of Algeria A, the intermediate team run by the Algerian Football Federation.

Season	Division	League		FA Cup		FL Cup		Total	
		A	G	A	G	A	G	A	G
2006-07 (R)	Premier	2 (3)	0	0	0	0	0	2 (3)	0
2007-08	Championship	24 (5)	2	2	0	2	0	28 (5)	2
Total		26 (8)	2	2	0	2	0	30 (8)	2

UK LEAGUE CAREER 152 games 8 goals

CHARLTON CAREER

Managers: *A Pardew*

Debut: *Preston North End (A) 05-08-2006*

V642

Finale: *Coventry City (H) 04-05-2008*

BOULTER Leslie Mervyn

1933 - 39

Forward   11st 5lbs   5' 9"
Born: 31-08-1913 - Ebbw Vale, Gwent
Died: 14-11-1975 - Pwllheli, Gwynedd

Les made 90 First Division appearances during the three-year period immediately prior to the Second World War when Charlton was enjoying its most successful period as a Football League club. He was the scorer of Charlton's first ever Division 1 goal at the Valley on 5th September 1936 against Liverpool. A creative inside forward, he has never received adequate recognition for his contribution to the cause and did not receive his one international cap for Wales until a month after being transferred to Brentford. He scored in a 3-1 win against Ireland on 15th March 1939, in a team that included his former Charlton colleagues George Green and Bert Turner. The outbreak of war effectively finished his career at the age of 25.

HONOURS

Wales International 1939 1 cap 1 goal

Ebbw Vale Schools & Welsh Schools

Charlton Athletic 1934-35 Winners Division 3 (S)

Charlton Athletic 1935-36 Runners Up Division 2

Charlton Athletic 1936-37 Runners Up Division 1

CLUBS

CWM Welfare 1931 (youth) ••Charlton Athletic 24.06.32 (pro) ••Brentford 08.02.39 (£5,950) ••Yeovil Town 27.06.47 (free) ••Pwllheli & District 1948 (player manager)

South Wales was a tough place to grow up during the 1930s and young Les worked as a pit boy while at the same time taking his first tentative steps as a footballer. He had already represented Welsh Schools when the opportunity came to join Charlton in 1932 and his move to South East London, which lasted nearly seven years, proved highly beneficial for all concerned. He featured at inside left as the club rose in consecutive seasons from the depths of Division 3 South to the runners-up spot in the First Division, a feat that never has and never will be equalled.

If not always an automatic choice for the team, he nevertheless played his part when called upon and by 1936-37 was featuring in the majority of games. One memorable match in which he participated took place at the Valley on 17th October 1936 against Arsenal. It resulted in a 2-0 defeat, but the official attendance of 68,160 remains a Charlton record for a league game. The gates were shut 15 minutes before kick off but many thousands are believed to have broken in without tickets and the true attendance probably exceeded 80,000.

As befitted their position as one of England's leading teams,

Charlton played many high profile friendlies either side of the war and on 11th April 1937, Les was in the side when they defeated the full strength French national team 5-2 in Paris. Two months later they toured USA and Canada and he appeared in several of those matches including the 12-2 demolition of Saskatchewan. His name appeared among the scorers, although George Tadman grabbed the headlines that day with seven goals.

In February 1939, Brentford, then a First Division team, paid a sizeable transfer fee to take Les to West London but the outbreak of war just seven months later meant there was little opportunity for them to gain value for their outlay. He made wartime guest appearances for both Manchester City and Blackpool and played one final season for Yeovil Town in 1947-48 before hanging up his boots.

In 1959 Les had a spell running Charlton's A team who at that time competed in the Aetolian League and he took a job in the insurance industry at Woolwich. Later he moved back to Wales and worked as a barman. At the time of his retirement he was a grocer and newsagent in Pwllheli and passed away in November 1975 at the age of 62.

Season	Division	League		FA Cup		D3 Cup		Total	
		A	G	A	G	A	G	A	G
1932-33 (R)	Division 2	14	5	0	0			14	5
1933-34	Divison 3 (S)	16	0	2	0	1	0	19	0
1934-35 (P)	Divison 3 (S)	18	6	0	0	0	0	18	6
1935-36 (P)	Division 2	29	2	1	0			30	2
1936-37	Division 1	34	6	1	0			35	6
1937-38	Division 1	34	5	3	1			37	6
1938-39	Division 1	22	3	1	0			23	3
Total		167	27	8	1	1	0	176	28

UK LEAGUE CAREER 183 games 28 goals

CHARLTON CAREER

Managers: *A MacFarlane, A Lindon, J Seed*

Debut: *Plymouth Argyle (H) 18-02-1933*

V166

Finale: *Arsenal (A) 21-01-1939*

BOVER IZQUIERDO Ruben   2011

Ruben spent 19 months at Charlton but only managed two first team appearances during his time in South London and both were League Cup matches at the Valley. He is a tidy and skilful midfielder but perhaps lacked the physical attributes needed to succeed in English football.

Midfield, Forward   10st 5lbs   5' 10"
Born: 24-06-1992 - Majorca, Spain

HONOURS

Charlton Athletic U21 2012-13 Winners PD League 2 South
New York Cosmos B 2015 Winners National Premier Soccer League

New York Cosmos 2015 Winners NASL Championship
FC Andorra 2018-19 Winners Primera Catalana

CLUBS

RCD Mallorca, Spain 2006 (youth) ••KIdderminster Harriers 2009 (youth) ••Halesowen Town 2010 (pro) •Charlton Athletic 01.07.11 (free) ••San Roque De Lepe, Spain 27.01.12 (loan) ••New York Red Bulls, USA 09.12.13 (free) ••New York Cosmos, USA 15.04.15 (free) ••Barnet 27.01.17 (free) ••FC Andorra, Spain 09.12.18 (free)

After moving to the UK at the age of 17, Ruben played a season with Halesowen Town in the Southern League and then joined Charlton following a trial period at the end of 2010-11. His first team debut came very soon thereafter in a closely contested game against a Reading side which included Simon Church. It resulted in a 2-1 victory thanks to goals by Paul Benson and Jason Euell, but three weeks later, a home defeat against Preston proved to be his swansong, Both Ruben and another young Charlton player, Tosan Popo, spent the second half of the campaign on loan at Lepe in Spain
With no further opportunities at the Valley for Ruben, he moved to the USA and in February 2013 signed for New

York Red Bulls where he played alongside both LLoyd Sam and Bradley Wright-Phillips. He later switched to New York Cosmos who finished NASL champions in 2015. A return to English football with Barnet proved less successful and he departed back to Spain after they were relegated from the Football League.
Since December 2018 Ruben has played for FC Andorra who in 2018-19 were winners of the Primera Catalana, the fifth tier of Spanish football. Unusually because another team were folding through financial difficulties, they were then permitted to pay 452,022 euros to the Spanish FA and buy themselves a place in the third tier for the following season.

Season	Division	League		FA Cup		FL Cup		FL Trophy		Total	
		A	G	A	G	A	G	A	G	A	G
2011-12 (P)	League One	0	0	0	0	2	0	0	0	2	0
Total		0	0	0	0	2	0	0	0	2	0

UK LEAGUE CAREER 27 games 0 goals

CHARLTON CAREER

Managers: *C Powell*

Debut: *Reading (H) 23-08-2011*

V734

Finale: *Preston North End (H) 13-09-2011*

BOWEN Mark Rosslyn   1997 - 99

Defender   11st 11lbs   5' 8"
Born: 07-12-1963 - Neath, West Glamorgan
Education: St Joseph's Comprehensive School, Port Talbot.

A Welsh international, Mark was a stylish full back who played the majority of his career with Norwich City and only joined Charlton at the age of 33.

He proved an excellent signing however and played regularly in the promotion season of 1997-98 and in the Wembley play off final against Sunderland took and scored the fifth penalty in front of a crowd of 77,739. Since retiring as a player Mark has enjoyed a variety of coaching and managerial roles with leading clubs, as well as a spell as assistant manager of Wales.

HONOURS

Wales International 1986-97 41 caps 3 goals
Wales U21 International 1982-83 3 caps 0 goals

Afan Nedd Schools & Welsh Schools
Charlton Athletic 1997-98 Promoted Play Offs Division 1

CLUBS

Tottenham Hotspur 08.79 (youth) 01.12.81 (pro) ••Norwich City 23.07.87 (£90,000) ••West Ham United 10.07.96 (free) ••Shimizu S-Pulse, Japan 01.97 (free) ••Charlton Athletic 16.09.97 (free) ••Wigan Athletic 06.08.99 (free) ••Wales 08.99 (coach) 2001 (ass manager) ••Reading 03.12.99 (free} ••Crystal Palace 27.06.01 (coach) ••Birmingham City 12.12.01 (coach) ••Blackburn Rovers 16.09.04 (ass manager) ••Manchester City 05.08 (ass manager) ••Fulham 04.08.10 (ass manager) ••Queens Park Rangers 10.01.12 (ass manager) ••Stoke City 01.06.13 (ass manager) ••Southampton 14.03.18 (ass manager) ••Reading 27.03.19 (tech consultant) 21.08.19 (sporting director) 14.10.19 (manager)

First team opportunities were limited for a young player at Tottenham in the eighties, so having completed his apprenticeship but not been able to command a regular spot, Mark moved to Norwich City in 1987 and enjoyed eight seasons in the top flight of English football, including 1992-93 when he was ever present as they competed for and nearly won the inaugural season of the Premier League. They led the table at the end of March but finished in third place, which is still the best in the club's history. An orthodox defender, he was an infrequent goalscorer but got the winner when on 19th October 1993 they won 2-1 at Bayern Munich in the UEFA Cup. This was an exciting time to be a Norwich player and he clocked up almost 400 league and cup matches for them before switching to West Ham in 1996.

His stay in East London was a good deal less memorable and after six months he accepted a lucrative offer to play in Japan for Shimizu S-Pulse before in September 1997 being snapped up by Alan Curbishley and joining Charlton's promotion drive. Mark's second season in SE7 was interrupted by injury and he only managed six matches. His place was taken by new signing Chris Powell and his playing career then wound down via brief encounters at Wigan and Reading.

Mark played 41 times for Wales, his final appearance being against Ireland on 11th February 1997. When his Welsh teammate Mark Hughes was brought in to manage the national side in 1999, Bowen was recruited as one of his coaching staff and over the next 20 years he followed Hughes from job to job, working as his assistant manager as they moved between one club and another. Mark finally landed his own managerial appointment at Reading in October 2019 but it only lasted 10 months before he was sacked on 31st August 2020.

Season	Division	League		FA Cup		FL Cup		Play Offs		Total	
		A	G	A	G	A	G	A	G	A	G
1997-98 (P)	Division 1	34 (2)	0	3	0	0	0	3	0	40 (2)	0
1998-99 (R)	Premier	2 (4)	0	0	0	0	0			2 (4)	0
Total		36 (6)	0	3	0	0	0	3	0	42 (6)	0

UK LEAGUE CAREER 403 games 27 goals

CHARLTON CAREER
Managers: *A Curbishley*
Debut: *Norwich City (A) (sub) 17-09-1997*
V569
Finale: *Sheffield Wednesday (H) (sub) 16-05-1999*

BOWERS Alfred George Walter　　　　　　　　　1924

Alf was an outstanding athlete and swimmer who is believed to have been signed in July 1919 when Charlton still had amateur status and if true he would possibly have taken part in the very earliest matches at the Valley, their newly acquired ground in Floyd Road. Appearance records for the amateur years are sadly incomplete but it can be confirmed with certainty that Alf lined up at centre half in Charlton's first league match as a professional club on 28th August 1920 against Norwich City. The Addicks got off to an encouraging start, with Cyril Smith scoring the deciding goal in a 2-1 win.

Defender　　12st 6lbs　　6′ 1″
Born: 02-04-1895 - Bethnal Green, London
Died: 22-03-1975 - Hackney, London

HONOURS

Charlton Athletic Reserves 1920-21 Winners Kent League　　　　Charlton Athletic A 1923-24 Winners Kent League

CLUBS

Hoffman Athletic 1912 ••Chelmsford 1913 ••Mile End Albion 1914 ••Bromley Celtic 1918 ••Charlton Athletic 07.19 ••Bristol Rovers 12.06.25 ••Queens Park Rangers 08.26

A tall, imposing central defender, Alf lived his early life in the East End, but by the age of 17 was playing football for Hoffman Athletic, the Chelmsford based works team for the Hoffman's Bearings Co, from where he later switched to Chelmsford FC, who were competing in the recently formed Athenian League.

By the time that he joined Charlton, he was in his mid-twenties and although he featured four times in the Southern League during season 1920-21, he was destined to spend most of his time at SE7 playing for the Reserves and was a regular in the side which won the Kent League that season. It was in fact four years before he got another opportunity in the first team and his Football League debut came at Ashton Gate on 24th September 1924 against a Bristol City side which was second in the table, but a goal from Alex Steele earned Charlton a welcome 1-1 draw. He remained in the squad for no more than five weeks however and a disappointing 2-0 defeat at Gillingham at the beginning of November signalled the end of his first team duties. As a professional footballer in 1924, Alf's earnings at Charlton were £3-10-0 a week.

He signed for Bristol Rovers in the summer of 1925 and managed three first team appearances, including a useful 2-0 victory on 5th September 1925 against a Gillingham team which included his former Charlton teammates Bert Goodman and Bill Berry. This was the first season since the offside law had been changed and an attacking player now needed two not three defenders ahead of him, which led to a feast of goals and initially made life very difficult for defenders. A final season with Queens Park Rangers wrapped up Alf's time in the Football League and he bowed out following a heavy 6-2 defeat at Bournemouth on 2nd October 1926.

Later in life he worked as a nightwatchman, but had retired when at the age of 79, he succumbed to coronary thrombosis at his home in Hackney Wick.

Season	Division	League		FA Cup		Total	
		A	G	A	G	A	G
1924-25	Divison 3 (S)	5	0	0	0	5	0
Total		5	0	0	0	5	0

UK LEAGUE CAREER 9 games 0 goals

CHARLTON CAREER
Managers: *W Rayner*
Debut: *Southern League Norwich City (A) 28-08-1920 Football League Bristol City (A) 24-09-1924*
V064
Finale: *Gillingham (A) 01-11-1924*

BOWMAN Richard David   1973 - 76

Midfield   10st 1lbs   5' 6"
Born: 25-09-1954 - Lewisham, London
Education: Ealdham Primary School and Crown Woods School, Eltham.

A very popular and dynamic midfield player, what Richie lacked in inches he made up for by non-stop running and a tremendous work rate. He was a key member of Andy Nelson's 1974-75 promotion side which finished in third place in Division 3 and was immediately recognisable because of his unruly mop of long blond hair. His style of play was infectious and he often seemed to inspire his teammates with his 'never say die' attitude. He was deservedly voted the Charlton Athletic Player of the Year in 1975.

HONOURS

Woolwich Schools & Kent Schools
Charlton Athletic 1975 Player Of The Year

Charlton Athletic 1974-75 Promoted Division 3
Reading 1978-79 Winners Division 4

CLUBS

Charlton Athletic 27.01.70 (youth) 07.03.73 (pro) ••Dover Athletic 22.07.74 (loan) ••Reading 16.12.76 (£5,000) ••Gillingham 24.08.81 (£25,000) ••Libra c1985 ••Santogee 66 c1988 ••Priory Vets c1990

Richie joined Charlton as an associated schoolboy at the age of 15 and was upgraded to an apprentice professional on 27th November 1970. He later trained with the England Youth squad and made his first team debut for Charlton in a 5-0 drubbing at Plymouth, shortly before signing his first professional contract on 14th March 1973. It was another year before he became a fixture in the team, but in 1974-75 he hardly missed a game. After promotion to Division 2 he was less influential but still popular with supporters who always appreciate a player who gives everything. Richie was substitute in the infamous game at Sunderland on 21st February 1976 when goalkeeper Graham Tutt was kicked in the head after only seven minutes. He was carried off the field and Derek Hales went in goal. The match was lost 4-1, but Richie did at least score the consolation goal.

By December 1976 he had lost his place at right half to Peter Hunt and was transferred to Reading for a modest fee of £5,000. His new club certainly got a bargain and Richie went on to play more than 200 matches for them over the next five years, which included promotion as champions of Division 4 in 1978-79 where his teammates included a young George Shipley. They finished that season with the then record of 11 straight matches without conceding a goal.

His third and final club was Gillingham where Keith Peacock was manager and he joined them for a transfer fee of £25,000 in August 1981 and played alongside Peter Shaw, Colin Powell and Dick Tydeman. By November, they were top of Division 3 and the future looked bright as Richie grabbed the only goal to eliminate Plymouth Argyle from the FA Cup on 24th November. The next round against non-league Barking was played three weeks later and during this match he picked up the knee injury which effectively finished his career. He did not play again for 15 months and although he managed a further eight games and even scored in his comeback match, he was unable to reach the required level and announced his retirement at the age of 29.

Although Richie played Sunday football for some time, including a spell with Priory Vets where he lined up alongside former Charlton reserve team player David Burke, he went on to earn his living in the hospitality sector. First though he spent three years working with his uncle in the building trade, but then became a restaurateur and for some 18 years ran a popular sandwich bar at London Bridge. He retired in 2020 and is now living at West Malling.

Season	Division	League		FA Cup		FL Cup		Total	
		A	G	A	G	A	G	A	G
1972-73	Division 3	4	0	0	0	0	0	4	0
1973-74	Division 3	8	0	0	0	0 (1)	0	8 (1)	0
1974-75 (P)	Division 3	44	4	2	0	2	0	48	4
1975-76	Division 2	26 (3)	2	1	0	7	2	34 (3)	4
1976-77	Division 2	11	1	0	0	1	0	12	1
Total		93 (3)	7	3	0	10 (1)	2	106 (4)	9

CHARLTON CAREER
Managers: *T Foley, A Nelson*
Debut: *Plymouth Argyle (A) 03-03-1973*
V379
Finale: *Bolton Wanderers (A) 27-11-1976*

UK LEAGUE CAREER 317 games 43 goals

BOWYER Lee David　　　　　　　　　　　　　　1994 - 96

Lee was Charlton's 'enfant terrible' and a massively talented midfielder who spent two years with the first team at the start of his

Midfield　10st 6lbs　5' 9"
Born: 03-01-1977 - Poplar, London
Education: Culloden Primary School & Langdon Park Secondary Modern School, Poplar.

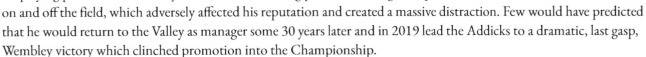

career. In 1996, he was sold to Leeds United in a big money transfer and at a time when they were one of the leading clubs in the country, but by then had already demonstrated that he had the ability to reach the very top in English football. Ultimately, his failure to fully achieve his playing potential was directly the result of a seemingly endless catalogue of problems both on and off the field, which adversely affected his reputation and created a massive distraction. Few would have predicted that he would return to the Valley as manager some 30 years later and in 2019 lead the Addicks to a dramatic, last gasp, Wembley victory which clinched promotion into the Championship.

HONOURS

England International 2002 1 cap 0 goals
England U21 International 1995-00 13 caps 4 goals
England U18 International 1994-95 6 caps 2 goals
FA Youth XI 1994 1 cap 0 goals

Hackney, Tower Hamlets & Inner London Schools
Charlton Athletic 1996 Young Player Of The Year
Birmingham City 2008-09 Runners Up Championship
Birmingham City 2010-11 Winners Football League Cup

HONOURS AS MANAGER

Charlton Athletic 2018-19 Promoted Play Offs League One

CLUBS

Asta 1983 (youth) ••Senrab Boys Club (youth) ••Hyde Rovers (youth) ••Charlton Athletic 03.91 (youth) 13.04.94 (pro) ••Leeds United 03.07.96 (£2,812,500) ••West Ham United 08.01.03 (£350,000) ••Newcastle United 22.05.03 (free) ••West Ham United 08.06.06 (£750,000) ••Birmingham City 09.01.09 (loan) 08.07.09 (free) ••Ipswich Town 11.07.11 (free) ••Charlton Athletic 01.17 (coach) 01.07.17 (ass,manager) 22.03.18 (manager) ••Birmingham City 16.03.21 (manager)

Something of a child prodigy, Lee first played for Asta, a junior club in Poplar, from the age of six. They were managed by his father and from there he moved to Senrab, the famous East End boys club which launched the careers of several well-known players, including Jonathan Fortune and Jermaine Defoe. Up to the age of 13 he had been a centre half, but did not have the height to make it as a central defender and was turned down after a trial with Arsenal because they considered him too small. Instead, it was to Charlton that he turned, signing associated schoolboy forms in March 1991 and becoming a full

professional on 13th April 1994.

His first team debut was against Swindon Town on 27th September 1994 and by then Lee was already an England U18 international. He eventually made six appearances at that level, including a 3-2 win over Norway, in which he scored the winning goal. Having got his career off to such a bright start, at the age of 18 he reached his first bump in the road when on 27th March 1995 it was announced that two Charlton players, Lee and Dean Chandler, had failed routine drugs tests and tested positive for marijuana. Adverse publicity and FA intervention sidelined him until the final game of the season, but he was back in the team on 7th May when Charlton went down 2-1 at Reading.

It was in his second season that Lee really stepped up to the plate and his no nonsense battling performances in midfield made it very clear that he was on his way to the top. There was a pulsating League Cup tie at Wimbledon in September which finished 5-4 and in which he scored a hat-trick, plus unexpected league success over Millwall. At the Den, Charlton got the result despite Lee being red carded in the first half, but back at the Valley in March, there were goals from Lee and Carl Leaburn and a 2-0 win to ensure a rare double over those noisy neighbours from New Cross. In all, Lee played 52 matches and scored 14 goals and was voted Charlton's Young Player of the Year for 1996.

Obviously Lee was destined for the Premier League, but it was still disappointing for Charlton supporters that he did not stay for more than the one full season. On 3rd July 1996 he was transferred to Leeds United for a fee of £2,815,500, a club record and more than double the amount received from Chelsea in 1994 from the sale of Scott Minto. A further £250,000 was to have been payable should he make 10 international appearances. His Premier League debut was on 17th August against a Derby County side which included Chris Powell, Gary Rowett and Christian Dailly and Lee scored the final goal as Leeds came away with a 3-3 draw.

Having got off to a good start, an ankle injury received against Manchester United sidelined him five games into the season and so he took the opportunity to return to Poplar to see family and friends. This excursion hit the headlines following an unruly incident on 3rd October 1996 in McDonald's on the Isle of Dogs, when Lee and two friends were not able to purchase cheeseburgers while the breakfast menu was still in operation. A row quickly escalated, chairs were thrown around and they were captured on video causing general mayhem within the restaurant. There were also allegations of a racial nature. Lee pleaded guilty to causing an affray and was fined £4,500. Leeds United were unimpressed and added a £4,000 club fine plus a stern warning as to future behaviour.

This unsavoury behaviour was just a taster for what was to come. On 12th January 2000 a late-night incident outside the Majestyk Club in Leeds ended with an Asian youth receiving severe injuries including a broken nose, a broken leg and serious facial damage after being attacked by five men, three of whom were identified as Leeds footballers. Lee was arrested on 18th January and charged with grievous bodily harm and causing an affray. The legal process

dragged on for over a year until the trial finally commenced at Hull Crown Court in February 2001. Two months later, it had to be aborted after the 'Sunday Mirror' committed a contempt of court by publishing an interview with the victim's father. A second trial was concluded in December 2001 and although three other defendants received guilty verdicts, Lee was cleared of all charges.

Throughout this two-year period, Leeds had followed the principal of 'innocent until proven guilty' and Lee carried on playing, despite travelling each day to court and the difficulty in maintaining any sort of regular training schedule. The FA did not take the same view and he was not therefore considered for international duty at a time when it is generally accepted that he was at the peak of his form. He seemed able to somehow block out the court pressures and channel all his energy into his football and it was England's loss that they were unable to harness his talent when he was playing so well. He had already played 12 times for England U21 (the first four caps while at Charlton) but only ever played one full international. This was against Portugal on 7th September 2002. He made the England goal in a 1-1 draw, but was never selected again. He came with just too much baggage.

Lee had not been awarded costs at the time of the criminal trials and the legal expenses, which had so far been funded by Leeds United, were estimated at up to £1 million. On top of everything else the club imposed a fine of four weeks wages, which he refused to pay. Having played for two years with this whole sorry business hanging over him and with his existing contract nearing an end, relations between player and club became somewhat strained. A payment plan to reimburse Leeds was put together and a transfer to West Ham became effective in January 2003. He joined a club already rooted at the foot of the Premier League, but with more than half the season already gone, his efforts proved insufficient to halt the downward slide. After only 10 matches for the Hammers, relegation was confirmed and Lee moved on to Newcastle United.

This should have meant a new start with the slate wiped clean, as well as an opportunity to re-gain his best form, but the trouble which pursued Lee throughout his career was never far behind him. On 2nd April 2005 a crowd of 52,306 were at St James's Park for the visit of Aston Villa. With eight minutes of the match remaining, Newcastle were 3-0 down when Lee, frustrated at not receiving the ball, squared up to his teammate Keiron Dyer. Words were spoken and as the red mist descended, Lee headbutted Dyer and followed up with a series of punches. They grappled together until other players could pull them apart. Both men were sent off, Lee with his shirt ripped and with rage still masking his face. The FA handed out a seven match suspension and a £30,000 fine, while the club stopped his wages for six weeks and issued a final warning. To make matters worse, Northumbria Police got involved and elected to additionally prosecute him for the Public Order offence of causing fear or provocation of violence. Meanwhile, the earlier fracas in Leeds had still not gone away, as both the victim in the assault case and his brother then brought a civil action claiming substantial compensation. This rumbled on for some time before an out-of-court settlement was agreed in November 2005. In reality, Lee could not afford to carry on running up still more legal costs, but made it clear that he was not accepting liability and that the payment made was substantially less than claimed. To again prove his innocence would incur further legal expense, far more than would be recovered even if he defeated the claim. The Dyer police case was heard at Newcastle Crown Court in July 2006 and after negotiation, he pleaded guilty to the lesser Public Order offence of causing harassment, alarm or distress and was handed another fine. The cost this time was £600 with £1,000 costs.

At last, he could concentrate on the football and his playing career continued via a second spell with West Ham, followed in 2009 by a transfer to Birmingham City which helped them secure promotion to the Premier League. The off-field distractions make it easy to forget what a good player Lee was, but up to this point, he had very little silverware to show for his years in the game. In 2010-11, Birmingham struggled throughout the league season and were relegated, yet had a marvellous run in the League Cup. After defeating both Aston Villa and West Ham, they met Arsenal in the Wembley final on 27th February 2011. The Birmingham side included both Lee and Roger Johnson and against all the odds they pulled off a shock 2-1 win. This was the 15th season that Lee had played in the Premier League and he stepped down having received a record 99 yellow cards. He played one further season in the Championship with Ipswich Town before hanging up his boots at the age of 34.

Away from football Lee had always been a keen fisherman and after purchasing two carp fishing lakes in Orconte, north-east France, turned his hobby into a business venture called 'Bows Fishing Lakes' which he still runs with his wife, Gemma. This is a far cry from the rough and

tumble of the Premier League and few would have envisaged him reappearing in the role of a football manager at any stage. It was a call from his former Leeds colleague Harry Kewell which caused the transformation. Kewell was in charge of the youth set-up at Watford and in the autumn of 2015, invited Lee to come and coach them for six weeks. He found the experience highly rewarding and in January 2017 joined the coaching staff at Charlton, working initially with the youth players. Progress was swift and in July 2017 he was promoted to assistant manager. Then when Karl Robinson departed for Oxford United, he moved into the manager's office, first in a caretaker role on 22nd March 2018 and then six months later as the permanent appointment.

When Lee took over at the Valley, promotion was looking unlikely. There were only 10 matches still to be played in 2017-18, but he got an instant response from the players and six wins proved enough to secure a play off place. However, the two semi-final ties against Shrewsbury Town were each lost 1-0, so the season concluded on something of an anti-climax. The club was up for sale during the summer of 2018 and it was much thanks to Head of Recruitment Steve Gallen, that from a limited budget, Lee was able to construct a squad mainly comprising short term free transfers and loans, but which was equipped to make another tilt for promotion. The side started slowly but as the season progressed, moved into the play off places and on 26th May 2019 Lee led his Charlton team out at Wembley for the Final against Sunderland and along with the Charlton contingent within the 76,155 crowd, enjoyed the exciting and nail-biting 2-1 victory. The euphoria was inevitably short-lived as the Belgian owner was still marking time awaiting a buyer for the club and despite a strong start to 2019-20, injuries piled up and after just one season back in the Championship, Charlton were relegated again on the final day of the Covid affected season. Lee resigned on 15th March 2021 and took over as manager of Birmingham City the following day.

Season	Division	League		FA Cup		FL Cup		Play Offs		Total	
		A	G	A	G	A	G	A	G	A	G
1994-95	Division 1	5	0	0	0	0 (1)	0			5 (1)	0
1995-96	Division 1	41	8	3	1	6	5	2	0	52	14
Total		46	8	3	1	6 (1)	5	2	0	57 (1)	14

UK LEAGUE CAREER 489 games 68 goals

CHARLTON CAREER

Managers: *A Curbishley/S Gritt, A Curbishley*

Debut: *Swindon Town (H) (sub) 27-09-1994*

V548

Finale: *Crystal Palace (A) 15-05-1996*

BRIGGS Arthur Horace   1922 - 24

Forward   5' 5"
Born: 30-08-1897 - Poplar, Middlesex
Died: 07-05-1960 - Smithfield, London
Education: Devons Road School, Bromley-by-bow.

Signed from struggling Kent League side Woolwich FC, Arthur spent most of his time at Charlton playing reserve team football. He was given chances with the first team both on the right wing and at inside forward, but failed to deliver the goods and in 1925 moved on to Guildford United.

HONOURS

Tower Hamlets District   Charlton Athletic A 1923-24 Winners Kent League

CLUBS

Woolwich 1920 ••Charlton Athletic 09.03.22 (amateur) 12.08.22 (pro) ••Chatham 02.25 (loan) ••Guildford United 13-07-25

An East End boy, Arthur worked as a labourer after leaving school until joining the Royal Navy at the age of 16, just three weeks after the start of World War 1. He served on the guard ship HMS Wallaroo out of Chatham and was discharged from the Navy in September 1919.

He was initially signed as an amateur by Charlton and only completed the paperwork on Thursday 9th March 1922 the very day of their away league match with Swansea Town. He was rushed straight into the team at outside right and must have been on the road before they knew for certain that he was eligible to play. The match ended 0-0 but the same eleven remained in Wales and played again two days later against Merthyr United. This must have been a baptism of fire for Arthur and although he had no more first team action for seven months, he progressed sufficiently to be signed on professional terms in August at the mouth watering wage of £3 a week.

In 1923-24 Charlton's A team stormed the Kent League and finished champions by nine clear points, only losing twice and Arthur was the leading goalscorer with 18 in the 30 matches. He scored a hat-trick against Tunbridge Wells Rangers on 23rd February 1924 and eventually earned a recall to first team duty but now as an inside forward rather

than a winger.

After 17 months out of the team, he was brought back in time for another trip to Merthyr on 11th October 1924. Player manager Albert Lindon was in goal for the home team and Arthur opened the scoring before Charlton slipped to a 2-1 defeat. He kept his place for three more matches, but a disappointing 2-0 defeat against a Gillingham side that included winger Bill Berry, proved to be his finale.

His contract with Guildford United meant a reduced wage of £2 10s 0d a week but included a clause whereby he was allowed to carry on his work in London but must pay his own travelling expenses to Guildford. A similar arrangement had applied at Charlton and both clubs allowed him to train on Tuesday and Thursday evenings only.

By 1939 Arthur was living in Ilford with his wife Gladys and son Arthur Jnr and working in the docks as a timber porter. Later they took up residence at 12 Bow Lane in the City of London where he was a lift man up to the time of his death in St Bartholomew's Hospital at the age of 62.

Season	Division	League		FA Cup		Total	
		A	G	A	G	A	G
1921-22	Divison 3 (S)	2	0			2	0
1922-23	Divison 3 (S)	3	0	0	0	3	0
1924-25	Divison 3 (S)	4	1	0	0	4	1
Total		9	1	0	0	9	1

UK LEAGUE CAREER 9 games 1 goal

CHARLTON CAREER
Managers: *W Rayner*
Debut: *Swansea Town (A) 09-03-1922*
V032
Finale: *Gillingham (A) 01-11-1924*

BRIGHT Mark Abraham   1997 - 99

Mark made over 500 league and cup appearances and spent much of his career competing in the top

Forward   12st 12lbs   6' 0"
Born: 06-06-1962 - Stoke-on-Trent, Staffordshire
Education: Dove Bank Primary School, KIdsgove, Abbey Hulton Junior School, Stoke and Maryhill Comprehensive, Kidsgrove.

division of English football for Crystal Palace and Sheffield Wednesday. He appeared in two Wembley FA Cup finals, (both of which were drawn and went to replays) as well as a Football League Cup final, but even so, in his 2019 autobiography, 'My Story', he conceded that his participation in the 1998 Mendonca final for Charlton was both 'an absolute classic and one of the most memorable games I played in during my career'.

HONOURS
England FA Over 35 XI 2003
Charlton Athletic 1997-98 Promoted Play Offs Division 1
Crystal Palace 1988-89 Promoted Play Offs Division 2
Crystal Palace 1989-90 Finalists FA Cup

Crystal Palace 1990-91 Winners Full Members Cup
Sheffield Wednesday 1992-93 Finalists FA Cup
Sheffield Wednesday 1992-93 Finalists League Cup
Charlton Athletic Reserves 1998-99 Winners Football Combination

CLUBS
Port Vale 1977 (youth) ••Masons Arms 1979 (amateur) ••Leek Town 1979 (amateur) ••Kidsgrove Athletic 1981 (amateur) ••Port Vale 15.10.81 (amateur) 05.83 (pro) ••Leicester City 19.07.84 (£66,666) ••Crystal Palace 13.11.86 (£75,000) ••Sheffield Wednesday 11.09.92 (£375,000 + player) ••Millwall 13.12.96 (loan) ••Sion, Switzerland 27.01.97 (£65,000) ••Charlton Athletic 04.04.97 (free) ••Crystal Palace 2009 (academy coach)

After his parents split up, Mark was fostered from the age of two and grew up with a burning ambition to be a professional footballer. He was training with Port Vale at the age of 15, but at that time was not considered good enough to be taken on to the staff. Instead, he played Sunday football for a pub side called Masons Arms and on Saturdays for Leek Town in the Cheshire County League. After leaving school he took a job as an apprentice in a hydraulics factory, but after scoring a hat-trick for Leek in a league match against Chorley Town in March 1982, he was given a second chance at Port Vale and this time his efforts were better appreciated.

He became a part-time pro in May 1982, the same month that he made his league debut, but it was another year before he signed a full time pro contract and not until season 1983-84 did he become established in the Port Vale team. He managed 10 goals in a relegated side, including the winner against Colin Appleton's Hull City on 7th May,

but then turned down the offer of a new contract. There was interest from Sheffield Wednesday, but Mark chose to join Leicester City instead, the transfer fee of £100,000 to be paid in three instalments. Only two thirds of the money was ever paid however as he failed to reach 50 appearances which is the point at which the balance would have been due.

The jump from Division 3 with Port Vale to Division 1 with Leicester took some adjustment and Mark spent most of his first season on the bench. The opening game of 1985-86 was at home to Everton and he scored twice in a 3-1 win but even though this led to a run of matches, he never really settled and in November 1986 signed for Crystal Palace at a cost of £75,000.

This is where his career really took off and he spent a very satisfying six years at Selhurst Park making a total of 227 league appearances. He was ever present in the 1989 promotion team (which also included Alan Pardew) and a year later was in the Palace side which was narrowly beaten by Manchester United over two games in the FA Cup final. They did win the Full Members Cup in 1991 though. A team including Mark, Pardew, John Salako and John Humphrey beat Everton 4-1 at Wembley, but it was not all cup finals and glory and John was also in the Palace team on 12th September 1989 when they were demolished 9-0 by Liverpool.

In September 1992 Mark left Selhurst and transferred to Sheffield Wednesday where this new challenge earned him three further Wembley cup final appearances. On 18th April 1983 they went down 2-1 against Arsenal in the League Cup and a month later were beaten again by the same opponents and by the same score, but this time after a drawn game in the FA Cup. Disappointing though this undoubtedly was, he played four seasons of Premier League football for Wednesday and would have stayed longer but for a change of manager which left him out in the cold. After a short spell on loan at Millwall, Mark tried his luck abroad with the Swiss team FC Sion in January 1997, but owing to a financial squabble between them and Wednesday, the whole thing went belly up after just a few weeks and he was then back in the UK, now aged 34 and looking for a new club.

Alan Curbishley was pleased to add an experienced campaigner like Mark to his squad, especially when he scored twice on his full debut against Portsmouth, when

Charlton ran out winners by 2-1 on 19th April 1997. His extensive experience proved invaluable both on and off the field and he was in the starting line-up for the three play off matches at the business end of the 1997-98 season. At Wembley, he played his part in Charlton's triumph against Sunderland, but did not participate in the nerve racking penalty shoot out, having been substituted for Steve Brown after 93 minutes. He stayed with the club for a further season, the final goal of his professional career helping to secure a 2-2 draw up at Newcastle on 17th January 1999. He announced his retirement on 4th May 1999.

With his playing career behind him, Mark became a summariser and analyst for the BBC and for a while fronted the 'Wright And Bright Show' on Radio 5 Live with Ian Wright. He has also made numerous appearances on 'Match Of The Day', 'Football Focus', 'The Big Breakfast' and the like and has run (or walked) marathons for various charities, including cancer research. He has coached at Crystal Palace and although they are now amicably divorced, was married to the singer and actress Michelle Gayle.

Season	Division	League		FA Cup		FL Cup		Play Offs		Total	
		A	G	A	G	A	G	A	G	A	G
1996-97	Division 1	4 (2)	2	0	0	0	0			4 (2)	2
1997-98 P)	Division 1	13 (3)	7	2 (1)	0	0 (2)	0	3	0	18 (6)	7
1998-99 (R)	Premier	1 (4)	1	0 (1)	0	0 (1)	0			1 (6)	1
Total		18 (9)	10	2 (2)	0	0 (3)	0	3	0	23 (14)	10

UK LEAGUE CAREER 461 games 166 goals

CHARLTON CAREER
Managers: *A Curbishley*
Debut: *Huddersfield Town (A) (sub) 09-04-1997*
V565
Finale: *Everton (A) 24-04-1999*

BRISLEY Terence William   1978 - 79

Midfield, Forward   10st 7lbs   5' 6"
Born: 04-07-1950 - Wapping, London
Education: Davenant Foundation School, Stepney.

An industrious midfield player, Terry spent 18 months at the Valley after helping Millwall to achieve promotion and establish themselves in Division 2. He was unable to achieve the same degree of success whilst at Charlton but did hit the headlines on 24th March 1978 when his second half goal ensured a popular 1-0 win in a hard fought game against Crystal Palace.

HONOURS

East London Schools 1964   Portsmouth 1979-80 Promoted Division 4
Millwall 1975-76 Promoted Division 3

CLUBS

Orient 03.64 (youth) 01.07.68 (pro) ••Southend United 01. 03.75 (loan) ••Millwall 15.07.75 (player exchange) ••Charlton Athletic 18.01.78 (£20,000) ••Portsmouth 20.07.79 (£25,000) ••Maidstone United 06.81 (free) ••Chelmsford City 1981 (free) ••Wealdstone 1983 (free)

An East End boy, Terry joined Leyton Orient at the age of 13, but by the time he signed his first professional contract in 1968, they had dropped 'Leyton' from their name and were known simply as Orient. (The name reverted back in 1987). In 1970-71 he made his league debut and by the time Orient played at the Valley on 3rd April 1971 he was a regular in the side. His teammates included full back Mick Jones, but two goals from Keith Peacock ensured a 2-0 victory for Charlton that day.

He clocked up over 150 competitive appearances for Orient before transferring to Millwall in July 1975 in a player exchange which sent Doug Allder in the opposite direction. In his first season they finished with an unbeaten run of 15 matches to clinch promotion to Division 2 and Terry played a full part in this success, probably playing the best football of his career over the next 18 months as Millwall performed comfortably at the higher level.

When Charlton paid £20,000 for his registration in January 1978, it looked like a quality signing, but in truth he struggled to maintain the same form with his new club. He did score twice on 4th November 1978 in a shock 4-1 away win against a Cardiff City side which included Alan Campbell, but by the end of that season he was no longer among the first names on the team sheet and Charlton cashed in their chips by selling him to Portsmouth for a profitable £25,000.

Down in Division 4 Terry thrived during 1979-80 and plundered 16 competitive goals as Portsmouth gained promotion. This was to be his last taste of success however and he played his final match for Pompey in October 1980, his career then winding down via spells with Maidstone United, Chelmsford and Wealdstone.

Terry prospered in his business life and by the mid-nineties was living in Brentwood and working in the City as a foreign exchange broker. He later moved on to a senior position with a Belgian bank.

Season	Division	League		FA Cup		FL Cup		Total	
		A	G	A	G	A	G	A	G
1977-78	Division 2	15 (1)	2	0	0	0	0	15 (1)	2
1978-79	Division 2	29 (3)	3	3	0	5	1	37 (3)	4
Total		44 (4)	5	3	0	5	1	52 (4)	6

UK LEAGUE CAREER 360 games 41 goals

CHARLTON CAREER

Managers: *A Nelson*

Debut: *Luton Town (H) 21-01-1978*

V409

Finale: *Oldham Athletic (H) (sub) 05-05-1979*

BROWN Henry 'Ernie'   1929 - 30

Ernie started out in the Welsh coal mining village of Aberaman and went on to play over 200 competitive matches for his seven Football League clubs. He spent a year with Liverpool, but despite appearing 26 times for their reserves in the Central League, he never featured in their first team. Instead, most of his career took place in the basement of Division 3 (South) with clubs who were fighting for their lives and despite his best efforts, almost every one of them crashed and burned, either during his watch or shortly thereafter. He was without question the footballing 'Jonah', but happily Charlton at least did escape unscathed after Ernie had left the building.

Forward   11st 0lbs   5' 7"
Born: 17-03-1902 - Aberaman, Glamorgan
Died: 17-07-1984 - Merthyr Tydfil, Glamorgan

HONOURS

Welsh League XI 1922   Aberdare Athletic 1922-23 Finalists Welsh FA Cup

CLUBS

Aberaman Athletic 05.21 ••Merthyr Town 05.11.21 ••Caerphilly 1922 ••Aberdare Athletic 13.11.22 ••Liverpool 19.06.24 (small fee) ••Southport 25.08.25 (free) ••Aberdare Athletic 25.08.26 ••Merthyr Town 23.06.28 ••Charlton Athletic 09.04.29 (£300) ••Newport County 11.09.30 ••Thames 09.07.31

During his year at The Valley, Ernie competed for the right wing position with Harry Wyper, Albert Legge and the amateur, George Watson. Such competition restricted him to just two league games, but he did play his part in an impressive 3-0 win at Queens Park Rangers in the third round of the FA Cup on 16th January 1930. He was retained for the next round against Middlesbrough where a goal from Jack Pugsley forced a 1-1 draw and in the replay at the Valley, a strike by Billy Lennox ensured the same scoreline. The third match was played at Maine Road, Manchester and was another tight affair but Charlton were finally beaten 1-0 and this proved to be Ernie's last outing in the first team.

The remainder of his career is such a tale of woe that it does not make for easy reading and perhaps a health warning should precede the next couple of paragraphs. Things first went wrong for Southern League club Caerphilly who imploded shortly after he arrived in 1922 and had their results expunged from the 1922-23 league table. Ernie moved on to Aberdare Athletic where he had two spells, culminating with the disastrous 1926-27 season. His final appearance was a 7-0 home defeat against Coventry City, shortly after which they were voted out of the Football League, never to return. He then spent a year with Merthyr Town who just about survived in 1928-29 but were themselves voted out twelve months later and replaced by the East London club Thames.

After leaving the Valley, Ernie signed for Newport County. His one season with them was another disaster. They finished second from bottom of Division 3 (South) and failed to survive the vote for re-election. They were duly expelled in favour of Mansfield Town. His final port of call was Thames and along with his former Charlton colleague Billy Lennox, he took part in their second and final season as a Football League club. They struggled through to the end of 1931-32 before disintegrating completely. His last seven matches were all heavy defeats including a 9-2 thrashing at Cardiff in February.

Ernie was a quiet, unassuming man who was twice widowed and never seemed to receive his fair share of good fortune. After his football career came to an end, he returned to Wales and worked down the pits and later for the coal mining company Powell Duffryn. He finished his working life with the NCB and passed away in Merthyr Tydfil at the age of 82.

Season	Division	League		FA Cup		Total	
		A	G	A	G	A	G
1929-30	Division 2	2	0	4	0	6	0
Total		2	0	4	0	6	0

UK LEAGUE CAREER 189 games 34 goals

CHARLTON CAREER
Managers: *A MacFarlane*
Debut: *Notts County (A) 21-09-1929*
VV129
Finale: *Middlesbrough (N) 03-02-1930*

BROWN Robert Albert John 'Sailor'   1938 - 46

Inside Forward   10st 5lbs   5' 8"
Born: 07-11-1915 - Great Yarmouth, Norfolk
Died: 27-12-2008 - Forres, Morayshire
Education: St Peter's Primary School, Gorleston & Priory School, Great Yarmouth

Like so many of his generation, Sailor lost the best years of his footballing life to the Second World War. He was one of the leading English players of the wartime era as can be confirmed by the unique and unbeatable achievement of he and Sam Bartram who both played in four consecutive Wembley Cup Finals. He almost won the 1946 final for Charlton when he dribbled past five defenders late in the game and with the score still 0-0 just failed with the final pass.

HONOURS

England Wartime International 1945-46, 7 caps 5 goals
Charlton Athletic 1942-43 Finalists FL South Cup
Charlton Athletic 1943-44 Winners FL South Cup
Charlton Athletic 1943-44 Joint Winners Alexander Cup
Charlton Athletic 1945-46 Finalists FA Cup Final

Charlton Athletic 2020 Hall Of Fame
Millwall (guest) 1944-45 Finalists FL South Cup
FA Tour of South Africa 1939
RAF Tour (captain) Sweden, Norway & Denmark

CLUBS

Gorleston Juniors c1930 (youth) ••Gorleston c1932 ••Charlton Athletic 25.08.34 (free) ••Nottingham Forest 07.05.46 (£6,750) ••Aston Villa 15.10.47 (£10,000) ••Gorleston 01.08.49 (player manager)

Bert Brown acquired his nickname 'Sailor' through his rolling gait and muscular build which reminded his teammates of the cartoon character, 'Popeye'. His career at the top of English football was affected not only by the war, but also through a falling out with Jimmy Seed. He was transferred to Second Division Nottingham Forest only days after the 1946 Cup Final thereby missing out on the chance of a place in the victorious Charlton team a year later. This also prevented him adding to his seven appearances for England which were all in post war Victory Internationals and are not therefore counted as full caps. A broken jaw put an end to his career in 1949, but he carried on playing non-league and later managing

Gorleston, his home town club, until 1956.
During the war he had been an RAF sergeant and when he retired from football worked variously as a sports equipment retailer, bookmaker (in business with Joe Jobling), sports organiser at the Gorleston Holiday Centre and timber merchant, eventually retiring in 1982. He remained in Norfolk, but after the death of his wife Daisy in 2001 moved up to Scotland for his final years to be close to his daughter, Julie. Sailor was an extremely gifted footballer and but for the war years may well have been remembered as one of Charlton's very best. In 2020, he was inducted into the Charlton Athletic Hall of Fame

Season	Division	League		FA Cup		Total	
		A	G	A	G	A	G
1937-38	Division 1	17	9	2	2	19	11
1938-39	Division 1	30	12	1	0	31	12
1945-46	Division 1			10	1	10	1
Total		47	21	13	3	60	24

UK LEAGUE CAREER 122 games 47 goals

CHARLTON CAREER
Managers: *J Seed*
Debut: *Birmingham City (H) 29-01-1938*
V199
Finale: *Derby County (FA Cup Final) 27-04-1946*

BROWN Steven Byron   1991 - 02

'Stevie Brown won't let you down' was the chant that regularly rang out from the Covered End during the

Defender   14st 4lbs   6' 1"
Born: 13-05-1972 - Brighton East Sussex
Education: Coldean Primary School, & Patcham Fawcett School, Brighton.

90s and what better acknowledgement could any player want. Supporters will always appreciate someone prepared to give everything for the shirt and Steve was very much in that category. In the early days his career was threatened by injury but through determination and hard work he overcame every obstacle placed before him and forced his way into the team. As popular as he was, surely nobody saw him as a top flight player, yet when Charlton finally achieved Premier League status, Steve remained very much in the frame and went on to appear in 60 matches at the highest level and without question never let anyone down.

HONOURS   Brighton Schools & Sussex Schools
Charlton Athletic 1997-98 Promoted Play Offs Division 1

Charlton Athletic Reserves 1998-99 Winners Football Combination
Charlton Athletic 1999-00 Winners Division 1

CLUBS

Whitehawk 1987 (youth) ••Charlton Athletic 12.09.88 (youth) 03.07.90 (pro) ••Reading 19.12.02 (free) ••Charlton Athletic c2004 (youth coach) ••West Ham United 11.06 (reserve team coach) ••Brighton & Hove Albion 08.09 (youth coach) ••Dover Athletic 09.11 (assistant manager) ••Ebbsfleet United 03.06.13 (manager) ••Lewes 04.03.15 (manager) ••Margate 11.16 (assistant manager) 06.17 (director of football) 21.05.18 (joint manager)

Steve spent the majority of his playing career at Charlton and on a daily basis would car share with Garry Nelson and

Johnny Robinson as they drove back and forth to training from their homes in the Brighton area. Those three men, who were such assets to the club, personified the wonderful spirit which built up during the Gritt and Curbishley regime and which helped so much in Charlton's recovery after the years in exile.

Steve was an old fashioned central defender and was always to be found at the heart of the battle. His sending off at the Valley on 29th September 2001 against Leicester City will never be forgotten by those present. After clashing with an opponent in front of the Covered End, Steve received treatment for an apparent injury and as he was being stretchered off the field, the referee brandished a red card at him. The club had kindly placed a merchandise catalogue on every seat before the game and as soon as the red card appeared so too did hundreds of catalogues, hurled on to the pitch by protesting fans.

Charlton were also able to utilise Steve as an emergency goalkeeper and his proud record shows that he never let the team down on the four occasions when he took over between the sticks. He was so good that on several occasions in the Premier League, Curbishley did not name a substitute goalie in the confident knowledge that Brown could do the job if required. This was put to the test on 8th May 1999 in a vital relegation battle at Aston Villa.

Andy Petterson was sent off and Steve took over in goal, survived an onslaught from the Villa forwards and left the field a hero after Danny Mills had snatched a last minute goal to secure a 4-3 win. Steve was granted a testimonial match on 12th August 2000 and a bad tempered affair against the Italian team, Vicenza, proved far from a 'friendly'. Charlton won 3-2. Chris Powell was sent off for fighting and the match ended with an 18-man brawl.

After more than 12 years of loyal service, he was transferred to Reading where his former teammate Alan Pardew was manager, but his playing career came to an end in March 2004 after a recurrence of an earlier anterior cruciate ligament injury. Since then, he has obtained his UEFA A coaching badge and for a year was head academy coach at the Pro Soccer Academy. As well as his coaching and managing activities, Steve has been a commentator and match summariser at BBC Radio London since July 2003 and scouted for Stoke City. In August 2017 he additionally became Football Coach at Lancing College. Steve was joint manager of Margate from May 2018 until February 2019. Since the introduction of Charlton TV, he has become familiar to a whole new generation of supporters via his detailed match commentaries.

Season	Division	League		FA Cup		FL Cup		FM Cup		AI Cup		Play Offs		Total	
		A	G	A	G	A	G	A	G	A	G	A	G	A	G
1991-92	Division 2	0 (1)	0	0	0	0	0	0	0					0 (1)	0
1993-94	Division 1	18 (1)	0	6	0	0	0			2	0			26 (1)	0
1994-95	Division 1	42	3	1	0	2	0							45	3
1995-96	Division 1	17 (2)	0	2	0	1	0					1	0	21 (2)	0
1996-97	Division 1	22 (5)	0	1	0	2	0							25 (5)	0
1997-98 (P)	Division 1	27 (7)	2	3	1	2	0					0 (2)	0	32 (9)	3
1998-99 (R)	Premier	13 (5)	0	0	0	0 (2)	0							13 (7)	0
1999-00 (P)	Division 1	29 (11)	2	4	0	2	0							35 (11)	2
2000-01	Premier	15 (10)	0	1	0	1	0							17 (10)	0
2001-02	Premier	11 (3)	2	1 (1)	0	2 (1)	1							14 (5)	3
2002-03	Premier	0 (3)	0	0	0	0 (1)	0							0 (4)	0
Total		194 (48)	9	19 (1)	1	12 (4)	1	0	0	2	0	1 (2)	0	228 (55)	11

UK LEAGUE CAREER 282 games 10 goals

CHARLTON CAREER
Managers: *L Lawrence, A Curbishley/S Gritt, A Curbishley*
Debut: *Watford (A) (sub) 21-09-1991*
V523
Finale: *Oxford United (H) (sub) 01-10-2002*

BROWN Thomas Law   1948 - 50

Midfield, Forward   12st 0lbs   5' 10"
Born: 17-04-1921 - Glenbuck, Scotland
Died: 10-05-1966 - Edinburgh, Scotland

Born in the small Ayrshire mining village of Glenbuck, Tommy started out with the South Lanarkshire club, Cambuslang Rangers. He was a Scottish Schoolboy international and progressed sufficiently to secure a trial with Rangers before moving on to Hearts in 1938. A highly skilful wing half, he always seemed destined for the top but sadly the first half of his football life was adversely affected by the onset of World War 2. Interestingly another future Charlton player, Matt Tees, would also commence his footballing journey with Cambuslang Rangers more than 20 years later.

HONOURS

Scotland Wartime International 1939-41 3 caps
Scottish League XI 1939 1 cap 0 goals
Scotland Schoolboy International 3 caps
London FA 1948 1 cap

Cambuslang Rangers 1937-38 Winners Scottish Junior Cup
Heart of Midlothian 1940-41 Finalists Southern League Cup (Scotland)
Millwall (guest) 1944-45 Finalists FL South Cup
Charlton Athletic Reserves 1949-50 Runners Up Football Combination Cup

CLUBS

Cambuslang Rangers, Scotland c1936 (youth) ••Heart of Midlothian, Scotland 1938 (pro) ••Millwall 01.45 (free) ••Charlton Athletic 01.10.48 (£8,500) ••Leyton Orient 04.08.50 (£300) ••Dartford 07.53 (player coach)

Shortly before the outbreak of war in 1939, Tommy played for the Scottish League in their first ever fixture against the League of Ireland and was also capped on three occasions for Scotland, including a 3-1 defeat against England at Hampden Park on 3rd May 1941 in front of a crowd of 78,000, although sadly these wartime internationals do not show up in the record books. He guested for Millwall during the later stages of the war and on 7th May 1945 appeared alongside fellow guest Robert 'Sailor' Brown at Wembley as Millwall went down 2-0 to Chelsea in the final of the Football League South Cup. This was the first club match ever attended by Princess Elizabeth, the future queen.

With the war at an end, Tommy signed officially for Millwall and made his debut at inside left against Northampton Town in the FA Cup on 5th January 1946. He proved very popular down the Old Kent Road and went on to captain them, before in October 1948 transferring to Charlton for a then club record fee of £8,500.

A crowd of 56,294 was at the Valley for his first game against Birmingham City and they enjoyed an early goal from Chris Duffy. However, the visitors equalised in the second half and the game ended 1-1. Tommy broke a small blood vessel in his leg during the second half and missed the next match against Manchester United. He soon settled into the side though and on his day was a quite brilliant player, featuring at either inside left or left half. Throughout his time at the club however, his fitness was always suspect and overall he did not really live up to the big transfer fee. He was known to enjoy nightclubbing, but happily for him players in those days did not come under the same media scrutiny in their private lives as in modern times.

Crystal Palace made a bid of £6,000 to sign both Brown and Duffy in June 1950 but no deal was ever concluded and only two months later he joined Leyton Orient for the cut-price fee of £300. He spent three steady but unspectacular seasons in East London before dropping into non-league with Dartford. Tommy Brown was working as a bus conductor back in Scotland when he was struck down by a fatal heart attack at the comparatively young age of 45.

Season	Division	League		FA Cup		Total	
		A	G	A	G	A	G
1948-49	Division 1	20	1	1	0	21	1
1949-50	Division 1	14	0	1	0	15	0
Total		34	1	2	0	36	1

UK LEAGUE CAREER 230 games 17 goals

CHARLTON CAREER
Managers: *J Seed*
Debut: *Birmingham City (H) 02-10-1948*
VV229
Finale: *Sunderland (H) 25-03-1950*

BROWNE Stephen Logan   1982

When Steve was called up to be a Charlton first team player he was still not the finished article. He had signed for the club in the category of an associated schoolboy on 5th March 1980 and been upgraded to an apprentice professional five months later on 21st August. He was only aged 17 and was four months short of becoming a full professional when on 20th February 1982 he replaced the injured Leighton Phillips during the home league match against Wrexham. The occasion was a happy one thanks to a goal from Steve Gritt which ensured a 1-0 win for the Addicks, but it proved to be the start and the finish of Steve's time as a Football League player.

Midfield
Born: 21-06-1964 - Hackney, London
Died: 01-01-2017 - Walthamstow, London

HONOURS

Charlton Athletic Reserves 1980-81 Winners Mid-Week League   Yeovil Town 1996-97 Winners Isthmian League Premier Division

CLUBS

Charlton Athletic 05.03.80 (youth) 21.06.82 (pro) ••Fulham 1983 (loan) •Reading 1983 (free) ••Maidstone United 1983 ••Dartford c1984 ••Grays Athletic c1984 ••Newmont Travel c1985 ••Wealdstone 1985 ••Barking c1986 ••Wealdstone 08.88 ••Sutton United 1992 (£9,000) ••KIngstonian c1993 ••Yeading c1993 ••Wealdstone 1994 ••Walton & Hersham c1995 ••Yeovil Town 09.95 ••Hendon 01.96 ••Yeovil Town 03.96 ••Chesham Town c1997 ••Slough Town 1998 (ass: manager) 1999 (manager) ••Boreham Wood 2003 (manager) ••Hemel Hempstead c2003 (manager) ••Dover Athletic 10.04 (manager) ••Aveley 02.06 (manager) ••Potters Bar Town 05.07 (manager) ••Enfield Town 12.08 (manager) ••Grays Athletic c2009 (ass: manager) ••Enfield Town c2010 (ass: manager) ••Billericay Town 05.10 (ass: manager)

Steve signed a professional contract on 21st June 1982 but spent much of the next year on loan at Fulham. There were no first team opportunities and after being freed by Charlton in May 1983 he linked up with Reading for whom he appeared in a reserve team match at the Valley on 25th October 1983. Shortly after this he turned his back on the Football League and the Steve Browne story really commenced, because over the next 25 years he played for or managed a staggering number of non-league clubs almost too numerous to mention. It is doubtful if the list contained here is complete, nor is it likely that even Steve himself would have been able to reel off the precise details of his many moves, but what is clear is that he contributed significantly to the non-league game during this period. Highlights include the time spent with Wealdstone, for whom he signed on three separate occasions, a costly transfer to Sutton United who paid a transfer fee reported at £9,000, and two spells with Yeovil Town. He was operating in their midfield when they won the Isthmian League, Premier Division in 1996-97 by a six point margin. In 1998, he moved into management, taking over as assistant at Slough Town and then a year later moving into the hot seat where he remained until 2003. He later held the reins with clubs including Boreham Wood, Dover Athletic, (sacked by a new owner after just three months), Potters Bar Town and Aveley.

Sadly Steve passed away at the age of 52 after a lengthy battle with bone cancer. There can be no better illustration of the respect in which he was held in footballing circles than the fact that following his death, a minute's silence was observed before the next match by more than one of his previous clubs. His son, Rhys Browne, played briefly for Charlton at youth level and has gone on to play in the Football League for among others, Yeovil Town and Port Vale, as well as being an Antigua & Barbuda international.

Season	Division	League		FA Cup		FL Cup		Total	
		A	G	A	G	A	G	A	G
1981-82	Division 2	0(1)	0	0	0	0	0	0(1)	0
Total		0(1)	0	0	0	0	0	0(1)	0

UK LEAGUE CAREER 1 game 0 goals

CHARLTON CAREER
Managers: *A Mullery, K Craggs, L Lawrence*
Debut: *Wrexham (11) (sub) 20-02-1982*
V434

BRUCK Dietmar Jurgen   1970 - 72

Defender   11st 6lbs   5' 8"
Born: 19-04-1944 - Danzig, Germany
Education: Bishop Ullathorne Roman Catholic School, Coventry

Dietmar was born in Germany but moved with his family to the UK at the age of four. He excelled as a schoolboy footballer and represented Coventry Schools, before joining Coventry City when he was 15. He made his first team debut aged 17 years and nine days and remained with them for a decade becoming part of Jimmy Hill's sky blue revolution in which this previously unfashionable and unsuccessful club rose from Division 3 to became established in the top strata of English football.

HONOURS

Coventry Schools & FA Youth Xl   Coventry City 1966-67 Winners Division 2
Coventry City 1963-64 Winners Division 3   Nuneaton Borough 1974-75 Runners Up Southern League Premier Division

CLUBS

Coventry City 07.59 (youth) 04.62 (pro) ••Charlton Athletic 15.10.70 (£11,000) ••Northampton Town 26.06.72 (£4,000) ••Nuneaton Borough 1974 (free) ••Weymouth 23.05.75 (player manager) •Redditch United 1977 (player manager) ••Coventry Sporting (manager) ••Racing Club Warwick (manager) ••Leamington 1985 (caretaker manager)

Charlton and Coventry met in league matches during the mid-sixties, but Dietmar made a losing start on his first visit to the Valley on 26th April 1966, when goals from wingers Len Glover and Mike Kenning ensured a 2-0 win for the Addicks. Things were very different on 18th February 1967, however. The Coventry team that day were excessively physical and it is remembered as being one of the dirtiest games for many years. Dietmar himself was not directly involved in the worst incidents, but Charlton were battered to a 2-1 defeat.

His two years at Charlton comprised one long struggle against relegation from Division 2. He performed reasonably well, especially in his first season, but in 1971-72

it all fell apart and the team finished second from bottom and was consigned to Division 3 for the first time since 1935. Relegation was confirmed after a 5-0 drubbing at Blackpool on the final day of the season and this proved to be Dietmar's last game for the club as he moved on to Northampton Town during the summer.

He later enjoyed limited success in football management and went on to become a financial consultant in the insurance industry. In 2003, he survived a horrific car crash in Malaga, in which his partner Sue Cherrington was killed. After retirement, Dietmar was employed as community champion for Tesco in Coventry, a role that he maintained until 2016.

Season	Division	League		FA Cup		FL Cup		Total	
		A	G	A	G	A	G	A	G
1970-71	Division 2	31	0	1	0	0	0	32	0
1971-72 (R)	Division 2	23 (2)	0	2	0	3	0	28 (2)	0
Total		54 (2)	0	3	0	3	0	60 (2)	0

UK LEAGUE CAREER 286 games 7 goals

CHARLTON CAREER
Managers: *T Foley*
Debut: *Sheffield Wednesday (H) 17-10-1970*
V357
Finale: *Blackpool (A) 29-04-1972*

BULLIVANT Terence Patrick   1982 - 83

After 123 years Sutton United gained a place in the Football League for the first time when they finished as champions of the National League in season 2020-21. On 25th June and in readiness for the new challenge which lay

Midfield   10st 11lbs   5' 7"
Born: 23-09-1956 - Lambeth, London
Education: Rutlish School, Morden.

ahead, they announced the appointment of 65-year-old Terry Bullivant as their new director of football. This was a sound move as Terry had almost 50 years experience in the professional game, having signed as an apprentice with Fulham in April 1972 and played, coached, managed and scouted for a whole variety of clubs since then.

HONOURS

Brentford 1984-85 Finalists Associate Members' Cup

CLUBS

Fortesque 1969 (youth) ••Fulham 1970 (youth) 05.74 (pro) ••Aston Villa 13.11.79 (£220,000) ••Charlton Athletic 30.07.82 (£100,000) ••Brentford 01.07.83 (free) ••Reading 03.84 (loan) ••Maidstone United 01.86 (free) ••Fulham 08.86 (player coach) ••Carshalton United 1983 (coach) •Barnet 10.93 (coach) 08.96 (manager) ••Reading 30.06.97 (manager) ••Brentford 07.98 (coach) ••Crystal Palace 04.01 (coach) ••Watford 10.04 (coach) ••Birmingham City 2005 (coach) ••Brentford 11.03.08 (ass manager) ••Aldershot 22.02.13 (ass manager) ••Millwall 07.15 (scout) ••Sutton United 25.06.21 (director of football)

The early part of Terry's career was spent with Fulham. He signed a pro contract in May 1974 and by season 1976-77 was becoming an established member of the team. He first came up against Charlton in a Division 2 league match at

the Valley on 28th August 1976 and scored a first half goal, only for it to be cancelled out by one from Keith Peacock, as a result of which the game ended in a 1-1 draw. Over the next couple of years the meetings between the two clubs invariably produced stalemates and both teams were generally to be found in the lower reaches of Division 2. Eventually they both got relegated in 1979-80 but by then Terry had been transferred to Aston Villa for a healthy fee of £220,000 and had been given the opportunity to test himself against First Division opposition.

The move to Villa did not really work out. His stay lasted nearly three years but during that time he only featured in 10 league games, normally playing on the left side of midfield. Villa cut their losses in the Summer of 1982 and Terry joined Charlton just a few days after Paul Walsh had departed for Luton Town. He inherited Paul's number eight shirt although another new signing, Steve White, took over his goal scoring duties. Terry played further back but was a tidy passer of the ball with a good positional sense. He played 30 league matches in 1982-83 as the team flattered to deceive, eventually finishing 17th in Division 2. In July 1983 he was on the move again, joining Brentford on a free transfer. They were in Division 3 at the time, but still proved too strong for Charlton in the League Cup at Griffin Park on 30th August. It was only Terry's second game for his new club but they won 3-0. It was a two legged tie and the Addicks came out on top in the return leg, but

were eliminated 4-2 on aggregate. He played regularly during the first half of that season, but only made one appearance after mid-February and ceased to be a fixture in the team in the remaining two years of his contract. One of his final games for the Bees was against Wolverhampton Wanderers on 17th August 1985. He scored the opening goal in a 2-1 win, but was sent off early in the second half. Terry's playing career was winding down by this point and he re-joined Fulham in 1986 primarily in a coaching capacity, although he did turn out in some reserve team games in 1988-89. He spent more than three years at Barnet, originally coaching under manager Alan Mullery, before two short spells as their manager. His only lengthy managerial engagement was at Reading in 1997-98 where his playing squad included Phil Parkinson and Linvoy Primus, but he lost his job in the March after a run of nine defeats in ten matches. At Crystal Palace he was twice the caretaker manager, while at both Brentford and Aldershot he had spells as assistant manager. More recently Terry has worked as chief scout for Millwall, but now faces new challenges with Sutton United.

Season	Division	League		FA Cup		FL Cup		Total	
		A	G	A	G	A	G	A	G
1982-83	Division 2	30	3	1	0	2	0	33	3
Total		30	3	1	0	2	0	33	3

UK LEAGUE CAREER 180 games 7 goals

CHARLTON CAREER
Managers: *K Craggs, L Lawrence*
Debut: *Leicester City (A) 28-08-1982*
V436
Finale: *Derby County (A) 13-04-1983*

BULOT WAGHA Frederic   2014 - 15

Forward, Midfield   11st 0lbs   5' 10"
Born: 27-09-1990 - Libreville, Gabon

Freddie spent a year in English football. He was one of the players loaned to Charlton from within the network of clubs owned by Roland Duchatelet and arrived at the Valley from Standard Liege in the Summer of 2014. He had not been keen to come to England and took time to settle in, but now looks back on his season with Charlton as having been one of the high points of his professional career. He made 10 international appearances for Gabon while in England and was a good technical player with plenty of energy and pace who could operate anywhere across the midfield, Mildly unpopular with Charlton supporters initially, his form improved steadily over the season and by the end of his loan, most would have happily retained him for a further period had the strange workings of the network permitted it.

HONOURS
Gabon International 2014-19 23 caps 2 goals
France U21 International 2010-12 9 caps 3 goals
France U19 International 2008-09 17 caps 0 goals
France U18 International 2007-08 5 caps 0 goals

France U17 International 2006-07 12 caps 2 goals
France U16 International 2005-06 12 caps 0 goals
Standard Liege 2013-14 Runners Up Belgian Pro League

CLUBS

FC Tours, France 1996 (youth) ••IFR Chateauroux, France 2002 (youth) ••AS Monaco, Monaco 2005 (youth) 18.07.06 (pro) ••SM Caen, France 09.06.11 (free) ••Standard Liege, Belgium 29.07.12 (£1.8 million) ••Charlton Athletic 30.08.14 (loan) ••Stade de Reims, France 13.07.15 (undisclosed) ••FC Tours, France 30.01.18 ••FC Gifu, Japan 10.07.18 ••Felda United, Malaysia 07.01.20 ••Doxa Katokopias, Cyprus 12.04.21

Born in the Central African port of Libreville, Freddie enjoyed dual nationality through having a French father. He entered the highly acclaimed youth academy at AS Monaco at the age of 15 and turned professional three years later, making his first team debut against Lyon in August 2010. He represented France up to U21 level, but his career really came alive after he moved to Standard Liege in the Summer of 2012.

During the two years that Freddie played in Belgium, Standard competed in the UEFA Europa League as well as challenging for honours in the Belgian Pro League. In 2013-14 the team which also included Tal Ben Haim and Yoni Buyens led for much of the league season only to slip back to second place during the play off phase of the Belgian season. It was during that period that he elected to switch his international allegiance to Gabon and made his debut in a 1-1 draw against Morocco on 5th March 2014. The African Cup of Nations was being contested during 2014-15 and his call-ups for the Gabon team proved somewhat disruptive and certainly did not help him to settle down in South London, although interestingly the

manager of the Gabon side during this period was none other than Jorge Costa. Freddie was mainly deployed by Charlton in a wide attacking role, but in the early part of the season he rather flattered to deceive. He was absent during January and played three internationals, including a 2-0 win against Burkina Faso, but when he returned to SE7, he seemed like a different player and performed consistently well for the rest of the campaign, in particular on 3rd March when he scored both goals as Nottingham Forest were defeated 2-1.

Freddie signed for Stade de Reims after returning home from the UK, but his hot streak had come to an end and they were relegated from the French Ligue 1 at the end of his first season. Things did not improve and a meniscus injury in 2016 required an operation and a long lay-off. Since that time his career has been unremarkable but has included spells playing in both Japan and Malaysia. On 12th April 2021 he joined the Cypriot First Division side Doxa Katokopias.

Season	Division	League		FA Cup		FL Cup		Total	
		A	G	A	G	A	G	A	G
2014-15	Championship	19 (9)	5	0	0	0	0	19 (9)	5
Total		19 (9)	5	0	0	0	0	19 (9)	5

UK LEAGUE CAREER 28 games 5 goals

CHARLTON CAREER
Managers: *B Peeters, G Luzon*
Debut: *Wolverhampton Wanderers (H) (sub) 16-09-2014*
V786
Finale: *AFC Bournemouth (H) 02-05-2015*

BUMSTEAD John   1991 - 93

John was a very fine yet underrated midfielder who played the majority of his football for Chelsea. He made more than 400 competitive appearances for

Midfield   10st 0lbs   5' 7"
Born: 27-11-1958 - Rotherhithe, London

them and twice featured in promotion sides as the club shuffled between the First and Second Divisions. This was in the 1980s and long before the arrival of Roman Abramovich. He joined Charlton on a two-year contract in 1991 at the age of 32, but injury brought his career to a premature close before his second season had been concluded.

HONOURS

FA Youth Xl 1975 2 caps 0 goals
Chelsea 1983-84 & 1988-89 Winners Division 2

Chelsea 1985-86 & 1989-90 Winners Full Members Cup

CLUBS

Oxford & Bermondsey (youth) ••Fisher Athletic (youth) ••Chelsea 1972 (youth) 12.76 (pro) ••Charlton Athletic 22.07.91 (free) ••Bromley 1993 (free) ••Metrogas Veterans c2003

A week before his 20th birthday John made his first team debut for Chelsea in a 2-1 defeat up at Leeds. They were heading for relegation from Division 1 at the time, but within a year he was nailed on at right half as they re-shaped the team ready for a promotion push. It took five years before this was achieved, but during this period John played against Charlton on a number of occasions, most memorably from his perspective being on 24th November 1981 when Chelsea edged a pulsating match at the Valley by 4-3 and he scored two goals, one a spectacular effort which simply flew into the corner of the net.

1985-86 was probably John's best season for Chelsea. They finished sixth in the First Division and he played 42 competitive games. In addition, they triumphed at Wembley in the Full Members Cup on 23rd March 1986, beating Manchester City 5-4 in front of a crowd of 67,236. The Chelsea side that day also included Colin Pates and Joe McLaughlin.

He played in the notorious 'Battle at the Bridge' on 7th May 1988, one of the dirtiest games involving a Charlton side for many years. Both teams were trying to hold off the threat of relegation and the bruising 1-1 draw was enough to give Charlton one more season in Division 1, whereas Chelsea were banished for a year before returning as Division 2 champions in 1989. John even enjoyed a second Full Members Cup triumph in 1990 with a win over Middlesbrough, but at the end of the 1990-91 season was given a free transfer and signed for Charlton on 22nd July. His debut, a 2-1 victory over Newcastle United, was the first home match played at the Boleyn Ground. The ground share with Crystal Palace was finally over and for

Charlton supporters the depressing journey to Selhurst Park was being replaced, at least for a short time, by the only slightly more pleasant experience of a trip through the Blackwall Tunnel every other weekend.

The most significant event during John's two years at Charlton was of course the return to the Valley on 5th December 1992. He had played in the six previous matches, so was understandably unhappy when he and Alan Pardew were left out for the encounter with Portsmouth, one of the places being taken by joint player manager Steve Gritt who up to that point had not started a match all season. However, he did finally get to play at the Valley for Charlton a fortnight later when he came on as a substitute and scored in the 1-1 draw with Oxford United. John's contribution to Charlton during this critical time in the club's history has often been overlooked. Everything was geared up for the return to SE7 but it was vital that results on the field were satisfactory as well. John was one of those who laid the foundation for the success which would follow over the next decade.

His second season with Charlton proved to be his last as a full time professional and his career finished as it had started, with a match against Leeds United. The Addicks earned a respectable 1-1 draw in the FA Cup on 2nd January 1993 thanks to a goal from Garry Nelson, but John was injured 10 minutes from the end and a protruding disc in his back forced him into retirement. He has since worked as a black cab taxi driver as well as serving as a match day host at both the Valley and at Stamford Bridge.

Season	Division	League		FA Cup		FL Cup		FM Cup		AI Cup		Total	
		A	G	A	G	A	G	A	G	A	G	A	G
1991-92	Division 2	36	0	3	0	0	0	1	0			40	0
1992-93	Division 1	18 (2)	3	1	0	2	0			1	0	22 (2)	3
Total		54 (2)	3	4	0	2	0	1	0	1	0	62 (2)	3

UK LEAGUE CAREER 395 games 41 goals

CHARLTON CAREER
Managers: *A Curbishley/S Gritt*
Debut: *Newcastle United (H) 18-08-1991*
V520
Finale: *Leeds United (A) 02-01-1993*

BURKETT Jack William   1968 - 69

Jack was a member of the most
successful West Ham side of all
time, winning the FA Cup in
1964 and then the European

Defender   11st 2lbs   5' 11"
Born: 21-08-1942 - Edmonton, London
Education: Downhills Junior School and Tottenham County High School.

Cup Winners Cup twelve months later. They beat Preston North End by 3-2 on 2nd May 1964
(having put paid to Charlton's chances at the Third Round stage in a somewhat one sided
contest) and then saw off the German team, TSV 1860 Munich, by 2-0 on 19th May 1965. Both
finals were played at Wembley and Jack featured at left back on each occasion.

HONOURS

England Youth International 1965 4 caps 0 goals
Tottenham Schools & Middlesex Schools
West Ham United U18 1958-59 Winners Southern Junior Floodlight Cup
West Ham United U18 1958-59 Finalists FA Youth Cup
West Ham United U18 1959-60 Finalists South East Counties League Cup
West Ham United 1963-64 Winners FA Cup

West Ham United 1964 Joint Winners FA Charity Shield
West Ham United 1964-65 Winners European Cup Winners Cup
West Ham United 1965-66 Finalists Football League Cup
Charlton Athletic Reserves 1968-69 Runners Up London Mid-Week League
St Patrick's Athletic 1971-72 Winners Leinster FA President's Cup
St Patrick's Athletic 1973-74 Finalists FAI Cup

CLUBS

Parkhurst (youth) ••West Ham United 07.58 (youth) 10.10.59 (pro) ••Charlton Athletic 12.06.68 (£10,000) ••Millwall 23.07.70 (player coach)
••Southend United 1971 (player coach) ••St Patrick's Athletic, Ireland 08.71 (player manager) ••Southend United 14.07.75 (player coach) ••Saudi Arabia
12.09.76 (youth coach) ••Orsta, Norway 01.80 (coach) ••Southend United c 07.82 (youth coach) ••Fulham 07.85 (youth coach) 1986 (ass manager)

In all, Jack spent 10 very enjoyable years at West Ham
where he had a reputation as a fast and tenacious full back
who sometimes played in an attacking role akin to a
modern day wing back. He suffered a very painful back
injury on Boxing Day 1964 against Birmingham City
which kept him encased in plaster and out of the game for
three months and although he regained his place in time for
the European final, he was left with a permanent weakness
in his back which shortened his playing career and has
caused him considerable discomfort in later life.

By the Summer of 1968 he had lost his place in the West
Ham side and after turning down a move to Wolves, signed
for Charlton on 12th June for a fee of £10,000.
Unfortunately he fell out with Eddie Firmani almost
immediately, not appreciating his strict, regimented, Italian
style of management. He hardly played in the first team and
his two years at the Valley must be viewed as a big
disappointment for all concerned. To make matters worse
there was an unacceptable delay in paying his signing-on
fee, as a result of which he demanded a meeting with
chairman Michael Gliksten and threatened the club with
legal action. The matter was resolved but Jack was by now
viewed as a troublemaker and left to rot in the Reserves
where increasingly he occupied his time coaching the young
players.

This unhappy interlude ended in May 1970 when he joined
Millwall primarily in a coaching role, although he did later

attempt a playing come-back in their Reserves. Benny
Fenton was manager during this period, but once again it
came to an abrupt conclusion after an unresolved wage
dispute.

Within days of leaving Millwall, Jack got a call from Theo
Foley who suggested that he consider a move to St Patrick's
Athletic, a League of Ireland club situated just outside
Dublin and in August 1971 they appointed him as player
manager. It proved to be a considerable culture shock as St
Pat's played on a ramshackle ground in front of crowds of
under a thousand, while to make matters worse the Irish
troubles had flared up again. Three of his teammates were
prone to sudden unexplained absences and it was only
when he spotted a gun and a balaclava among their training
kit that he realised they were active members of the IRA.
He got stuck into his new role and during his four years at
the helm they adopted a more professional approach and
were rewarded by improved league placings and in 1974
reached the final of the FAI Cup only to lose 3-1 to Finn
Harps. During his time in Dublin Jack also worked as a
part-time coach to the Republic of Ireland team as they
attempted unsuccessfully to qualify for the 1974 World
Cup.

After a spell coaching at cash strapped Southend United,
Jack travelled out to Saudi Arabia on 12th September 1976
to work with that country's U20 squad. This was a highly
paid position and he was flown to matches in a private jet,

but in contrast he also witnessed a man being beheaded in a public execution at Jeddah. In 1980, he moved to a remote part of Norway as player manager of Orsta, before finally returning home for coaching jobs with Southend (again) and then Fulham, where he stayed long enough to be promoted to assistant manager.

In January 1991, Jack accepted the position of Regional Youth Co-ordinator with the PFA and worked in that role for 14 years up to retirement. He has since endured extensive health problems in the form of skin cancer, a heart attack and the long term effects of his old back injury. He contributed towards a biography, 'The Jack Burkett Story' by Terry Roper, that was published in 2009.

Season	Division	League		FA Cup		FL Cup		Total	
		A	G	A	G	A	G	A	G
1968-69	Division 2	5	0	0	0	0	0	5	0
1969-70	Division 2	3	0	0	0	0	0	3	0
Total		8	0	0	0	0	0	8	0

UK LEAGUE CAREER 150 games 4 goals

CHARLTON CAREER
Managers: *E Firmani, T Foley*
Debut: *Millwall (H) 10-08-1968*
V341
Finale: *Cardiff City (A) 20-12-1969*

BURLISON Robert Lyle   1946

Forward
Born: 29-03-1920 - Elswick, Northumberland
Died: 16-02-1987 - Barnet, Hertfordshire

A right winger who signed for Charlton shortly before the outbreak of war in 1939., Bob's only first team appearance came more than seven years later in a 2-0 win at Leeds, a match in which he lined up alongside eight of the team that would bring home the FA Cup at the end of 1946-47. There were several contenders for the outside right slot at the start of that, the first post-war league season, including Les Fell who had played in the Cup Final of 1946. Unfortunately Bob was unable to convince Jimmy Seed that he was the man for the job and it was Gordon Hurst who went on to wear the number seven shirt and share the headlines when Charlton enjoyed their greatest success just seven months later.

CLUBS
Horden Colliery Welfare c1938 ••Charlton Athletic 03.06.39 (pro)

Horden Colliery was situated 13 miles to the east of Durham and in the 1930s they had a thriving football team which competed in the North Eastern League where the opposition included the reserve teams of clubs such as Sunderland and Middlesbrough. Bob's father was employed as a stone man at the colliery, whilst he worked as a plumber and also turned out on the wing for Horden Colliery Welfare FC. Charlton manager Jimmy Seed still had strong family connections in the area and when Bob signed for Charlton in June 1939, a donation of £10 was made to his former club.

Bob made three second team appearances before the war

intervened and later went on to be leading goalscorer for Charlton Reserves in 1947-48, but never got another chance with the first team. Freed by the club in June 1948, there were arrangements in hand for a move to Crystal Palace, but a cartilage operation a month later scuppered the deal and appears to have finished his football career. He had married in 1942 and settled in Barnet where he remained for the rest of his life, working as a telecommunications packing supervisor. Bob passed away in Barnet General Hospital at the age of 66.

Season	Division	League		FA Cup		Total	
		A	G	A	G	A	G
1946-47	Division 1	1	0	0	0	1	0
Total		1	0	0	0	1	0

UK LEAGUE CAREER 1 game 0 goals

CHARLTON CAREER
Managers: *J Seed*
Debut: *Leeds United (A) 04-09-1946*
V216

BURMAN Anthony Paul   1976 - 78

It has been stated that Tony Burman has been at Dartford for longer than the Queen Elizabeth Bridge and in truth he has proved to be an even more permanent structure. A promising young forward who did not quite make the grade at Charlton, he went on to become 'Mr Dartford' and after playing in excess of 500 matches for the club, had two spells as manager, including a period of nearly 14 years between 2005 and 2018 when he became one of the longest serving managers in the UK. In all he has been connected with Dartford for more than 30 years and a director continuously since 2004.

Forward   11st 0lbs   5' 8"
Born: 03-06-1958 - Stockwell, London
Education: Beaufoy School, Lambeth.

HONOURS

Dartford 1980-81 Winners Southern League Southern Division   Dartford 1983-84 Winners Southern League Premier Division

HONOURS AS MANAGER

Dartford 1994-95 Finalists Kent League Cup   Dartford 2009-10 Winners Isthmian League Premier Division
Dartford 1995-96 Runners Up Kent League   Dartford 2010-11 & 2015-16 Winners Kent Senior Cup
Dartford 1995-96 Winners Kent Senior Trophy   Dartford 2011-12 Promoted Play Offs Conference South
Dartford 2007-08 Winners Isthmian League Division 1 North

CLUBS

Queens Park Rangers (youth) ••Charlton Athletic 26.08.76 (pro) ••Dartford 02.02.79 (£2,000) ••Leytonstone- Ilford 1987 (free) ••Bromley 1988 (free) ••Erith & Belvedere 1989 (free) ••Dartford 1990 (free) 02.93 (manager) •Phoenix Sports 01.02 (player coach) ••Dartford 25.01.05 (manager) ••Dartford 08.19 (interim manager)

Before Dartford there was Charlton however and Tony made his first team debut at the Den in a less than festive local derby on 27th December 1976. Derek Hales had been sold to Derby County two weeks earlier and his were very large boots for the youngster to fill. He lined up at inside right and in front of an excitable holiday crowd, scored the equalising goal in the 88th minute against Gordon Jago's Millwall. The final score was 1-1 and this was an almost dream like debut for Tony who did enough to retain his place for a run of 10 matches. It was a difficult time for Charlton and by mid-February the more experienced Peter Hunt was switched into the number 8 shirt, but Tony did play in the return fixture against Millwall at the Valley on Good Friday which resulted in a nervy 3-2 home win.

He saw less first team action in 1977-78 and certainly had no luck at all in front of goal. The arrival of Martin Robinson from Tottenham in February probably sealed his fate and he made his last two first team appearances in April, eventually completing the transfer to Dartford in February 1979.

From then on he was a permanent fixture for the Darts as they gained two promotions, the most notable of which came in 1983-84 when they topped the Premier Division of the Southern League and moved up to just one division below the Football League. They did even better the

following season, finishing third in the Alliance Premier League, but were prevented from entering the ballot for election into the Football League as their ground did not meet the required standard. This was the highest league placing achieved by Dartford in their entire history.

Tony's first year as Dartford manager could not have been more traumatic. The club had become financially insolvent. They had been forced to sell off their ground at Watling Street to pay creditors and had to withdraw from the Southern League just four matches into the 1992-93 season. He took over in February 1993 and steered the club back up the football pyramid, while obliged to spend more than 13 years in exile until their new stadium at Princes Park was completed in November 2006.

Among the league and cup honours clocked up by Dartford during Tony's time at the helm were two wins in the Kent Senior Cup in 2010-11 and 2015-16. Their opponents in the 2016 final were Charlton, who fielded a young, inexperienced but highly talented eleven, which included Joe Aribo, Anfernee Dijksteel and Brendan Hanlan. The Dartford side were physically stronger and more savvy and ran out comfortable winners 3-1, Charlton having only a goal from Josh Umerah to show for their efforts.

A resident of Crayford, Tony has successfully mixed his

football activities with his business running a transport company. He officially stood down as Dartford manager in May 2018, but remains a club director and filled in as

caretaker boss for two months in 2019. Nobody would bet against him getting further involved again in the future.

Season	Division	League		FA Cup		FL Cup		Total	
		A	G	A	G	A	G	A	G
1976-77	Division 2	11	3	2	1	0	0	13	4
1977-78	Division 2	5 (3)	0	0	0	0	0	5 (3)	0
Total		16 (3)	3	2	1	0	0	18 (3)	4

UK LEAGUE CAREER 19 games 3 goals

CHARLTON CAREER
Managers: *A Nelson*
Debut: *Millwall (A) 27-12-1976*
V400
Finale: *Brighton & Hove Albion (A) 25-04-1978*

BURNS Anthony John   1969 - 70

Goalkeeper   12st 11lbs   6' 0"
Born: 27-03-1944 - Edenbridge, Kent

Nobody who saw Tony Burns play during his short stay at Charlton would fail to remember him. He was a competent goalkeeper, but what stayed in the memory was his enormous throw which was as long and as accurate as a kicked clearance. He would regularly throw to the feet of a teammate positioned beyond the halfway line and would turn defence into attack in the blink of an eye. He enjoyed a long and varied career as player, coach and manager and was still working as a goalkeeping coach with Gillingham well beyond his 70th birthday.

HONOURS

South West Kent Schools

Crystal Palace 1976-77 Promoted Division 3

HONOURS AS MANAGER

Gravesend & Northfleet 1988-89 Runners Up Southern League Southern

Division

CLUBS

Crystal Palace (youth) ••Tonbridge 1961 (youth) ••Arsenal 14.03.63 (pro) ••Brighton & Hove Albion 22.07.66 (£3,000) ••Charlton Athletic 08.03.69 (free) ••Tonbridge 07.70 (free) ••Durban United, South Africa 01.71 (free) ••Maritzburg, South Africa 1973 (free) ••Crystal Palace 16.10.73 (free) ••Brentford 13.01.77 (loan) ••Memphis Rogues, USA 28.03.78 (loan) ••Plymouth Argyle 14.08.78 (free) ••Tonbridge Angels 01.79 (free) ••Dartford 1979 (free) ••Hastings Town 09.79 (loan) ••Tonbridge Angels 08.80 (manager) ••Gravesend & Northfleet 12.82 (manager) ••Tonbridge Angels 08.89 (manager) ••Millwall 07.92 (coach) ••Tonbridge Angels 2000 (director of football) 11.01 (caretaker manager) ••Millwall 20. 04.06 (caretaker manager) ••Crystal Palace 07.06 (coach) ••Millwall 11.07 (coach) ••Gillingham 02.07.14 (coach)

The start of Tony's career was probably unique. Spotted while playing for Tonbridge, he was offered an under 18 youth contract to join Arsenal, but was aged almost 19 at the time. Not wanting to lose his chance, he falsified the documents and signed anyway. By the time this deception was spotted, he had proved his worth and the matter was overlooked by the club. He made his debut in a 3-2 win against Burnley on 17th October 1964 and went on to make another 30 appearances before competition for places squeezed him out and he transferred to Brighton, where he remained for nearly three years.

His next move brought him to the Valley and when interviewed in 2020 he wrongly recalled having 'Won every game. Might have drawn one'. In fact his memory was well off track, because of the 11 matches played for Charlton, he

was only on the winning side once and that was on his debut, a 4-0 victory over a Blackburn Rovers team that included Eamonn Rogers and in which Dennis Booth, Matt Tees, Bob Curtis and Alan Campbell were the scorers. After that he played in four drawn games and six defeats, his final outing being a 5-1 drubbing at Portsmouth. In the same interview, Tony recalled being offered a new contract by Theo Foley, but turned it down as he would not accept only a £5 per week increase in wages.

Instead, he appeared briefly for Tonbridge, but only played two games for them before joining the exodus of English players heading out to play in South Africa. He first joined Durban United where his teammates included Rodney Green and then moved on to Maritzburg in the province of KwaZulu-Natal. He was part of the UK All Stars, who were the first all-white team to play in the township of Soweto under manager Malcolm Allison and through him, he landed a contract to join Crystal Palace when he returned to the UK in October 1973.

This was the most successful period in Tony's playing career and he helped Palace to promotion from Division 3 in 1976-77, before eventually following Allison out to the USA where he played in the North American Soccer League for the newly formed Memphis Rogues. A broken leg kept him away from the action and when he returned home he signed for Plymouth Argyle which turned out to be his final Football League club. He played eight games, but was second choice 'keeper and in January 1979 went

back to Tonbridge, (now re-named Tonbridge Angels), for a third time.

His managerial career commenced the following year and included more than six years with Gravesend & Northfleet, during which he guided them to promotion from the Southern League, Southern Division in 1989. Tony spent the best part of 20 years as goalkeeping coach at Millwall and for a month in 2006, he and Alan McLeary held the reins as joint caretaker managers. Early on he had worked for an engineering company in Edenbridge and later ran his own painting and decorating business, but football always seemed to come first for the man with the amazing throw.

Season	Division	League		FA Cup		FL Cup		Total	
		A	G	A	G	A	G	A	G
1968-69	Division 2	2	0	0	0	0	0	2	0
1969-70	Division 2	8	0	1	0	0	0	9	0
Total		10	0	1	0	0	0	11	0

UK LEAGUE CAREER 199 games 0 goals

CHARLTON CAREER
Managers: *E Firmani, T Foley*
Debut: *Blackburn Rovers (H) 15-04-1969*
V344
Finale: *Portsmouth (A) 31-01-1970*

BURNS Leslie George Henry   1967 - 68

Coincidentally there were two defenders named Leslie Burns playing football in the South London / Kent area

Defender   11st 12lbs   6' 1"
Born: 22-06-1944 - Shepherds Bush, London
Education: Park Walk Primary School, Chelsea & Henry Compton School, Fulham.

during the 1960s. One made more than 600 appearances and captained Dartford during an impressive 14-year career, but our Les played just eight games after signing from Carshalton United in February 1967. He turned professional a month after joining Charlton on amateur terms and as a result, a donation of £250 was paid to Carshalton in compensation.

HONOURS
West London Schools

CLUBS
Tooting & Mitcham United ••Carshalton United ••Charlton Athletic 10.02.67 (amateur) 16.03.67 (pro) ••Guildford City

Charlton were having a torrid time in the lower reaches of Division 2 when Les arrived. He performed well in the Reserves during a 1-0 win at Leyton Orient and was rushed into the first team only two days into his professional career for a very important relegation battle at Bury on 18th March. He was tasked with man marking the highly experienced Alex Dawson and did a fine job, despite the match ending in a 2-1 defeat. Ian King, the regular centre half, was injured during the later stages of the season which gave Les further opportunities to play in what were very much high-pressure games.

With two league matches remaining, Charlton were only one point above second from bottom Northampton Town when the two clubs met at the Valley on 6th May 1967. Included in the Cobblers' team were both Theo Foley and Graham Moore, but with the tall, fair haired Burns playing alongside John Keirs at the heart of the Addicks defence, they triumphed 3-0, courtesy of two goals from 33-year-old Eddie Firmani and one from Alan Campbell. Les helped Charlton keep another clean sheet in the final fixture, a 1-0 victory against Birmingham City, so the club ended up in the comparative safety of 19th place, five points clear of the drop.

Having made such an exciting start to his professional career, it would have been reasonable to have expected more of the same, but in fact it was all but over. He did play in a Kent Challenge Cup match against Millwall at the Valley on 8th May in which both clubs fielded strong teams. Unusually Charlton defeated their South London rivals on this occasion, the 3-2 scoreline featuring goals from Rodney Green (2) and Keith Peacock.

Season	Division	League		FA Cup		FL Cup		Total	
		A	G	A	G	A	G	A	G
1966-67	Division 2	7	0	0	0	0	0	7	0
1967-68	Division 2	1	0	0	0	0	0	1	0
Total		8	0	0	0	0	0	8	0

UK LEAGUE CAREER 8 games 0 goals

In June 1967 Charlton signed Paul Went from Leyton Orient and that spelled the end for Les. Went became the mainstay of the defence for the next five years and in the whole of 1967-68 Les only got two more chances in the first team. One came in a friendly match against the Swedish club, I F Kamraterna and the other at Huddersfield filling in for an injured Brian Kinsey.

He was granted a free transfer in May 1968 and departed to Guildford City. His later activities are unknown.

CHARLTON CAREER
Managers: *R Stokoe, E Firmani*
Debut: *Bury (A) 18-03-1967*
V329
Finale: *Huddersfield Town (A) 30-03-1968*

BURRIDGE Peter John   1965 - 67

Forward, Midfield   11st 6lbs   5' 9"
Born: 30-12-1933 - Harlow, Essex
Education: Fawbert & Barnard School, Harlow.

The 35 league goals that Peter scored for Millwall in season 1960-61 created a post-war club record that has now stood for more than 60 years. Short and wiry in build, he was surprisingly good in the air, but would often seem to amble aimlessly around the pitch until suddenly bursting to life with a deft pass or a blistering shot on goal. He spent 18 months at the Valley later in his career and was still capable of pulling off something unexpected, but had moved back from inside forward to wing half by then and was no longer the goal scoring predator of his youth.

HONOURS

Essex Youth XI
Millwall 1961-62 Winners Division 4

Crystal Palace 1963-64 Runners Up Division 3

CLUBS

Harlow Town c 1946 (youth) ••Bishop's Stortford (youth) ••Tottenham Hotspur (youth) ••Walthamstow Avenue (amateur) ••Hitchin Town (amateur) ••Bishop's Stortford (amateur) ••Barnet 1957 (amateur) ••Leyton Orient 12.04.58 (pro) ••Millwall 12.08.60 (£2,000) ••Crystal Palace 01.07.62 (£8,000) ••Charlton Athletic 25.11.65 (£5,500) ••Bedford Town 05.67 (free)

Peter did not become a professional footballer until the age of 24. By then he had learned his craft in the amateur game, having started out in the Spartan League with Harlow Town when he was just 13 and then after leaving school had attracted the attention of Tottenham, whilst at the same time training as an apprentice plumber. He played one season with Walthamstow Avenue and during his National Service in the RAF, turned out for Hitchin Town or Bishop's Stortford whenever available. He spent most of the 1957-58 season playing for Barnet in the Athenian League and finally arrived as a professional in April 1958 by signing for Leyton Orient.

His Football League debut came on 27th December 1958

at Stoke City and although Orient went down 3-2, Peter announced his arrival by scoring in the very first minute of the match. Despite such a promising start, first team opportunities were few and far between and in August 1960 he was sold to Millwall. Orient's manager at the time was Les Gore, who later served as caretaker manager at Charlton for a few matches.

After his record breaking first season with Millwall, Peter hit a further 23 league goals in 1961-62, including seven in one spell of four games. They stormed to the Division 4 title but then rather surprisingly sold their leading scorer to Crystal Palace, which proved a somewhat foolish move. He continued to find the net regularly and when Palace gained promotion from Division 3 in 1963-64, Peter finished up joint leading scorer alongside Cliff Holton, on 20 goals apiece. That Palace side also included Don Townsend, Fred Lucas, John Sewell, Eddie Werge and Brian Whitehouse. By the time he moved to Charlton in November 1965, Peter's best days were behind him but he was still capable of some classy displays and the occasional goal. After going one down to Birmingham City on 19th February 1966, Peter and Keith Peacock changed the game with first half

strikes that turned defeat into a 2-1 victory. He played less in his second season though and left for a final playing season at Bedford Town in May 1967.

For 21 years Peter was the publican at the Bull in Sawbridgeworth, but later came out of the pub trade to work at a friend's printing company in Hackney. Now retired, he remains active and in 2020 was in the news after receiving an award for 50 years membership of Bishop's Stortford Golf Club.

Season	Division	League		FA Cup		FL Cup		Total	
		A	G	A	G	A	G	A	G
1965-66	Division 2	25	3	1	0	0	0	26	3
1966-67	Division 2	17 (2)	1	1	0	1	0	19 (2)	1
Total		42 (2)	4	2	0	1	0	45 (2)	4

UK LEAGUE CAREER 250 games 106 goals

CHARLTON CAREER
Managers: *R Stokoe*
Debut: *Southampton (H) 04-12-1965*
V314
Finale: *Hull City (H) 22-04-1967*

BURRILL Frederick   1923 - 24

Frank represented East London Schools and in 1911 joined his local team, West Ham United, making his debut for them in the Southern League on 2nd March 1912 against Queens Park Rangers. He stayed with the Hammers for nearly five years playing alongside teammates Bronco Burton and Joe Hughes. After the war he switched to Southend United, another Southern League club, where his fellow striker was Dick Upex. All of Burrill, Burton, Hughes and Upex would turn out in the colours of Charlton Athletic before too long.

Forward
Born: 20-04-1894 - Manor Park, London
Died: 07-04-1962 - Whitechapel, London
Education: Fourth Avenue School, East Ham.

HONOURS

East London Schools   Wolverhampton Wanderers 1920-21 Finalists FA Cup

CLUBS

South Weald (youth) ••West Ham United 1911 ••Southend United 1919 ••Wolverhampton Wanderers 05.20 (£800) ••Charlton Athletic 23.07.23 (£200) ••Walsall 07.24

In May 1920 Frank was transferred to Wolverhampton Wanderers, then a Second Division club, for a fee of £800. The league form was indifferent, although he scored all three goals against Stoke in a 3-3 draw on 26th February 1921, but it was in the FA Cup that they enjoyed a season to remember. Two First Division clubs were dispatched as they advanced to the final and on 23rd April he lined up before a crowd of 72,805 at Stamford Bridge, against Tottenham Hotspur, who included Jimmy Seed in their star studded team. Wembley would not be built for a further two years. Wolves fought hard but went down 1-0, but Frank did have some consolation as the medals that day were presented by King George V.
He remained with Wolves for three seasons before joining

Charlton in July 1923 and went straight into the first team at inside right. He started well enough, scoring on his debut against Aberdare Athletic and notching two against Southend in September, but as the season progressed he appeared less and less often. Charlton left the Valley just before Christmas but Frank only played once at the Mount, his final game for the club against Brighton in March. Interestingly an FA Cup tie against his old club Wolves had been switched back to the Valley on 2nd February by special permission of the FA, as it was felt that the Mount could not accommodate the crowd of 20,057. Frank was in the Charlton team which battled to a 0-0 draw that day, only to lose the replay 1-0.
After just one season in SE7, he transferred to Walsall and

enjoyed a successful final season in the Football League, scoring 14 goals in 39 league matches. Frank, who was also a useful club cricketer with Leigh on Sea CC, passed away back in East London at the age of 67.

Season	Division	League		FA Cup		Total	
		A	G	A	G	A	G
1923-24	Divison 3 (S)	13	4	2	0	15	4
Total		13	4	2	0	15	4

UK LEAGUE CAREER 113 games 34 goals

CHARLTON CAREER
Managers: *W Rayner*
Debut: *Aberdare Athletic (H) 25-08-1923*
V047
Finale: *Brighton & Hove Albion (H) 22-03-1924*

BURSTOW Mason Paul James   2021 -

Forward   12st 6lbs   6' 2"
Born: 04-08-2003 - Woolwich, London
Education: Woolwich Polytechnic School, Thamesmead.

It would be hard to improve upon Mason's introduction to senior football. Just 18 years old and two months into his professional career, the young striker was named among the substitutes for the Football League Trophy tie against Crawley Town at the Valley on 31st August 2021. After 80 minutes and with the Addicks in a comfortable 4-1 lead, He was brought on in place of Elliot Lee. Just two minutes later he stooped and adroitly steered Charles Clayden's cross into the net with his very first touch of the ball. As if that was not sufficient and as the clock was moving towards stoppage time, he drove forward and laid off a precision pass to Josh Davison who then scored his second of the match and wrapped up an impressive 6-1 victory.

HONOURS
Blackheath District Schools
Charlton Athletic U18 2020-21 Winners PD League 2 South

Charlton Athletic U18 2020-21 Runners Up PD National League 2

CLUBS
Welling United 2019 (youth) ••Maidstone United 08.19 (youth) ••Charlton Athletic 26.09.20 (youth) 02.07.21 (pro) ••Chelsea 31.01.22 (£1.6 million) ••Charlton Athletic 01.02.22 (loan)

Mason has already made quite an impact in his young footballing life. At the age of 17, he was competing for Maidstone United in their U23 team and during February 2020 twice had trials for Chelsea at their Cobham training ground. After joining Charlton in the September, it soon became clear that he is a hard-working forward with an eye for goal and he established himself in the U18 side during the second half of 2020-21 as they won the Professional Development League 2 South by a 10 point margin. In the play off semi-final he scored twice as Birmingham City were defeated 3-2 and he did so while showing great composure in front of goal.

Undoubtedly Mason's first team debut came sooner than expected and he took his chance with considerable maturity but it was still a shock when after only seven league appearances, he was sold to Chelsea on transfer deadline day in January 2022 for an undisclosed fee, believed to be £1.6 million plus add-ons. Time will tell how far he can go in the game, but a loan agreement with Chelsea allowed him to remain with Charlton until the end of 2021-22.

UK LEAGUE CAREER 0 games 0 goals

CHARLTON CAREER
Managers: *N Adkins, J Jackson*
Debut: *Crawley Town (H) (sub) 31-08-2021*
V932

BURTON Deon John   2008 - 10

Phil Parkinson had only been Charlton's caretaker manager for four days when he completed the signing of much travelled striker, Deon Burton. The club had not

Forward   11st 6lbs   5' 8"
Born: 25-10-1976 - Reading, Berkshire
Education: Meadway Comprehensive School, Reading.

won for nine league matches and were already looking like candidates for relegation. Despite Deon's best efforts they then failed to win the next nine as well, by which time they were rock bottom of the Championship where they remained for the rest of the season. He was only able to contribute two goals (one a penalty) until the final match of the campaign, when on 3rd May 2009 he grabbed a hat-trick against Norwich City in an unexpected 4-2 win at the Valley. Unfortunately it was too little and too late.

HONOURS

Jamaica International 1997-09 62 caps 13 goals
Jamaica Sportsman Of The Year 1997
Stoke City 2001-02 Promoted Play Offs Division 2

Portsmouth 2002-03 Winners Division 1
Gillingham 2012-13 Winners League Two
Scunthorpe United Runners Up League Two

CLUBS

Portsmouth (youth) 15.02.94 (pro) ••Cardiff City 24.12.96 (loan) ••Derby County 09.08.97 (£1 million) ••Barnsley 14.12.98 (loan) ••Stoke City 21.02.02 (loan) ••Portsmouth 09.08.02 (loan) 12.12.02 (£250,000) ••Walsall 12.09.03 (loan) ••Swindon Town 17.10.03 (loan) ••Brentford 04.08.04 (free) ••Rotherham United 01.08.05 (free) ••Sheffield Wednesday 02.01.06 (£110,000) ••Charlton Athletic 27.11.08 (loan) 02.01.09 (free) ••Gabala FK, Azerbaijan 15.07.10 (free) ••Gillingham 07.08.12 (free) ••Scunthorpe United 22.07.13 (free) ••York City 30.10.14 (loan) ••Eastleigh 05.02.15 (free) ••Brackley Town 08.08.15 (free) ••Birmingham City 08.15 (coach) ••Worcester City 12.09.15 (free) ••West Bromwich Albion 07.18 (coach)

Deon's erratic career commenced at Portsmouth where he signed professional in 1994, at the age of 17. By season 1995-96 he was in their first team and single handedly sank Charlton 2-1 with goals either side of half-time when they met at Fratton Park on 2nd March. A young striker will always attract attention and the following year he joined Derby County in exchange for a £1 million fee and this ushered in the most satisfying period of his footballing life. Derby had just moved into their new Pride Park stadium and for a time there was a buzz about the place as they competed in the top half of the Premier League. When Charlton were the visitors on 20th February 1999, things went less well for Deon however and goals from Andy Hunt and Martin Pringle ensured an unanticipated 2-0 scoreline for the then relegation threatened Addicks. As time went on, Deon got less and less game time at Derby. He spent a couple of months on loan with Stoke City at the tail-end of 2001-02 season and played upfront for them, along with Chris Iwelumo, when they defeated Brentford 2-0 in the Division 2 Play Offs final at Cardiff on 11th May, netting the opening goal himself. In 2002, he moved back to Portsmouth, initially on loan, but after the move was made permanent he found goals hard to come by and was a marginal player as they clinched promotion to the Premier League in 2002-03. He moved on again and spent 2004-05 with Brentford where he re-discovered his

goal scoring form.
A free transfer took him to Rotherham United in August 2005, but despite a hat-trick against Blackpool, he did not settle and agitated for another move, eventually joining Sheffield Wednesday, where he appeared more settled and played regularly, at least for the next couple of years. 2006-07 was his most successful season and playing in the same side as Madjid Bougherra he finished joint leading goalscorer, but from then on found the net less often and in November 2008 he signed for Charlton, initially on loan, with the move converted to a permanent transfer two months later.
A seasoned international, Deon had played for Jamaica since 1997, including the FIFA World Cup finals in France and it had been his four goals in five WC qualifying games that earned him the accolade of Jamaican Sportsman of the Year in 1997. In all he gained 62 international caps, but only the final one came after his move to London SE7. If his first season as a Charlton player was scarred by relegation, he did have an altogether better time in 2009-10 when he netted 13 league goals (the best return of his entire career) and finished as the club's leading goalscorer.
His next move was a surprise to everyone and saw Deon join Gabala FK in the Azerbaijan Premier League which must have been something of a culture shock after the delights of South East London. This was followed by brief

encounters with both Gillingham and Scunthorpe, where his vast experience helped to secure promotions for both clubs. After that his playing career started to wind down and in 2015 he accepted a coaching role with Birmingham

City. Three years later he switched to West Bromwich Albion where he is currently in charge of their U23 side as well as running the Deon Burton Training Academy.

Season	Division	League		FA Cup		FL Cup		FL Trophy		Play Offs		Total	
		A	G	A	G	A	G	A	G	A	G	A	G
2008-09 (R)	Championship	12 (8)	5	3	0	0	0					15 (8)	5
2009-10	League One	35 (4)	13	0 (1)	0	0 (1)	0	0 (1)	0	2	1	37 (7)	14
Total		47 (12)	18	3 (1)	0	0 (1)	0	0 (1)	0	2	1	52 (15)	19

UK LEAGUE CAREER 544 games 125 goals

CHARLTON CAREER
Managers: *P Parkinson*
Debut: *Southampton (H)*
29-11-2008
V677
Finale: *Swansea Town (H)*
17-05-2010

BURTON Frank James 'Bronco'   1921 - 24

Defender   12st 0lbs   6' 1"
Born: 07-09-1890 - Cheadle, Cheshire
Died: 06-07-1967 - Auckland, New Zealand

The first thing to know about Frank 'Bronco 'Burton is that he was not born in Luapango, Mexico as has been claimed down the years in a whole series of reference books and websites. If true, it would have made him Charlton's first overseas player, but unfortunately no such place exists in Mexico, nor anywhere else for that matter. It was only in recent years that this mystery was finally solved after his family was consulted and his birth certificate produced. He was in fact born in Cheadle, maybe a little less romantic, but probably more believable. One other non-event relates to a modest but strategically placed road called Frank Burton Close which is to be found within walking distance of the Valley. Despite claims to the contrary, it was named, not after our Frank, but in homage to an eminent Labour councillor with the same name who is remembered for his generous charity work.

HONOURS

Charlton Athletic 1922-23 Winners London Challenge Cup
West Ham United 1919 & 1920 Winners London FA Professional Charity

Fund Cup
Real Oviedo 1927-28 Winners Asturian Championship

CLUBS

Kilburn (amateur) ••Queens Park Rangers 1910 (amateur) ••West Ham United c07.12 (pro) ••Charlton Athletic 22.08.21 ••Grays Thurrock United 05.25 (player trainer) ••Real Oviedo, Spain 20.08.27 (player manager)

Frank was a long legged, slightly ungainly full back who joined West Ham United in the Summer of 1912. He made his debut on 5th October against Plymouth Argyle and appeared in 50 Southern League matches during the next three seasons. He was very popular with the crowd who bestowed upon him the nickname of 'Bronco' because of his loping gait and on-field contortions which were likened to the bucking of a cowboy's horse.

When the Great War came, he served in the 1st Royal Fusiliers between December 1914 and July 1920 reaching the rank of sergeant and fought at Ypres, the Somme and Cambrai. Frank was wounded six times and in 1916 was treated for shrapnel wounds at the Welsh Metropolitan War Hospital in Whitworth. He eventually received the Victory and General Service medal, and the French decorations,

Medaille Militaire and the Croix de Guerre, yet still found the time to turn out for West Ham in 40 wartime matches in the London Combination.

West Ham were elected into the Football League for season 1919-20 but did not get off to a very promising start, losing their second match 7-0 to Barnsley. Six changes were made for their next fixture at Lincoln City on 6th September 1919 with Frank coming in at centre half. He scored a late penalty as the Hammers secured a much improved 4-1 victory, their first as a Football League club. He was soon switched to left back though and racked up a total of 64 post-war league appearances by the end of 1920-21.

He was transferred to Charlton in August 1921 and made his debut in the third match of their first season as a Football League club, just as he had done at West Ham.

The match on 3rd September 1921 was at Exeter City but ended 1-0 to the Grecians. Frank nailed down his place in the Charlton defence though and went on to play more than 100 league and cup games, usually at right back, over the next four seasons. He fell out with manager Walter Rayner early on and was briefly transfer listed at a proposed fee of £500, but they soon made up and he was a key member of the FA Cup giant killing side in 1922-23, when they defeated three First Division clubs before narrowly falling to Bolton Wanderers 1-0 in the quarter final.
In May 1925 he joined Grays Thurrock United as player-trainer along with goalkeeper Freddy Wood and two years later at the age of 37 became manager (and occasional

player) with Spanish club Real Oviedo, steering them to the Regional Championship of Asturias in 1927-28.
Frank's first wife Florence had died in 1918 at the age of 22, but by 1939 he and his second wife Amy were living in the Hornchurch area of Essex while he worked for a sugar distribution company. He later emigrated to New Zealand where he died in 1967 at the age of 76. His remains were interred at the Birkenhead-Glenfield Cemetery in Auckland, where today a plaque makes proud reference to his time as a Royal Fusilier.

Season	Division	League		FA Cup		Total	
		A	G	A	G	A	G
1921-22	Divison 3 (S)	25	0			25	0
1922-23	Divison 3 (S)	37	0	6	0	43	0
1923-24	Divison 3 (S)	19	0	4	0	23	0
1924-25	Divison 3 (S)	15	0	0	0	15	0
Total		96	0	10	0	106	0

UK LEAGUE CAREER 160 games 2 goals

CHARLTON CAREER
Managers: *W Rayner*
Debut: *Exeter City (A) 03-09-1921*
V015
Finale: *Bournemouth & Boscombe Athletic (H) 08-11-1924*

BUTLER Charles Reginald   1930

Charlton were sitting comfortably in the top half of Division 2 at the end of January 1930. In fact, they were on a seven game unbeaten run in cup and league, but were obliged to travel to Reading on 1st February without both Dai Astley and Jack Pugsley, the latter on international duty for Wales. This did however provide the opportunity for inside forward Charlie Butler to replace Astley in what turned out to be his only appearance for the first team. The match finished 3-1 in favour of the home team, with Charlton's goal being scored by Fred Whitlow. Seven days later when they lined up against Millwall, both Pugsley and Astley had returned and Charlie's time as a Charlton first team player was over.

Forward, Midfield   10st 10lbs   5' 10"
Born: 20-03-1908 - Barry, South Glamorgan
Died: 07-07-1983 - Hendon, London

HONOURS
Wales Schoolboys

CLUBS
Barry 1926 ••Charlton Athletic 25.02.28 (pro) ••Chatham Town 1928 (loan) •Sittingbourne 12.09.29 (loan) ••Cardiff City 31.07.30 ••Thames 10.10.30 ••Bath City 08.31 ••Blackburn Rovers 30.11.31 ••Bath City 1932 (loan) ••New Brighton 11.08.33 ••Oldham Athletic 04.07.35 (£200) ••Tranmere Rovers 01.07.36 ••Tunbridge Wells Rangers 03.37 ••Cork, S Ireland 15.07.37 ••South Liverpool 12.37

He arrived from South Wales in February 1928 and joined Charlton on a weekly wage of £3 10s 0d, (£3.50), but appears to have spent at least part of his time playing on loan in the Southern League for first Chatham Town and then Sittingbourne. He left the club in 1930 and after a brief flirtation with Cardiff City, signed for the East

London side, Thames in October 1930. They were struggling at the foot of Division 3 (South) and threw him straight into the team for their next three matches, but despite netting in a 4-3 defeat at Exeter, he was not called on again.
His career did not really stabilise until he moved to New

Brighton in August 1933, where he got a run of matches, mainly at left half. They had a somewhat porous defence however and let in six against both Gateshead and Crewe and endured a whopping 8-0 thrashing from Accrington Stanley, which was the biggest win in their history. Both Billy Lennox and Tommy Wyper were playing for Stanley that day and Lennox got two of the goals. In Charlie's second season they tightened up at the back and had a less traumatic time and he scored the winner when they finally disposed of Southport 2-1 in an FA Cup second replay at Goodison Park.

After two seasons his stock must have risen because Oldham Athletic paid a fee of £200 to take him to Boundary Park, but only a year later in July he was on the move again to his final Football League club, Tranmere

Rovers. where he played just once, a 2-1 defeat against Hartlepools United on 5th September 1936. Charlie spent five months with League of Ireland club Cork, but arrived as they were sinking financially and struggling to even pay for travel to away games. He stuck it out until December 1937, but only two months after he departed, the club was forced into voluntary liquidation.

A career as a professional footballer in the years between the wars was hard and there was no big money to be earned. Little is known about Charlie's later life, but he had married in Bath during 1931 and eight years later was living in Greenwich and earning his living as a car wash worker. He died in Edgware General Hospital at the age of 75 and was cremated in Barnet on 14th July 1983.

Season	Division	League		FA Cup		Total	
		A	G	A	G	A	G
1929-30	Division 2	1	0	0	0	1	0
Total		1	0	0	0	1	0

CHARLTON CAREER
Managers: *A Lindon, A MacFarlane*
Debut: *Reading (A) 01-02-1930*
V132

UK LEAGUE CAREER 87 games 1 goal

BUTT Harold Herbert   1933 - 35

Forward   10st 0lbs   5' 6"
Born: 03-03-1910 - Bristol
Died: 10-11-1988 - Bristol

The signing of Harry Butt was a classic example of Jimmy Seed's dynamic managerial style. Charlton played two FA Cup ties against Bath City in the last week of November 1933 and Harry featured at inside left in both games. He must have shown up well in contrast to George Biswell, the Charlton number 10, as a deal was quickly struck and a fee of £160 agreed between the clubs. Harry signed for Charlton on 30th November, the day after the second match, at a weekly wage of £5 plus a signing on fee of £10. The transfer was registered with the Football League, effective 1st December and the following day he made his Charlton debut in the 3-1 away win against Clapton Orient.

HONOURS
Bath City 1932-33 Winners Southern League, Western Division

CLUBS
Bath City 1929 ••Charlton Athletic 01.12.1933 £160) ••Aldershot 03-12-36 (£40) ••Cheltenham Town 1938 ••Bristol Rovers 1939

Harry spent time as a teenager with Southern League club Bath City. He was a regular goalscorer for their reserves and eventually made around 100 competitive appearances at first team level. He participated in the first match at their Twerton Park ground in September 1932 and played his part when they finished as champions of the Southern League, Western Division in 1932-33. Nevertheless, the sudden transfer to Charlton and the move from his home in Bristol to South London must have been a shock to the

system.

He kept his place in the team for the remainder of 1933-34 and managed to score six league goals, including the winner at the Valley on 23rd April 1934 when Bristol City were beaten 2-1. However, his second season was when Jimmy Seed really showed that he meant business with the introduction of Sam Bartram, Don Welsh and the goal machine, Ralph Allen. The inside left position was shared between Les Boulter and another newcomer, George

Stephenson, leaving Harry out in the cold and restricted to just seven league appearances as Charlton raced to the Division 3 (South) title. His first team opportunities had come to an end and he finally departed to Aldershot in December 1936, which was the same month that Charlton took over the lead in Division 1.

Life at Aldershot could not have been a greater contrast. While Charlton were continuing their meteoric rise, Harry's new club were heading in the opposite direction. His debut was an uninspiring home defeat against Luton Town on 5th December and they had already commenced a winless run in the league that eventually stretched for 17 matches. They hit the bottom of Division 3 (South) on 2nd January and stayed there. Despite Harry's best efforts they

finished nine points adrift and had to seek re-election. The next season was only marginally better.

By 1939 he was back living in Bristol along with his wife Clarice and their baby daughter and had found employment as an aircraft woodworker. He signed for Bristol Rovers in time for the 1939-40 season but had not played when competition was aborted in September following the outbreak of war and this brought Harry's playing career to a close. He did scout for Bristol Rovers during the fifties but for the remainder of his working life was employed as a production engineer in the aircraft industry. He died in 1988 at the age of 78.

Season	Division	League		FA Cup		D3 Cup		Total	
		A	G	A	G	A	G	A	G
1933-34	Divison 3 (S)	21	6	0	0	0	0	21	6
1934-35 (P)	Divison 3 (S)	7	2	0	0	1	1	8	3
Total		28	8	0	0	1	1	29	9

UK LEAGUE CAREER 68 games 15 goals

CHARLTON CAREER
Managers: *J Seed*
Debut: *Clapton Orient (A) 02-12-1933*
V176
Finale: *Aldershot (A) 19-04-1935*

BUTTERFIELD Daniel Paul   2009

Danny played over 500 league and cup matches as a defender, yet will probably be remembered as much for the one occasion when he become a makeshift striker for the afternoon. Crystal Palace were skint and in administration and with no recognised striker available he was picked to play up front for their FA Cup Round 4 replay on 2nd February 2010. Amazingly he scored a six-minute second half hat-trick to clinch a 3-1 victory against Wolverhampton Wanderers.

Defender   11st 3lbs   5' 11"
Born: 21-11-1979 - Boston, Lincolnshire
Education: Boston Grammar School.

HONOURS
Crystal Palace 2003-04 Promoted Division 1
Southampton 2010-11 Runners Up League 1

Southampton 2011-12 Runners Up Championship

CLUBS
Grimsby Town 1993 (youth) 07.08.97 (pro) ••Crystal Palace 05.07.02 (free) ••Charlton Athletic 02.03.09 (loan) ••Southampton 17.07.10 (free) ••Bolton Wanderers 28.03.13 (loan) ••Carlisle United 23.08.13 (non contract) ••Exeter City 21.09.13 (free) 10.05.15 (player coach) ••Southampton 16.09.16 (youth coach) ••Milton Keynes Dons 10.08.18 (coach) ••Macclesfield Town 16.01.20 (ass manager)

Danny commenced his career at Grimsby Town and made his league debut aged 18. He soon became a regular in the first team and during the period when Lennie Lawrence was their manager, featured (along with Bradley Allen) in an unexpected League Cup win at Anfield on 9th October 2001 when a strong Liverpool side were defeated 2-1 after extra time. He moved on to Crystal Palace during the Summer of 2002 and played more than 250 games for them in an eight-year stay.

In season 2008-09 Charlton were engaged in a desperate relegation battle in the Championship. They dropped to the foot of the league table on Boxing Day and would stay there right through to May. With no funds available for new players, manager Phil Parkinson was increasingly reliant on loan signings and when veteran loanee Graeme Murty suffered a calf injury against Swansea City, a replacement right back became a top priority.

Danny signed on 2nd March and was thrown straight into

the team against Doncaster Rovers the following day. When everything on the field is going wrong, obtaining a loan player from Crystal Palace is not a move guaranteed to appease the crowd and Danny felt the full brunt of their frustration. He performed adequately, but could add nothing that would remove the inevitability of relegation. The only home win during his time at the Valley was saved until the final day of the season when Norwich City were dispatched 4-2, but it was all too late.

He moved on to Southampton in Summer 2010 and played regularly during their League One promotion season, competing with Frazer Richardson for the right back spot.

Season	Division	League		FA Cup		FL Cup		Total	
		A	G	A	G	A	G	A	G
2008-09 (R)	Championship	12	0	0	0	0	0	12	0
Total		12	0	0	0	0	0	12	0

UK LEAGUE CAREER 488 games 9 goals

He played less often in 2011-12, when a second promotion took the Saints back to the Premier League and finally wrapped up his playing career at Exeter City, announcing his retirement in September 2016, while at the same time re-joining Southampton as a youth team coach. From there he had 15 months as first team coach of MK Dons.

In January 2020 he became assistant manager of troubled League 2 club Macclesfield Town. They had horrendous problems on and off the field and debts approaching £750,000. A seven point deduction for failing to pay wages was confirmed on appeal and Danny left the club in August 2020. They went into liquidation a month later.

CHARLTON CAREER
Managers: *P Parkinson*
Debut: *Doncaster Rovers (H) 03-03-2009*
V684
Finale: *Norwich City (H) 03-05-2009*

BUTTON David Robert Edmund   2013

Goalkeeper   13st 10lbs   6' 3"
Born: 27-02-1989 - Stevenage, Hertfordshire
Education: Monk's Walk School, Welwyn Garden City.

David has had a most unusual career. Having signed pro for Tottenham Hotspur at the age of 17, he then spent the next six years on a seemingly endless procession of short term loans, Even he would probably be pushed to remember all the 11 different clubs for whom he appeared during this period and the list does not include his parent club, for whom he made just one solitary appearance off the substitute's bench in a League Cup tie at Doncaster in August 2009. It is often the plight of a goalkeeper to spend long periods on the sidelines, awaiting the chance to play, but few if any will have suffered as long as David and when he finally left Tottenham in the Summer of 2012, he still had another year to wait for a decent run of games.

HONOURS
England U20 International 2009 1 cap 0 goals
England U19 International 2006-08 11 caps 0 goals
England U17 International 2004-06 18 caps 0 goals

England U16 International 2003-04 3 caps 0 goals
Brentford 2013-14 Runners Up League 1
Fulham 2017-18 Promoted Play Offs Championship

CLUBS
Stevenage Borough (youth) ••Tottenham Hotspur 2003 (youth) 03.03.06 (pro) ••Grays Athletic 10.01.08 (loan) ••Rochdale 27.03.08 (loan) ••Grays Athletic 19.09.08 (loan) ••AFC Bournemouth 16.01.09 (loan) ••Luton Town 06.03.09 (loan) ••Dagenham & Redbridge 16.04.09 (loan) ••Crewe Alexandra 22.07.09 (loan) 01.09.09 (loan) ••Shrewsbury Town 20.11.09 (loan) ••Plymouth Argyle 03.08.10 (loan) ••Leyton Orient 25.08.11 (loan) ••Doncaster Rovers 01.01.12 (loan) ••Barnsley 20.03.12 (loan) ••Charlton Athletic 28.08.12 (£500,000) ••Brentford 31.07.13 (undisclosed) ••Fulham 19.07.16 (£2 million) ••Brighton & Hove Albion 16.07.18 (£4 million) ••West Bromwich Albion 05.09.20 (£1 million)

Other than his time with Shrewsbury and Plymouth, David only played a handful of matches on each of his loans, yet initially his career had started so brightly. He played for England at U16, U17 and U19 levels and on 31st March 2009 played for England U20's at Loftus Road against Italy. He started the match but was later substituted in favour of Ben Amos. They both must have been satisfied

with their contribution as the final score was 2-0 to England, but possibly because of his unstable club situation this proved to be the final chapter in David's international career.

It was to Charlton that David moved in August 2012 and he must have hoped that the transfer would provide some stability at last, not to mention the opportunity to play every week after spending so long on the fringes. Unfortunately he had first to dislodge Ben Hamer from the team, but Ben had played a significant role in the 2011-12 promotion from League One and was safely ensconced as first choice goalkeeper. David did not make his debut until a highly forgettable FA Cup tie at the Valley on 5th January 2013. Huddersfield scored an early goal. Dorian Dervite was red carded and the match fizzled out to a limp 1-0 defeat. He was not called upon again until March, when his four game run in the team ended abruptly after a 2-0 home defeat to Millwall. He did at least finish on the winning team, however. His final match against Bristol City in May ended 4-1, courtesy of goals by Yann Kermorgant (2), Jon Obika and Johnnie Jackson, but he had still been no more than a back-up 'keeper and so after only 11 months at the Valley, it was time to move on again. At last David's career came alight after he transferred to Brentford in July 2013 and over the next three years he made 134 league appearances, including their promotion season of 2013-14 when they finished as runners-up in League One. They almost made it two straight promotions,

but lost out to Middlesbrough in the Championship play offs of 2015. One memorable match came at Griffin Park on 5th March 2016 when a relegation threatened Charlton pulled off an unexpected 2-1 win thanks to two goals from Callum Harriott.

A big money transfer fee, believed to have been around £2 million, took David to Fulham in July 2016 and he played regularly until mid-way through 2017-18 when he lost his place in the team, so was an unused substitute when they gained promotion to the Premier League via a Wembley play off win against Aston Villa. An even bigger fee took him to Brighton and he finally got to play in the Premier League, debuting alongside Dale Stephens in a 1-0 win over Everton on 29th December 2018. However, he was destined to be merely a back-up goalie once again and made no more than four league and a handful of cup appearances before joining West Bromwich Albion in September 2020, where he is again usually to be found on the substitute's bench.

Season	Division	League		FA Cup		FL Cup		Total	
		A	G	A	G	A	G	A	G
2012-13	Championship	5	0	1	0	0	0	6	0
Total		5	0	1	0	0	0	6	0

UK LEAGUE CAREER 294 games 0 goals

CHARLTON CAREER
Managers: *C Powell*
Debut: *Huddersfield Town (H) 05-01-2013*
V755
Finale: *Bristol City (H) 04-05-2013*

BUYENS Yoni   2014 - 15

Yoni has spent almost his whole career in Belgium. The only exception was 2014-15 when he became new Charlton manager Bob Peeters' first signing and spent a season on

Midfield   11st 11lbs   6' 0"
Born: 10-03-1988 - Duffel, Belgium

loan from Standard Liege. A defensive midfield player, he steadily acclimatised to English football, but his time in SE7 will be best remembered for his return of seven penalties scored in league matches, a total only exceeded by Mark Reid back in 1986 and by Lyle Taylor in the promotion season of 2018-19.

HONOURS
Belgium U21 International 2009-10 2 caps 0 goals
Belgium U20 International 2007-08 3 caps 0 goals
Belgium U19 International 2006-07 8 caps 0 goals

Lierse SK 2008-09 Runners Up Belgian Second Division
Standard Liege 2013-14 Runners Up Belgian Pro League

CLUBS
Lierse SK, Belgium 2004 (youth) 2006 (pro) ••KV Mechelen, Belgium 07.09 (free) ••Standard Liege, Belgium 01.07.11 (1.5 million euros) ••Charlton Athletic 21.06.14 (loan) ••KRC Genk, Belgium 30.06.15 (undisclosed) ••KVC Westerlo, Belgium 26.08.16 (loan) ••Lierse SK, Belgium 17.01.18 (free) ••Lierse Kempenzonen, Belgium 10.06.18 (free) ••KVV Zepperen-Brustem, Belgium 06.20 (free)

During three years spent with Standard Liege immediately before coming to England, Yoni participated in more than

100 games in the Belgian Pro League. In season 2013-14 they finished in first place after the 30 match 'regular

season', but under the somewhat strange Belgian rules, had to compete in a further 10 match 'play off,' following which they dropped back to second spot.

When Yoni signed for Charlton, he had the difficult job of replacing Diego Poyet who had just left the club after a magnificent run of form in the previous season. It took a little time for him to win over the Charlton supporters, but his own form in the second half of 2014-15 ensured almost universal disappointment when he was not retained beyond the period of his loan. Much of the criticism that was levelled at the club's owner could have been avoided if players like Yoni Buyens had been used to build a team rather than as part of an ill advised revolving door policy which could never bring lasting success.

Returning to Belgium after his sabbatical in London, Yoni

joined KRC Genk for a year and then was loaned to KVC Westerlo for season 2016-17, where he again linked up with manager Bob Peeters. All did not go well, however. Peeters was sacked in September and a dismal run of form saw them finish bottom of the newly re-constructed Belgian First Division A.

In January 2018 he signed for Lierse SK, the club where he had started out in the first team as a 17-year-old back in 2005, but further disaster awaited him. Only four months later Lierse went into bankruptcy after 112 years and two rival clubs were formed out of the wreckage, one of which was Lierse Kempenzonen. Yoni signed for them but in 2020 announced that at age 32, his pro career was at an end and he would in future only play for enjoyment.

Season	Division	League		FA Cup		FL Cup		Total	
		A	G	A	G	A	G	A	G
2014-15	Championship	38 (2)	8	1	0	1 (1)	1	40 (3)	9
Total		38 (2)	8	1	0	1 (1)	1	40 (3)	9

UK LEAGUE CAREER 40 games 8 goals

CHARLTON CAREER
Managers: *B Peeters, G Luzon*
Debut: *Brentford (A) 09-08-2014*
V781
Finale: *AFC Bournemouth (H) 02-05-2015*

BYRNE Nathan William   2017

Defender, Midfield   10st 1lbs   5' 10"
Born: 05-06-1992 - St Albans, Hertfordshire

Nathan performed admirably during his time on loan at Charlton where he was deployed as either an attacking full back or further up the pitch as a winger. During his four months in SE7 he did little wrong, but this was not a happy period and the club were struggling both on and off the field. He scored one goal for Charlton and it proved to be the winner in an explosive match at the Macron Stadium on 28th January 2017. Lewis Page had been sent off as early as the 11th minute and the Bolton Wanderers side, which included both Ben Alnwick and Lawrie Wilson, soon took the lead only for first Patrick Bauer and then Nathan himself to find the net for the Addicks and claim an unlikely victory by 2-1.

HONOURS
Wigan Athletic 2017-18 Winners League One

CLUBS
St Albans City (youth) ••Tottenham Hotspur 2008 (youth) 06.10 (pro) ••Brentford 21.02.11 (loan) ••AFC Bournemouth 28.07.11 (loan) ••Crawley Town 24.09.12 (loan) ••Swindon Town 29.03.13 (loan) 09.07.13 (free) ••Wolverhampton Wanderers 01.09.15 (£1 million) ••Wigan Athletic 31.08.16 (£400,000) ••Charlton Athletic 09.01.17 (loan) ••Derby County 10.09.20 (£250,000)

Although viewed as a promising young player at Tottenham, there were no first team opportunities and the early part of Nathan's career comprised a series of loans, including a spell at Brentford where he played under caretaker manager Nicky Forster. Eventually he settled at Swindon Town where he appeared regularly for two seasons, but really made people sit up and take notice on

the opening day of 2015-16 with a second half hat trick against Bradford City in a 4-1 victory, the other goal being scored by Jonathan Obika.

The following month he was transferred to Wolverhampton Wanderers for £1 million, but despite a three-year contract was unable to justify the fee and moved on again to Wigan Athletic only 12 months later for an undisclosed fee that has been variously claimed as between £400,000 and £551,000.

That Nathan was a good player was never really in question, but it was not until he returned from his loan spell at Charlton that his career really blossomed and he was a key member of the Wigan side which secured promotion from League One in 2017-18. He later maintained his place in the team as they adapted to life in the Championship. In April 2019 after scoring a late equaliser against Bristol City,

he was forced to endure racial abuse on social media. The police became involved and the perpetrator, who had bet on the match result, was charged and subsequently found guilty in the courts. Nathan was praised for standing out against this unacceptable behaviour.

Since September 2020 he has been playing for troubled Derby County in their seemingly endless struggle to keep the club afloat in the face of points deductions and financial meltdown.

Season	Division	League		FA Cup		FL Cup		FL Trophy		Total	
		A	G	A	G	A	G	A	G	A	G
2016-17	League One	16 (1)	1	0	0	0	0	0	0	16 (1)	1
Total		16 (1)	1	0	0	0	0	0	0	16 (1)	1

UK LEAGUE CAREER 331 games 16 goals

CHARLTON CAREER
Managers: *K Robinson*
Debut: *Millwall (H) 14-01-2017*
V835
Finale: *Swindon Town (H) 30-04-2017*

CAIG Antony   2001

Tony enjoyed just one afternoon in the spotlight during his time in London SE7 and that occurred on 30th January 2001. He had been signed specifically to provide goalkeeping cover and had taken up his usual place on the substitute's bench when Dean Kiely picked up an injury against Derby County and had to be replaced at half time with the score finely balanced at 1-1. He put in a solid display in the second half and Scott Parker scored to give Charlton a 2-1 win. Owing to Kiely's consistency, this proved to be Tony's only first team appearance during his six months at the club.

Goalkeeper   13st 4lbs   6' 1"
Born: 11-04-1974 - Cleator Moor, Cumbria
Education: Ehenside School, Cleator Moor.

HONOURS

Carlisle United 1994-95 Winners Division 3
Carlisle United 1996-97 Promoted Division 3

Carlisle United 1996-97 Winners Football League Trophy
Vancouver Whitecaps 2006 Winners USL First Division

CLUBS

Cleator Moor Celtic (youth) ••Carlisle United 1990 (youth) 10.07.92 (pro) ••Blackpool 25.03.99 (£40,000) ••Charlton Athletic 03.11.00 (loan) 09.01.01 (free) ••Hibernian, Scotland 27.07.01 (free) ••Newcastle United 31.01.03 (free) ••Barnsley 16.01.04 (loan) ••Vancouver Whitecaps, Canada 13.04.06 (player coach) ••Gretna, Scotland 06.10.07 (amateur) ••Houston Dynamo, USA 29.01.08 (free) ••Chesterfield 10.03.09 (free) ••Workington 08.07.09 (free) ••Carlisle United 09.07.10 (player coach) ••Hartlepool United 02.06.15 (player coach) ••Newcastle United 03.17 (coach) ••Bury 06.17 (coach) ••Livingstone, Scotland 01.18 (coach) ••Falkirk, Scotland 17.06.21 (coach) ••Dundee United, Scotland 22.07.21 (coach)

Most of the action in Tony's career came at the beginning. He made 272 league appearances for his first two clubs, Carlisle United and Blackpool, but then only 25 in total for the other seven English and Scottish League clubs for whom he played. His seven seasons with Carlisle included two promotions and a dramatic Wembley final in the Football League Trophy on 20th April 1997 when a crowd of 45,077 witnessed a 0-0 draw between Carlisle and Colchester United. The match was decided by kicks from the penalty spot and he saved twice to win the cup for Carlisle.

A move to Blackpool came at the wrong time. The club was in disarray and his only full season with them ended with relegation, following which he drifted from Hibernian where he hardly played, to Newcastle where he didn't play at all. A spell in Canada with Vancouver Whitecaps proved more memorable. They came through to win the United Soccer League First Division in 2006 after a thrilling 2-0 play off win against New York club, the Rochester Raging Rhinos. Tony kept a club record 11 clean sheets throughout that season.

He returned early from Canada and was initially prevented from playing because the Scottish Premier League would not sanction his transfer to Gretna whilst he was still under contract to the Whitecaps. Eventually he signed for them as an amateur and made seven SPL appearances before returning to the US to play for Houston Dynamo. This was another brief encounter and his next port of call was Workington where he played throughout 2009-10 earning the accolade of 'National Conference Keeper of the Year'. From then on Tony played less and concentrated more on coaching. Returning to Carlisle in 2010, he took on the role of goalkeeping coach and even acted as interim manager for four games in 2014. He runs a coaching school for young goalies in Cumbria and also operates as a freelance for the Scottish FA. By 2020 he was working part-time for Livingston and had set up 'The Goalkeeping Consultants' to provide every conceivable area of training, mentoring and education and making full use of his UEFA A goalkeeper coaching qualification. In July 2021 he accepted a full-time coaching position with Dundee United.

Season	Division	League		FA Cup		FL Cup		Total	
		A	G	A	G	A	G	A	G
2000-01	Premier	0 (1)	0	0	0	0	0	0 (1)	0
Total		0 (1)	0	0	0	0	0	0 (1)	0

UK LEAGUE CAREER 297 games 0 goals

CHARLTON CAREER
Managers: *A Curbishley*
Debut: *Derby County H) (sub) 30-01-2001*
V598

CAIRNS John

1926

Forward
Born: 14-11-1902 - Glasgow, Lanarkshire
Died: 24-06-1965 - Shooters Hill, London

The early years of John's football career are somewhat confusing, There were quite a few 'Cairns' playing in Scotland in the 1920s and at least two different forwards named John Cairns played for Broxburn United during the period 1921 to 1926 when this tiny West Lothian town was hosting a club in Division 2 of the Scottish League. Charlton's John Cairns was a centre forward who made his name playing in the Glasgow Junior League for St Roch's and as well as Broxburn he also turned out for Scottish League clubs Bathgate and Dunfermline Athletic

CLUBS

Kirkintilloch Rob Roy, Scotland 01.23 ••St Roch's, Scotland 07.23 ••Port Vale 10.23 ••St Roch's, Scotland 12.23 ••Broxburn United, Scotland 04.24 ••Bathgate, Scotland 01.25 ••Dunfermline Athletic, Scotland 16.07.25 •Kettering Town 10.25 ••Charlton Athletic 06.05.26 ••Brentford 09.27 ••Leicester City 18.05.28 ••Margate 1929 ••Portsmouth 1931 ••Toronto Scottish, Canada 07.32 •Crystal Palace 12.32 ••Rochdale 08.33 ••Ramsgate Press Wanderers 1933 ••Hay's Wharf 1934

John came down to England in October 1923 and spent two months with Port Vale playing in the Cheshire League for their reserve team. This did not lead to a longer contract, so he returned to Scotland and it was almost two years before he tried his luck again south of the border. A short trial period at Southern League club Kettering Town led nowhere but in May 1926 he finally got his chance and joined Charlton, where he got off to the best possible start with a hat-trick in a 1926-27 pre-season trial match.

He went straight into the team at centre forward for the opening match against Watford but did not find the net in any of his first three games, all of which were lost. Another chance came on 6th November and this time he scored the winner as Northampton Town were beaten 1-0 at the County Ground. He followed with goals in his next two games as well, including the decider in a tight FA Cup encounter with non-league Woking which finished 3-2, but by the end of December his brief time in the first team was

over and he left the club at the end of the season.

His next port of call was Brentford where John was selected for just one league game but scored in a 5-1 win over Bristol Rovers on 7th April 1928. His team-mates included Bill Berry. From then on he shuffled from club to club without establishing himself anywhere and even tried his luck out in Canada, but along with his wife Isabel and young son William, returned to the UK aboard the ocean liner RMS Aurania on 28th November 1932. At that time he was living in Ordnance Road, Greenwich.

Five games for Rochdale at the start of the 1933-34 signalled the end of John's time as a professional footballer but by 1939 he was still resident in Greenwich and employed as a lorry driver. He passed away at the age of 62 whilst working as head groundsman at Sutcliffe Park in Kidbrooke and was cremated at Greenwich on 30th June 1965.

Season	Division	League		FA Cup		Total	
		A	G	A	G	A	G
1926-27	Divison 3 (S)	7	2	1	1	8	3
Total		7	2	1	1	8	3

UK LEAGUE CAREER 28 games 6 goals

CHARLTON CAREER
Managers: *A MacFarlane*
Debut: *Watford (A) 28-08-1926*
V092
Finale: *Gillingham (A) 27-12-1926*

CAMPBELL Alan James   1965 - 70

Immediately recognisable by his mop of
dark hair, Alan was a key figure in the
Charlton side of the late sixties. A hard
tackling, all action midfield player, he

Midfield   10st 7lbs   5' 8"
Born: 21-01-1948 - Arbroath, Scotland
Education: Hayshead Primary School & Arbroath High School.

appeared in 109 consecutive league matches commencing on 10th February 1968. Working in
tandem with Welsh International Graham Moore, he was the engine room of an entertaining if
erratic team which at its best came tantalisingly close to gaining a place in Division 1. His ability
was acknowledged when he played for the Scottish U23's against Wales U23's in a 1-1 draw at
Aberdeen on 14th January 1970 and it is perhaps surprising that he never went on to win full
international honours later in his career.

HONOURS

Scotland U23 International 1970 1 cap 0 goals
Scotland Youth International 1965-66 4 caps
London FA Youth XI 1964 -65 2 caps
Charlton Athletic Youth 1965-66 Winners South East Counties League Cup

Birmingham City 1971-72 Runners Up Division 2
Cardiff City 1975-76 Runners Up Division 3
Cardiff City 1976-77 Finalists Welsh Cup

HONOURS AS MANAGER

CLUBS

Arbroath Lads, Scotland (youth) ••Charlton Athletic 04.07.64 (amateur) 08.02.65 (pro) ••Birmingham City 14.10.70 (£70,000) ••Cardiff City 03.03.76
(£20,000) ••Carlisle United 07.11.80 (£30,000) ••Redditch United 1982 ••Olton Royale 1986 ••Highgate United 1989 (ass manager) 1992 (manager)
••Stratford Town 1992 (ass manager) 1993 (manager)

Charlton's match at Burnden Park on 21st August 1965 is
famous for being the first occasion when a substitute was
used in the Football League. Keith Peacock took the field
when goalkeeper Mike Rose was injured (as every quiz
enthusiast is fully aware), but less well known is the fact
that this match which ended up as a 4-2 win for Bolton
Wanderers, also saw Alan Campbell's debut for Charlton at
the age of 17. Seven days later he scored his first goal as
Ipswich Town were beaten 2-0 at the Valley.
His hard-working and all action style made him a firm
favourite with supporters and never more so than on 6th
January 1968 when his spectacular individual goal earned a
1-0 win against Millwall. It is a great shame that the
promotion ambitions of the team fell just short the
following season when Alan was in fine form, as he
deserved the opportunity to perform at the highest level.
He was ever present in both the 1968-69 and 1969-70
seasons and on 4th April 1970 became the youngest
Charlton player to play 200 senior games at the age of 22
years and 240 days.
There were bumps in the road, however. In October 1969
Alan appeared at Woolwich Magistrates Court on a charge
of Careless Driving and having more than the permitted
level of alcohol in his blood following a motor accident in
Kidbrooke. In an attempt to get a lower fine he misled the

police, claiming that he was a £25 a week labourer and not a
footballer earning twice that amount. A month later he put
in a transfer request, having fallen out with manager, Eddie
Firmani, but it was rejected by the Charlton directors and
then in May 1970 he became embroiled in difficult contract
negotiations which resulted in him staying at the club for
an increased weekly wage of £55 plus £10 per game.
In October 1970 Charlton accepted an offer of £70,000
and Alan moved to Birmingham City where he played for
five years, including their promotion season of 1971-72
when he was ever present. They came close to reaching the
FA Cup Final as well that year but went down to Leeds
United in the semi-final. He played 104 matches in the First
Division before moving on to Cardiff City in time to play a
hand in their promotion from Division 3 in 1976.
His goal-scoring had almost completely dried up by that
stage but he continued to play regularly until eventually
dropping down into Division 3 with Carlisle United. Five
months later Alan took part in the fondly remembered
match on 25th April 1981 when Charlton clinched
promotion back to Division 2, thanks to a 2-1 win at
Carlisle and goals by Paul Walsh and Martin Robinson.
He played non-league for Redditch United before trying
his hand in management and later worked in Solihull as an
audit engineer for Land Rover. Now retired, Alan is an

enthusiastic bowls player and a season ticket holder at

Season	Division	League		FA Cup		FL Cup		Total	
		A	G	A	G	A	G	A	G
1965-66	Division 2	23 (1)	4	0	0	1	0	24 (1)	4
1966-67	Division 2	39 (1)	7	1	0	1	0	41 (1)	7
1967-68	Division 2	40	9	1	0	2	1	43	10
1968-69	Division 2	42	4	3	0	1	0	46	4
1969-70	Division 2	42	4	3	0	1	0	46	4
1970-71	Division 2	10	0	0	0	2	0	12	0
Total		196 (2)	28	8	0	8	1	212 (2)	29

UK LEAGUE CAREER 571 games 43 goals

Birmingham City where he attends matches with his son.

CHARLTON CAREER
Managers: *F Hill, R Stokoe, E Firmani, T Foley*
Debut: *Bolton Wanderers (A) 21-08-1965*
V309
Finale: *Bolton Wanderers (A) 10-10-1970*

CAMPBELL David Alistair   1976 - 80

Defender   11st 8lb   6' 1"
Born: 02-11-1958 - Edinburgh, Scotland
Education: Roan Grammar School, Greenwich. University of London, BSc
Economics !st Class

David was the first schoolboy to appear for Charlton in the Football League when he interrupted his A level studies to play against Blackburn Rovers at the age of 17. In November 1976 he appeared for an Anglo Scottish Youth XI against a Scottish Youth XI at St Mirren. He signed pro terms upon leaving school in the summer of 1977, but was really only ever a part time professional, dividing his time between football and studying Economics at the University of London, eventually achieving a First Class Honours degree.

HONOURS
Blackheath & Kent Schools
Anglo Scottish Youth XI 1976

Charlton Athletic Reserves 1979-80 Runners Up Mid-Week League

CLUBS
Charlton Athletic 26.11.73 (youth) 27.06.77 (pro) ••Barking 18.07.80 (free)

David did well during his time at Charlton, especially in season 1978-79 when he was first choice for one or other of the full back positions and played in nearly every game. Relegation in 1980 brought his Football League career to an end and he left Charlton shortly before graduating from university. He had a spell playing for Barking in the Isthmian League under manager Harry Cripps, a former teammate at the Valley, but from then on chose to concentrate on his business career.

He spent 15 years with banker's JP Morgan, rising to the position of managing director, became CEO of Tilney Investment Management, one of Britain's oldest wealth management firms and had two spells, totalling seven years, as MD of the Deutsche Bank. By 2018 his glittering business career showed no sign of ending and it was announced in the Times that he had been appointed managing partner of Vestra Wealth, providing a wealth management service to private clients and financial intermediaries.

Season	Division	League		FA Cup		FL Cup		Total	
		A	G	A	G	A	G	A	G
1975-76	Division 2	1 (2)	0	0	0	0	0	1 (2)	0
1977-78	Division 2	13 (3)	1	1	0	1	0	15 (3)	1
1978-79	Division 2	39	2	3	1	4	0	46	3
1979-80 (R)	Division 2	18	0	0	0	2	0	20	0
Total		71 (5)	3	4	1	7	0	82 (5)	4

UK LEAGUE CAREER 76 games 3 goals

CHARLTON CAREER
Managers: *T Foley, A Nelson, M Bailey*
Debut: *Blackburn Rovers (H) (sub) 20-03-1976*
V398
Finale: *Fulham (A) 22-04-1980*

CAMPBELL David Anthony   1987 - 89

The second David Campbell to wear a Charlton shirt was an Irishman from Londonderry who enjoyed a run in the first team during the Selhurst Park years. He was

Midfield   12st 2lbs   5' 10"
Born: 02-06-1965 - Eglinton, Londonderry

already a Northern Ireland international when he was signed from Nottingham Forest in October 1987 and had played for his country against Brazil in the 1986 World Cup finals. He had also featured twice against England during the qualifying tournament for the UEFA Euro 1988 Championship and went on to make a further four international appearances during his time at Charlton, including the 1-0 win over Turkey on 11th November 1987 in which his teammates included former Charlton loanee Alan McDonald.

HONOURS

Northern Ireland International 1986-88 10 caps 0 goals   League Of Ireland X1 1991 1 cap 0 goals
Northern Ireland Youth International

CLUBS

Oxford Boys Club, N Ireland (youth) ••Nottingham Forest 06.81 (youth) 07.83 (pro) ••Notts County 12.02.87 (loan) ••Charlton Athletic 09.10.87 (£75,000) ••Plymouth Argyle 09.03.89 (loan) ••Bradford City 17.03.89 (£75,000) ••Derry City, N Ireland 14.12.90 (loan) ••Shamrock Rovers, Ireland 15.01.91 (loan) 08.91 (free) ••Cliftonville, N Ireland, 02.92 (loan) ••Rotherham United 11.11.92 (free) ••West Bromwich Albion 10.02.93 (free) ••Burnley 19.03.93 (free) ••Lincoln City 07.02.94 (loan) ••Portadown, N Ireland 03.94 (loan) ••Wigan Athletic 29.07.94 (free) ••Cambridge United 27.01.95 (free) ••Tamworth 1995 (free) ••Sutton Coldfield Town 1996 (loan) ••Paget Rangers 1996 (loan)

David started out at Brian Clough's Nottingham Forest and did remarkably well to make 41 league appearances for them in the period 1985-87 when they were one of the leading sides in the country and when there was considerable competition for places. He came up against Charlton on two occasions and was victorious both times, including a 4-0 spanking at the City Ground on 27th August 1986. He was a very skilful player, well able to dribble into attacking positions, but liable to misplace the final pass or fail to make enough of a scoring opportunity. Ultimately this inconsistency cost him his place at Forest and he joined Charlton for a transfer fee of £75,000 in October 1987.

The club was rock bottom of Division 1 when he arrived and a useful 1-1 draw at West Ham on his debut was much needed. However, results did not really improve and for a long time they looked relegation certainties. One bright moment came on 13th December 1987 when David scored

at White Hart Lane in a 1-0 win over Tottenham Hotspur, but this proved to be his only goal for the club and after a run in the side that extended from October up to the end of February, he was dropped after a disappointing display at Highbury which ended in a 4-0 defeat to Arsenal. Happily the side rallied and finished unbeaten in the last six matches of the season thereby avoiding the drop, but for David his time as a Charlton player was drawing to a close.

When season 1988-89 got underway, he was no longer a regular in the team and although he played at least some part in a further nine Division 1 matches, he failed to be on the winning side in any of them and in March a loan spell at Plymouth was cut short so that he could sign for Bradford City. A little over a year later they were relegated from Division 2, after which David's career seemed to lurch out of control. He bounced from club to club, but never settled anywhere, despite brief encounters that extended to include spells in both the North and South of Ireland. While playing for Shamrock Rovers he represented the League of Ireland in a match against the Irish League (South v North) that was played in Dublin in November 1991

After that there were monthly contracts with Rotherham and West Bromwich Albion, an injury ravaged period at Burnley and yet more loan deals at Lincoln City and Portadown. He played seven league games for Wigan Athletic in 1994-95 but was never once on the winning side and his haphazard career came to a dramatic close when he broke his leg on 28th January 1995 while making his debut for Cambridge United, alongside Danny O'Shea, in a 6-0

defeat at Brentford.

David carried on a little longer in non-league but his future lay in the foundation of David Campbell Soccer which since 1995 has provided coaching and sports education to over one million children from age four upwards and among their successful graduates is Charlton player Marvin Sordell. This immensely successful operation has been featured on ITV's holiday programme, 'Wish You Were Here'. David holds a UEFA Pro Licence as well as the British Citizens Award for outstanding contribution to Education.

Season	Division	League		FA Cup		FL Cup		FM Cup		Total	
		A	G	A	G	A	G	A	G	A	G
1987-88	Division 1	21	1	1	0	1	0	1	0	24	1
1988-89	Division 1	5 (4)	0	0 (1)	0	2	0	1	0	8 (5)	0
Total		26 (4)	1	1 (1)	0	3	0	2	0	32 (5)	1

UK LEAGUE CAREER 146 games 11 goals

CHARLTON CAREER
Managers: L Lawrence
Debut: *West Ham United (A) 10-10-1987*
V494
Finale: *Sheffield Wednesday (A) 04-03-1989*

CAMPBELL James 'Jock'   1947 - 57

Defender   11st 1lb   5' 10"
Born: 11-11-1922 - Thorntonhall,, South Lanarkshire
Died: 17-07-1983 - Trumpington, Cambridgeshire
Education: Cumbernauld High School

Hard man Scottish full back Jock Campbell was a regular in the Addicks defence for more than a decade and it is doubtful if there has been any other Charlton player who was more physically intimidating. He played in an era when tackling was a good deal more primitive than in the modern game and Jock was the ideal man to slow down a tricky winger with the sort of eye watering slide tackle that would be totally unacceptable today. He made 255 league appearances for Charlton, his only Football League club and all but one were in the First Division.

HONOURS

London FA 1948-51 2 caps 0 goals

Charlton Athletic Reserves 1949-50 Runners Up Football Combination Cup

Charlton Athletic Reserves 1950-51 Winners London FA Challenge Cup

Charlton Athletic Reserves 1951-52 Finalists London FA Challenge Cup

CLUBS

Allandale Juveniles (youth) ••RAF Brize Norton c1940 ••Charlton Athletic 18.01.45 (amateur) 31.01.45 (pro) ••Cambridge United 30.06.58 (free)

Jock was born in the tiny village of Thorntonhall, just eight miles south of Glasgow. During World War 2 he was stationed with the RAF at Brize Norton at the same time as Sailor Brown who recommended him to Charlton. He signed as an amateur in January 1945 and then on professional terms a fortnight later, earning £2 a week, but it was not until he was demobbed from the RAF in July 1946 that the club got a real look at their new acquisition. His first team debut came in the 1946-47 season and he played in the first four FA Cup matches of that campaign, including the Sixth Round against Preston North End, when goals from Chris Duffy and Gordon Hurst ensured a

2-1 victory. First choice right back Peter Croker returned for the semi-final and final, however. By the next season the full back pairing of Jock and Frank Lock had come together and the combination of the fearsome Scotsman and the more elegant Londoner served the club admirably for several years to come.

He was twice capped by the London FA, the first occasion being on 1st November 1948 against the Belgian national team, known as Les Diables Rouges. The match took place in Brussels and the LFA line-up also included Roy Bicknell, Bill Whittaker, Benny Fenton and Tommy Brown, the latter having transferred from Millwall to

Charlton the previous month. The LFA side won 4-3. Three years later on 21st November 1951 the London FA, with Jock and Frank Lock as full backs, drew 1-1 in Germany against the Berlin FA.

Jock toured Turkey with Charlton in May 1949 where they encountered very aggressive and unruly crowds and some quite frightening situations. Before their match against Fenerbahce, it became known that two of the opposing players were currently serving jail sentences, but were being let out specifically to play in this prestigious match. One, the outside left, had only recently been imprisoned for stabbing a man to death and there was considerable speculation within the Charlton camp as to how his personal battle with their dour Scottish right back would pan out. Five minutes into the match the convict broke through but Jock held his ground and in the ensuing collision saw him fly head first over his shoulder and land on the bone-hard ground. He was carried off on a stretcher, still unconscious and on his way back to jail. Charlton won 3-0 with two goals from Charlie Vaughan and one from Jimmy D'Arcy.

The Charlton team was gradually declining during the fifties but there were still some magnificent displays to savour and Jock played his part when Liverpool were dispatched 6-0 and Middlesbrough 8-1 in 1953. He helped annihilate Everton 6-0 the following year and Aston Villa 6-1 in 1955, but the great days were becoming less frequent. Jock scored only one goal in his career and it came on 12th February 1955 at Roker Park. Sunderland were defeated 2-1 with the winner coming from the versatile John Hewie who was playing at centre forward that day.

On two occasions there was talk of a transfer but he stayed and reached age 34 during the relegation season of 1956-57 when he was clearly past his best. His final match came in December 1957 when two goals from Stuart Leary sealed a 4-1 win. At the end of that season Jock moved on to non-league Cambridge United where he linked up again with Frank Lock, Kevin Barry and Bert Johnson.

He later worked for the Traffic Commissioners in Cambridge and ran Campbell's Hardware shop in Anstey Way, Trumpington before passing away in that Cambridgeshire village at the age of 60.

Season	Division	League		FA Cup		Total	
		A	G	A	G	A	G
1946-47	Division 1	5	0	4	0	9	0
1947-48	Division 1	23	0	3	0	26	0
1948-49	Division 1	28	0	1	0	29	0
1949-50	Division 1	22	0	2	0	24	0
1950-51	Division 1	14	0	0	0	14	0
1951-52	Division 1	4	0	1	0	5	0
1952-53	Division 1	28	0	0	0	28	0
1953-54	Division 1	31	0	2	0	33	0
1954-55	Division 1	38	1	3	0	41	1
1955-56	Division 1	39	0	3	0	42	0
1956-57 (R)	Division 1	22	0	2	0	24	0
1957-58	Division 2	1	0	0	0	1	0
Total		255	1	21	0	276	1

CHARLTON CAREER
Managers: *J Seed, J Trotter*
Debut: *Rochdale (H) 11-01-1947*
V221
Finale: *Ipswich Town (H) 07-12-1957*

UK LEAGUE CAREER 255 games 1 goal

CAMPBELL Tyreece Anthony Tupac Shakur   2022 -

Tyreece Campbell became the 942nd Charlton first team player when he replaced Elliott Lee in the later stages of the home

Forward   11st 13lbs   5' 10"
Born: 14-09-2003 - Camberwell, London
Education: St Thomas The Apostle School, Peckham & Harris Academy, Greenwich.

match with Oxford United on 19th February 2022. His appearance was just in time to take his place in this book and will hopefully be the start of a worthwhile football career for the young man. Shoot for the stars, Tyreece.

HONOURS

Charlton Athletic U18 2020-21 Winners PD League 2 South

Charlton Athletic U18 2020-21 Runners Up PD National League 2

CLUBS

United All Stars 2011 (youth) ••Charlton Athletic 2012 (youth) 21.07.21 (pro)

Tyreece was born in Camberwell to Jamaican parents and has been part of the Charlton Athletic academy since Under 9. He was one of the mainstays of the U18 team in 2020-21 and was ever present as they won the Professional

Development League 2 South and were narrowly beaten in the national final. A winger who loves to dribble and looks for one on ones with a defender, he has an exciting future ahead of him.

UK LEAGUE CAREER 0 games 0 goals

CHARLTON CAREER
Managers: *N Adkins, J Jackson*
Debut: *Oxford United (H) (sub) 19-02-2022*
V942

# CAMPBELL-RYCE Jamal Julian					2003

Forward, Midfield   12st 3lbs   5' 6"
Born: 06-04-1983 - Lambeth, London
Education: St Joseph's Catholic School, Hendon.

Enthusiastic Charlton supporters who attended a Premier League Reserve fixture at the Valley in 2002 were entertained during the half time break by a display of extraordinary ball juggling and football skill from one of the substitutes who had been left warming up in readiness for the second half. Teenager Jamal Campbell-Ryce was then at the dawn of a playing career which stretched out to nearly 20 years and involved as many as 15 Football League clubs, five of which he served on more than one occasion. At one time referred to as the 'Black Ronaldo', he was blessed with outstanding natural ability and was highly popular with crowds wherever he went.

HONOURS

Jamaica International 2003-09 17 caps 0 goals
Jamaica U23 International 2003 1 cap 0 goals
Charlton Athletic Reserves 2003-04 Winners Premier Reserve League (South)

Charlton Athletic 2003 Young Player Of The Year
Southend United 2005-06 Winners League One
Interwood Vets 2019-20 Winners London FA Veterans Cup

CLUBS

Millwall c1998 (youth) ••Charlton Athletic 03.04.00 (youth) 02.05.02 (pro) ••Leyton Orient 10.08.02 (loan) ••Wimbledon 06.02.04 (loan) ••Chesterfield 20.08.04 (loan) ••Rotherham United 26.11.04 (free) ••Southend United 27.09.05 (loan) ••Colchester United 23.03.06 (loan) ••Southend United 30.05.06 (£90,000) ••Barnsley 31.08.07 (£270,000) ••Bristol City 19.01.10 (£203,000) ••Leyton Orient 08.03.12 (loan) ••Notts County 03.07.12 (free) ••Sheffield United 19.05.14 (free) ••Notts County 26.02.15 (loan) ••Chesterfield 19.03.16 (loan) ••Barnet 04.08.16 (free) ••Carlisle United 31.01.18 (free) ••Stevenage 29.05.18 (free) ••Colchester United 19.08.19 (player-coach) ••Interwood Vets 2020 ••Peterborough United 03.10.21 (coach)

Despite all his obvious ability, there were only limited opportunities for Jamal in SE7. He made cameo appearances in just five competitive matches, but they did include an exciting League Cup encounter with Luton Town on 23rd September 2003 which was eventually won 8-7 on penalties after a pulsating 4-4 draw. He also came off the bench to replace Jonatan Johansson when Arsenal were held to a 1-1 draw at the Valley a month later, but the strength in depth of the Charlton team around this time

made it extremely difficult for a young player to break into the side and after loan spells with Leyton Orient, Wimbledon and Chesterfield he made a permanent move to Rotherham in November 2004.
In fact nothing proved very permanent in Jamal's career and he was soon locked into a recurring pattern. Always a crowd favourite, he would shine brightly on the field for a time, but within a couple of years move on to pastures new. Reportedly it was homesickness which caused him to come

back south in September 2005 for a loan spell with a Southend United side which included Mark Gower. They stormed to the top of League One and he featured in 13 games for them but by March 2006 was lining up alongside Billy Clarke, Chris Iwelumo and Greg Halford at Colchester, where his four appearances helped them over the line as League One runners-up, thereby completing a very unusual promotion double for himself.

Jamal earned his first international cap for Jamaica while still at Charlton when he came on as a substitute in an away fixture against Australia on 7th September 2003, but did not have far to travel as the match was played at Reading. Two months later he appeared for Jamaica U23's in an Olympic qualifier against Guatemala, while later in his career he was in the Jamaica side that played England at Old Trafford on 3rd June 2006. His teammates included Deon Burton, Jason Euell and Ricardo Fuller, but they were soundly beaten 6-0.

He played more than 200 games at Championship level, but nearly always in struggling sides. Both Rotherham and Southend were relegated during his tenure and later spells with Barnsley and Bristol City were mainly spent struggling at the wrong end of the table. As time passed, the teenage winger had evolved into an experienced and mature midfielder and he captained Barnet during their relegation from League Two in 2018 at the age of 35. He finally called a halt to his playing career in 2020 and settled into a coaching role with Colchester United, another of his former clubs.

Season	Division	League		FA Cup		FL Cup		Total	
		A	G	A	G	A	G	A	G
2002-03	Premier	0 (1)	0	0	0	0	0	0 (1)	0
2003-04	Premier	0 (2)	0	0	0	0 (2)	0	0 (4)	0
Total		0 (3)	0	0	0	0 (2)	0	0 (5)	0

UK LEAGUE CAREER 491 games 41 goals

CHARLTON CAREER
Managers: *A Curbishley*
Debut: *Blackburn Rovers (A) (sub) 12-04-2003*
V609
Finale: *Leeds United (H) (sub) 29-11-2003*

CANN Sidney Thomas   1935 - 39

Sidney (not Sydney) Cann enjoyed a long and varied career in football, tasting success in each of five successive decades, first as a Schoolboy International, then as a top player and finally, after becoming disillusioned with the professional game, as a very successful manager of leading amateur clubs, Wycombe Wanderers and Sutton United. He reached five Wembley finals, two as a player with Manchester City and Charlton and three times as a manager, but sadly ended up on the losing side on each occasion. During the fifties he was briefly called up to give special football tuition to Prince Charles at Cheam School, but with no noticeable success.

Defender
Born: 30-10-1911 - Torquay, Devon
Died: 01-11-1996 - New Malden, Surrey
Education: Babbacombe School, Torquay.

HONOURS

England Schoolboy International 1925-26 2 caps
Charlton Athletic 1942-43 Finalists Football League (South) Cup

Manchester City 1932-33 Finalists FA Cup

HONOURS AS MANAGER

Wycombe Wanderers 1955-56 & 1956-57 Winners Isthmian League
Wycombe Wanderers 1956-57 Finalists FA Amateur Cup
Wycombe Wanderers 1957-58 & 1959-60 Runners Up Isthmian League

Sutton United 1962-63 & 1968-69 Finalists FA Amateur Cup
Sutton United 1962-63 Winners Athenian League Challenge Cup
Sutton United 1966-67 Winners Isthmian League

CLUBS

Babbacombe (youth) ••Torquay United 1927 (youth) 11.28 (pro) ••Manchester City 14.03.30 ••Charlton Athletic 12.06.35 (£400) ••Southampton 05.46 (physio) 08.49 (manager) 12.51 (secretary) ••Wycombe Wanderers 07.07.52 (manager) ••Norwich City 06.61 (coach) ••Sutton United 07.62 (manager)

Sid was still just a 16-year-old schoolboy when he made his   debut for his local League club Torquay United in

September 1928 but by the end of that first season he had made the right back spot his own. He was soon attracting the attention of the bigger clubs and signed for Manchester City in March 1930, his final appearance for Torquay being an overwhelming 7-0 thrashing of Bournemouth. Competition for places was intense, but he got a good run in the first team during his second full season in Manchester and played at Wembley on 29th April 1933 in the FA Cup Final. Their opponents were a very strong Everton team which included Dixie Dean who was among the scorers as City went down 3-0. They got back to Wembley and emerged victorious 12 months later, but Sid had lost his place by then and was not involved. A year later Sid signed for Charlton, but although he remained with the club until the end of the war, he was never more than a reserve, as first Norman Smith and later Bert Turner blocked his path to the first team. A paltry 15 League appearances seems a poor return for his years of service, but at least he signed off in style as his final peacetime match was the 7-1 defeat of Manchester United at the Valley on 11th February 1939. In this match George Tadman and Monty Wilkinson ran amok through the

United defence and scored six of the Charlton goals between them.

During the War, Sid served in the Army Physical Training Corps, reaching the rank of warrant officer and continued to turn out for Charlton whenever possible. He clocked up a further 57 Wartime League matches and on 1st May 1943 returned to Wembley when Charlton played Arsenal in the final of the Football League (South) Cup. Sid had the job of marking Denis Compton, but their North London rivals had scored four by half-time and eventually won 7-1. He also made wartime guest appearances for Torquay, Aldershot and Bristol City.

He qualified as a masseur at the British College of Physiotherapy and in 1946 joined Southampton as trainer and later spent two years as their manager. In 1952, he turned his back on the professional game and for 20 years enjoyed success in amateur football as his teams won three Isthmian League titles and reached three Wembley finals in the FA Amateur Cup. Sid finally left Sutton United in September 1973 and passed away in New Malden at the age of 85.

Season	Division	League		FA Cup		Total	
		A	G	A	G	A	G
1935-36 (P)	Division 2	9	0	0	0	9	0
1936-37	Division 1	4	0	0	0	4	0
1938-39	Division 1	2	0	0	0	2	0
Total		15	0	0	0	15	0

UK LEAGUE CAREER 101 games 3 goals

CHARLTON CAREER
Managers: *J Seed*
Debut: *Fulham (H) 26-12-1935*
V187
Finale: *Manchester United (H) 11-02-1939*

CARSON Scott Paul   2006 - 07

Goalkeeper   13st 7lbs   6' 3"
Born: 03-09-1985 - Whitehaven, Cumbria
Education: Ehenside School, Cleator Moor.

It was in 2006-07 that Charlton secured the services of the young Liverpool goalkeeper Scott Carson on a season's loan. He arrived at the Valley three months after the departure of Alan Curbishley and was one of the signings made during the brief managerial tenure of Iain Dowie. This was the year when it all seemed to fall apart for Charlton and they lurched from crisis to crisis until relegation engulfed the club. There were few highlights in this miserable season but the consistent form of Scott was a revelation and he was deservedly named as Player of the Year thereby becoming the first loan player to be so honoured.

HONOURS

England International 2007-11 4 caps 0 goals
England B International 2006-07 2 caps 0 goals
England U21 International 2004-07 29 caps 0 goals
England U18 International 2003 2 caps 0 goals

Charlton Athletic 2007 Player Of The Year
West Bromwich Albion 2009-10 Runners Up Championship
Bursaspor 2011-12 Finalists Turkish Cup
Wigan Athletic 2013 Runners Up FA Community Shield

CLUBS

Cleator Moor Celtic 2000 (youth) ••Workington 2001 (youth) ••Leeds United 07.02 (youth) 05.09.02 (pro) ••Liverpool 21.01.05 (£750,000) ••Sheffield Wednesday 10.03.06 (loan) ••Charlton Athletic 14.08.06 (loan) ••Aston Villa 10.08.07 (loan) ••West Bromwich Albion 18.07.08 (£3.25 million) ••Bursaspor, Turkey 01.07.11 (£2 million) ••Wigan Athletic 04.07.13 (£700,000) ••Derby County 12.06.15 (undisclosed) ••Manchester City 08.08.19 (loan) 19.08.20 (loan) 20.07.21 (free)

By a strange quirk of fate two Charlton goalkeepers of the future received their education at Ehinside School in the small Cumbrian town of Cleator Moor. Tony Caig, being nine years older, would have completed his schooling by the time Scott arrived but it would be interesting to know whether the same sports master taught both boys. Certainly they each progressed to play for Cleator Moor Celtic before moving on to more prominent footballing destinations. For a young goalkeeper at a big club, it is often more about learning his craft than playing matches and this was certainly the case for Scott. Appearances at first Leeds and then Liverpool were limited although he did play alongside Djimi Traore at Anfield on 5th April 2005, which resulted in a 2-1 win against Juventus in the quarter final of the Champions League. In the end though, he needed the time out on loan to gain match experience and after his season in SE7, he had an even more productive year with Aston Villa who finished 6th in the Premier League in 2007-08. Scott's form led to international recognition and on 16th November 2007 he made his full England debut against Austria, keeping a clean sheet in a 1-0 win. Five days later came the match which would haunt him for years to come. He conceded a howler as England lost at home to Croatia 3-2 and thereby failed to qualify for the finals of UEFA Euro 2008. The press and media showed no mercy and his England career was virtually finished before it had got going, with just two further substitute appearances over the next four years.

His club career found a measure of stability at West Bromwich Albion where he played regularly for three seasons which included both relegation from and promotion to the Premier League, before spending two years with the Turkish club Bursaspor. They reached the final of the Turkish FA Cup on 16th May 2012 but went down 4-0 to Fenerbahce.

In July 2013 Scott came back to the UK and joined the FA Cup holders Wigan Athletic, They almost repeated this achievement in his first season, but lost out to Arsenal at the semi-final stage. He returned to the Valley with Wigan on 16th August 2014 but was beaten by a stoppage time goal from Frank Moussa which earned Charlton a 2-1 win. The second half of Scott's career was all played at Championship level, including four years with Derby County, until surprisingly in August 2019 and aged almost 34, he was loaned to Manchester City to fill the position of third choice goalkeeper. After 12 months he had not played a single match but continued to be extremely well paid and so the arrangement was extended for a second season. He finally made his City debut on 14th May 2021 in a 4-3 win against Newcastle United and two months later, having been freed by Derby, signed up for a third season in Manchester.

Season	Division	League		FA Cup		FL Cup		Total	
		A	G	A	G	A	G	A	G
2006-07 (R)	Premier	36	0	0	0	2	0	38	0
Total		36	0	0	0	2	0	38	0

UK LEAGUE CAREER 406 games 0 goals

CHARLTON CAREER
Managers: *I Dowie, L Reed, A Pardew*
Debut: *West Ham United (A) 19-08-2006*
V633
Finale: *Tottenham Hotspur (H) 07-05-2007*

CARTER Matthew James   2017

Midfield   10st 10lbs   5' 9"
Born: 02-10-1997 - Canning Town, London

On 5th December 2017 Matt made it into the record books when he both started and finished his first team career with Charlton during one uninspiring evening. He entered the field of play as a substitute for Leon Best with just two minutes plus stoppage time remaining in a League Trophy match against Swansea U21's. There was only a derisory crowd of 501 present to witness this auspicious occasion and as he was never called up for first team duties again, it must be assumed that this briefest of cameos made little impact on the result, a 3-2 win for the Addicks. His may be the shortest appearance aggregate in Charlton's history, but he did at least cross that white line in the famous red shirt. How many others among us would have loved that privilege?

HONOURS

Charlton Athletic U23 2016-17 Winners PD League 2 South   Charlton Athletic U23 2017-18 Runners Up PD League 2 South

CLUBS

West Ham United 2003 (youth) 01.06.16 ••Charlton Athletic 19.08.16 (free) ••Hashtag United 2018 (free)

Matt is a box to box midfield player with a good awareness and range of passing. An East End boy, he spent 13 years with West Ham commencing at the age of five, until in June 2016 he earned himself his first professional contract. He had played regularly up to and including U18 level, so it was something of a surprise when only two months later he moved to Charlton. He must have considered his prospects were more favourable in SE7 and certainly he forged a place for himself in the U23 team which contested league honours in each of his two seasons with the club. But for his two minutes in the spotlight at Swansea, Matt would be just another youngster who came close but did not quite make it to the first team. He was released at the end of season 2017-18 and has so far made little impact elsewhere. He joined Hashtag United, the newly formed YouTube inspired club, but only appeared sporadically for them in the Eastern Counties League.

Season	Division	League		FA Cup		FL Cup		FL Trophy		Play Offs		Total	
		A	G	A	G	A	G	A	G	A	G	A	G
2017-18	League One	0	0	0	0	0	0	0(1)	0	0	0	0(1)	0
Total		0	0	0	0	0	0	0(1)	0	0	0	0(1)	0

UK LEAGUE CAREER 0 games 0 goals

CHARLTON CAREER
Managers: *R Slade, K Robinson, L Bowyer*
Debut: *Swansea City U21 (A) (sub) 05-12-2017*
V853

CASTLE Sidney Ernest Roland   1921 - 23

Forward   11st 2lbs   5' 9"
Born: 12-03-1892 - Basingstoke, Hampshire
Died: 27-01-1978 - Basingstoke, Hampshire

In addition to football, Sid was a natural athlete and a successful county standard competitor at both sprinting and hurdling. He did not however fully establish his football career until 1920, when at the age of 28 he signed for Tottenham and spent two seasons around the first team which at that time also included Jimmy Seed. He made a handful of first team appearances but was largely a reserve as they clinched the Division 2 Championship and then in 1921, won the FA Cup for the first time as a Football League club.

HONOURS

Charlton Athletic 1922-23 Winners London Challenge Cup

CLUBS

Basingstoke Town 1913 ••Thornycrofts 1914 ••Reading ••Crystal Palace ••Guildford United 1919 ••Tottenham Hotspur 03.20 (pro) ••Charlton Athletic 05.21 ••Chelsea 08.05.23 ••Guildford United 1926 • Ajax, Netherlands 1927 (coach) ••Zwolsche AC, Netherlands 1928 (coach) ••PEC Zwolle, Netherlands 1930 (coach) ••Heerenveen, Netherlands 1932 (manager) ••Meppel SC, Netherlands 1933 (manager) ••Heerenveen, Netherlands 1936 (manager)

Sid made his Charlton debut against Exeter City in the club's first game in the Football League and played regularly for two years, mainly in the outside right position. He scored the winner at the Den on New Year's Eve 1921 in a rare victory against Millwall and the following season appeared in five of the FA Cup matches as the Addicks progressed to the quarter final stage. It was his perfectly placed corner kick in the 83rd minute which enabled skipper Arthur Whalley to head the winner at Hyde Road and eliminate Manchester City, one of three First Division teams to be knocked out as Charlton became one of the FA Cup's first real giant killers.

Sid moved on to Chelsea and played regularly in 1923-24 until a 6-0 drubbing by Notts County in February cost him his place and they sunk towards relegation from Division 1. He reappeared from time to time the following season but his playing career was nearing its end and in 1927 he obtained a coaching position with Ajax in the Netherlands. He later had two spells managing the West Friesian club Heerenveen, where he worked with the legendary Dutch striker Abe Lenstra, then only starting out on his playing career.

Sid eventually returned to live in the UK and by 1953 was running a works canteen in Basingstoke. He passed away in Basingstoke Hospital at the age of 85.

Season	Division	League		FA Cup		Total	
		A	G	A	G	A	G
1921-22	Divison 3 (S)	30	4			30	4
1922-23	Divison 3 (S)	36	6	5	0	41	6
Total		66	10	5	0	71	10

UK LEAGUE CAREER 103 games 12 goals

CHARLTON CAREER
Managers: *W Rayner*
Debut: *Exeter City (H) 27-08-1921*
V007
Finale: *Swindon Town 03-05-1923*

CATON Thomas Stephen   1988 - 91

The story of Tommy Caton makes very sad reading. An outstanding young player who made his First Division debut for Manchester City at the age of 16 years 10 months, he went on to appear in an FA Cup final at 18 and had already played over 100 league matches well before his 20th birthday, making him the youngest player in Football League history to achieve this feat. After such a spectacular start, his career levelled off, but was cut short by a foot injury incurred while playing for Charlton on Boxing Day 1990. He was forced to retire at the age of 30 and tragically died only a month later.

Defender   13st 7lbs   6' 2"
Born: 06-10-1962 - Kirkby, Liverpool
Died: 30-04-1993 - Bampton, Oxfordshire
Education: St Kevin's RC School, Kirkby.

HONOURS

England U21 International 1981-84 14 caps 0 goals
England Youth International 1979-80 4 caps 0 goals
England Schoolboy International 1977-78 10 caps

Liverpool Boys & Merseyside Schools
Manchester City U18 1978-79 & 1979-80 Finalists FA Youth Cup
Manchester City 1980-81 Finalists FA Cup

CLUBS

KIrkby Boys {youth} ••Manchester City 1978 (youth) 10.79 (pro) ••Arsenal 01.12.83 (£500,000) ••Oxford United 30.01.87 (£180,000) ••Charlton Athletic 17.11.88 (£100,000)

Manchester City manager and former Charlton centre half Malcolm Allison gave Football League debuts to Tommy and to 17-year-old Steve MacKenzie against Crystal Palace on 18th August 1979. It was a bold move and Tommy was tasked with marking the experienced Mike Flanagan, but both youngsters grabbed their opportunity and played their parts in a 0-0 draw. So well did Tommy perform at centre half that he went on to be ever present in all 42 league matches in that 1979-80 season.

He was also an important member of the international set-up, having already captained England Schoolboys and in May 1980, along with Andy Peake, Steve MacKenzie and Colin Pates helped the U18's to capture the UEFA Youth Tournament in Germany. Two years later he saw England to victory in the UEFA U21 Championship and in 1984 did so again, although not playing in the two legged final against Italy.

Manchester City reached the FA Cup Final in 1981 and came within 10 minutes of victory before an own goal forced the tie into a replay. Tommy played in both matches but it was the Tottenham Hotspur team, including Garth Crooks and Paul Miller, which triumphed 3-2 in the replay. Two years later City were relegated to Division 2 and in December 1983 he accepted a big money transfer to Arsenal where he initially did well, but after his second season found his place under threat. He made his final appearance for the Gunners in February 1986 although it was another year before he moved on to Oxford United, then a First Division club.

Tommy's career was now slipping below the very high standard of his early years. Oxford were certainly overachieving as they tried to compete with the top clubs of the day and on 24th March 1987 Tommy was in the side when they ground out a point in a dour 0-0 draw against Charlton at Selhurst Park. In 1987-88 they battled to the semi-final of the League Cup, but were finally relegated after a disastrous run of league results in which they failed to win any of their last 26 games.

On 17th November 1988 he signed for Charlton and headed straight into another relegation struggle. Lennie Lawrence's team were able to keep their heads above water however and occasional results like the 1-0 win against Manchester United on 22nd April proved vital. Interestingly on that day, the Charlton team included Peake, MacKenzie, Pates and Caton, all four of whom had helped England win that UEFA U18 Championship almost nine years earlier.

Relegation could not be avoided the next season, but Tommy remained at the club through into 1990-91 as Charlton battled against rising financial problems. The return to the Valley had become the top priority but football matches still had to be won. He played in the 1-0 defeat to West Bromwich Albion on Boxing Day 1990 and broke a bone in his foot. The severity of the injury was not immediately apparent and he finished the match and played in the next four as well. This included a breath-taking 4-4 draw at Ipswich on 29th December in which Tommy netted the late penalty which levelled the scores, but before long the foot injury had to be addressed. It led to a long lay-off and three operations, but he was never able to regain his fitness and eventually in March 1993 he announced his retirement.

It was known within the game that Tommy had suffered difficulties with both alcohol and depression, going back to his time with Arsenal, but his sudden death on 30th April 1993 was still a terrible shock. It was reported in the media that he had died of a heart attack at his home in Bampton, Oxfordshire and left behind a wife and three young children. His son Andy Caton later played for Swindon Town.

Season	Division	League		FA Cup		FL Cup		FM Cup		Total	
		A	G	A	G	A	G	A	G	A	G
1988-89	Division 1	13	1	0	0	0	0	0	0	13	1
1989-90 (R)	Division 1	23 (1)	1	3	0	0	0	1	0	27 (1)	1
1990-91	Division 2	20	3	1	0	2	0	0	0	23	3
Total		56 (1)	5	4	0	2	0	1	0	63 (1)	5

UK LEAGUE CAREER 356 games 18 goals

CHARLTON CAREER
Managers: *L Lawrence, A Curbishley/S Gritt*
Debut: *Wimbledon (A) 19-11-1988*
V502
Finale: *Everton (H) 05-01-1991*

CEBALLOS PRIETO Cristian   2015 - 16

When Cristian signed for Charlton in the summer of
2015, he seemed an ideal addition to the squad, having
learnt his craft at the Barcelona youth academy and then
spent four years with Tottenham Hotspur. His name had first become known when he featured
in a video while juggling a football alongside Ronaldinho at age 14 and had demonstrated
considerable promise when he first arrived in England, but was now in need of first team
football if his career was to progress. Sadly he never really got going during his time in SE7 and
perhaps unfairly, is now remembered for little other than what has been described as,
'Charlton's worst ever corner'.

Midfield, Forward   10st 10lbs   5' 9"
Born: 03-12-1992 - Santander, Spain

CLUBS

Barcelona, Spain 2004 (youth) ••Tottenham Hotspur 11.07.11 (pro) ••FC Arouca, Portugal 02.09.13 (loan) ••Charlton Athletic 23.07.15 (free) ••Sint-
Truiden, Belgium 01.08.16 (loan) 19.07.17 (free) ••Al-Wakrah, Qatar 07.19 (undisclosed) ••Qatar Sports, Qatar 10.03.21 (free) ••Sabah, Azerbaijan
08.08.21 (free)

Cristian featured in just seven matches during his year at
Charlton, but did not complete 90 minutes in a single one.
The infamous corner came during a 1-1 draw at Derby
County on 15th August 2015. He had come on as a second
half substitute for Zakarya Bergdich and right in front of
the travelling supporters, completely mis-hit the ball which
rolled off for a goal kick without even reaching the 18 yard
box. Unfortunately for Cristian, the incident is preserved
for posterity on YouTube.

After an encouraging start to the 2015-16 season, Charlton
gradually slid down the Championship table and Cristian
was just one of several players who were unable to halt the
decline. His appearances all came in the first half of the
campaign and his swansong was the truly appalling FA Cup
defeat against Colchester United on 9th January. Karel

Fraeye, Charlton's hapless Interim Manager, lost his job less
than a week later and Cristian was removed from the firing
line as the team sunk back towards League One.
He spent 2016-17 on loan at Sint-Truiden, another club
owned by Roland Duchatelet, which played in the top
division of the Belgian Pro League. He returned to the
Valley the following summer and showed up well in pre-
season before making permanent his transfer to Sint-
Truiden on 19th July 2017, where his teammates included
Jordan Botaka, Igor Vetokele and Jorge Teixeira. By 2019
Cristian was playing for Al-Wakrah in the Qatar Stars
League, but is currently to be found in the Azerbaijani
Premier League with Sarbah. It is not known whether he
takes their corners.

Season	Division	League		FA Cup		FL Cup		Total	
		A	G	A	G	A	G	A	G
2015-16 (R)	Championship	3 (2)	0	1	0	1	0	5 (2)	0
Total		3 (2)	0	1	0	1	0	5 (2)	0

UK LEAGUE CAREER 5 games 0 goals

CHARLTON CAREER
Managers: *G Luzon, K Fraeye, J Riga, R Slade, K Robinson*
Debut: *Queens Park Rangers (H0 08-08-2015*
V803
Finale: *Colchester United (A) 09-01-2016*

CHAMBERLAIN Kenneth Russell   1952 - 57

One of the South Africans brought over by Jimmy
Seed to play for Charlton in the early fifties, Ken
spent five and a half years in South London and
although he never achieved the heights of Leary,
Firmani or Hewie, he was nevertheless a solid and
reliable centre half who featured mainly in the Reserves, but was called upon for first team
duty whenever England international Derek Ufton was unavailable through injury.

Defender   12st 0lbs   6' 0"
Born: 30-06-1926 - Durban, South Africa
Died: 25-11-2002 - Johannesburg, South Africa
Education: Mansfield High School, Durban.

HONOURS

South Africa XI 1956 1 cap 0 goals   Charlton Athletic Reserves 1952-53 Runners Up Football Combination Cup
Province of Natal 1948

CLUBS

Thistle, South Africa ••Parkhill, South Africa ••Glenwood, South Africa ••Parkhill, South Africa ••Charlton Athletic 10.10.51 (pro) ••Johannesburg Wanderers, South Africa 1957 (free)

Ken came to prominence during 1951 when he twice played for a South African representative XI against a touring Wolverhampton Wanderers side and that same year signed a professional contract with Charlton. Before travelling to England he had been working as an apprentice boilermaker with Dorman Long Engineering.

He got his first team chance somewhat by default after Derek Ufton was injured in just the second league fixture of the 1952-53 season. Derek was replaced for the next match by Jimmy Walls who himself got injured against Wolves three days later and this proved to be Jimmy's final appearance in the first team. With two central defenders in the medical room, Ken was called up for his debut at Portsmouth on 3rd September and helped earn a respectable 1-1 draw thanks to an equalising goal from Billy Kiernan. He held his place until Ufton was fit again in October, which included an extraordinary game at Blackpool which finished with Charlton on the wrong end of an 8-4 scoreline. Bartram was also missing that day and fellow South African Albert Uytenbogaardt had the dubious pleasure of joining Ken in the Addicks defence.

The pattern continued right through Ken's time in English football. He remained Ufton's understudy, but with Derek's recurring shoulder injuries giving increasing cause for concern as the years went by, he seemed assured of at least some first team action every season. He did get to play in an unofficial international between Scotland and South Africa at Maine Road, Manchester on 12th March 1956 to raise funds for the British Olympic Appeal and the South African side was managed by Jimmy Seed.

By the time that Ufton's grip on the number five shirt loosened, it was the relegation season of 1956-57 and Gordon Jago was now also in contention. Ken was tried at wing half over Christmas and the New Year but the results did not improve. There was talk of a move to Wisbech Town as player manager in February 1957, but instead he was freed from his contract and returned home to South Africa on 24th April.

He initially found work as a travelling salesman for a Johannesburg wine company but by 1959 was selling motor tyres. Later Ken worked as a brewery representative. He passed away at the age of 76.

Season	Division	League		FA Cup		Total	
		A	G	A	G	A	G
1952-53	Division 1	15	0	0	0	15	0
1953-54	Division 1	5	0	0	0	5	0
1954-55	Division 1	8	0	0	0	8	0
1955-56	Division 1	5	0	0	0	5	0
1956-57 (R)	Division 1	9	0	2	0	11	0
Total		42	0	2	0	44	0

UK LEAGUE CAREER 42 games 0 goals

CHARLTON CAREER
Managers: *J Seed, J Trotter*
Debut: *Portsmouth (A) 03-09-1952*
V251
Finale: *Manchester City (A) 19-01-1957*

CHAMPION Ernest Frank   1923

Defender
Born: 23-05-1894 - Lewisham, London
Died: 16-01-1974 - Bromley, Kent

Shortly after Frank moved from Catford Southend to Charlton in the Summer of 1923, the two clubs engaged in secret talks to set up a ground share arrangement whereby the Valley would be abandoned in favour of the more compact Catford stadium, the Mount. Charlton were in a dire financial state and this unpopular manoeuvre was a desperate attempt to keep them afloat. Against such an unsettling atmosphere full back Frank Champion had to try and establish himself with his new club.

HONOURS

Charlton Athletic A 1923-24 Winners Kent League

CLUBS

Catford Southend 1922 ••Charlton Athletic 19.08.23 (amateur) 11.23 (pro) ••Catford Southend 07.24 ••Tunbridge Wells Rangers 1925

Frank got his chance in the first team during December and played two matches on consecutive Saturdays, each against Swansea Town and both ended in defeat. The home game was a particularly sombre occasion as it was to be the final match at the Valley and a crowd of around 5000 saw Kosha Goodman score a consolation goal as they went down 3-1 against their promotion chasing opponents

Frank's own contribution must have been considered modest as he was never picked again and was therefore absent two weeks later when Charlton played their first home game at the Mount decked out in the light and dark blue strip of Catford Southend. At least, six decades later, when Charlton were foolish enough to try an equally unpopular ground share, they did not do so wearing the claret and blue of Crystal Palace.

The move to the Mount was quickly seen to have been a mistake and they returned to the Valley at the end of that 1923-24 season, but without Frank who re-signed for his old club, his Football League career at an end. By 1939 he was resident in Bourne Road, Bromley and working as a plumber and fitter.

Season	Division	League		FA Cup		Total	
		A	G	A	G	A	G
1923-24	Divison 3 (S)	2	0	0	0	2	0
Total		2	0	0	0	2	0

UK LEAGUE CAREER 2 games 0 goals

CHARLTON CAREER
Managers: *W Rayner*
Debut: *Swansea Town (A) 01-12-1923*
V054
Finale: *Swansea Town (H) 08-12-1923*

CHANDLER Dean Andrew Robert   1995 - 96

Charlton signed two young players on professional terms on 13th April 1994. One was Dean Chandler and the other was Lee Bowyer. The subsequent careers of both men headed off in very different directions, but it would not be unfair to say that they both shared one thing in common, namely the ability throughout their playing days to attract the headlines and in many cases for the wrong reasons.

Defender   11st 5lbs   6' 0"
Born: 06-05-1976 - Ilford, Essex

HONOURS

Redbridge Schools
England Learning Disability X1 2004

Charlton Athletic Reserves 1995-96 Finalists Kent Senior Cup

CLUBS

Tottenham Hotspur 20.08.91 (youth) ••Charlton Athletic 25.02.92 (youth) 13.04.94 (pro) ••Torquay United 27.03.97 (loan) ••Lincoln City 04.08.97 (free) ••Yeovil Town 28.11.97 (loan) ••Chesham United 28.08.98 ••Slough Town 26.11.98 ••Yeovil Town 27.11.00 (£3,500) ••Slough Town 09.00 ••Woking 10.08.01 (free) ••Purfleet 11.01 ••Thurrock 2003 ••Ford United 08.03 ••East Thurrock United 06.04 ••Leyton 11.05 ••Heybridge Swifts 04.06 ••East Thurrock United 04.07 ••Redbridge 12.07

Dean was a centre half who in total spent more than five years with Charlton. His name first came to the attention of the general public when as an 18-year-old on 27th March 1995, it was reported that both he and Lee Bowyer had given a positive reading for marijuana in a routine drug test. The FA became involved in the subsequent discussions and

both players were stopped from playing, although not formally suspended. However, by 7th May they appear to have been forgiven as they each appeared against Reading in a league fixture at Elm Park. This was Dean's debut and he scored what appeared to be the equalising goal, only for the home side to grab a late winner.

In the following season Lee became a first team regular, but Dean had to wait seven months before he was called upon again and then it was only as a substitute in the 90th minute of a game at the Valley against Ipswich Town and there was hardly even time for his legs to get muddy. However, there was a reason for the long gap between his two first team appearances. Following a day allegedly spent smoking cannabis and drinking lager, Dean had been charged with raping a teenage girl in her flat and had to face a trial at the Old Bailey in July 1995. The jury were unable to reach a verdict and a re-trial took place three months later when this time he was unanimously acquitted.

Sent out on loan to Torquay United in March 1997, he joined Garry Nelson in a relegation battle in Division 3, but injured an ankle just 22 minutes into his debut and only managed a total of four appearances. He was given a free transfer by Charlton at the end of that season and signed for Lincoln City, where he played one solitary League Cup match against Burnley on 26th August 1997 before dropping into non-league where he moved from club to club with alarming regularity.

Dean signed with Slough Town in November 1998, but was allowed to switch to Yeovil just a day later. Here all went well for a time, but he was eventually released after reportedly turning out in a testimonial cricket match while supposedly injured. By 2002 he was with Purfleet playing in the Isthmian League, but this too came to an abrupt end when he was sacked for a breach of club discipline. In 2004, he was selected for the England Learning Disability team to compete in the INAS Global Games, but got sent off against Brazil in the quarter final for violent conduct. He had a spell with East Thurrock United playing alongside Paul Linger and by 2008 was competing in the Isthmian League for Redbridge. Later reports indicated that he was working as a site manager for a construction company.

Season	Division	League		FA Cup		FL Cup		Play Offs		Total	
		A	G	A	G	A	G	A	G	A	G
1994-95	Division 1	1	1	0	0	0	0			1	1
1995-96	Division 1	0 (1)	0	0	0	0	0	0	0	0 (1)	0
Total		1 (1)	1	0	0	0	0	0	0	1 (1)	1

UK LEAGUE CAREER 6 games 1 goal

CHARLTON CAREER
Managers: *A Curbishley/S Gritt, A Curbishley*
Debut: *Reading (A) 07-05-1995*
V553
Finale: *Ipswich Town (H) (sub) 09-12-1996*

CHAPPLE Philip Richard　　　　　　　　　　　1993 - 98

Defender　12st 7lbs　6' 2"
Born: 26-11-1966 - Norwich, Norfolk
Education: The Hewett School, Norwich.

A no nonsense central defender, Phil made his name at Cambridge United during that heady period when under the managerial guidance of John Beck this small and unfashionable club achieved two consecutive promotions and in 1992 came tantalisingly close to achieving a place in the newly formed Premier League. This unlikely scenario was achieved through Beck's extreme coaching methods and his commitment to the long ball game. Phil was a key member of this the most successful Cambridge team of all time and when the bubble inevitably burst and others worked out how to counter Beck's tactics, he was transferred to Charlton for a fee initially set at £100,000, but which with add ons eventually increased to £125,000.

HONOURS
Norwich Schools & Norfolk Schools
Charlton Athletic 1997-98 Promoted Play Offs Division 1
Cambridge United 1989-90 Promoted Play Offs Division 4

Cambridge United 1990-91 Winners Division 3
Peterborough United 1999-00 Promoted Division 3

CLUBS
Norwich City 05.83 (youth) 10.07.85 (pro) ••Cambridge United 29.03.88 (£10,000) ••Charlton Athletic 13.08.93 (£125,000) ••Peterborough United 07.08.98 (free) 2001 (coach) ••West Ham United 2003 (youth coach) ••Newmarket Town 05.05 (coach) ••Charlton Athletic 07.01.07 (chief scout & coach) ••Fulham 28.09.15 (scout) ••Brighton & Hove Albion 12.16 (european scout) ••Stoke City 19.09.19 (head of recruitment) ••Luton Town 15.02.21 (scout)

The first time Charlton encountered Phil Chapple was　　　　when Cambridge visited the Boleyn Ground on 23rd

November 1991. Their pre-match preparation involved all their team, (which included John Vaughan, Gary Rowett and Alan Kimble), hitting long ball passes to each other across the full width of the pitch in readiness for the onslaught that was to follow. Charlton were battered to a 2-1 home defeat, with only a late goal from Paul Gorman to show for their efforts.

Phil got off to the best possible start at Charlton, scoring on his debut in a 1-0 victory over Birmingham City. He was a formidable physical presence and enjoyed an excellent first season before a succession of injuries restricted his appearances and gradually affected his form. There was a hernia operation in 1994, while on 5th December 1995 he picked up a serious knee ligament injury at Millwall which kept him out of the side for nine months. He never seemed quite the same player after that but did maintain his place in the team up to and including the 1997-98 promotion season and the fact that he played in 35 league games that term has now been overlooked by many, because he did not feature after the 5-0 win against West Bromwich Albion on

5th March and was just a spectator for the Wembley promotion decider against Sunderland.

He moved on to Peterborough United in the summer but his injury problems were worsening and he only managed one league appearance during the whole of 1998-99. So rarely did he turn out for his new club that he became referred to as the 'Chapple of Rest'. He was able to participate in the first part of Peterborough's promotion campaign of 1999-00, but his playing contribution ended in January after which he moved over to assist with coaching.

Since hanging up his boots Phil has had a number of jobs in football and returned to Charlton in 2007, initially in a scouting capacity. He coached for a time when Phil Parkinson was in the manager's chair, but held the role of chief scout through until 2015 when he found that new owner Roland Duchatelet held different views on player recruitment and so departed for a similar position with Fulham. He joined the scouting team at Luton Town in February 2021.

Season	Division	League		FA Cup		FL Cup		AI Cup		Play Offs		Total	
		A	G	A	G	A	G	A	G	A	G	A	G
1993-94	Division 1	40 (4)	5	3	0	2	0	5	0			50 (4)	5
1994-95	Division 1	21	2	1	0	2	0					24	2
1995-96	Division 1	13 (3)	2	0	0	3	0			0	0	16 (3)	2
1996-97	Division 1	25 (1)	2	2	0	3	0					30 (1)	2
1997-98 (P)	Division 1	29 (6)	4	3	0	1	0			0	0	33 (6)	4
Total		128 (14)	15	9	0	11	0	5	0	0	0	153 (14)	15

UK LEAGUE CAREER 346 games 35 goals

CHARLTON CAREER
Managers: *A Curbishley/S Gritt, A Curbishley*
Debut: *Birmingham City (H) 14-08-1993*
V540
Finale: *Crewe Alexandra (A) 21-03-1998*

CHARLES-COOK Regan Evans   2015 - 17

Regan was a graduate of Charlton's excellent youth academy and a member of the championship winning Under 21 side of 2015-16. Usually a midfield player, he was rewarded with a first team debut at right back as deputy for Chris Solly in the League Cup match against Dagenham & Redbridge on 11th August 2015 and gave a solid performance in a 4-1 victory. His brothers Reice Charles-Cook and Anthony Cook are both professional footballers, while his uncle James Cook MBE is the former European super middleweight boxing champion.

Midfield, Defender   10st 12lbs   5' 9"
Born: 14-02-1997 - Beckenham, Kent
Education: Forest Hill School, London.

HONOURS
Charlton Athletic U18 2013-14 & 2014-15 Winners PD League 2 South
Charlton Athletic U21 2014-15 Winners Kent Senior Cup
Charlton Athletic U21 2015-16 Winners PD League 2 South
Charlton Athletic U21 2015-16 Finalists Kent Senior Cup
Charlton Athletic U23 2016-17 Winners PD League 2 South

CLUBS
Arsenal 2007 (youth) ••Charlton Athletic 2013 (youth) 2015 (pro) ••Solihull Moors 04.02.17 (loan) •Woking 01.09.17 (loan) 08.03.18 (loan)
••Gillingham 30.05.18 (free) •Ross County, Scotland 30.06.20 (free)

Having enjoyed a taste of first team football in 2015-16, Regan spent much of the next two years on loan with National League sides Solihull Moors and Woking, where he performed adequately, but without quite being able to persuade any of the constantly changing procession of Charlton managers to give him a decent run in the side. At the end of 2017-18, he was offered a further contract for one year and initially it was reported that he would remain with the club, but on 30th May he signed for League One rivals Gillingham instead. He joined a squad which included both Brandon Hanlan and Josh Parker and over the next two seasons featured in 41 league games, but invariably from the bench, as the Gills maintained a safe mid-table presence in League One. In June 2020 Regan uprooted and signed for Scottish Premier League club Ross County.

Based in Dingwall, the Staggies are comparative newcomers to the Scottish League. They were promoted to the top division in 2019 for only the second time in their history and struggle to compete at that level. In his first season, Regan again spent much of his time warming the bench and did not score in any of the 26 league matches in which he participated. In 2021-22 however he has been a revelation. On 27th October 2021 he scored twice when Ross County recorded an unexpected 5-0 Premier League win away against Dundee and although they remained near to the foot of the division, his goals have been keeping the club afloat. Converted to a wide, more attacking role, on 26th February 2022 he scored another brace as St Johnstone were defeated 3-1 and his 13 league goals for the season up to that point, then placed him top goalscorer in the Scottish Premier League.

Season	Division	League		FA Cup		FL Cup		FL Trophy		Total	
		A	G	A	G	A	G	A	G	A	G
2015-16 (R)	Championship	0 (1)	0	1	0	2	0			3 (1)	0
2016-17	League One	0	0	0	0	0	0	0 (1)	0	0 (1)	0
2017-18	League One	0	0	0	0	2	1	2	0	4	1
Total		0 (1)	0	1	0	4	1	2 (1)	0	7 (2)	1

UK LEAGUE CAREER 68 games 6 goals

CHARLTON CAREER
Managers: *C Powell, J Riga, B Peeters, G Luzon, K Fraeye, J Riga, R Slade, K Robinson, L Bowyer*
Debut: *Dagenham & Redbridge (H) 11-08-2015*
V804
Finale: *Swansea City U23 (A) 05-12-2017*

CHICKSEN Adam Thomas   2016 - 17

Defender, Midfield   11st 9lbs   5' 8"
Born: 27-09-1991 - Milton Keynes, Buckinghamshire
Education: St Paul's Catholic School, Milton Keynes.

In August 2008, Adam became the first Milton Keynes born player to appear for them in the Football League when he made his debut as a 16-year-old substitute against Leicester City. A tidy full back, he is of English, Zimbabwean and Chinese descent and on 21st March 2018 obtained his first full international cap for Zimbabwe in the semi final of the Four Nations Cup against Zambia.

HONOURS
Zimbabwe International 2018-20 2 caps 0 goals

CLUBS
Milton Keynes Dons 07.06 (youth) 05.10 (pro) ••Leyton Orient 01.01.12 (loan) ••Brighton & Hove Albion 14.07.13 (free) ••Gillingham 14.11.14 (loan) ••Fleetwood Town 27.02.15 (loan) ••Leyton Orient 02.10.15 (loan) ••Gillingham 27.01.16 (loan) ••Charlton Athletic 30.08.16 ((free) ••Bradford City 19.06.17 (free) ••Bolton Wanderers 14.09.19 (free) ••Notts County 10.09.20 (free)

Adam spent time on the fringe of the first team at Milton Keynes but did feature in the play off semi finals against Huddersfield in May 2012, when the Dons, including Charlie MacDonald, narrowly missed out on a trip to Wembley and promotion from League One. A move to Brighton did not improve things and he had little involvement at first team level during his three years on the Sussex coast.

After signing for Charlton on the last day of the August 2016 transfer window, Adam made a positive impact as a substitute at Bristol Rovers on 22nd November, in what was a very one sided contest. It ended 5-1 and he scored the fourth goal, but found it hard to displace Chris Solly and Morgan Fox from the full back positions. The club did not renew his contract at the end of the season and he moved on to Bradford City in June 2017 and to Bolton Wanderers two years later. Both clubs were in a financial mess and he played through an unsuccessful relegation battle with Bradford in 2018-19 and then again with Bolton a year later,

It could be argued that Adam's choice of clubs was questionable, but after being released by Bolton, he eventually joined Notts County who had just been relegated into the National League. Two years later he is looking to reverse the fortunes of both himself and the club by regaining a place in the Football League.

Season	Division	League		FA Cup		FL Cup		FL Trophy		Total	
		A	G	A	G	A	G	A	G	A	G
2016-17	League One	15 (6)	1	1	1	0	0	2 (1)	0	18 (7)	2
Total		15 (6)	1	1	1	0	0	2 (1)	0	18 (7)	2

UK LEAGUE CAREER 194 games 3 goals

CHARLTON CAREER
Managers: *R Slade, K Robinson*
Debut: *Southampton U21 (A) (sub) 30-08-2016*
V831
Finale: *Peterborough United (A) 01-04-2017*

CHIN Richard Li   2021 -

Richard is an all-action box to box midfield player who is viewed as an exciting prospect. He made his debut in the Football League Trophy match at Leyton Orient on 9th November 2021. It was the final group game and as both teams had already qualified for the knockout stage of the competition, was something of a dead rubber. It was however an ideal opportunity to blood some of the young players who have performed so well in the academy and who were now knocking at the first team door. Richard was given his full debut and although the match was narrowly lost 1-0, he did enough to show that he is very much one to watch for the future.

Midfield   11st 0lbs   5' 8"
Born: 18-10-2002 - Sidcup, Kent
Education: Beths Grammar School, Bexley.

HONOURS
Kent Schools   Charlton Athletic U18 2020-21 Winners PD League 2 South

CLUBS
Charlton Athletic 2008 (youth) 07.21 (pro)

Born in Sidcup to Seychellois-Malaysian parents, Richard attended Beths Grammar School in Bexley where he played in the same team as another future Addick, Euan Williams. He had spells training with both Charlton and Crystal Palace, but his family chose Charlton as the academy where they felt comfortable and where there is a well-defined pathway to the first team for those youngsters that attain

the necessary standard. He has represented Kent Schools and at Charlton has been consistently playing a year above his age group. After captaining the U18's to league honours in 2020-21 and now having made his first team debut, the future looks bright as long as he continues to work hard and keep clear of injuries.

UK LEAGUE CAREER 0 games 0 goals

CHARLTON CAREER
Managers: *N Adkins, J Jackson*
Debut: *Leyton Orient (A) 09-11-2021*
V935

CHIPPERFIELD John James   1923 - 24

Forward   11st 4lbs   5' 9"
Born: 04-03-1894 - Bethnal Green, London
Died: 06-09-1966 - Wandsworth, London

No Charlton supporter alive ever saw Jimmy play for the club, as it is now almost 100 years since the last of his three matches and in truth very few would have seen him in action even at the time. All three games were played away from home, all were lost and not a single goal was scored by the team, which hardly makes for a very memorable contribution. Born in Lymon Street, Bethnal Green, he had moved to Luton by 1911 and at the age of 17 was working as an iron turner for Commercial Cars. It was with them that he commenced his footballing life the following year.

HONOURS

Charlton Athletic A 1923-24 Winners Kent League   Tottenham Hotspur 1919-20 Winners Division 2
Luton Clarence 1913-14 Runners Up Athenian League

CLUBS

Commercial Cars 1912 ••Luton Clarence 1913 ••Luton Town 1914 (pro) ••Arsenal 1915 (wartime) ••Tottenham Hotspur 19.06.19 (£1,000) ••Notts County 13.12.21 (£1,500) ••Northfleet United 01.12.22 ••Charlton Athletic 05.23 ••Chatham Town 08.24

Jimmy played regularly for Arsenal during the First World War. League football during that period was regionalised to reduce travel and they competed in the London Combination. He played up front with the famous Kent cricketer, Wally Hardinge and made more than 100 appearances. He twice scored hat tricks and finished as Arsenal's leading goalscorer in both the 1916-17 and 1918-19 seasons.

After the war, he signed for Tottenham and made his debut at outside left on 30th August 1919, scoring twice as Coventry City were battered 5-0. The hapless Coventry goalkeeper that day was future Charlton player and manager Albert Lindon. Spurs led Division 2 from start to finish in the 1919-20 season and Jimmy contributed 15

games and six goals. His teammate during the later stages was Jimmy Seed, newly signed from Mid-Rhondda. Jimmy spent season 1921-22 with Notts County in Division 2. Although their league form was unremarkable, they had an exciting FA Cup run and he scored both goals as they held Aston Villa to a 2-2 draw in the quarter final on 4th March. They won the replay, but he missed the semi final defeat against Huddersfield Town a few weeks later. His final season in the Football League was 1923-24 for Charlton, but with both Steve Smith and Bill Berry preferred for the outside left berth ahead of him, his career was allowed to quietly fade away, Jimmy later worked as a maintenance man and died in Wandsworth at the age of 72.

Season	Division	League		FA Cup		Total	
		A	G	A	G	A	G
1923-24	Divison 3 (S)	3	0	0	0	3	0
Total		3	0	0	0	3	0

UK LEAGUE CAREER 36 games 8 goals

CHARLTON CAREER
Managers: *W Rayner*
Debut: *Millwall (A) 29-09-1923*
V051
Finale: *Brighton & Hove Albion (A) 15-03-1924*

CHURCH Simon Richard   2013 - 15

Without doubt, it was his success in international football with Wales which provided the greatest career satisfaction for

Striker   13st 2lbs   6' 0"
Born: 10-12-1988 - Amersham, Buckinghamshire

Simon. Although born in Buckinghamshire, he qualified through his Welsh grandfather and captained Wales U21's before making his full debut in 2009. He went on to form the most unlikely of strike partnerships with Gareth Bale and appeared at UEFA Euro 2016, including the memorable semi final against Portugal in which Wales came closer than ever to reaching a major tournament final.

HONOURS

Wales International 2009-16 38 caps 5 goals   Reading 2011-12 Winners Championship
Wales U21 International 2007-10 15 caps 8 goals

CLUBS

Wycombe Wanderers 1998 (youth) ••Reading 2003 (youth) 04.07.07 (pro) ••Crewe Alexandra 19.10.07 (loan) ••Yeovil Town 30.01.08 (loan) ••Wycombe Wanderers 28.08.08 (loan) ••Leyton Orient 17.02.09 (loan) ••Huddersfield Town 08.11.12 (loan) ••Charlton Athletic 01.08.13 (free) ••MIlton Keynes Dons 30.06.15 (free) ••Aberdeen, Scotland 01.02.16 (loan) ••Roda JC Kerkrade, Netherlands 24.08.16 (free) ••Scunthorpe United 21.10.17 (free) ••Plymouth Argyle 19.01.18 (free)

The early part of Simon's career was spent with Reading, but before being given a first team chance, he was tested through loans at Crewe Alexandra, Yeovil Town and Wycombe Wanderers. His time finally arrived in season 2009-10 and he delivered 10 league goals in the Championship, more than he ever achieved in the years ahead. Two seasons later when Reading won promotion to the Premier League, he only scored seven, but two of them came on 10th December 2011 in the 3-0 defeat of West Ham.

Simon joined Charlton as an established Welsh international, but it is fair to say that his two-year stay was disappointing for all concerned. Nobody could fault his effort, however. He was constantly looking for the ball and no matter how badly things went for him, he would never hide and for this alone he must be given credit. He was capable of dribbling long distances and the occasional defence splitting ball, but as soon as he got close to goal he

seemed to lack a striker's instinct and chance after chance went begging. He became visibly frustrated and after a while the crowd started to get at him as well.

Simon managed seven Welsh caps and one international goal during his time at Charlton but eventually he moved on to MK Dons seeking a new start at club level. In 2016, he decided to try his luck overseas, but after only four games with Dutch team Roda JC Kerkrade exacerbated an earlier hip injury which was made worse by their artificial pitch. He struggled to get fit and resume his career but after false starts with Scunthorpe and Plymouth announced his retirement from the game on 9th May 2018.

Back in 2009 and at the age of 20, Simon had set up his own company titled Simon Church Property Investment Co Ltd and with his playing days now behind him, he announced that he would be pursuing this as his new career path aimed specifically to cater for professional sports people.

Season	Division	League		FA Cup		FL Cup		Total	
		A	G	A	G	A	G	A	G
2013-14	Championship	28 (10)	3	5	2	1	2	34 (10)	7
2014-15	Championship	3 (14)	2	1	0	0 (1)	1	4 (15)	3
Total		31 (24)	5	6	2	1 (1)	3	38 (25)	10

UK LEAGUE CAREER 244 games 42 goals

CHARLTON CAREER
Managers: *C Powell, J Riga, B Peeters, G Luzon*
Debut: *AFC Bournemouth (H) (sub) 03-08-2013*
V761
Finale: *AFC Bournemouth (H) (sub) 02-05-2015*

CHURCHOUSE Gary   1979 - 80

Midfield   11st 8lbs   5' 9"
Born: 01-02-1957 - Wembley, Middlesex
Education: Evelyn's Secondary School, West Drayton.

The Valley was not a very tranquil place when Gary was signed from non-league Windsor & Eton in March 1979. Andy Nelson was entering what turned out to be his final year as Charlton manager and on the field both performances and results were worsening. It was only weeks since the infamous sending off of two players for fighting each other. Derek Hales had been sacked and then reinstated, while Mike Flanagan had walked out and would later be sold to Crystal Palace. Team spirit had inevitably been affected by all this upheaval and it was going to be a monumental task for Gary or anyone else to come into the team and halt the downward spiral.

HONOURS

Charlton Athletic Reserves 1979-80 Winners Mid-Week League Cup   Charlton Athletic Reserves 1979-80 Runners Up Mid-Week League

CLUBS

Viking Sports (youth) ••Brentford 1972 (youth) ••Uxbridge 1973 (youth) ••Windsor & Eton 1978 (pro) ••Charlton Athletic 22.03.79 (£2,000) ••Herfolge BK, Denmark 1981 ••Maidenhead United 1982 ••Wealdstone 1982 ••Uxbridge 1982 ••Southall 1982 ••Woking 1984 ••Takapuna City, New Zealand 1985 ••Hayes 1986 ••Waitakrie City, New Zealand 1989

His debut came in a home game against Crystal Palace and finished 1-1 thanks to a first minute strike from Colin Powell. This was the seventh consecutive winless match and already the Valley faithful were getting restless. The club had been 10th in the league on the day that Gary signed, but tumbled downwards as the run continued. Defender Peter Shaw was the victim of some vicious barracking around this time and it is fair to say that Gary's efforts in midfield were not wholly appreciated either. Charlton did not register a victory in any of his first nine matches and it needed a long overdue result against Oldham Athletic on the final day of the season to avoid the drop and to produce the first win in 16 matches. Two goals from Martin Robinson ensured a 2-0 scoreline and probably kept Andy Nelson in his job for a little longer.

Season 1979-80 proved even worse and Charlton were bottom of Division 2 by mid-September. Gary was in and out of the side early on, but was gradually phased out and hardly played at all after Mike Bailey took over as manager in March. He was given one last opportunity on 5th May 1980. It was the final match of the season and Charlton in

22nd place were already confirmed for relegation. The opponents were West Ham and they scored after just 17 seconds and went on to register a 4-1 win. Tony Hazell was sent off for Charlton in the second half and for Gary Churchouse, this brought his time in the Football League to a close.

He left Charlton in 1981 and spent a year playing in Denmark for Herfolge Boldklub, before returning for a series of short spells with senior non-league clubs in the London area. The exception was Isthmian League Southall where he stayed for two years leading up to an even more distant move to New Zealand where he turned out first for Takapune City and later Waitakrie City. In between he managed two seasons with Hayes back in the Isthmian League.

Gary had worked as a plasterer before joining Charlton, but by 2005 had settled in Queensland, Australia and since then has been working in the electrical and communications industry for Rainbow Engineering and residing in the small town of Nerang.

Season	Division	League		FA Cup		FL Cup		Total	
		A	G	A	G	A	G	A	G
1978-79	Division 2	9	0	0	0	0	0	9	0
1979-80 (R)	Division 2	4 (5)	0	0	0	1 (1)	0	5 (6)	0
Total		13 (5)	0	0	0	1 (1)	0	14 (6)	0

UK LEAGUE CAREER 18 games 0 goals

CHARLTON CAREER
Managers: *A Nelson, M Bailey*
Debut: *Crystal Palace (H) 27-03-1979*
V413
Finale: *West Ham United (A) 05-05-1980*

CLARE Sean James Kweku   2021 -

A box to box midfield player and occasional full
back, Sean signed for Charlton ahead of the 2021-22
season. The club was re-building for the first full
campaign under new owner Thomas Sandgaard and

Midfield, Defender   6' 3"
Born: 18-09-1996 - Hackney, London
Education: Nike Academy, Burton on Trent.

he arrived from Oxford United for an undisclosed fee. For Sean this was a return to his roots
as he had started out with the Charlton academy in the same Under 11 team as Joe Gomez
and he looked upon this fresh challenge in SE7 as unfinished business.

HONOURS

Heart Of Midlothian 2018-19 Finalists Scottish FA Cup

CLUBS

Charlton Athletic 2007 (youth) ••Shenfield High c 2014 (youth) ••Nike Academy c 2015 (youth) ••Sheffield Wednesday 02.16 (pro) ••Bury 05.03.16
(loan) ••Accrington Stanley 20.01.17 (loan) ••Gillingham 31.08.17 (loan) ••Heart Of Midlothian, Scotland 16.09.18 (free) ••Oxford United 06.08.20
(undisclosed) ••Burton Albion 12.01.21 (loan) ••Charlton Athletic 20.07.21 (undisclosed)

A Londoner born into a Ghanaian family, Sean initially
stepped away from football in his teens because of concerns
that his school work was beginning to suffer. After his A-
levels, he was accepted into the Nike Academy and from
there earned a pro contract with Sheffield Wednesday. Not
deemed ready for the first team, he had spells out on loan
first with Bury and Accrington Stanley and then with
Gillingham where in 2017-18 he played alongside Scott
Wagstaff and Josh Parker and twice defeated Charlton in
league encounters. He finally made his full league debut for
Sheffield Wednesday in the Championship on 13th
February 2018 and scored against Aston Villa the following
week.

In September 2018 he signed a three-year deal to join
Hearts and in his first season north of the border they
enjoyed a run in the Scottish Cup. Sean scored in the semi-
final win over Inverness Caledonian Thistle and played in
the Final at Hampden Park on 25th May 2019, but Celtic

proved too strong and Hearts went down 2-1. The
following season proved disastrous for the Edinburgh club
and they were relegated from the Scottish Premier League
at the end of the Covid interrupted season of 2019-20. Sean
and his teammate Conor Washington both departed, Sean
joining Oxford United on 6th August 2020 and Conor
signing for Charlton seven days later.

Oxford played him mainly at full back and it was in that
position that he lined up at the Valley on 27th October
2020, but Charlton ran out as winners 2-0, courtesy of
goals from Conor Washington and Andrew Shinnie. He
reverted to midfield after joining Burton Albion on loan in
January 2021. They were bottom of League One when he
arrived but a remarkable spell of eight wins in nine matches
saw them safe from relegation. Hoping to see some action
at the other end of the division he joined Charlton on a
two-year contract in July 2021.

UK LEAGUE CAREER 129 games 11 goals

CHARLTON CAREER
Managers: *N Adkins, J Jackson*
Debut: *Sheffield Wednesday (H) 07-08-2021*
V924

CLARKE Allen Frederick   1971

Goalkeeper   12st 8lbs   5' 11"
Born: 02-12-1952 - Crayford, Kent
Education: Slade Green School.

Allen was a promising goalkeeper who as a teenager represented North Kent Schools and first appeared for the Charlton Colts in season 1969-70. He played in three first team matches during October 1971 as replacement for Derek Bellotti, but was unable to convince manager Theo Foley that he had a long term future with the club and was given a free transfer in May 1973.

HONOURS
Slade Green Athletic 1968-69 Runners Up Greater London League

CLUBS
Slade Green Athletic 1967 (amateur) ••Charlton Athletic 02.12.69 (youth) 04.012.70 (pro) ••Margate 03.71 (loan) ••Bristol Rovers 09.71 (loan) ••Ramsgate 1972 (loan) ••Exeter City 23.02.73 (loan) 18.05.73 (free) ••Dartford 1974 (free) ••Slade Green Athletic c1975 (free)

Before featuring in Charlton's first team, Allen had gone on loan to Margate in March 1971 and played 14 games for them in the Southern League. It would have been 15 appearances, but he missed the home match with Dover after getting on the wrong train. Otherwise, however he made a favourable impression and excelled in a 2-0 victory against Worcester City in April.

Another loan transfer took him to Bristol Rovers where he made his Football League debut in a 3-2 win at Notts County on 25th September 1971 but the following month he was recalled by Charlton where he was given his first team chance, ironically against Bristol Rovers in the

Football League Cup. He played two further games before his time in SE7 came to an end, his final first team appearance coming in a somewhat bizarre encounter at Hull where Paul Went and Allen himself were credited with own goals, but a fine hat trick by Ray Treacy earned the Addicks a 3-2 win, the first in an away match for almost a year.

His short career in the Football League ended following two years with Exeter City, after which he returned to North Kent, having earlier trained as a hairdresser at the Erith College of Technology. In 2006, he was living in Vigo Village.

Season	Division	League		FA Cup		FL Cup		Total	
		A	G	A	G	A	G	A	G
1971-72 (R)	Division 2	2	0	0	0	1	0	3	0
Total		2	0	0	0	1	0	3	0

UK LEAGUE CAREER 19 games 0 goals

CHARLTON CAREER
Managers: *E Firmani, T Foley*
Debut: *Bristol Rovers (A) 05-10-1971*
V363
Finale: *Hull City (A) 16-10-1971*

CLARKE Leon Marvin   2012

Forward   14st 1lb   6' 2"
Born: 10-02-1985 - Wolverhampton, Staffordshire
Education: Deansfield School, Wolverhampton.

The old adage, 'more clubs than Jack Nicklaus', is a perfect description for the career of Leon Clarke. A big, old fashioned centre forward, he rarely settled for long in one place and was viewed by many as being extremely high maintenance. He came to Charlton after a public falling out with manager Paolo Di Canio at Swindon Town and the transfer involved a player swap, with fellow striker Paul Benson travelling in the other direction.

HONOURS
Wolverhampton Schools 1995-00
West Midlands Schools 1997-00

Queens Park Rangers 2010-11 Winners Championship
Wolverhampton Wanderers 2013-14 Winners League One

Sheffield United 2016-17 Winners League One   Sheffield United 2018-19 Runners Up Championship

CLUBS

Wolverhampton Wanderers (youth) 2003 (pro) ••Kidderminster Harriers 25.03.04 (loan) ••Queens Park Rangers 31.01.06 (loan) ••Plymouth Argyle 23.03.06 (loan) ••Sheffield Wednesday 16.01.07 (£300,000) ••Oldham Athletic 01.03.07 (loan) ••Southend United 31.08.07 (loan) ••Queens Park Rangers 02.06.10 (free) ••Preston North End 28.01.11 (loan) ••Swindon Town 19.08.11 (free) ••Chesterfield 08.09.11 (loan) ••Charlton Athletic 01.01.12 (player exchange) ••Crawley Town 17.03.12 (loan) ••Scunthorpe United 07.09.12 (loan) ••Coventry City 01.01.13 (loan) 07.01.13 (free) ••Wolverhamptonj Wanderers 30.01.14 (£750,000) ••Wigan Athletic 02.02.15 (loan) ••Bury 02.06.15 (free) •Sheffield United 27.07.16 (undisclosed) ••Wigan Athletic 30.01.19 (loan) ••Shrewsbury Town 25.09.20 (free) ••Bristol Rovers 31.08.21 (free)

Leon's long and erratic footballing journey commenced with local team Wolverhampton Wanderers and has stretched out through no less than 18 Football League clubs to date. Presumably they were all anxious to acquire a big target man, yet with unfailing regularity he would play no more than a handful of games before being packed off on loan or to pastures new.

He did spend three and a half years as a Sheffield Wednesday player but took time to establish himself in the team. On 25th August 2007 he played at the Valley in a Wednesday side that also included Richard Wood and Deon Burton, but a goal from Andy Reid and two from Chris Iwelumo sent them back to Yorkshire empty handed. By season 2009-10 he was playing regularly but could not find the net often enough to prevent relegation to League One. He did score in his final match, but then broke his toe while kicking an advertising board and had to be substituted. He was released at the end of his contract.

A switch to Queens Park Rangers brought an immediate change of fortune as his new club won the Championship in 2001-11, but his own contribution was modest and he moved on for a short and best forgotten spell with Swindon Town, prior to joining Charlton in January 2012. Leon has

subsequently admitted that his head was not in the right place during this period and he appeared to be just going through the motions, failing to score in any of the seven matches in which he participated.

Three months on loan at Scunthorpe helped him to re-discover some form and this good run continued after he transferred to Coventry City, 15 league goals being scored for them in 2013-14. Still he kept moving on with mixed fortunes until he reached Sheffield United and this proved to be the high point of his somewhat patchy career. He was part of the team that won two promotions in three years and scored an impressive 19 league goals in 2017-18, including all four against Hull City on 4th November. Finally, at the age of 34, Leon made his Premier League debut against Liverpool in September 2019, but it proved to be his final appearance for United and he was transfer listed shortly after. There was even vague talk of him re-signing for Charlton during the January 2020 transfer window but he chose to sit out his contract along with his injured colleague Ricky Holmes and received criticism from Sheffield United manager Chris Wilder for not seeking yet another new club. He is currently with Bristol Rovers, but now aged 37, his career seems to be winding down.

Season	Division	League		FA Cup		FL Cup		FL Trophy		Total	
		A	G	A	G	A	G	A	G	A	G
2011-12 (P)	League One	1 (6)	0	0	0	0	0	0	0	1 (6)	0
Total		1 (6)	0	0	0	0	0	0	0	1 (6)	0

UK LEAGUE CAREER 468 games 139 goals

CHARLTON CAREER
Managers: *C Powell*
Debut: *Brentford (H) (sub) 02-01-2012*
V742
Finale: *Colchester United (H) (sub) 06-03-2012*

CLARKE William Charles   2017 - 18

Despite his lack of inches, Billy was a clever, skilful footballer with an eye for goal and he performed well for Charlton until he ruptured an anterior cruciate ligament at Blackburn on 16th December 2017. This was the second such injury of his career and kept him out of action for 11 months. Understandably he needed time to regain his previous form and with an unusual abundance of attacking midfield players available, he was allowed to re-sign for his old club, Bradford City at the end of the January 2019 transfer window as, in the short term at least, his first team opportunities at Charlton were limited.

Forward   10st 3lbs   5' 7"
Born: 27-12-1987 - Cork, Ireland

HONOURS

Republic of Ireland U21 International 2007-08 11 caps 1 goal
Republic of Ireland U19 International 2005-06 8 caps 6 goals
Republic of Ireland U17 International 2003 2 caps 0 goals

Blackpool 2009-10 Promoted Play Offs Championship.
Crawley Town 2011-12 Promoted League Two

CLUBS

Leeds AFC, Ireland (youth) ••Ipswich Town 27.12.03 (youth) 01.07.05 (pro) ••Colchester United 23.03.06 (loan) ••Falkirk, Scotland 31.01.08 (loan) ••Darlington 08.08.08 (loan) ••Northampton Town 20.01.09 (loan) ••Brentford 23.03.09 (loan) ••Blackpool 01.07.09 (free) ••Sheffield United 14.10.11 (loan) ••Crawley Town 31.01.12 (free) ••Bradford City 01.07.14 (free) ••Charlton Athletic 08.06.17 (free) ••Bradford City 31.01.19 (free) ••Plymouth Argyle 19.10.19 (free) ••Grimsby Town 09.01.20 (free) ••Bradford City 16.07.20 (free) ••Hull City 20.09.21 (coach)

Although born in Cork, Billy's childhood included spells in Tanzania and Bahrain, but it was in East Anglia where his footballing journey really began after he signed for Ipswich Town on his 16th birthday. Highly rated but never fully established as a first team regular, the early part of his career involved a series of loans which included a brief and unhappy period in Scotland with Falkirk and half a season with Darlington where on 30th August 2008 he scored four times in a 6-0 win at Macclesfield Town.

Eventually he moved on to Blackpool where, playing alongside Jason Euell and Hameur Bouazza, he was in time to play a part in their unlikely promotion from the Championship, but just as he was poised to test himself against Premier League opposition, he damaged his knee in a pre-season friendly and missed the whole of the 2010-11 season. By the time he returned a year later Blackpool had been relegated again and his chance to play in the top division was gone forever.

A move to Crawley Town in January 2012 led to promotion from League Two and later to three productive seasons with Bradford City where he was especially popular. Following his all too brief spell at Charlton, Billy rejoined the Bantams only to find himself in a desperate relegation struggle that they were unable to survive. He and Adam Chicksen were among 11 players freed by Bradford City at the end of 2018-19. Short term deals took him to Plymouth and Grimsby but eventually in the Summer of 2020 he found himself back at Bradford for a third time and with his injury worries apparently behind him. Season 2020-21 proved to be his final campaign and he announced his retirement on 30th August. Billy is currently coaching within the Hull City youth academy.

Season	Division	League		FA Cup		FL Cup		FL Trophy		Play Offs		Total	
		A	G	A	G	A	G	A	G	A	G	A	G
2017-18	League One	16 (1)	1	0 (1)	0	1 (1)	1	1	0	0	0	18 (3)	2
2018-19 (P)	League One	0	0	2 (1)	0	0	0	1	0	0	0	3 (1)	0
Total		16 (1)	1	2 (2)	0	1 (1)	1	2	0	0	0	21 (4)	2

UK LEAGUE CAREER 390 games 73 goals

CHARLTON CAREER
Managers: *K Robinson, L Bowyer*
Debut: *Bristol Rovers (H) 05-08-2017*
V840
Finale: *Doncaster Rovers (H) 01-12-2018*

CLAYDEN Charles James   2021 -

Forward   11st 5lbs   5' 8"
Born: 16-11-2000 - Harold Wood, Essex
Education: Brentwood School, Essex

In 2019 when Leyton Orient were cutting back on their youth academy, one of the players looking for a new club was former Brentwood School boy, Charles Clayden. He made his debut for Charlton as a trialist on 23rd February 2019 in an U18 league match at Watford and played out the remainder of that season with the Addicks, including a goal in a 2-0 victory up at Hull in April. The young left winger made sufficient impact that on 30th May 2019 he was rewarded with a well-deserved professional contract.

HONOURS

Charlton Athletic U18 2020-21 Winners PD League 2 South

CLUBS

Leyton Orient 2017 (youth) ••Charlton Athletic 02.19 (youth) 30.05.19 (pro) ••Dulwich Hamlet 24.10.20 (loan)

Charles has spent two seasons with the Charlton U23 side and by 2020-21 was a regular starter. That season he scored seven goals and by the next pre-season was pushing to be involved with the first team. He was named as a substitute for the opening league match on 7th August 2021 against Sheffield Wednesday and came on as replacement for Conor

Washington. His exciting wing play in this and subsequent cup appearances, drew comparison with the then recently departed Alfie Doughty. He is not yet the finished article but his progress will be closely monitored and despite several players vying for the attacking places in the Charlton side, Charles is very much one for the future.

UK LEAGUE CAREER 0 games 0 goals

CHARLTON CAREER
Managers: *L Bowyer, N Adkins, J Jackson*
Debut: *Sheffield Wednesday (H) (sub) 07-08-2021*
V925

CODD Henry

1927 - 28

Defender Harry Codd was one of the victorious Ebbw Vale team who in 1926 pulled off an unlikely victory in the Welsh FA Cup Final, defeating Swansea Town by 3-2. The Cowboys, to use their nickname of the time,

| Midfield, Defender | 11st 4lbs | 5' 10" |

Born: 18-01-1903 - Aberdare, Wales
Died: 31-08-1975 - Northampton, Northants

were at the end of a season in which they had finished mid-table in the Southern League, Western Division so it was a major upset for them to beat their Football League opponents who had been battling for promotion to Division 1. This was the only occasion on which Ebbw Vale ever won the Welsh Cup and it certainly bolstered Harry's CV prior to his move to South London a year later.

HONOURS
1925-26 Ebbw Vale Winners Welsh FA Cup

CLUBS
Aberdare Athletic 06.23 ••Ebbw Vale 1925 ••Charlton Athletic 10.05.27 ••Wigan Borough 09.07.29 ••Connah's Quay & Shotton 1930

Harry already had Football League experience before he arrived in London, having played nine games for his hometown club Aberdare Athletic during their short tenure in Division 3 South. He had appeared for them mainly as a full back but was converted to right half by Charlton manager Alex 'Sandy' MacFarlane as both full back positions were already occupied by stalwarts Norman Smith and Baden Herod.

He was given a run in the side during season 1927-28 and appeared in nearly half of the matches, taking over from Scotsman Willie Paterson in February. The club had started that season brightly and initially there were thoughts of promotion until a series of bad results and three consecutive defeats which culminated in a 5-0 thumping at Millwall. MacFarlane had departed and been replaced by Albert Lindon as manager and he persevered with Harry for the remainder of the campaign. Charlton finished up in mid-table but there were some entertaining moments and he was in the side when goals from Billy Welsh, Billy

Lennox and Jackie Horton earned a 3-0 win against Brighton on 14th April 1928.

By the start of 1928-29 MacFarlane was back in charge and the number four shirt was passed to another Scotsman Alex Hird. Harry was only called upon once more, a disappointing 4-1 defeat at Northampton Town in August and although the club went on to earn their first Football League promotion, his time was up and he moved north to Wigan Borough at the end of the season where the manager was ex-Charlton player Angus McKinnon.

Back in defence for much of his time at Wigan, Harry played in an 8-0 league win against Carlisle United on 25th September 1929, with two of the goals scored by his former Charlton colleague Billy Welsh. Overall however the team struggled in the lower reaches of Division 3 North and his final match was a 5-0 defeat in which Carlisle gained revenge for their earlier humiliation.

When his playing days were at an end Harry returned to Aberdare where he worked as an insurance agent. He died in Northampton at the age of 72.

Season	Division	League		FA Cup		Total	
		A	G	A	G	A	G
1927-28	Divison 3 (S)	18	0	2	0	20	0
1928-29 (P)	Divison 3 (S)	1	0	0	0	1	0
Total		19	0	2	0	21	0

UK LEAGUE CAREER 54 games 0 goals

CHARLTON CAREER
Managers: *A MacFarlane, A Lindon, A MacFarlane*
Debut: *Merthyr Town (H) 30-11-1927*
V112
Finale: *Northampton Town (A) 25-08-1928*

COLE Carlton Michael George   2003 - 04

Striker   13st 3 ibs   6' 3"
Born: 12-10-1983 - Croydon, Surrey

Carlton Cole was picked out at an early age and tipped to become a Chelsea star of the future. A big, strong target man with a superb physique, he appeared to have it all, but although he played for England and nearly all of his 340 League appearances were at Premier League level, he reached the end of his career leaving the impression that perhaps he should have achieved even more. His seven full England caps came during his time with West Ham and were all as substitute, the most appearances by an England player without getting to start a game. He played twice for England at U21 level during his time at Charlton.

HONOURS

England International 2009-10 7 caps 0 goals
England U21 International 2003-05 19 caps 6 goals
England U20 International 2002-03 2 caps 0 goals

Eng;land U19 International 2002 5 caps 1 goal
West Ham United 2011-12 Promoted Play Offs Championship

CLUBS

Chelsea (youth) 23.10.00 (pro) ••Wolverhampton Wanderers 28.11.02 (loan) ••Charlton Athletic 20.08.03 (loan) ••Aston Villa 12.07.04 (loan) ••West Ham United 06.07.06 (free) 14.10.13 (re-signed) ••Celtic, Scotland 22.10.15 (free) ••Sacramento Republic, USA 23.08.16 (free) ••Persib Bandung, Indonesia 03.17 (free) ••West Ham United 12.18 (youth coach)

Carlton was still just 19 and had only played a handful of first team games when he joined Charlton on a season's loan on 20th August 2003, making his debut at the Valley three days later. He was used sparingly and mainly as a substitute but had some success, including the winner against Tottenham at White Hart Lane on 28th December, after coming on as a substitute for Jonatan Johansson. The downside was that during games he often appeared lethargic and seemed to lack concentration. Lack of consistency is a common fault with young players, but when things were going wrong, that did not endear him to supporters.

Alan Curbishley was sufficiently impressed with Carlton however, that he tried to extend the loan into the next season, but the two clubs got into a dispute which at one stage looked likely to involve the lawyers. Happily it was all sorted out quite quickly, Carlton went off for a loan with Aston Villa and Charlton received an unspecified sum in compensation.

It was West Ham who eventually signed him from Chelsea

and he spent a total of nine years with them, although never quite scoring enough goals to satisfy the fans. He was given a free transfer at the end of season 2012-13, but when they failed to acquire an adequate replacement, was re-signed a few months later. He left for the second time and joined Celtic in October 2015, but a knee injury restricted him to just four appearances. An equally brief spell in Sacramento followed and then in March 2017 he moved to West Java to play for the leading Indonesian club, Persib Bandung. This was another rocky period as there was an apparent power struggle going on within the club and the manager would not play him. Harsh words were spoken in the media and his contract terminated on 4th August 2017.

Carlton was declared bankrupt in June 2018, despite having earned millions during his playing career. He reacted by expressing regret at not having taken a closer interest in his business affairs and proceeded to set up CC Twelve Football Academy in East London to mentor young footballers, especially in financial matters. He joined West Ham's coaching staff in December 2018.

Season	Division	League		FA Cup		FL Cup		Total	
		A	G	A	G	A	G	A	G
203-04	Premier	8 (13)	4	1	1	0	0	9 (13)	5
Total		8 (13)	4	1	1	0	0	9 (13)	5

UK LEAGUE CAREER 340 games 67 goals

CHARLTON CAREER

Managers: *A Curbishley*

Debut: *Wolverhampton Wanderers (H) (sub) 23-08-2003*

V614

Finale: *Southampton (H) (sub) 15-05-2004*

COLLINS Nicholas   1927

Nick was a left winger who spent the 1926-27 season with Charlton. He only got one chance in the first team and that came in the final match of the campaign when he replaced Jackie Horton for the home game against Exeter City. Horton had been ever present up to that point and had been a key member of the team, but the Addicks finished in style with a 1-0 win, thanks to a goal from leading scorer David Sherlaw.

Forward

Born: 06-04-1901 - Hamilton, Lanarkshire

Died: 1978 - Hamilton, Lanarkshire

HONOURS

Blantyre Celtic 1924-25 Winners Lanarkshire Junior League Division 2

CLUBS

Greenford Colliery, Scotland c 1923 ••Blantyre Celtic, Scotland 1924 ••Charlton Athletic 17.06.26 ••Alloa Athletic, Scotland 03.06.27

A Scotsman from Hamilton, Nick made his reputation playing for Blantyre Celtic in the Lanarkshire Junior League. This was adult not youth football and success at this level could often attract the big clubs who were always on the lookout for talent. Blantyre had a successful season in 1924-25 winning Division 2 and this put their players in the shop window. During 1925-26 and now playing in the top division, Raith Rovers and Coventry City were reportedly interested in the young winger and he even got as far as a trial with Cowdenbeath. In the end however it was Charlton with their strong Scottish contacts through manager Sandy Macfarlane who landed the prize. Nick travelled down to London and scored in a trial match at the Valley on 21st August 1926 having already been registered with the Football League on 17th June.

He made his debut in the Reserves against Millwall and scored in a 6-1 defeat. He did well enough to play regularly at outside left in the second team throughout the 1926-27 season and was on the scoresheet again in the 2-2 draw with Fulham on New Year's Day, but received a negative mention in the programme after missing an easy chance against Tottenham. His finest game was probably against Clapton Orient in April when he scored both goals in a 2-0 win, but despite his eventual elevation to the first team on 7th May, Nick was not retained and returned to Scotland where he signed for Alloa Athletic on 3rd June.

Alloa were competing in the Scottish League Division 2 and he managed 20 league appearances and two goals for them in 1927-28 but did not build upon his two years in Senior football and disappeared from sight at the end of the season. He does not appear to have been re-instated into Junior football either. He passed away in Hamilton at the age of 76.

Season	Division	League		FA Cup		Total	
		A	G	A	G	A	G
192627	Divison 3 (S)	1	0	0	0	1	0
Total		1	0	0	0	1	0

UK LEAGUE CAREER 21 games 2 goals

CHARLTON CAREER

Managers: *A MacFarlane*

Debut: *Exeter City (H) 07-05-1927*

V103

COOK Jordan Alan   2012 - 14

Forward, Midfield   12st 5lbs   5' 9"
Born: 20-03-1990 - Hetton-Le-Street, Tyne & Wear
Education: Hetton School, Sunderland.

Jordan made a career for himself in the lower reaches of the Football League without ever threatening to set the world alight. He spent two years at Charlton but rarely appeared in the first team. A pacey forward who is comfortable on either wing, he spent most of his time in SE7 either injured or on the fringes of the side. He made a total of 14 appearances in a Charlton shirt but never lasted for the full 90 minutes. He was however one of the U21 team who were victorious in the Kent Senior Cup Final on 1st May 2013, scoring the opening goal in the 7-1 rout of Tonbridge Angels.

HONOURS

Charlton Athletic U21 2012-13 Winners PD League 2 South
Charlton Athletic U21 2012-13 Winners Kent Senior Cup

Walsall 2014-15 Finalists Football League Trophy
Luton Town 2017-18 Runners Up League Two

CLUBS

Hetton Juniors 1996 (youth) ••Sunderland 1997 (youth) 30.05.08 (pro) ••Darlington 18.08.09 (loan) ••Walsall 24.03.11 (loan) ••Carlisle United 16.01.12 (loan) ••Charlton Athletic 09.07.12 (free) ••Yeovil Town 18.03.13 (loan) ••Walsall 07.07.14 (free) ••Luton Town 05.07.16 (free) ••Grimsby Town 22.06.18 (free) ••Gateshead 20.10.20 (free) ••Hartlepool United 16.09.21 (free)

Raised in a football mad Mackem family, Jordan spent around 15 years with Sunderland, progressing through their academy and finally making his first team debut alongside Darren Bent against Manchester United on 26th December 2010. His early career comprised a series of short term loans, but in July 2012 he signed a two-year contract with Charlton as Chris Powell sought to strengthen his squad following promotion from League One.

Although there were ample opportunities at the Valley, Jordan was never able to nail down a regular spot in the team and his Charlton career came to an abrupt halt on 18th January 2014 following a disappointing 1-0 defeat at Middlesbrough. The club had just been sold to a new Belgian owner and this was the game in which the French goalkeeper Yohann Thuram-Ulien made his debut on his

specific orders and against the wishes of the manager Chris Powell, who was dismissed shortly thereafter. His successor Jose Riga, made no further use of Jordan who left the club on 22nd May.

After signing for Walsall, he did at last find some first team action and a trip to Wembley on 22nd March 2015, where he contested the final of the Football League Trophy, only to go down 2-0 against Preston North End in front of a crowd of 72,315. The following season was largely spent on the bench and in July 2016 he moved to Luton Town where he suffered a similar fate, but did play at least a peripheral part in their promotion from League Two in 2017-18. Since September 2021 he has been a Hartlepool United player although a groin injury has kept him away from the action.

Season	Division	League		FA Cup		FL Cup		Total	
		A	G	A	G	A	G	A	G
2012-13	Championship	1 (6)	0	1	0	1	0	3 (6)	0
2013-14	Championship	1 (2)	0	1	0	1	0	3 (2)	0
Total		2 (8)	0	2	0	2	0	6 (8)	0

UK LEAGUE CAREER 190 games 22 goals

CHARLTON CAREER
Managers: *C Powell, J Riga*
Debut: *Leyton Orient (H) 14-08-2012*
V747
Finale: *Middlesbrough (A) 18-01-2014*

COOK Lee

2008 - 12

Lee spent almost his entire footballing career in the London area but is best remembered for his performances for Queens Park Rangers, the team he

Forward, Midfield   12st 1lbs   5' 10"
Born: 03-08-1982 - Hammersmith, London

had supported since childhood. A talented and pacey winger, he made nearly 200 competitive appearances for the West London club and when in 2007 he had the opportunity to move into the Premier League with Fulham, he donated his signing on fee of £250,000 to them, at a time when Rangers were financially desperate and in danger of closure - a quite extraordinary act of generosity. At his best he was a potential match winner, but his effectiveness declined through the years as a result of injuries. Lee is second cousin to former Olympic gold medallist and world boxing champion, James DeGale.

HONOURS

Barnet 2014-15 Winners Conference Premier Division

CLUBS

Southampton c1998 (youth) ••Aylesbury United 01.99 (youth) ••Watford 19.11.99 (pro))))•York City 02.10.02 (loan) ••Queens Park Rangers 20.12.02 (loan) ••Queens Park Rangers 03.07.04 (£125,000) ••Fulham 19.07.07 (£2,5 million) ••Charlton Athletic 31.01.08 (loan) ••Queens Park Rangers 01.08.08 (loan) 08.01.09 (£850,000) ••Leyton Orient 24.11.11 (loan) ••Charlton Athletic 19.03.12 (loan) ••Leyton Orient 24.08.12 (free) ••Apollon Smyrnis, Greece 07.01.14 (free) ••Barnet 05.08.14 (free) ••Eastleigh 29.06.15 (free)

There was no instant success for Lee after signing for Watford at the age of 17 and it took him more than four years to establish himself in their first team. He enjoyed a four-month spell on loan with Queens Park Rangers in 2002-03 and eventually turned down a new contract with Watford in favour of a permanent move to Loftus Road in the summer of 2004.

For the next three seasons, Lee was probably at his peak and was a constant fixture in the Rangers team. The big money transfer to Fulham in 2007 should have provided the opportunity to test himself against Premier League opposition, but a serious knee injury put paid to such ambition and he never managed even a single game for his new club who received little reward for their £2.5 million transfer fee.

By early 2008, Lee was finally recovering from his injury but had not played a first team game for 10 months. It was a critical time for Charlton who were chasing a quick promotion back to the Premier League and were in fifth place in the Championship. Manager Alan Pardew signed Lee on loan in the hope that he would provide the necessary impetus to complete the job, but he was far from

match fit and unable to make any real impact as the side stuttered and eventually sank back to a disappointing mid-table finish.

He soon found himself back at Queens Park Rangers, first on loan and then in January 2009 with a three and a half year contract, but continually plagued by knee problems, he was no longer able to maintain the same level of performance as in the past. He returned to Charlton and played a further four matches during the later stages of the 2011-12 promotion season, but never managed the full 90 minutes in any of them. His career was now drawing to a gradual conclusion, although he enjoyed a brief spell with Apollon Smyrnis in Athens that came to an abrupt end when they were relegated from the Greek Super League 1. Lee dropped into non-league football in 2014-15 and helped Barnet to win promotion back to the Football League but finally retired from the game after a short spell with Eastleigh. His first venture into the world of business did not prove successful. He launched a football agency, Select Soccer Management Ltd in 2016, but it was placed into administration three years later.

Season	Division	League		FA Cup		FL Cup		FL Trophy		Total	
		A	G	A	G	A	G	A	G	A	G
2007-08	Championship	4 (5)	0	0	0	0	0			4 (5)	0
2011-12 (P)	League One	3 (1)	0	0	0	0	0	0	0	3 (1)	0
Total		7 (6)	0	0	0	0	0	0	0	7 (6)	0

UK LEAGUE CAREER 308 games 26 goals

CHARLTON CAREER
Managers: *A Pardew, C Powell*
Debut: *Sheffield Wednesday (A) (sub) 12-02-2008*
V663
Finale: *Preston North End (A) 28-04-2012*

COQUELIN Francis   2014

Midfield   11st 13lbs   5' 10"
Born: 13-05-1991 - Laval, France
Education: Ambroise-Pare High School, Laval.

He may only have been a Charlton player for little more than one month commencing 3rd November 2014, but Francis used his time wisely and demonstrated considerable skill and the ability to break down opposition attacks through a series of interceptions and tackles in his role as the modern defensive midfield player. Up to that point he had been unable to secure a regular place for himself in the Arsenal first team, but the loan was cut short as a result of the North London club's sudden injury crisis and he was thrust straight into the Arsenal squad on 13th December, where he remained until the end of the season and beyond. His form became a revelation and much credit was given for the treatment that he received during his brief time in SE7.

HONOURS

France U21 International 2011-12 7 caps 0 goals	Arsenal U18 2008-09 Winners FA Youth Cup
France U20 International 2010-11 12 caps 0 goals	Arsenal 2013-14 & 2016-17 Winners FA Cup
France U19 2010 Winners UEFA Euro U19 Championship	Arsenal 2015 Winners FA Community Shield
France U19 International 2009-10 16 caps 0 goals	Valencia 2018-19 Winners Copa Del Rey
France U18 International 2008-09 5 caps 0 goals	Villarreal 2020-21 Winners UEFA Europa League
France U17 International 2007-08 3 caps 0 goals	

CLUBS

AS Du Bourny, France 2000 (youth) ••Stade Lavallois, France 2005 (youth) ••Arsenal 18.07.08 (pro) ••Lorient, France 21.06.10 (loan) ••SC Friburg, Germany 05.07.13 (loan) ••Charlton Athletic 03.11.14 (loan) ••Valencia, Spain 11.01.18 (£12.6 million) ••Villarreal, Spain 12.08.20 (£7.2 million)

A highly promising young player, Francis was plucked from Stade Lavallois during a period when Arsenal became infamous for cherry picking from the best of the emerging French talent. He was aged 17 when he arrived in London and was rewarded with his first team debut against Sheffield United on 23rd September 2008, but further progress became difficult owing to the array of talented midfield players available to the Gunners during that period. At the end of his first season, he was, along with Emmanuel Frimpong, part of the Arsenal team that defeated Liverpool over two legs in the final of the FA Youth Cup. Hugh McAuley was manager of the Liverpool youth team.
He spent season 2010-11 back in France competing in Ligue 1 for Lorient and was a semi-regular in their side which finished in a comfortable mid-table position, even scoring a rare goal, the winner in a 2-1 victory over Rennes. However, a later loan period in Germany proved tough as he was asked to play out of position on the left wing for

much of his time with SC Friburg.
Francis never looked back after returning from Charlton and became a regular fixture in the Arsenal midfield. That season ended at Wembley with the FA Cup Final and an emphatic 4-0 victory over Aston Villa. A knee ligament injury restricted his appearances in 2015-16, but he contributed to another FA Cup win on 27th May 2017 when he came on as substitute as Chelsea were dispatched 2-1.
In the following season he lost his place in the Arsenal team and was transferred to Valencia in January 2018 for a fee variously reported as somewhere between £12.6 million and £14 million. Further cup success came with a 2-1 victory over Barcelona on 25th May 2019 in the final of the Copa del Rey.
On 26th May 2021 he was a second half substitute when Villarreal defeated Manchester United on penalty kicks in the final of the Europa League.

Season	Division	League		FA Cup		FL Cup		Total	
		A	G	A	G	A	G	A	G
2014-15	Championship	3 (2)	0	0	0	0	0	3 (2)	0
Total		3 (2)	0	0	0	0	0	3 (2)	0

UK LEAGUE CAREER 110 games 0 goals

CHARLTON CAREER
Managers: *B Peeters*
Debut: *Leeds United (A) (sub) 04-11-2014*
V788
Finale: *Nottingham Forest (A) 06-12-2014*

CORT Leon Terence Anthony   2011 - 14

A solid and experienced central defender, Leon came
to Charlton during the latter part of his career, arriving
in time to join the promotion side of 2011-12.

Defender   13st 0lbs   6' 4"
Born: 11-09-1979 - Bermondsey, London

However, injury and the consistent form of Michael Morrison and Matt Taylor prevented
him from playing more than a supporting role. During his time at the Valley Leon was called
up to play international football for Guyana and he appeared in six 2014 FIFA World Cup
qualifiers, scoring in the 2-1 win over Trinidad & Tobago on 11th November 2011. His
older bother is the former Wolves striker Carl Cort while Ruben Loftus-Cheek of Chelsea is
a half brother.

HONOURS

Guyana International 2011-12 6 caps 1 goal   Hull City 2004-05 Runners Up League One
Charlton Athletic 2011-12 Winners League One   Stoke City 2007-08 Runners Up Championship

CLUBS

Dulwich Hamlet 07.97 (youth) ••Millwall 14.01.98 (pro) ••Forest Green Rovers 15.12.00 (loan) •Stevenage Borough 29.03.01 (loan) ••Southend
United 11.07.01 (free) ••Hull City 07.07.04 (free) ••Crystal Palace 30.06.06 (£1.25 million) ••Stoke City 30.10.07 (loan) 15.01.08 (£1.2 million)
••Burnley 27.01.10 (£1.5 million) ••Preston North End 25.11.10 (loan) ••Charlton Athletic 29.08.11 (loan) 12.01.12 (free)

After more than three years at Millwall without a first team
appearance, Leon's career took off following his switch to
Southend United in the Summer of 2001 and he played
130 consecutive league games for the Shrimpers over the
next three seasons. Turning down the offer of a new
contract, he then moved to Hull City and figured
prominently as they won promotion to the Championship
in 2004-05.

An interesting confrontation arose on 25th February 2006
when Hull hosted Wolverhampton Wanderers in a league
fixture. Leon, at centre half, lined up in direct opposition to
his brother, who was playing up front for the visitors. Leon
scored the opening goal, only for Carl to grab the winner
in the final minute of the match which ended 3-2 to Wolves
The first half of Leon's career was notable for his
consistency and he missed just three league games between
August 2001 and November 2006. By the end of this
impressive run he was a Crystal Palace player and along
with Mark Hudson, the cornerstone of their defence. After
transferring to an upwardly mobile Stoke City a year later,

he helped them to gain promotion to the Premier League
and chipped in with a useful eight goals in addition to his
defensive duties.

Competition for places intensified at Stoke in 2008-09 and
this plus a groin injury kept Leon out of the team for most
of the second half of that season. Unable to get back into
the side he eventually moved on to Burnley in January 2010
but could not prevent them from dropping out of the
Premier League. One of the few bright moments came on
10th April when they scored an unexpected 4-1 away
victory at Hull City. The Burnley team included another
future Charlton defender, Andre Bikey-Amougou.

Leon's next transfer brought him to Charlton where he
eventually replaced Matt Taylor in the centre of the defence
and for a few months in 2012-13 was able to perform to his
full potential. Sadly this situation did not last and he was
forced to retire on 18th July 2014 after an injury affected
final season at the Valley. He has since worked as a
commentator for Sky TV and in 2018 joined the Stellar
Group as a football agent.

Season	Division	League		FA Cup		FL Cup		FL Trophy		Total	
		A	G	A	G	A	G	A	G	A	G
2011-12 (P)	League One	10 (5)	0	1	0	1	0	0	0	12 (5)	0
2012-13	Championship	30	2	0	0	1	0			31	2
2013-14	Championship	1 (2)	0	0	0	1 (1)	0			2 (3)	0
Total		41 (7)	2	1	0	3 (1)	0	0	0	45 (8)	2

UK LEAGUE CAREER 396 games 38 goals

CHARLTON CAREER
Managers: *C Powell, J Riga*
Debut: *Preston North End (H) 13-09-2011*
V735
Finale: *Yeovil Town (H) (sub) 08-04-2014*

COSTA ALMEIDA Jorge Paulo   2001 - 02

Defender   6' 2"
Born: 14-10-1971 - Porto, Portugal

Jorge Costa was a top class central defender who spent the majority of his career with his local club, Porto. Apart from one brief loan spell, he featured in their first team for 14 seasons during which they were immensely successful and he accumulated a vast array of honours both in domestic and European competitions. Jorge burst on to the world stage in the 1991 FIFA World Youth Championships in which he was named as one of the 'rising stars' of the tournament. On 30th June 1991 Portugal met Brazil in the Final before a crowd of 127,000 and won 4-2 on penalties after a goalless draw. Jorge Costa scored the first penalty.

HONOURS

Portugal International 1995-02 50 caps 2 goals
Portugal U21 & U20 International
Portugal 1991 Winners FIFA World Youth Championships
FC Porto 1993-94, 1997-98, 1999-00, 2000-01 & 2002-03 Winners Taca de Portugal
FC Porto 1993-94, 1999-00, 2000-01 Runners Up Portuguese Primeira Divisao
FC Porto 1994-99 (5 seasons), 2002-03 & 2003-04 Winners Portuguese Primeira Divisao

FC Porto 1994-95 & 1999-00 Runners Up Portuguese Supertaca
FC Porto 1995-96, 1997-98, 1998-99, 2000-01 Winners Portuguese Supertaca
FC Porto 2002-03 Winners UEFA Cup
FC Porto 2003-04 Winners UEFA Champions League
FC Porto 2003-04 Runners Up Taca de Portugal
FC Porto 2004 Winners FIFA Intercontinental Cup
Standard Liege 2005-06 Runners Up Belgian First Division A

HONOURS AS MANAGER

SC Olhanense 2008-09 Winners Portugal Segunda Divisao
CFR Cluj 2011-12 Winners Romania Liga 1

AEL Limassol 2012-13 Runners Up Cypriot Cup

CLUBS

FC Foz, Portugal (youth) ••FC Porto, Portugal 1987 (youth) 1989 (pro) ••Penafiel, Portugal 1990 (loan) ••CS Maritimo, Portugal 08.91 (loan) ••Charlton Athletic 04.12.01 (loan) ••Standard Liege, Belgium 12.12.05 (free) ••SC Braga, Portugal 01.07.06 (ass. coach) 19.02.07 (manager) ••SC Olhanense, Portugal 16.06.08 (manager) ••Academica, Portugal 08.06.10 (manager) ••CFR Cluj, Romania 2011 (manager) ••AEL Limassol, Cyprus 24.10.12 (manager) ••Anorthosis Famagusta, Cyprus 18.08.13 (manager) ••FC Pacos de Ferreira, Portugal 26.02.14 (manager} ••Gabon 07.14 (manager) ••CS Sfaxien, Tunisia 30.03.17 (manager) ••FC Arouca, Portugal 29.06.17 (manager) ••Tours, France 22.11.17 (manager) ••Mumbai City, India 14.08.18 (manager) ••Gaz Metan Medias, Romania 29.09.20 (manager) ••SC Farense, Portugal 04.02.21 (manager) ••CS Sfaxien, Tunisia 03.02.22 (manager)

Porto dominated Portuguese football throughout the nineties and after Jorge became established in the first team, won the Primeira Liga for five consecutive years starting in 1994-95. He was a massive presence at the heart of their defence and his tough tackling style earned him the nicknames 'Tank' and 'Animal'. By 1997 he was captain and a hugely popular figure with Porto supporters. It is unlikely that he would ever have left but for a feud with manager Octavio Machado which became so intense that he signed on a loan deal with Charlton in December 2001 and remained at the Valley for the remainder of that season.

His debut came as a substitute in a tough away match at Stamford Bridge where he replaced Mark Fish and helped steady the ship and hold off the marauding Chelsea forwards until Kevin Lisbie could score a late winner for an unlikely 1-0 scoreline. He proved a real asset as Charlton achieved the double over both Tottenham and Chelsea and recorded an impressive 3-0 win at Everton.
Sadly there was never any prospect of Jorge remaining at Charlton and with Machado having been sacked, he returned to Porto for season 2002-03 where he was reinstated as captain by their new manager, Jose Mourinho.

Together they led the club to even greater success, winning the UEFA Cup that season, beating Celtic 3-2 in the Final and a year later defeating Monaco 3-0 on 26th May 2004 in the Final of the UEFA Champions League. The ultimate was achieved in December when in Yokohama, Japan, Porto overcame the Colombian club Once Caldas (8-7 on penalties) after a goalless draw, to win the FIFA Intercontinental Cup and the right to call themselves the best team in the world. Jorge was captain and scored one of Porto's penalties.

He played 50 times for Portugal, including appearances in UEFA Euro 2000 and the 2002 FIFA World Cup. Three of his caps for Portugal were earned in 2002, whilst a Charlton player and he scored one of his only two international goals against Spain in Barcelona on 13th February 2002.

Jorge finally left Porto for Standard Liege in December 2005 and retired from playing seven months later. He has since held a whole range of managerial jobs, with differing degrees of success. For two years he was in charge of the Gabon national team but was sacked following poor results ahead of the African Cup of Nations tournament in 2016. In August 2018 he took over as manager of the Indian Super League side, Mumbai City where he remained until leaving by mutual consent in March 2020.

After initially agreeing to accept the role of coach to the Portuguese national team, Jorge changed his mind and six days later on 29th September 2020 was appointed as manager of the Portuguese club Gaz Metan Medias. By February 2022 he was in Tunisia and managing CS Sfaxien for the second time.

Season	Division	League		FA Cup		FL Cup		Total	
		A	G	A	G	A	G	A	G
2001-02	Premier	22 (2)	0	2	0	0	0	24 (2)	0
Total		22 (2)	0	2	0	0	0	24 (2)	0

UK LEAGUE CAREER 24 games 0 goals

CHARLTON CAREER
Managers: *A Curbishley*
Debut: *Chelsea (A) (sub) 05-12-2001*
V603
Finale: *Manchester United (A) 11-05-2002*

COUSINS Jordan Paul   2013 - 16

When Jordan stepped on to the Valley's hallowed turf as a late substitute for Dale Stephens on 6th August 2013, it was the start of a three-year period in which he dominated the Charlton midfield and his high energy, non stop running, earned him first the accolade of Young Player of the Year in 2014 and then Player of the Year in both 2015 and 2016. He played three times for England U20's alongside Jake Forster-Caskey during the Toulon Tournament in May 2014 and scored on his debut in a 3-0 win over Qatar. His cousin Kerrea Gilbert played for Arsenal and Leicester City.

Midfield   12st 12lbs   6' 1"
Born: 06-03-1994 - Greenwich, London
Education: James Wolfe School, Greenwich.

HONOURS

England U20 International 2014 3 caps 1 goal
England U18 International 2011 1 cap 0 goals
England U17 International 2009-11 22 caps 0 goals
England U16 International 2008-10 11 caps 1 goal
Charlton Athletic U23 2012-13 Winners PD League 2 South

Charlton Athletic U21 2012-13 Winners Kent Senior Cup
Charlton Athletic U21 2012-13 Winners PD National League 2
Charlton Athletic 2014 Young Player Of The Year
Charlton Athletic 2015 & 2016 Player Of The Year

CLUBS

Charlton Athletic 2006 (youth) 2011 (pro) ••Queens Park Rangers 13.07.16 (£1.25 million) ••Stoke City 25.06.19 (free) •Wigan Athletic 15.06.21 (free)

Having been the backbone of the Charlton team for three seasons, Jordan considered it time to move on following relegation from the Championship in 2015-16 and was eagerly snapped up by Queens Park Rangers manager and ex-Charlton player Jimmy Floyd Hasselbaink. He had scored at Loftus Road in April and the move to West

London seemed a logical one at a time when Charlton were in decline on the field and the controversial Belgian ownership was almost universally unpopular among the supporters.

It turned out however that QPR were also a club in conflict and struggling to maintain their place in the

Championship. Jordan suffered a string of injuries that restricted both the number and quality of his appearances and in 2019 was not offered a new contract when his initial three-year deal expired. Instead, he moved to Stoke City where the manager Nathan Jones was a familiar face, having worked with Jordan during the 2012-13 season while employed as development coach for the Charlton U21's.

Again he found it hard to break into the side and although he fulfilled his two-year contract, too much of his time was spent on the sub's bench.

In June 2021 Jordan dropped into League One for the first time with Wigan Athletic and returned to the Valley on 21st August in a side that also included Ben Amos. Charlton were outplayed that day and went down 2-0.

Season	Division	League		FA Cup		FL Cup		Total	
		A	G	A	G	A	G	A	G
2013-14	Championship	37 (5)	2	3 (1)	0	0 (1)	0	40 (7)	2
2014-15	Championship	43 (1)	3	1	0	2	0	46 (1)	3
2015-16 (R)	Championship	39 (2)	0	1	0	2	0	42 (2)	0
Total		119 (8)	5	5 (1)	0	4 (1)	0	128 (10)	5

UK LEAGUE CAREER 206 games 8 goals

CHARLTON CAREER
Managers: *C Powell, J Riga, B Peeters, G Luzon, K Fraeye, J Riga, R Slade*
Debut: *Oxford United (H) (sub) 06-08-2013*
V763
Finale: *Burnley (H) 07-05-2016*

COX Keith   1956 - 59

Midfield   11st 0lbs   5' 9"
Born: 26-01-1936 - Heanor, Derbyshire
Died: 09-09-2015 - Derby, Derbyshire
Education: Codner Secondary Modern School, Somercotes.,

Keith had a short spell in the first team as replacement for Cyril Hammond, but it unfortunately came at a time when results on the field were nothing short of disastrous. The club was careering headlong towards relegation from Division 1 and 10 of the 13 games in which he participated during season 1956-57, ended in defeat. This included a 7-3 hiding at Wolverhampton plus five goals conceded against each of the Manchester clubs. Bobby Charlton scored the first hat-trick of his career at the Valley on 18th February 1957 and Keith's run as left half came to an end after the 6-2 thumping by Tottenham on 22nd April.

HONOURS

Ilkeston & District
FA Youth X1 1952-53
Southern Transvaal XI

Charlton Athletic A 1957-58 & 1959-60 Winners London Mid-Week League
Charlton Athletic A 1959-60 Winners Aetolian League Cup
Arcadia United 1965 Finalists NFL (South Africa) Cup

CLUBS

Heanor Town (youth) ••Charlton Athletic 05.11.51 (youth) ••Bexleyheath & Welling 09.53 (pro) ••Charlton Athletic 13.04.54 (free) ••Marist Brothers, South Africa 07.60 (free) ••Arcadia United, South Africa 1964 (player manager) ••Heanor Town 1967 (player coach)

It was almost certainly a family connection that precipitated Keith's arrival at the Valley in 1951 at the age of 15. He was the nephew of Charlton's assistant manager George Robinson and had already captained his school team as well as representing Ilkeston and District U15's. He worked in the office at Charlton and later on the ground staff, before turning professional with Bexleyheath & Welling in September 1953.
Keith rejoined Charlton at the end of that season but ten days later was called up for his National Service and during the next two years was stationed at Uxbridge, where he played for Technical Training Command and represented

the RAF, one of his teammates being Stuart Leary
He was never really able to build on that run of first team appearances in 1956-57 and his progress was badly affected by a dislocated shoulder incurred on 7th September 1957 against Tottenham Reserves. He was eventually recalled to the side for three games over the 1958 Christmas period, but a disappointing home defeat against Brighton brought down the curtain on his time as a Charlton first team player. Keith qualified as an FA Coach in 1959, but sensing that his future prospects were uncertain, he requested and was granted a transfer request in February 1960. He was listed for a fee of £2,000, but four months later decided to

try his luck out in South Africa. On 7th July, he sailed, along with Peter Firmani and John Hewie, with the club retaining his FA registration in case he should return in the future.

Initially Keith played semi-professionally for Marist Brothers in the newly established National Football League, while at the same time working in the dispatch department of a Johannesburg drug store, but by 1964 was player manager of the Pretoria based Arcadia United where he played alongside his former Charlton colleague Eddie

Werge. The following year he returned home and spent one final season as player coach of Midland League club Heanor United before an injury to his right knee forced him into retirement.

After football, Keith worked for a packing company, then alongside his brother in a fruit and veg business. For a time he was spinning yarn for Coulthard's and finished his working life as a window framer. A keen snooker player, he was very active in the British Legion and passed away in Derby Hospital from lung disease, at the age of 79.

Season	Division	League		FA Cup		Total	
		A	G	A	G	A	G
1956-57 (R)	Division 1	11	0	2	0	13	0
1958-59	Division 2	3	0	0	0	3	0
Total		14	0	2	0	16	0

UK LEAGUE CAREER 14 games 0 goals

CHARLTON CAREER
Managers: *J Seed, J Trotter*
Debut: *Luton Town (A) 22-12-1956*
V274
Finale: *Brighton & Hove Albion (H) 03-01-1959*

COX William Charles   1921 - 26

Billy lined up at centre forward for much of the 1921-22 season and his two goals against Bristol Rovers on his debut was the first occasion when a Charlton player had scored twice in a single match during this, their debut season as a Football League

Forward
Born: 19-03-1899 - Watford, Hertfordshire
Died: 09-03-1987 - Shanklin, Isle of Wight
Education: Callowland School, Watford

club. He finished that campaign with seven goals but never managed to exceed that figure in his five years with the Addicks but instead turned from goal scorer to goal provider, making many of his later appearances on the left wing.

HONOURS
England Schoolboy International 1913 3 caps 9 goals
Watford Schools
Charlton Athletic 1922-23 Winners London Challenge Cup

Charlton Athletic A 1923-24 Winners Kent League
Leavesden Hospital 1919-20 Winners Herts County League, Western Division
Sittingbourne 1926-27 Runners Up Kent League

CLUBS
Leavesden Hospital 1918 ••Watford 1920 (pro) ••Charlton Athletic 09.21 ••Sittingbourne 08.26 ••Hampstead 01.31

Nine goals in three matches against Scotland and Wales (twice), was the outstanding record of Billy Cox as an England Schoolboy International in 1913. However before he could build upon this extraordinary achievement, the First World War intervened and at the age of 16 he joined the army and served for three and a half years with the Herts Yeomanry in Mesopotamia (now Iraq).
Back home again, he signed for Watford in 1920, the same year that they were elected to the Football League, but he had no first team experience at that level until switching to Charlton a year later. Football League records date the transfer from 24th September 1921, but something is clearly amiss as his debut against Bristol Rovers came seven

days earlier.
He was a semi-regular in the Charlton team for five seasons and featured in all the attacking positions, but it was from the left wing that he scored the very late equaliser to ensure a 1-1 draw against Millwall on 3rd October 1925 before a crowd of 25,337 rowdy South Londoners. Billy was earning £5 a week during his time with Charlton, although this figure was reduced to £4 during the summer.
In August 1926 he joined Sittingbourne, where he played four years in the Kent League, before switching to Athenian League club Hampstead (now known as Hendon). He only appears to have played one match for them and this was a league fixture that took place on 10th

January 1931 against Uxbridge Town but it was abandoned by the referee after 50 minutes through extreme weather conditions and this seems to have heralded the end of Billy's football career. By 1939 he was living in Ruislip

and employed as a foreman painter. Later he moved to the Isle of Wight with his wife Alice and they ran a guest house from 1951 to 1974. Billy passed away at Shanklin shortly before his 88th birthday.

Season	Division	League		FA Cup		Total	
		A	G	A	G	A	G
1921-22	Divison 3 (S)	26	7			26	7
1922-23	Divison 3 (S)	10	0	2	1	12	1
1923-24	Divison 3 (S)	14	0	0	0	14	0
1924-25	Divison 3 (S)	24	5	0	0	24	5
1925-26	Divison 3 (S)	24	6	2	0	26	6
Total		98	18	4	1	102	19

UK LEAGUE CAREER 98 games 18 goals

CHARLTON CAREER
Managers: *W Rayner, A MacFarlane*
Debut: *Bristol Rovers (H) 17-09-1921*
V024
Finale: *Watford (A) 10-04-1926*

CRANIE Martin James 2008

Defender   12st 2lbs   6' 0"
Born: 26-09-1986 - Yeovil, Somerset
Education: Birchfield Community Primary School, Yeovil and Bucklers Mead School, Yeovil.

Martin was aged just 17 when he made his league debut at right back for Southampton on 4th May 2004 and although they went down 4-0 and he scored an own goal, it was generally felt that he had a promising future in the game. He had already represented England U17's and continued to receive international recognition at each level up to and including U21, for whom he was capped 16 times, including two matches in 2008 against the Czech Republic and Portugal, while on loan at Charlton.

HONOURS
England U21 International 2007-09 16 caps 1 goal
England U20 International 2003-05 2 caps 0 goals
England U19 International 2004-05 12 caps 0 goals
England U18 & U17 International
Southampton Youth 2004-05 Finallists FA Youth Cup
Huddersfield Town 2016-17 Promoted Play Offs Championship
Sheffield United 2018-19 Runners Up Championship

CLUBS
Southampton 2003 (youth) 29.09.04 (pro) ••AFC Bournemouth 29.10.04 (loan) ••Yeovil Town 08.11.06 (loan) 02.03.07 (loan) ••Portsmouth 26.06.07 (free) ••Queens Park Rangers 08.10.07 (loan) ••Charlton Athletic 01.09.08 (loan) ••Coventry City 13.08.09 (£500,000) ••Barnsley 20.08.12 (free) ••Huddersfield Town 22.07.15 (free) ••Middlesbrough 31.01.18 (free) ••Sheffield United 01.09.18 (free) •Luton Town 28.06.19 (free)

Despite his early start in the game, Martin was unable to carve out a regular first team place for himself with either Southampton or Portsmouth to whom he was transferred in 2007.
He had several spells out on loan, one of which brought him to Charlton in September 2008 at the tail end of manager Alan Pardew's term of office and his four-month stay covered a very difficult period for the club. From his debut against Wolves, a 3-1 home defeat, to his final game, a similar scoreline at Sheffield United, the team could only scrape together two wins. Pardew was sacked in November and by the time Martin departed back to Portsmouth, the

club were rock bottom of the Championship where they would remain for the remainder of the season.
His career really only took off after joining Coventry City in August 2009, where he played regularly for three years while they struggled and were finally relegated from the Championship in 2012. The same pattern emerged after he moved to Barnsley, who crashed out of the Championship two years later as Martin recorded a hat trick of relegations. Subsequent moves to Huddersfield under Chris Powell and to Middlesbrough were less traumatic, although he was released by the latter at the end of the 2017-18 season and during September 2018 joined Chris Wilder's Sheffield

United in time to play a part in their unexpected promotion to the Premier League.

Martin's most recent club was Luton Town and he was a semi-regular in their team for two seasons. His contract

Season	Division	League		FA Cup		FL Cup		Total	
		A	G	A	G	A	G	A	G
2008-09 (R)	Championship	19	0	0	0	0	0	19	0
Total		19	0	0	0	0	0	19	0

UK LEAGUE CAREER 407 games 4 goals

expired at the conclusion of 2020-21 but he declined an extension and is currently unattached, although there has been some interest from Coventry City.

CHARLTON CAREER
Managers: *A Pardew, P Parkinson*
Debut: *Wolverhampton Wanderers (H) 13-09-2008*
V672
Finale: *Sheffield United (A) 28-12-2008*

CRAWFORD Raymond   1969

Ray was a top class striker who scored goals wherever he played. The son of a heavyweight boxer, he was a key member of the Ipswich Town side that won the Second and First Division titles

Forward   11st 10lbs.   5' 11"
Born: 13-07-1936 - Portsmouth, Hampshire
Education: Hilsea Modern School, Portsmouth.

in consecutive years in the early sixties and a teammate of future Charlton manager Andy Nelson. Ray missed only one game during the two championship seasons, during which he contributed a staggering 73 league goals. He played twice for England, scoring in the 3-1 win over Austria at Wembley on 4th April 1962 and bagged all three goals when the Football League defeated the Irish League by the same score six months later.

HONOURS
England International 1961-62 2 caps 1 goal
Portsmouth Schools
Football League XI 1961-62 3 caps 5 goals
Malaya International XI 1956
Ipswich Town 1960-61 & 1967-68 Winners Division 2
Ipswich Town 1961-62 Winners Division 1

CLUBS
Portsmouth 06.54 (amateur) 28.12.54 (pro) ••Ipswich Town 06.09.58 (£6,500) ••Wolverhampton Wanderers 16.09.63 (£55,000) ••West Bromwich Albion 17.02.65 (£35,000) ••Ipswich Town 10.03.66 (£15,000) ••Charlton Athletic 05.03.69 (£12,500) ••Kettering Town 10.69 (free) ••Colchester United 04.06.70 (£1,000) ••Durban City, South Africa 08.71 (free) ••Brighton & Hove Albion 09.11.71 (coach) ••Portsmouth 1973 (coach) ••F C Eden, New Zealand 08.74 (coach) ••Portsmouth 1976 (coach) 1977 (ass. manager) ••Fareham Town 1978 (manager) ••Winchester City 05.81 (manager)

Ray represented Portsmouth Schools and signed for his hometown club at the age of 17. He spent his National Service with the British Army out in the jungle of South East Asia, during which time he played for the Malayan International team. His debut for Portsmouth came in August 1957 and he scored twice against Tottenham in only his second match.

He never failed to score goals at any club lucky enough to employ him and it was a great shame that he did not move to Charlton sooner, as he was approaching the age of 33 when he signed in March 1969. Even then it was fortunate that Ipswich deemed him surplus to their requirements, as he had scored both goals in a 2-0 victory at Arsenal only a fortnight earlier.

Ray came into a Charlton side chasing promotion from Division 2, although initially his presence seemed to disrupt

rather than aid the cause as it broke up the popular Tees/Tracey strike partnership. He did claim the winning goals against both Norwich and Sheffield United but the team eventually fell short of their target, finishing in third place. Season 1969-70 was less successful, despite Ray contributing a spectacular overhead kick for Charlton's equaliser in a 1-1 draw at Millwall on 16th August. Following a dispute with manager Eddie Firmani, his brief stay in SE7 ended when he departed to non league Kettering two months later, but Charlton shrewdly retained his Football League registration and were suitably rewarded with a transfer fee when he joined Colchester the following Summer. He managed 31 goals in 1970-71 including two in their shock FA Cup win against high flying Leeds United on 13th February.

After retirement, Ray held a number of coaching positions,

most notably back with Portsmouth and also tried his hand at management. He worked as a merchandise representative and in 2007 brought out his autobiography, 'Curse Of The Jungle Boy'. He is patron of the charity, 'Football For Cancer'.

Season	Division	League		FA Cup		FL Cup		Total	
		A	G	A	G	A	G	A	G
1968-69	Division 2	9	3	0	0	0	0	9	3
1969-70	Division 2	12	4	0	0	1	0	13	4
Total		21	7	0	0	1	0	22	7

UK LEAGUE CAREER 476 games 290 goals

CHARLTON CAREER
Managers: *E Firmani*
Debut: *Carlisle United (H) 08-03-1969*
V343
Finale: *Hull City (A) 27-09-1969*

CRIPPS Henry Richard   1974 - 75

Defender, Midfield   13st 8lbs   5' 10"
Born: 29-04-1941 - East Dereham, Norfolk
Died: 29-12-1995 - Wanstead, London
Education: Faraday Secondary Modern School, Canning Town

Harry is rightly considered a legend at Millwall where he made in excess of 440 competitive appearances in more than 13 years. A likeable and charismatic character and an inspiration on the field, he played in two promotion teams while at the Den and became a great favourite with their fans. His popularity extended to a somewhat embarrassing record 'The Ballad Of Harry Cripps' which was released by Decca in 1972, and a much more acceptable tribute at the New Den, where one of their lounges has been named 'Arry's Bar' in his memory.

HONOURS

West Ham Boys & Essex County Boys
London Boys & Southern England Boys
West Ham United Youth 1958-59 Finalists FA Youth Cup

Millwall 1964-65 Runners Up Division 4
Millwall 1965-66 Runners Up Division 3
Charlton Athletic 1974-75 Promoted Division 3

CLUBS

West Ham United 1956 (youth) 06.58 (pro) ••Millwall 17.06.61 (free) ••East Ham United (coach) ••Charlton Athletic 03.10.74 (free) 04.76 (coach) 21.02.78 (ass. manager) ••Norwich City 1979 (scout) ••Barking 1980 (manager) ••Crystal Palace 08.83 (coach) ••Southend United 1984 (ass. manager) ••Crown & Manor 1988 (manager) ••Purfleet 06.02.90 (manager)

Harry's potential as a footballer was spotted at an early age and he represented West Ham Boys, Essex Schools, London Boys and Southern England. By the age of 15 he was with West Ham United and in 1958-59 they reached the final of the FA Youth Cup, losing in a two legged final against Blackburn Rovers. The Hammers team included not only Harry, Bobby Moore and Geoff Hurst, but also two other future Charlton players, Derek Woodley and Jack Burkett. He was released without making a league appearance and his debut for Millwall came on 19th August 1961 against Wrexham. Excepting injuries, he was rarely missing from their line-up until 1974 and during that period they established themselves in the Second Division, maintaining their status until the season after Harry departed when they sunk back to Division 3.

Considering his iconic status with their local rivals, it might

have proved a controversial signing when Harry joined Charlton in October 1974, but thanks to his personality and all action playing style, he was readily accepted and became a useful addition to Andy Nelson's promotion side. Either lining up at left back or in a marauding midfield role, he chipped in with some useful goals, including the winner in a 2-1 scoreline at Bournemouth.

As his playing days drew to a close Harry took on a coaching role and in February 1978 became assistant manager to Andy Nelson, a position that he retained until September 1979. He later managed Isthmian League club Barking for two years and maintained a presence in the game with several other coaching and managerial positions, even becoming a coach at Winchester College for a time. He found employment in the insurance industry with Royal London Assurance and lived at Upminster in Essex.

Harry was recovering from a stroke in Wanstead Hospital when he suffered a fatal heart attack and passed away on

29th December 1995 at the age of 54.

Season	Division	League		FA Cup		FL Cup		Total	
		A	G	A	G	A	G	A	G
1974-75 (P)	Division 3	17 (2)	4	2	0	0	0	19 (2)	4
1975-76	Division 2	0 (1)	0	0	0	0	0	0 (1)	0
Total		17 (3)	4	2	0	0	0	19 (3)	4

UK LEAGUE CAREER 419 games 41 goals

CHARLTON CAREER
Managers: *A Nelson*
Debut: *Peterborough United (H) 05-10-1974*
V390
Finale: *Notts County (H) (sub) 16-08-1975*

CROFTS Andrew Lawrence   2016 - 17

A combative midfield player, Andrew qualified to play international football for Wales through his grandparents. His debut came in a FIFA World Cup qualifier on 12th October 2005 against Azerbaijan, playing alongside John Robinson in a 2-0 win. He went on to earn a total of 29 caps but none during his year as a Charlton player. By then it had seemed as if his international career was at an end, but on 14th November 2017 he was recalled for his final appearance in the 1-1 draw with Panama.

Midfield 11st 4lbs 5' 8"
Born: 29-05-1984 - Chatham, Kent

HONOURS
Wales International 2005-17 29 caps 1 goal
Wales U21 International 2005 6 caps 1 goal
Wales U19 International 2002 3 caps 0 goals
Norwich City 2010-11 Runners Up Championship

CLUBS
Chelsea (youth) ••Gillingham 08.00 (youth) 05.01 (pro) ••Dover Athletic 11.03 (loan) ••Peterborough United 19.11.08 (loan) ••Wrexham 16.02.09 (loan) ••Brighton & Hove Albion 29.06.09 (free) ••Norwich City 21.05.10 (£300,000) ••Brighton & Hove Albion 02.08.12 (free) ••Gillingham 19.03.16 (loan) ••Charlton Athletic 22.07.16 (free) ••Scunthorpe United 31.08.17 (free) ••Newport County 26.06.18 (free) ••Yeovil Town 27.06.19 (player coach) ••Brighton & Hove Albion 27.07.19 (player coach)

Although Andrew spent almost nine years with his local club, Gillingham, for most of that period they were having a tough time and were relegated from both the Championship in 2005 and then from League One three years later. He was a consistent performer however and did manage to grab the limelight on 20th September 2005 when his stoppage time goal disposed of Premier League Portsmouth 3-2 in a League Cup match at the Priestfield Stadium.

After a year with Brighton, he signed for Norwich City in May 2010 for an undisclosed fee that was believed to be in the region of £300,000 and went on to enjoy the most successful period in his career as they clinched promotion from the Championship in 2010-11 and followed this up with a mid-table finish the following season. He featured in 24 matches in the Premier League before returning to Brighton in the Summer of 2012.

Andrew was badly affected by injury during his second spell on the Sussex coast and had to undergo two knee ligament

operations during 2014. He joined Charlton at the beginning of Russell Slade's short managerial reign and featured in all but one of the league matches in 2016-17. His year's contract had an option for a further year and initially he exercised his right to remain at the Valley. When however it became clear that new manager Karl Robinson did not see him as more than a squad player, he changed his mind and switched to Scunthorpe United on the last day of the August 2017 transfer window.

Always a leader on the field, Andrew was invariably made captain wherever he went and by November 2018 was skipper of Newport County as his career moved towards its conclusion. Interestingly and possibly with the future in mind, he along with Rob Elliot and Chris Solly, set up the Players Elite Academy to provide coaching and development for children in the Gillingham area which perhaps hints at the direction his life will take when his playing days are over. Since 2019 he has been coaching in the Brighton & Hove Albion youth academy.

Season	Division	League		FA Cup		FL Cup		FL Trophy		Total	
		A	G	A	G	A	G	A	G	A	G
2016-17	League One	41 (4)	1	2	0	1	0	3	0	47 (4)	1
2017-18	League One	0 (1)	0	0	0	1	0	1	0	2 (1)	0
Total		41 (5)	1	2	0	2	0	4	0	49 (5)	1

UK LEAGUE CAREER 431 games 36 goals

CHARLTON CAREER
Managers: *R Slade, K Robinson*
Debut: *Bury (A) 06-08-2016*
V821
Finale: *Crawley Town (A) 29-08-2017*

CROKER Edgar Alfred   1950

Defender   11st 3lbs   5' 10"
Born: 13-02-1924 - Kingston Upon Thames, Surrey
Died: 25-12-1992 - Cheltenham, Gloucestershire
Education: Malden West School, New Malden. KIngston Technical School, Kingston.

Ted was the younger brother of Peter Croker who was the right back in Charlton's FA Cup winning team of 1947 and although he failed to emulate Peter's achievements on the field, he did go on to become a top football administrator and held the positions of Secretary and Chief Executive of the Football Association between 1973 and 1989. He was a Life Vice President of the FA, a Vice President of the South East Counties League and in 1991 was elected to FIFA's Disciplinary panel. In the 1989 Queen's Birthday Honours List he was awarded the CBE, for services to football.

HONOURS

Dartford 1946-47 Winners Kent Senior Cup

Charlton Athletic Reserves 1949-50 Winners Football Combination

Charlton Athletic Reserves 1949-50 Runners Up Football Combination Cup

Charlton Athletic Reserves 1950-51 Winners Football Combination Cup

CLUBS

RAF 04.42 (amateur) ••Charlton Athletic 03.10.45 (amateur) ••Kingstonian 1946 (amateur) ••Dartford 02.47 (amateur) ••Kingstonian 01.48 (amateur) ••Charlton Athletic 15.04.48 (pro) ••Kidderminster Harriers 06.12.51 (free) ••Headington United 07.53 (free) ••Cheltenham Town (coach)

At different times, a footballer, an administrator and a businessman, Ted enjoyed a varied and interesting life. After gaining a scholarship to Kingston Technical School, he undertook a business management course, then progressed to working as a junior draughtsman before joining the RAF in April 1942 and training to be a pilot. He spent the later part of World War 2 stationed in South Africa as a pilot instructor.

Like his brother Peter, he showed talent on the football field and joined Charlton as an amateur in October 1945, but a horrific plane crash in the Pennines two months later put paid to his early footballing ambitions. He was piloting a twin-engined Air Speed Oxford and crashed into a hillside at 120 mph. Needless to say he was fortunate to survive at all and with both ankles broken, crawled for two miles to summon help for his two companions who were still trapped inside the plane. It took a year before Ted could resume his football career and he had spells playing for both Kingstonian and Dartford before finally signing a professional contract with Charlton in April 1948.

First team opportunities were scarce during Ted's time at the Valley. Harold Phipps held on tightly to the centre half shirt, as he had done continuously since the war. Ted played well in the reserves but it was not until November 1950 that he finally got his chance after Phipps injured his ankle at Burnley. He managed a run of eight matches, but in all honesty things did not go well for him nor the team. Only one victory was recorded during this period and he twice scored own goals, one at Middlesbrough on 9th December in a heavy 7-3 defeat and by the end of that month Harold had returned to the team bringing Ted's first team days to an end.

He continued in the non-league game after leaving Charlton in December 1951, but married shortly thereafter and soon turned his attention to more lucrative ways to earn his living than the £9 a week he had at one stage received as a professional footballer. For two years he ran a garage in Chipping Norton, but later invented an industrial snow blower called the 'Croker Sno-Blo' and by 1973 was chairman of Liner Croker Ltd, employing 500 staff and with an annual turnover of £10 million.

Ted's time at the Football Association made him a public

figure, but spanned a difficult time for the game, encompassing various stadium disasters and the rise of football hooliganism although he stood up to prime minister Margaret Thatcher over her opposition to professional football and her desire to introduce draconian measures such as identity cards. His autobiography, 'The First Voice You Hear Is...' was published in 1987. Ted Croker passed away on Christmas Day 1992, following a long battle with cancer. His grandson is Tottenham footballer Eric Dier.

Season	Division	League		FA Cup		Total	
		A	G	A	G	A	G
1950-51	Division 1	8	0	0	0	8	0
Total		8	0	0	0	8	0

UK LEAGUE CAREER 8 games 0 goals

CHARLTON CAREER
Managers: *J Seed*
Debut: *Chelsea (H) 04-11-1950*
V242
Finale: *Aston Villa (A) 26-12-1950*

CROKER Peter Harry Lucas   1946 - 51

At the end of World War 2, the Football League remained on a regional basis for the first year and only appearances in the FA Cup are officially recognised for season

Defender   13st 4lbs   6' 1"
Born: 21-12-1921 - Kingston Upon Thames, Surrey
Died: 07-12-2011 - Bexley, Kent
Education: Malden West Central School, New Malden and Kingston Technical School, KIngston.

1945-46. Peter played 72 games for Charlton during the war years and was a key member of the defence during that first post-war campaign. Sadly for him, he broke his right leg during a match against Tottenham on 17th April 1946 and this kept him out of the Cup Final which was played just 10 days later. His place at right back went to Harold Phipps. There was to be a happy ending to this personal tragedy however as Charlton, beaten finalists in 1946, fought their way through to the second post-war Cup Final as well and on 26th April 1947 Peter was in the side that defeated Burnley 1-0 to bring the trophy back to South London for the first and so far only time.

HONOURS

Surbiton & District Schools (as goalkeeper) c1933	Charlton Athletic Reserves 1949-50 Winners Football Combination
South Eastern Combination 1942-44 2 caps	Charlton Athletic Reserves 1950-51 Winners Football Combination Cup
FA XI v Oxford United 11.45	Charlton Athletic 2014 Hall Of Fame
Charlton Athletic 1946-47 FA Cup Winners	

CLUBS

Kingston YMCA (youth) ••Leyland Motors (Kingston) (youth) ••Charlton Juniors 01.40 (U18's) ••Bromley 1940 (loan) ••Charlton Rovers c1941 (amateur) ••Charlton Athletic 19.03.41 (amateur) 20-11-45 (pro) ••Watford 09.06.52 (£300) ••Gravesend & Northfleet 07.53 (free) •Harvey's Sports 11.54 (free) ••Charlton Athletic 08.56 (scout) (colts manager) 25.10.65 (ass: manager) ••Blackpool 1972 (scout) ••Sunderland 1973 (scout)

Peter was playing for Leyland Motors when goalkeeper Syd Hobbins introduced him to Charlton and he cut his teeth in a newly formed U18 league commencing in January 1940. He was still playing as an amateur when he made his first team debut on 30th October 1943 against Brighton in a below strength side that contained four guest players. This was common practice during the war years and Peter himself turned out for Brentford as a guest on occasions. His first Charlton match was perhaps not surprisingly a home defeat by 4-1 and with only a consolation goal from Sailor Brown to stir the Valley crowd. He signed a professional contract on 20th November 1945 and played

in each of the nine FA Cup ties prior to his broken leg. To make matters worse Peter had been heavily tipped to play for England in the forthcoming matches with France and Switzerland until his injury put paid to those ambitions. The broken leg kept Peter out of action until September 1947 after which time he returned to the team but now faced competition for his position at right back in the rugged shape of hard man Jock Campbell. Jimmy Seed gave Jock his debut in the FA Cup against Rochdale in January and he went on to play in each of the first four Cup games. With the team through to the semi-final, Peter must have been worried that he would miss out on the Cup Final for a second year running, but he was recalled in March and lined up in front of 47,821 against Second Division Newcastle United in the semi final on 29th March 1947. Charlton may have been favourites but on the day of the game, Peter was one of five players who were suffering from food poisoning. Despite this handicap, the game was won 4-0 and a month later Burnley were vanquished and Charlton were FA Cup winners.

The FA Cup win was undoubtedly the high point of Peter's career and by 1948 his first team appearances were becoming less frequent as not only Campbell but also Jack Shreeve was being preferred for the number two shirt. He was transferred to Watford in June 1952 where he linked up with his former Charlton teammate Harold Phipps, but after just one season he dropped into non-league and found work as an estimator with Harvey's in Greenwich. He remained closely linked to Charlton and in August 1956 started scouting for the club and later managed the Colts team. It was Peter who drove Derek Ufton to hospital on the occasion of the famous 7-6 match against Huddersfield but made it back to the Valley in time for the second half.

In April 1963 he became chief scout and then for nine months in 1965-66 acted as assistant manager to Bob Stokoe.

Like his younger brother Ted Croker, Peter got involved in football administration and for 35 years held a variety of posts with the South East Counties League, finishing up as Chairman. In addition, he served on the committee of the Metropolitan League, was Assistant Secretary of the London Mid-Week League and a Vice President of the Spartan South Midlands League. He was a fine cricketer and golfer and carried on working in a solicitor's office until the age of 73.

In 1995, he suffered a fall in his garden and severed the main artery in his left hand on a milk bottle which required extensive treatment at Queen Victoria Hospital, East Grinstead and by November 2003 he had lost the sight in his left eye and only had limited vision in his right. Three years later he moved into sheltered accommodation and passed away in Bexley shortly before his 90th birthday, having been the last survivor of the FA Cup winning team. Peter's great nephew is Tottenham footballer Eric Dier.

Season	Division	League		FA Cup		Total	
		A	G	A	G	A	G
1945-46	Wartime			9	0	9	0
1946-47	Division 1	29	0	2	0	31	0
1947-48	Division 1	4	0	0	0	4	0
1949-50	Division 1	15	0	2	0	17	0
1950-51	Division 1	11	0	2	1	13	1
Total		59	0	15	1	74	1

UK LEAGUE CAREER 82 games, 0 goals

CHARLTON CAREER
Managers: *J Seed*
Debut: *Wartime Brighton & Hove Albion (H) 30-10-1943 FA Cup Fulham (H) 05-01-1946*
V207
Finale: *Arsenal (A) 24-02-1951*

CROOKS Garth Anthony   1986 - 90

Forward   12st 1lb   5' 8"
Born: 10-03-1958 - Bucknall, Staffordshire
Education: St Peter's Comprehensive, Stoke-on-Trent.

A top class striker, Garth spent nearly four years at Charlton during the Selhurst period and in season 1987-88 scored 10 vital league goals which went a long way towards keeping the club in Division 1. Relegation at that stage would have been economically disastrous and as no other player managed more than six, a lot of credit must go to Garth. With small crowds and little reason for optimism, the club just managed to stay up on goal difference and buy themselves some much-needed breathing space. In June 1988 new owners took over at Charlton and the long journey back home to the Valley commenced.

HONOURS

England U21 International 1979-80 4 caps 3 goals	Tottenham Hotspur 1980-81 & 1981-82 Winners FA Cup
Stoke & Staffordshire Schools	Tottenham Hotspur 1981-82 Finalists Football League Cup
Stoke City 1978-79 Promoted Division 2	Tottenham Hotspur 1982 Runners Up FA Charity Shield

Stoke City (youth) 03.76 (pro) ••Tottenham Hotspur 25.07.80 (£600,000) ••Manchester United 11.83 (loan) •West Bromwich Albion 18.07.85 (£100,000) ••Charlton Athletic 27.03.87 (£75,000)

Garth joined Stoke City while still at school, but by the time he established himself in the first team they were facing relegation from the First Division in 1976-77. He contributed both goals when Leeds United were beaten 2-1 on 12th April 1977 and got the winner in the home match with Birmingham City, but was unable to prevent them from the drop. Over the next two years he became increasingly important to Stoke, his devastating pace and shooting prowess resulting in 30 league goals and after they regained their First Division place, he scored another 12 in 1979-80, including a hat-trick against West Bromwich Albion.

On 20th November 1979, Garth grabbed another hat-trick, this time on his international debut at Leicester, when England U21 defeated Bulgaria U21 by 5-0. He went on to earn four caps and was unlucky never to receive a call-up to the full England side. He did however attract the attention of Tottenham who in July 1980 paid a fee of £650,000 to bring him to North London.

The five years that Garth spent at Spurs represent the pinnacle of his career, especially the first two seasons when they won the FA Cup both times. In the 1981 final against Manchester City, they drew the first game, but won the replay 3-2, Garth scoring the second Spurs goal. His teammates included Paul Miller, while in the City side were Tommy Caton and Steve MacKenzie. A year later Miller and Crooks featured again in the FA Cup final, this time against a Queens Park Rangers team which had Mike Flanagan in their line-up. As before it went to two games, but Tottenham retained the Cup with a 1-0 win. Garth continued to score goals at a highly acceptable rate until injuries kept him sidelined in 1983-84 and having lost his place in the team, he spent two months on loan at Manchester United. He returned to the Spurs side and had another fine season in 1984-85, at one stage scoring in seven consecutive matches, including the 1-1 FA Cup tie against

Charlton on 5th January 1985. Two months later he scored the only goal at Anfield to give Spurs their first away win against Liverpool since 1912.

In July 1985 Garth moved on to West Bromwich Albion, but after a good start, missed the later part of 1985-86 through injury as they flopped to the bottom of Division 1. After relegation, he got back among the goals and in March 1987 Lennie Lawrence brought him down to London for another similar battle. His experience was invaluable when Charlton had to play their way through five play off matches to preserve their First Division status and over the next year, until the emergence of Paul Williams, he was the club's primary striker. Sadly as time went on a persistent back injury caused him to miss more and more games until on 8th November 1990 he took the decision to hang up his boots.

Always an active figure off the field, Garth had become the first black Chairman of the Professional Footballers' Association in December 1988, a post that he held for nearly two years. He became Chairman of the Institute of Professional Sport in 1993 and was a founder of the charity SCAR (Sickle Cell Anaemia Relief). He also chaired the Football Foundation's Grassroots Advisory Group and served as special advisor on football to the Commission for Racial Equality. He has worked extensively in the media as both analyst and interviewer and his talk and music show 'Garth Crooks In Conversation' on GLR Radio won a Sony Award. He also had an acting role in a BBC production 'It's A Stick Up' and often appeared on 'Match Of The Day'. He was part of the BBC TV team covering the Atlanta Olympics in 1996. He remains an active campaigner for racial equality and lectures on discrimination and diversity.

Garth Crooks was awarded the OBE in the Queen's Birthday Honours list of 1999, for Services to Professional Sport.

Season	Division	League		FA Cup		FL Cup		Play Offs		FM Cup		Total	
		A	G	A	G	A	G	A	G	A	G	A	G
1986-87	Division 1	5 (2)	2	0	0	0	0	5	0	0	0	10 (2)	2
1987-88	Division 1	24 (4)	10	0 (1)	0	2	2			1	0	27 (5)	12
1988-89	Division 1	10 (4)	2	3	1	0	0			0	0	13 (4)	3
1989-90 (R)	Division 1	0	0	0	0	0	0			1	0	1	0
1990-91	Division 2	2 (5)	1	0	0	1 (1)	0			0	0	3 (6)	1
Total		41 (15)	15	3 (1)	1	3 (1)	2	5	0	2	0	54 (17)	18

UK LEAGUE CAREER 375 games 129 goals

CHARLTON CAREER
Managers: *L Lawrence*
Debut: *Oldham Athletic (H) 04-10-1986*
V490
Finale: *Watford (H) (sub) 20-10-1990*

CULLEN Joshua Jon   2018 - 20

Midfield   11st 0lbs   5' 9"
Born: 07-04-1996 - Hackney, London
Education: St Thomas More High School, Westcliff-on-Sea.

It was Josh who crossed the ball in the dying seconds of the 2019 play off decider at Wembley and from which Patrick Bauer scored the goal which clinched Charlton's promotion to the Championship. For those present, this created a memory that will stay with them forever, as the victory over Sunderland was a pivotal moment in the history of the club. The young midfielder was completing his year as a Charlton player and was expected to go back to his parent club, West Ham, after a highly successful spell on loan. Surprisingly however they agreed to renew the loan for a further season and in August 2019 Josh returned to the Valley to take his place in Lee Bowyer's team as they prepared to compete back at the higher level.

HONOURS

Republic of Ireland International 2019-21 15 caps 0 goals
Republic of Ireland U21 International 2015-19 17 caps 1 goal
Republic of Ireland U19 International 2014-17 3 caps 0 goals

Republic of Ireland U18 International 2014 2 caps 0 goals
England U16 International 2011 1 cap 0 goals
Charlton Athletic 2018-19 Promoted Play Offs League One

CLUBS

Rayleigh Boys (youth) ••West Ham United 2005 (youth) 2013 (pro) ••Bradford City 11.02.16 (loan) 08.08.16 (loan) ••Bolton Wanderers 01.08.17 (loan) ••Charlton Athletic 30.08.18 (loan) 07.08.19 (loan) ••Anderlecht, Belgium 05.10.20 (£450,000)

Josh was born in London's East End, but grew up in the Southend area. He joined West Ham at the age of nine, but despite flourishing as a young player, found first team opportunities few and far between. His Premier League debut came on 29th August 2015 and this proved a memorable occasion for the Hammers as it was the first time that they had won a league match at Anfield for over 50 years. Josh made a very late appearance from the bench as the team, which had Darren Randolph in goal, beat Liverpool 3-0.
His first two spells out on loan were each with Bradford City and in two successive seasons he helped them progress to the League One play offs, only to lose to Millwall on each occasion. On 20th May 2017 they did at least make it to Wembley, but the team which also included Billy Clarke and Mark Marshall, went down 1-0. He spent the first half of 2017-18 at Bolton Wanderers before returning to the Boleyn Ground, but again he was given little chance to

progress his career and West Ham let him join Charlton on yet another loan in August 2018.
Josh's tackling, non-stop running and energetic midfield play had a lot to do with the success of the Addicks in 2018-19 and he was a popular and much appreciated member of the promotion side. He had first enjoyed a taste of international football in May 2011 when he helped the England U16 side to a 3-0 win against Wales in the Victory Shield, but later changed his allegiance to the Republic of Ireland for whom he qualified via his grandfather. He played and eventually skippered the Ireland U21 team in the UEFA Championship qualifiers, earning five caps while at Charlton and early in his second loan spell at the Valley was rewarded with a full cap on 10th September 2019 when Ireland beat Bulgaria 3-1. His second cap was also during his time with Charlton and he has now become an established member of the Irish team, with hopefully many more international appearances to come.

In October 2020 Josh was transferred to Anderlecht, who compete in the Belgian First Division and after only twelve matches was made captain.

Season	Division	League		FA Cup		FL Cup		FL Trophy		Play Offs		Total	
		A	G	A	G	A	G	A	G	A	G	A	G
2018-19 (P)	League One	29	1	0	0	0	0	0		0	3	0	32	1
2019-20 (R)	Championship	34	1	0	0	0	0					34	1
Total		63	2	0	0	0	0	0		0	3	0	66	2

UK LEAGUE CAREER 133 games 3 goals

CHARLTON CAREER
Managers: L Bowyer
Debut: Southend United (A) 01-09-2018
V865
Finale: Leeds United (A) 22-07-2020

CULLUM Riley Granville   1949 - 52

In October 1947 Fred Alexander and Riley Cullum were transferred to Charlton for a combined fee of £6,000 which at the time was a Football League record paid to a non-league club. It allowed Southern League side Dartford to clear all their debts and outstanding liabilities. Alexander, a centre half, never appeared for Charlton at first team level, and became better known as a Middlesex cricketer, but Riley went on to spend nearly six years at the Valley and although his time was mainly spent in the reserves, he became a popular figure with supporters and was probably unlucky not to have seen more first team action.

Forward   10st 6lbs   5' 7"
Born: 02-04-1923 - West Ham, Essex
Died: 31-12-1996 - Barking, Essex
Education: Storey Street School, North Woolwich.

HONOURS
Kent FA 1946-47 1 cap (v London FA)
Dartford 1946-47 Winners Kent Senior Cup
Charlton Athletic Reserves 1949-50 Winners Football Combination
Charlton Athletic Reserves 1949-50 & 1952-53 Runners Up Football

Combination Cup
Charlton Athletic Reserves 1950-51 Winners Football Combination Cup
Charlton Athletic Reserves 1951-52 Finalists London FA Challenge Cup

CLUBS
Storey Athletic ••Dartford 02.46 (amateur) 02.47 (pro) ••Charlton Athletic 04.10.47 (£3,000) ••Gravesend & Northfleet 06.08.1953 (free) ••Dartford 05.54 (free) ••Argyle Sports 1959

A skilful inside forward, Riley was a consistent scorer in the reserves and scored three or more goals on six separate occasions. Fulham must have been sick of the sight of him after he hit four against them on 23rd March 1951 and then followed up with another three only a few days later in the return fixture. He was less prolific while on first team duty but did get a decent run in the side during 1950-51 and contributed the opening goal against Sheffield Wednesday in an important Division 1 encounter on 13th January. The club had just gone eight matches without a win and were sliding into relegation trouble, but an 89th minute strike from Hans Jeppson ensured a 2-1 win and eased the pressure considerably.

Riley's final appearance for the Addicks came against Arsenal and was a memorable one. On 13th September 1952 they won 4-3 at Highbury in front of a crowd of 60,102, thanks to goals from Billy Kiernan (2), Charlie Vaughan and Gordon Hurst. At the end of that season he moved on to Gravesend and later returned to finish his career back with Dartford.

By 1957 he was living in Bexley and working as a milkman but still keeping his boots close at hand. In February 1959 along with Malcolm Allison and Kevin Barry, he turned out for Metropolitan Sunday League side Argyle Sports in a charity cup match. He moved to live in Silverland Street, Woolwich before getting married at East Ham in 1964 and later worked as an engineer at a Barking pumping station. Riley passed away in Barking at the age of 73. His father, also Riley Cullum, played for Norwich City in 1919-20, the season before they became a Football League club.

Season	Division	League		FA Cup		Total	
		A	G	A	G	A	G
1949-50	Division 1	6	0	0	0	6	0
1950-51	Division 1	21	4	0	0	21	4
1951-52	Division 1	4	2	1	0	5	2
1952-53	Division 1	1	0	0	0	1	0
Total		32	6	1	0	33	6

UK LEAGUE CAREER 32 games 6 goals

CHARLTON CAREER
Managers: *J Seed*
Debut: *Manchester City (A) 24-12-1949*
VV238
Finale: *Arsenal (A) 13-09-1952*

CUMMINGS Joseph Theodore   2017 - 18

Defender   11st 9lbs   6' 2"
Born: 08-09-1998 - Sheffield, Yorkshire
Education:

A tall, imposing central defender, Jo progressed through the Sheffield United youth academy, but was released in 2017 without the offer of a pro contract. Charlton invited him down for a trial and were sufficiently impressed to sign him for the Development squad. He enjoyed two years at the Valley without being able to force his way into the first team and made just two appearances in cup matches before his time was up.

HONOURS

Charlton Athletic U23 2017-18 Runners Up PD League 2 South

CLUBS

Sheffield United (youth) ••Charlton Athletic 09.05.17 (pro) ••Guiseley 17.10.18 (loan) ••Scunthorpe United 08.07.19 (free) ••Radcliffe 06.03.20 (loan) 20.06.20 (free)

The Football League Trophy is used by many clubs as an opportunity to blood young players, especially as those from the Premier and Championship are permitted to field Under 21 sides in what is supposedly a first team fixture. Charlton were no exception and on 1st November 2017 Jo was part of a much weakened first eleven who took the field at the Valley against Fulham U21 in front of a crowd of only 741. Perhaps unexpectedly, the small crowd witnessed an exciting contest as the home team came from behind with two very late goals from Joe Dodoo and Joe Aribo to snatch a 2-1 win.

Jo's second appearance at first team level came in similar circumstances in a Football League Cup encounter at MK Dons in which a team of mainly youngsters was fielded against more experienced opposition. This did not go so well although Jo played the full 90 minutes at centre half. Two early goals were conceded and during the second half he was unfortunate enough to concede an own goal as the home side gained a somewhat flattering 3-0 scoreline.

At the end of the 2018-19 season he was freed by Charlton and joined Scunthorpe United, but has since dropped down into non-league football with Northern Premier League side Radcliffe.

Season	Division	League		FA Cup		FL Cup		FL Trophy		Play Offs		Total	
		A	G	A	G	A	G	A	G	A	G	A	G
2017-18	League One	0	0	0	0	0	0	1	0	0	0	1	0
2018-19 (P)	League One	0	0	0	0	1	0	0	0	0	0	1	0
Total		0	0	0	0	1	0	1	0	0	0	2	0

UK LEAGUE CAREER 0 games 0 goals

CHARLTON CAREER
Managers: *K Robinson, L Bowyer*
Debut: *Fulham U21 (H) 01-11-2017*
V850
Finale: *Milton Keynes Dons (A) 14-08-2018*

CURBISHLEY Llewellyn Charles 'Alan'   1984 - 93

In April 2021 it was announced that the East Stand at the Valley would be re-named the Alan Curbishley Stand. This was

Midfield   11st 4lbs   5' 10"
Born: 08-11-1957 - Forest Gate, London
Education: Gainsborough School, West Ham, Trinity College School E16 &
West Ham Technical School.

in honour of Charlton's most successful manager since Jimmy Seed whose reign ended 65 years earlier and after whom the South Stand has been re-branded. Few would dispute that Alan has earned this special recognition and the names of both men are now proudly displayed at the stadium. They are visible to everyone who attends a match and long into the future will serve as a reminder of their outstanding achievements for Charlton Athletic.

HONOURS

England U21 International 1980 1 cap 0 goals
England Youth International 1975-76 9 caps 1 goal
England U15 Schoolboy International 1973 8 caps 1 goal
Newham Schools & Essex Schools
Forest Gate Boys 1972

Charlton Athletic 1985-86 Runners Up Division 2
West Ham United U18 1974-75 Finalists FA Youth Cup
Birmingham City 1979-80 Promoted Division 2
Brighton & Hove Albion 1987-88 Runners Up Division 3

HONOURS AS MANAGER

Charlton Athletic 1997-98 Promoted Play Offs Division 1

Charlton Athletic 1999-00 Winners Division 1

CLUBS

Senrab Boys Club (youth) ••West Ham United c1973 (youth) 07.75 (pro) ••Birmingham City 06.79 (£225,000) ••Aston Villa 03.83 (£100,000 + player) ••Charlton Athletic 24.12.84 (£38,000) ••Brighton & Hove Albion 21.08.87 (£30,000) ••Charlton Athletic 03.07.90 (player/coach) 24.07.91 (joint player/manager) 15.06.95 (manager) ••West Ham United 18.05.06 (manager) ••Fulham 24.12.13 (technical director) 05.03.15 (coach)

Alan first visited the Valley in 1974. He was a 16- year old apprentice at West Ham and earning £8 a week at the time, but this occasion had nothing to do with football. His brother Bill was manager of the Who and they were headlining a major concert at the ground. He spent the day selling memorabilia within the vast arena, which a quarter of a century later would be transformed into a proud modern stadium, at least partly due to his managerial efforts.

However, first came Alan Curbishley the player and there was never any doubt that West Ham United was the club most likely to attract the attention of this cultured young midfielder who lived only a mile or so from Upton Park. He played eight times for England Schoolboys in the under 15 age group and was soon signed up as an associated schoolboy by the Hammers. He was upgraded to an apprentice professional on 22nd July 1974 and was an unused sub for the first team against Everton a month later while still only 16. Alan was capped nine times for England U18's, which included victory in the UEFA U18 Youth Tournament of 1975. (Some sources show 10 caps, but the 4-2 win over Las Palmas on 23rd January 1975 and Alan's goal in the same match, were not granted official

international status).

His West Ham debut came on 29th March 1975 in a 1-0 home defeat against a Chelsea side that included Marvin Hinton and his first goal ensured a 2-1 win against Newcastle United on 11th October. He was in and out of the Hammers side until season 1977-78, but this proved to be the year when they dropped out of the old First Division, despite fielding a team that included Billy Bonds, Derek Hales and Mervyn Day. Alan figured in 32 league matches and his one goal of the campaign was a late 1-0 winner against Birmingham City on Boxing Day. He remained for one more season before in June 1979 transferring to Birmingham for what was probably the high point of his playing career.

The Birmingham team of 1979-80 won promotion from Division 2 and Alan was ever-present. They beat Charlton 1-0 in both league games, even though they were reduced to 10 men in the match at the Valley on 2nd February 1980. This was Alan's first Football League match at the venue where he would enjoy so much success in the future. On 18th November 1980 he played for England U21's who won 5-0 against Switzerland in a UEFA U21 Tournament qualifier. It proved to be his last international appearance.

In the next three years he helped Birmingham to hold on in Division 1, before moving to the then current European Cup holders Aston Villa in March 1983 for a fee of £100,000, plus winger Robert Hopkins who moved across to Birmingham in part-exchange. In contrast to Alan's time in the blue half of the city, his days as an Aston Villa player were spent competing safely in the middle of Division 1 and away from the threat of relegation.

Eventually a change of manager left him out of favour and out of the team, plus in addition he was becoming concerned at the rise in house prices. He felt that if he did not do something soon he would be priced out of a return to the London area, so was receptive when Charlton came calling and on Christmas Eve 1984 headed for SE7 in exchange for a transfer fee of £38,000. His initial impressions were strictly negative. Lennie Lawrence had been careful to keep him away from the Valley while negotiating the transfer and when he saw the rundown state of the stadium and realised the extent of the financial problems at the Valley, he thought that he had just made the worst decision of his life. Happily for all concerned, he soon settled down and got stuck into the fight to avoid relegation into Division 3

Charlton finished 1984-85 in 17th place, but things were about to change. Somehow the directors managed to find a modest transfer budget and Lennie used it well, constructing a new team that would go on to win the most unlikely promotion in the club's history. Alan missed the early weeks of the season through injury and therefore avoided the furore when it was announced in September that the club were to leave the Valley and ground share with Crystal Palace. His first home match of the season was against Sunderland on 5th October 1985. It was also the first 'home' game played at Selhurst Park. Bob Bolder was in goal for the visitors, but at least Charlton came out on top via a 2-1 scoreline and thanks to goals from Mark Reid and Mark Stuart. Alan went on to play 30 league games in the promotion season, but was missing for the run in through a troublesome Achilles injury, which eventually required surgery.

With the Achilles still a problem, Alan missed the start of 1986-87 and then had to contend with new arrivals Andy Peake and Colin Walsh who provided stiff competition for his place in midfield. He only started nine league matches in the whole season and desperate to get playing again, accepted the opportunity to join Brighton & Hove Albion in August 1987. With Charlton surviving in Division 1, the move appeared a backward step for Alan, but he was eager to play regularly and slotted quickly into the midfield and

along with teammates Garry Nelson and Steve Gatting he helped Brighton to promotion and a place in Division 2. Lennie Lawrence had regretted his decision to let Alan leave and kept him very much on his radar during the three years that he played for Brighton. The injury problems had been overcome and he played 116 league matches during that period, but it was still something of a surprise when he re-joined Charlton in July 1990, now with the additional responsibility of being not only a player but also reserve team coach. The club was still at Selhurst Park but, after battling the odds for four years, had dropped back into the Second Division. All available funds were now being channelled towards a return to the Valley, but this was still some way in the future. Alan was upgraded to first team player-coach on 4th October 1990 following the departure of Mike Flanagan, but still featured in 25 league games that term

The exile at Selhurst was finally at an end by the 1991-92 season, but the financial crisis had left the building work at the Valley unfinished and so home matches were temporarily switched to West Ham's ground. A bigger shock however was the departure of Lennie Lawrence who, after nine years driving Charlton through some unbelievably choppy waters, had left to take over as manager of Middlesbrough. The cheapest option was to replace him from within the club and effective 24th July 1991 Alan and Steve Gritt became joint player-coaches. (The job description was later amended to player-manager). Their real job was to keep the club afloat until the return to the Valley could be achieved and despite their management inexperience they showed themselves well up to the task. It was 5th December 1992 when Charlton finally ended seven years of exile and returned home to the Valley, although Alan did not play in the match against Portsmouth, which took place in almost a carnival atmosphere. His playing career was being allowed to fade away as both he and Gritt concentrated on slowly re-building the club after the years of neglect. Alan played his last game on 17th August 1993, a 2-1 away win at Portsmouth, courtesy of goals from Garry Nelson and Colin Walsh.

The two young managers gradually laid the foundations for the future success at Charlton, but on 15th June 1995 it was announced that the joint arrangement would be discontinued and from that point Alan became the sole manager of Charlton Athletic. The ground was being slowly re-built and transformed into a modern stadium and in 1995-96 when the team reached the play-offs, supporters were finally able to dream that perhaps a promotion to the

Premier League was becoming a possibility.

Two further years passed before Alan led his Charlton team out on 25th May 1998 for the Division 1 play off final against Sunderland. Clive Mendonca's hat-trick plus the drama of extra time and the penalty shoot out place this match as one of the greatest seen at Wembley and when Sasa Ilic saved the 14th penalty of the day, Charlton were duly promoted to the Premier League. After a valiant struggle which lasted until the final round of games, they just failed to maintain their new status in 1998-99 and were relegated again after only one year. With largely the same squad, Alan then returned the club to the Premier League twelve months later, this time finishing as champions of Division 1.

Over the next six seasons, Alan maintained Charlton's Premier League status and earned the right to be viewed as one of the club's greatest managers. Probably only Jimmy Seed would edge him out of the top spot, but what Alan achieved was quite remarkable, operating as he did with a much smaller budget than his opposition. Throughout this period the club always punched far above its weight and not only did they maintain their place at the Premier League table, he kept them firmly positioned in the middle of the division with no great fear of relegation. Indeed, in 2003-04 they came close to qualifying for Europe, before slipping back to 7th.

By February 2006 Alan was becoming restless at Charlton and starting to question whether he was ready for a change. A small minority of brainless supporters were airing the view that he had taken the club as far as he could and it was time to find someone who would 'take it to the next level'. This phrase came back to haunt them in the years ahead. By now, Alan was being spoken of as a possible England manager. He met with the Football Association on 10th March and had a second interview on 20th April, but was never offered the post. The press were all over the story right from the start and this further unsettled him, as well as alerting the directors to the crisis ahead. There was one more year remaining on Alan's contract and he turned down the offer of an extension, so after a meeting with Charlton's Chairman Richard Murray and Chief Executive Peter Varney, it was decided that he would not see out his final year, but leave at the end of the season by mutual agreement. His last home match came on 29th April 2006 against Blackburn Rovers and a crowd of 26,254 gave him a wonderful send-off on an occasion full of emotion. Everybody at Charlton knew that this was the end of an era.

Seven months after his dramatic departure from Charlton, Alan was appointed manager of West Ham United. Both clubs were staring into the abyss and relegation from the Premier League was a real possibility, with West Ham 18th and Charlton 19th (out of 20) when he took over. They met at the Valley on 24th February and the Addicks triumphed 4-0 with goals from Darren Ambrose, Jerome Thomas (2) and Darren Bent. A week later, another four goals were conceded and the Hammers dropped to the bottom of the table. At that point few would have given them a hope of survival, but Alan pulled them to safety in 15th place and it was Charlton who were relegated. The next season, West Ham had a much better time and finished in the top half of the Premier League, yet many of their supporters were critical of the playing style and unappreciative of Alan's brand of management. 2008-09 was his third season in charge and West Ham started well enough. They were sitting 4th in the Premier League when Alan unexpectedly resigned on 3rd September. The club had sold two players without consulting him and in breach of his contract. He sued claiming constructive dismissal and 14 months later was awarded compensation of £2.2 million.

It is extraordinary that Alan never got another manager's job and it is hard not to conclude that his claim against West Ham frightened away potential employers. In the years since, he has worked extensively on both TV and radio, but in December 2013 finally landed the job of Technical Director at Fulham. It didn't last long though and he was sacked again just two months later, although he did rejoin their coaching staff for a time in 2015.

15 years after resigning as Charlton's manager, he finally came home to the Valley ,where his efforts were always fully appreciated by the majority. He is now a regular host on Charlton TV along with Scott Minto and this basically shy (or is it reserved?) man has seemed visibly more relaxed of late. Perhaps realisation has dawned that he will always be regarded as a legend in London SE7.

Season	Division	League		FA Cup		FL Cup		FM Cup		AI Cup		Total	
		A	G	A	G	A	G	A	G	A	G	A	G
1984-85	Division 2	23	2	2	0	0	0					25	2
1985-86 (P)	Division 2	30	4	1	0	0	0	0	0			31	4
1986-87	Division 1	9 (1)	0	0	0	1	0	2	0			12 (1)	0
1990-91	Division 2	20 (5)	0	1	0	0	0	0	0			21 (5)	0
1991-92	Division 2	1	0	0	0	0	0	0	0			1	0
1992-93	Division 1	1	0	0	0	0	0			0	0	1	0
1993-94	Division 1	0 (1)	0	0	0	0	0			0	0	0 (1)	0
Total		84 (7)	6	4	0	1	0	2	0	0	0	91 (7)	6

UK LEAGUE CAREER 458 games 36 goals

CHARLTON CAREER
Managers: *L Lawrence, A Curbishley/S Gritt*
Debut: *Crystal Palace (A) 26-12-1984*
V462
Finale: *Portsmouth (A) (sub) 17-08-1993*

CURRIE Glassford   1925 - 26

Midfield, Defender   11st 12lbs   5ft 7ins
Born: 08-11-1898 - Innerleithen, Peeblesshire
Died: 03-1967 - Richmond, Surrey

The exotically named Glassford Currie came from the Scottish Border town of Innerleithen. He spent one season at Charlton in 1925-26 and played largely for the reserves, but was called up for a handful of first team games mainly towards the end of the campaign as the team struggled to keep away from the foot of Division 3 South.

HONOURS
Vale Of Leithen 1920-21 Winners East Of Scotland Qualifying Cup
Vale Of Leithen 1920-21 Finalists King Cup
Vale Of Leithen 1921-22 Runners Up Eastern League (Scotland)
Vale Of Leithen 1921-22 Winners King Cup

CLUBS
Vale Of Leithen, Scotland ••Arsenal c1922 ••Charlton Athletic 25.06.25

Ford, as he was known, started out playing for his local team, Vale Of Leithen. They competed in the Eastern League in Scotland and enjoyed considerable success in the non-league game in the years following World War I. This prompted Scottish League clubs to sign some of their better players, although both goalkeeper Jock Robson and Ford himself were transferred to Arsenal. Robson became the Gunners shortest ever 'keeper at just 5 ft 8 ins, but went on to play over 100 league games for them and proved an excellent signing for a transfer fee of only £5. Whether Currie commanded a similar outlay, or was thrown in at no extra cost, is now lost in the mists of time
Unlike Robson however, Ford did not make the grade at Arsenal and switched to the Addicks on 25th June 1925,

never having been given a chance at first team level throughout his time in North London. He managed seven games for Charlton, all but one at wing half, but lined up at centre forward against Crystal Palace at Selhurst Park on 27th March 1926. He scored his only goal for the club on 6th April against Bristol Rovers and only once finished on a winning team. That came on the previous day, Easter Monday 5th April, when Luton Town were beaten 2-1. Ford left Charlton at the end of the season, but he and his wife Minnie remained in the London area and at the outbreak of war in 1939 were living in Barnes where he worked as a builder's handyman. He passed away in Richmond at the age of 68.

Season	Division	League		FA Cup		Total	
		A	G	A	G	A	G
1925-26	Divison 3 (S)	7	1	0	0	7	1
Total		7	1	0	0	7	1

UK LEAGUE CAREER 7 games 1 goal

CHARLTON CAREER
Managers: *A MacFarlane*
Debut: *Swindon Town (A) 05-09-1925*
V074
Finale: *Watford (A) 10-04-1926*

CURTIS Paul Anthony Ernest   1982 - 85

Paul was a steady if unspectacular defender who was a semi-regular in the Charlton defence for three seasons in the eighties when

Defender   11st 2lbs   5' 10"
Born: 01-07-1963 - Woolwich, London
Education: St Margaret's Primary School, Plumstead and Eaglesfield School, Shooters Hill.

the club was usually to be found scrambling for points at the wrong end of Division 2. He was never quite able to nail down the right back spot as his own and initially had to fight off competition from Steve Gritt and Danny O'Shea. Eventually he lost out to Paul Friar and moved on to Northampton Town where he later became assistant manager.

HONOURS

Woolwich District Schools & London Schools FA
Charlton Athletic Reserves 1979-80 Winners Mid-Week League Cup
Charlton Athletic Reserves 1979-80 Runners Up Mid-Week League

Charlton Athletic Reserves 1981-82 Winners Mid-Week League
Nexday (Northampton) 1987-88 Winners FA Sunday Cup

CLUBS

Kestral Rangers (youth) ••Charlton Athletic 06.08.79 (youth) 03.07.81 (pro) ••Northampton Town 03.07.85 (free) ••Corby Town 16.10.86 (free) ••Kettering Town 31.07.87 (free) ••Nexday (Northampton) 1987 (free) ••Corby Town 31.07.89 (free) ••Northampton Town 07.92 (player coach) c 1998 (ass manager) ••Corby Town 1994 ••Rothwell Town 1995 ••Buckingham Town 1998 ••Aylesbury United 01.04 (player manager)

A local boy who went to school on Shooters Hill, Paul joined Charlton in August 1979 and became an apprentice professional three months later on 22nd November. His first team debut came during the short managerial reign of Ken Craggs on 5th October 1982 in a disappointing League Cup tie at Luton. The home side, which included Paul Walsh, won comfortably 3-0 but Curtis did enough to become a regular member of the squad for the remainder of the season.

1982-83 was memorable for the extraordinary signing of Allan Simonsen and the contrast between the Danish international and the rest of Charlton's very average team was never more noticeable than on 5th March 1983 when Chelsea were put to the sword via a 5-2 scoreline. Paul performed well at right back that afternoon, but the little Dane was virtually unplayable.

The following season started positively and for a time the club looked settled in the top half of Division 2, before eventually drifting down to 13th place. However, one bright spot occurred on 10th December 1983 in front of a disappointingly small crowd of 6,140 at Craven Cottage.

Fulham were defeated 1-0 and it was Paul who scored, what for him was a rare goal, three minutes from time.

He moved on to Northampton Town in July 1985 and played a year in Division 4 before dropping down into non-league football, while at the same time working as a sales negotiator for an estate agency. With his full time football career seemingly at an end, Paul also turned out for Nexday, a Northampton based club who in 1988 won the FA Sunday Cup with a 2-0 win up at Newcastle. He returned to Northampton Town in 1992 as coach for the youth team, but with the league side struggling on the field he was unexpectedly recalled for first team duty in October 1992 and made 22 further appearances which helped keep them away from the foot of Division 4. He went on to serve as assistant manager before a stint as player manager with Aylesbury Town who failed to win in any of his first 21 matches in charge.

More recently Paul has worked as Football Development Officer for Corby Borough Council and since 2011 has been doing a similar job at Tresham College in Kettering. Paul's parents were English Ballroom Dance champions.

Season	Division	League		FA Cup		FL Cup		Total	
		A	G	A	G	A	G	A	G
1982-83	Division 2	19 (1)	1	0	0	2	0	21 (1)	1
1983-84	Division 2	23 (1)	3	2	0	1 (1)	0	26 (2)	3
1984-85	Division 2	27 (1)	1	2	0	0	0	29 (1)	1
Total		69 (3)	5	4	0	3 (1)	0	76 (4)	5

UK LEAGUE CAREER 121 games 7 goals

CHARLTON CAREER

Managers: *A Mullery, K Craggs, L Lawrence*

Debut: *Luton Town (A) 05-10-1982*

V438

Finale: *Wimbledon (H) 13-04-1985*

CURTIS Robert Dennis   1967 - 78

Defender, Utility   11st 0lbs   5' 9"
Born: 25-01-1950 - Langwith, Derbyshire
Died: 19-03-2010 - Langwith, Derbyshire
Education: Whaley Thorns School, Langwith.

The 11,840 crowd who attended the Valley on 11th March 1967 had no idea of the significance of the occasion. Charlton were playing Preston North End in a routine Division 2 fixture which was settled in their favour with a score of 2-0, thanks to a pair of goals from Matt Tees. What made this match of special interest is that it was the only occasion when their two home produced full backs, Billy Bonds and Bob Curtis, played together at first team level. It was Bob's debut as deputy for the injured Brian Kinsey and he played at left back, while Billy was in his usual place at right back. Bonds departed for West Ham at the end of that season, after which Bob quickly made the right back position his own.

HONOURS

FA XI 1968

Charlton Athletic Youth 1965-66 Winners London FA Youth Cup

Charlton Athletic Youth 1965-66 Winners South East Counties League Cup

Charlton Athletic Youth 1966-67 Winners South East Counties League

Charlton Athletic Youth 1966-67 Finalists South East Counties League Cup

Charlton Athletic 1974-75 Promoted Division 3

CLUBS

Shirebrook Miners Welfare (youth) ••Charlton Athletic 12.05.64 (youth) 25.01.67 (pro) ••Mansfield Town 10.02.78 (£8,000) ••Kettering Town 1980 (free) ••Long Willows (manager)

Bob was a Derbyshire lad from the village of Langwith who signed schoolboy terms with Charlton at the age of 14, later upgrading to an apprentice. He made his first team debut shortly after becoming a professional on 1st February 1967, following which the club made a donation of £50 to Shirebrook Miners Welfare FC for whom he had been playing, mainly as a forward. There was never much doubt that he had the ability to succeed and he was selected for the England youth squad against Ireland in February 1968 but was obliged to withdraw through injury. He did however play for an FA XI against Guernsey later that year, in a match to celebrate 75 years of the Guernsey FA.

He very quickly became a great favourite with the Valley crowd and his emergence as a swashbuckling full back went a long way towards overcoming the disappointment felt by all Charlton supporters at the departure of Billy Bonds. It was a great compliment to him that there was genuine debate as to whether he or Bonds was the better player.

Bob was an integral part of the Charlton team that came close to achieving promotion to Division 1 in 1968-69 and

although they narrowly missed out, there was still much to enjoy, not least the FA Cup replay at Selhurst Park on 8th January 1969 where a crowd of 39,404 witnessed the 2-0 win against Crystal Palace and two goals from Ray Treacy. That season apart, Charlton struggled on the field and were finally relegated in 1972, when Bob hardly played through injury. However, he remained loyal to the club and was a mainstay within the side when three years later they reclaimed their Division 2 status.

Bob had become the preferred penalty taker and had the perfect temperament for the job, amassing 20 successful strikes in cup and league, which remains a Charlton record to this day. He was very much a footballer of his time with a long straggly mane of hair which at one stage was briefly restyled peroxide blond. Hard as nails in the tackle, he nonetheless liked nothing more than to mix with supporters in the British Oak on Blackheath, where he was regularly to be found after a match.

He could and should have played at the top level but chose to remain at Charlton for most of his career, eventually departing for Mansfield Town in February 1978. The club granted him a Testimonial Match which was played against Queens Park Rangers at the end of that season.

Largely thanks to his penalty kicks, Bob achieved the position of top goalscorer for Mansfield in season 1978-79, but his time with the East Midlands club was cut short by a serious Achilles injury. He managed a final year with Kettering before retiring in 1981.

After football, Bob worked for a time as a builder, but suffered badly with arthritis in his knees and ankles. He died at the age of 60 after a long battle with motor neurone disease and his funeral, which was attended by Theo Foley, took place at St Luke's Church, Langwith on 16th March 2010. His son, Robbie Curtis, played briefly for Northampton Town in 1994-95.

Season	Division	League		FA Cup		FL Cup		Total	
		A	G	A	G	A	G	A	G
1966-67	Division 2	1	0	0	0	0	0	1	0
1967-68	Division 2	25	3	1	0	2	0	28	3
1968-69	Division 2	40	3	3	0	1	0	44	3
1969-70	Division 2	30 (1)	0	0	0	1	0	31 (1)	0
1970-71	Division 2	41	6	1	0	2	0	44	6
1971-72 (R)	Division 2	8 (1)	1	0	0	0	0	8 (1)	1
1972-73	Division 3	37 (4)	3	3	1	4 (1)	0	44 (5)	4
1973-74	Division 3	35 (4)	4	1	0	2	0	38 (4)	4
1974-75 (P)	Division 3	43	8	2	0	2	1	47	9
1975-76	Division 2	24 (2)	1	4	1	0	0	28 (2)	2
1976-77	Division 2	36 (1)	6	2	0	3	0	41 (1)	6
1977-78	Division 2	4	0	0	0	0	0	4	0
Total		324 (13)	35	17	2	17 (1)	1	358 (14)	38

UK LEAGUE CAREER 410 games 42 goals

CHARLTON CAREER

Managers: *F Hill, R Stokoe, E Firmani, T Foley, A Nelson*
Debut: *Preston North End (H) 11-03-1967*
V328
Finale: *Luton Town (H) 21-07-1978*

D'ARCY Seamus Donal

1948 - 51

Seamus D'Arcy, known as 'Paddy' or more usually 'Jimmy,' played his football in Southern Ireland during World War 2, including three seasons with Limerick., but moved back home to the North in November 1946 and joined Ballymena United. They had just returned to Senior football after a wartime hiatus and Jimmy, a gifted ballplayer, made an immediate impact with 19 goals in 30 league matches, thereby attracting the attention of Charlton who in February 1948 brought him to England in a £5,000 deal. Ballymena's manager was former Charlton forward Bob McKay.

Forward   12st 0lbs   5' 11"
Born: 14-12-1921 - Newry, Northern Ireland
Died: 22-02-1985 - Harrow, Middlesex

HONOURS

Northern Ireland International 1952-53 5 caps 1 goal
Irish FA Xl Tour of USA & Canada 1953
Charlton Athletic Reserves 1949-50 Winners Football Combination
Charlton Athletic Reserves 1949-50 Runners Up Football Combination Cup

Charlton Athletic Reserves 1950-51 Winners Football Combination Cup
Charlton Athletic Reserves 1950-51 Winners London FA Challenge Cup
Limerick 1943-44 & 1944-45 Runners Up League Of Ireland

CLUBS

Waterford, Ireland 1943 ••Limerick, Ireland 1943 ••Dundalk, Ireland 1946 ••Ballymena United, N Ireland 11.46 (free) ••Charlton Athletic 28.02.48 (£5,000) ••Chelsea 26.10.51 (£6,300) ••Brentford 21.10.52 (player exchange)

Jimmy spent over three years at Charlton but never played more than a supporting role. His one real moment in the spotlight came on 11th January 1950 when he netted the winner against Fulham in an FA Cup replay at Craven Cottage which finished 2-1. The majority of his time was however spent in the reserves where he recorded a highly impressive tally of 80 goals in 112 matches and it is a reflection of Charlton's strength in depth during the early post war years that such impressive goal scoring was still not enough for him to earn a run in the first team.

He was transferred to Chelsea in October 1951 and enjoyed a successful first season, scoring two goals against Manchester United and a hat trick against Middlesbrough who were thrashed 5-0 on 16th February. He finished up as Chelsea's joint top scorer with 12 goals in only 21 League matches and made his debut for Northern Ireland during March, in a 3-0 defeat against Wales.

Jimmy switched to Brentford the following season in a player exchange deal that saw future England manager Ron

Greenwood move in the other direction. He remained part of the Northern Ireland team and scored his one international goal against Scotland in a 1-1 draw in Glasgow on 5th November 1952.

He was selected for an Irish FA tour of the USA and Canada in the Summer of 1953 and five games into the tour took part in the 10-0 thrashing of a Saskatchewan XI in Moose Jaw, during which he badly damaged his right ankle on the rutted pitch. Jimmy never fully recovered from the injury and was forced to retire in January 1954. Brentford successfully sued the Irish FA through the High Court over the injury.

In March 1955 Jimmy returned to Charlton for eight months in the role of Development Association Liaison Officer, before moving to Sudbury in Suffolk where he worked as quality inspector for a local glass manufacturer. He passed away in Northwick Park Hospital at the age of 63.

Season	Division	League		FA Cup		Total	
		A	G	A	G	A	G
1947-48	Division 1	4	0	0	0	4	0
1949-50	Division 1	6	1	2	1	8	2
1950-51	Division 1	3	0	1	0	4	0
Total		13	1	3	1	16	2

UK LEAGUE CAREER 49 games 16 goals

CHARLTON CAREER
Managers: *J Seed*
Debut: *Huddersfield Town (H) 20-03-1948*
V228
Finale: *Newcastle United (H) 14-04-1951*

DADLEY Benjamin James 'Jas'   1922

Midfield   11st 11lbs   5' 11"
Born: 01-06-1898 - Great Baddow, Essex
Died: 18-01-1962 - Carshalton, Surrey

Jas Dadley was a combative wing half. His first team debut came in the Southern League at Gillingham on 9th April 1921 when Charlton, who had comfortably beaten the same opponents at the Valley only a week earlier, went down 4-0. Dadley played at left half in place of Bertram Dunn, which was only one of nine changes to the team, so the heavy defeat was perhaps not unexpected. For most of his four years with the club he was a reserve team player, but Jas did also enjoy a brief run in the side during 1921-22 when he replaced the more experienced Walker Hampson at left half. Charlton's Irish International Alex Steele married his sister, Hetty Dadley, in 1925.

HONOURS

Charlton Athletic Reserves 1920-21 Winners Kent League   Charlton Athletic A 1923-24 Winners Kent League

CLUBS

Croydon Boys (youth) ••Croydon Juniors 1919 ••Charlton Athletic 1920 ••Chatham c1924

Private Benjamin Dadley served in the 22nd London Regiment in both France and Palestine during World War 1 and signed for Charlton in 1920. A wholehearted player and a ferocious tackler, it was said of him that he 'plays hard, tackles hard and only knows defeat when the final whistle has sounded'.

His run of eight games came towards the end of Charlton's first season as a Football League club. They included a 1-0 win at the Valley on 4th March 1922 against a Merthyr Town team which included Sammy Langford and future Charlton manager Albert Lindon, plus a welcome 2-1 away win at Reading thanks to goals from Arthur Whalley and Sid Castle.

Jas remained a regular in the Reserves and featured on both occasions when they won the Kent League although he was sent off against Northfleet on 6th March 1924, an unusual occurrence in those far off days. Later that year he left for Kent League side Chatham and by 1939 was living in Fellowes Road, Carshalton with his wife Edith and working as a carpenter and joiner. He passed away in 1962 at the age of 63.

Season	Division	League		Total	
		A	G	A	G
1921-22	Divison 3 (S)	8	0	8	0
Total		8	0	8	0

UK LEAGUE CAREER 8 games 0 goals

CHARLTON CAREER
Managers: *W Rayner*
Debut: *Southern League Gillingham (A) 09-04-1921 Football League Portsmouth (A) 25-02-1922*
V030
Finale: *Newport County (A) 27-04-1922*

DAILLY Christian Eduard   2009 - 11

Defender, Utility   6' 0"
Born: 23-10-1973 - Dundee, Scotland
Education: Manchester Metropolitan University

Christian's career as a professional footballer lasted close to 22 years, commencing on 2nd August 1990, when he signed for Dundee United and that same month became the youngest first team player to make his debut for them. He was called up for Scotland U21's at the age of 16 and made a record 35 appearances at that level. He went on to become a Scottish international, earning 67 full caps and captaining his country on 12 occasions. His son Harvey Dailly is also a footballer and appeared briefly for Dundee United.

HONOURS

Scotland International 1997-08 67 caps 6 goals   Scotland Youth International
Scotland U21 International 1990-96 35 caps 5 goals   Charlton Athletic 2010 Player Of The Year

Dundee United 1993-94 Winners Scottish Cup
Dundee United 1995-96 Winners Play Offs Scottish Division 1
West Ham United 2004-05 Winners Play Offs Championship
West Ham United 2005-06 Finalists FA Cup

Rangers 2007-08 Runners Up Scottish Premier League
Rangers 2007-08 Winners Scottish League Cup
Rangers 2008-09 Winners Scottish Cup
Rangers 2008-09 Finalists Scottish League Cup

CLUBS

Sporting Club, Scotland (youth) ••Dundee United, Scotland 02.08.90 (pro) ••Derby County 12.08.96 (£500,000) ••Blackburn Rovers 22.08.98 (£5.35 million) ••West Ham United 18.01.01 (£1.75 million) ••Southampton 21.09.07 (loan) ••Rangers, Scotland 30.01.08 (free) ••Charlton Athletic 31.07.09 (free) ••Portsmouth 05.08.11 (free) ••Southend United 16.03.12 (non contract)

Although he later settled down as a cultured central defender, Christian was able to play in almost any outfield position and featured on the right wing for Dundee United on 21st May 1994 when they won the Scottish Cup for the first time, defeating Rangers 1-0 at Hampden Park. After switching to Derby County he further showed his versatility starting 31 Premier League matches in seven different positions during his first season with the club. A big money transfer to Blackburn Rovers followed in 1998, but three years on from their Premier League title, the team were struggling and with Christian injured for much of the campaign, they were relegated and it took two years to regain their place in the top division. He spent much of the promotion season out of the team and finally moved on to West Ham in January 2001.

His fortunes at the Boleyn Ground were equally mixed. West Ham were relegated in 2002-03 and two seasons later injury kept him sidelined until the very end when he reappeared in the play offs and on 30th May 2005 came on as a substitute at Wembley as the Hammers, including Chris Powell and Shaun Newton, clinched promotion 1-0 against Preston North End. He again featured from the bench 12 months later when a reshaped West Ham team, now including Paul Konchesky, reached the FA Cup Final, only to go down 1-0 to Liverpool.

Christian spent 18 months back in Scotland with Rangers and was an unused sub in both the finals of the 2008 UEFA Cup and Scottish Cup. He did however gain some silverware that year when they won the Scottish League Cup and on 30th May 2009 he again came off the bench as Falkirk were dispatched 1-0 in the Scottish Cup Final. In this match he was kept out of the starting line up by another centre half with Charlton connections, Madjid Bougherra.

He joined Charlton in July 2009, but unlike other players of a certain age, had lost none of his desire to win and had an excellent first season at the heart of the defence making 44 league appearances and being voted Player of the Year. His second season, now aged 36, proved more of a struggle and was notable for a Charlton record of three red cards, the third of which was collected in his final game against Oldham Athletic. However, there were still many who were sorry when he was freed by the club in the Summer of 2011 as he had never given less than his best in a Charlton shirt. Since retiring in July 2012 Christian has studied for a first class honours degree in Sports Science and although resident in Essex worked informally as a coach with Dundee United. He is now working as an athletics coach as well as broadcasting for Sky Sports as part of their coverage of Scottish football.

Season	Division	League		FA Cup		FL Cup		FL Trophy		Play Offs		Total	
		A	G	A	G	A	G	A	G	A	G	A	G
2009-10	League One	44	1	1	0	0	0	2	0	2	0	49	1
2010-11	League One	32	0	3	0	0	0	3 (1)	0			38 (1)	0
Total		76	1	4	0	0	0	5 (1)	0	2	0	87 (1)	1

CHARLTON CAREER
Managers: P Parkinson, C Powell
Debut: *Wycombe Wanderers (H) 08-08-2009*
V688
Finale: *Oldham Athletic (A) 09-04-2011*

UK LEAGUE CAREER 548 games 30 goals

DARLINGTON Jermaine Christopher Marcellus   1992

Defender, Midfield   10st 10lbs   5' 7"
Born: 11-04-1974 - Hackney, London
Education: Homerton House School, Hackney.

Jermaine played more than 100 times for Wimbledon. He featured in the very last game before the move to Milton Keynes on 30th August 2003 and scored the only goal in a 1-0 win over Derby County at the end of that troubled season.

HONOURS
Hackney Schools & London Schools

CLUBS
Crown & Manor (youth) ••Chelsea (youth) ••Watford (youth) ••Tottenham Hotspur 1989 (youth) ••Charlton Athletic 12.07.90 (youth) 24.07.92 (pro) ••Dover Athletic 07.93 (loan) ••Hendon 10.96 ••Dulwich Hamlet 1997 ••Heybridge Swifts 1997 ••Aylesbury United 04.98 ••Queens Park Rangers 25.03.99 (£25,000) ••Wimbledon 02.08.01 (£200,000) ••Watford 09.08.04 (free) ••Cardiff City 02.08.05 (free) ••AFC Wimbledon 11.06 (free) ••Maidstone United 10.09 (free) ••Whitstable Town 03.11 (free) ••Sittingbourne 2015 (U21 manager) ••Herne Bay 05.17 (joint manager)

February 1992 was a very important month for 17-year-old Jermaine Darlington. He made his Football League debut for Charlton as a substitute at Brighton on the 1st and then only a little over three weeks later was named in the starting line up for the local derby at Millwall, when ten of the first team squad were injured. Sadly he was out of his depth and struggled to make an impact in the highly charged atmosphere of the Den and was substituted after 77 minutes. This brought his Charlton career to an end before it had properly started and he disappeared into non-league football for seven years before getting his second chance with Queens Park Rangers.

On a personal level, his first year at Loftus Road was possibly the high point of Jermaine's career. He was voted the QPR player of the year, although they did not fare very well against Charlton who put them out of the FA Cup on 8th January 2000, courtesy of a Charlie MacDonald goal. He also played in the two league encounters, which produced a 0-0 draw in the first game, but another Charlton victory by 2-1 at the Valley on 31st March, courtesy of strikes by Shaun Newton and Scott Parker. In the second season he maintained his place in the team, but

they struggled throughout and were relegated from Division 1.

He switched to Wimbledon in August 2001, but his three years with them were overshadowed by the unforgivable decision to move to Milton Keynes which hastened the death of that fine old club. Ground sharing at Selhurst Park nearly did the same for Charlton, so nobody in SE7 could have anything but sympathy for their plight. Jermaine only missed one league match in 2003-04, but Wimbledon did not have a Lennie Lawrence to perform miracles for them and they soon slid to the bottom of Division 1.

By 2006 he was at Cardiff where a persistent knee injury effectively ended his professional career and Jermaine became the first former Wimbledon player to play a competitive match for the newly formed AFC Wimbledon. They showed their inexperience by failing to obtain his international clearance from the FA of Wales and were fined, deducted league points and expelled from two cup competitions as a result. He continued in the non-league game and in 2017 became joint manager of Isthmian League club, Herne Bay, a position that he held for 10 months.

Season	Division	League		FA Cup		FL Cup		FM Cup		Total	
		A	G	A	G	A	G	A	G	A	G
1991-92	Division 2	1 (1)	0	0	0	0	0	0	0	1 (1)	0
Total		1 (1)	0	0	0	0	0	0	0	1 (1)	0

UK LEAGUE CAREER 213 games 5 goals

CHARLTON CAREER
Managers: *A Curbishley/S Gritt*
Debut: *Brighton & Hove Albion (A) (sub) 01-02-1992*
V526
Finale: *Millwall (A) 26-02-1992*

DASILVA Jay Rhys   2017 - 18

Despite his diminutive stature, Jay enjoyed an outstanding time as a teenage footballer, but first hit the headlines in January 2012 when it was announced that Chelsea had signed not only 13-year-old Jay, but also his 12-year-old twin brothers Cole and Rio. All three boys were added to their burgeoning roster of young talent, although very few of these young players had any realistic chance of progressing into the first team squad. Jay fared better than most and his two periods on loan at Charlton undoubtedly helped him on his way. Time will tell whether he will make the grade at Premier League level.

Defender   5' 4"
Born: 22-04-1998 - Luton, Bedfordshire

HONOURS

England U21 International 2018-19 13 caps 0 goals
England U20 International 2017-18 6 caps 0 goals
England U19 International 2016-17 15 caps 0 goals
England U18 International 2015-16 4 caps 0 goals
England U17 International 2013-15 21 caps 1 goal

England U16 International 2012-13 4 caps 0 goals
Charlton Athletic 2018 Player Of The Year
Chelsea U18 2013-14, 2014-15 & 2015-16 Winners FA Youth Cup
Chelsea U18 2014-15 Winners UEFA Youth League

CLUBS

Luton Celtic c2005 (youth) ••Luton Town 2007 (youth) ••Chelsea 01.12 (youth) 07.15 (pro) ••Charlton Athletic 01.01.17 (loan) 21.07.17 (loan) ••Bristol City 09.08.18 (loan) 26.06.19 (undisclosed)

The young Jay Dasilva made his international debut at the age of 14, when on 29th November 2012 the England U16's, (which included Joe Gomez), defeated Scotland 1-0 to win the Victory Shield. Over the next seven years he made a total of 63 appearances for his country, including the UEFA U19 Championships in 2017 which were won by England and the U21 Toulon Tournament in 2018 during which England remained unbeaten in their five matches and beat Mexico 2-1 in the final.

Jay was progressing almost as well at club level. For three years running Chelsea U18's won the FA Youth Cup between 2014 and 2016 and he played throughout. They also triumphed in the UEFA Youth League winning the 2014-15 tournament by beating Shakhtar Donetsk 3-2 in the final match. They repeated this feat the following season but Jay did not play in the finals.

Despite such an impressive start to his career, he had still got nowhere near to Chelsea's first team and it needed a period out on loan to move his career forward, He joined Charlton in January 2017 and at first there were concerns whether he was physically suited to life in League One. His debut came against Millwall in a 0-0 draw at the Valley when he entered the field as replacement for the injured Lewis Page after 28 minutes. It was the usual bruising local derby and a real baptism of fire. He lasted until the 80th minute before being himself replaced by Ricky Holmes as

Charlton tried in vain to find a goal. He was not elevated to the starting eleven until 4th April but then played in the last six games of the season and did enough to show that he was ready for the rigours of life at the third level of the football pyramid.

A second loan was agreed which kept Jay at the Valley for the whole of the 2017-18 season and he had an excellent campaign at left back, showing defensive consistency and the ability to overlap into attacking positions whenever the opportunity arose. He was voted Player of the Year in 2018 and shares with Scott Carson (the 2007 winner) the honour of being the only loan players to have won this award. During his time at Charlton, Jay made three England U19 appearances and four at U20, including the 2-1 defeat against Germany in the match which determined the winners of the Euro Elite League in November 2017.

In August 2018 he joined Bristol City in another loan deal and quickly demonstrated that he was able to perform to Championship standard. At the end of the season, the move was converted into a permanent transfer and he signed a four-year contract for an undisclosed fee. Jay returned to the Valley on Boxing Day 2019 and came on as a half-time substitute, but could not stop his Bristol City side from a 3-2 defeat thanks to a pair of goals from Macauley Bonne and a late winner by Alfie Doughty.

Season	Division	League		FA Cup		FL Cup		FL Trophy		Play Offs		Total	
		A	G	A	G	A	G	A	G	A	G	A	G
2016-17	League One	6 (4)	0	0	0	0	0	0	0			6 (4)	0
2017-18	League One	34 (4)	0	2	0	0 (1)	0	1	0	2	0	39 (5)	0
Total		40 (8)	0	2	0	0 (1)	0	1	0	2	0	45 (9)	0

UK LEAGUE CAREER 111 games 1 goal

CHARLTON CAREER
Managers: *K Robinson, L Bowyer*
Debut: *Millwall (H) (sub) 14-01-2017*
V836
Finale: *Shrewsbury Town (A) 13-05-2018*

DAVIES Alan   1986

Forward   10st 4lbs   5' 8"
Born: 05-12-1961 - Manchester, Lancashire
Died: 04-02-1992 - Horton, West Glamorgan
Education: North Manchester High School

The high point in the career of Alan Davies came in May 1993. After toiling all season in Manchester United's reserves, he was suddenly thrust into the first team limelight, played the last three league games and then retained his place for the FA Cup final against a Brighton team which included Steve Gatting. The game was a 2-2 draw, but in the replay on 26th May, United triumphed 4-0 and young Alan, with only a handful of senior appearances to his name, had a hand in two of the goals and now had an FA Cup winners medal to his name. To make things even better, just five days later he made his full international debut for Wales in a 1-0 victory over Northern Ireland at Windsor Park.

HONOURS

Wales International 1983-90 13 caps 0 goals

Wales U21 Internaional 6 caps 0 goals

Manchester United 1982-83 Winners FA Cup

Swansea City 1987-88 Promoted Play Offs Division 4

CLUBS

Mancunian Juniors (youth) ••Manchester United 09.77 (youth) 12.78 (pro) ••Newcastle United 29.07.85 (£50,000) ••Charlton Athletic 20.03.86 (loan) ••Carlisle United 29.11.86 (loan) ••Swansea City 06.08.87 (free) ••Bradford City 29.06.89 (£135,000) ••Swansea City 23.08.90

The FA Cup success did not prove a breakthrough for Alan who broke his ankle in the following pre-season and eventually featured in just three league games for Manchester United over the next two years. The only bright spot was an appearance off the bench on 11th April 1994 against Juventus in the semi-final of the European Cup Winners Cup. He scored in a 1-1 draw at Old Trafford but was not selected for the second leg in Italy.

It eventually became clear that he had no future at Manchester and in July 1985 was transferred to Newcastle United where he started the 1985-86 season in the first team. By Christmas however he was out of the side and on 20th March made a loan move to Charlton where Lennie Lawrence was chasing an unlikely promotion to Division 1. Alan was selected for the away fixture with Shrewsbury Town, a game that needed to be won, but already 2-0 down by half time, he was pulled off in favour of Robert Lee. The team performance did improve and George Shipley pulled a goal back, but Alan was never called upon again and soon returned to Newcastle.

He joined Swansea City in the Summer of 1987 and finally held down a regular place as they battled through to the two legged final of the Division 4 Play Offs against Torquay United. He scored a vital goal in the second game which earned them promotion by an aggregate score of 5-4 and kept his place throughout the following campaign, before switching to Bradford City for 1989-90.

Alan came up against Charlton in the FA Cup when his Bradford team forced a 1-1 draw at Selhurst Park on 7th January 1990, but the Addicks convincingly won the replay three days later with a 3-0 scoreline and goals by Robert Lee, Paul Williams and Andy Jones. Two other former Charlton players, David Campbell and Mark Aizlewood played for Bradford that day.

Alan re-joined Swansea in August 1990 and played consistently for them throughout that season. Results were disappointing however and by 1991-92 he found first team opportunities limited. His final match was on 25th January when they recorded a 3-2 away win against West Bromwich Albion. Ten days later after taking his four-year-old daughter to school, he drove the 15 miles to the village of Horton and was later found slumped at the wheel of his car having committed suicide through carbon monoxide poisoning. His wife Deborah was eight months pregnant. A Benefit match was played at Swansea in August 1992 in

his memory with Manchester United the opponents.

Season	Division	League		FA Cup		FL Cup		FM Cup		Total	
		A	G	A	G	A	G	A	G	A	G
1985-86 (P)	Division 2	1	0	0	0	0	0	0	0	1	0
Total		1	0	0	0	0	0	0	0	1	0

UK LEAGUE CAREER 186 games 15 goals

CHARLTON CAREER
Managers: L Lawrence
Debut: *Shrewsbury Town (A) 05-04-1986*
V477

DAVIES Cyril　　　　　　　　　　　　　　1970 - 73

There are far too many instances where the footballing career of a talented player is cut short through injury and sadly Cyril Davies falls into that category. He was identified early as being an

Midfield　10st 8lbs　5' 7"
Born: 07-09-1948 - Swansea, Glamorgan
Education: Dynevor Grammar School, Swansea.

outstanding prospect and represented Wales first as a Schoolboy International and then at Under 23 level. On 24th November 1971, (not in 1972 as has been repeatedly claimed) and at the age of 23, he overcame his fear of flying and travelled to Bucharest and played in the Euro '72 qualifying match in which Wales lost 2-0 to Romania. It was to be his only full international and 18 months later his career was effectively over.

HONOURS

Wales International 1971 1 cap 0 goals
Wales U23 International 1971-72 4 caps

Wales Schoolboy International 1964
Swansea Schools & Welsh Schools

CLUBS

Swansea Town 1965 (youth) 16.09.66 (pro) ••Carlisle United 07.06.68 (free) ••Yeovil Town 07.69 (free) ••Charlton Athletic 06.05.70 (£5,000) ••Tonbridge 1973 (free) ••Libra 1974 (player manager) ••Old Roan 1981 ••Petts Wood ••Grove ••Staplehurst Monarchs 1990 (player manager)

Charlton discovered Cyril playing in the Southern League for Yeovil Town and in May 1970 agreed a transfer fee of £3,000 which would rise to £5,000 if he proved able to make the jump in standard to Division 2 of the Football League and make 10 first team appearances. So quickly did he adapt, that the balance of £2,000 became payable before the end of September and Cyril went on to play 31 games in that first season.

His time at Charlton overlapped with that of Alan Campbell, another creative midfielder, who departed for Birmingham City in October 1970. From a distance there was a physical similarity between the two men and in the games they played together it was sometimes difficult to tell them apart in the heat of battle. Cyril's second season was a good deal less successful as Charlton were relegated to

Division 3, although on a personal level he featured in nearly every match.

The next season proved to be his last and two cartilage operations in the summer only delayed the inevitable. By the end of season 1972-73 it was accepted that his body could no longer stand the strain of full time training and he dropped down into non-league football for a brief spell with Tonbridge.

After retirement, Cyril did play some Sunday football in the Metropolitan League and turned out for Old Roan in the Spartan League while at the same time being employed as their groundsman, a position he held until 1984. Later he became groundsman at Bethany School, near Goudhurst.

Season	Division	League		FA Cup		FL Cup		Total	
		A	G	A	G	A	G	A	G
1970-71	Division 2	23 (5)	1	1	0	2	1	26 (5)	2
1971-72 (R)	Division 2	40	4	2	0	3	1	45	5
1972-73	Division 3	7 (1)	1	0	0	0	0	7 (1)	1
Total		70 (6)	6	3	0	5	2	78 (6)	8

UK LEAGUE CAREER 78 games 6 goals

CHARLTON CAREER
Managers: *T Foley*
Debut: *Sheffield Wednesday (A) 15-08-1970*
V352
Finale: *Halifax Town (H) (sub) 06-03-1973*

DAVIES Frank Palmer   1926 - 28

Defender, Midfield   12st 8lbs   5' 10"
Born: 01-08-1903 - Swansea, Glamorgan
Died: 01-01-1970 - Northampton, Northants

Although Frank made almost 250 competitive appearances with Bristol City, Northampton Town and Charlton during his 11-year Football League career, there were very few memorable moments. No promotions or cup finals feature on his CV and he saved up his one big achievement for his very last season. On 27th January 1934, a mediocre Northampton side were tasked with an away FA Cup tie at Huddersfield Town, at that point one of the strongest clubs in the land who had enjoyed a decade of cup and league success and were destined to finish 1933-34 as runners-up in Division 1. Nobody gave the visitors a chance, but with Frank at right half, they pulled off an incredible 2-0 win which is now viewed as one of the great FA Cup giant killing feats.

CLUBS
Swansea Town (amateur) ••Bath City ••Bristol City 1923 ••Charlton Athletic 14.10.26 ••Portsmouth 23.07.28 ••Nantwich 08.08.29 ••Northampton Town 03.07.30 ••Burton Town 1934 ••Scunthorpe & Lindsey United

The son of a Welsh boilermaker, Frank commenced his Football League career with Bristol City and featured in and around their first team for three seasons before joining Charlton in October 1926. They had made a horrendous start to the season and after nine matches were at the very bottom of Division 3 (South). England international centre half George Armitage was absent through injury, so Frank was pitched straight in at the deep end as his replacement, just two days after signing. The 2-2 draw against Swindon Town was a welcome improvement thanks to goals from David Sherlaw and Jazzo Kirk, but Frank's efforts against the Swindon centre forward were not wholly successful as he scored both of the visitors' goals.
He kept his place until Armitage returned to the side in December and was even tried at centre forward in two

matches. He scored in one of them as Gillingham were defeated on Christmas Day, but hardly played during the second half of the campaign. His second season followed a similar pattern and he was mainly called up when first choice Armitage was absent.
Frank moved on to Northampton in August 1930 and did well for them making more than 150 league and cup appearances, mainly at wing half. He played when Charlton were the visitors to the County Ground on 21st October 1933, but a scoreline of 2-1 and goals from Cyril Pearce and Monty Wilkinson ensured that the league points travelled safely back to South London. When his playing days were over, Frank remained in Northampton and passed away there at the age of 66.

Season	Division	League		FA Cup		Total	
		A	G	A	G	A	G
1926-27	Divison 3 (S)	11	1	2	0	13	1
1927-28	Divison 3 (S)	14	0	4	0	18	0
Total		25	1	6	0	31	1

UK LEAGUE CAREER 223 games 8 goals

CHARLTON CAREER
Managers: *A MacFarlane, A Lindon, A MacFarlane*
Debut: *Swindon Town (H) 16-10-1926*
VV099
Finale: *Swindon Town (H) 30-04-1928*

DAVIES James

Jimmy's entire career was played out in the north of England except for season 1926-27 when he ventured down to South London and spent a year at Charlton. Initially his form provoked negative comment in the club programme, which is not normally the most critical of publications, but during the second half of the season he performed better and enjoyed a run of first team games at left half.

Midfield, Defender   11st 0lbs   5' 9"
Born: 20-11-1897 - Northwich, Cheshire
Died: 1970 - Warrington, Cheshire

HONOURS
Gateshead 1931-32 Runners Up Division 3 (North)

CLUBS
Gnome Saltney c1922 ••Huddersfield Town 10.23 ••Charlton Athletic 15.06.26 ••South Shields 20.07.27 ••Gateshead 09.07.30 ••Chesterfield 1932 ••Eden Colliery Welfare 09.33 ••Crawcrook Albion 1933 ••Clara Vale 1934

After spending three seasons with Huddersfield Town without making a single first team appearance, Jimmy was soon involved in the action for his new club. He played five matches early on, which included three at centre half as deputy for Charlton's England international, George Armitage, who was absent through injury. The team had started the season badly but it was the home defeat to Bournemouth on 9th October 1926 which provoked the sharp criticism. The Addicks had only a late consolation goal by David Sherlaw to show for their efforts in a 3-1 defeat and the visitors' centre forward had scored a hat-trick. Furthermore, the defeat dumped Charlton into bottom spot in the league and Jimmy's performance was described as 'lamentably weak' as he was 'caught napping' on an 'off day'.

Unsurprisingly he was removed from the front line after such a chastening experience and his namesake Frank Davies was signed from Bristol City five days later. Jimmy played on in the Reserves and did much better, gaining praise for his efforts on a mud heap of a pitch against Crystal Palace. He was recalled to first team duties in March and held his place for the remainder of the campaign. The season, which had started so badly, concluded with Charlton safely in mid-table.

He moved back up north in the summer of 1927 and joined South Shields where he suffered relegation from Division 2 in his first season. In 1928-29 however he was ever-present and back at centre half as they stabilised again and even managed a 10-1 demolition of Rotherham United. He remained a key part of the defence until financial pressures and apathy within the town forced South Shields to uproot and re-invent themselves as nearby Gateshead in 1930. Jimmy stayed on and played two further years. He appeared less frequently in 1931-32 but did contribute to a second place finish in Division 3 (North).

By 1939 he was back in Cheshire and working as a clerk in Warrington. He passed away in 1970 at the age of 72.

Season	Division	League		FA Cup		Total	
		A	G	A	G	A	G
1926-27	Divison 3 (S)	17	0	0	0	17	0
Total		17	0	0	0	17	0

UK LEAGUE CAREER 174 games 0 goals

CHARLTON CAREER
Managers: *A MacFarlane*
Debut: *Queens Park Rangers (H) 18-09-1926*
V095
Finale: *Exeter City (H) 07-05-1927*

DAVIES Paul   1972 - 74

Striker   11st 5lbs   5' 10"
Born: 10-10-1952 - Holywell, Flintshire

Paul was a Welsh Schoolboy International and his obvious potential was spotted by Arsenal. He was part of their team which won the FA Youth Cup in 1971 and the following January was an unused substitute for Wales U23's against Scotland. His older brother was Ron Davies, the Southampton and Wales striker, one of the leading forwards of his generation.

HONOURS

Wales Schoolboy International 5 caps   Arsenal 1970-71 Winners FA Youth Cup
Flintshire Boys & North Wales Boys

CLUBS

Arsenal 01.69 (youth) 10.69 (pro) ••Charlton Athletic 18.08.72 (loan) 01.12.72 (£7,000) ••Romford 07.03.75 (free)

Paul came to Charlton initially on a three-month loan and made enough of an impact that the move was made permanent and in his first season he was near ever-present in the side. A skilful target man with a decent first touch and neat passing ability but no great pace, he proved a little lightweight for the physical demands of Division 3. He was used less often in his second season and eventually dropped into non-league football with Romford after a two and a half year stay at the Valley.

His career was cut short by injury and he retired from the game in May 1976 at the age of 23. Paul later worked as a black cab driver and lived in Hatfield, Hertfordshire.

Season	Division	League		FA Cup		FL Cup		Total	
		A	G	A	G	A	G	A	G
1972-73	Division 3	41 (3)	7	4	1	4	1	49 (3)	9
1973-74	Division 3	9 (2)	2	0	0	2	0	11 (2)	2
1974-75 (P)	Division 3	1 (1)	0	0	0	0	0	1 (1)	0
Total		51 (6)	9	4	1	6	1	61 (6)	11

UK LEAGUE CAREER 58 games 9 goals

CHARLTON CAREER
Managers: *T Foley, A Nelson*
Debut: *Shrewsbury Town (H) (sub) 19-08-1972*
V371
Finale: *Preston North End (A) (sub) 17-09-1974*

DAVIS David Lowell   2020

Midfield   12st 1lbs   5' 9"
Born: 20-02-1991 - Smethwick, West Midlands

In January 2020 the Roland Duchatelet era appeared to be at an end and the new owners, East Street Investments, announced that funds would be available for Charlton to strengthen the playing squad during the transfer window. They omitted to mention however that the club had been placed under a transfer embargo and that the anticipated marquee signings were never going to happen. Instead, on 31st January, the final day before the window closed, three loan players were brought in, namely injury troubled Aiden McGeady from Sunderland, a youngster Matt Smith from Manchester City and with the clock showing 22.59, David Davis, a journeyman midfielder who was deemed surplus to requirements at BIrmingham City.

HONOURS

Wolverhampton Wanderers 2013-14 Winners League One

CLUBS

Walsall (youth) ••Tividale 2007 (youth) ••Wolverhampton Wanderers 2007 (youth) 07.07.09 (pro) ••Darlington 22.10.09 (loan) ••Walsall 09.09.10 (loan) ••Shrewsbury Town 31.01.11 (loan) ••Inverness Caledonian Thistle, Scotland 31.08.11 (loan) ••Chesterfield 13.01.12 (loan) ••Birmingham City 11.08.14 (£100,000) ••Charlton Athletic 31.01.20 (loan) ••Shrewsbury Town 15.01.21 (free)

David made his name as a hard tackling defensive midfielder with Wolverhampton Wanderers. He was a semi-regular in the Wolves side which won League One in 2013-14 but never quite established himself as a fixture in the starting line-up during his time at Molineux. Earlier he had performed well during a loan spell with Shrewsbury Town and helped steer them into the 2011 League Two play-offs only to fall just short of a Wembley appearance when they were beaten over two legs by Torquay United. Another loan took him up to Scotland and he played 14 games for Inverness Caledonian Thistle in the Scottish Premier League during 2011-12, but although he was offered the chance to extend his stay for the second half of that season, he preferred another temporary move, this time to Chesterfield.

He finally transferred to Birmingham City in August 2014 and became an important player for them during six years mainly spent struggling to stay afloat in the lower reaches of the Championship, where his team-mates included Michael Morrison, Jonathan Spector, Andrew Shinnie and Omar Bogle. He finished 2016-17 with the worst disciplinary record in the division but his uncompromising style meant that his services were always in demand and several other clubs tried to sign him, including Derby County who allegedly offered £1.5 million.

In 2018-19 a knee injury, picked up in pre-season, reduced David's first team appearances, but he was back for the following campaign and played in the Birmingham side that won 1-0 at the Valley on 14th September 2019. When he packed his bags for his loan move to SE7 at the end of January, he had been playing regularly and appeared to have just the sort of experience Charlton needed at that point to strengthen the midfield whilst various key players were missing through injury.

Sadly David never really got going during his time with Charlton, although his five matches did include wins against Luton Town and Nottingham Forest. The Covid pandemic brought the Football League to a halt in March 2020 and when play finally re-started 15 weeks later, he refused to see out the remainder of his contract and brought his brief time as a Charlton player to an abrupt and unsatisfactory conclusion. He was without a club until January 2021 but then signed a short term contract with Shrewsbury Town up to the end of the 2020-21 season when he was released. Two months later Shrewsbury did an about turn and re-signed him for a further year.

Season	Division	League		FA Cup		FL Cup		Total	
		A	G	A	G	A	G	A	G
2019-20 (R)	Championship	5	0	0	0	0	0	5	0
Total		5	0	0	0	0	0	5	0

UK LEAGUE CAREER 315 games 13 goals

CHARLTON CAREER
Managers: *L Bowyer*
Debut: *Stoke City (A) 08-02-2020*
VV893
Finale: *Sheffield Wednesday (A) 26-02-2020*

DAVISON Joshua Michael Blainey

2019 -

Josh received his first professional contract whilst with Peterborough United, but it was after he moved on to Enfield Town in 2018 that his career really came alive. Although still a teenager, he scored an impressive 16 goals in 21 matches in the Isthmian League, Premier Division during season 2018-19 and these figures swelled to 21 in 25 games when cup matches were included. This inevitably attracted the attention of other clubs and on 18th October 2019 he signed for Charlton without ever dreaming that in only eight days he would make his first team debut in the Championship.

Forward   6' 2''
Born: 16-09-1999 - Middlesbrough, North Yorkshire

CLUBS

Peterborough United (youth) 2017 (pro) ••St Neots Town 10.17 (loan) ••Wisbech Town 04.18 (loan) ••Enfield Town 07.18 (free) ••Barking 27.10.18 (loan) ••Charlton Athletic 18.10.19 (free) ••Woking 24.10.20 (loan) ••Forest Green Rovers 19.01.21 (loan) ••Swindon Town 24.01.22 (loan)

When Josh arrived at the Valley, he was joining a club in crisis. The long -running ownership saga was dragging on and manager Lee Bowyer had been forced to put together a squad to compete in the Championship which comprised a mixture of free transfers and loan players. They had made an excellent start to the 2019-20 season but by October were suffering from an ever increasing injury list. Eight days after his registration he found himself on the bench for the match at West Bromwich Albion and then as the game drew to a close he was brought on to replace Jason Pearce as Charlton pressed for an equalising goal. The home team were already down to ten men and with the Londoners dominating play, Naby Sarr was fouled in the area and in the fourth minute of stoppage time Josh Cullen scored the

penalty which earned them a 2-2 draw.

The jump of five divisions up the football pyramid was enormous but Josh held his place in the first team squad and in no way disgraced himself as he was repeatedly called upon to play as the injury list worsened. He even got his name on the scoresheet in the return fixture against West Bromwich in January. His efforts were rewarded with a new two-year contract which he signed in June 2020.

With the new owner in place and a more experienced squad of players available for selection, Josh was sent out on loan, first to Woking and then in January 2021 to Forest Green Rovers. The intention was to further aid his development and give him valuable game time. In January 2022 he went out for a further loan spell, this time to Swindon Town.

Season	Division	League		FA Cup		FL Cup		FL Trophy		Total	
		A	G	A	G	A	G	A	G	A	G
2019-20 (R)	Championship	5 (4)	1	1	0	0	0			6 (4)	1
2020-21	League One	0	0	0	0	0	0	2	0	2	0
Total		5 (4)	1	1	0	0	0	2	0	8 (4)	1

UK LEAGUE CAREER 29 games 4 goals

CHARLTON CAREER
Managers: *L Bowyer, N Adkins, J Jackson*
Debut: *West Bromwich Albion (A (sub)) 26-10-2019*
V887

DAWSON Thomas   1939 - 47

Forward, Midfield   11st 6lbs   5' 9"
Born: 06-02-1915 - Middlesbrough, North Yorkshire
Died: 20-12-1972 - Middlesbrough, North Yorkshire

At first glance, Tommy's football career seems unremarkable, comprising 162 league and cup matches but no divisional titles nor representative honours to show for his efforts. There is however one single event which elevates him to hero status for any Charlton supporter. His 29 games for the club includes the 1947 FA Cup Final and for that alone he will never be forgotten.

HONOURS
Charlton Athletic 1946-47 Winners FA Cup

CLUBS
South Bank 1932 ••Cargo Fleet 1933 ••Spennymoor United 1934 ••Whitby United 1934 ••Darlington 12.36 ••Spennymoor United 1938 ••Charlton Athletic 03.03.39 (£500) ••Brentford 12.08.47 (£5,000) ••Swindon Town 14.05.48 (free) ••Chippenham Town 1950 (player manager) ••Bishop Auckland Auto Spares 1951 ••Adamstown Rosebud, Australia 1960 (coach)

Tommy started out with South Bank, now defunct, but then one of the oldest known football clubs in England. He also spent time with Whitby Town before making his Football League debut for Darlington on 5th December 1936 against Tranmere Rovers. He played on the right wing and scored in a 3-1 win which helped him retain his place for the remainder of the 1936-37 season.
In 1938, he switched to Northern League club, Spennymoor United, from where he signed for Charlton on 3rd March 1939 in exchange for a transfer fee of £400,

which increased by a further £100 after 10 appearances. His debut came up at Sunderland in a 1-1 draw and the record books show this as his only pre-war game, but he in fact played twice at the start of 1939-40, before that season's results were expunged after the outbreak of hostilities. Wartime guest appearances were made for York City, Middlesbrough, Bradford PA and Sunderland.
Tommy returned to the Charlton side against Stoke City on 31st August 1946 and was used initially at right half. By the time they met Blackburn Rovers on 8th February in the

FA Cup Round 5, he had been moved up to inside right and although never a prolific goalscorer, netted the only goal of the game just 13 seconds before the final whistle. This was the first FA Cup tie, other than the final, to be shown live on television. Seven weeks later he scored the opening goal as Newcastle were beaten 4-0 in the semi final at Leeds.

The Cup Final was far from a classic and although Charlton secured victory in extra time, Jimmy Seed's personal notes on the game recorded Tommy's contribution as 'poor'. Indeed, his misplaced pass late in the match might have handed Burnley an equaliser. He did retain his place for the outstanding league fixtures which

followed the final, but was transferred to Brentford before the start of the 1947-48 season, the first of the Cup winning team to depart.

The remainder of his career was fairly routine and he finished up as player manager of Western League club, Chippenham Town, before returning home to the north-east. He later spent time in Australia as coach and physiotherapist for the New South Wales team, Adamstown Rosebud. Tommy was working as a football coach in 1972 when he suffered a coronary and passed away in North Ormesby Hospital at the age of 57.

Season	Division	League		FA Cup		Total	
		A	G	A	G	A	G
1938-39	Division 1	1	0	0	0	1	0
1946-47	Division 1	22	2	6	2	28	4
Total		23	2	6	2	29	4

UK LEAGUE CAREER 147 games 30 goals

CHARLTON CAREER
Managers: *J Seed*
Debut: *Sunderland (A) 01-04-1939*
V205
Finale: *Blackburn Rovers (A) 26-05-1947*

DEMPSEY Ben Michael   2018-

A hard-working box to box midfield player, Ben joined Charlton at age eight and progressed through the youth academy, making his first team debut in the Football League Cup match at MIlton Keynes in August 2018. Highly rated as a real prospect for the future, he was unexpectedly thrust into the league side for four matches in 2019-20 during an injury crisis which left manager Lee Bowyer with more than a dozen of his first team squad in the treatment room.

Midfield 5' 10"
Born: 25-11-1999 - Mitcham, London

HONOURS

Charlton Athletic U23 2017-18 Runners Up PD League 2 South   Charlton Athletic U18 2017-18 Runners Up PD League 2 South

CLUBS

Charlton Athletic 2008 (youth) 05.18 (pro) ••Kingstonian 07.12.18 (loan) ••Dulwich Hamlet 08.11.19 (loan) ••Woking 10.02.20 (loan) 12.10.20 (loan) ••Ayr United, Scotland 24.01.22 (loan)

Having captained the U18's with distinction, Ben made the step-up to U23 level and in 2017-18 made appearances for both sides as they each finished runners-up in their respective divisions. With no reserve team football available any longer he went out on loan, first to Kingstonian, where he played alongside fellow Charlton loanee Alfie Doughty and then to Dulwich Hamlet.

After the first team squad's injury crisis had cleared and

with the bonus of four league matches under his belt, Ben commenced a new loan with National League side Woking. By January 2022 however, he had fallen back in the pecking order at Charlton and accepted a loan transfer to Scottish Championship side Ayr United for the rest of the season and with the option to then make the arrangement permanent.

Season	Division	League		FA Cup		FL Cup		FL Trophy		Play Offs		Total	
		A	G	A	G	A	G	A	G	A	G	A	G
2018-19 (P)	League One	0	0	0	0	1	0	0(1)	0	0	0	1(1)	0
2019-20 (R)	Championship	3(1)	0	0	0	0	0					3(1)	0
2020-21	League One	0	0	0	0	0	0	1	0			1	0
Total		3(1)	0	0	0	1	0	1(1)	0	0	0	5(2)	0

UK LEAGUE CAREER 4 games 0 goals

CHARLTON CAREER
Managers: *L Bowyer, N Adkins, J Jackson*
Debut: *Milton Keynes Dons (A) 14-08-2018*
V860

DERVITE-VAUSSOUE Dorian Pierre   2012 - 14

Defender, Midfield   14st 0lbs   6' 3"
Born: 25-07-1988 - Lille, France

Dorian was primarily a central defender, but could also play a holding role in midfield as he demonstrated against Leeds United on 23rd October 2012. It was the occasion of his first appearance in the starting eleven for Charlton and he capped a fine performance with a spectacular long range goal which earned them a point in a hard fought 1-1 draw.

HONOURS

France U21 International 2009 8 caps 1 goal
France U19 International 2006-07 9 caps 1 goal
France U18 International 2005-06 8 caps 0 goals
France U17 International 2004-05 17 caps 2 goals

France U16 International 2003-04 17 caps 1 goal
France U15 International
Bolton Wanderers 2016-17 Runners Up League One

CLUBS

LA Madeleine, France 1994 (youth) ••Lille OSC, France 1999 (youth) 2005 (pro) ••Tottenham Hotspur 06.06 (free) ••Southend United 29.01.09 (loan) ••Villarreal B, Spain 18.08.10 (free) ••Charlton Athletic 17.08.12 (free) ••Bolton Wanderers 01.07.14 (free) ••Royal Charleroi SC, Belgium 23.07.18 (free) ••NAC Breda, Netherlands 31.01.19 (loan) •Doxa Katokopias, Cyprus 12.07.19 (free) ••KSV Roeselare, Belgium 27.07.20 (free) ••Renaissance Mons 44, Belgium 30.10.20 (free)

The International career of Dorian Dervite got off to an impressive start and he played regularly for France at each age group through his teenage years. He was captain of the French U18 team in 2006 when Tottenham Hotspur came calling and successfully negotiated his transfer from Lille, they having identified him as a young man with the potential to succeed at the top level. Later on 31st March 2009, he was in the French U21 side that beat England U21 by 2-0 at Nottingham in a warm-up for the Euro 2009 U21 Championships.

In contrast, however, his progress at club level proved more difficult. Having moved to London, Dorian played regularly for Spurs Reserves until a serious knee injury in January 2007 put him out of action for the remainder of that season and his only first team game during his four-year stay at White Hart Lane was a League Cup encounter in which the Tottenham side, which also included Danny Murphy, won 3-1 against Port Vale, who had future Charlton striker Akpo Sodje leading their attack.

After failing to break through at Tottenham, Dorian moved to Spain in August 2010 and played two seasons in the Segunda Division for Villarreal B, before joining Charlton, who were newly promoted and looking to re-establish themselves in the Championship. He had to compete with Michael Morrison and Leon Cort for a place in the team and spent much of his first season as third choice centre half, although his versatility made him more than a useful squad player.

In his second season he played more regularly especially in the later stages and chipped in with vital goals against both Yeovil and Bournemouth. The team had flirted with relegation but improved and did at least finish strongly, winning the final two matches of 2013-14. A new contract was offered to Dorian, but he declined and instead signed for Bolton Wanderers on 27th May 2014.

He returned to the Valley on 21st October 2014 with a Bolton team which also included Darren Pratley, but they were beaten 2-1 thanks to goals from George Tucudean and Johnnie Jackson. His stay at Bolton lasted four years and included both relegation and promotion back to the

Championship, but in May 2018 the club announced that he would not be retained and he later joined Belgian Pro League team, Royal Charleroi. In 2020, he signed for Renaissance Mons, a Belgian club which had been declared bankrupt in 2015 but was now busily re-inventing itself again.

Season	Division	League		FA Cup		FL Cup		Total	
		A	G	A	G	A	G	A	G
2012-13	Championship	20 (10)	3	1	0	0	0	21 (10)	3
2013-14	Championship	33 (7)	2	2 (1)	0	1	0	36 (8)	2
Total		53 (17)	5	3 (1)	0	1	0	57 (18)	5

UK LEAGUE CAREER 175 games 6 goals

CHARLTON CAREER
Managers: *C Powell, J Riga, B Peeters*
Debut: *Ipswich Town (A) (sub) 22-09-2012*
V749
Finale: *Blackpool (A) 03-05-2014*

DEVINE John   1926 - 27

Jock was given a lengthy run in the Charlton side at left back during the first half of season 1926-27, but results were poor and only two wins were recorded in his first dozen matches.

Defender   11st 0lbs   5' 8"
Born: 10-06-1899 - Twechar, East Dunbartonshire
Died: 08-07-1949 - Glasgow, Lanarkshire

Things did start to improve but by February both Jock and centre forward Harry Kirk had become the target of some cruel barracking by a minority of supporters and it was felt that their confidence had been adversely affected. The matter was discussed at a formal Directors Meeting and the decision taken that both players should be released as soon as possible. Jock never played in the first team again and departed for Dundee on 15th March.

HONOURS
Plymouth Argyle 1922-23 Runners Up Division 3 (S)

CLUBS
Kilsyth Rangers, Scotland 1920 ••Plymouth Argyle 11.06.21 (pro) ••Exeter City 1923 ••East Stirlingshire, Scotland 15.08.24 ••Kettering Town 06.25 ••Charlton Athletic 08.05.26 ••Dundee, Scotland 15.03.27 ••Southport 16.06.27 ••Crewe Alexandra 28.07.28 ••Kilsyth Rangers, Scotland 1929 ••Croy Celtic, Scotland 1930

Born in the tiny Scottish mining village of Twechar, Jock started his footballing journey at nearby Kilsyth Rangers which was only a short bus ride away and a sharp contrast to his next club which was Plymouth Argyle at a distance of 486 miles.

He made his Football League debut in December 1921 and by the following season was a semi-regular in the Plymouth team. He played at the Valley on 23rd October 1922 when a Sid Castle penalty was enough to clinch a 1-0 win for Charlton, but although Argyle finished in second place they were denied promotion. Only the winners of Division 3 South were promoted in those days. Jock moved on to Exeter City but never featured at first team level and ironically a playing colleague at both of the Devon clubs was his future Charlton team-mate Harry Kirk.

In August 1924 Jock came back to Scotland and enjoyed a run of 20 games with East Stirlingshire, before another long journey south eventually led him to the Valley where his efforts were to prove so unpopular with Charlton supporters. His abrupt departure to Dundee only extended to a single match and was followed by a more successful season at Southport where his topsy turvy career at least stabilised for a while. A single FA Cup appearance for Crewe Alexandra in 1928-29 proved to be his finale and he then returned home to Kilsythe and found employment as a labourer while also working at the local gun range.

Jock died in Glasgow Royal Infirmary at the age of 50 as a result of a stroke during an impromptu lunchtime football game at work.

Season	Division	League		FA Cup		Total	
		A	G	A	G	A	G
1926-27	Divison 3 (S)	19	0	1	0	20	0
Total		19	0	1	0	20	0

UK LEAGUE CAREER 88 games 5 goals

CHARLTON CAREER
Managers: *A MacFarlane*
Debut: *Watford (A) 28-08-1926*
V088
Finale: *Queens Park Rangers (A) 05-02-1927*

DI CANIO Paolo   2003 - 04

Forward   11st 9lbs   5' 10"
Born: 09-07-1968 - Rome, Italy
Education: Duca d'Aosta School, Rome.

One of the most gifted, exciting and charismatic players of his generation, Paolo spent the 2003-04 season with Charlton. Aged 35 when he signed from West Ham, his best days were behind him, yet he still had plenty to offer and his total dedication to training and insistence that everyone around him gives of their absolute best at all times, had a tremendous impact in the dressing room, especially among the younger players. The team finished seventh in the Premier League that season and Paolo was an important factor in that achievement. High maintenance he undoubtedly was, yet when he changed his mind about a second season in SE7 and returned to his beloved Lazio, it was a real loss to Charlton. Characters like Paolo Di Canio do not come around very often.

HONOURS

Italy B International 1989 1 game 0 goals
Italy U21 International 1988-90 9 caps 2 goals
SS Lazio Youth 1985-86 Winners Campionato Nazionale Primavera
Juventus 1991-92 Finalists Coppa Italia
Juventus 1992-93 Winners UEFA Cup

AC Milan 1994-95 Winners European Super Cup
AC Milan 1995-96 Winners Serie A
Celtic 1996-97 Runners Up Scottish Premier League
West Ham United 1999 Winners UEFA Intertoto Cup

HONOURS AS MANAGER

Swindon Town 2011-12 Winners League Two

Swindon Town 2011-12 Finalists Football League Trophy

CLUBS

Pro Tevere Roma, Italy 1980 (youth) ••SS Lazio, Italy 1981 (youth) 1985 (pro) ••Ternana, Italy 1986 (loan) ••Juventus, Italy 1990 (£450,000) ••SSC Napoli, Italy 1993 (loan) ••AC Milan, Italy 16.09.94 (£1.5 million + player exchange)) ••Celtic, Scotland 07.96 (£1.5 million) ••Sheffield Wednesday 08.08.97 (£4.2 million) ••West Ham United 28.01.99 £2 million) ••Charlton Athletic 12.08.03 (free) ••SS Lazio, Italy 10.08.04 (free) ••AS Cisco Calcio Roma, Italy 07.06 (free) ••Swindon Town 20.05.11 (manager) ••Sunderland 31.03.13 (manager)

Born in Quarticciola, a tough working-class suburb of Rome, Paolo grew up on the streets. He auditioned unsuccessfully as a child actor, but otherwise spent his early life playing football. He was a fanatical supporter of Lazio and for six years would attend their matches home and away as one of the infamous Lazio ultras, known as the Irriducibili (meaning unyielding). They travelled in a gang and fought with both opposing supporters and the police, causing mayhem wherever they went. For Paolo, this dark side of his life ran parallel to his burgeoning talent as a young footballer. Lazio had signed him at age 13 and had they at any time known about his association with the Irriducibili, he would have been immediately dismissed. He attended a trade school for electro-mechanics but showed little interest in the course. Paolo wanted to be a professional footballer and was prepared to train longer and

harder than everyone else to achieve his goal.
Lazio's youth team captured the Italian title in 1985-86 by beating Cesena at the Stadio Olimpico, but despite this victory, he had yet to make his first team debut and was loaned out to Serie C2 side Ternana for a year. During this period of absence, Lazio regained their place in Serie A and when Paolo returned from his loan, he was more than ready to perform at the highest level. He made a spectacular debut in 1988-89 and further endeared himself to the Lazio supporters by scoring against Roma in his first derby match. For two seasons he was in outstanding form, but it gradually dawned on him that the chairman was looking to sell his best players to balance the books. For a long while he refused to be sold, but the club eventually forced him out against his will and in 1990 he joined Juventus.
It is hard to believe that Paolo was never called up for a full

international as his form certainly justified selection and it is reasonable to assume that it was his confrontational behaviour rather than any lack of ability which held him back. During his time at Juventus, they reached the final of the 1992 Coppa Italia, losing out to Parma, but a year later captured the UEFA Cup, beating Borussia Dortmund over a two legged final. At the beginning of 1993-94 he had a big bust up with manager Giovanni Trapattoni in which a verbal attack turned physical and in his anger he pushed him over. Soon after, he was despatched on loan to Napoli for a year.

This temporary transfer worked well for all concerned. Paolo played 26 matches in Serie A and Napoli finished in sixth place, while his parent club, Juventus, were runners-up to AC Milan. It was planned for the transfer to be made permanent, but Napoli ran out of money and a proposed new contract with Juventus had already been rejected. Paolo was caught up in an unsavoury contract dispute and fell out big time with the Juventus manager, Luciano Moggi. When the dust settled, he became an AC Milan player at a cost of £1.5 million, plus a player exchange involving defender Alessandro Orlando, who was valued at another £1.5 million, making £3 million in all.

The two years that Paolo spent with Milan were quite successful for the club, but the quality of players within the squad and a debilitating bout of mononucleosis kept him out of the side for too long. In February 1995 they beat Arsenal 2-0 on aggregate to claim the European Super Cup but he only made cameo appearances in the dying minutes of each game and missed the UEFA Champions League final against Ajax completely. He did feature in 22 of Milan's 34 league games in 1995-96 as they stormed to the top of Serie A, winning by an eight point margin, but conflict was never far away and it all blew up during an end of season tour of the Far East. A verbal exchange with Milan manager Fabio Capello accelerated into a fist fight and the two men had to be pulled apart. 'I'm not going to hang around here and look at your ugly penis face any longer', was Paolo's comment as he stormed off to the hotel. His time with AC Milan was at an end and he was now ready to follow up an enquiry to play his football in the UK.

His next port of call was Celtic with whom he agreed a modest financial package for 1996-97, but on the basis that if he played well, improved terms would be available for the second and subsequent years. This was a period of great dominance by Rangers who had won the Scottish Premier League in each of the previous eight seasons and Celtic still proved unable to overhaul their Glasgow rivals. They

eventually finished five points adrift, although Paolo himself had enjoyed an outstanding campaign and was voted Player of the Year by the Scottish PFA. Unfortunately when it came time to discuss terms for the new season, previous promises were forgotten and after a massive row, Paolo walked out and flew home to Italy.

When it became clear that he would not be returning, Celtic cut their losses and Paolo joined Sheffield Wednesday in August 1997. This was his introduction to the Premier League and in his first season things went relatively smoothly, except for a training ground punch-up with manager Ron Atkinson. He played well, netting 12 league goals and Wednesday finished clear of relegation. Something was always going to happen though and it all kicked off on 26th September 1998 in a home game against Arsenal. Just before half-time and after an altercation between Di Canio and Keown, Paul Alcock the referee, red carded Paolo, who wrongly thought that the Arsenal player was going to escape punishment. He lunged at the official and pushed him with both hands. It was not a violent attack but Alcock was off balance and fell to the ground. This was probably the incident that the media had been waiting for and seemingly all hell broke loose. Paolo flew back to Italy while Sheffield Wednesday tried to distance themselves from the whole incident. The hearing took place on 23rd October and Paolo received an 11 match ban (3 for the sending off and 8 for the push). He never played for Wednesday again and in January 1999 joined West Ham United and perhaps the one manager, Harry Redknapp, with the man management skills to take on such a formidable challenge.

In fact the period of nearly five years when Paolo was a Hammer proved to be among the most memorable of his career. He played consistently well and by and large let his football speak for him. On 26th March 2000 his sumptuous volley against Wimbledon was voted Premier League Goal of the Season and there were countless other occasions when his mercurial skill and tremendous energy were a joy to behold. Another side of this most complex character appeared on 16th December 2000 at Goodison Park. With time running out and the Everton goalie injured on the ground, he spurned the chance to score the winning goal and caught the ball instead, an act of sportsmanship that few would have duplicated. His action was officially recognised when he was awarded the FIFA Fair Play Award. West Ham's ten-year stay in the Premier League came to an end when they were relegated in 2002-03 and Paolo was given a free transfer at the end of that season.

The Paolo Di Canio who played more than 30 matches for

Charlton in 2003-04 was still a very good player and the final league placing of seventh in the Premier League the best since the days of Jimmy Seed. Particularly memorable were his corner kicks which were all struck with devastating accuracy. Paolo may have been in the autumn of his career but he remained a very fit and enthusiastic competitor. He seemed happy at Charlton and had a good relationship with his manager, Alan Curbishley. He re-signed for a second season, but before the first match asked to be released as Lazio wanted to bring him home. In theory Charlton could have forced him to honour his contract, but the prospect of an unhappy Paolo in the building did not bear thinking about. He thanked Charlton profusely and said 'I can only apologise to Alan Curbishley and the supporters of Charlton, for whom I have the greatest affection. I have often said I wished I joined Charlton earlier in my career and whatever has happened, I will always believe this to be so.'

At first things went well for Paolo back at Lazio. He scored a goal in the Roma derby just as he had done back in 1988 and was lauded by the local supporters. Gradually however the stories of his connection to the Lazio ultras and his extreme political views caused embarrassment to the club, especially when on a number of occasions he celebrated goals with a fascist salute. He was freed by the club in summer 2006, but carried on playing for Serie C2 club Cisco Roma until finally hanging up his boots at the age of 39.

Paolo's dream was to manage West Ham and he applied unsuccessfully for the job in 2008, but nevertheless did have two spells in management. His first position with Swindon Town went well and his squad, which included Alan McCormack and Paul Benson, won promotion from League Two in 2011-12 and also reached the final of the Football League Trophy. Financial restraints kicked in during the next season and he resigned in February 2013. He was appointed manager of Sunderland six weeks later, but only survived for 13 matches before being unceremoniously sacked.

Season	Division	League		FA Cup		FL Cup		Total	
		A	G	A	G	A	G	A	G
2003-04	Premier	23 (8)	4	0 (1)	0	1	1	24 (9)	5
Total		23 (8)	4	0 (1)	0	1	1	24 (9)	5

UK LEAGUE CAREER 216 games 78 goals

CHARLTON CAREER
Managers: *A Curbishley*
Debut: *Wolverhampton Wanderers (A) (sub) 23-08-2003*
V615
Finale: *Southampton (H) 15-05-2004*

DIARRA Alou   2015 - 16

Midfield, Defender   12st 4lbs   6' 3"
Born: 15-07-1981 - Villepinte, France

Born in the north-east suburbs of Paris, Alou was part of the French international set-up for more than a decade, starting at U20 level and making his senior debut against the Republic of Ireland in 2004. He represented his country in two World Cups and came on as substitute for Patrick Vieira in the 2006 final in Berlin. They eventually lost the match to Italy after extra time and a penalty shoot out. Four years later on 22nd June 2010 and during the next World Cup, Alou received the honour of captaining his country against the host nation, South Africa. In all he earned 44 full international caps and was one of the leading French players of his generation.

HONOURS

France International 2004-12 44 caps 0 goals
France U21 International 2002-04 14 caps 1 goal
France U20 International 2001-02 5 caps 0 goals
RC Lens 2005 Winners UEFA Intertoto Cup
Olympique Lyonnaise 2006-07 Winners Ligue 1
Bordeaux Girondins 2007-08 Runners Up Ligue 1

Bordeaux Girondins 2008 & 2009 Winners Trophee des Champions
Bordeaux Girondins 2008-09 Winners Ligue 1
Bordeaux Girondins 2009-10 Finalists Coupe de La Ligue
Olympique de Marseille 2011 Winners Trophee des Champions
Olympique de Marseille 2011-12 Winners Coupe de La Ligue

CLUBS

Aulnay, France 1987 (youth) ••Villepinte, France 1993 (youth) ••Louhans-Cuiseaux, France 1997 (youth) 1999 (pro) ••Bayern Munich, Germany 2000 (free) ••Liverpool 09.07.02 (free) ••Le Havre, France 01.08.02 (loan) ••SC Bastia, Corsica 21.07.03 (loan) ••RC Lens, France 20.07.04 (loan) 2005 (£2.7 million) ••Olympique Lyonnais, France 23.08.06 (£4.7 million) ••Bordeaux Girondins, France 20.07.07 (£5 million) ••Olympique de Marseille, France 02.07.11 £4.75 million) ••West Ham United 10.08.12 (£2.25 million) ••Stade Rennais, France 31.01.13 (loan) ••Charlton Athletic 23.02.15 (free) ••AS Nancy, France 01.09.16 (free) ••RC Lens, France 24.08.18 (ass: manager)

After two years learning his craft in the reserves at Bayern Munich, Alou signed for Liverpool shortly before his 21st birthday. Even at this stage he had been identified as a young player who was heading for the top, but he only got to play one match, a pre-season friendly, before he was packed off first to Le Havre and then Bastia for extended loans which occupied much of the period of his Liverpool contract. By 2005 and with Liverpool still not prepared to give him a first team chance, he converted another loan, this time with Lens, into a permanent transfer. He remained a hot property and there was even talk of interest from Arsenal (looking for a successor for Patrick Vieira), but instead his next move was to Lyon in August 2006.

This led into a highly successful period when Alou captured the French Ligue 1 title twice, once with Lyon and then again in 2008-09 after transferring to Bordeaux. There was cup glory as well and on 18th April 2012, having moved on again, this time to Marseille, he played alongside Rod Fanni in the exciting final of the Coupe de la Ligue, where more than 80,000 people saw Lyon defeated 1-0. His powerful tackling and quality performances in the centre of midfield were inspirational as were his leadership qualities.

In August 2012 he returned to the UK and signed for West Ham, but again the transfer did not really work out. He played very infrequently and when moved into the back of the Hammers defence alongside Roger Johnson during the two legged League Cup semi-final against Manchester City in January 2014, had to accept his share of the blame for the resultant 0-9 aggregate scoreline. Alou's playing style appeared ideally suited to the English game, yet his best days seemed to all take place on the other side of the English Channel.

He was 34 by the time that he ventured back to the UK for the third time and signed for a Charlton team which was not without merit, but which was decidedly unbalanced as a result of the peculiar transfer policy adopted by the new Belgian owner. He scored his one and only goal in English football at the New Den on 3rd April 2015, but any hope of immortality in SE7 was dashed when Millwall scored two late goals to scrape a 2-1 victory.

The one full season that he spent at the Valley was the wretched campaign of 2015-16 which ended up with a needless relegation from the Championship. Bizarre managerial appointments and muddled thinking in the boardroom, plus increasing unrest among the supporters, led to the inevitable outcome, although Alou was one of the few players who came through this period with any great credit. His obvious class was apparent as he battled to hold Charlton's back line intact and his efforts were acknowledged at the annual Presentation Dinner when he was runner-up in the Player of the Year vote for the season. He was inked in to remain at the club after relegation, but was released from his contract after he requested to return home to France for family reasons.

He concluded his playing career with a final season in Ligue 1 with newly promoted Nancy and in August 2018 was appointed assistant manager of his old club, Lens.

Season	Division	League		FA Cup		FL Cup		Total	
		A	G	A	G	A	G	A	G
2014-15	Championship	8 (4)	1	0	0	0	0	8 (4)	1
2015-16 (R)	Championship	31 (1)		0	0	1	0	32 (1)	0
Total		39 (5)	1	0	0	1	0	40 (5)	1

UK LEAGUE CAREER 50 games 1 goal

CHARLTON CAREER
Managers: *G Luzon, K Fraeye, J Riga*
Debut: *Derby County (A) (sub) 24-02-2015*
V797
Finale: *Burnley (H) 07-05-2016*

DIAWARA Souleymane   2006 - 07

Defender   11st 9lbs   6' 2"
Born: 24-12-1978 - Gabou, Senegal

One of several expensive signings made during the short but eventful period when Iain Dowie was Charlton manager, Souley spent one largely unfulfilled season in South London while the club was in turmoil and was crashing towards relegation from the Premier League. He served under three separate managers and would probably view his time at the Valley as the least successful chapter in an otherwise glittering career which saw him accumulate multiple league and cup honours in France. An experienced international defender, he was rather disparagingly described by Charlton Chairman Richard Murray as 'the best centre half you have never heard of'.

HONOURS

Senegal International 2002-12 48 caps 0 goals	Olympique de Marseille 2008-09 Winners Coupe de La Ligue
Sochaux 2003-04 Winners Coupe de La Ligue	Olympique de Marseille 2009-10 Winners Ligue 1
Bordeaux Girondins 2007-08 Runners Up Ligue 1	Olympique de Marseille 2010 & 2011 Winners Trophee des Champions
Bordeaux Girondins 2008 & 2009 Winners Trophee des Champions	Olympique de Marseille 2010-11 Runners Up Ligue 1
Bordeaux Girondins 2008-09 Winners Ligue 1	Olympique de Marseille 2010-11 Winners Coupe de La Ligue

CLUBS

Le Havre, France 1998 (pro) ••Sochaux-Montbeliard, France 04.08.03 (free) ••Charlton Athletic 30.08.06 (£3.7 million) ••Bordeaux Girondins, France 07.08.07 (£3.5 million) ••Olympique de Marseille, France 02.07.09 (£5.85 million) ••OGC Nice, France 05.08.14 (free)

Although born in Gabou in the Tambacounda region of Senegal, Souley played the majority of his football in France. He turned professional in 1998 and had his first cup success with Sochaux-Montbeliard in 2004 when they defeated Nantes to win the Coupe de la Ligue after extra time and penalties.

It is fair to say that his transfer to Charlton in August 2006, for a massive fee of £3.7 million, was a surprise to everyone. The signing was announced at a sponsor's event at Lingfield Racecourse and had been completed at speed, as being a holder of a French passport, he did not require a work permit. Souley made his debut at Chelsea on 9th September, but the match was lost 2-1 and Charlton had only a consolation goal from Jimmy Floyd Hasselbaink to show for their efforts. By the end of that month, the club was firmly placed at the bottom of the Premier League and it was clear that survival would be difficult to achieve. Souley was far from being the worst performer in the Charlton defence during that miserable season, but was unable to make the difference that was expected by many as a result of the big transfer fee. He was also forced to accept some light-hearted ribbing because regardless of the weather he always wore gloves when playing.

At the end of the 2006-07 season and with relegation confirmed, Charlton were forced to shed players as a result of the financial pressures from their reduced status. Birmingham City expressed interest in signing Souley, but

instead he returned to France and in August 2007 joined Bordeaux. From this point his career really took off and in his second season with Les Girondins, (as Bordeaux are known), they won both Ligue 1 and the Coupe de la Ligue, triumphing against Vannes 4-0 in the final.

He transferred to Marseille in July 2009 and immediately repeated the same cup and league double for a second time. Then 12 months later on 23rd April 2011 the Marseille team, including both Souley and Rod Fanni, beat Montpellier 1-0 to again win the Coupe de la Ligue. This was the fourth time and with three different clubs that he had won that competition.

Senegal capped Souley on 48 occasions over a ten-year period, but none of his international football came during his year in South London as he had at that time fallen out with the national coach over a breach of discipline. He did however play in the Africa Cup of Nations finals in 2006 when Senegal reached the semi-final stage. His final cap was in 2012 and he retired from all football in 2015.

In April 2015 Souley was arrested by French police and spent two and a half months in custody. He had been sold a Porsche Cayenne that turned out to be stolen and in an attempt to recover his money from the car dealer had been the instigator of a 'commando operation' to obtain 50,000 euros from him in compensation. It came to court in 2019 when he was found guilty of complicity in an extortion. The prosecution pressed for a prison sentence, but luckily he escaped with a fine of 10,800 euros.

Season	Division	League		FA Cup		FL Cup		Total	
		A	G	A	G	A	G	A	G
2006-07 (R)	Premier	18 (5)	0	0 (1)	0	2	0	20 (6)	0
Total		18 (5)	0	0 (1)	0	2	0	20 (6)	0

UK LEAGUE CAREER 23 games 0 goals

CHARLTON CAREER
Managers: *I Dowie, L Reed, A Pardew*
Debut: *Chelsea (A) 09-09-2006*
V638
Finale: *Tottenham Hotspur (H) 07-05-2007*

DICKENSON Kevin James   1980 - 84

An East London boy who made up in effort for what he lacked in inches, Kevin was the pocket sized blond bomber who for a time held down the left back spot in the Charlton defence during the early eighties. He

Defender   10st 6lbs   5' 6"
Born: 24-11-1962 - Hackney, London
Education: Bedfords Park School, Harold Hill.

had started out at Tottenham, but never got close to a first team outing and after switching to the Valley made his debut against Swansea City on 3rd May 1980. It was a disappointing 2-1 home defeat with only a consolation goal from Martin Robinson to show for the afternoon's work. Kevin was aged 17 and looked even younger, but even in his first game he let the opposition know that he was able to stand up to the physical aspects of professional football.

HONOURS

East London & Havering Schools
Charlton Athletic Reserves 1979-80 Winners Mid-Week League Cup

Charlton Athletic Reserves 1981-82 Winners Mid-week League
Leyton Orient 1988-89 Promoted Play Offs Division 4

CLUBS

Tottenham Hotspur 1978 (youth) ••Charlton Athletic 01.05.80 (amateur) 21.05.80 (pro) ••Orient / Leyton Orient 01.07.85 (free) ••Leyton Orient Cavaliers 1992 (player manager)

Kevin spent five years at Charlton and achieved the feat of being ever present in 1983-84. It was a difficult season, played out against the financial drama that found the club within 30 minutes of being wound up in the High Court, before the rescue package put together by Sunley Holdings saved the day. Kevin was in the team which went down 1-0 at Swansea on 25th February, thought at the time to have possibly been Charlton's final match and then again at the Valley on 10th March after the club had been saved and when the new chairman John Fryer was introduced to the crowd. It was very difficult to concentrate on the football during this worrying period.
In all he played 70 consecutive league and cup matches between 4th April 1983 and 3rd November 1984. It was far from a vintage period on the field as Charlton flirted with relegation and put in some truly forgettable displays, culminating in the awful performance at Brighton on 1st

October 1983 which finished 7-0 and in which the home team seemed to score every time they approached the Charlton goal. A happier occasion was at Layer Road in the FA Cup on 7th January 1984 when it was Kevin's run and cross which forced a Colchester defender into a late own goal and secured a largely undeserved 1-0 victory. Kevin's run of games finally came to an end and he was left out in favour of Paul Friar after a home defeat by Leeds and he never regained his place in the side, moving to Orient at the end of the 1984-85 season on a free transfer (They changed their name back to Leyton Orient two years later). He did well with his new club, making more than 200 appearances and featuring in their promotion campaign in 1988-89. He brought down the curtain on his Football League career in 1992, but was back at Leyton Orient in August 2017 as one of their match day hosts.

Season	Division	League		FA Cup		FL Cup		Total	
		A	G	A	G	A	G	A	G
1979-80 (R)	Division 2	1	0	0	0	0	0	1	0
1981-82	Division 2	5 (2)	0	0	0	1	0	6 (2)	0
1982-83	Division 2	11 (1)	0	0	0	0	0	11 (1)	0
1983-84	Division 2	42	1	2	0	2	0	46	1
1984-85	Division 2	13	0	0	0	2	0	15	0
Total		72 (3)	1	2	0	5	0	79 (3)	1

UK LEAGUE CAREER 267 games 4 goals

CHARLTON CAREER
Managers: *M Bailey, A Mullery, K Craggs, L Lawrence*
Debut: *Swansea Town (H) 03-05-1980*
V423
Finale: *Leeds United (H) 03-11-1984*

DICKSON Christopher Alexander Kofi   2007 - 10

Forward   13st 3lbs   5' 11"
Born: 28-12-1984 - Plumstead, London

On 27th March 2021 Isthmian League side Hornchurch unexpectedly defeated Notts County from the National League to reach the final of the FA Trophy. Their team included former Charlton players Oliver Muldoon and 36-year-old veteran striker Chris Dickson and it was the latter who held his nerve and scored the decisive kick from the penalty spot which ensured victory and a trip to Wembley. Back in 2008 Chris had briefly been hailed by some as Charlton's next scoring sensation and when this had not proved to be the case he had moved from club to club, mainly within the non-league game but also including spells in both Cyprus and China. Finally, he was able to grab the headlines for a day.

HONOURS

Ghana International 2008-09 2 caps 0 goals   Hornchurch 2020-21 Winners FA Trophy
Pafos 2014-15 Runners Up Cyprus League Division 2

CLUBS

Erith & Belvedere 2004 ••Dulwich Hamlet c07.06 (free) ••Charlton Athletic 12.03.07 (£35,000) ••Crewe Alexandra 17.08.07 (loan) ••Gillingham 21.09.07 (loan) ••Bristol Rovers 17.09.09 (loan) ••Gillingham 15.02.10 (loan) ••Nea Salamis Famagusta, Cyprus 23.07.10 (free) ••AEL Limassol, Cyprus 26.01.12 (undisclosed) ••Shanghai Dongya, China 29.01.13 (free) ••Dagenham & Redbridge 03.10.13 (free) ••Pafos, Cyprus 01.07.14 (free) ••Enosis Neon Paralimni, Cyprus 13.07.15 (free) ••Ermis Aradippou, Cyprus 04.01.16 (free) ••Sutton United 31.07.16 (free) ••Chelmsford City 06.01.17 (free) ••Hampton & Richmond Borough 01.07.18 (free) ••Hornchurch 19.07.19 (free) ••Dartford 21.11.20 (loan) ••Erith & Belvedere 09.10.21 (free0 ••Cray Wanderers 20.10.21 (free)

Chris made his name at Dulwich Hamlet where 26 goals in 34 games attracted the attention of Charlton manager Alan Pardew, who had himself played for the Hamlet at the dawn of his career. He proved to be a larger than life character, brimming with self-confidence but uncoached in the finer details of football tactics at this higher level. Having signed in March 2007, he was quickly sent out on loan in an attempt to fine tune him ready for first team duty and he made a tremendous impact during a three-month stay at Gillingham, delivering 11 goals including a hat-trick against Luton Town and finishing up as their leading goalscorer for 2007-08.

Once recalled to the Valley there were demands for him to be played in Charlton's first team and he was rewarded with various cameo appearances from the sub's bench, from one of which he scored a late equaliser past Dean Kiely in an FA Cup replay against West Bromwich Albion at the

Hawthorns. As results got worse and with the team positioned firmly at the foot of the Championship, so the calls for Chris to play increased and he finally got a run of six starts commencing at the end of January 2009. Sadly however he was unable to live up to the hype that had become attached to his name and he failed to score a single league goal.

The bubble had burst by then but earlier he had played the first of two international matches for Ghana, for whom he qualified through his Ghanaian father. His debut came on 20th August 2008 in a 1-1 away draw with Tanzania. Chris also did some important work off the field for Charlton by fronting up the 'Street Violence Ruins Lives' campaign. He was allowed to leave the club at the conclusion of the 2009-10 season and next had spells with two clubs competing in the Cypriot First Division. First he appeared for Famagusta and then at Limassol where he played under manager Jorge Costa and appeared in the Europa League, even scoring against Marseilles. Chris then tried his luck in the Chinese Super League with Shanghai Dongya before returning to the UK for a final try at the Football League with Dagenham & Redbridge.

Since 2014 he has moved restlessly between clubs without staying anywhere for any length of time nor achieving

anything significant until the FA Trophy final of 2020-21 placed him on centre stage. The match was played at Wembley on 22nd May and after going behind to an early goal, Hornchurch came back and defeated Hereford United by 3-1. Chris and Oliver Muldoon were both in the team.

Season	Division	League		FA Cup		FL Cup		FL Trophy		Play Offs		Total	
		A	G	A	G	A	G	A	G	A	G	A	G
2007-08	Championship	0 (2)	0	0 (2)	1	0 (1)	0					0 (5)	1
2008-09 (R)	Championship	6 (15)	0	0 (2)	1	0 (1)	0					6 (18)	1
2009-10	League One	1 (4)	0	0	0	0	0	0	0	0	0	1 (4)	0
Total		7 (21)	0	0 (4)	2	0 (2)	0	0	0	0	0	7 (27)	2

UK LEAGUE CAREER 91 games 13 goals

CHARLTON CAREER
Managers: *A Pardew, P Parkinson*
Debut: *Swindon Town (A) (sub)*
14-08-2007
V654
Finale: *Leyton Orient (H) (sub)*
25-01-2010

DIJKSTEEL Anfernee Jamal   2017 - 19

Anfernee made an immediate impact after joining Charlton's development squad in January 2016 and only two months later played for the Netherlands U20 team in a 1-1 draw against Portugal. He was

Defender, Midfield   11st 5lbs   6' 0''
Born: 27-10-1996 - Amsterdam, Netherlands
Education: Nike Academy, Burton on Trent.

fast tracked into the Charlton first team early in the 2017-18 season, playing at right back rather than his accustomed position in the middle of the midfield. So well did he perform that he soon became a regular member of the squad and an important component in the promotion side of 2018-19. His younger brother Malik, had trials with Oxford United in October 2019.

HONOURS

Netherlands U20 2016 1 cap 0 goals
Charlton Athletic U21 2015-16 Finalists Kent Senior Cup
Charlton Athletic U23 2016-17 Winners U23 PD League 2 South

Charlton Athletic U23 2017-18 Runners Up PD League 2 South
Charlton Athletic 2018-19 Promoted Play Offs League One

CLUBS

Amsterdamsche, Netherlands 2014 (youth) ••Nike Academy 2015 (youth) ••Charlton Athletic 01.16 (pro) ••Middlesbrough 07.08.19 (£2 million)

The play off final in May 2019 was not Anfernee's first appearance at Wembley as he had played there in November 2015 for the Nike Academy against Barcelona U19's. By the time of his second appearance, he had matured into a solid and reliable full back and gave a good account of himself against Sunderland as Charlton regained their place in the Championship.

From then on however it became increasingly clear that he was not going to accept the terms of his proposed new contract and although he featured in the opening match of 2019-20, it was no surprise when the club accepted a fee, believed to be in the region of £2 million, for his transfer to

Middlesbrough.

He took time to settle in at his new club and was not assisted by a serious knee injury incurred against Barnsley on 27th November 2019. This would normally have ended his season, but after games were suspended during the Covid pandemic, he was eventually fit to return in July 2020 and participated in the remaining four matches which helped Middlesbrough preserve their Championship status. Since then, he has cemented his place in the Borough side and was in the team on 4th February 2022 when they travelled to Old Trafford and knocked a full strength Manchester United side out of the FA Cup.

Season	Division	League		FA Cup		FL Cup		FL Trophy		Play Offs		Total	
		A	G	A	G	A	G	A	G	A	G	A	G
2017-18	League One	8 (2)	0	1	0	2	0	5	0	1	0	17 (2)	0
2018-19 (P)	League One	21 (9)	1	3	0	1	0	2	0	3	0	30 (9)	1
2019-20 (R)	Championship	1	0	0	0	0	0					1	0
Total		30 (11)	1	4	0	3	0	7	0	4	0	48 (11)	1

UK LEAGUE CAREER 86 games 1 goal

CHARLTON CAREER
Managers: *J Riga, R Slade, K Robinson, L Bowyer*
Debut: *Exeter City (A) 08-08-2017*
V843
Finale: *Blackburn Rovers (A) 03-08-2019*

DMITROVIC Marko   2015

Goalkeeper   14st 11lbs   6' 4"
Born: 24-01-1992 - Subotica, Yugoslavia (now Serbia)

Marko had little opportunity to shine during his brief spell as a Charlton player as he was only ever viewed as a back-up goalkeeper, but had circumstances been different, he may well have proved a very worthwhile signing. He was already a Serbian U21 International and acquired three further caps at that level while in England, including the 1-1 draw against Germany in the European U21 Championships on 17th June 2015. He has since gone on to become Serbia's first choice goalkeeper with every chance of retaining that position for several years to come.

HONOURS

Serbia International 2017-21 18 caps 0 goals

Serbia U19 International 2010-12 9 caps 0 goals

Serbia U21 International 2012-15 15 caps 0 goals

CLUBS

Red Star Belgrade, Serbia 2006 (youth) 2010 (pro) ••Ujpest, Hungary 03.09.13 (free) ••Charlton Athletic 06.01.15 (undisclosed) ••AD Alcorcon, Spain 27.07.15 (loan) 07.07.16 (undisclosed) ••SD Elbar, Spain 23.06.17 (£700,000) ••Sevilla, Spain 04.07.21 (free)

The signing by Charlton of Marko Dmitrovic came at the time of the network experiment by Belgian Owner Roland Duchatelet. His plan was for the clubs that he owned across Europe to be able to move players between themselves for their mutual benefit and the giant young goalkeeper arrived at the Valley from Ujpest of Hungary on 6th January 2015, the same day that Tony Watt was signed from Standard Liege., both Duchatelet owned clubs.

Manager Bob Peeters welcomed Marko to SE7 as cover was urgently needed for the injured Stephen Henderson. Rookie goalkeeper Nick Pope was still not deemed quite ready and was packed off on loan to Bury that same day, but before the newcomers had even laced up their boots, Peeters was dismissed and on 13th January Guy Luzon was installed as the new Charlton manager. Marko made his debut against Wolverhampton Wanderers on 24th January 2015 which was Luzon's first match in charge and

acquitted himself well in a 0-0 draw. The Wolves team had a former Charlton loanee goalkeeper Carl Ikeme, in their side.

Marko played in the next three games and then made one final appearance on 7th March when Henderson was again injured and had to be replaced at half time against Cardiff City. He conceded in the 56th minute, but an equaliser from Tony Watt and a late penalty by Yoni Buyens were enough to clinch a useful 2-1 away victory.

In July 2015 Marko moved on loan to Alcorcon, another of the network clubs and the deal was made permanent a year later. He now seems settled in Spain having spent four years playing in La Liga for the Basque club, SD Elbar. They had a disastrous season in 2020-21 however and finished bottom of the league, but Marko escaped relegation to the Segunda Division and moved that summer to Sevilla on a free transfer.

Season	Division	League		FA Cup		FL Cup		Total	
		A	G	A	G	A	G	A	G
2014-15	Championship	4 (1)	0	0	0	0	0	4 (1)	0
Total		4 (1)	0	0	0	0	0	4 (1)	0

UK LEAGUE CAREER 5 games 0 goals

CHARLTON CAREER
Managers: *B Peeters, G Luzon, K Fraeye, J Riga*
Debut: *Wolverhampton Wanderers (A) 24-01-2015*
V792
Finale: *Cardiff City (A) (sub) 07-03-2015*

DOBSON George David   2021 -

George signed for Charlton during the summer of 2021 tasked with taking over the defensive midfield role that had previously been the territory of Darren Pratley. This is one of the least glamorous positions, but one that is vitally important as it provides both a shield in front of the defence and a link with the more creative players ahead of him. He had been well-taught, having spent ten years in the youth academy at Arsenal and all Charlton supporters, buoyed by the confident predictions of new owner, Thomas Sandgaard, had high expectations and were looking forward to a successful season in 2021-22.

Midfield, Defender   6' 1"
Born: 15-11-1997 - Harold Wood, Essex
Education: Brentwood School.

CLUBS

Arsenal 2005 (youth) ••West Ham United 27.07.15 (pro) ••Walsall 29.06.16 (loan) •Sparta Rotterdam, Netherlands 16.07.17 (undisclosed) ••Walsall 03.01.18 (free) ••Sunderland 25.07.19 (undisclosed) ••AFC Wimbledon 22.01.21 (loan) ••Charlton Athletic 01.07.21 (free)

Although signing professional for West Ham in 2015, George did not make his league debut until the following year when on loan at Walsall. One of his first appearances in a side that also included Frank Moussa, Neil Etheridge and Erhun Oztumer, was at the Bescot Stadium against Charlton on 20th August 2016, but a brace of goals from Nicky Ajose ensured a 2-1 win for the Addicks. A year later George moved abroad and spent the early part of the 2017-18 season with Sparta Rotterdam, but only played a handful of matches as they sunk to relegation from the Dutch Eredivisie.

Back in the UK, he signed a permanent contract with Walsall and played in 60 league matches for them up to the end of the 2018-19 season when they were relegated to League Two, but at that point he jumped ship and joined Sunderland on a three-year deal. They were a deeply troubled club, although he had a reasonable first season and even scored on 28th August 2019 when they defeated Premier League Burnley 3-1 in the League Cup. His next campaign did not go so well until he spent three months on loan with AFC Wimbledon, (playing alongside Joe Pigott). His impressive display against Charlton at the Kingsmeadow Stadium on 20th March 2021 may well have contributed to his transfer to the Addicks some five months later.

UK LEAGUE CAREER 139 games 3 goals

CHARLTON CAREER
Managers: *N Adkins, J Jackson*
Debut: *Sheffield Wednesday (H) 07-08-2021*
V923

DODD George Frederick   1921

Forward   11st 7lbs   5' 7"
Born: 07-02-1885 - Whitchurch, Shropshire
Died: 01-01-1960 - Whitchurch, Shropshire
Education: Whitchurch Council School.

George was Charlton's first born, entering this life on 7th February 1885 and no other of their Football League players has an earlier date of birth. He had already enjoyed a long and varied football career before the arrival of World War 1 but by the time he signed for Charlton a week before their opening game as a Football League club, he was aged 36 and his best days were very definitely behind him. It was understandable that the league new boys should target a few experienced players as they sought to consolidate in their first season and both Harold Halse and Arthur Whalley (mere youngsters at 35 years) were inspired choices. However, it is less easy to understand why George was brought in as he would only ever play one first team game.

HONOURS
Chelsea 1911-12 Runners Up Division 2

CLUBS
Wallasey Town 1903 ••Rock Ferry 1904 ••Stockport County 08.05 ••Workington 07.07 ••Notts County 12.07 ••Tunbridge Wells Rangers 1910 ••Chelsea 25.08.11 ••Millwall Athletic 02.13 ••Brighton & Hove Albion 12.13 ••Darlington 06.14 ••West Ham United 1914 ••Luton Town 10.19 ••Treherbert 05.20 (player manager) ••Charlton Athletic 22.08.21 ••Catford Southend 07.24 (secretary/manager)

Intriguingly George's name appears in most but not all record books as being the very first man to score a goal against Chelsea after they were elevated to the status of a Football League club. This memorable feat occurred during their opening fixture on 2nd September 1905 at Edgeley Park when in the 60th minute Stockport County were awarded a penalty. It was partially saved by Willie Foulke, the giant Chelsea goalkeeper, only for two Stockport players, Dodd and Manson, to bundle the ball home for a 1-0 victory. The home side tried to claim that both men had scored the goal and with no 'dubious goals panel' in existence at that time the matter was never satisfactorily resolved, although most sources now accept George Dodd as the goalscorer. He featured at inside left for Stockport through much of the 1905-06 season before moving to Workington who at that time were competing in the Lancashire Combination.

George re-appeared in the Football League for Notts County on Christmas Day 1907 in a 2-1 win against Everton and he clocked up nearly 100 games for them in Division 1 over the next four seasons as well as taking part in an 11-day tour of Denmark in May 1910. His somewhat nomadic career then brought him to Chelsea where he

participated in their 1911-12 Division 2 promotion team, contributing eight league goals, including a hat-trick in a 4-0 win against Birmingham City on 11th November. Bob Thomson, another Charlton player of the future, scored the other goal.

George's final game for Chelsea came in December 1913 against Manchester United, after which he drifted around a series of then non-league clubs, before signing for Charlton nearly eight years later. His one outing in the first team came in the third fixture of the season when he was picked to play up front at Exeter alongside his old Chelsea comrade Bob Thomson. The result was a 1-0 defeat and despite a heavy turnover of players in that first season, he was never again called upon to play. George did however remain at Charlton for almost three years and was even sent off in a reserve match against West Ham in February 1923. After Charlton's ill fated move to the Mount had been tried and failed and they had returned to the Valley, George took over as secretary manager of Catford Southend in July 1924, where his squad included Albert 'Mosky' Mills. A very fine golfer all his life, he passed away in his home town of Whitchurch at the age of 75.

Season	Division	League		Total	
		A	G	A	G
1921-22	Divison 3 (S)	1	0	1	0
Total		1	0	1	0

UK LEAGUE CAREER 148 games 33 goals

CHARLTON CAREER
Managers: *W Rayner*
Debut: *Exeter City (A) 03-09-1921*
V018

DODGIN William

Season 1934-35 was the start of the greatest period in Charlton's history. In just three years manager Jimmy Seed led the club from the Third Division to just one place short of the Division 1 championship, an

Midfield, Defender   5' 10"
Born: 17-04-1909 - Gateshead, Co Durham
Died: 16-10-1999 - Godalming, Surrey

achievement that has never been equalled, let alone beaten. Bill was signed in August 1934 and throughout that first campaign contested the left half position with Joe Jobling and latterly with Bert Turner, thereby earning himself a Division 3 (South) winners medal, the only tangible success in his long career as both a player and a manager. His brother Norman played for Newcastle United in the 1940s, while his son Bill Dodgin Jnr, made more than 200 appearances for Arsenal. Both also managed at Football League clubs.

HONOURS
Gateshead Schools & Newcastle Schools   Charlton Athletic 1934-35 Winners Division 3 (S)

CLUBS
Gateshead High Fell (youth) ••Kirkley & Waveney (youth) ••Wallsend (youth) ••Lowestoft Town ••Huddersfield Town 16.11..29 ••Lincoln City 03.33 ••Charlton Athletic 03.08.34 ••Bristol Rovers 04.05.36 (free) ••Clapton Orient 07.37 ••Southampton 05.39 (free) 01.46 (manager) ••Fulham 08.49 (manager) ••Brentford 10.53 (manager) ••Sampdoria, Italy 05.57 (manager) ••Yiewsley 03.59 (manager) ••Bristol Rovers 08.61 (scout) 08.69 (manager) 07.72 (scout)

Born in the North East, Bill turned professional with Huddersfield Town in 1929 but did not get much first team football until he moved to Lincoln City three years later. He came up against Charlton on 1st April 1933 when both clubs were battling relegation from Division 2 and the league table showed Charlton in bottom place, but the match at Sincil Bank finished 1-1 courtesy of a Les Boulter goal for the Addicks. Bill had become captain of the Lincoln side at the age of 24 and perhaps it was his leadership qualities that persuaded Seed to add him to the playing staff at the Valley for a wage of £7 per week. After clinching promotion back to Division 2, Charlton carried on where they had left off in 1935-36, but unfortunately for Bill he was left out of the first team after the first few matches, his place at left half being taken by Don Welsh. However, he did re-appear for three games shortly after Christmas, including the 3-0 win over Doncaster Rovers on 4th January 1936 when goals by Monty Wilkinson, George Stephenson and Stan Prior fired Charlton to the top of Division 2 for the very first time. This proved to be Bill's final league outing and he departed to Bristol Rovers at the end of the season. One year with Rovers was followed by two with Clapton Orient, all spent in the lower half of Division 3 (South), but

in June 1939 Bill's fortunes appeared to be back in the ascendancy thanks to a move to Southampton, then a Second Division club. He got to play in two league games alongside Charlton's former winger Gerry Kelly, only for the outbreak of war to bring the 1939-40 season to an abrupt halt in September. Regional matches were played throughout the conflict and Bill appeared 84 times for Southampton and a further 26 guesting for Orient but by the end of the war his playing days were over and in March 1946 he became Southampton manager, a post that he held for more than three years.

He went on to enjoy a long managerial career which embraced time with Fulham, Brentford and Bristol Rovers (where he took over from Fred Ford), plus a spell out in Italy with Sampdoria, where his playing squad included Eddie Firmani. Viewed as a safe pair of hands and an astute judge of footballing ability, Bill was universally respected within the game and continued as a scout for Bristol Rovers until 1983. Away from football, Bill's life was varied, having been employed as a coal miner before turning pro and during the war working in an aircraft factory. He later ran a tobacconist shop in Byfleet and passed away in Robertson Nursing Home, Godalming at the age of 90.

Season	Division	League		FA Cup		D3 Cup		Total	
		A	G	A	G	A	G	A	G
1934-35 (P)	Divison 3 (S)	24	0	2	0	0	0	26	0
1935-36 (P)	Division 2	5	0	1	0			6	0
Total		29	0	3	0	0	0	32	0

UK LEAGUE CAREER 177 games 3 goals

CHARLTON CAREER
Managers: *J Seed*
Debut: *Southend United (H) 15-09-1934*
V181
Finale: *Clapton Orient (A) 11-01-1936*

DODOO Joseph   2017

Forward   11st 1lb   6ft 0ins
Born: 29-06-1995 - Kumasi, Ghana

Joe was born in Ghana but came to live in Nottingham with his grandmother at the age of eight. He showed considerable promise as a young footballer and joined the Leicester City academy in 2006. He was capped by England at U18 level in March 2013 against Belgium and made his first team debut for Leicester in the League Cup on 25th August 2015. He celebrated with a sparkling hat trick as Bury were defeated 4-1, but found further progress difficult at Leicester during that amazing season when they were crowned Premier League champions.

HONOURS

England U18 International 2013 1 cap 0 goals

CLUBS

AFC Vernon (youth) ••Leicester City 2006 (youth) 2013 (pro) ••Bury 19.11.15 (loan) ••Rangers, Scotland 19.07.16 (£250,000) ••Charlton Athletic 31.08.17 (loan) ••Blackpool 13.06.18 (loan) ••Bolton Wanderers 03.10.19 (free) ••Ankara Keciorengucu, Turkey 12.09.20 (free) ••Wigan Athletic 09.02.21 (free) ••Doncaster Rovers 06.09.21 (free)

A transfer fee of £250,000 took Joe to Ibrox and he made his Rangers' debut on 22nd July 2016 in a Scottish League Cup win at East Stirlingshire, celebrating with an injury time goal in a 3-0 victory. He featured in 20 Scottish Premier League matches that season, but mainly was restricted to cameo appearances from the substitute's bench. His most memorable display came on 26th November against Partick Thistle with two late goals that clinched a 2-1 win.

By season 2017-18 Joe had fallen out of favour at Rangers and joined Charlton on loan during the final hours of the August transfer window. It was wrongly claimed that he had scored on debut at each of his previous clubs, but in fact he had failed to do so while on a short loan spell at Bury where his best effort had been deemed an own goal from an opponent. At Charlton however, he hit the jackpot at Oldham in his first outing, replacing Karlan Ahearne-Grant as a second half substitute and scoring in a topsy turvy 4-3 win. He never really settled at the Valley however and was not given an extended run in the side at any stage.

With one more year remaining on his Rangers' contract, Joe went on loan to Blackpool for the 2018 19 season and did get a run of games without really establishing himself. Back in May 2016 he had been invited to train with the Ghana squad, but had been unable to make his international debut as FIFA had yet to clear his change of nationality and since then he has been given no further opportunity to play international football for the country of his birth.

Since leaving Charlton, Joe has still not settled and has spent time with both Bolton Wanderers and Wigan Athletic as well as four months out in Turkey playing for Ankara Keciorengucu. He is currently tasked with keeping Doncaster Rovers in League One.

Season	Division	League		FA Cup		FL Cup		FL Trophy		Total	
		A	G	A	G	A	G	A	G	A	G
2017-18	League One	0 (5)	1	1	0	0	0	2	1	3 (5)	2
Total		0 (5)	1	1	0	0	0	2	1	3 (5)	2

UK LEAGUE CAREER 92 games 14 goals

CHARLTON CAREER
Managers: *K Robinson*
Debut: *Oldham Athletic (sub) 02-09-2017*
V848
Finale: *Portsmouth (H) 07-11-2017*

DOHERTY Gary Michael Thomas　　　　　　2010 - 11

After his April 2000 transfer from Luton to Spurs, Gary was described by the Telegraph as 'a snip at a million pounds'. He never quite lived up to such star billing but did score in an FA Cup semi final against Arsenal and represent his country with distinction on 34 occasions. He spent nearly six years at Norwich and when finally released by them turned down the chance to join New York Red Bulls before eventually signing for Charlton.

Defender, Forward　13st 13lbs　6'2"
Born: 31-01-1980 - Carndonagh, Ireland
Education:

HONOURS
Republic of Ireland International 2000-05 34 caps
Republic of Ireland U20 ,U19 & U18 International

Norwich City 2009-10 Winners League One

CLUBS
Luton Town (youth) 02.07.97 (pro) ••Tottenham Hotspur 22.04.00 (£1 million) ••Norwich City 20.08.04 ••Charlton Athletic 06.07.10 (free) ••Wycombe Wanderers 24.02.12 (loan) 03.07.12 (free)

Gary's career kicked off at Luton Town and he made his debut as a second half substitute on 2nd September 1997. The opponents were a Millwall team that included Kim Grant, Paul Sturgess and Alan Mcleary and they were too strong for Luton who went down 2-0. It took him a couple of years to find his feet but in season 1999-00 he was almost ever present until on 22nd April, Tottenham spent their million and made him a Premier League player.
He never got a long run in the Spurs side but was a more than useful squad player, mainly in attack. On 25th January 2004 he was playing alongside a young Johnnie Jackson against Manchester City in the FA Cup and scored the equalising goal in a hard fought 1-1 draw. During his final year at Tottenham, he was used mainly in defence and after he switched to Norwich City in August 2004, it was as a centre half that he flourished. He endured two relegations and the euphoria of promotion back into the Championship in 2009-10 fully earning his reputation as a never say die warrior. He played six seasons for Norwich, but in July 2010 was given a free transfer and became a Charlton player.

The Ginger Pele was 30 years old when he signed for Charlton. Viewed as a no nonsense defender who had played at the highest level, his experience was much needed in what was a pretty mediocre season. Although his commitment and effort were never in question, he lacked pace and was generally unable to play to the standard that he had reached during the early years of his career.
The following summer new manager Chris Powell was building his promotion side and from then on Gary was no more than a squad player. In February 2012, he and Paul Hayes were loaned to League One strugglers, Wycombe Wanderers and although they were unable to prevent relegation, Gary impressed sufficiently that he joined them permanently and did well until a serious knee injury brought his career to an end in December 2014.
Very much a cult figure, Gary's popularity was demonstrated in 2010 when the indie-punk band We Can't Dance recorded a song dedicated to him, titled 'Gary Doherty'. He moved to the USA in 2020 and is setting up his own soccer school in Boston.

Season	Division	League		FA Cup		FL Cup		FL Trophy		Total	
		A	G	A	G	A	G	A	G	A	G
2010-11	League One	35 (3)	0	3 (1)	0	0 (1)	0	3	0	41 (5)	0
2011-12	League One	0 (3)	0	0	0	2	0	1	0	3 (3)	0
Total		35 (6)	0	3 (1)	0	2 (1)	0	4	0	44 (8)	0

UK LEAGUE CAREER 433 games 31 goals

CHARLTON CAREER
Managers: *P Parkinson, C Powell*
Debut: *AFC Bournemouth (H) 07.08.2010*
V704
Finale: *Brentford (H) 05.10.11 05-10-2011*

DOHERTY John   1933 - 34

Forward, Midfield
Born: 12-04-1908 - Belfast, Northern Ireland
Died: Unknown -

Jack Doherty, nicknamed 'Dot', was a top Irish amateur footballer in the 1920s and whilst a Portadown player took part in the highly controversial international fixture that was played between Northern Ireland and France at the Buffalo Stadium, Paris on 21st February 1928. It ended in a comfortable 4-0 win for the French and was watched by a crowd of 27,000. It was deemed controversial because the Irish team was selected from a mixture of amateur and professional players and for this reason there were opposing views on whether it could count as an official match. The professionals had been paid a fee of £2 2s 0d each so it could not be classed as an amateur contest, but after much debate it has now been accepted by FIFA and appears in the record books as a full Northern Ireland International.

HONOURS
N Ireland International 1928-32 3 caps 0 goals　　　　　　N Ireland Amateur International 1927-31 7 caps 0 goals

CLUBS
Park End, N Ireland (youth) ••Belfast Celtic, N Ireland (amateur) ••Park End, N Ireland (amateur)) ••Woodburn, N Ireland 1926 (amateur) ••Portadown, N Ireland 1927 (amateur) ••Ards, N Ireland 1930 (amateur) ••Cliftonville, N Ireland 1932 (amateur) ••Charlton Athletic 17.12.32 (amateur) 14.01.33 (pro)

Whilst a teenager Jack was scouted by Middlesbrough, but declined the opportunity to join them, preferring instead to remain at home and sign for Belfast Celtic. By 1927 he was playing regularly at inside left for the Irish League side Portadown and attracted sufficient attention that he earned the first of his seven Northern Ireland Amateur caps on 12th November against England in a 1-1 draw at Blackpool. He was called up for his country in each of the next five years and in 1932, whilst a Cliftonville player, played twice for the full Northern Irish side, the first occasion being a narrow 1-0 defeat against a strong England team which included the legendary Dixie Dean and the second a 4-1 defeat to Wales in Wrexham on 7th December.
12 days later Jack signed for Charlton and made his debut at inside forward in the 1-0 win over Oldham Athletic in January. This was a rare bright spot in a troubled season as

Charlton were already languishing at the foot of Division 2. The situation did not improve and relegation was confirmed when five of the last six games were all lost. By the start of 1933-34 Jimmy Seed had taken over as secretary manager, but Jack had to wait until April before returning to the side, this time at left half and he featured on the winning side in each of his four appearances. Evidently his contribution was not enough to impress Seed however and he was never called up to the first team again.
In May 1935 Charlton gave Jack a free transfer and initially there was interest from New Brighton, but when nothing came of it, he is believed to have turned his back on football and returned home to Ireland. A man named J Doherty did serve on the club management committee at Cliftonville for several years in the 1960s and may have been our Jack.

Season	Division	League		FA Cup		D3 Cup		Total	
		A	G	A	G	A	G	A	G
1932-33 (R)	Division 2	4	0	0	0			4	0
1933-34	Divison 3 (S)	4	0	0	0	0	0	4	0
Total		8	0	0	0	0	0	8	0

UK LEAGUE CAREER 8 games 0 goals

CHARLTON CAREER
Managers: *A Lindon, J Seed*
Debut: *Oldham Athletic (H) 21-01-1933*
V165
Finale: *Swindon Town (H) 02-05-1934*

DOUGHTY Alfie Henry Harman　　　　2018 - 20

A versatile and energetic young footballer, Alfie enjoyed the full experience of Charlton's outstanding youth academy and by the age of 17 was competing in not only the U18 but also the U23 side, both of which finished as runners-up in their respective leagues in 2016-17. He made his first team debut as a substitute in the League Cup at MK Dons on 14th August 2018 and although on that night the young Charlton side were shown to be somewhat out of their depth against more experienced opposition, he did enough to leave the impression that there was a lot more to come from him.

Midfield　6' 0"
Born: 21-12-1999 - Hatfield, Hertfordshire

HONOURS
Charlton Athletic U18 2015-16, 2016-17 & 2017-18 Runners Up PD League 2 South
Charlton Athletic U18 2015-16 Winners PD National League 2
Charlton Athletic U23 2016-17 Winners PD League 2 South
Charlton Athletic U23 2017-18 Runners Up PD League 2 South
Charlton Athletic 2020 Young Player Of The Year

CLUBS
Charlton Athletic (youth) 05.18 (pro) ••Kingstonian 19.10.18 (loan) ••Bromley 07.09.19 (loan) ••Stoke City 22.01.21 (undisclosed) ••Cardiff City 29.01.22 (loan)

Alfie made his full debut against Forest Green Rovers at the Valley in another League Cup match on 13th August 2019. It was an uninspiring 0-0 draw and Charlton made their usual early exit from the competition via the penalty shoot out. Alfie played the whole 90 minutes at full back and clearly enhanced his reputation because three months later when the first team were decimated by injury, he was given his chance as a second half substitute in the Championship game with Cardiff City on 23rd November and he impressed with a spirited display in a much more attacking role. That was the start of a run of games in which he continued to shine and by the end of that season he was a shoo-in for the first team and was becoming an increasingly important member of the squad.
He played in ten matches at the start of 2020-21 and was

becoming a potent attacking threat thanks to his extreme pace and crossing ability. Alfie scored in the 2-0 away win against a Crewe Alexandra side which included Charlie Kirk on 12th September, but tore a hamstring during the match at Northampton on 24th October 2020 and never played for Charlton again. There had already been enquiries from Celtic and in January 2021 the still injured player signed for Stoke City for an undisclosed fee.
It was not until 7th August 2021 when fit again Alfie could make his Stoke debut. He was a second half substitute against Reading and this was to be his role for much of the early season. He never played 90 minutes in any of Stoke's league matches and on 29th January was sent out on loan to Cardiff City for the rest of 2021-22.

Season	Division	League		FA Cup		FL Cup		FL Trophy		Play Offs		Total	
		A	G	A	G	A	G	A	G	A	G	A	G
2018-19 (P)	League One	0	0	0	0	0 (1)	0	0	0	0	0	0 (1)	0
2019-20 (R)	Championship	20 (9)	2	0	0	1	0					21 (9)	2
2020-21	League One	7	1	0	0	2	0	0 (1)	0			9 (1)	1
Total		27 (9)	3	0	0	3 (1)	0	0 (1)	0	0	0	30 (11)	3

UK LEAGUE CAREER 36 games 3 goals

CHARLTON CAREER
Managers: *L Bowyer*
Debut: *Milton Keynes Dons (A) (sub) 14-08-2018*
V862
Finale: *Northampton Town (A) 24-10-2020*

DOWLING Thomas

1921 - 23

Midfield, Forward   12st 5lbs   5' 9"
Born: 1893 - Ireland
Died: 14-08-1945 - Plumstead, London
Education: St Patrick's School, Plumstead.

Tommy was the man for the big occasion and twice wrote his name into the record books. He made his debut for Charlton in their home league match on 4th September 1920 and scored twice, including the opening goal, in a 3-1 win against Brighton & Hove Albion. It was a Southern League fixture and their first at the Valley since becoming a professional club. It was also the only match in which he scored throughout the 1920-21 season. A year later he repeated the trick. Lining up at right half, he scored Charlton's first goal as a Football League club in the opening fixture against Exeter City on 27th August 1921. It secured them a 1-0 win and proved to be his only goal that season as well.

HONOURS

Woolwich League XI
Kent FA 1920-21, 1 cap (against London FA)

Charlton Athletic A 1923-24 Winners Kent League

CLUBS

Plumstead Hibernians 1907 ••Woolwich 1913 ••Charlton Athletic 1919 ••Indiana Flooring, USA 1924 ••Newark Skeeters, USA 1925 ••Calpe American, USA 1926

An Irishman whose family moved to South London in 1903, Tommy was brought up in Plumstead and played six years of local football before joining Kent League side Woolwich FC in 1913. They had leased the Manor ground after Arsenal had re-located to North London and were trying to fill the void caused through their departure. The outbreak of war put paid to this ambition however and in December 1915 Tommy was enlisted in the army, serving for four years in the Egyptian Expeditionary Force in Egypt, Palestine and Syria.

He joined Charlton after the war and played 23 Southern League and FA Cup games in the 1920-21 season including the 6-0 hammering of Catford Southend on 25th September in which Dick Upex scored a hat trick and he remained involved as the club fought to establish themselves in the Football League. However, first team appearances for Tommy became few and far between during his final two seasons with the club and he left on a free transfer at the end of 1923-24.

That signalled the end of Tommy's short career in English football but he moved out to the USA and played in the American Soccer League during the now forgotten period when Association Football briefly threatened the popularity of their own game and when crowds sometimes exceeded those for NFL matches.

These were the golden years of American Soccer but for Tommy who played for clubs such as Newark Skeeters and Indiana Flooring, it was only a brief interlude because when he returned home he had a leg amputated in the Brook Hospital on Shooters Hill. Charlton granted him a Benefit Match, a reserve team fixture played against Hounslow on Christmas morning 1928 and an exciting game finished 5-5 and produced gate receipts of £97.

Tommy Dowling was residing in Conway Road, Plumstead and working at the Royal Ordnance Factory in Woolwich at the time of his death through heart failure at the age of 52 and was buried on 18th August 1945.

Season	Division	League		FA Cup		Total	
		A	G	A	G	A	G
1921-22	Divison 3 (S)	17	1			17	1
1922-23	Divison 3 (S)	3	0	0	0	3	0
1923-24	Divison 3 (S)	1	0	0	0	1	0
Total		21	1	0	0	21	1

UK LEAGUE CAREER 21 games 1 goal

CHARLTON CAREER
Managers: *W Rayner*
Debut: *Southern League Brighton & Hove Albion (H) 04-09-1920 Football League Exeter City (H) 27-08-1921*
V004
Finale: *Swindon Town (A) 10-11-1923*

DOWMAN Stephen John

1983 - 85

Steve enjoyed four successful seasons in Colchester United's first team including their Division 4 promotion season of 1976-77, when he helped them clinch third place in the final game of the season. It was on 14th May and having defeated Bradford City 2-1 and thanks to their superior defensive record, they moved above them on goal average. Steve's contribution to the season also included 12 league goals, an unusually high return for a central defender.

Defender   12st 4lbs   5' 11"
Born: 15-04-1958 - Manor Park, Essex

HONOURS

Havering District Schools & Essex Youth
Essex FA Xl

Colchester United 1976-77 Promoted Division 4
Wrexham 1982-83 Finalists Welsh Cup

CLUBS

Colchester United (youth) 04.76 (pro) ••Wrexham 29.07.80 (£75,000) ••Charlton Athletic 26.08.83 (loan) 06.02.84 (£15,000) ••Newport County 08.85 (free) ••Cambridge United 10.85 (free) ••Brightlingsea United 1987 (player manager) ••Wivenhoe Town 1991 (free) ••Heybridge Swifts 1993 (free) ••Braintree Town 1994 (free0 ••Wivenhoe Town 1997 (manager)

A transfer fee of £75,000 took Steve to Wrexham in the Summer of 1980, but after hardly playing in his first year, he was obliged to endure a torrid two seasons in which the club crashed and burned, a double relegation dropping them straight from the Second into the Fourth Division. He was rescued from this nightmare by signing for Charlton and spent two years as a regular in the Addicks defence, although he would undoubtedly wish to forget the match at the Goldstone Ground on 1st October 1983 when a Brighton team, including Steve Gatting, handed them a 7-0 drubbing. Generally though, he held his own as a Second Division defender and a far happier occasion occurred on 2nd January 1984 when he scored the winner in a tough 1-0 victory at Derby.
It was the following season that Lennie Lawrence put together the side that took Charlton back to the First

Division after an absence of 29 years, but Steve was no longer at the club, having been swiftly moved on after a dispute with the manager. He finished his Football League career with Newport and Cambridge before dropping into non-league football and later had spells managing at Brightlingsea United and Wivenhoe Town
He took over running his father in law's carpet business in Brightlingsea and was later elected Vice Chairman of Brightlingsea United. In 2015, he was back at Colchester at the age of 57 to demonstrate the virtues of walking football.

Season	Division	League		FA Cup		FL Cup		Total	
		A	G	A	G	A	G	A	G
1983-84	Division 2	35	3	2	0	1	0	38	3
1984-85	Division 2	25 (1)	2	0 (1)	0	0	0	25 (2)	2
Total		60 (1)	5	2 (1)	0	1	0	63 (2)	5

UK LEAGUE CAREER 356 games 32 goals

CHARLTON CAREER
Managers: *L Lawrence*
Debut: *Brentford (A) 30-08-1983*
V447
Finale: *Manchester City (A) 11-05-1985*

DRINKWATER Charles John
1938

Forward   5' 4"
Born: 25-06-1914 - Willesden, London
Died: 08-04-1998 - Denham, Buckinghamshire

Charlie was part of the Willesden team who won the English Schools Shield in 1927 and this led to a trial for England Schoolboys. While still a teenager he featured regularly for Golders Green (now known as Hendon), where he amassed nearly 80 competitive appearances and in August 1934 toured the Netherlands with Middlesex Wanderers including fixtures against Ajax and Sparta Rotterdam. The following year he was capped by England Juniors against Scotland.

HONOURS

England Junior International 1935 1 cap
Willesden 1926-27 Winners English Schools Shield

Middlesex Wanderers XI 1934 Tour of Netherlands
Ruislip Manor 1951-52 Runners Up London League

CLUBS

Willesden 1927 (youth) ••Hampstead 1932 (amateur) ••Northfleet United 1933 (amateur) ••Golders Green 05.33 (amateur) ••Middlesex Wanderers 1934 (touring team) ••Brentford 24.08.34 (amateur) ••Walthamstow Avenue 1935 (amateur) ••Aston Villa 08.35 (amateur) 10.35 (pro) ••Charlton Athletic 30.07.38 (free) ••Walsall c 1939 ••Gillingham 1939 ••Watford 02.41 ••Pinner 02.48 (trainer) ••Ruislip Manor 04.52 (player manager)

It was after joining Aston Villa in 1935 that Charlie turned professional and he made what was a dream debut on 16th November in a Division 1 match against Chelsea, lining up at outside left alongside former Charlton marksman Dai Astley. Only three minutes into the game he scored with almost his first kick and Villa went on to earn a much needed 2-2 draw as they battled against relegation. He held his place the following week when Astley scored twice against Birmingham, but got no further chances in the first team.

He signed for Charlton in July 1938 and was given an early debut because regular left winger Harold Hobbis was recovering from a broken leg. Goals from George Tadman and Monty Wilkinson gave Charlton a 2-0 win against

Leeds United on 3rd September, but after just two further appearances Hobbis returned from his injury and there was no more room for Charlie in a team which would finish the season third in the First Division and as the top London club.

During World War 2 he served in the Royal Navy as a physical training instructor but also played some matches for Watford during this period. His final Football League appearance came for Watford in October 1946 after which he concentrated on his career as a remedial gymnast, eventually working for 30 years at Mount Vernon Hospital in Northwood. Charlie passed away in Denham at the age of 83.

Season	Division	League		FA Cup		Total	
		A	G	A	G	A	G
1938-39	Division 1	3	0	0	0	3	0
Total		3	0	0	0	3	0

UK LEAGUE CAREER 6 games 1 goal

CHARLTON CAREER
Managers: *J Seed*
Debut: *Leeds United (H) 03-09-1938*
V202
Finale: *Wolverhampton Wanderers (H) 10-12-1938*

DUDLEY William Ernest

1924

Erith & Belvedere had only been formed in 1922 and during just their second season in the Kent League battled through to the final of the FA Amateur Cup. They defeated London Caledonians in a marathon semi-final which stretched to three matches and their centre half Billy Dudley was a key figure in this unlikely scenario. He scored in the first match which ended 1-1 and then after a goalless replay, was among the scorers as Caledonians were finally put to the sword, 3-1 in the second replay at Stamford Bridge. The final took place on 5th April 1924, but they were well-beaten by Clapton and went down 3-0. This cup final capped an exciting month for Billy as he had earlier played two Football League matches for Charlton Athletic as well.

Defender   12st 7lbs   6' 0"
Born: 12-08-1893 - Luton, Bedfordshire
Died: 04-06-1960 - Dartford, Kent

HONOURS
Erith & Belvedere 1923-24 Finalists FA Amateur Cup

CLUBS
Erith & Belvedere 08.23 (amateur) ••West Ham United (amateur) ••Charlton Athletic 02.24 (amateur) ••Bradford City 12.04.24 (pro)

Billy was still serving in the army at Woolwich, when at the age of 30 he made his debut for Erith & Belvedere on 28th August 1923 in a Kent League fixture against Northfleet. During his time with the Deres he also made occasional appearances for West Ham and for the Army. In one memorable week in October 1923 he turned out for an Army XI against Aston Villa on the Wednesday, for West Ham Reserves on the Thursday and for Erith on the Saturday. He probably came to the attention of Charlton when the two clubs met on Christmas Day. At that point Charlton's Kent League side (reserves) were in excellent form and had won all their first ten matches, only to come unstuck when Erith unexpectedly beat them 2-1.
After signing as an amateur, Billy made his Charlton debut in a reserve fixture against Crystal Palace on 28th February 1924. After two reserve outings he was promoted to the first team for the away fixture with Bristol Rovers on 8th March and although this resulted in a 2-0 defeat, did well enough to hold his place for the home game with Portsmouth two days later. This was played at the Mount in Catford and a goal from Bobby Thomson enabled the Addicks to salvage a 1-1 draw. The reason for Billy's swift acceleration into the first team was the untimely exit of former skipper Arthur Whalley who had been granted a free transfer at his own request and his sudden absence

created an urgent need for a centre half.
Two days after Billy played his second and final first team match for Charlton, the club signed another central defender, namely George Armitage from Wimbledon, who was already an England Amateur international and being more than four years younger must have been viewed as the better prospect. With his army days behind him, Billy was free to sign a professional contract and seven days after the FA Amateur Cup final joined, not Charlton as had been expected, but Bradford City, who also snapped up his Erith teammate, inside forward Stan Hillier.
Hillier went on to enjoy a modest career with Bradford City and Gillingham, but Billy failed to make the grade in the pro game and never appeared in a first team match for the Bantams. He was already a married man having wed Emily Seabrook in 1913, but instead of a football career, he found work as a long distance lorry driver. By 1939 he was living in Dunstable and also operating as a special constable in the police. He passed away in Dartford at the age of 66.

Season	Division	League		FA Cup		Total	
		A	G	A	G	A	G
1923-24	Divison 3 (S)	2	0	0	0	2	0
Total		2	0	0	0	2	0

UK LEAGUE CAREER 2 games 0 goals

CHARLTON CAREER
Managers: *W Rayner*
Debut: *Bristol Rovers (A) 08-03-1924*
V056
Finale: *Portsmouth (H) 10-03-1924*

DUFF William

1956 - 62

Goalkeeper   12st 6lb   5' 11"
Born: 06-02-1935 - Winchburgh, West Lothian
Died: 30-08-2004 - Edinburgh, Scotland
Education: Corstorphine Primary School & Boroughmuir High School,
Edinburgh.

Willie started life as a full back
and became a goalkeeper by
accident when a teammate
failed to turn up for a match.
He was spotted by Hearts

while playing in the East of Scotland League for Easthouses Lily and working as a joiner. Within two years he was their first choice between the sticks, collecting two cup winners medals and representing the Scottish League in a 5-0 win over the League of Ireland.

HONOURS

Scotland U23 International 1955 1 cap
Scotland League v League of Ireland 1954
British Army 1957-58 2 caps

Hearts 1954-55 Winners Scottish League Cup
Hearts 1955-56 Winners Scottish FA Cup

CLUBS

Juniper Green YMCA, Scotland 1950 (youth) ••Slateford Athletic, Scotland 1950 (youth) ••Easthouses Lily, Scotland 1951 (youth) ••Heart Of Midlothian, Scotland 08.52 (£200) ••Charlton Athletic 15.12.56 (loan) 06.02.58 (£6,500) ••Peterborough United 14.05.63 (£2,000) ••Dunfermline Athletic, Scotland 1967 (free) ••Raith Rovers, Scotland 1971 (non contract) ••East Stirlingshire, Scotland 1971 (non contract) ••Albion Rovers, Scotland 1973 (non contract)

Willie was called up for his National Service in 1956 and was posted to London with the Royal Horse Artillery. It became too difficult for him to commute to Edinburgh and play for Hearts, as a result of which he was loaned to Charlton at the very time that they were struggling to fill the void left by the retirement of Sam Bartram earlier that year. He fitted in so well that he became first choice goalkeeper for nearly six years and a firm favourite with the fans, his permanent transfer from Hearts being completed after his Army commitments were concluded.

Very much a larger than life character, Willie was playing in a highly charged FA Cup tie at the Valley on 24th January 1959 and taking a physical battering from the opposing forwards until eventually he sought his own justice and laid out Everton's Dave Hickson with a well aimed punch. Without waiting for the referee's whistle he peeled off his jersey and headed for the tunnel. Players were rarely sent off in those days and his actions led to a 14-day suspension during which his wages were stopped by the club.

In season 1959-60 he was ever present in league and cup matches, but eventually Willie lost his place in the Charlton team to Peter Wakeham and moved on to a successful spell with Peterborough for whom he made more than 100 appearances.

He then returned to Scotland with Dunfermline and appeared for them in the semi final of the European Cup Winners Cup against Slovan Bratislava in 1968-69. He retired the following year, but still found himself in demand making brief comebacks with Raith Rovers, East Stirlingshire and Albion Rovers as cover for goalkeeping injuries.

When he was finally allowed to retire, Willie ran a joinery business in Edinburgh for several years before emigrating to the USA in the eighties to be near his son who lived in Washington. He returned to Scotland in 2003 in time for he and his wife Elma to celebrate their golden wedding anniversary. Willie Duff died suddenly at the age of 69, after collapsing during a game of bowls.

Season	Division	League		FA Cup		FL Cup		Total	
		A	G	A	G	A	G	A	G
1956-57 (R)	Division 1	20	0	2	0			22	0
1957-58	Division 2	41	0	3	0			44	0
1958-59	Division 2	33	0	3	0			36	0
1959-60	Division 2	42	0	2	0			44	0
1960-61	Division 2	39	0	1	0	1	0	41	0
1961-62	Division 2	38	0	3	0	3	0	44	0
Total		213	0	14	0	4	0	231	0

UK LEAGUE CAREER 447 games 0 goals

CHARLTON CAREER
Managers: *J Trotter, F Hill*
Debut: *Aston Villa (H) 15-12-1956*
V272
Finale: *Liverpool (A) 30-04-1962*

DUFFIELD Martin John   1984

Martin played in the same Queens Park Rangers youth team as Alan McDonald and early on both men also had spells on loan at Charlton. He showed considerable promise as a young player, even representing England at youth level against Scotland, but unlike McDonald who went on to enjoy a long and productive career, Martin never came close to establishing himself and managed in total, less than 10 league and cup appearances for his three Football League clubs.

Forward   11st 3lbs   5' 8"
Born: 28-02-1964 - Park Royal, London

HONOURS
England Youth International 1982 1 cap 0 goal;s
Enfield 1985-86 Winners Alliance Premier League
St Albans City 1992-93 Runners Up Isthmian League Premier Division

CLUBS
Tottenham Hotspur 21.08.79 (youth) ••Queens Park Rangers 27.02.80 (youth) 01.82 (pro) ••AFC Bournemouth 09.83 (loan) ••Charlton Athletic 15.11.84 (loan) ••Enfield 07.85 ••Hendon 06.88 ••Sutton United 10.91 ••St Albans City 03.92 ••Hendon 12.95

When Martin arrived at Charlton they were on a run of six league games without a win and manager Lennie Lawrence put him straight into the side at right back for the home match with Birmingham City. Unusually he wore the number 8 on his back as this was still the era when shirt numbers signified the position of the wearer. Goals from Mark Aizlewood and Robert Lee helped clinch a 2-1 victory, but Martin did not make sufficient impact to justify a second appearance and soon returned to Queens Park Rangers leaving utility player Steve Gritt to fill the void at right back.

This was his last match in the Football League, but he did achieve some success in the non-league game, especially with Enfield and St Albans City, the latter finishing runners-up in the Isthmian League in season 1992-93, only to be denied promotion into the Football Conference for health and safety reasons because of a 140-year-old oak tree that occupied part of the terracing behind one goal.
Martin left St Albans at the start of the 1995-96 season and took a coaching job in the USA, later returning and finding work with a hire company.

Season	Division	League		FA Cup		FL Cup		Total	
		A	G	A	G	A	G	A	G
1984-85	Division 2	1	0	0	0	0	0	1	0
Total		1	0	0	0	0	0	1	0

UK LEAGUE CAREER 8 games 1 goal

CHARLTON CAREER
Managers: *L Lawrence*
Debut: *Birmingham City (H) 17-11-1984*
V460

DUFFY Christopher   1946 - 52

Forward   10st 7lbs   5' 5"
Born: 21-10-1918 - Wemyss, Fife.
Died: 20-02-1978 - Bangor, County Down

A diminutive Scottish winger, Chris wrote himself large in Charlton's history on 26th April 1947 at Wembley Stadium in front of a crowd of 98,215. The occasion was the 1946-47 FA Cup Final against Burnley and in the 24th minute of extra time and with the score goalless, he volleyed the ball into the top of the net to clinch victory. This remains the club's only FA Cup win and is one of the pivotal moments in the Charlton Athletic story. The match itself was far from a classic, but Chris ensured that it was a day to savour, especially as even now more than 70 years later, Charlton remains the only one of the three South East London league clubs to enjoy FA Cup glory.

HONOURS

Charlton Athletic (guest) 1943-44 Winners FL South Cup
Charlton Athletic (guest) 1943-44 Joint Winners Alexander Cup
Charlton Athletic 1945-46 Finalists FA Cup
Charlton Athletic 1946-47 Winners FA Cup
Charlton Athletic Reserves 1949-50 Winners Football Combination

Charlton Athletic Reserves 1949-50 Runners Up Football Combination Cup
Charlton Athletic Reserves 1950-51 Winners London FA Challenge Cup
Charlton Athletic Reserves 1950-51 Winners Football Combination Cup
Leith Athletic 1938-39 Winners Rosebery Charity Cup
Glenavon (guest) 1939-40 Finalists Irish FA Cup

CLUBS

Wemyss Strollers, Scotland 1933 (youth) ••Wellesley Juniors, Scotland 1934 (semi-pro) ••Leith Athletic, Scotland 1936 (semi-pro) ••Charlton Athletic 04.09.45 (£530) ••Bangor, N Ireland 04.53 (player manager)

Born in the parish of Wemyss, on the South coast of Fife, Chris's father Patrick Duffy was chairman of the Fife & Lothians Junior Football Association and a respected local football administrator. He was also secretary/manager of Wellesley Juniors for whom young Chris played for three seasons commencing in 1934-35. Slight of build, he stood just a fraction over five foot five, but despite this obvious physical handicap, he was a talented winger with pace and tricks to concentrate the mind of any opposing defender. His brother Bertie Duffy was a full back who played in the same Wellesley team and during 1935 played for Scotland Juniors against England at the Hawthorns. However, in January 1937 it was Chris who had trials with both Hibernian and Leith Athletic, before signing for the latter on the 18th of that month

Leith is a port area to the north of Edinburgh and in the years leading up to World War 2 was home to a semi-professional team which competed in the Scottish League Division 2. Chris slotted straight into their first team and although their results did not set the world alight, he gained valuable experience and made 63 league appearances and scored 13 goals up to the end of 1938-39.

He signed up for the Royal Welsh Fusiliers and spent the first part of the war posted to Northern Ireland where he made guest appearances for both Linfield and Glenavon. The latter reached the final of the Irish FA Cup and on

20th April 1940 Chris was in the Glenavon side that went down 2-0 to Ballymena United at Windsor Park, Belfast. He represented the NI Army against the British Army in September 1941 and turned out as a guest for Walsall in 1942. He remained a Leith player however and while back in Scotland made a couple of wartime appearances for them in 1941-42.

Stationed at Maidstone for the second half of the war, Chris played his first game for Charlton in October 1942 against Brighton. He was one of four guest players that day and the team did not play well, but he continued to be called up with increasing regularity and on 30th January 1943 added to strikes by Jackie Dryden and Charlie Revell as Millwall were defeated 3-0. Charlton reached the final of the Football League (South) Cup that season but Chris was not in the side that was hopelessly outplayed 7-1 by Arsenal. In 1943-44 they made it to Wembley again and this time he played in the final, Chelsea being vanquished 3-1 in front of 85,000 people, courtesy of goals from Charlie Revell (2) and Don Welsh. The winners of the FL South and FL North Cups then met at Stamford Bridge to contest the Alexander Cup. The Charlton team was unchanged and the opponents Aston Villa. The match ended 1-1 and the cup was shared.

After playing nearly 50 wartime matches for Charlton in his first two seasons, Chris did not play at all in 1944-45 and the reason was a self-imposed injury that occurred at the time of the D-Day landings. As the plane in which he was travelling prepared its descent, he accidentally shot himself, but happily he recovered and in September 1945 was finally transferred from Leith Athletic for a fee of £330. The arrangement was that Charlton would also play a match against Leith, but when that could not be arranged they paid a further £200 in compensation which raised the total transfer fee to £530, (excellent value as it turned out). In all he made 81 wartime league and cup appearances, none of which are counted as official matches, but with the re-introduction of the FA Cup for 1945-46 he finally got to make his official debut against Fulham in January 1946. He scored the opening goal in a 3-1 win.

Any self-respecting Charlton supporter is aware of Duffy's goal in the Cup Final of 1947, but considerably fewer people appreciate his personal contribution to the FA Cup run in the first post-war season of 1945-46. Charlton played a total of 10 FA Cup ties, and he played in them all and scored 10 goals, the most ever by a Charlton player in a single season in that competition. In the 2-0 semi-final win over Bolton Wanderers he scored both goals and his second strike came after he had dribbled past five defenders and was described by Jimmy Seed as the best he had ever seen. The final against Derby County was a big disappointment,

but 12 months later Chris's winning goal at Wembley made up for it. His form during 1946-47 was excellent and he was the only player who was ever present throughout.

Chris was a regular in the Charlton team for two further years and shared in some memorable wins, such as the 4-0 hammering of Sunderland on 30th October 1948 and a very exciting 4-3 win over Arsenal six weeks later. He scored twice that day, including the winner 10 minutes from time, while the other Charlton goals came from Harold Phipps and Sid O'Linn. It was the arrival of Billy Kiernan in July 1949 that was the beginning of the end for Chris and from then on he ceased to be first choice at outside left (although they both played for much of 1950-51).

He remained at the club until April 1953 when he accepted a post as player manager of Bangor in the Irish League. Charlton had earlier turned down a combined fee of £6,000 from Crystal Palace for both Duffy and Tommy Brown in June 1950. In reality however his playing days were almost over and he had to undergo a cartilage operation after just one game in Ireland. He resigned in 1955 and became a publican for many years. His pub was bombed on two occasions, with fatalities, during the Irish troubles. Chris passed away on 20th February 1978 at the age of 59.

Season	Division	League		FA Cup		Total	
		A	G	A	G	A	G
1945-46	Division 1			10	10	10	10
1946-47	Division 1	42	10	6	5	48	15
1947-48	Division 1	35	8	3	0	38	8
1948-49	Division 1	37	7	1	0	38	7
1949-50	Division 1	2	1	0	0	2	1
1950-51	Division 1	5	1	0	0	5	1
1951-52	Division 1	32	5	1	0	33	5
1952-53	Division 1	9	1	0	0	9	1
Total		162	33	21	15	183	48

UK LEAGUE CAREER 225 games 46 goals

CHARLTON CAREER
Managers: *J Seed*
Debut: *Wartime Brighton & Hove Albion (H) 31-10-1942 FA Cup Fulham (H) 05-01-1946*
V211
Finale: *West Bromwich Albion (H) 25-10-1952*

DUGDALE Alan   1977 - 78

Defender   12st 8lbs   5' 8"
Born: 11-09-1952 - Kirkby, Liverpool

Born in the Kirkby area of Liverpool, Alan was a hard man central defender who never shirked a challenge. He represented Kirkby Boys and after leaving school was signed by Coventry City at the age of 15. He was in the Coventry side which took part in the amazing FA Youth Cup final of 1970 against a Tottenham team which included Mike Flanagan. The score was all square after the two legs and stretched to not one but two replays, before they were finally defeated in the fourth match. The Coventry goalkeeper was David Icke, who went on to fame as the eccentric sports broadcaster and philosopher. Alan came from a footballing family. His uncle Jimmy had won the FA Cup with Aston Villa in 1957 while his brother Ken later managed the New Zealand national team.

HONOURS

England Youth International 1971 7 caps 0 goals

Kirkby Boys

Charlton Athletic Reserves 1979-80 Runners Up Mid-Week League

Coventry City Youth 1969-70 Runners Up FA Youth Cup

Bulova SA 1981-82 Winners Hong Kong FA Cup

CLUBS

Coventry City 1968 (youth) 06.11.69 (pro) ••Charlton Athletic 27.10.77 (£50,000) ••Barnsley 17.08.79 (loan) ••Tulsa Roughnecks, USA 1980 ••Bulova SA, Hong Kong 1981 ••Happy Valley, Hong Kong c1982

Despite being capped at right back for England at youth level, Alan found it hard to break into the Coventry first team and did not make his debut until September 1972, almost three years after turning professional. He gradually established himself as a 'no nonsense' centre half and was known affectionately, (although probably not to his face), as Alan 'Thugdale.' In an era of tough guy centre halves, he was among the most effective and despite his lack of inches, was surprisingly good in the air.

After five years, he lost his place in the Coventry team and dropped down to the Second Division with Charlton where he played regularly and effectively during the rather odd 1977-78 season, in which they managed to transform from promotion candidates in December to narrowly avoid relegation in the May.

Alan got into dispute with manager Andy Nelson and was transfer listed for a time, before eventually settling his

differences with the club. He was playing in a reserve team match at Brentford on 31st October 1978 when he broke his leg and although he recovered sufficiently to play a handful of games on loan at Barnsley, he never returned to first team duty with Charlton and turned down a £15,000 transfer to Hereford. His contract was cancelled in November 1979.

He then moved out to the USA and played a season of indoor soccer in the NASL for the Tulsa Roughnecks before joining the Hong Kong club, Bulova SA. They enjoyed a successful season, finishing third in Division 1, as well as winning the Hong Kong FA Cup Final of 1982 with a 2-1 victory over See Bee.

Alan remained in Tulsa, Oklahoma for several years after his playing days were over and worked as a salesman for Coca-Cola, but by 2014 had gone full circle and was back living in Kirkby.

Season	Division	League		FA Cup		FL Cup		Total	
		A	G	A	G	A	G	A	G
1977-78	Division 2	30	0	1	0	0	0	31	0
1978-79	Division 2	4	0	0	0	3	0	7	0
Total		34	0	1	0	3	0	38	0

UK LEAGUE CAREER 183 games 0 goals

CHARLTON CAREER

Managers: *A Nelson*

Debut: *Crystal Palace (A) 29-10-1977*

V407

Finale: *Luton Town (A) 02-09-1978*

DUNN Bertram Scott   1921 - 22

Bert was a Surrey boy and should not be confused with the
Scottish winger of the same name from Montrose, who
appeared in four League matches for Clapton Orient in 1925,
whereas our Bert, known as Scottie, played for Carshalton
Athletic either side of the First World War. Charlton Athletic were his only Football League club.

Midfield 11st 6lbs 5' 9"	
Born: 29-09-1893 - Carshalton, Surrey	
Died: 09-1976 - Merton, London	

HONOURS
Football League XI v Army FA XI 1921   Carshalton Athletic 1913-14 Finalists London FA Junior Cup

CLUBS
Carshalton United 1911 ••Charlton Athletic 1920

World War 1 was declared in July 1914 and Scottie enrolled
with the King's Royal Rifles the following month. After a
period in Ireland, his regiment was deployed to France and
they took part in the second and third battles of Ypres. He
was wounded and sent home to England in 1915 but
happily made a full recovery and in 1917 was able to return
to football with Carshalton Athletic.

He signed for Charlton in 1920 when they were still
competing in the Kent League and was just in time to
participate in the club's sudden rise from local fame to
national prominence as a member of the Football League.
He appeared in the opening game in season 1920-21 when,
as a professional club, they competed for the first time in
the Southern League making an impressive start, winning
2-1 at Norwich City.

Scottie was a regular member of the side throughout that
first campaign, appearing in all five of the FA Cup matches,
including the very first one played at the Valley on 25th
September 1920, when Catford Southend were dispatched
6-0. He and Johnny Mitchell were the only two who played
in that first Southern League fixture to also line up 12
months later against Exeter City, when Charlton made
their debut as a Football League club. He did not however
survive long and found intense competition for his spot at
left half from the veterans Walker Hampson and Harold
Halse. The disappointing home defeat against Luton
Town in April proved to be his swan song and he was given
a free transfer the following month.

Season	Division	League		Total	
		A	G	A	G
1921-22	Divison 3 (S)	8	0	8	0
Total		8	0	8	0

UK LEAGUE CAREER 8 games 0 goals

CHARLTON CAREER
Managers: *W Rayner*
Debut: *Southern League Norwich City (A) 28-08-1920 Football League Exeter City (H) 27-08-1921*
V006
Finale: *Luton Town (H) 22-04-1922*

DUNN John Alfred   1971 - 74

John was a popular figure at Charlton and in 1974
became one of the first winners of the club's
Player Of The Year award. Originally discovered
by Terry Venables' father who was scouting for
Chelsea, he represented Essex Schools and eventually spent nine years at Stamford Bridge. He
worked his way through the youth system and turned professional at the age of 17, but was
never able to hold down a regular first team place, although he performed well enough when
opportunities did arise, such as the FA Cup replay against Tottenham on 8th January 1964.
That day the Chelsea side, which included Marvin Hinton, won 2-0 in front of a crowd of
70,123.

Goalkeeper 12st 5lbs 6' 0"	
Born: 21-06-1944 - Barking, Essex	
Education: Eastbury Secondary School,. Barking.	

HONOURS

Barking Schools, Essex & London Schools
Charlton Athletic 1974 Player Of The Year

Aston Villa 1970-71 Finalists Football League Cup

CLUBS

Chelsea (youth) c1957 (youth) 30.01.62 (pro) ••Torquay United 21.10.66 (free) ••Aston Villa 19.01.68 (£8,000) ••Charlton Athletic 17.07.71 (free) ••Ramsgate 07.12.74 (loan) ••Tooting & Mitcham United 02.75 (free) ••Woking 1975 (player coach) ••Grays Athletic 1976 (player coach) ••Craven 1977

With his progress at Chelsea blocked by the excellent form of Peter Bonetti, John was obliged to seek his fortune elsewhere and moved on, first to Torquay United and then Aston Villa where he joined a club in decline. They crashed to relegation from Division 2 in 1969-70, a season when Charlton were facing a similar possibility and this made the league encounter at the Valley on 14th March 1970 all the more important. A tight game finished 1-0 and was decided by a Keith Peacock goal which ultimately proved vital as the Londoners finished the season one place and just two points above Villa.

The following season Villa were expected to stroll through Division 3 but could only manage 4th place, John played in almost every game but their promotion prospects were not helped by an amazing run in the League Cup which added 10 matches to their schedule. They defeated a star studded Manchester United in the semi-final and John played at Wembley in the final before a capacity crowd of 100,000 on 27th February 1971, but an impressive Tottenham Hotspur ran out winners 2-0.

After switching to the Valley in July 1971, he found himself back in the same relegation struggle as two years before, but this time Charlton's luck ran out and John was relegated from Division 2 for the second time in three years. He retained his place in goal for two further seasons as the club looked to regain Second Division status, but ironically his eventual fall from grace came just as Andy Nelson's promotion side was coming together.

He started the promotion season of 1974-75 as first choice 'keeper and chalked up four consecutive clean sheets during August but it was the trip to Manchester United in the League Cup on 11th September when it all went wrong. Despite taking an early lead, Charlton took an awful mauling that day, eventually losing 5-1 and John's confidence seemed badly affected by the experience. He only made three further appearances in the first team before being replaced first by Mike Franklin and then by the impressive teenager Graham Tutt. By the end of that season, as Charlton celebrated the return to Division 2, John had already departed to non-league Tooting & Mitcham, his career in the Football League at an end.

In 1986, he was refereeing in the Essex Business Houses League and later worked as a PE teacher at Stewards Comprehensive School in Harlow. More recently he was living in Basildon and a PE teacher at Barking Abbey Sports College.

Season	Division	League		FA Cup		FL Cup		Total	
		A	G	A	G	A	G	A	G
1971-72 (R)	Division 2	30	0	2	0	0	0	32	0
1972-73	Division 3	37	0	4	0	5	0	46	0
1973-74	Division 3	30	0	1	0	0	0	31	0
1974-75 (P)	Division 3	7	0	0	0	2	0	9	0
Total		104	0	7	0	7	0	118	0

UK LEAGUE CAREER 262 games 0 goals

CHARLTON CAREER
Managers: *T Foley, A Nelson*
Debut: *Sunderland (H) 19-10-1971*
V365
Finale: *Swindon Town (H) 21-09-1974*

DUNPHY Eamonn Martin   1973 - 75

Starting out as a 'Busby Babe' at Manchester United, Eamonn was a skilful and intelligent player. When he failed to break into their first team, he switched to York City where he

Midfield   8st 13lbs   5' 8"
Born: 03-08-1945 - Dublin, Ireland
Education: St Patrick's National School, Drumcondra.

earned the first of his 23 Irish International caps, but it was at Millwall where he spent the lion's share of his career, making over 300 competitive appearances in a stay of nearly eight years. He was part of the Millwall side that won promotion from Division 3 in 1966.

HONOURS

Republic of Ireland International 1965-71 23 caps 0 goals
Republic of Ireland U23 International 1966 1 cap 0 goals
Charlton Athletic 1974-75 Promoted Division 3

Millwall 1965-66 Runners Up Division 3
Reading 1975-76 Promoted Division 4
Shamrock Rovers 1977-78 Winners FAI Cup

CLUBS

Stella Maris, Ireland (youth) ••Manchester United 1960 (youth) 07.08.62 (pro) ••York City 12.08.65 (£4,000) ••Millwall 20.01.66 (£6,000) ••Charlton Athletic 29.11.73 (£16,666) ••Reading 02.07.75 (free) ••Shamrock Rovers, Ireland 07.77 (player coach)

Eamonn spent the best part of two seasons at the Valley and was a member of Andy Nelson's 1975 promotion side that finished third in Division 3, appearing regularly up to Christmas before losing his place, only to be recalled for three crucial games late in the season. A special train and 20 coaches travelled to Chesterfield on 26th April hoping to see Charlton clinch promotion, but it all went wrong after Arthur Horsfield conceded a penalty and this 2-0 defeat proved to be Eamonn's last match for the club. Promotion was finally confirmed three days later at the Valley against Preston.

After two seasons with Reading, which included promotion from Division 4 in 1976, Eamonn finished his playing career back in Ireland. He joined Shamrock Rovers and helped the Dublin club to a 1-0 victory in the FAI Cup against Sligo Rovers. It was played at Dalymount Park on 30th April 1978 and the goal was scored by Ray Treacy, another ex-Charlton player.

Since retiring as a player, he has remained very much in the public eye, appearing regularly on Irish television as a football pundit and analyst on programmes like 'Premier

Soccer Saturday', as well as in 2001 hosting the popular quiz show 'The Weakest Link'. Among several other TV projects, he was even granted his own Friday night chat show, 'The Dunphy Show' on TV3 which ran for a short time in 2003. The following year he took over as host of 'The Breakfast Show' on the Dublin radio station Newstalk 106.

Eamon, (somewhere along the way he mislaid an N), has for many years written newspaper columns on both football and current affairs in a variety of journals including the 'Sunday Independent' and the' Irish Daily Star'. He is author of numerous books. His 'Only A Game? Diary Of A Professional Footballer' received critical acclaim and he has also written a best selling biography of the rock band, U2. He was the ghostwriter of Roy Keane's autobiography, wrote 'A Strange Kind Of Glory' about Matt Busby and in 2013 published his own life story 'The Rocky Road'.

Now retired, he and his second wife Jane divide their time between homes in Ranelagh, near Dublin and Deauville in France.

Season	Division	League		FA Cup		FL Cup		Total	
		A	G	A	G	A	G	A	G
1973-74	Division 3	22 (2)	2	0	0	0	0	22 (2)	2
1974-75 (P)	Division 3	17 (1)	1	2	0	2	0	21 (1)	1
Total		39 (3)	3	2	0	2	0	43 (3)	3

UK LEAGUE CAREER 415 games 33 goals

CHARLTON CAREER

Managers: *T Foley, A Nelson*
Debut: *Port Vale (H) 01-12-1973*
V386
Finale: *Chesterfield (A) 26-04-1975*

DURANDT Clifford Michael

1963 - 64

Forward
Born: 16-04-1940 - Johannesburg, South Africa
Died: 03-10-2002 - Johannesburg, South Africa
Education: Edward VII School, Johannesburg

As a youngster Cliff excelled at sport, representing Transvaal at both swimming and rugby and in May 1957 appearing for a South Africa XI against a touring Wolverhampton Wanderers team. Although Wolves won the match 7-3, Cliff scored two goals and made such an impression that a month later they signed him. Competition for places proved intense as Wolves went on to win the Division 1 Championship in each of the next two years but he finally made his debut against Manchester United on 4th October 1958 in the first Saturday evening game played in the Football League.

HONOURS

Wolverhampton Wanderers 1957 Winners FA Charity Shield
Wolverhampton Wanderers 1957-58 Winners FA Youth Cup

Charlton Athletic A 1963-64 Winners Metropolitan League

CLUBS

Marist Brothers, South Africa 1956 (youth) ••Wolverhampton Wanderers 17.06.57 (pro) ••Charlton Athletic 26.03.63 (£15,000) ••Germiston Callies, South Africa 12.02.65 (£4,000) ••Highlands Park, South Africa 1967 ••State House Tornados, Rhodesia 1968 ••Durban United, South Africa 1969 ••Maritzburg, South Africa 1969

Charlton were in serious danger of relegation when Cliff was signed from Wolves in March 1963 and despite his contributing the winning goals against both Cardiff City and Huddersfield Town, a run of seven games for only one point soon made the position look hopeless. With only two games remaining, the match at the Valley against Southampton on 18th May was a do-or-die affair and with only a minute left and the score locked at 1-1, he completed his Roy of the Rovers act with a freak, seemingly mishit winner that kept Charlton afloat and the great escape was completed at Walsall six days later.

Cliff only scored one further goal for the club and

eventually expressed the wish to return to South Africa When the transfer negotiations stalled, his mother flew over from South Africa and paid £4,000 to buy his registration from Charlton in what must be a quite unique football transfer.

Back home, Cliff continued his career with Germiston Callies and for a short spell played for State House Tornados in Rhodesia. He passed away following a heart attack at the age of 62. His son, Nick Du Randt, who was born in England during Cliff's time at Charlton, went on to become a world famous boxing promoter.

Season	Division	League		FA Cup		FL Cup		Total	
		A	G	A	G	A	G	A	G
1962-63	Division 2	13	3	0	0	0	0	13	3
1963-64	Division 2	11	0	0	0	0	0	11	0
1964-65	Division 2	12	1	0	0	0	0	12	1
Total		36	4	0	0	0	0	36	4

UK LEAGUE CAREER 79 games 14 goals

CHARLTON CAREER

Managers: *F Hill*

Debut: *Portsmouth (H) 30-03-1963*
V299
Finale: *Cardiff City (A) 07-11-1964*

DWYER Noel Michael   1965 - 66

Noel's footballing journey commenced at Stella Maris, the famous Dublin club which over the years has found and developed several top players, including another Charlton footballer, Eamonn Dunphy. His break came when he joined Wolverhampton Wanderers and during 1957-58 was given a run of five first team games which included the 4-0 victory over a weakened Manchester United, this coming only weeks after the Munich air crash. Wolves were Division 1 champions that season but with no immediate prospect of displacing regular goalie, Malcolm Finlayson, he moved to West Ham in December 1958.

Goalkeeper   12st 10lbs   5' 11"
Born: 30-10-1934 - Dublin, Ireland
Died: 27-12-1992 - Wolverhampton, Staffordshire

HONOURS

Republic of Ireland International 1959-64 14 caps 0 goals
Republic of Ireland B international 1957 1 cap 0 goals

Swansea Town 1960-61 Winners Welsh Cup

CLUBS

Stella Maris, Ireland (youth) ••Ormeau United, Ireland 1952 ••Wolverhampton Wanderers 13.08.53 (pro) ••West Ham United 18.12.58 ••Swansea Town 02.08.60 (£3,500) ••Plymouth Argyle 02.01.65 (£7,500) ••Charlton Athletic 07.12.65 (free) ••Ammanford 07.69

During 1959, Noel became an established first team player at West Ham and earned the first of his 14 Irish international caps. His career appeared to be progressing well until a disastrous home match against Newcastle United on 20th February 1960 when everything fell apart. A scoreline of 5-3 to the visitors was bad enough, but it was his errors that were largely responsible and some wild allegations of match fixing were made in the media although never substantiated. However, he did not play for the West Ham first team again and joined Swansea Town at the end of the season.

Noel's time with Swansea was much less controversial and included victory in the Welsh Cup final of 1960-61 when Bangor were beaten 3-1, but his next move to Plymouth Argyle was again far from smooth. Signed by their manager Malcolm Allison, he became very unpopular with the Plymouth fans and when Allison was forced to resign and replaced by another ex-Charlton figure, Derek Ufton, he was rapidly jettisoned off to London SE7 after less than a

year in the West Country.

Charlton were experiencing a goalkeeping crisis throughout season 1965-66 and ended up using no less than five different custodians in an attempt to steady the defence. Noel got his chance in December, but only managed four further appearances before being sidelined following a cartilage operation as the club battled against relegation. Happily this was avoided, but with Charlie Wright taking over in goal during April, Noel's chance was gone and he announced his retirement in the summer of 1966 on medical grounds.

He reappeared briefly for Ammanford in the Welsh League during 1969 and for a time became licensee of the Trafalgar pub in the village of Wimblebury, near Cannock. Noel died in 1992 at the age of 58, after a long battle with cancer. His son-in-law Frank Worthington was an England International during the 1970s, while his father-in-law Charlie Phillips played extensively for Wolves and was a Welsh International in the 1930s.

Season	Division	League		FA Cup		FL Cup		Total	
		A	G	A	G	A	G	A	G
1965-66	Division 2	6	0	1	0	0	0	7	0
Total		6	0	1	0	0	0	7	0

UK LEAGUE CAREER 213 games 0 goals

CHARLTON CAREER
Managers: *R Stokoe*
Debut: *Derby County (A) 11-12-1965*
V315
Finale: *Ipswich Town (A) 05-02-1966*

DYER Alexander Constantine   1990 - 93

Forward, Utility.   11st 12lbs   5' 11"
Born: 14-11-1965 - Forest Gate, London
Education: Forest Gate High School.

In a career that has lasted more than 40 years, Alex has been associated with more than a dozen Football League clubs and has been employed as both player, coach, sports scientist and manager. He signed his first contract as an apprentice at Watford in July 1982 and by 2021 was manager of Scottish Premier League club Kilmarnock and one of the scandalously small number of black footballers who have been able to attain a senior management position within the sport. He is universally popular and has twice worked at Charlton, first as a player when the club were re-building during and after the exile years and then as assistant to manager Chris Powell when they achieved promotion from League One in 2012.

HONOURS

Blackpool 1984-85 Runners Up Division 4
Crystal Palace 1989-90 Finalists Full Members Cup Southern Area

FC Maia 1996-97 Winners Segunda Divisao B
Notts County 1997-98 Winners Division 3

CLUBS

Watford 1977 (youth) ••Blackpool 20.10.83 (pro) ••Hull City 13.02.87 (£37,000) ••Crystal Palace 11.11.88 (£250,000) ••Charlton Athletic 29.09.90 (loan) 30.11.90 (£100,000) ••Oxford United 26.07.93 (free) ••Brighton & Hove Albion 1995 (free) ••Lincoln City 21.08.95 (free) ••Barnet 01.09.95 (free) ••FC Maia, Portugal 09.05.96 (free) ••Huddersfield Town 13.08.97 (free) ••Notts County 02.03.98 (free) ••Reading 2000 (youth coach) ••KIngstonian 01.12.00 (free) ••Hayes 11.01.01 (free) ••Dulwich Hamlet 28.03.01 (free) ••West Ham United 04.04 (sports scientist) 07.07 (coach) ••Charlton Athletic 31.01.11 (ass manager) ••Huddersfield Town 03.09.14 (ass manager) ••Welling United 07.07.17 (manager) ••KIlmarnock, Scotland 16.10.17 (ass manager) 17.12.19 (manager) ••Colchester United 15.06.21 (ass. manager)

Alex signed professional terms with Blackpool in 1983 and while still a teenager found a place in their first team, He featured on the left wing and scored eight invaluable goals when a year later they won promotion from Division 4 and continued to progress after moving to Hull City where he was sometimes played as a centre forward. A big money transfer to Crystal Palace came in November 1988 but did not really work out and after two years, during which he was unable to secure a regular place in the Palace team, he accepted a loan move to newly relegated Charlton in September 1990.

This was during the exile years and home games were being played at Crystal Palace's Selhurst Park ground where the team had made a poor start to the season. Alex went straight into the side at centre forward and played so well that the loan was quickly converted to a permanent transfer. He had an excellent first season with the club and scored seven goals as results steadily improved. They moved safely away from the threat of a further relegation but by 1991 Carl Leaburn had made the centre forward position his own and Alex went back out on the wing, although injury kept him away from the team for much of 1991-92. He featured more regularly after that but never quite re-captured the same level of performance and was given a free transfer in May 1993.

The second half of his playing career included a relegation

with Oxford United, but was largely unmemorable. He did spend a year in Portugal with FC Maia and contributed 12 goals in 28 matches as they topped the Segunda Divisao B, but after returning home, played mainly as a defender. He joined Notts County in March 1998 and along with Mark Robson and Andy Hughes helped them secure promotion from Division 3, but this proved to be his last League club as a player.

Two years were spent as a personal trainer and as a sports coach at Stockwell High School before in 1994 the opportunity arose to join West Ham United and work as assistant to their sports scientist. Alex had been a West Ham supporter all his life and with his former Charlton colleague Alan Pardew in the manager's chair, jumped at the chance to get back into the game. By September 2008 he was coaching the Reserves, but in January 2011 when Chris Powell was appointed Charlton manager, Alex returned to the Valley as his assistant.

This new partnership worked a treat as Powell led Charlton to the League One Championship in 2012 but two years later when owner Roland Duchatelet took over the club and dismissed Powell, Alex left shortly thereafter, only for the two men to pair up again as the management team at Huddersfield Town. In 2017, he was appointed assistant manager at Kilmarnock and in December 2019 he took over as manager. This lasted until January 2021 and he has since had a spell as assistant manager at Colchester United which came to an end on 18th January 2022.

Season	Division	League		FA Cup		FL Cup		FM Cup		AI Cup		Total	
		A	G	A	G	A	G	A	G	A	G	A	G
1990-91	Division 2	34 (1)	7	1	1	0	0	1	0			36 (1)	8
1991-92	Division 2	3 (10)	1	0	0	2	0	1	0			6 (10)	1
1992-93	Division 1	23 (7)	6	0	0	0 (1)	0			1 (1)	0	24 (9)	6
Total		60 (18)	14	1	1	2 (1)	0	2	0	1 (1)	0	66 (20)	15

UK LEAGUE CAREER 465 games 64 goals

CHARLTON CAREER
Managers: *L Lawrence, A Curbishley/S Gritt*
Debut: *Wolverhampton Wanderers (A)*
02-10-1990
V512
Finale: *Birmingham City (A) 08-05-1993*

EAGLES Christopher Mark   2015

Chris was a highly rated young player at Manchester United where he was at one time earmarked for stardom. He

Forward, Midfield   11st 0lbs   6' 0"
Born: 19-11-1985 - Hemel Hempstead, Hertfordshire
Education: Ashton on Mersey School, Manchester and University of Bolton. (honorary degree).

had natural ability, speed and a great awareness of the players around him, He even scored on his Premier League debut at Everton on 28th April 2007, but could not force his way into the team on a regular basis and eventually turned down a five-year contract extension and opted to seek his fortune elsewhere. This was a brave decision, but one which did not prove wholly successful. His exciting wing play was not always matched by sufficient attention to his defensive duties and in the end his footballing achievements fell short of those early expectations.

HONOURS

Manchester United 2004 Runners Up FA Community Shield
Watford 2005-06 Promoted Play Offs Championship

Burnley 2008-09 Promoted Play Offs Championship

CLUBS

Watford 1998 (youth) ••Manchester United 2000 (youth) 25.07.03 (pro) ••Watford 21.01.05 (loan) ••Sheffield Wednesday 04.08.05 (loan) ••Watford 06.01.06 (loan) ••NEC Nijmegen, Netherlands 31.08.06 (loan) ••Burnley 29.07.08 (£1.2 million) ••Bolton Wanderers 29.07.11 (£3 million) ••Blackpool 18.11.14 (free) ••Charlton Athletic 19.02.15 (free) ••Bury 19.10.15 (free) ••Accrington Stanley 05.08.16 (free) ••Port Vale 11.01.17 (free) ••Ross County, Scotland 23.11.17 (free) ••Oldham Athletic 27.07.19 (free)

Chris did not make many first team appearances during his time at Manchester United but did feature as a substitute in the FA Community Shield match held at the Millennium Stadium in Cardiff on 8th August 2004, where along with future Charlton loanee Jonathan Spector, they were well beaten 3-1 by Arsenal. Loans with Watford, Sheffield Wednesday and even a frustrating period with NEC, playing in the Dutch Eredivisie League, were all designed to prepare him for a career at the top, but somehow it never quite happened.

There were two big money transfers, first to Burnley and then Bolton and each resulted in promotions to the Premier League. Once there however, it quickly went wrong and the only two seasons when Chris featured regularly in the top flight ended in relegation and from 2014 he seemed set on a tour of the lesser Lancashire clubs, stopping off for increasingly short periods at the likes of Blackpool, Bury and Accrington.

Sandwiched in between was his brief spell in London and he signed for Charlton as a free agent in February 2015, having left Blackpool the previous month. Guy Luzon had only recently taken over as manager and was steering Charlton away from relegation danger in the Championship, so Chris's debut goal, added to earlier efforts by Frederic Bulot and Igor Vetokele, helped towards a very important 3-0 win at Wigan. He scored again at Blackpool the following month but although the side settled into a comfortable mid-table league position, he did not show enough for his contract to be extended beyond the end of the season.

The downward spiral continued via an unsuccessful relegation battle at Port Vale and a brief outing in the Scottish Premier League with Ross County, before his playing career was concluded with Oldham Athletic in the lower reaches of League Two.

In March 2021 Chris was arrested after being found slumped over the steering wheel of his £70,000 Audi near Altrincham in the early hours of the morning. He pleaded guilty to being 'drunk in charge' and received a three-month ban and a £1,250 fine.

Season	Division	League		FA Cup		FL Cup		Total	
		A	G	A	G	A	G	A	G
2014-15	Championship	5 (10)	2	0	0	0	0	5 (10)	2
Total		5 (10)	2	0	0	0	0	5 (10)	2

UK LEAGUE CAREER 349 games 53 goals

CHARLTON CAREER
Managers: *G Luzon*
Debut: *Wigan Athletic (A) (sub) 20-02-2015*
V796
Finale: *AFC Bournemouth (H) (sub) 02-05-2015*

ECCLESTON Nathan Geoffrey Junior   2011

Forward   10st 2lbs   5' 10"
Born: 30-12-90 - Newton Heath, Manchester

Once viewed by some as the 'future of Liverpool', Nathan's loan signing for Charlton was finalised just days after Phil Parkinson departed from the manager's office. Keith Peacock had been placed in temporary charge of the squad by the new owners and the team had crashed out of the FA Cup, losing 3-0 at Tottenham only four days earlier. Nathan arrived in SE7 on 13th January 2011 and a day later came the unexpected but exciting news that Chris Powell was to be the new Charlton manager. It is fair to say that Nathan's signing was overshadowed by these other events and his low key arrival set the scene for the remainder of his time at the club.

HONOURS

England U17 International 2007 1 game 0 Goals

LIverpool U18 2006-07 Winners FA Youth Cup

Liverpool U18 2008-09 Runners Up FA Youth Cup

CLUBS

Bury 2005 (youth) ••Liverpool 2006 (youth) 2009 (pro) ••Huddersfield Town 28.01.10 (loan) ••Charlton Athletic 13.01.11 (loan) ••Rochdale 20.10.11 (loan) ••Blackpool 31.08.12 (free) ••Tranmere Rovers 25.10.12 (loan) ••Carlisle United 04.10.13 (loan) ••Coventry City 26.03.14 (loan) ••Partick Thistle, Scotland 01.09.14 (free) ••Kilmarnock, Scotland 14.02.15 (free) ••Bekescsaba 1912 Elore, Hungary 09.02.16 (free) ••Nuneaton Borough 28.03.19 (free)

Signed by Liverpool at the age of 15, Nathan was viewed as an exciting prospect. He featured in the FA Youth Cup winning team that defeated Manchester United in 2007 and two years later was part of the squad beaten in the final by an Arsenal side that contained both Cedric Evina and Francis Coquelin. He made his Premier League debut in October 2009 and gained further experience in European games, mainly from the bench, including a 1-1 draw at Steaua Bucharest in December 2010.

Nathan featured in 21 league matches during his time with Charlton and scored during the 2-0 win against Plymouth Argyle in only his second game. Things started brightly as the new manager enjoyed a honeymoon period that stretched for five matches without defeat, but the team only managed two further wins during the last three months of the season and Nathan was not alone in making a very limited impact during this period. He was mainly used as a substitute and seemed physically unsuited to the robust treatment to be found in League One.

By the time he returned to Liverpool, they'd had a change of manager and he was never recalled for first team duty, moving to Blackpool in August 2012. Again he failed to

establish himself in the first team, but one of his few games for the Seasiders was at the Valley on 12th January 2013. He was a second half substitute and scored a stoppage time goal, but earlier strikes from Johnnie Jackson and Scott Wagstaff ensured a 2-1 scoreline in favour of Charlton. Nathan spent the 2014-15 season in Scotland, first with Partick Thistle where he played alongside Danny Seaborne and then for Kilmarnock where he competed for a first team spot with Josh Magennis. He hardly featured for either club, spending most of his time on the bench and became disillusioned by his lack of progress. In February 2016, after a break from the game, he accepted a short term contract to play in Hungary, but this interlude proved equally frustrating as Bekescsaba 1912 struggled all season and finished bottom of the top tier of Hungarian football, while his own contribution was affected by injury.

In September 2014 Nathan had set up an e-commerce business, Peaches Sports Wear, supplying women's fashion sports clothes and this now became his main priority. He had trials with Rochdale but could not agree terms and effectively retired in 2016 at the age of 25, only returning briefly three years later as a part time pro in the National

League North with Nuneaton Borough.

Season	Division	League		FA Cup		FL Cup		FL Trophy		Total	
		A	G	A	G	A	G	A	G	A	G
2010-11	League One	8 (13)	3	0	0	0	0	0	0	8 (13)	3
Total		8 (13)	3	0	0	0	0	0	0	8 (13)	3

UK LEAGUE CAREER 78 games 8 goals

CHARLTON CAREER
Managers: *C Powell*
Debut: *Sheffield Wednesday (A) (sub) 15-01-2011*
V715
Finale: *Hartlepool United (H) (sub) 07-05-2011*

EDMUNDS Charles Trevor   1931 - 32

Nobody ever managed a more spectacular start to his Football League career than Welsh striker Trevor Edmunds who made his debut for Bradford City in a league game against Rotherham United on 25th August 1928. It was the opening day of the season and the crowd of 12,356 witnessed an almost unbelievable spectacle as Bradford pulverised their opponents 11-1. This extraordinary scoreline remains in the record books nearly 100 years later than their biggest league or cup victory and Trevor, the new boy, scored three goals.

Forward   10st 10lbs   5' 9"
Born: 07-12-1903 - Merthyr Tydfil, Wales
Died: 07.1975 - Worcester, Worcestershire

HONOURS
Bradford City 1928-29 Winners Division 3 (N)

CLUBS
Aberdare Athletic 1926 ••Aberaman Athletic 1927 ••Bradford City 06.28 ••Chesterfield 10.05.29 ••Yeovil & Petters United 14.07.30 ••Charlton Athletic 07.05.1931 ••Red Star Olympique, France 1932 ••Worcester City 08.35 ••Redditch Town 05.36 ••Worcester City 01.37

Looking back it is difficult to understand why Trevor played so few matches in the Football League. Whatever shortcomings he may have had as a footballer, there is always a demand for a predatory goalscorer and his record of 16 in just 33 matches is impressive and was worthy of further games.

He started out with Aberdare Athletic, who spent six seasons in Division 3 South during the 1920s, but did not feature at first team level until moving to Bradford City. After such an explosive start, they went on to win Division 3 North in 1928-29 and scored an amazing 128 league goals. Trevor contributed 11 in less than half the games but hardly played in the second half of the season and when promotion was assured, was moved on to Chesterfield.

It was in May 1931 that he arrived at the Valley and in the same week leading goalscorer Fred Whitlow departed for Exeter City. Welsh international striker Dai Astley was then sold to Aston Villa in June, so with both of the main goal scorers gone, there was a golden opportunity for Trevor to stake his claim for a place in the Charlton team. He netted

three goals in a trial match on 15th August and then made his debut against Nottingham Forest in the opening league match of 1931-32. It ended 3-1 and he scored twice and nine days later got two more in a 2-2 draw with Bradford Park Avenue.

However, another amazing start soon fizzled out for Trevor and he played only a handful of games, following which the number nine shirt was moved around between George Kidd, Ernie Watkins and James Yardley with varying degrees of success. He was not retained at the end of the season and moved to France where he joined Red Star Olympique who had been one of their first clubs to embrace professionalism (only introduced in France in 1930) and were now founder members of the newly formed Ligue 1.

Trevor finished his career with spells at Worcester City and Redditch Town but was never granted a further opportunity to play in the Football league. He passed away in Worcester at the age of 71.

Season	Division	League		FA Cup		Total	
		A	G	A	G	A	G
1931-32	Division 2	6	4	0	0	6	4
Total		6	4	0	0	6	4

UK LEAGUE CAREER 33 games 16 goals

CHARLTON CAREER
Managers: *A MacFarlane*
Debut: *Nottingham Forest (H) 29-08-1931*
V144
Finale: *Bradford City (H) 27-02-1932*

EDWARDS Dennis   1959 - 64

Forward   12st 10lbs   5' 11"
Born: 19-01-1937 - Slough, Berkshire
Died: 13-09-2019 - Denmead, Hampshire
Education: Lea Junior School, Slough & Slough Grammar School.

A goal scoring inside forward, Dennis was a regular member of the Charlton side during the early sixties and was affectionately nicknamed Daisy, because of the amount of time he spent on the ground (down among the daisies). Although sometimes frustrating, on his day he was a very effective striker, being strong in the air and possessing a lethal left foot. He came to Charlton from Isthmian League club Wycombe Wanderers and only three days later on 27th September 1958 earned the first of two England Amateur International caps when Northern Ireland were defeated 6-2 at Bournemouth in the British Amateur Championships. His personal contribution was three goals.

HONOURS

England Amateur International 1958 2 caps 3 goals
Football Combination X1 1962
Slough Schools
Charlton Athletic A 1963-64 Finalists Metropolitan League Cup

Slough Town 1954-55 Winners Berks & Bucks Senior Cup
Wycombe Wanderers 1957-58 Runners Up Isthmian League
Wycombe Wanderers 1957-58 Winners Berks & Bucks Senior Cup

CLUBS

Old Paludians 1953 (amateur) ••Slough Town 1954 (amateur) ••Arsenal 1954 (amateur) ••Royal Air Force 1955 (amateur) ••Wycombe Wanderers 1957 (amateur) ••Charlton Athletic 24.09.58 (amateur) 19.02.59 (pro) ••Portsmouth 15.01.65 (£15,500) ••Brentford 09.67 (loan) ••Aldershot 13.12.67 (£5,000)

Dennis left school in 1953 and found work as a clerk with ICL in Slough, while at the same time playing for Old Paludians, the old boys of Slough Grammar School. He progressed to Corinthian League club Slough Town and even made occasional appearances for Arsenal Reserves before spending two years National Service in the RAF. From there he joined Wycombe Wanderers and was an immediate hit, scoring a hat-trick against Clapton on 8th March 1958 as they made a late surge to secure the runners-up spot in the Isthmian League under manager Sid Cann, himself a former Charlton defender. He started 1958-59 in excellent form and plundered 11 goals in the first five matches which attracted the attention of Charlton manager Jimmy Trotter and he signed Dennis as an amateur on 24th September 1958. His final tally for Wycombe Wanderers was an outstanding 31 goals in 28 matches. The second of Dennis's international appearances came on 11th October 1958 when Finland fielded their full national side at Dulwich Hamlet, but were still beaten 3-2 by England's

amateurs.
In February 1959 he signed professional terms and made his Charlton first team debut a month later. His first goals came in his fifth appearance when he hit two past Sunderland's Peter Wakeham, (later to be his teammate), in a 3-1 win at the Valley on 7th November. Dennis went on to become a fixture at inside forward and in season 1960-61 scored an impressive 24 goals in 37 league matches, including a hat trick against Middlesbrough in the amazing 6-6 draw on 22nd October 1960.
He was unable to repeat that level of success in front of goal, but on 4th October 1961 bagged three against Stoke City and went into the record books as the first Charlton player to score a hat trick in the Football League Cup. There was another treble four months later against Luton Town, but it is probably the exciting exploits of 1963-64 for which he is best remembered. This was the season when Eddie Firmani returned from Italy and Charlton, although failing to gain promotion, served up a series of exciting

performances not least of which was the 5-2 win on 26th October 1963 against Cardiff City, in which all the forward line of Kenning, Matthews, Firmani, Edwards and Glover got among the goals.

By 1965 Dennis was suffering with a recurring knee injury and was not getting on with manager Frank Hill, so took the opportunity to move to Portsmouth, who at that time were managed by former Charlton defender George Smith. He was signed as a replacement for Ron Saunders, who would himself join Charlton only seven months later, but found him a difficult act to follow. He did well enough in 1965-66 and scored for the Pompey side that also included Frank Haydock, as Charlton were beaten 3-1 on 28th December 1965, but increasing knee problems and

declining form led to a final move to Aldershot, before he retired from the game in 1968.

Dennis had coached football at Crown Woods School during his time at Charlton, but after retirement settled at Denmead in Hampshire and from 1973 ran a wholesale business, Dennis Edwards Frozen Foods. He was a keen golfer and long time member of Waterlooville Golf Club. He passed away at the age of 82, a cardiac arrest having been brought on following a bad fall some days earlier.

Season	Division	League		FA Cup		FL Cup		Total	
		A	G	A	G	A	G	A	G
1958-59	Division 2	3	0	0	0			3	0
1959-60	Division 2	20	6	1	0			21	6
1960-61	Division 2	37	24	1	0	1	0	39	24
1961-62	Division 2	42	16	3	0	3	4	48	20
1962-63	Division 2	20	3	1	0	1	0	22	3
1963-64	Division 2	34	8	1	0	1	0	36	8
1964-65	Division 2	15	4	0	0	3	1	18	5
Total		171	61	7	0	9	5	187	66

CHARLTON CAREER
Managers: J Trotter, F Hill
Debut: *Ipswich Town (H) 21-03-1959*
V283
Finale: *Leyton Orient (A) 26-12-1964*

UK LEAGUE CAREER 267 games 78 goals

EDWARDS Leonard Trevor   1957 - 60

Trevor's football career got off to an exciting start when he was unexpectedly picked to play for Wales against Northern Ireland in Belfast on

Defender   10st 10lbs   5' 8"
Born: 24-01-1937 - Penygraig, Glamorgan
Education: Tai Junior School and Craig yr Eos School, Penygraig.

10th April 1957. At this stage he had made only eight league appearances for Charlton, but despite his inexperience, the Welsh team managed a 0-0 draw and he played again a month later in a World Cup qualifier in Leipzig in front of a crowd in excess of 110,000. This time they were defeated 2-1 by a strong East German side but went on to participate in the 1958 World Cup finals. Trevor was part of the Welsh squad which progressed to the last eight in this their only appearance in the finals of a World Cup but never did add to his two international caps.

HONOURS
Wales International 1957 2 caps 0 goals
Wales U23 International 1958-59 2 caps 0 goals
Australia B International 1964 1 cap 0 goals
RAF v Royal Navy 1957

Kent Youth Xl
New South Wales Rep X1 1965
Sydney X1 1965 2 caps

CLUBS
Ystrad Boys (youth) ••Charlton Athletic 29.10.52 (youth) 02.05.55 (pro) ••Bexleyheath & Welling 1952 (loan) ••Biggleswade Town 1955 (loan) ••Cardiff City 09.06.60 (£5,500) ••Sydney Hakoah, Australia 1964 (free) ••Melita Eagles, Australia 1969 (player coach) ••Club Marconi, Australia 1970 (player coach)

Recommended to Charlton by Hadyn Price, a long time   contact of Jimmy Seed from his playing days with the Welsh club, Mid-Rhondda, Trevor made his first team debut against Manchester United at the Valley on 18th February 1957 as replacement for Jock Campbell, the team having conceded seven goals at Wolverhampton just two days earlier. It proved a baptism of fire as they were again overwhelmed, this time by a 5-1 scoreline and a young Bobby Charlton scored a hat-trick. Almost exactly a year later six of that United side perished in the Munich air disaster.

Trevor kept his place for the remainder of the 1956-57 relegation season and the first half of the next campaign, but shortly after playing in the famous 7-6 match with Huddersfield, lost his position at right back to Peter Firmani and did not re-appear in the first team for eight months, although during this period he played for the victorious Wales U23's, who on 23rd April 1958 triumphed 2-1 against an England side that included Maurice Setters.

Despite spending three and a half years as a first team player with Charlton, Trevor's place in the side never seemed totally secure and for long periods of time he also appeared to be at odds with the club. As early as May 1957 there were press reports that he was unhappy and had re-signed under protest at the terms offered to him. He denied the stories, but in February 1958 put in a written transfer request

citing the reduction in his wages to the basic £14 a week whilst out of the side, as the cause of his discontent. By November the matter was still not resolved and although not formally transfer listed, it was then made known that Charlton were open to offers for the player.

It was not until the conclusion of the 1959-60 season that he finally departed and it was to Cardiff City for a £5,500 transfer fee, much less than the £12,000 that had originally been hoped for by the club. He played four seasons at Ninian Park, but just as before he seemed to be in and out of the side. He did play on 18th February 1963 when Cardiff were visitors at the Valley in the FA Cup, but despite a tight match, a Lenny Glover goal saw the Addicks safely through to the next round.

The curtain fell on Trevor's Football League career when he emigrated to Australia in 1964, but he carried on playing as a semi-pro, first with Hakoah Sydney for five years and later he played and coached at Melita Eagles and Club Marconi. He hung up his boots in 1972 and worked for a men's clothing company and then moved on to Brisbane where he became manager of a company importing frozen foods. By 2009 he was retired as a result of high blood pressure and was resident in Hervey Bay, Queensland and working on his golf handicap.

Season	Division	League		FA Cup		Total	
		A	G	A	G	A	G
1956-57 (R)	Division 1	12	0	0	0	12	0
1957-58	Division 2	21	0	0	0	21	0
1958-59	Division 2	15	0	0	0	15	0
1959-60	Division 2	16	0	2	0	18	0
Total		64	0	2	0	66	0

UK LEAGUE CAREER 137 games 3 goals

CHARLTON CAREER
Managers: *J Seed, J Trotter*
Debut: *Manchester United (H) 18-02-1957*
V276
Finale: *Lincoln City (A) 09-04-1960*

EGGLETON James Arthur Edward   1922 - 23

Defender
Born: 29-08-1897 - Heston, Middlesex
Died: 13-01-1963 - Hillingdon, Middlesex

Queens Park Rangers was Jimmy's final club. He joined them in 1926 and remained for the rest of his days, nearly 37 years to be precise. 'Eggie' hung up his boots at the end of the 1929-30 season and took on the position of trainer. Rangers became his whole life and during World War 2 his duties involved him at once being trainer, assistant secretary, groundsman, boiler man and general maintenance man. He sometimes had to wash the kit because of laundry problems and in his spare time was in charge of fire watching. Now that is a 'utility player'.

HONOURS
Middlesex & London Schools
British Army International 1921

Charlton Athletic 1922-23 Winners London Challenge Cup

CLUBS

British Army 1920 ••Slough 1921 ••Charlton Athletc 28. 09.21 (amateur) 19.10.22 (pro) ••Watford 12.23 (£500) ••Lincoln City 09.26 (free) ••Queens Park Rangers 23.10.26 (free) 1930 (trainer) 1947 (ass. manager)

Jimmy was a strong tackling centre half and played for both Middlesex and London Schools. During World War I he served as a gunner in the Royal Artillery and was gassed while in combat. Later in life he suffered with bad health as a result of this, but by 1920 he was fit enough to play representative football for the Army.

He joined the Charlton ground staff in April 1922 and played two games for the first team in their debut season as a Football League club deputising for regular centre half, Arthur Whalley. He signed professional terms six months later and saw more first team action in 1922-23, but mainly during the first half of the season.

In December 1923 Jimmy was transferred to Watford for a fee of £500 and went straight into their team in Division 3 (South). He scored a rare goal against Newport County in an 8-2 thrashing on 5th January and featured in the 1-0 defeat of First Division Middlesbrough in the FA Cup at Ayresome Park seven days later. He eventually moved on to Queens Park Rangers where he played a further 42 league games before injury ended his playing career.

Jimmy was a well liked character and an enthusiastic pigeon fancier. He and his father had their own roost and their birds won many important races. He came back to Charlton with QPR as their reserve team manager in 1954, yet another of the duties which he carried out for them. By 1960 his health was failing and he eventually died in Hillingdon at the age of 65.

Season	Division	League		FA Cup		Total	
		A	G	A	G	A	G
1921-22	Divison 3 (S)	2	0			2	0
1922-23	Divison 3 (S)	15	0	2	0	17	0
1923-24	Divison 3 (S)	9	0	0	0	9	0
Total		26	0	2	0	28	0

UK LEAGUE CAREER 116 games 2 goals

CHARLTON CAREER
Managers: *W Rayner*
Debut: *Newport County (A) 27-04-1922*
V035
Finale: *Swansea Town (A) 01-12-1923*

EL KARKOURI Talal   2004 - 07

A fine example of the modern footballer, Talal plied his trade wherever his talent led him, be it Casablanca, Paris, Thessaloniki or Doha. His first taste of the English game came during a loan spell at Sunderland in which the Black Cats had no good luck whatsoever and contrived to lose every one of the nine league and cup matches in which he participated as they crashed to relegation from the Premier League with a miserly 19 points.

Defender   12st 9lb   6' 3"
Born: 08-07-1976 - Casablanca, Morocco

HONOURS

Morocco International 2000-09 53 caps 6 goals
Morocco 2004 Runners Up Africa Cup of Nations
Morocco 2005 Runners Up Islamic Solidarity Games
Raja Casablanca 1996-99 (4 times) Winners Moroccan Premier League
Raja Casablanca 1997 Winners CAF Champions League

Paris Saint-Germain 1999-00 & 2003-04 Runners Up France Ligue 1
Paris Saint-Germain 1999-00 Runners Up France Coupe De La Ligue
Paris Saint-Germain 2001 Winners UEFA Intertoto Cup
Paris Saint-Germain 2003-04 Winners Coupe De France

CLUBS

Raja Casablanca, Morocco 07.95 ••Paris Saint- Germain, France 20.01.00 ••Aris Salonika, Greece 21.01.01 (loan) ••Sunderland 31.01.03 (loan) ••Charlton Athletic 11.07.04 (£1million) ••Al- Gharafa, Qatar 06.04.06 (loan) ••Qatar Sporting Club, Qatar 14.06.07 (free) ••Umm-Salal, Qatar 01.08.11 (free) 26.02.13 (ass manager) ••Raja Casablanca, Morocco 07.07.15 (ass manager) ••Al- Shabab, Saudi Arabia 03.01.16 (ass manager) ••Umm-Salal, Qatar 04.02.18 (manager)

Talal brought to Charlton a vast experience of top level   football, having played in the Champions League with Paris

Saint-Germain and in 1997 been a winner of the African equivalent, the CAF Champions League, when Raja Casablanca defeated the Ghanaian side Obuasi Goldfields on penalties. He fitted in well at the Valley, a solid central defender with the knack of serving up the occasional goal, none of which was more spectacular than the 35 yard free kick which flew into the Arsenal net on New Year's Day 2005.

He was used more sparingly in his second season, often being absent on international duty and even moving to Qatar for a loan spell with Al-Gharafa, but regained his

place in the Charlton team for the ill fated relegation season of 2006-07. Talal appeared 53 times for Morocco (21 caps and two of his international goals came during his time at Charlton) but probably the high point of his career was when Morocco reached the final of the Africa Cup of Nations on 14th February 2004, although they were narrowly beaten 2-1 by Tunisia.

After leaving Charlton, he returned to Qatar, eventually retiring as a player on 25th May 2012. He later moved into management and on 4th February 2018 was briefly appointed manager of Umm-Salal in Qatar.

Season	Division	League		FA Cup		FL Cup		Total	
		A	G	A	G	A	G	A	G
2004-05	Premier	28 (4)	5	3	0	1	0	32 (4)	5
2005-06	Premier	4 (6)	0	0	0	2	0	6 (6)	0
2006-07 (R)	Premier	36	3	1	0	2	0	39	3
Total		68 (10)	8	4	0	5	0	77 (10)	8

UK LEAGUE CAREER 86 games 8 goals

CHARLTON CAREER
Managers: *A Curbishley, I Dowie, L Reed, A Pardew*
Debut: *Portsmouth (H) (sub) 21-08-2004*
V622
Finale: *Tottenham Hotspur (H) 07-05-2007*

EL KHALEJ Tahar   2003

Defender, Midfield   13st 8lbs   6' 3"
Born: 16-06-1968 - Marrakesh. Morocco

Tahar was a Moroccan international who was signed by Alan Curbishley in January 2003 to provide cover in the centre of the defence. Nearly 35 years old when he arrived at the Valley, he was nearing the end of his career, but remained an imposing figure and was highly experienced at the top level. As it turned out he only figured in three matches, the most memorable of which was the 3-0 win against an Aston Villa side which included Mark KInsella, on 22nd February 2003. Already leading from a Jason Euell goal early in the second half, two late strikes by Jonatan Johansson ensured a decisive victory for the Addicks.

HONOURS
Morocco International 1990-01 69 caps 2 goals
Kawkab Marrakech 1990-91 & 1992-93 Winners Moroccan Throne Cup
Kawkab Marrakech 1991-92 Winners Moroccan League Division 1

Benfica 1996-97 Finalists Taca de Portugal (cup)
Benfica 1997-98 Runners Up Portuguese Primeira Divisao

CLUBS
Kawkab Marrakech, Morocco 1990 ••UD Leiria, Portugal 1994 ••Benfica, Portugal 1996 ••Southampton 10.03.00 (£350,000) ••Charlton Athletic 28.01.03 (free) ••Kawkab Marrakech, Morocco 2005 (president)

A Moroccan international for more than a decade, Tahar featured in two World Cups (1994 and 1998) and on 23rd June 1998 played in his country's famous 3-0 victory over a Scotland side which included Christian Dailly. He also played in two Africa Cup of Nations tournaments (1998 and 2000).

In club football, he enjoyed four years of league and cup success with Kawkab Marrakech before moving to Europe and joining Uniao Leiria, newly promoted to Portugal's Primeira Divisao. From there he switched to Benfica and on

10th June 1997 played in the final of their national cup competition, the Taca de Portugal, which ended in a narrow defeat (3-2) against Boavista.

Tahar came to England in March 2000 and joined Southampton. He played at the Valley on 6th September 2000 in a Premier League match which ended in a 1-1 draw, Charlton's cause not being improved by the sending off of Steve Brown for two yellow cards. In the same fixture the following season, Tahar's late equaliser cancelled out Richard Rufus's opener, for another 1-1 draw, but his time at Southampton was drawing to a close and he signed off with a red card against Newcastle on 11th May 2002. After his brief stay with Charlton, Tahar announced his retirement on 27th May 2003 and returned to Morocco

where in 2005 he was elected president of his old club, Kawkab Marrakech and guided them to promotion back into the Moroccan First Division.

Season	Division	League		FA Cup		FL Cup		Total	
		A	G	A	G	A	G	A	G
2002-03	Premier	2 (1)	0	0	0	0	0	2 (1)	0
Total		2 (1)	0	0	0	0	0	2 (1)	0

UK LEAGUE CAREER 61 games 3 goals

CHARLTON CAREER
Managers: *A Curbishley*
Debut: *Aston Villa (H) 22-02-2003*
V608
Finale: *Birmingham City (H) 19-04-2003*

ELEREWE Ayodeji Joshua Oluwapelumi Akinola   2021 -

Both Joe Gomez and Ezri Konsa are recent graduates of the Charlton youth academy who have gone on to enjoy successful careers in the Premier League and many people are already looking at

Defender   13st 8lbs   6' 4"
Born: 14-09-2003 - Croydon, Surrey
Education: Royal Russell School, Addington.

another young defender, Deji Elerewe and wondering if he may be the next one off the production line. Composed and confident on the ball and an impressive aerial presence, along with Nazir Bakrin he formed the backbone of the U18 team which in 2020-21 stormed to the Professional Development League South title by a massive 10 point margin and only just fell short of becoming national champions when they lost 2-0 to Wigan Athletic in the final match.

HONOURS
Charlton Athletic U18 2020-21 Winners PD League 2 South   Charlton Athletic U18 2020-21 Runners Up PD National League 2

CLUBS
Crystal Palace 2012 (youth) ••KInetic Foundation 2016 (youth) ••Charlton Athletic 12.16 (youth) 04.11.21 (pro)

English born of Nigerian descent, Deji joined Charlton at U13 level, having earlier been released by Crystal Palace. In the summer of 2021 he was fast-tracked into the first team squad at the age of 17 and performed most impressively in pre-season. He made his debut in the League Cup against AFC Wimbledon on 10th August 2021 and although the

match was lost 1-0, his performance was considered one of the successes of an otherwise disappointing display. A week later he made his first league appearance off the bench as replacement for Ryan Inniss and having now shown that he is not out of place at this level, much is expected from him in the future.

UK LEAGUE CAREER 0 games 0 goals

CHARLTON CAREER
Managers: *N Adkins, J Jackson*
Debut: *AFC Wimbledon (H) 10-08-2021*
V927

ELLIOT Robert

2008 - 11

Goalkeeper   13st 7lbs   6' 2"
Born: 30-04-86 - Greenwich, London

English by birth, Rob qualified to play football for the Republic of Ireland because his father's family came from Cork. During his time with Charlton he was capped at U19 level and then later, after his move to Newcastle, made his full international debut on 25th May 2014 against Turkey in Dublin. His final game for Ireland was in a 2-2 draw against Slovakia on 29th March 2016 and a serious knee injury picked up while trying to prevent the opening goal sidelined him for six months and put paid to any chance of competing in UEFA Euro 2016

HONOURS

Ireland International 2014-16 4 caps 0 goals
Ireland U19 International 2004 1 cap 0 goals
Charlton Athletic U19 2003-04 Runners Up FA Premier Academy U19 League

Charlton Athletic Reserves 2007-08 Runners Up Premier Reserve League (South)
Accrington Stanley 2005-06 Winners Football Conference

CLUBS

Erith Town 2001 (youth) ••Charlton Athletic 2003 (youth) 27.01.05 (pro) ••Erith & Belvedere 2003 (loan) ••Bishop's Stortford 08.04 (loan) ••Notts County 28.01.05 (loan) ••Accrington Stanley 24.11.05 (loan) 02.08.06 (loan) ••Newcastle United 30.08.11 (£100,000) ••Watford 28.01.21 (free)

Rob is a local boy who grew up as a Charlton supporter and season ticket holder. At the age of 15 he was playing for Erith Town as an outfield player, when a teammate failed to turn up for a match. He filled in as goalkeeper and discovered that he had a natural talent in that position. Two years later he wrote off to more than 20 league clubs seeking a trial but ironically it was only Charlton who gave him a chance.

His Football League debut came during a loan spell at Notts County. Their regular goalkeeper received a red card during their match against Kidderminster Harriers on 12th March 2005 and Rob took over and made a further three appearances during his suspension. This was quite a baptism of fire for the youngster, especially as each of the four matches ended in defeat.

Things went a good deal better during his first of two loan spells with Accrington Stanley and he had an outstanding season in 2005-06 as they ran away with the Football Conference and gained entry into the Football League, finishing 11 points clear of the runners-up.

His Charlton debut came somewhat unexpectedly on 5th April 2008 when Nicky Weaver was sent off at Plymouth after only three minutes, but two second half goals from Leroy Lita made it 2-1 and an afternoon to remember for

Rob and the travelling supporters. It was not until the following season that he became a regular in the team, but he held his place through a turbulent period for the club, until in August 2011 he got the opportunity to step up to the Premier League and join Newcastle United.

Rob's decision to move to the North East made perfect sense financially, but must have proved frustrating as his first team chances were initially very limited. In his first four years at Newcastle, he only featured in 15 league games. It was not until October 2015 that the chance finally came for a run in the side and he did well until injury forced him back on to the sidelines. He was eventually released in June 2020 having been at St James's Park for almost nine years but had still only played 68 competitive matches.

For seven months Rob was without a club and at one stage returned to train at Charlton, although there never seemed any realistic prospect of him re-signing. He eventually agreed a contract with Watford, but did not get to make his debut until 21st September 2021 when he featured in a disappointing 3-1 home defeat against a Stoke City side that included Alfie Doughty. This was his first competitive match since 2017.

Season	Division	League		FA Cup		FL Cup		FL Trophy		Play Offs		Total	
		A	G	A	G	A	G	A	G	A	G	A	G
2007-08	Championship	0 (1)	0	0	0	0	0					0 (1)	0
2008-09 (R)	Championship	23	0	2	0	1	0					26	0
2009-10	League One	33	0	0	0	1	0	1	0	0	0	35	0
2010-11	League One	35	0	5	0	0	0	3	0			43	0
2011-12 (P)	League One	4	0	0	0	0	0	0	0			4	0
Total		95 (1)	0	7	0	2	0	4	0	0	0	108 (1)	0

UK LEAGUE CAREER 162 games 0 goals

CHARLTON CAREER
Managers: *A Curbishley, I Dowie, L Reed, A Pardew, P Parkinson, C Powell*
Debut: *Plymouth Argyle (A) (sub)*
05-04-2008
V666
Finale: *Scunthorpe United (H) 20-08-2011*

ELLIOTT Matthew Stephen   1988

Matt Elliott enjoyed a long and productive career as a professional footballer, making over 700 competitive appearances for six clubs, as well as representing Scotland on 18 occasions. However only the first of these matches was in the colours of Charlton Athletic where he spent a little under a year learning his trade as a teenage centre half. The occasion was an inauspicious League Cup match against Northampton Town at Selhurst Park on 11th October 1988, played in front of a crowd of just 2,782. A penalty from Mark Reid and a goal by Andy Jones ensured victory for the Addicks and set Matt's career off to a positive start.

Defender   13st 6lbs   6' 3"
Born: 01-11-1968 - Wandsworth, London

HONOURS

Scotland International 1997-01 18 caps 1 goal
Torquay United 1989-90 Finalists Football League Trophy
Torquay United 1990-91 Promoted Play Offs Division 4
Oxford United 1995-96 Runners Up Division 2

Leicester City 1998-99 Finalists League Cup
Leicester City 1999-00 Winners League Cup
Leicester City 2002-03 Runners Up Division 1

CLUBS

Crystal Palace Youth} ••Leatherhead (youth) ••Epsom & Ewell 08.87 (semi pro) ••Charlton Athletic 09.05.88 (£50,000) ••Torquay United 23.03.89 (loan) 18.04.89 (£11,500) ••Scunthorpe United 26.03.92 (loan) 19.06.92 (£50,000) ••Oxford United 05.11.93 (£160,000) ••Leicester City 17.01.97 (£1.6 million) ••Ipswich Town 16.03.04 (loan) ••Hednesford Town 09.06.08 (ass manager) ••Oadby Town 08.09 (ass manager) ••Stafford Rangers 20.10.10 (ass manager) 11.01.11 (manager) ••Army United, Thailand 11.13 (manager)

With experienced defenders like Shirtliff, Caton and Pates contesting the centre half spot at Charlton, opportunities for Matt were limited and he moved on to Torquay United in March 1989. This gave him first team football and only two months later the bonus of a Wembley final in the Football League Trophy (sponsored that year by Sherpa Vans). They were beaten 4-1 by Bolton Wanderers, but Matt was now a fixture in the side where he remained for three seasons and which included a promotion from Division 4 in 1990-91.

Spells with Scunthorpe and Oxford United found him to be a model of consistency and he rarely missed a match. He came up against Charlton again on 12th February 1994, but the outcome was a resounding 4-0 win for the Addicks and two goals from Carl Leaburn. There was another promotion in 1996 while at Oxford, but it was the transfer to Leicester City in January 1997 which really elevated

Matt on to centre stage and the fee of £1.6 million was the record paid by the Foxes up to that time.

Over the next seven years Matt played close to 200 Premier League matches and captained Leicester with great distinction, but perhaps his finest hour came at Wembley in the 1999-00 League Cup final, when he turned in a Shirtliff like performance, scoring both goals in a 2-1 victory in front of a crowd of 74,313. Although a Londoner by birth, he qualified to play for Scotland through his Scottish grandmother and as well as his 18 international caps, he earned a trip to the 1998 World Cup in France where frustratingly he was not called upon to play.

After enjoying a largely injury free career, Matt eventually succumbed to a damaged knee and his final appearance for Leicester came on 30th October 2004 in an uninspiring 0-0 draw against Lennie Lawrence's Cardiff City, the same manager who had kick-started his career at Charlton some

16 years earlier. He announced his retirement in January 2005.

Since then Matt has remained remarkably active via a series of managerial roles in the non-league game. He has worked as an analyst for BBC Radio Leicester, was first team coach at De Montford University and an academy coach with Leicester City. In 2011, he launched the Matt Elliott Football Development Scheme and by 2020 was working as an after dinner speaker, as a match day host for Leicester and as Sports Director of ME Training & Development.

Season	Division	League		FA Cup		FL Cup		FM Cup		Total	
		A	G	A	G	A	G	A	G	A	G
1988-89	Division 1	0	0	0	0	1	0	0	0	1	0
Total		0	0	0	0	1	0	0	0	1	0

UK LEAGUE CAREER 588 games 71 goals

CHARLTON CAREER
Managers: *L Lawrence*
Debut: *Northampton Town (H) 11-10-1988*
V498

ELLIOTT Paul Marcellus   1981 - 83

Defender   11st 11lbs   6' 2''
Born: 18-03-1964 - Lewisham, London
Education: Woodhill Primary School, Woolwich and Blackheath Bluecoat School.

A quality centre half who earned six England Youth caps while at Charlton, Paul always seemed destined for the top and it was a great pity that he only made 63 league appearances before following Paul Walsh to Luton Town in March 1983. That must have seemed an upward move at the time, yet only three years later Lennie Lawrence led Charlton back to the top flight. Had the club been in a more stable condition, perhaps Paul could have been part of that promotion adventure instead of being sold far too early and for what seemed a giveaway fee of £95,000.

HONOURS

England B International 1991 1 cap 0 goals	Blackheath Schools
England U21 International 1984-86 3 caps 1 goal	Charlton Athletic 1981 Young Player Of The Year
England Youth International 1981-82 6 caps 0 goals	Celtic 1989-90 Finalists Scottish FA Cup
Scottish Player Of The Year 1990-91	Celtic 1990-91 Finalists Scottish League Cup

CLUBS

Highmead 1979 (youth) ••Charlton Athletic 23.08.79 (youth) 20.03.81 (pro) ••Luton Town 09.03.83 (£95,000) ••Aston Villa 02.12.85 (£400,000) ••AC Pisa, Italy 07.87 £400,000) ••Celtic, Scotland 20.06.89 (£600,000) ••Chelsea 04.07.91 (£1.4 million) 1996 (coach)

A Charlton supporter from the age of eight, Paul signed a professional contract in March 1981 and made his first team debut six months later in a 2-0 defeat at Crystal Palace. Once in the team, he never looked likely to lose his place and as time went on his level of performance steadily increased until he became a key member of a somewhat unbalanced Charlton side. Results fluctuated, but there were good days such as 4th December 1982 when the defence kept a clean sheet and goals from Don McAllister and the mercurial Allan Simonsen ensured a 2-0 win against Newcastle United. There were bad days as well though and few came worse than Paul's final outing in a Charlton shirt on 26th February 1983. Both Derek Hales and Mark Aizlewood were sent off at Turf Moor as Burnley handed out a 7-1 hiding, five of their goals coming in the

last 15 minutes when the Addicks were down to nine men. The transfer to Luton Town took Paul into the First Division and despite the fact that his new club was initially engaged in a struggle against relegation, he handled the step-up in standard and gradually the league position improved. On 16th October 1984 he was called up for the first of three England U21 caps. It was a home fixture in the UEFA U21 Championships and Finland were defeated 2-0. In the future Paul's career would be shortened through injury and he suffered a prequel on 30th October 1984 when he broke a leg in a League Cup tie against Leicester City which kept him out of action for 10 months. When fit again, he transferred to Aston Villa and in 1985-86 they reached the semi-final stage of the League Cup, only to lose out to Oxford United. He twice played against Charlton during the following campaign and although successful in the first game, his Villa side were well beaten at the Valley on 20th April 1987 when goals from Peter Shirtliff, Mark Reid and Jim Melrose cemented a 3-0 victory for Charlton. In July 1987 he was sold to the Italian club AC Pisa and spent the next two years competing in Serie A against some of the finest players of the day. In only his third match, he was sent off after clashing with Maradona, but he settled in and made a success of his time in Italy before moving to Scotland for two years with Celtic. They were experiencing one of their less dominant periods but Paul was far from a weak link and was voted Scottish Player of the Year in 1990-91 as well as captaining England B to a 2-1 win against Switzerland in May.

His final transfer took him back to the First Division when he signed for Chelsea in July 1991 and as with all his previous moves, he slotted effortlessly into the side, which also contained Graham Stuart and eventually became the London club's first black captain. However, his playing career came to an abrupt end at Anfield on 5th September 1992 when he suffered serious damage to the ligaments in his right knee as a result of a brutal challenge by Liverpool's Dean Saunders. Despite several operations he never regained match fitness and later unsuccessfully sued Saunders for negligence.

From a Jamaican family, Paul's grandmother had been one of the post-war Windrush generation and he suffered terribly from racial taunts and abuse throughout his career, especially at Celtic and in Italy. After retiring in 1994, he devoted much of his time to anti-racism for which he was awarded an MBE in 2003. He had an active role in the 'Kick It Out' campaign and in 2012 received a CBE for services to equality and diversity in football. However, the following year he was obliged to resign from the FA after sending a racially insulting text to another former Charlton player, Richard Rufus, in a row over a failed business venture which escalated into a libel action between the two men.

Even though he was successful in the libel case, this unsavoury incident between the two Charlton defenders undoubtedly affected Paul's reputation for a time, but in 2014 he was re-elected on to the FA's Inclusion Advisory Board and has since gone on to become the FA representative on the board of UEFA and advisor to the European Parliament on issues of racial prejudice. After nearly 30 years he remains one of the most important figures in the fight for equality and diversity in football.

Season	Division	League		FA Cup		FL Cup		Total	
		A	G	A	G	A	G	A	G
1981-82	Division 2	36 (2)	1	0 (1)	0	3	1	39 (3)	2
1982-83	Division 2	25	0	1	0	2	0	28	0
Total		61 (2)	1	1 (1)	0	5	1	67 (3)	2

UK LEAGUE CAREER 282 games 17 goals

CHARLTON CAREER
Managers: *M Bailey, A Mullery, K Craggs, L Lawrence*
Debut: *Crystal Palace (A) 12-09-1981*
V432
Finale: *Burnley (A) 26-02-1983*

ELLIS Alan   1970 - 72

Alan was a promising wing half, who in 1971 was the first ever winner of Charlton's annual award for Young Player of the Year. He made his first team debut at the Valley on 19th September 1970 against a Leicester City team that included Len Glover, but this was not an easy time and results on the field were not going well. The match ended in a 1-0 home defeat and left Charlton positioned at the very foot of the Division 2 table. Alan was viewed at the time as being very much 'one to watch', but sadly his career never kicked on, as hoped.

Midfield   10st 2lbs   5' 6"
Born: 17-11-1951 - Somercotes, Derbyshire

HONOURS
Alfreton District Schools   Charlton Athletic 1971 Young Player Of The Year

CLUBS
Ridding St James' Colts (youth) ••Charlton Athletic 10.02.68 (youth) 21.11.69 (pro) ••Mansfield Town 11.10.72 (loan) ••Ilkeston Town 1973

Born in the Derbyshire village of Somercotes. Alan signed   as an apprentice with Charlton in February 1968 and although small in stature, made encouraging progress during his first three years with the club. After his initial breakthrough into the first team he featured in a total of 13 matches in the 1970-71 season, most memorably on 3rd October 1970 at the Valley, when Swindon Town were defeated 2-1 thanks to goals by Dick Plumb and Gordon Riddick.

The next campaign should have seen him cement his place in the side, but he was injured during a pre-season match in the Netherlands and sidelined for a long period. An operation for a ruptured thigh muscle was carried out at the Miller Hospital on 7th December 1971, after which a second operation became necessary and this did not take place until March 1972, effectively wiping out his entire

season. From then on things went rapidly downhill and he received a club fine in September 1972 for absenting himself without permission. A further absence led to a two-week suspension.

It seemed as if a loan move to Mansfield Town, just 10 miles from his home and effective 11th October 1972, might get his career back on track, but he returned without making any first team appearances and in November Charlton cancelled his contract. Alan's football career was effectively over at the age of 21.

Prior to his time in London, he had been employed as an apprentice engineer at a Derby locomotive works, but Alan did not pursue this line of work and instead became a lorry driver for White Peaks Transport in Alfreton.

Season	Division	League		FA Cup		FL Cup		Total	
		A	G	A	G	A	G	A	G
1970-71	Division 2	9 (4)	0	0	0	0	0	9 (4)	0
1972-73	Division 3	0 (1)	0	0	0	0	0	0 (1)	0
Total		9 (5)	0	0	0	0	0	9 (5)	0

UK LEAGUE CAREER 14 games 0 goals

CHARLTON CAREER
Managers: *E Firmani, T Foley*
Debut: *Leicester City (H) 19-09-1970*
V354
Finale: *York City (H) (sub) 02-09-1972*

ELLIS Sydney Carey   1953 - 57

Defender   10st 2lbs   5' 8"
Born: 16-08-1931 - Charlton, London
Died: 26-03-2001 - Greenwich, London
Education: Charlton Central School.

There was an urban myth often passed around the terraces at the Valley, namely that Syd had been the only defender to tame the great Stanley Matthews. Closer examination however shows that the two men played in direct opposition on only four occasions and that Blackpool were victorious in all but one, a 4-2 home win for Charlton on 10th October 1953 and this was the occasion when Syd played probably the game of his life. His career had started in spectacular fashion and he made his debut in Charlton's biggest ever victory, 8-1 against Middlesborough and this started a run of six straight wins, including a 6-0 crushing of Liverpool. No Charlton player can ever have made a better start, so it is all the more surprising that he failed to build upon this early promise.

HONOURS
England U23 International 1954 1 cap 0 goals
Royal Army Ordnance Corps 1949-50 Winners Army FA Challenge Cup
London Boys 1947-48

Charlton Athletic Reserves 1952-53 Runners Up Football Combination Cup
Brighton & Hove Albion 1957-58 Winners Division 3 (S)

CLUBS
Greenwich United (youth) ••Crystal Palace 1948 (amateur) ••Charlton Athletic 03.49 (amateur) 10.05.49 (pro) ••Tonbridge 18.09.51 (loan) ••Brighton & Hove Albion 22.11.57 (£2,000) ••Guildford City 08.59 (free)

Syd was born in Charlton and went to school within walking distance of the Valley. He represented London Boys in 1947-48 and later during his National Service played alongside goalkeeper Eric Gill for the 3rd Battalion, Royal Army Ordnance Corps. They were 2-1 winners of the Army FA Cup in 1950 and both men were presented

with their medals by King George VI.

He was selected, along with Stuart Leary, for the first ever England U23 International, which was played in Bologna on 20th January 1954. The visitors were however comprehensively outplayed and the Italian team won 3-0. Charlton still had a strong playing squad during this period so competition for places was intense and despite his England call up, Syd lost out to Don Townsend for the left back spot early in 1954-55 and only managed 10 first team appearances over the next two seasons.

His chance came again in the ill fated campaign of 1956-57 when 30 different players were utilised, but his contribution proved almost a mirror image of his first season when everything had gone so well. His final seven appearances in Division 1 netted one draw and six straight defeats, including a 5-0 thumping at Everton on 9th February, as Charlton were relegated having conceded an embarrassing 120 league goals.

Syd was transferred to Brighton in November 1957 and

helped them to promotion from Division 3 (South) in his first season, but the downward spiral continued and he very quickly dropped into the Southern League with Guildford City where he played alongside another ex-Charlton colleague, Mickey Stewart.

By the mid-sixties he was coaching youngsters at Charlton and working as an advertising salesman in the publishing industry and also for a time ran a Boys Brigade football team. He was invited to Sir Stanley Matthews' 75th birthday Dinner in 1990 and the great man generously acknowledged his one time adversary. Syd passed away in Greenwich at the age of 69.

Season	Division	League		FA Cup		Total	
		A	G	A	G	A	G
1953-54	Division 1	26	0	1	0	27	0
1954-55	Division 1	3	0	0	0	3	0
1955-56	Division 1	6	0	1	0	7	0
1956-57 (R)	Division 1	12	0	0	0	12	0
1957-58	Division 2	1	0	0	0	1	0
Total		48	0	2	0	50	0

UK LEAGUE CAREER 90 games 0 goals

CHARLTON CAREER
Managers: *J Seed, J Trotter*
Debut: *Middlesbrough (H) 12-09-1953*
V255
Finale: *West Bromwich Albion (A) 06-04-1957*

EMBLEN Paul David   1997 - 98

During his time with Wycombe Wanderers, Paul scored the vital goal in their last match of the 1998-99 season, which ensured that they avoided relegation. His older brother Neil Emblen also played League football, most notably for Wolves. They both started their careers with Tonbridge Angels for whom Paul made over 150 league appearances.

Midfield, Forward   12st 5lbs   5' 11"
Born: 03-04-1976 - Bromley, Kent

HONOURS
Charlton Athletic Reserves 1997-98 Winners Football Combination

CLUBS
Tonbridge Angels (youth) 1993 (pro) ••Charlton Athletic 16.05.1997 (£7,500) ••Brighton & Hove Albion 04.11.97 (loan) ••Wycombe Wanderers 28.08.98 (loan) 18.09.98 (£60,000) ••Tonbridge Angels 03.02 (free)

Paul was a squad member during the exciting promotion season of 1997-98, but was not involved at Wembley for the play off final. His contribution was modest but he did make four substitute appearances. Most of his football was played for the Reserves and he made 22 league appearances as the club also finished winners of the Football Combination. His first team chances would have been even more limited

the following season and so he was moved on to Wycombe Wanderers where he enjoyed some measure of success before injuries and a change of manager put an end to his Football League career.

Since 2004 Paul has worked as a self employed carpet fitter and in 2015 it was reported that he had become a sports management consultant.

Season	Division	League		FA Cup		FL Cup		Play Offs		Total	
		A	G	A	G	A	G	A	G	A	G
1997-98 (P)	Division 1	0 (4)	0	0	0	0	0	0	0	0 (4)	0
Total		0 (4)	0	0	0	0	0	0	0	0 (4)	0

UK LEAGUE CAREER 82 games 7 goals

CHARLTON CAREER
Managers: *A Curbishley*
Debut: *Stockport County (H) (sub) 27-09-1997*
V570
Finale: *Port Vale (A) (sub) 13-04-1998*

ENDEAN Barry   1971

Forward   11st 11lbs.   5' 10"
Born: 22-03-1946 - Chester-Le-Street, County Durham

Barry's time at Charlton lasted only a little over seven months, yet nearly 50 years later his name is still mentioned whenever a striker fails to score an acceptable number of goals and the resigned accusation is always that 'he is another Barry Endean'. The facts do however support the legend, as he failed to find the net in a league match from his debut on 13th February 1971 until his 20th game on 28th August. Even this breakthrough did not open the floodgates and when he departed for Blackburn Rovers two months later, despite no end of effort and some measure of bad luck, the cold hard facts revealed one league goal in 27 games. Charlton have endured several non-striking strikers since Barry's time but he remains the standard against which they are always measured.

HONOURS
Watford 1968-69 Winners Division 3

CLUBS
Pelton Fell (youth) ••Everton 1962 (youth) ••Black Horse (amateur)) ••Watford 03.09.68 (pro) ••Charlton Athletic 09.02.71 (£11,111) ••Blackburn Rovers 26.10.71 (player exchange) ••Huddersfield Town 13.03.1975 (player exchange) ••Workington 31.10.75 (loan) ••Hartlepool 13.03.76 (free) ••Workington 1977 (free) 04.79 (manager) ••Chester-le-Street c1981 (youth coach) 03.88 (player manager)

Barry left school at 15 and was working as an apprentice welder when the opportunity came for a trial with Everton. He signed a youth contract, but being unable to settle in the city, soon returned home to County Durham. It was not until four years later that a second chance presented itself and by then he was knocking in the goals for Black Horse FC, a Sunday morning pub team based in Chester-Le-Street. He received an offer from Watford and on 7th September 1968 became a professional footballer and was pitched straight in the deep end, making his Football League debut up at Hartlepool nine days later.

All the high points in Barry's career came in the first couple of years. He played regularly for Watford in the season 1968-69 and scored 18 league goals as they topped Division 3. At one stage he netted eight goals in five games, including three in a 5-0 win at Gillingham on 11th January. He held his place the following season and on an unforgettable afternoon in February 1970 scored the header which knocked Liverpool out of the FA Cup at the Sixth Round stage. From then on things went rapidly downhill and Barry's final league goal for Watford came on 21st March 1970, to be followed by a dry spell that lasted

for 16 matches up to his transfer to Charlton nearly a year later. The only crumb of comfort during this period was a hat trick against Reading in an FA Cup match.

For most of Barry's time at Charlton, the crowd were supportive of a player who was clearly giving everything to the team, but as the barren spell grew ever longer, there were some who queried his continued selection and ironically when the goal finally came, it was scored against his old team, Watford. With the threat of relegation looming, a deal was completed in October 1971 and he was transferred to Blackburn Rovers in exchange for Eamonn Rogers.

Initially things did not improve at Blackburn and they had to wait until his 16th League game on 19th August 1972 before he scored for them, finally bringing to an end a 57 game run involving three clubs, lasting two years five months and producing one solitary goal.

A further player exchange in March 1975 took Barry to Huddersfield with Bobby Hoy travelling in the opposite direction and he also had short spells with Workington and Hartlepool before eventually hanging up his boots. After football, he returned to Chester-Le-Street where he worked for many years as a builder.

Season	Division	League		FA Cup		FL Cup		Total	
		A	G	A	G	A	G	A	G
1970-71	Division 2	17	0	0	0	0	0	17	0
1971-72 (R)	Division 2	10	1	0	0	2	1	12	2
Total		27	1	0	0	2	1	29	2

UK LEAGUE CAREER 228 games 55 goals

CHARLTON CAREER
Managers: *T Foley*
Debut: *Sheffield United (H) 10-02-1971*
V361
Finale: *Cardiff City (A) 23-10-1971*

EPHRAIM Hogan Phillip   2011

Hogan was a talented young footballer who earned international recognition whilst a teenager and went on to enjoy a moderately successful career in the professional game without perhaps quite fulfilling that early promise. He played nine times for England U19's, including three matches in the UEFA U19 Championships qualifying round in 2007 and scored in the 2-1 defeat by the Netherlands on 17th May, when his teammates included Elliot Omozusi and Danny Haynes.

Forward   11st 0lbs   5' 9"
Born: 31-03-1988 - Holloway, London
Education: Highbury Grove School, London

HONOURS
England U19 International 2005-07 9 caps 3 goals
England U18 International 2005-06 3 caps 0 goals
England U17 International 2004-05 13 caps 6 goals

England U16 International 2003-04 3 caps 0 goals
Queens Park Rangers 2010-11 Winners Championship

CLUBS
West Ham United 07.04 (youth) 15.04.05 (pro) ••Colchester United 23.11.06 (loan) ••Queens Park Rangers 10.08.07 (loan) 02.01.08 (£800,000) ••Leeds United 26.11.09 (loan) ••Charlton Athletic 15.11.11 (loan) ••Bristol City 22.03.12 (loan) ••Toronto, Canada 27.02.13 (loan) ••Peterborough United 08.11.13 (loan) ••Wycombe Wanderers 28.10.14 (free) ••Whitehawk 10.03.17 (free)

Hogan's senior debut was for West Ham in a League Cup match at Hillsborough on 20th September 2005. He was only aged 17, but played his part in the 4-2 win over Sheffield Wednesday. However, this was to be his one opportunity with the Hammers and in January 2008 and after a successful spell on loan, he signed for Queens Park Rangers, the fee of £800,000 a clear sign that he was considered a useful prospect.

He spent five seasons at Loftus Road and played over 100 games without ever really being among the first names on the team sheet, but did feature prominently during their Championship promotion season of 2010-11. He dropped down the pecking order the following season and never got the chance to play in the Premier League so in November 2011 accepted the opportunity to kick-start his career via a short period loan with Chris Powell's promotion chasing Charlton team.

Hogan played five matches and never once appeared on a losing side. Although not a prolific goalscorer, he did find the net at the Valley against Huddersfield Town on 28th

November, adding to Yann Kermorgant's opener in a 2-0 win, but the loan period ended on 3rd January without any permanent deal being drawn up.

With no real future at Queens Park Rangers, further loans went ahead including a three-month spell in Major League Soccer with Toronto, until eventually he joined Wycombe Wanderers in October 2014. Yet again his first team chances were limited but he was in the starting eleven along with Paul Hayes when they met Southend United in the League Two play off final at Wembley on 28th May 2015.

Wycombe appeared to have the game in the bag until Joe Pigott, on loan from Charlton, scored the equaliser in the final minute of extra time and Southend clinched promotion 7-6 on penalties.

This effectively brought Hogan's football career to an end at the age of 27. He left Wycombe in May 2015, turning down a new contract and although there were offers to play elsewhere, he chose not to pursue them. On 10th March 2017 he did make a half- hearted attempt at a comeback when he and his former England colleague Elliot Omozusi both signed for National League South side Whitehawk, on the same day. He only lasted three matches however and a further comeback seems unlikely.

Always active on social media, Hogan has had his own Apple Podcast since January 2016 along with former

Wycombe Wanderers player Marcus Bean. Titled 'Two Pros and a Pod', it is a monthly internet discussion where the two men give their views on footballing issues and perhaps this may in time lead him to a new career in the media.

Season	Division	League		FA Cup		FL Cup		FL Trophy		Total	
		A	G	A	G	A	G	A	G	A	G
2011-12 (P)	League One	4 (1)	1	0	0	0	0	0	0	4 (1)	1
Total		4 (1)	1	0	0	0	0	0	0	4 (1)	1

UK LEAGUE CAREER 164 games 11 goals

CHARLTON CAREER
Managers: *C Powell*
Debut: *Brentford (A) (sub) 19-11-2011*
V740
Finale: *Yeovil Town (A) 26-12-2011*

ETHERIDGE Neil Leonard Dula   1970 - 15

Goalkeeper   14st 2lb   6' 2"
Born: 07-02-1990 - Enfield, Middlesex
Education: Court Moor School, Fleet

It took a long time for Neil's career to really get going and he was aged 25 by the time that he finally got a run of games with Walsall, the seventh Football League club with whom he had been attached. This was a sharp contrast to his international career where he was capped by England U16's against Northern Ireland on 5th November 2005, before switching his allegiance to the Philippines, for whom he qualified through his Filipino mother. By the time he turned 25, he already had some 50 Philippines international caps in his locker.

HONOURS
Philippines International 2008-19 65 caps 0 goals   Cardiff City 2017-18 Runners Up Championship
England U16 International 2005 1 cap 0 goals

CLUBS
Cuffy Chiefs (youth) ••Hart Boys (youth) ••Chelsea 2003 (youth) ••Fulham 2006 (youth) 2008 (pro) ••Leatherhead 09.08 (loan) ••Charlton Athletic 06.03.11 (loan) ••Bristol Rovers 20.09.12 (loan) ••Crewe Alexandra 22.11.13 (loan) ••Oldham Athletic 30.10.14 (free) ••Charlton Athletic 27.11.14 (loan) 05.01.15 (free) ••Walsall 02.07.15 (free) ••Cardiff City 30.05.17 (free) ••Birmingham City 11.09.20 (undisclosed)

Neil signed a professional contract with Fulham in 2008 but in the next six years only appeared once in their first team. His sole moment of glory came on 14th December 2011 when he lined up against the Danish club, Odense BK in a Europa Cup match, but the occasion was spoiled when victory was snatched away after he conceded a last minute goal for a 2-2 draw.

Charlton had a minor goalkeeping crisis after Rob Elliot was injured against Tranmere on 5th March 2011 and the following day Neil was summoned to the Valley as cover for rookie 'keeper Ross Worner. He had hardly unpacked his bag when he was recalled by Fulham who had their own injury concerns and his first loan in SE7 lasted just six days. Having failed to make the breakthrough with Fulham, Neil was on the point of giving up, but signed a short term contract with Oldham Athletic in October 2014, during which he was obliged to sleep on a friend's sofa. The following month he returned to Charlton where he

remained until the end of the 2014-15 season. His first appearance was at the Valley on Boxing Day 2014 and after Callum Harriott was sent off in the first half, the team did well to salvage a 1-1 draw thanks to an equalising goal by Johann Gudmundsson. His short run in the Charlton side came to an abrupt end after a 5-0 mauling by Watford on 17th January.

With little to show for his seven years as a professional footballer, Neil joined Walsall in Summer 2015 and finally got a run of games as they battled through to the League One play offs. He returned to the Valley on 11th March 2017 when his Walsall side, which included Erhun Oztumer, forced a 1-1 draw, the Charlton goal coming from Tony Watt.

Neil turned down a new contract and was transferred to Cardiff City where he became their first choice goalkeeper and in 2017-18 only missed one match as they clinched promotion to the Premier League, their first time in the top flight since 1962. They were unable to maintain this status, but he was ever present for Cardiff during 2017-18 despite suffering with mental health issues and continued in goal

Season	Division	League		FA Cup		FL Cup		Total	
		A	G	A	G	A	G	A	G
2014-15	Championship	4	0	1	0	0	0	5	0
Total		4	0	1	0	0	0	5	0

UK LEAGUE CAREER 243 games 0 goals

for the Bluebirds until he eventually lost his place at the end of 2019. The following September he signed for Birmingham City for an undisclosed fee.

CHARLTON CAREER
Managers: *C Powell, B Peeters, G Luzon*
Debut: *Cardiff City (H) 26-12-20114*
V790
Finale: *Watford (A) 17-01-2015*

EUELL Jason Joseph   2001 - 12

Striker Jason Euell was transferred from Wimbledon to Charlton on 16th July 2001 for a club record fee of £4.75 million. He received a five-year contract and proved a resounding success, finishing as Charlton's leading goalscorer in each of his first three seasons. After five years away, he returned in 2011 and from the sub's bench made a handy contribution to the League One promotion side Since hanging up his boots, Jason has been a massively important figure within the youth academy, coaching and mentoring successive generations of future Charlton players, until on 1st April 2021 he was promoted to the position of first team coach to work alongside new manager Nigel Adkins. This provided conclusive proof that the club had got value for money from that big transfer fee almost 20 years earlier. He was elected into the Hall of Fame in 2021.

Forward, Midfield   12st 7lbs   6' 0"
Born: 06-02-1977 - Lambeth, London

HONOURS

Jamaica International 2004-06 3 caps 1 goal

England U21 International 1996-98 4 caps 0 goals

England Youth International

Charlton Athletic Reserves 2004-05 Winners Reserve League (South)

Charlton Athletic 2011-12 Winners League One

Charlton Athletic 2021 Hall Of Fame

Blackpool 2009-10 Promoted Play Offs Championship.

CLUBS

Merrow Rovers (youth) ••Wimbledon 1989 (youth) 01.06.95 (pro) ••Charlton Athletic 16.07.01 (£4.75 million) ••Middlesbrough 31.08.06 (£300,000) ••Southampton 31.08.07 (free) ••Blackpool 21.07.09 (free) ••Doncaster Rovers 17.02.11 (loan) ••Charlton Athletic 10.08.11 (free) 09.13 (coach) ••AFC Wimbledon 10.01.12 (loan) ••England 02.09.19 (U20 coach) ••Charlton Athletic 01.04.21 (1st team coach)

Jason started out as a member of the infamous 'crazy gang' who for more than a decade kept Wimbledon in the top strata of English football. Continually punching above their weight, they regularly beat the more fancied clubs, despite having limited resources and by the time he reached their first team in 1995, the added disadvantage of ground sharing at Selhurst Park, a concept only too familiar to anyone connected with Charlton. He scored on his league debut against Southampton, but took time to earn a regular place. Along with Chris Perry and Alan Kimble, he helped beat Liverpool 2-1 on 6th May 1997 and contributed the opening goal. By season 1997-98 he was well established and he and Carl Leaburn were spearheading the Wimbledon attack. On 9th February 1998 Carl scored twice and Jason got the third as Crystal Palace were

convincingly beaten 3-0 in an 'away' match at Selhurst Park.

Wimbledon's bubble finally burst and they were relegated from the Premier League in 1999-00 but Jason remained with the club and had his best season the following year, scoring 20 league and cup goals before making the move across London to join Charlton. Alan Curbishley's team were, (like Wimbledon before them), succeeding in the Premier League against the odds and he fitted in perfectly, scoring twice against West Ham, plus the winner in an exciting game against Ipswich Town. On 2nd March 2002 he scored both goals as Chelsea were defeated 2-1 and was by now an important member of this Charlton side that was performing so admirably.

For the next two seasons he continued in the same way,

claiming a brace in the 2-2 draw at Tottenham on Boxing Day 2002 and a further two, (hat-tricks always seemed to elude him), against Wolves in January 2004. By the later stages of that season however, he was moved back into midfield and spent much of his final two years with Charlton on the sub's bench.

Jason left upon the expiry of his contract in the Summer of 2006 and by then was a Jamaican international, having three caps, including one against Ghana on 29th May 2006 in which he scored in a 4-1 win. He moved to Middlesbrough and then on to Blackpool before returning to the Valley for the 2011-12 season in which he made a number of cameo appearances from the bench. He called a halt to his playing career in 2012.

A move into the business world had devastating effects when his property company failed and Jason suffered financial hardship, but his coaching activities were flourishing and he quickly became a much respected figure working with the young players in Charlton's academy. In 2019 as further evidence of his excellent reputation, he was selected to work as a coach for England's U20 age group as part of the FA's coach placement programme. With his elevation to first team coach at Charlton, there are many who would back Jason to become a future Charlton manager.

Season	Division	League		FA Cup		FL Cup		FL Trophy		Total	
		A	G	A	G	A	G	A	G	A	G
2001-02	Premier	31 (5)	11	2	1	2	1			35 (5)	13
2002-03	Premier	35 (1)	10	2	1	1	0			38 (1)	11
2003-04	Premier	24 (7)	10	0 (1)	0	1 (1)	0			25 (9)	10
2004-05	Premier	7 (19)	2	1 (2)	0	0 (2)	0			8 (23)	2
2005-06	Premier	5 (5)	1	0 (1)	0	0	0			5 (6)	1
2011-12 (P)	League One	0 (11)	0	1 (1)	1	2	1	0 (1)	0	3 (13)	2
Total		102 (48)	34	6 (5)	3	6 (3)	2	0 (1)	0	114 (57)	39

UK LEAGUE CAREER 427 games 87 goals

CHARLTON CAREER
Managers: *A Curbishley, I Dowie, C Powell*
Debut: *Everton (H) 18-08-2001*
V600
Finale: *Hartlepool United (H) (sub) 05-05-2012*

EVANS John   1950 - 53

Forward   10st 11lbs   6' 0"
Born: 28-08-1929 - Tilbury, Essex
Died: 08-1999 - Brentwood, Essex
Education: St Mary's Catholic School, Tilbury.

John was a superb header of a football and a quality goalscorer. A crowd of 48,056 was at the Valley on 22nd September 1951 to witness the 3-0 demolition of a strong Newcastle United side and Charlie Vaughan had already scored the first of his two goals, when in the 55th minute, Gordon Hurst fired in a cross from the right. It was hit with considerable venom and in the hope that a defender might cause a deflection in the crowded goal mouth. Instead, John rose with perfect timing and the ball simply flew into the net. Until Matt Tees arrived at Charlton more than a decade later, Evans was viewed as the greatest header of a football that the club had ever seen and in the end it was simply a matter of personal opinion as to which of these two special talents was the best.

HONOURS

Football League XI 1955 I cap I goal   Thurrock District Schools
RAF Coastal Command XI c1948   Bata Sports c1948 Winners South Essex League

CLUBS

Bata Sports 1947 (amateur) ••Tilbury 1948 (amateur) ••Watford 1948 (amateur) ••Charlton Athletic 31.05.49 (amateur) 10.05.50 (pro) ••Liverpool 26.12.53 (£12,500) ••Colchester United 21.11.57 (free) ••Romford 07.60 (free) ••Ford's Works 11.62 ••Grays Athletic 1965 (manager)

John played for Thurrock District Schools and after completing his education worked at the Bata shoe factory in East Tilbury. Their works team, Bata Sports, competed in the South Essex League and the 56 goals that he scored for them in one season alone, had a lot to do with their success during the early post war period. He was stationed in Hertfordshire with the RAF during his National Service and turned out briefly for Watford at reserve level as well as representing RAF Coastal Command.

He joined Charlton in May 1949 and a year later signed on

as a professional. He scored on his debut at Hillsborough in the 2-1 defeat of Sheffield Wednesday and in each of his first three league outings. His hat trick against Portsmouth on 11th November 1950 ensured a 3-3 draw in a hard fought match at Fratton Park and he very quickly became an important member of the Charlton side.

John scored in six consecutive Division 1 league matches during the 1951-52 season, including the winner in a 2-1 victory at Blackpool. By the start of his fourth campaign however, his strike rate was falling away and when his old teammate Don Welsh came calling in his capacity as manager of Liverpool, the Charlton directors accepted an offer of £12,500 for John and a further £7,500 for full back Frank Lock, the deals being agreed on Christmas Day and the transfers effective from 26th December 1953.

As it turned out, this was not a good time to be joining Liverpool and results were disappointing. When Charlton visited Anfield in February, John fired an early goal to put them ahead but the Addicks returned home with both league points thanks to a pair of goals from Eddie Firmani and a late winner from Sid O'Linn. Things did not improve and John only managed five goals as relegation became a certainty, but he more than made amends during the following season, collecting 33 cup and league goals in 42

games.

The stand-out performance during this feast of goals came on 15th September 1954 when he scored all five in a 5-3 win against Bristol Rovers and he almost repeated the feat later in the season with four against a Bury team that included ex-Charlton defender Norman Nielson. He played for a Football League XI and scored in a 3-2 defeat against the Scottish League at Hampden Park on 16th March 1955, having been a late selection when Bobby Ayre withdrew through injury.

John remained at Liverpool until November 1957, when he switched to Colchester United who were managed by another former Charlton colleague, Benny Fenton. The following season they reached the FA Cup round 4 and John netted the equaliser as the Essex team, which also included Cyril Hammond, held Arsenal to a 2-2 draw. His playing career wound down with a short spell in the Southern League for Romford.

He found employment at Fords Spare Parts Division in Aveley and turned out for their works team (not for Ford United as has been reported) and for three seasons managed Athenian League club, Grays United. He passed away in 1999 at the age of 70.

Season	Division	League		FA Cup		Total	
		A	G	A	G	A	G
1950-51	Division 1	31	14	1	0	32	14
1951-52	Division 1	34	12	0	0	34	12
1952-53	Division 1	13	5	0	0	13	5
1953-54	Division 1	12	7	0	0	12	7
Total		90	38	1	0	91	38

UK LEAGUE CAREER 243 games 109 goals

CHARLTON CAREER
Managers: *J Seed*
Debut: *Sheffield Wednesday (A) 09-09-1950*
V240
Finale: *Burnley (A) 19-12-1953*

EVANS Reginald   1959

Reg was an outside left who joined Newcastle United straight from school. He earned himself a professional contract but found it difficult to break into the first team, eventually getting his

Forward
Born: 18-03-1939 - Consett, County Durham
Education: Stanley Grammar School, Co. Durham

chance on 20th September 1958 in the 3-1 defeat of Wolverhampton Wanderers. This was a big match as Wolves went on to win the First Division title that season, but it did not lead to an extended run in the side for Reg and just over five months later he was deemed surplus to requirements and was transferred to Charlton in a straight swap for John 'Buck' Ryan.

HONOURS
Durham Youth

CLUBS
Newcastle United c1955 (youth) 18.03.56 (pro) ••Charlton Athletic 06.03.59 (player exchange) ••Ashington 07.60

Reg was thrust straight into the Charlton team and made his debut the day after his arrival and as a Geordie would have been pleased to see Sunderland dispatched 3-1, two of the goals being scored by the versatile John Hewie. Reg himself was among the scorers in his second game, a 3-3 draw at Lincoln, but despite this promising start to his Charlton career, he was not destined to stay long in London.

First team opportunities were less frequent in his second season when either Eddie Werge or Johnny Summers were preferred on the left wing and a £750 move to York City was rejected, Reg preferring to seek employment outside the game.

He had worked in an accountant's office when he first left school, but now found employment as a brewer with Scottish & Newcastle, a position that he maintained for nearly 40 years, eventually, upon retirement, being retained as a brewery tour guide.

Season	Division	League		FA Cup		Total	
		A	G	A	G	A	G
1958-59	Division 2	12	1	0	0	12	1
1959-60	Division 2	2	1	0	0	2	1
Total		14	2	0	0	14	2

UK LEAGUE CAREER 18 games 2 goals

CHARLTON CAREER
Managers: *J Trotter*
Debut: *Sunderland (H) 07-03-1959*
V282
Finale: *Leyton Orient (A) 28-11-1959*

EVINA-SI David Cedric Yannick   2011 - 14

Defender, Midfield   10st 6lbs   5' 7"
Born: 16-11-1991 - Douala, Cameroon
Education: The Compton School, North Finchley.

Cedric spent his early life in Paris before his family re-located to North London. He joined Arsenal at the age of nine and although he did well to advance through their academy, sign professional terms and even captain their youth team, the competition was so intense that he never got the opportunity to progress further and was released without playing a single game in the first team.

HONOURS

Doncaster Rovers 2016-17 Promoted League Two

CLUBS

Arsenal 2001 (youth) 08.09 (pro) ••Oldham Athletic 05.10.10 (loan) 28.01.11 (free) ••Charlton Athletic 21.06.11 (free) ••Doncaster Rovers 30.07.14 (free) ••Crawley Town 30.06.17 (loan) ••Notts County 14.09.18 (free) ••Romford 15.01.20 (free)

After leaving Arsenal, Cedric spent a season with Oldham Athletic where he played mainly on the left side of midfield. He was offered a contract for a second season but chose instead to seek out a club nearer to his family in London. Chris Powell was busily recruiting his promotion team during the summer of 2011 and saw him as a useful prospect, but he ended up in the shadow of Rhoys Wiggins who was viewed as first choice for the left back spot and despite his pace there were no first team chances in a more attacking role either. During his second season Wiggins was absent for a time through injury and Cedric deputised well enough but was never able to cement a regular place in the team.

He left Charlton after three years and moved to Doncaster Rovers where he tasted both relegation and promotion, followed by a season on loan at Crawley, which brought him to the end of his contract. No fresh offers were immediately forthcoming and he struggled to find a new club until on 14th September 2018 he signed for crisis team Notts County, bottom of the Football League and in desperate need of new blood to improve their fortunes. Despite his best efforts they failed to halt the decline and dropped out of the Football League for the first time since becoming founder members in 1888.

After leaving County in May 2019, Cedric was without a club for eight months. He did eventually sign for Romford in January 2020, but only lasted for a few training sessions before deciding to work on projects away from football.

Season	Division	League		FA Cup		FL Cup		FL Trophy		Total	
		A	G	A	G	A	G	A	G	A	G
2011-12 (P)	League One	2 (1)	0	2 (1)	0	2	0	1	0	7 (2)	0
2012-13	Championship	10 (2)	0	1	0	1	0			12 (2)	0
2013-14	Championship	4 (4)	0	2	0	2	0			8 (4)	0
Total		16 (7)	0	5 (1)	0	5	0	1	0	27 (8)	0

UK LEAGUE CAREER 178 games 3 goals

CHARLTON CAREER
Managers: *C Powell, J Riga*
Debut: *Reading (H) 23-08-2011*
V733
Finale: *Birmingham City (H) 08-02-2014*

FAMEWO Akinlolu Richard Olamide   2020 -

Young central defender Akin Famewo could hardly have made a more positive start to his first season's loan at Charlton. He made his debut on 27th September 2020 in a

Defender   6' 2"
Born: 09-11-1998 - Lewisham, London

2-0 defeat at Lincoln City, but had only completed his move from Norwich City the previous day. In the next six matches not a single goal was conceded and the blossoming partnership of Akin and another new signing, Ryan Inniss, at the heart of the defence, was a major factor in this impressive run of results. Unfortunately Akin damaged his hamstring in the 2-0 win at Portsmouth on 31st October and Inniss picked up a quad injury in training soon after. There was a noticeable downturn in Charlton's fortunes while both men were absent.

CLUBS

Luton Town 2008 (youth) 19.07.16 (pro) ••Grimsby Town 06.07.18 (loan) ••Norwich City 29.01.19 (undisclosed) ••St Mirren, Scotland 08.01.20 (loan) ••Charlton Athletic 26.09.20 (loan) 08.07.21 (loan)

Akin spent over 10 years with Luton Town and after progressing through each age group within their academy, was granted his first team debut on 16th August 2016. The manager who gave him his chance was Nathan Jones, who had previously worked for a year at Charlton as Development Coach. A Londoner by birth, Akin is of Nigerian descent. His mother's family come from the Norwich area and like himself are Norwich City supporters. It was therefore an easy decision for him to make when in January 2019 the opportunity came for him to sign for them.

Highly rated by his new club, he was not however deemed

ready for more than the occasional first team outing. He captained the Norwich U23's and spent the second half of the 2019-20 season competing in the Scottish Premier League with St Mirren, until the campaign was cancelled in May because of the Covid crisis. His next opportunity came with the loan move to Charlton, but injuries restricted him to just 22 league appearances in 2020-21. His form, when he did play, was very encouraging and it was a universally popular decision among Charlton supporters when in July 2021, he re-signed for a second season's loan with an option for the move to eventually be made permanent.

Season	Division	League		FA Cup		FL Cup		FL Trophy		Total	
		A	G	A	G	A	G	A	G	A	G
2020-21	League One	20 (2)	0	0	0	0	0	0	0	20 (2)	0
Total		20 (2)	0	0	0	0	0	0	0	20 (2)	0

UK LEAGUE CAREER 48 games 0 goals

CHARLTON CAREER
Managers: *L Bowyer, N Adkins, J Jackson*
Debut: *Lincoln City (A) 27-09-2020*
V900

FAMILIA-CASTILLO Juan Carlos   2022 -

The January 2022 transfer window was the first opportunity for new Charlton manager Johnnie Jackson to make adjustments to his playing squad. Popular striker Chuks Aneke was re-signed, but the

Defender, Midfield   5' 9"
Born: 13-01-2000 - Amsterdam, Netherlands
Education: Bindelmeer College, Amsterdam.

first new face to arrive at the Valley, was highly rated Dutch defender Juan Castillo on loan from Chelsea until the end of the 2021-22 season. He had just come off a less than successful loan at Birmingham City where the manager, Lee Bowyer, had initially criticised him for being overweight and out of shape when he first arrived at St Andrews. At the age of 22 and now both in shape and in need of first team action, the next phase of his football development was important for both club and player.

HONOURS

Netherlands U20 International 2020 6 caps 0 goals	Netherlands U15 International 2014-15 8 caps 0 goals
Netherlands U19 International 2018-19 9 caps 3 goals	Chelsea U18 2016-17 & 2017-18 Winners FA Youth Cup
Netherlands U18 International 2017-18 5 caps 2 goals	Chelsea U18 2016-17 National Winners PD League
Netherlands U17 International 2016-17 10 caps 3 goals	Chelsea U19 2018 & 2019 Finalists UEFA Youth League
Netherlands U16 International 2015-16 11 caps 1 goal	

CLUBS

AVV Zeeburgia, Netherlands (youth) ••Ajax, Netherlands 2009 (youth) ••Chelsea 2016 (youth) 13.01.19 (pro) ••Jong Ajax, Netherlands 30.08.19 (loan) ••AZ Alkmaar, Netherlands 06.10.20 (loan0 ••ADO Den Haag, Netherlands 11.01.21 (loan) ••Birmingham City 06.07.21 (loan) •Charlton Athletic 21.01.22 (loan)

Juan spent seven years in the youth academy at Ajax before being signed by Chelsea at the age of 16. He was in their U18 team that won the FA Youth Cup in both 2017 and 2018 and his teammates in the second year included Conor Gallagher. He was also a regular participant when Chelsea U18's became the national winners of the Professional U18 Development League in 2016-17. This enabled them to participate in the UEFA U19 Youth League the following season. Playing at wing back, he scored twice against Atlético Madrid in the group stage and featured along with Gallagher in the final when they went down 3-0 to Barcelona. They reached the final again in April 2019, but were again beaten, this time 3-1 by Porto. The Chelsea team that day included Juan, Conor and Ian Maatsen.

In 2019 Juan was deemed ready to have a spell out on loan and he returned home and spent season 2019-20 playing for Jong Ajax, the reserve team of Ajax who play in the Eerste Divisie, the second level of football in the Netherlands. Since then his progress has been Covid interrupted, but he did manage 16 games while on loan with ADO Den Haag, prior to his time with Birmingham. He has played international football with the Netherlands since 2014 and with such an impressive pedigree in youth football, is now ready to really make his mark in the adult game. His debut as a substitute, replacing Ben Purrington in the Football League Trophy against Hartlepool United, gave Charlton supporters their first glance at this exciting new signing.

UK LEAGUE CAREER 0 games 0 goals

CHARLTON CAREER
Managers: *J Jackson*
Debut: *Hartlepool United (A) (sub) 25-01-2022*
V939

FANNI Rod Dodji 2016

Defender   12st 2lbs   6' 1"
Born: 6-12-1981 - Martigues, France.
Education: Bachelors Degree in Industrial Science and Technology

Although born in France, Rod's family originated from Benin in West Africa. He was linked with moves to several Premier League clubs including Everton, Newcastle and West Ham at different times in his career. In 2014 when Leicester City tried to sign him from Marseilles, crucial e-mails were wrongly routed into their junk folder as a result of which the transfer was never concluded.

HONOURS

France International 2008-10 5 caps 0 goals	Olympique de Mareille 2011 & 2012 Winners Coupe de La Ligue
Olympique de Marseille 2011 Winners Trophee des Champions	

CLUBS

FC Martigues, France 1999 (youth) 2000 (pro) ••RC Lens, France 01.07.02 ••LB Chateauroux, France 2004 (loan) ••OGC Nice, France 06.05 ••Stade Rennes, France 2007 ••Olympique de Marseille, France 17.12.10 ••Al-Arabi SC, Qatar 11.07.15 (free) ••Charlton Athletic 01.02.16 (loan) ••Olympique de Marseille, France 31.08.16 ••Montreal Impact, Canada 05.03.18

Rod was a very classy defender as was demonstrated during   his loan spell at Charlton. It was just unfortunate that his stay in SE7 was so short and that he came to the club during a period of great turbulence both on and off the field. Had he been available for Charlton during the whole of the 2015-16 season, perhaps a quite needless relegation could have been avoided. During his time in France, Rod was named in the UNFP Team of the Year in both 2009 and 2010 while playing for Rennes and was unfortunate not to earn more than five international caps.

On 28th July 2011, Marseilles and Lille contested the Trophee des Champions at the Tangier Stadium in Morocco. The Marseilles team contained not only Rod but also Souleymane Diawara and Alou Diarra and the match

turned out to be a classic, finally ending 5-4 after Marseilles converted two penalties in second half stoppage time.

Any hope of keeping him at Charlton after his loan period expired was dashed when relegation became a certainty and he returned to France and re-signed for Marseilles. In March 2018 Rod joined the Canadian club, Montreal Impact, where he concluded his career playing in Major League Soccer. His contract was not renewed in the December and although he wanted to carry on playing, he was unable to find an acceptable opening and was forced to retire at the age of 37.

Season	Division	League		FA Cup		FL Cup		Total	
		A	G	A	G	A	G	A	G
2015-16 (R)	Championship	13 (1)	0	0	0	0	0	13 (1)	0
Total		13 (1)	0	0	0	0	0	13 (1)	0

UK LEAGUE CAREER 14 games 0 goals

CHARLTON CAREER
Managers:
Debut: *Preston North End (sub) (A) 23-02-2016*
V817
Finale: *Burnley (H) 07-05-2016*

FAYE Amdy Mustapha   2006 - 07

Senegal born Amdy Faye made his name with the French club, Auxerre, for whom he played consistently in Ligue 1 as well as in the UEFA Champions League. On 31st May 2003 he was in the Auxerre team that defeated Paris St Germain 2-1 in the final of the Coupe de France in front of 78,316 people and by then was also a Senegalese International. He made a total of 34 appearances for his country, all before he joined Charlton and took part in the 2002 FIFA World Cup in Japan, where Senegal progressed to the quarter final stage, as well as the African Cup of Nations in 2002 and 2006.

Midfield, Defender 6' 0"
Born: 12-03-1977 - Dakar, Senegal

HONOURS
Senegal International 2001-06 34 caps 0 goals   AJ Auxerre 2002-03 Winners Coupe de France

CLUBS
AS Monaco, France 1994 (youth) ••ES Frejus, France 1995 ••AJ Auxerre, France 07.02.98 (free) ••Portsmouth 14.08.03 (£1.5 million) ••Newcastle United 25.01.05 (£2 million) ••Charlton Athletic 08.08.06 (£2 million) ••Rangers, Scotland 31.08.07 (loan) ••Stoke City 15.08.08 (free) ••Leeds United 09.09.10 (free)

8th August 2006 was not a great day in the history of Charlton Athletic, as it was then that manager Iain Dowie announced his two new signings, Amdy Faye from Newcastle and Djimi Traore from Liverpool at a cool £2 million each.

Portsmouth manager Harry Redknapp had brought Amdy to England three years earlier and the story goes that he was worried that another club would get wind of the signing and de-rail the transfer, so his player was checked into a hotel under the name of 'Andy Henry' and kept locked in a room under guard of a big dog until the paperwork could be completed. Despite the hefty transfer fees Amdy had not

been a great success at either Portsmouth or his next club, Newcastle and by Summer 2006 was deemed surplus to requirements on Tyneside.

The 2006-07 season was a disaster for Charlton as they crashed out of the Premier League and Faye was one of the big money signings who flopped during that dismal period. He did manage one goal, his only one in English football and it was the winner against his old club, Portsmouth on 20th January 2007, but overall his contribution was below the standard required to preserve Premier League status. After relegation, the club became desperate to get his not inconsiderable salary off the books and he was loaned out to

Scottish giants, Rangers, but made no impact north of the border and only started two league games. The downward spiral continued with less than impressive spells at Stoke and Leeds before he eventually hung up his boots in 2011. Earlier Amdy had been arrested by City of London Police in November 2007 as part of the investigations into

corruption within football, as his transfer between Portsmouth and Newcastle was the subject of close examination by the Lord Stevens Enquiry. He was however never charged with any wrong doing and allegations against various Portsmouth officials were also dropped.

Season	Division	League		FA Cup		FL Cup		Total	
		A	G	A	G	A	G	A	G
2006-07 (R)	Premier	25 (3)	1	1	0	2 (1)	0	28 (4)	1
2007-08	Championship	0 (1)	0	0	0	1	0	1 (1)	0
Total		25 (4)	1	1	0	3 (1)	0	29 (5)	1

UK LEAGUE CAREER 140 games 1 goal

CHARLTON CAREER
Managers: *I Dowie, L Reed, A Pardew*
Debut: *West Ham United (A) 19-08-2006*
V635
Finale: *Stockport County (H) 28-08-2007*

FELL Leslie James   1946 - 51

Forward   10st 10lbs   5' 6"
Born: 16-12-1920 - Leytonstone, London
Died: 09-10-2010 - Rochester, Kent
Education: Brook Road School and Maynard Road School, Walthamstow and Central School, Margate.

Les represented Kent Schools and at the age of 15 was invited for a trial with Margate who were Arsenal's nursery team in those days. He was at the same time working in the office of Hewson & Brooke, heating engineers in Cliftonville. When war broke out he became a draughtsman with Short Brothers at Rochester Airport where they were building Stirling bombers and Sunderland flying boats and his footballing ambitions took a back seat for a time. Les played for Erith & Belvedere in the final of the London Senior Cup on 12th May 1945 which was the Saturday after VE Day. They beat Tooting & Mitcham 5-3 and he had a hand in three of the goals. A very speedy and tricky winger, he was known as 'Lightning Les' or 'The Pimpernel'

HONOURS
London FA v Diables Rouges (in Brussels) 01.11.47
Margate Boys & Kent Boys
Charlton Athletic 1945-46 Finalists FA Cup
Charlton Athletic Reserves 1949-50 Winners Football Combination
Charlton Athletic Reserves 1949-50 Runners Up Football Combination Cup
Charlton Athletic Reserves 1950-51 Winners Football Combination Cup
Charlton Athletic Reserves 1950-51 Winners London FA Challenge Cup
Charlton Athletic Reserves 1951-52 Finalists London FA Challenge Cup
Erith & Belvedere 1944-45 Winners London Senior Cup

CLUBS
Margate 1936 (youth) ••Canterbury Waverley 1937 (youth) ••Margate 1939 (amateur) ••Shorts Sports 1942 (amateur) ••Gravesend United 1943 (amateur) ••Charlton Athletic 28.08.44 (amateur) 04.12.45 (pro) ••Erith & Belvedere 05.45 (amateur) ••Crystal Palace 03.10.52 (£2,500) ••Margate 1954 (free)

Les made his Charlton debut in a rather bizarre Wartime Football League (South) fixture at the Valley on 28th October 1944 against Luton Town which resulted in a scoreline of 9-4 and six goals for Charlie Revell. He went on to play 20 games during that season and a further 45 in 1945-46, although only the FA Cup games counted as 'official' appearances during that first post-war season. Les was first choice at outside right and played throughout the Cup run, his biggest contribution coming in the semi-final at Villa Park when he laid on the opening goal for

Chris Duffy in a 2-0 victory over Bolton Wanderers in front of a crowd of 70,819. Defeat in extra time in the final was of course a big disappointment, but Les Fell is still to this day one of only 16 men who have represented Charlton in an FA Cup Final.
For him the bad news came when Gordon Hurst was signed the following season and took over his place on the right wing. Les remained with the club for a further six years but was never again first choice for selection and after two seasons playing in Division 3 with Crystal Palace, he

headed back to Margate in 1954. He continued to work as a layout draughtsman for Swifts, near Rochester Airport

and remained there until his retirement in 1985.

Season	Division	League		FA Cup		Total	
		A	G	A	G	A	G
1945-46	Wartime			10	3	10	3
1946-47	Division 1	5	2	0	0	5	2
1949-50	Division 1	5	0	0	0	5	0
1950-51	Division 1	2	0	0	0	2	0
1951-52	Division 1	1	0	0	0	1	0
Total		13	2	10	3	23	5

UK LEAGUE CAREER 78 games 8 goals

CHARLTON CAREER
Managers: *J Seed*
Debut: *Wartime Luton Town (H) 28-10-1944 FA Cup Fulham (H) 05-01-1946*
V209
Finale: *West Bromwich Albion (A) 15-09-1951*

FENTON Benjamin Robert Vincent   1947 - 55

Season 1952-53 was Charlton's most successful post-war league campaign. On 3rd April and with seven games remaining they stood 2nd on goal average

Midfield, Forward   11st 5lbs   5' 8"
Born: 28-10-1918 - Forest Gate, London
Died: 29-07-2000 - Poole, Dorset
Education: Odessa Road School & Godwin Road School, Forest Gate.

and with a good chance of finishing as Division 1 champions until three straight defeats made this impossible and they had to settle for an otherwise creditable 5th place. Benny Fenton was Charlton's inspirational captain and was ever present throughout the entire season. He enjoyed a highly productive eight years at the Valley and later spent a similar period as manager of Millwall, before returning to Charlton, first as secretary and then general manager. His brother Ted Fenton played for West Ham and also enjoyed a long managerial career.

HONOURS

Essex Youth and London Boys
Army v FA XI
London FA 1948 1 cap

FA XI v Army 1950
Charlton Athletic Reserves 1949-50 Runners Up Football Combination Cup

HONOURS AS MANAGER

Colchester United 1961-62 Runners Up Division 4

CLUBS

Colchester Town 1934 (youth) ••West Ham United 28.10.35 (pro) •Millwall 16.03.39 (£3,000) •Charlton Athletic 17.01.47 (£5,000) ••Colchester United 28.02.55 (£1,450 player manager) 05.58 (manager) ••Leyton Orient 17.11.63 (manager) ••Millwall 02.05.66 (manager) ••Charlton Athletic 10.01.77 (secretary) 07.79 (euro rep) 29.03.80 (ass manager) 23.06.81 (gen manager)

Benny had a trial for England Schools before turning pro on his 17th birthday and he clocked up more than 20 appearances for West Ham before, in March 1939, moving to Millwall where they offered a greater prospect of first team football. However, the outbreak of war saw the temporary re-organisation of the game on to a regional basis and when his army commitments permitted, he appeared in matches over the next few years, not just for Millwall, but on occasions as a guest player for West Ham, York City, Manchester City, Cardiff City and Charlton. His first game for Charlton was at the Valley on 14th November 1942 when a very weak side containing five

guest players went down 5-1 against Brentford with only a Charlie Revell goal to show for their efforts. Another of the guests that day was Chris Duffy of Leith Athletic. Benny made a total of 11 wartime appearances for Charlton and scored four goals, but when the FA Cup re-started in season 1945-46 he was back with Millwall and along with Tommy Brown and Fred Ford was part of the team humiliated by Aston Villa in a 4th Round tie on 28th January 1946. The result of 9-1 remains the biggest defeat in their history. Jimmy Seed knew all about Benny's ability as a wing half or in a more attacking role at inside forward and shelled out £5,000 to bring him to the Valley in January 1947. He went straight into the team, made his debut the following day and played consistently in the league side for the remainder of the season. However, he was already cup-tied (as was Charlie Vaughan), his final game for Millwall having been a dismal FA Cup defeat at home to Port Vale and this cost him dearly. He played for Charlton in the matches either side of the Cup Final, but both men had to be replaced for the trip to Wembley.

As time passed and the pre-war players gradually fell away, Benny became a key member of the Charlton side and almost a permanent fixture at right half. The team played attractive and exciting football during this period and he was an influential leader both on and off the field. When Jimmy Seed was sacked in 1956, it was Benny Fenton whom he recommended to the directors as his successor, but they, having already panicked into a managerial change, now compounded their error by ignoring him in favour of long time trainer Jimmy Trotter.

Benny had already departed by this time, having joined Colchester United as player manager in February 1955, when at the age of 36, his playing days were nearing an end. He hung up his boots in May 1958 but carried on as manager and guided the Essex club to promotion from Division 4 in 1962. He spent a difficult year managing Leyton Orient which ended with the sack and then moved back to Millwall where ironically Jimmy Seed was now a director, Benny held the reins at the Den for over eight years, and still remains their longest serving manager since the 1930s.

He returned to Charlton in 1977 and took over as club secretary and then did spells as both assistant manager and general manager before finally departing in May 1982 following the arrival of new chairman Mark Hulyer. He retired down to Dorset and passed away in July 2000 at the age of 81.

Season	Division	League		FA Cup		Total	
		A	G	A	G	A	G
1946-47	Division 1	17	3	0	0	17	3
1947-48	Division 1	28	5	1	0	29	5
1948-49	Division 1	39	7	1	0	40	7
1949-50	Division 1	16	0	1	0	17	0
1950-51	Division 1	41	0	2	0	43	0
1951-52	Division 1	40	2	1	0	41	2
1952-53	Division 1	42	2	1	0	43	2
1953-54	Division 1	31	2	1	0	32	2
1954-55	Division 1	10	1	3	0	13	1
Total		264	22	11	0	275	22

UK LEAGUE CAREER 409 games 53 goals

CHARLTON CAREER
Managers: *J Seed*
Debut: *Wartime Brentford (H) 14-11-1942 Football League Preston North End (H) 18-01-1947*
V222
Finale: *Wolverhampton Wanderers (A) 19-02-1955*

FERGUSON Iain John 1989

Forward, Midfield   10st 7lbs   5' 7"
Born: 04-08-1962 - Newarthill, North Lanarkshire
Education: Braidhurst High School, Motherwell.

Much has been made of Tony Watt's spectacular goal against Barcelona whilst playing for Celtic. Yet another player with Charlton connections can at least equal this feat and without it having become a career defining moment. Iain Ferguson headed the last minute winner for Dundee United at Camp Nou on 18th March 1987 in the quarter final of the UEFA Cup. They then progressed right to the final only to be narrowly beaten over two legs by IFK Göteborg. Iain was among the leading Scottish strikers of his generation and although never a full International, did appear for the Scotland U21's against East Germany in a UEFA U21 qualifier on 12th October 1982. They won 2-0, the first goal being scored by Colin Walsh.

HONOURS
Scotland U21 International 1982
Scotland Youth International
Scotland Schoolboy International 4 caps
Rangers 1984-85 Winners Scottish League Cup

Dundee United 1986-87 Finalists UEFA Cup
Dundee United 1986-87 Finalists Scottish FA Cup
Dundee United 1987-88 Finalists Scottish FA Cup
Motherwell 1990-91 Winners Scottish FA Cup

Portadown 1995-96 Winners Irish League

CLUBS

••Fir Park Boys Club, Scotland (youth) ••Dundee, Scotland 1978 (youth) 1979 (pro) ••Rangers, Scotland 07.84 (£200,000) •Dundee, Scotland 1986 (loan) ••Dundee United, Scotland 07.86 (£140,000) ••Heart Of Midlothian, Scotland 19.07.88 (£325,000) ••Charlton Athletic 29.11.1989 (loan) ••Bristol City 21.03.90 (loan) ••Motherwell, Scotland 12.90 (£100,000) •Airdrieonians, Scotland 09.93 (£50,000) ••Portadown, N Ireland 1994 (£20,000) ••Dundee, Scotland 1996 ••Dundalk, Ireland 1997 •Gretna 1998

Iain's career commenced at Dundee where he signed as a 16 year old and made his debut on 15th December 1979, scoring in a 3-1 win over Kilmarnock. He went on to be their leading scorer for three seasons before joining Rangers, somewhat accidentally, after a heavy drinking session. He was obliged to double check later as to whether he had actually signed or not.

He had a good first season at Rangers, scoring the only goal against Dundee United in the League Cup Final and holding down a regular place in the first team, but was less involved after that and moved on to Dundee United in the summer of 1986. His two years at Tannadice Park saw the club reach three cup finals, but sadly on each occasion they ended in disappointment. Iain was a natural goalscorer, but one who never seemed to score a simple tap in. He specialised in the spectacular and none more so than a thunderbolt for his next club, Hearts, which on 28th February 1989 put paid to Bayern Munich in the first leg of their UEFA Cup tie.

Lennie Lawrence brought Iain down to England for the first time and his Charlton debut on 2nd December 1989 at Derby was as replacement for Carl Leaburn. The game was

lost 2-0, but had Iain's loan period run it's course, perhaps his proven ability as a goalscorer could have helped in that season's relegation struggle. Unfortunately he picked up an injury and never got the chance to play for Charlton again, returning to Scotland shortly thereafter.

Twice a beaten finalist in the Scottish FA Cup while with Dundee United, Iain again reached the final in 1990-91, now playing for his hometown club, Motherwell. He scored the opening goal in one of the most open and exciting finals that anyone could remember. It finished 4-3, with Motherwell victorious against, ironically enough, Dundee United.

Iain later had a spell playing for Portadown and appeared 25 times for them in 1995-96 as they won the Irish League and eventually finished his playing career at Gretna, who although based in Scotland, were at that time competing in the Northern District League.

After retiring, Iain lived in Spain for some while and set up in business retailing replica shirts. He later had a stall in the Forge, an indoor market in Glasgow selling sportswear, worked as a car salesman and ran a sports bar in Hamilton.

Season	Division	League		FA Cup		FL Cup		FM Cup		Total	
		A	G	A	G	A	G	A	G	A	G
1989-90 (R)	Division 1	1	0	0	0	0	0	0	0	1	0
Total		1	0	0	0	0	0	0	0	1	0

CHARLTON CAREER
Managers: *L Lawrence*
Debut: *Derby County (A) 02-12-1989*
V507

UK LEAGUE CAREER 389 games 105 goals

FERNS Philip David   1981 - 82

Phil was born in Liverpool but raised in Poole, Dorset. He represented his county from U13 to U18 level and came close to national

Defender, Utility   11st 4lbs   5' 11"
Born: 12-09-1961 - Liverpool
Education: Turlin Moor Primary School & Herbert Carter Secondary Modern School, Poole.

recognition. He was called up for the England Youth squad, but never capped. His father, also Phil Ferns, played for Liverpool in the 1964-65 side that won the Division 1 title and later for both Bournemouth and Mansfield Town. Phil Jnr followed in his father's footsteps and signed for AFC Bournemouth at the age of 17.

HONOURS

Yeovil Town 1986-87 Runners Up Isthmian League Premier Division	Yeovil Town 1987-88 Winners Isthmian League Cup
Yeovil Town 1987-88 Winners Isthmian League Premier Division	Poole Town 1989-90 Runners Up Southern League Division 1 South

CLUBS

Turlin Moor c1971 (youth) ••Langland Street Boys Club (youth) ••Strouden Rangers (youth) ••Charminster Saints c1978 (youth) ••Poole Town 1978 (youth) ••AFC Bournemouth 07.78 (youth) 01.79 (pro) ••Charlton Athletic 27.07.81 (£20,000) ••Wimbledon 12.82 (loan) ••Blackpool 08.83 (free) ••Aldershot 07.85 (free) ••Yeovil Town 07.86 (free) ••Poole Town 10.89 (£3,000) ••Yeovil Town 07.91 (free) ••Trowbridge Town 03.95 (free)

He made his Bournemouth debut only four months after his 17th birthday and in his second match was part of a resounding 7-1 win against Doncaster Rovers on 3rd February 1979. He quickly established himself at left back and by the end of season 1980-81 had clocked up more than 100 league and cup games. He came up against Charlton in an FA Cup tie at the Valley on 13th February 1980 but the visitors were beaten 2-1, thanks to goals by Paul Walsh and Derek Hales.

Charlton had just regained their place in Division 2 in the Summer of 1981 when new manager Alan Mullery rather surprisingly decided to dismantle the promotion team and when the new season kicked off on 29th August at Luton Town, there were six newcomers, including Phil Ferns, in the Charlton team. He played pretty regularly that first season, except for a six-week absence following an ankle injury sustained against Cambridge United on 23rd January, but by 1982-83 his place had come under attack and his final match was on 30th October, the left back spot eventually being filled by new signing Mark Aizlewood.

A five-week loan spell at Wimbledon went well, apart from a red card up at Swindon, but there was no longer a place for Phil at Charlton and after two years at the Valley, he

moved on first to Blackpool and then Aldershot, where he played his last Football League game on 15th April 1986. Having commenced his career so young, it had all come to an end by age 24.

He did however enjoy considerable success in the non-league game and along with teammate Alan Pardew, helped Yeovil Town to the runners-up spot in the Premier Division of the Isthmian League in 1986-87. The following season, after Pardew had moved on to Crystal Palace, they did even better, completing the league and cup double. In his second spell with Yeovil, Phil was part of the giant killing side, which on 15th November 1993 dispatched Fulham (1-0) from the FA Cup.

In 1996, he joined the police force and served for many years in the Dorset constabulary, as well as working as a freelance football coach. Phil holds a UEFA A coaching licence as well as being an FA Level 2 tutor/assessor.

Season	Division	League		FA Cup		FL Cup		Total	
		A	G	A	G	A	G	A	G
1981-82	Division 2	26 (2)	0	1	0	3	0	30 (2)	0
1982-83	Division 2	9 (1)	1	0	0	0 (1)	0	9 (2)	1
Total		35 (3)	1	1	0	3 (1)	0	39 (4)	1

UK LEAGUE CAREER 211 games 9 goals

CHARLTON CAREER
Managers: *A Mullery, K Craggs, L Lawrence*
Debut: *Luton Town (A) 29-08-1981*
V431
Finale: *Blackburn Rovers (H) 30-10-1982*

FIELD Samuel Edward

2019 - 20

Sam joined Charlton on a season's loan from West Bromwich Albion in August 2019 and as a highly promising holding midfield player, he was expected to be a useful addition to the squad following

Midfield   10st 3lbs   5' 10"
Born: 08-05-1998 - Wordsley, West Midlands
Education: Haybridge High School, Hagley.

promotion from League One. Initially he lacked match fitness, but was just starting to settle into the side when a knee injury at Bristol City on 23rd October pulled him out of the action. Two months later he was a week away from returning when his knee let him down again and by February manager Lee Bowyer reported that he was unlikely to play again during the period of his loan. When the Covid epidemic caused the season to be extended into July, he reappeared unexpectedly and featured in the remaining matches after lockdown.

HONOURS
England U20 International 2017-19 12 caps 0 goals
England U19 International 2016-17 8 caps 1 goal

England U18 International 2016 2 caps 0 goals

CLUBS
West Bromwich Albion 2007 (youth) 29.06.16 (pro) ••Charlton Athletic 08.08.19 (loan) ••Queens Park Rangers 01.02.21 (loan) 20.05.21 (undisclosed)

A graduate of the youth academy at West Bromwich Albion, Sam made his Premier League debut against Liverpool on 15th May 2016 and was clearly identified as a young player with a big future. He scored against Newcastle the following season but found his first team opportunities limited despite playing consistently for the England youth

teams. He was sent off on his debut for England U18's against South Korea after picking up two yellow cards in the match.
After a spell on loan at Queens Park Rangers, Sam signed a three-year deal with them in May 2021.

Season	Division	League		FA Cup		FL Cup		Total	
		A	G	A	G	A	G	A	G
2019-20 (R)	Championship	10 (7)	0	0	0	1	0	11 (7)	0
Total		10 (7)	0	0	0	1	0	11 (7)	0

UK LEAGUE CAREER 70 games 3 goals

CHARLTON CAREER
Managers: *L Bowyer*
Debut: *Forest Green Rovers (H) 13-08-2019*
V880
Finale: *Leeds United (A) 22-07-2020*

FILLISTON Joseph William

1922 - 23

Joe came from the Kingsland Road in Shoreditch and as well as his ability on the football field, was also an accomplished cricketer. A specialist batsman, he spent five years at Lords and in 1921 was playing as a professional at Penzance in Cornwall. His father, also

Forward
Born: 12-05-1894 - Shoreditch, London
Died: 06-1981 - Enfield, London.
Education: Page Green School, Tottenham.

Joe Filliston, was himself a prominent figure in the cricketing world, played in matches with WG Grace and umpired at Lords when aged over 100.

HONOURS
Charlton Athletic 1923-24 Finalists London Challenge Cup
Mildmay Athletic Winners Tottenham Charity Cup

London League v London Combination 1922

CLUBS
Mildmay Athletic 1912 ••Woking ••Barnet ••Redhill ••Clapton Orient 1920 ••Charlton Athletic 03.22 (amateur) 08.22 (pro)

Joe made his debut for Charlton as an amateur and played at centre forward in the last five matches of the 1921-22 season, their first as a Football League club, He did reasonably well, netting against both Newport and Swindon and signed professional terms during the summer of 1922.

The following season started well enough and he scored both goals against Luton Town in a 2-1 victory at the Valley on 2nd September 1922, but gradually the goals dried up and he lost his place up front to Kosha Goodman when the team was re-shuffled during November. From then on Joe was never a regular in the side and his final appearance came just before Christmas 1923 in a goalless draw with Northampton. At the end of that season he was given a free transfer.

He had a trial with Luton Town in November 1924, presumably off the back of his two goals a couple of years earlier, but it did not lead to anything, leaving Joe to concentrate on his cricket. He worked as a cabinetmaker and was resident in Morton Way, Southgate up to the time of his death in Highlands Hospital shortly after his 87th birthday.

Season	Division	League		FA Cup		Total	
		A	G	A	G	A	G
1921-22	Divison 3 (S)	5	2	0	0	5	2
1922-23	Divison 3 (S)	20	5	0	0	20	5
1923-24	Divison 3 (S)	5	1	0	0	5	1
Total		30	8	0	0	30	8

UK LEAGUE CAREER 30 games 8 goals

CHARLTON CAREER
Managers: *W Rayner*
Debut: *Reading (A) 17-04-1922*
V033
Finale: *Northampton Town (H) 22-12-1923*

FIRMANI Edwin Ronald   1951 - 67

Forward   12st 0lbs   5' 11"
Born: 07-08-1933 - Cape Town, South Africa
Education: Marist Brothers School & Cape Town High School.

Approaching 1,000 players have represented Charlton Athletic since they were elected to the Football League in 1921 and Eddie Firmani would probably be placed in the top 10 if they were to be judged on their overall contributions to the club. He had three separate spells as a player between 1950 and 1967, followed by two and a half years as manager and was enormously influential throughout his time at the Valley. It is hard to imagine that Jimmy Seed ever had a better day as Charlton manager than the occasion in February 1950 when he travelled to Cape Town to watch Stuart Leary play in a trial match. Eddie scored five goals that afternoon and Seed was inspired to sign both men. Now that was a good day's work.

HONOURS
Italy International 1956-58 3 caps 2 goals
Italy B International 1957 1 cap 0 goals
London FA 1955 1 cap 2 goals
Western Province Schools

Charlton Athletic A 1950-51 Winners London Mid-Week League
Charlton Athletic Reserves 1951-52 Finalists London FA Challenge Cup
Charlton Athletic 2017 Hall OF Fame

HONOURS AS MANAGER
Tampa Bay Rowdies 1975 Winners NASL Soccer Bowl
Tampa Bay Rowdies 1975 & 1976 Winners NASL Eastern Division
Tampa Bay Rowdies 1975 Runners Up NASL Indoor Tournament
Tampa Bay Rowdies 1976 Winners NASL Indoor Tournament
New York Cosmos 1977 & 1978 Winners NASL Soccer Bowl
New York Cosmos 1977 Runners Up NASL Eastern Division
New York Cosmos 1978 Winners NASL Eastern Division

Montreal Manic 1981 & 1982 Runners Up NASL Eastern Division
Montreal Manic 1981-82 Winners NASL Indoor Season Eastern Division
Kazma SC 1985-86 & 1986-87 Winners Kuwaiti Premier League
Kazma SC 1985, 1987 & 1988 Runners Up Kuwaiti Emir Cup
Kazma SC 1987 Winners Gulf Club Champions Cup
Kazma SC 1988 Runners Up Gulf Club Champions Cup
Sur SC 1992-93 Winners Omani League Division 2

CLUBS

Clyde, South Africa ••Charlton Athletic 21.02.50 (pro) ••Sampdoria, Italy 18.07.55 (£35,000) ••Internazionale, Italy 06.58 (£88,000) ••Genoa, Italy 1961 (£65,000) ••Charlton Athletic 04.10.63 (£12,500) ••Southend United 26.05.65 (£8,500) ••Charlton Athletic 07.03.67 (£2,000) 11.09.67 (manager) ••Bromley 11.73 (manager) ••Tampa Bay Rowdies, USA 1974 (manager) ••New York Cosmos, USA 1977 (manager) ••New Jersey Americans, USA 19.06.79 (manager) ••Philadelphia Fury, USA 11.10.79 (manager) ••Montreal Manic, Canada 1981 (manager) ••New York Cosmos, USA 1984 (manager) ••Kazma SC, Kuwait 1985 (manager) ••Khaitan SC, Kuwait 08.90 (manager) ••Al-Talaba SC, Iraq 1990 (manager) ••Montreal Supra, Canada 06.91 (manager) ••Sur SC, Oman 1992 (manager) ••Montreal Impact, Canada 1993 (manager) ••New York/New Jersey MetroStars, USA 04.01.96 (manager) ••Al-Seeb, Oman 09.96 (manager)

His grandfather was an Italian fisherman from the small coastal town of Ortona on the Adriatic coast, which is the reason why growing up in Cape Town, Eddie carried such an unusual sounding surname. He played football for his local team, Clyde, where the star player was another soccer crazy youngster named Stuart Leary and the two boys soon became close friends and would practice together after school on nearby Green Point Common. Clyde was highly successful and won several local tournaments and Leary in particular soon came to the attention of Jimmy Seed. Charlton had earlier identified South Africa as a largely untapped market and with Sid O'Linn already in the Charlton first team and others like John Hewie in the wings, he was very much on the lookout for more talent. Leary and Firmani were aged 16 when they left their families and travelled by ship to Southampton They were met by O'Linn and assistant manager George Robinson and Eddie moved into digs in Norfolk Gardens, Bexleyheath. It took a considerable time to acclimatize to British conditions and after a year at Charlton, he was still a long way short of a first team place. Seed kept faith in him however and during the 1951-52 season asked him to move from inside forward to full back. This experiment seemed to work and his form markedly improved so when left back Frank Lock went down with flu in November 1951, Eddie made his debut in a 3-3 draw against Derby County.

His first real run in the side came in September 1952 but after three further games at full back, he was moved into the attack. His second match as a forward ended with Stoke City on the end of a 5-1 beating thanks to a hat-trick from Eddie and goals from John Hewie and Billy Kiernan. From that point on the two South Africans, Leary and Firmani, led the Charlton attack and had a lot to do with the club finishing as high as fifth in Division 1. The following season both men kept the goals coming, but it was 1954-55 which proved to be Eddie's time. He just couldn't stop scoring. There were hat-tricks in consecutive matches during November, then another on Christmas Day when Sheffield Wednesday were dispatched 3-0. On 5th February 1955 Aston Villa arrived at the Valley and were demolished 6-1, courtesy of a goal by Billy Kiernan and five from Eddie. He

had wed Pat, the daughter of George Robinson in March 1954 and with impeccable timing, their son Paul was born the day after the Aston Villa match.

On 4th June 1955 a London FA team went out to Switzerland to play Basle in the Inter Cities Fairs Cup and both Eddie and Billy Kiernan were selected for the match. Firmani scored twice and Cliff Holton grabbed a hat-trick in a convincing 5-0 victory.

It seemed that things could not get much better for Eddie, but out of the blue an approach was made during the close-season by the Italian club Sampdoria who offered a transfer fee of £35,000, then a record for the Football League, plus for the player a signing on fee of £5,000, an enormous amount in those days. Charlton accepted the offer in July 1955, but without that Italian grandfather it would not have been possible as only foreign players with traceable Italian origins could be signed from abroad at that time. Eddie took the transfer very seriously and started to learn the Italian language, but for the first two months found goals hard to come by, not being used to the bone hard pitches. He finally scored the winner against Roma to remove the pressure and from then on his form improved and for the remainder of his time with Sampdoria he averaged almost a goal a game. On 11th November 1956 he made his international debut out in Switzerland and scored the equaliser for Italy in a 1-1 draw. He was unable to retain his place because a knee injury kept him out for three months, including 45 days in hospital, but he did eventually get two further caps and scored another goal against Austria on 23rd March 1958. Interestingly, by then the former Charlton wing half Bill Dodgin had taken over as Sampdoria manager.

In June 1958 Eddie was transferred to Internazionale for a fee reported to be £88,000 and three years later when he joined Genoa, a further £65,000 changed hands. These were huge fees and a sharp contrast to the financial structure in England where in 1958 there was still a maximum wage of £20 a week. He was successful at all his three Italian clubs and by the end of his career held the unique record of being the only player to have scored 100 league goals in both Serie A and the Football League. An autobiography, 'Football With The Millionaires' was published in 1959.

Perhaps he was always destined to return, but when it happened it was a major event in London SE7. His second debut was up at Maine Road on 5th October 1963 and Eddie scored twice. Mike Kenning added another and Manchester City were swept away 3-1. The whole club were re-energised and promotion back to Division 1 suddenly seemed a real possibility. He scored three at Norwich in November and finished the season with 16 league goals in 24 matches. although the club had to settle for fourth place. The next season the team fell away but Eddie scored a further 16 goals, before inexplicably being transferred to Southend United in June 1965. He was still aged only 31 and had more goals in him as he demonstrated by netting 24 in 55 games during his interlude on the Essex coast.

By March 1967 Charlton were staring at possible relegation from Division 2 when manager Bob Stokoe brought Eddie back to the Valley for a third time and although he was starting to show his age, the goalscorer's instincts remained and he managed six crucial goals. Two of them came in the penultimate game, when a 3-0 win over Northampton Town consigned them to Division 3 instead of Charlton. He made one final appearance as a player in August 1967 against Preston North End, but when Stokoe was sacked the following month, he announced his retirement as a

player and moved into the manager's office.

Eddie enjoyed mixed fortunes during his two and a half years as Charlton manager. His strict, military style was not to everyone's liking but was obviously a product of his years in Italy. 1968-69 was a glorious season. The team played attractive, attacking football and should really have clinched promotion, but just fell short. The following campaign it all went wrong again and on 28th March 1970 Eddie made the monumental error of naming winger Mike Kenning at left back for the home game with Leicester City. Two days after that 5-0 debacle, he was fired and his 20-year association with Charlton finally came to an end.

This was however only the start of Eddie's managerial career and over the next decade he found great success in the USA, first with Tampa Bay Rowdies and later with New York Cosmos, winning the NASL Soccer Bowl on three occasions. In 1985, he re-located to Kuwait and won their Premier League two years running with Kazma SC. He and his wife even got caught up in the first Gulf War and were held hostage for a time, but happily came to no harm. Eddie also managed in Canada, Iraq and Oman before finally calling a halt in 1996, He now lives in retirement in sunny Florida. In 2017, he was voted into the Charlton Athletic Hall of Fame.

Season	Division	League		FA Cup		FL Cup		Total	
		A	G	A	G	A	G	A	G
1951-52	Division 1	1	0	0	0			1	0
1952-53	Division 1	29	13	1	0			30	13
1953-54	Division 1	34	12	2	0			36	12
1954-55	Division 1	36	25	3	1			39	26
1963-64	Division 2	24	16	1	0	0	0	25	16
1964-65	Division 2	31	16	2	0	3	0	36	16
1966-67	Division 2	9	6	0	0	0	0	9	6
1967-68	Division 2	1	0	0	0	0	0	1	0
Total		165	88	9	1	3	0	177	89

UK LEAGUE CAREER 220 games 112 goals

CHARLTON CAREER
Managers: *J Seed, F Hill, R Stokoe*
Debut: *Derby County (H) 03-11-1951*
V247
Finale: *Preston North End (H) 26-08-1967*

FIRMANI Peter   1956 - 58

Peter was the younger brother of Charlton legend Eddie Firmani and he followed him to the Valley from South Africa in 1953 at the age of 17. Eddie was already a first team regular by this time, but Peter had to wait until April 1956 before he made

Defender, Utility   12st 4lbs   5' 10"
Born: 14-02-1936 - Cape Town, South Africa
Died: 26-11-2004 - Durban, South Africa
Education: Marist Brothers School, Cape Town.

his debut in a 0-0 draw against Cardiff City. He was primarily a full back but was occasionally used in attack and extraordinarily also featured as a goalkeeper from time to time while in England. Other sources have erroneously recorded his full name as Peter Walter Firmani, but although that was his intended name, his father celebrated his arrival rather too much and forgot to include Walter when registering the birth.

HONOURS

Western Province
Charlton Athletic A 1957-58, 1958-59 & 1959-60 Winners London Mid-Week

League
Charlton Athletic A 1959-60 Winners Aetolian League Cup

CLUBS

Marist Brothers, South Africa 1952 (youth) ••Charlton Athletic 01.09.53 (pro) ••Highlands Park, South Africa 1960 ••Johannesburg Wanderers, South Africa c1962 ••Robertsham Callies United, South Africa (manager)

By the time that Peter was ready to contest a first team spot at Charlton, the golden era was at an end. Brother Eddie was playing out in Italy, Sam Bartram had retired, while many of the other star names from the early fifties had either moved on or were past their best. He made three appearances in 1956-57 and the first was up at Sunderland on 1st September. It was an unmitigated disaster. The team lost 8-1 and manager Jimmy Seed was sacked two days later after 23 years loyal service. Peter retained his place at right back for the visit of Sheffield Wednesday a week later, with former trainer Jimmy Trotter now at the helm, but the team was all over the place and it took late goals from Stuart Leary and John Hewie to scramble a 4-4 draw. He returned to the Reserves, but got one further outing on 22nd April, by which time the hopelessly outclassed Charlton team were already relegated and had been rock bottom of Division 1 since early December. They were well beaten 6-2 by Tottenham and Peter's three games had leaked 18 goals. His most productive season at Charlton came in 1957-58 as the club battled to regain their place in Division 1 at the first attempt. They nearly did it and Peter occupied the right back spot for the second half of the campaign. In the end it all came down to the last game of the season at the Valley on 26th April 1958 and Charlton only needed to draw to clinch promotion. He perhaps surprisingly spent

part of the match at centre forward, had an outstanding game and was voted man of the match, but sadly his efforts were not rewarded as Blackburn Rovers were victorious 4-3. The Charlton goals came courtesy of Fred Lucas, John Hewie and Peter himself.

He featured less often after that and in June 1960 was transfer listed at a fee of £1,500. He did not hang about though and returned home to South Africa shortly after. Charlton retained his registration to preserve their right to a transfer fee in the event that he came back, but his football days were nearing an end. He found work outside the game as a typesetter in the printing industry although much of 1961 was spent ill in a Johannesburg hospital, Some contact with Charlton was retained and in 1969 Peter was announced as their scout in South Africa.

A natural sportsman, he was an avid cricketer who later in life took up both golf and bowls. A devoutly Christian man, he married three times and after retiring from the print lived on a golf estate called Mount Edgecombe in Natal. Peter made a trip back to the UK in 1998 to attend the Charlton Old Players Reunion and met up with his brother Eddie (now a US resident) for the first time in years. He passed away at the age of 68 after being struck down by a fatal heart attack while driving to Durban.

Season	Division	League		FA Cup		Total	
		A	G	A	G	A	G
1955-56	Division 1	1	0	0	0	1	0
1956-57 (R)	Division 1	3	0	0	0	3	0
1957-58	Division 2	19	2	4	0	23	2
1958-59	Division 2	8	0	0	0	8	0
Total		31	2	4	0	35	2

UK LEAGUE CAREER 31 games 2 goals

CHARLTON CAREER
Managers: *J Seed, J Trotter*
Debut: *Cardiff City (H) 21-04-1956*
V267
Finale: *Lincoln City (H) 25-10-1958*

FISH Mark Anthony   2000 - 05

Defender   12st 11lbs   6' 4"
Born: 14-03-1974 - Cape Town, South Africa
Education: Sunnyside Primary School, Pretoria and Pretoria High School.

Mark was an iconic figure in post apartheid South Africa and is considered by some to have been among their greatest players. He made 62 appearances for his country, the last two of his caps coming during his time at Charlton. On 3rd February 1996, along with Shaun Bartlett, he was in the South African team that defeated Tunisia 2-0 to win the African Cup of Nations and had his personal contribution recognised when he was voted into the Team of the Tournament. Two years later they reached the final again, but this time were beaten 2-0 by Egypt. Mark was again a key member of the team.

HONOURS

South Africa International 1993-04 62 caps 2 goals
South Africa U16 & Youth International
South Africa 1996 Winners African Cup Of Nations
South Africa 1998 Finalists African Cup Of Nations
Charlton Athletic Reserves 2004-05 Winners Premier Reserve League (South)
Orlando Pirates 1994 Winners South African League (NSL)

Orlando Pirates 1995 Winners South African Charity Cup
Orlando Pirates 1995 Winners African Cup Of Champions
Orlando Pirates 1996 Winners South African Top Eight Cup
Orlando Pirates 1996 Winners African Super Cup (CAF)
Bolton Wanderers 2000-01 Promoted Play Offs Division 1

CLUBS

Arcadia Shepherds, South Africa 1980 (youth) 12.91 (semi-pro) ••Jomo Cosmos, South Africa 09.92 (R30,000) ••Orlando Pirates, South Africa 02.94 ••SS Lazio, Italy 08.96 (£1.2 million) ••Bolton Wanderers 19.09.97 (£2 million) ••Charlton Athletic 10.11.00 (£700,000) ••Ipswich Town 08.08.05 (loan) ••Jomo Cosmos, South Africa 2007 (free) ••Thanda Royal Zulu, South Africa 07.09 (manager)

Mark was playing football almost as soon as he could walk and turned out for Arcadia Shepherds at U7 level, gradually working his way through the various age groups until at 16, he was considered good enough to play for their first team. In 1992, he turned professional and transferred to Jomo Cosmos where he was coached and mentored by former Charlton player Roy Matthews. Up to this point he had been a forward and it was Roy who converted him into a centre half.

His career really came alive after he joined Orlando Pirates in February 1994, winning not only domestic trophies but in 1995 the prestigious African Cup Of Champions, when they defeated ASEC Abidjan of the Ivory Coast in a two legged final. A year later the Pirates were victorious in the CAF Super Cup beating the Algerian team JS Kabylie by 1-0 in a tense encounter at the FNB Stadium in Johannesburg.

Inevitably Mark's success led to interest from Europe and he came close to joining Manchester United prior to signing for the Italian club, SS Lazio in 1996, where he competed for one season in Serie A, the first South African to do so since Eddie Firmani.

This was followed by a move to Bolton Wanderers, but his introduction to their team was not enough to stop the slide to relegation from the Premier League in season 1997-98. He played alongside Claus Jensen when they reached the FA Cup semi final in 2000 and they finally regained their place at the top table a year later, but by the time that promotion was assured, Mark had left for Charlton for a fee of £700,000.

What Charlton got for their money was a classy, confident and highly popular central defender. He shared the centre half duties with Jon Fortune and Chris Perry in 2003-04, the club's most successful league season for 51 years and was a tower of strength during epic battles such as the 1-0 victory on 28th December 2003 at White Hart Lane against a Tottenham side that included a young Johnnie Jackson. The cry of 'Feesh' could regularly be heard ringing out from the Valley faithful throughout his five years at the club.

In March 2004, an accident at home in which he fell through a glass table, resulted in 39 stitches and forced him to miss the remainder of that dramatic campaign and the following year the games missed through injury started to mount up. He went out on loan to Ipswich Town, but only lasted 45 minutes and announced his retirement shortly after as a result of a severe cruciate ligament injury. He did have one last try at resurrecting his playing career in 2007, rejoining Jomo Cosmos, but could not regain the level of fitness needed to play even one further match for them. Since retiring, Mark has had his share of bad luck. In 2005, he and his family were tied up by four burglars and expensive jewellery and valuables stolen from his Kent home, while in 2014 he suffered a heart attack. Happily he has recovered and remains a popular figure in South Africa where he is now employed as a television commentator and sports pundit. His story can be found in the 2001 book, 'Madiba's Boys', with a forward by Nelson Mandela. His great uncle, Ken Fish, played for Port Vale in 1937.

Season	Division	League		FA Cup		FL Cup		Total	
		A	G	A	G	A	G	A	G
2000-01	Premier	24	1	3	0	0	0	27	1
2001-02	Premier	25	0	0	0	1	0	26	0
2002-03	Premier	23	1	1	0	1	0	25	1
2003-04	Premier	23	0	0	0	2	0	25	0
2004-05	Premier	6 (1)	0	0 (1)	0	0	0	6 (2)	0
Total		101 (1)	2	4 (1)	0	4	0	109 (2)	2

UK LEAGUE CAREER 206 games 5 goals

CHARLTON CAREER
Managers: *A Curbishley*
Debut: *Ipswich Town (A) 11-11-2000*
V595
Finale: *Manchester City (H) 02-04-2005*

FLANAGAN Michael Anthony   1971 - 86

For much of the 70s and early 80s Charlton played exciting and entertaining football. There were often defensive frailties, but the attacking trio of Flanagan, Powell and Hales was the guarantee of thrills and spills galore in the offensive third of the pitch and the architect of many memorable goals. Mike had three spells at Charlton, two as a player and then later in a coaching role and made a massive contribution, scoring 120 goals in 396 cup and league appearances while creating a whole lot more 'assists'. His best season was 1976-77 when he was ever present and scored 23 league goals. He was overwhelmingly voted Player of the Year in 1977 and in 2020 was elected into the Hall of Fame.

Forward, Midfield   12st 3lbs   5' 10"
Born: 09-11-1952 - Ilford, Essex
Education: Clark's College, Romford.

HONOURS

England B International 1978-79 3 caps 0 goals
England Amateur Youth International 1971 3 caps 1 goal
Charlton Athletic 1974-75 Promoted Division 3
Charlton Athletic 1985-86 Runners Up Division 2
Charlton Athletic 1977 Player Of The Year

Charlton Athletic 2020 Hall Of Fame
Tottenham Hotspur U18 1969-70 Winners FA Youth Cup
New England Teamen 1978 Winners NASL Eastern Division
Queens Park Rangers 1981-82 Finalists FA Cup
Queens Park Rangers 1982-83 Winners Division 2

CLUBS

Ford United (youth) ••Tottenham Hotspur 1965 (youth) 11.70 (non-contract) ••Charlton Athletic 09.08.71 (pro) ••New England Tea Men, USA 09.04.78 (loan) ••Crystal Palace 01.08.79 (£650,000) ••Queens Park Rangers 15.12.80 (£150,000) ••Charlton Athletic 12.01.84 (£50,000) ••Cambridge United 12.09.86 (free) ••Charlton Athletic 10.87 (coach) ••Grays Athletic 1988 (free) ••Margate 09.90 (free) ••Billericay Town 03.91 (free) ••Southend United 08.91 (coach) ••Gillingham 01.93 (ass: manager) 12.07.93 (manager) ••Hornchurch 03.95 (free) ••Millwall 08.97 (coach) ••Waterford United, Ireland 10.98 (manager) ••Hastings United 08.02 (coach) ••Margate 04.06 (ass: manager) ••Maldon & Tiptree 11.11 (manager) ••Brentwood Town 12.15 (manager) 07.20 (coach)

From the age of 12, Mike played for Tottenham Hotspur at youth level and in 1970 featured in the marathon FA Youth Cup final which stretched to four matches, (a two legged final and two replays), before they finally overcame Coventry City. He was not offered professional terms at that point and for a short while found employment in the Civil Service while at the same time, continuing to play occasional matches for Spurs, below first team standard and on a non-contract basis. He played in three England Youth Internationals, including a match with Northern Ireland on 6th March 1971, in which he scored in a 1-1 draw.

He was introduced to Charlton by scout Les Gore and after trials in July 1971 signed as a professional on 9th August, before making his debut at Bristol Rovers two months later. Initially he played as an orthodox winger, but despite his skill on the ball, he lacked the pace for that role and would eventually be moved inside where he became considerably more effective. Mike did not score at all in his first season but in 1972-73 got among the goals, including four against Notts County who suffered a 6-1 thumping at the Valley on 19th September 1972. Charlton's other scorers that day were Bobby Hunt and Arthur Horsfield.

Injury restricted his appearances during the promotion season of 1974-75, but in the following campaign he was in outstanding form as a goal provider. The club consolidated their place back in Division 2 with Derek Hales plundering 28 league goals. A forward line which included Flanagan, Peacock, Hales and Powell made for exciting, attacking football and when Hales was sold to Derby County in December 1976, Mike took over the main striking role. One of his finest performances was against Chelsea on 11th April 1977 when he scored three goals in a 4-0 victory at the Valley and during this period he was averaging the highly impressive return of a goal every two matches. In February 1978 he played the first of three games for England B, a 2-1 victory in West Germany. (two of his three caps fell while he was a Charlton player).

In April 1978 Mike and Colin Powell were loaned for the summer to the New England Tea Men, who were based in Boston, Massachusetts and they, along with Lawrie Abrahams, helped the Tea Men to win the Eastern Division of the North American Soccer League. Mike himself was a great success, scoring 30 goals and eight assists in only 28 matches. By the time he flew back to SE7, he was ranked as the second-best player in the NASL.

Derek Hales was re-signed by Charlton in July 1978, following which comments in the press hinted that Mike was not keen about relinquishing the main striking role which had been bestowed upon him in his absence. True or

not, the issue flared up on 9th January 1979 in an FA Cup tie at the Valley against non-league Maidstone United. The visitors took an early lead and despite Mike grabbing an equaliser, the search for a further goal was proving elusive as chance after chance was squandered. With four minutes remaining, punches were thrown by both men and the surprised referee had no choice but to send them off, leaving the remaining nine Charlton players to hang on for the draw. After serving his suspension and paying a £250 club fine, Mike submitted a written transfer request on 1st February. He returned to the side against Notts County two days later, while Hales, deemed to be the instigator of the fight, had his contract cancelled but his league registration retained by the club. The incident was still far from over though. On 9th February Hales was reinstated, but the two men did not play together again at this stage, as Mike walked out shortly after as a protest about his unresolved transfer.

He eventually signed for Crystal Palace for £650,000, at that time a record fee between two London clubs. The move did not really work out however as they were a declining force, slipping towards relegation from Division 1 during his second season. Mike did lift the gloom on 21st October 1980 however, scoring all three goals in the 3-2 defeat of Southampton. Two months later he switched to Queens Park Rangers where he embarked upon a more rewarding period, as they reached the FA Cup final in 1982 and clinched promotion to the First Division in season 1982-83, beating Charlton twice in the process.

In January 1984 Mike returned to Charlton and the ever popular strike force of Flanagan and Hales was re-united, at least for a short while, time having apparently healed the old wounds. His second spell with the club was less spectacular, but he remained a fine player and even after he dropped back to play mainly in midfield, he still retained his eye for a goal, as demonstrated when he notched the winner against Bradford City on 19th March 1986. After being given a free transfer, Mike linked up with Cambridge United for 1986-87, which proved to be his final season in the Football League. He then rejoined Charlton in a coaching capacity while at the same time making occasional appearances in the non-league game for Grays Athletic. Departing from Charlton for a third time in August 1980, Mike signed on as a player with Margate where Colin Powell was manager and made a spectacular debut, scoring from 50 yards in his first match. Since then, he has moved between clubs in a variety of roles. After coaching at Southend United, he had 19 months managing Gillingham and spent a similar period in charge at League of Ireland club, Waterford United and a year coaching at Millwall. He still kept lacing up his boots however and in 1995 turned out for Isthmian League club, Hornchurch at the age of 42. Mike has worked for a company installing swimming pools and more recently as a maintenance man for the Corporation of London, but another job in football is

never far away. Further coaching and managerial positions have taken him to Hastings, Maldon & Tiptree and back to Margate. In July 2020 he was appointed coach at Brentwood Town where his son Adam Flanagan was manager.

Season	Division	League		FA Cup		FL Cup		FM Cup		Total	
		A	G	A	G	A	G	A	G	A	G
1971-72 (R)	Division 2	7 (11)	0	0 (1)	0	1	0			8 (12)	0
1972-73	Division 3	42	12	4	1	5	2			51	15
1973-74	Division 3	40 (2)	11	1	0	2	0			43 (2)	11
1974-75 (P)	Division 3	15	4	2	0	0	0			17	4
1975-76	Division 2	38	6	4	1	7	2			49	9
1976-77	Division 2	42	23	2	0	3	0			47	23
1977-78	Division 2	32	16	1	0	1	1			34	17
1978-79	Division 2	25	13	2	1	4	2			31	16
1983-84	Division 2	18	2	1	0	0	0			19	2
1984-85	Division 2	38	11	2	0	2	0			42	11
1985-86 (P)	Division 2	33 (4)	11	1	0	2	1	1	0	37 (4)	12
Total		330 (17)	109	20 (1)	3	27	8	1	0	378 (18)	120

UK LEAGUE CAREER 490 games 140 goals

CHARLTON CAREER
Managers: *T Foley, A Nelson, L Lawrence*
Debut: *Bristol Rovers (A) 05-10-1971*
V364
Finale: *Wimbledon (H) (sub) 06-05-1986*

FLEETWOOD Stuart Keith Wakley   2009

Charlton were in free fall when they signed Stuart from Forest Green Rovers in the Summer of 2008 for a fee that was

Forward   11st 2lbs   5' 10"
Born: 23-04-1986 - Gloucester
Education: Newent Community School, and St Davids College, Cardiff.

reported to be £100,000. It was twelve months on from their Premier League departure and they were about to drop out the bottom of the Championship as well. He had scored 28 league goals and finished as the leading goalscorer in the Football Conference in 2007-08 yet strangely was never given a proper first team opportunity after arriving at the Valley.

HONOURS

Wales U21 International c2005 5 caps
Wales U17 International

Hereford United 2005-06 Promoted Play Offs Conference National
Sutton United 2015-16 Winners National League South

CLUBS

Newend (youth) ••Cardiff City 1998 (youth) 08.03 (pro) ••Hereford United 31.01.06 (free) ••Accrington Stanley 31.01.07 (loan) ••Forest Green Rangers 29.06.07 (free) ••Charlton Athletic 16.06.08 (£100,000) ••Cheltenham Town 26.09.08 (loan) ••Brighton & Hove Albion 31.10.08 (loan) ••Exeter City 18.03.09 (loan) ••Hereford United 02.07.10 (£110,000) ••Luton Town 31.08.11 (£45,000) ••Eastleigh 18.07.13 (free) ••Forest Green Rangers 04.01.15 (loan) ••Sutton United 28.06.15 (free) ••Rosey Athletic 04.16 (non contract) ••Bath City 07.06.16 (free) ••Weymouth 20.10.16 (loan) ••Merthyr Town 19.05.17 (free) ••Redditch United 20.11.17 (free) ••Swindon Supermarine 06.18 (free) ••Yate Town 10.07.20 (player coach)

Stuart was a pacey forward with a high work rate who liked to play in tandem with a big centre forward. He scored goals consistently over his long career which makes it all the more odd that he was never given a real chance in a struggling Charlton side and was instead farmed out on loan, first to Cheltenham and later to Brighton and Exeter. His only first team appearance was when he came off the

bench as replacement for Izale McLeod during an unmemorable League Cup match which was lost 1-0 in extra time.
His career had started out with Cardiff City with whom he had made his Football League debut, as well as being capped by Wales at Under 21 level. Then at Hereford he had played his part as they gained promotion from the

Conference in 2005-06 and the following season scored a memorable hat-trick when Championship side Coventry City were beaten 3-1 in the League Cup. It was however his goals for Forest Green Rovers that had brought him to Charlton, but after Alan Pardew was dismissed as manager, he saw no future for himself in SE7 and was happy to return to Hereford.

The second half of Stuart's career has been played out in the non-league game where he has switched clubs with considerable regularity. There has always been someone eager to sign him and unusually he does not have an agent, preferring to negotiate his own contracts. Both his attitude and fitness levels have allowed him to keep playing well into his thirties and he currently divides his time between a full time job as a personal trainer and as player coach for Southern League side Yate Town.

Season	Division	League		FA Cup		FL Cup		FL Trophy		Play Offs		Total	
		A	G	A	G	A	G	A	G	A	G	A	G
2009-10	League One	0	0	0	0	0 (1)	0	0	0	0	0	0 (1)	0
Total		0	0	0	0	0 (1)	0	0	0	0	0	0 (1)	0

CHARLTON CAREER
Managers: *A Pardew, P Parkinson*
Debut: *Hereford United (A) 11-08-2009*
V692

UK LEAGUE CAREER 139 games 27 goals

FOLEY Kevin Patrick   2016 - 17

Full Back, Midfield   12st 2lbs   5' 9"
Born: 01-11-1984 - Luton, Bedfordshire

Irish International Kevin Foley spent five months at Charlton late in his career. At his peak, he had played for Wolverhampton Wanderers in the Premier League, but was troubled with injuries and clearly past his best by the time that he arrived in SE7. It was also at the height of the troubles between supporters and the Belgian owners and on one occasion he was summoned to attend an open forum chaired by the CEO, Katrien Meire.

Many of those attending the meeting were angry about the way the club was being run and a heated exchange took place which just about kept within acceptable boundaries. Kevin sat through the whole proceedings in silence and looking highly embarrassed.

HONOURS
Republic of Ireland International 2009-12, 8 caps 0 goals
Republic of Ireland B International 2006 1 game 0 goals
Republic of Ireland U21 International 2004-06 8 caps 1 goal
FAI U21 Player of The Year 2005

Luton Town 2004-05 Winners League One
Wolverhampton 2008-09 Winners Championship
Billericay Town 2017 18 Winners Isthmian League, Premier Division
Billericay Town 2017-018 Winners Essex Senior Cup.

CLUBS
Luton Town 1994-04 (youth) 08.03.04 (pro) ••Wolverhampton Wanderers 14.08.07 (free) •Blackpool 27.02.14 (loan) & 27.11.14 (loan) ••FCK Copenhagen, Denmark 12.01.15 (free) ••Ipswich Town 22.01.16 (free) ••Charlton Athletic 05.08.16 (free) ••Coventry City 06.01.17 (free) ••Billericay Town 02.08.17 (free) ••Tampa Bay Rowdies, USA 02.01.20 (coach)

Kevin was born in Luton and started out with his local club. He signed pro at the age of 18 and made his league debut in a 2-2 draw against Bristol City on 19th April 2003. (the Luton Town team included Matthew Spring, Alan Kimble and Kevin Nicholls). Five months later he came up against Charlton in the Football League Cup and scored the opening goal in a frantic 4-4 draw at the Valley, which was eventually settled in Charlton's favour, 8-7 on penalties. In 2004-05, Luton finished champions of League One and Kevin was a key member of the defence, as he was over the next two seasons, before moving on to Wolves at the expiry of his contract in 2007.

A steady rather than spectacular player, Kevin remained with Wolves for seven years and played over 200 league matches. In 2008-09 they gained promotion into the Premier League and survived for two seasons before crashing downwards via two relegations into League One. There was great upheaval at Wolves towards the end of Kevin's stay and in Summer 2014 he was one of 10 players banished from the rest of the squad. They were deemed surplus to requirement and obliged to train on their own, which was cruel treatment after his length of service Gradually their numbers dwindled as transfers were arranged, until only he and ex-skipper Roger Johnson, his future Charlton teammate, remained. Finally, he signed a short term contract to re-activate his career in Denmark with FCK Copenhagen.

Kevin was never properly appreciated by Charlton fans during his short stay at the club. His signing one day before the start of the 2016-17 season looked like a panic move by manager Russell Slade and in his early matches he was obliged to share midfield duties with Johnnie Jackson and Andrew Crofts, all three being over age 30 and the collective lack of pace seemed apparent to all. He was a good deal more effective at full back and showed glimpses of the form that had earned him eight full caps for the Republic of Ireland. He had been eligible because his parents came from County Kerry. Kevin left the club when his short term contract expired in January 2017.

His playing career wound down via a handful of games for Coventry City and a final season in which he helped Billericay Town gain promotion to the National League South. In January 2020 he accepted a coaching position in the USA for Tampa Bay Rowdies.

Season	Division	League		FA Cup		FL Cup		FL Trophy		Total	
		A	G	A	G	A	G	A	G	A	G
2016-17	League One	12 (3)	0	2	0	1	0	2	0	17 (3)	0
Total		12 (3)	0	2	0	1	0	2	0	17 (3)	0

UK LEAGUE CAREER 389 games 8 goals

CHARLTON CAREER
Managers: *R Slade, K Robinson*
Debut: *Bury (A) 06-08-2016*
V820
Finale: *Bristol Rovers (H) (sub) 02-01-2017*

FOLEY Theodore Cornelius   1967 - 68

A tough tackling full back who captained Northampton Town as they rose to the top level of English football for the only time in their history, Theo finished his playing career at Charlton in

Defender   12st 2lbs   5' 11"
Born: 02-04-1937 - Inchicore, Dublin
Died: 26-06-2020 - Blackheath, London
Education: Inchicore School & St Michael's School, Dublin

1968 and then two years later followed Eddie Firmani as manager. His four years in charge at the Valley were not overly successful on the field, but he will always be remembered for his extraordinary knack of talent spotting and for signing the likes of Hales, Flanagan, Horsfield and Powell at bargain basement prices. With hindsight, it is a great pity that he was not allowed longer in the job as the team that Theo built went on to gain promotion twelve months after his departure and his successor Andy Nelson gained the full benefit of his excellent groundwork.

HONOURS
Republic of Ireland International 1964-67 9 caps 0 goals
Northampton Town 1962-63 Winners Division 3
Northampton Town 1964-65 Runners Up Division 2

CLUBS
Richmond Rangers, Ireland 1949 (youth) ••Bulfin United, Ireland 1950 (youth) ••Ormeau, Ireland c1950 (youth) ••Home Farm, Ireland 1951 (youth) ••Burnley 1954 (youth) ••Home Farm, Ireland 1954 (youth) ••Exeter City 02.55 (trial) 28.03.55 (pro) ••Nothampton Town 19.05.61 (small fee) ••Charlton Athletic 09.08.67 (free) 01.12.67 (player coach) 01.70 (ass; manager) 01.04.70 (manager) ••Dulwich Hamlet 1974 (coach) ••Dartford 17.02.75 (coach) ••Millwall 07.04.75 (coach) ••Queens Park Rangers 12.77 (coach) ••Millwall 12.82 (ass: manager) ••Arsenal 05.86 (ass: manager) ••Northampton Town 29.05.90 (manager) ••Fulham 1993 (coach) •Southend United 20.06.94 (ass: manager) ••Leeds United 1997 (scout) ••Tottenham Hotspur 1998 (coach) ••Greenwich Borough 11.03 (coach) •Stevenage Borough 2004 (coach) ••VCD Athletic c2007 (coach)

Born in the Dublin suburb of Inchicore, Theo started out with Home Farm, a club that has long been renowned for producing international footballers and from where Mark Kinsella would commence his career nearly 40 years later. He developed a reputation as a reliable and committed defender and at the age of 17 spent a month on trial with Burnley playing for their U18's, but was released on the grounds that he was too small. Despite this obvious disappointment, he persevered with his football while at the same time driving a tractor at the local railway depot. In 1955, he was given a second chance with Exeter City and signed professional terms on 28th March. His Football League debut came against Norwich City six months later. Moving to Devon was an upheaval for the young Theo and he took time to settle. He decided to take up golf but inadvertently bought a left-handed set of clubs, so taught himself to play left-handed. Exeter City were usually to be found in the lower reaches of Division 3 (South) and there was little glamour to be found as every week was a battle for survival. However, one bright spot came when he met Sheila, his future wife, at an Exeter dance hall and they remained together for more than 60 years. After finishing bottom of the league in 1957-58, Exeter became founder members of the new Division 4 and briefly flirted with promotion the following year, but fell short and finished fifth. Eventually, in May 1961 he transferred to Northampton Town after having played in excess of 150 league matches for Exeter.

Northampton was another small club, but one that had ambitions to becoming upwardly mobile. Situated in Division 3, Theo's teammates included Pat Terry and Cliff Holton and the latter scored 36 league goals in 1961-62, while Theo was ever present in the defence. They finished a creditable eighth that year, but the following season won the division by four points and thrashed Wrexham 8-0 and Halifax Town 7-1 in the process. The Northampton team became renowned for their fearsome defence and Theo, who was now captaining the side, was generally in the thick of things. His nose was broken on three separate occasions, including once by a fan during a ruck against Queens Park Rangers.

By 1964-65 Holton had moved on to Crystal Palace, but the Cobblers had gradually strengthened the squad and were now candidates for a second promotion. Theo was again ever present and they went to the top of the Second Division after beating Charlton 1-0 on 10th October, but in the end had to settle for second place. Incredibly, this small club with the most limited of resources had now reached the top division in English football, which was a quite remarkable achievement. It was a very proud Theo Foley who as captain led them out against Everton at Goodison Park on 21st August 1965 for their first match in Division 1. Bobby Hunt was now a Northampton player and he scored that day, but Everton proved too strong and were run away winners by 5-2. Sadly this was the pattern going forward, as they were regularly outplayed and it was not until 23rd October that they gained their first win, a 2-1 scoreline against West Ham. Theo scored the opening goal from the spot and in fact never missed a penalty throughout his career. Even after Welsh international Graham Moore was signed in December, the results did not improve enough to save Northampton and they finished second from bottom, so this remains the only season that

they have ever competed in the top flight throughout their history.

Theo made his international debut for Ireland on 11th March 1964 in Seville. It was the quarter-final of the European Nations Cup and although they were beaten 5-1 by Spain, the eventual champions, he performed well enough to remain part of the Irish squad for three years and when he made his ninth and final appearance against Czechoslovakia, a 2-0 defeat in Dublin on 21st May 1967, he did so as captain. Later in 1975 he was short-listed for the Irish manager's job. International football may have been the glamorous side of life, but it was still a struggle to bring up a young family on a footballer's wages during that period, so he launched 'Foley's Bake 'n' Take Pie Shop' which provided some welcome additional income during his time with Northampton.

It was during the First Division season that Theo developed ongoing problems with his left knee, which caused him to miss 11 matches. He played on as best he could but in 1966-67, as Northampton tumbled to a second consecutive relegation, he played less than half the games and realised that his career was in jeopardy. The club gave him a free transfer in view of his loyal service and Michael Gliksten, presumably sensing a bargain, snapped him up without insisting upon the thorough medical that would have highlighted the injury. The Foley family moved into a clubhouse at Blackheath, which he later purchased from Charlton and which remained his residence for the rest of his life.

There is no doubt that Charlton got a raw deal when they signed Theo the player. He was already injured by the time that the 1967-68 season got underway and they were obliged to blood the inexperienced Bob Curtis at full back in his absence. Manager Bob Stokoe had already been sacked before Theo finally debuted for his new club on 21st October 1967 in a 2-2 draw against Carlisle United. Alan Campbell and Harry Gregory built a 2-0 lead before half-time, only for it to be squandered in the last 10 minutes. It was that kind of season, but Theo's suspect leg prevented him from playing more than six games as the club loitered just above the relegation zone and his time was increasingly spent coaching, having been elevated to player-coach in December after the resignation of Malcolm Musgrove. During 1968 he passed his FA coaching badge (on the same course as Malcolm Allison) and clearly this was the direction in which his future lay.

By the end of March 1970, Charlton were again facing the threat of relegation. Theo had by now been elevated to assistant manager and so when the directors decided to sack

Stokoe's successor, Eddie Firmani, the seemingly poisoned chalice fell into his lap and he became acting manager tasked with negotiating the final four matches and keeping Charlton in Division 2. A win and two draws did the trick and his appointment was made permanent on 8th May 1970. This was the start of Theo's four-year reign as Charlton's manager and it is difficult to dispute his own assessment that he got the job simply because he was the 'cheap option'. Michael Gliksten was facing heavy losses season on season and the enthusiastic yet inexperienced Theo was prepared to operate with almost a nil budget. Results on the field did not improve, but Theo was at least able to make some headway with his transfer dealings. Players were sold and some fees were re-invested in replacements, while the balance was used to reduce the overdraft at the bank. Relegation could not be avoided indefinitely though and in 1972-73 Charlton lined up in Division 3 for the first time since 1935. New signing Arthur Horsfield bagged 25 league goals and Mike Flanagan was starting to impose himself on the wing, despite which the club only finished mid-table, but still managed to turn a profit for the first time in years thanks to Theo's transfer activities. The following season he pulled off his greatest coup with the signing of Derek Hales from Luton and with Colin Powell also now established in the side, the future looked bright if only the defensive frailties could be addressed. Unfortunately for Theo however, his time had run out and on 23rd April 1974 he was sacked as Charlton manager.

Suddenly unemployed, he found work as a PE teacher at Eaglesfield School in Woolwich and coached at both Dulwich Hamlet and Dartford until in April 1975 he was appointed in a similar role at Millwall, where initially the manager was Gordon Jago. In fact, he served two spells at the Den (linked by a three-year stint with Queens Park Rangers) and ended up as assistant manager to George Graham, having twice stepped up to serve as caretaker manager. (At that time, Millwall were changing managers with some frequency). Together they got Millwall promoted from Division 3 and when Graham accepted the manager's job at Arsenal in May 1986, Theo went with him as his assistant.

The next four years were undoubtedly the high point of his working life, when together they re-established Arsenal at the forefront of English football after some years in decline. They won the League Cup in 1986-87 and then clinched the First Division title in spectacular fashion on the final day of the 1988-89 season. This was only the start of a successful period for the Gunners, but to Theo's regret he left in May 1990 after a behind the scenes shake-up at Highbury saw him relegated to coaching the reserves. His next job was a real contrast as he returned to Northampton as their manager, but financial pressures made the job near impossible. He lasted less than two years before being sacked when the club went into administration. After a short period coaching at Fulham, he joined Southend United as assistant manager. The playing squad included Chris Powell, Ricky Otto and Simon Royce, but the problems were the same. He worked with three managers in a spell of less than three years, including former Charlton defender Steve Thompson, but with no money to spend, the sack in February 1997 became inevitable.

Theo's last full-time job saw him link up again with George Graham, now at Tottenham, as coach for their reserves and this lasted until 2003. He passed away in 2020 at the age of 83 and during the last years of his life was again a familiar face back at the Valley where he was a popular match day host. His life-story, 'Theo, Give Us A Ball' was co-written with his son Paul and published in 2018. Another son, Adrian Foley, played for Charlton up to reserve team level in the late seventies.

Season	Division	League		FA Cup		FL Cup		Total	
		A	G	A	G	A	G	A	G
1967-68	Division 2	6	0	0	0	0	0	6	0
Total		6	0	0	0	0	0	6	0

UK LEAGUE CAREER 365 games 9 goals

CHARLTON CAREER
Managers: R Stokoe, E Firmani
Debut: *Carlisle United (H) 21-10-1967*
V334
Finale: *Huddersfield Town (A) 30-03-1968*

FORBES Dudley Douglas

1949 - 51

Midfield   11st 3lbs   5' 8"
Born: 19-04-1926 - Johannesburg, South Africa
Died: 15-05-2009 - Johannesburg, South Africa
Education: Sir John Adamson High School, Johannesburg.

Sid O'Linn and Dudley Forbes were two of the South African squad who toured Australia and New Zealand for two months between May and July 1947 and Dudley played in all the nine Internationals that took place, including a thrilling 2-1 victory over Australia at Sydney Cricket Ground in front of a crowd estimated at 40,000.

HONOURS

South Africa International 1947 9 caps
Charlton Athletic Reserves 1949-50 Runners Up Football Combination Cup
Charlton Athletic Reserves 1951-52 Finalists London FA Challenge Cup

CLUBS

Marist Brothers, South Africa ••Charlton Athletic 06.12.47 (free) ••Marist Brothers, South Africa 05.53

Dudley had started out as a goalkeeper, but by the time he was playing for the Johannesburg club Marist Brothers, he had found his role as a defensive wing half. When Jimmy Seed made his first visit to South Africa as Charlton's manager in 1947, he was on the lookout for footballing talent and his first signings were both members of the national team, Dudley Forbes and Sid O'Linn. By then Dudley had gained the reputation of being the strongest half back in South Africa, tireless, energetic and very fast. They arrived by sea at the beginning of December, but for Dudley there was to be a wait of over a year until he got his chance in the first team in a hard fought 1-0 win at Blackpool. He was part of the Charlton squad that toured Turkey in May 1949 and played in the victories against

Galatasaray and an Istanbul Combined XI. He only scored one goal for the Addicks and that came at the Valley on 21st October 1950 against Everton. Charlie Vaughan got the second half winner to ensure a 2-1 victory.

Never a first team regular, Dudley did nevertheless amass nearly 60 competitive appearances during his time at Charlton, before eventually heading home to Johannesburg on the ship 'Caernarvon Castle' on 14th May 1953, his fare of £69 having been paid by Charlton. He re-signed for his local team, Marist Brothers, where he remained for several years. After his playing days were over he worked for Shell Petroleum in South Africa and passed away in Johannesburg at the age of 83.

Season	Division	League		FA Cup		Total	
		A	G	A	G	A	G
1948-49	Division 1	1	0	0	0	1	0
1949-50	Division 1	29	0	0	0	29	0
1950-51	Division 1	27	1			27	1
Total		57	1	0	0	57	1

UK LEAGUE CAREER 57 games 1 goal

CHARLTON CAREER
Managers: J Seed
Debut: *Blackpool (A) 26-03-1949*
V233
Finale: *Liverpool (H) 27-01-1951*

FORD Frederick George Luther   1936 - 37

Charlton retained Fred's registration for almost 10 years, but his playing career was decimated by the six seasons lost during World War 2, as a result of which he was restricted to just 22 league appearances throughout his time in London SE7. The war years were spent serving with the Royal Engineers with whom he lost his right index finger in an accident, but nevertheless he went on to enjoy his share of success as both a coach and a manager in a career that eventually spanned around 40 years.

Midfield   12st 0lbs   6' 0"
Born: 10-12-1916 - Belvedere, Kent
Died: 16-10-1981 - KIdlington, Oxfordshire

HONOURS

Erith & Belvedere 1934-35 Finalists Kent Amateur Cup

HONOURS AS MANAGER

England U23 manager 1955-60   Swindon Town 1969 Winners Anglo-Italian League Cup
Bristol City 1964-65 Runners Up Division 3   Swindon Town 1969-70 Winners Anglo-Italian Cup

CLUBS

Erith Schoolboys 18.01.30 (youth) ••Park View (youth) ••Erith & Belvedere 08.34 (amateur) ••Arsenal 12.34 (amateur) ••Charlton Athletic 19.02.36 (amateur) 11.03.36 (pro) ••Millwall 21.11.45 (£1,400) ••Carlisle United 07.08.47 (player coach) ••Bristol Rovers 05.55 (coach) ••Bristol City 14.06.60 (manager) ••Swindon Town 1967 (coach) ••Bristol Rovers 04.68 (manager) ••Swindon Town 08.69 (manager) ••Torquay United c1972 (coach) ••Oxford United 1975 (coach/scout)

A promising wing half, Fred signed for Charlton in 1936 for the princely sum of £3-10-0 (£3.50) a week. He was primarily a reserve team player during the three pre-war seasons, but did enjoy brief periods when he was elevated to first team duty. On 5th December 1936 the team was flying when he made his debut against Huddersfield and two goals from Monty Wilkinson not only ensured a useful 2-1 away victory, but also positioned the club one point below leaders Sunderland in the Division 1 league table. This proved to be the club's most successful season and they finished in second place behind Manchester City
Fred was given a run in the side during the early weeks of 1937-38 when he took possession of the number six shirt for a period of three months, which included a fine 1-0 win at Preston on 13th September. Harold Hobbis scored the only goal of the game and at that point Charlton, who were unbeaten after the first six matches, were leaders in Division 1. Unfortunately they were unable to sustain the title challenge and Fred's time was up after a disappointing 3-0 home defeat against Arsenal on 20th November. The crowd of 55,078 saw Charlton comprehensively beaten and Fred himself score an own goal for Arsenal's third. The club embarked upon a lengthy trip to the USA and Canada in the Summer of 1937 and he was included in the 17 man playing squad. 13 matches were completed and Charlton remained unbeaten throughout with Fred featuring in several games, including the 9-1 defeat of a

team from Manitoba on 19th June. Don Welsh hit four goals that day and even Fred himself scored one.
He continued to make occasional appearances for the club during the war (21 games and 2 goals) and also guested for Tottenham, but in November 1945 was transferred to Millwall where initially he appeared alongside Tommy Brown and Benny Fenton prior to their transfers to Charlton. His playing days were coming to an end however and by the time he switched to Carlisle United in August 1947, coaching was becoming his main priority. For five years in the fifties he coached at Bristol Rovers during which time they attained their highest ever league placing. They were at that time managed by former Charlton player Bert Tann. During this period he also managed the England U23 team. In 1956, he toured South Africa and Rhodesia as the trainer with an FA party which included Bobby Ayre. By 1964-65 Fred was manager of Bristol City. He led them to promotion from Division 3 and came close to achieving a further promotion a year later. There was further success while he was manager at Swindon Town, They won the inaugural Anglo-Italian cup competition in 1969, defeating AS Roma over two legs with a team that included both Arthur Horsfield and Roger Smart. Horsfield scored a hat-trick in the second leg to ensure an aggregate score of 5-2. The following year they triumphed again but in more controversial circumstances. They were 3-0 up in the final against Napoli and Arthur Horsfield had again found the

net, when the Italian supporters rioted and the referee abandoned the contest after 79 minutes. The trophy was awarded to Swindon.

The war may have adversely affected Fred's playing career

but he remained in the game far longer than most and was still coaching well into the 1970s. He passed away in the Oxfordshire village of Kidlington at the age of 64.

Season	Division	League		FA Cup		Total	
		A	G	A	G	A	G
1936-37	Division 1	8	0	0	0	8	0
1937-38	Division 1	14	0	0	0	14	0
Total		22	0	0	0	22	0

UK LEAGUE CAREER 59 games 0 goals

CHARLTON CAREER
Managers: *J Seed*
Debut: *Huddersfield Town (A) 05-12-1936*
V193
Finale: *Arsenal (H) 20-11-1937*

FORSTER Derek   1973 - 74

Goalkeeper   11st 2lbs   5′ 9″
Born: 19-02-1949 - Newcastle upon Tyne
Education: Manor Park School, Newcastle.

Derek became the youngest goalkeeper to play in the Football League when on 22nd August 1964 he made his debut for Sunderland against Leicester City. He was aged just 15 years and 185 days, The match ended 3-3 and the opposing goalkeeper, Gordon Banks, spoke kindly of his future prospects in the game, but unfortunately for Derek, he was competing for the Sunderland jersey with the outstanding Jim Montgomery, who performed so consistently well that his opportunities at first team level would be restricted to only 18 League matches over the next nine years.

HONOURS

England Schoolboy U15 International 1964 5 caps 0 goals

Newcastle Schools

Sunderland 1965-66 Finalists FA Youth Cup

Sunderland 1966-67 Winners FA Youth Cup

CLUBS

Sunderland 07.64 (youth) 19.12.65 (pro) ••Charlton Athletic 19.07.73 (free) •Brighton & Hove Albion 23.07.74 (free) ••Gateshead United 1975 (free) ••Peterborough United 12.03.77 (non contract) ••Roker 1980 (free)

Already an England Schoolboy International, Derek was part of the outstanding Sunderland team which twice reached the FA Youth Cup final, losing to Arsenal in 1966, before finding success 12 months later against Birmingham City, twice winning 1-0 in the two legged final.

In the summer of 1967, he was a member of the Sunderland first team squad which competed in an extraordinary tournament designed to increase the North American public's awareness of football. A dozen overseas clubs participated, each being assigned to a US or Canadian city. Sunderland became the Vancouver Royal Canadians and played a series of matches across the American continent. However, the reports that filtered back home concentrated less on the football and more on the sometimes boozy parties, one in Vancouver involving rock'n'roll legend Little Richard.

After so long as second choice keeper, Derek finally left Sunderland in July 1973 and joined Charlton, where he now came into competition with John Dunn for the first

team jersey. He managed only nine league appearances during 1973-74 and sadly failed to cement his place in the team. By March the young Graham Tutt had been introduced and this signalled the end for both Forster and Dunn, Derek moving on to Brighton after only a year at the Valley.

Things did not go any better on the Sussex coast and by 1976 his career was over. With hindsight, he believes that he spent too long at Sunderland and should have left sooner to establish a first team place elsewhere.

Finally, he returned to the North East and played locally in the Wearside Football league while working at the Washington Leisure Centre in County Durham. He remained in this job for 30 years until in 2007 he was forced into early retirement after losing his left eye through cancer. He survived and remains resident in Sunderland where he is a keen golfer.

Season	Division	League		FA Cup		FL Cup		Total	
		A	G	A	G	A	G	A	G
1973-74	Division 3	9	0	0	0	2	0	11	0
Total		9	0	0	0	2	0	11	0

UK LEAGUE CAREER 30 games 0 goals

CHARLTON CAREER
Managers: *T Foley, A Nelson*
Debut: *York City (H) 25-08-1973*
V382
Finale: *Chesterfield (A) 09-02-1974*

FORSTER Matthew   1934

Matt was a stylish full back who spent the majority of his career with Tottenham Hotspur, for whom he played 244 competitive matches in a stay of more than a decade. He made his league debut on 26th February 1921 at home to West Bromwich Albion in a 1-0 victory for a Spurs team that also included Jimmy Seed. They won the FA Cup that season and were runners-up in Division 1 the following year, but by the time Matt established himself as a regular in the side, they were into a period of decline, eventually slumping to relegation in 1927-28.

Defender   11st 7lbs   5' 10"
Born: 24-08-1900 - Newburn, Northumberland
Died: 18-10-1976 - St Albans, Hertfordshire

HONOURS
Football League X1 1926   Reading 1931-32 Runners Up Division 3 (S)
Northumberland Schools

CLUBS
Scotswood ••Newburn 1918 ••Tottenham Hotspur 10.19 ••Reading 05.07.30 (£750) ••Charlton Athletic 12.10.33 ••Bexleyheath & Welling 01.11.35 ••Fulham 1938 (scout)

At one time Matt came close to international recognition and played in a couple of England trial matches and for the Football League against The Army in October 1926. He stayed loyal to Spurs after relegation and played two further seasons for them in Division 2 before eventually transferring to Reading in the summer of 1930.
Despite a 2-0 win over Charlton on 15th November in which Matt featured at right back, his new club were not faring any better and it was their poor away form which eventually sealed Reading's fate as they dropped into Division 3 (South) at the end of season 1930-31. Two years later he joined Charlton, where of course he already knew Jimmy Seed from their playing days together at Tottenham. Most of his time in SE7 was spent in the reserves as Norman Smith and Teddy Ivill contested the right back spot, but he did get one call up for first team duty against his other former club, Reading in April 1934, appearing at left back, but this ended in disappointment and a 0-1 scoreline. During his second season at the Valley, Matt made one further appearance for the first team in the now largely forgotten Third Division Southern Section Cup but

Charlton were hammered 6-1 at Aldershot and that proved to be his swansong as far as first team outings were concerned and he eventually moved on to Bexleyheath & Welling.
Matt did make one other important contribution during his time at Charlton as he is credited with having encouraged Seed to sign Sam Bartram at the conclusion of his trial period in 1934. He coached at Goldsmiths College in New Cross and acted as a scout for Fulham up to the war, as well as being a fine all round sportsman who excelled at billiards, golf, bowls and tennis and also a talented pianist.
Matt Forster worked for a time in the fur trade and later for the electronics firm Marconi Instruments in St Albans and passed away at the age of 76.

Season	Division	League		FA Cup		D3 Cup		Total	
		A	G	A	G	A	G	A	G
1933-34	Divison 3 (S)	1	0	0	0	0	0	1	0
1934-35 (P)	Divison 3 (S)	0	0	0	0	1	0	1	0
Total		1	0	0	0	1	0	2	0

UK LEAGUE CAREER 307 games 0 goals

CHARLTON CAREER
Managers: *J Seed*
Debut: *Reading (A) 02-04-1934*
V178
Finale: *Aldershot (A) 12-09-1934*

FORSTER Nicholas Michael   2010

Forward   5' 9"
Born: 08-09-1973 - Caterham, Surrey
Education: Oxted County School, Oxted.

Nicky is step father to another Charlton player, Jake Forster-Caskey. For most of his career he was a steady goalscorer but probably hit his peak during his time at Reading, when in one two year period he registered 35 league goals as they moved up to and established themselves in the second tier of English football.

HONOURS

England U21 International 1995 4 caps 1 goal   Reading 2001-02 Runners Up Division 2

CLUBS

Horley Town 1991 ••Gillingham 22.05.92 (free) ••Margate 1992 (loan) ••Hythe Town !992 (loan) ••Brentford 17.06.94 (£100,000) ••Birmingham City 31.01.97 (£700,000) ••Reading 23.06.99 (£650,000) ••Ipswich Town 01.08.05 (free) ••Hull City 31.08.06 (£250,000) ••Brighton & Hove Albion 06.07.07 (£75,000) ••Charlton Athletic 25.03.10 (loan) ••Brentford 01.07.10 (free) 03.02.11 (caretaker manager) ••Lingfield Vets 2011 ••Dover Athletic 27.09.11 (player manager) ••Staines Town 08.01.15 (manager)

It was at Gillingham where Nicky made his name. He scored 18 goals in 1993-94 for what was a mediocre side which finished 16th in Division 3. This earned him a move to Brentford where he did even better, hitting 24 (including a hat-trick at Chester), as his new club narrowly failed in the Division 2 play offs. He played four times for England U21's and scored the goal on 10th June 1995 when Angola were defeated 1-0. Birmingham City laid out £700,000 for him in 1997 and Reading almost as much a couple of years later.

A proven scorer is always in demand and his six years with Reading produced 60 goals at a time when the club were widening their horizons and settling in at the new Madejski Stadium. On the field they progressed from being one of football's 'also rans' into an established Championship side with an eye on a place in the Premier League. He left on a free transfer after the 2004-05 season when they finished 7th in the Championship.

After an injury affected spell with Ipswich Town, Nicky moved to Hull City, where the manager was Phil Parkinson, a former teammate at Reading, but neither man prospered in East Yorkshire. Parkinson left by mutual agreement in December 2006 and Nicky, who remained until the end of that season, only managed five league goals. However his next club was Brighton where he spent a fruitful four years. His goal touch returned and he was made club captain. It was only after a change of manager that the possibility of a loan move came up.

Phil Parkinson was now managing Charlton and being eager to add to his strike force, jumped at the opportunity to take Nicky on loan in March 2010. Charlton were chasing promotion from League One and a proven goalscorer was a priority. It looked like an inspired signing as he had been in fine form, but was out of favour through a contract dispute. Sadly he only managed two further goals during the remainder of the season and returned to Brighton after the play off semi finals

As his playing career wound down, Nicky had a brief spell as caretaker manager at Brentford, did a stint as a reporter and analyst for Sky TV and eventually found employment in the Insurance industry.

Season	Division	League		FA Cup		FL Cup		FL Trophy		Play Offs		Total	
		A	G	A	G	A	G	A	G	A	G	A	G
2009-10	League One	8	2	0	0	0	0	0	0	0 (2)	0	8 (2)	2
Total		8	2	0	0	0	0	0	0	0 (2)	0	8 (2)	2

UK LEAGUE CAREER 614 games 190 goals

CHARLTON CAREER
Managers: *P Parkinson*
Debut: *Huddersfield Town (A) 27-03-2010*
V703
Finale: *Swindon Town (H) 17-05-2010*

FORSTER-CASKEY Jake Dane　　　　　　　　2017 -

Jake started early and made his first team debut for Brighton & Hove Albion against Yeovil Town on 8th May 2010. He was playing in the same side as Andrew Crofts and the Seagulls were victorious 1-0. At only 16 years and 13 days, this made him the youngest player ever to represent Brighton in a competitive match. His father is former Reading midfielder Darren Caskey and up until 2011 he was known by that surname, but in homage to his step-father, the former Charlton striker Nicky Forster, he then extended his name to Forster-Caskey.

Midfield　10st 1lbs　5' 10"
Born: 25-04-1994 - Southend-on-Sea, Essex

HONOURS

England U21 International 2014-15 14 caps 0 goals
England U20 International 2014 5 caps 1 goal
England U18 International 2011 1 cap 0 goals
Eng;land U17 International 2010-11 17 caps 1 goal
England U16 International 2009-10 2 caps 0 goals
Charlton Athletic 2021 Player Of The Year

CLUBS

Brighton & Hove Albion 2007 (youth) 01.07.11 (pro) ••Oxford United 06.07.12 (loan) ••Milton Keynes Dons 22.09.15 (loan) 08.01.16 (loan) ••Rotherham United 20.07.16 (loan) ••Charlton Athletic 05.01.17 (undisclosed)

An attacking midfielder who likes to unleash the killer pass, Jake was often a rival to Jordan Cousins as they both progressed through the various age groups with England. He appeared in the FIFA U17 World Cup in 2011 and remained part of the International set up all the way to U21. His early arrival at club level was followed by a loan spell with Oxford United but by 2013 he was a regular member of the first team squad at Brighton.
Jake scored a late goal against Charlton at the Community Stadium on 12th April 2014. His Brighton side, which included Dale Stephens, managed an emphatic 3-0 win, but by the following year he was no longer featuring in the first team and his career seemed to be losing momentum. After an unhappy loan period at Rotherham, he was ready for a change and on 5th January 2017 signed for Charlton. Not having played much for several months, Jake took a little time to recapture his best form, but came good in season 2017-18, his skill and energy contributing to a

campaign which ended just short of promotion from League One. A knee injury during training in August 2018 dealt a serious blow to the club and to Jake himself when an MRI scan confirmed that he had ruptured an anterior cruciate ligament and would be sidelined for up to a year. He returned in time to make a cameo appearance in the 4-0 drubbing of Scunthorpe United on 22nd April 2019 but still had some way to go before he regained his old form. It was not until season 2020-21 that he finally shook off his injury problems and after re-gaining his place in the centre of Charlton's midfield, went on to be one of the outstanding successes of a somewhat disjointed campaign. He was overwhelmingly voted Player of the Year, but in the penultimate game of the season against Lincoln City on 4th May, he suffered another ACL injury which signalled a further long spell on the sidelines. In March 2022 he was finally able to return to full training and prepare for his second comeback.

Season	Division	League		FA Cup		FL Cup		FL Trophy		Play Offs		Total	
		A	G	A	G	A	G	A	G	A	G	A	G
2016-17	League One	12 (3)	2	0	0	0	0	0	0			12 (3)	2
2017-18	League One	40 (1)	5	2	0	0	0	0	0	2	0	44 (1)	5
2018-19 (P)	League One	0 (1)	0	0	0	0	0	0	0	0	0	0 (1)	0
2019-20 (R)	Championship	7 (4)	0	0	0	1	0					8 (4)	0
2020-21	League One	32 (2)	6	1	0	1	0	1 (1)	0			35 (3)	6
Total		91 (11)	13	3	0	2	0	1 (1)	0	2	0	99 (12)	13

UK LEAGUE CAREER 211 games 22 goals

FORTUNE Jonathan Jay   2001 - 11

Defender   12st 2lbs   6' 2''
Born: 23-08-1980 - Islington, London

15th May 2005 was a memorable day for Jon and one that Charlton supporters have never forgotten. The occasion was the final league game of the season when rivals Crystal Palace arrived at the Valley needing to win at all costs. After 71 minutes and with the score 1-1, he conceded a penalty through handball and this gave the lead to the visitors, but in an afternoon of high tension, made amends 11 minutes later when he rose at the far post and headed home a free kick for the equaliser. The match ended 2-2 and Iain Dowie's Palace, which included Danny Butterfield, Tom Soares and Ben Watson, was relegated from the Premier League.

CHARLTON CAREER
Managers: *K Robinson, L Bowyer, N Adkins, J Jackson*
Debut: *Bolton Wanderers (A)*
28-01-2017
V837

HONOURS

Charlton Athletic Reserves 1997-98 & 1998-99 Winners Football Combination   South
Charlton Athletic Reserves 1999-00 Runners Up FA Premier Reserve League   Charlton Athletic 2002 Young Player Of The Year

CLUBS

Senrab Boys Club (youth) ••Charlton Athletic 11.95 (youth) 05.98 (pro) ••Mansfield Town 18.02.00 (loan) 31.08.00 (loan) ••Stoke City 31.01.07 (loan) 03.07 (loan) ••Sheffield United 18.09.09 (free) ••Charlton Athletic 31.08.10 (free) ••Exeter City 09.03.12 (free) ••Barnet 26.07.12 (free) ••Chatham Town 08.02.13 (free) ••Dagenham & Redbridge 28.03.13 (free)

It is more than a little unfair that Jon Fortune's name is rarely mentioned when listing the successful graduates from Charlton's fantastic youth academy. True his career did not quite reach the heights of contemporaries like Scott Parker and Paul Konchesky who became England internationals, but it should not be forgotten that he made more than 100 Premier League appearances during the Curbishley years and competed with considerable success against the very best forwards of that era.

Jon started out with the famous East London club, Senrab and first played for Charlton as a 15-year-old on 11th November 1995, in a South East Counties League fixture against Bristol City. At that stage he was a striker and it was only later that Terry Westley, the youth team manager, converted him into a centre half. A professional contract followed in May 1998 and the next stage in his development was a one-month loan with Third Division Mansfield Town in February 2000, which provided a taste of first team football. A second spell with Mansfield, this

time for three months, followed in August.

He broke into the Charlton first team at the start of 2001-02 but could not have had a harder baptism. Brought on as a half-time substitute at the Valley, he spent an educational 45 minutes trying to defend against the physical presence of Everton's Duncan Ferguson. His first full match came on 12th September 2001, the day after the 9/11 terrorist atrocity in New York and he scored the opening goal in a 2-1 League Cup win against Port Vale, before going on to play his part in clean sheet defensive performances against the likes of Leeds, Chelsea and Tottenham.

While Charlton were playing in the Premier League, Jon had to contend with competition from players of the calibre of Rufus, Fish, Perry, El Karkouri and Jorge Costa, so his own place in the team was rarely secure for long, However he played enough matches to demonstrate that he was certainly up to Premier League standard.

2006-07 was when it all started to fall apart. Alan

Curbishley left the club and Jon very nearly signed for Stoke City in August 2007 after having been on loan in the Potteries for much of the relegation season. In the end he decided to stay with Charlton despite all the upheaval and remained for another two campaigns, until the home fixture against Crystal Palace on 27th January 2009, when it was as if the footballing gods were finally able to exact revenge for that infamous header almost four years earlier. Charlton won the match 1-0 thanks to a goal from Matt Spring, but Jon snapped his Achilles after an hour and did not play again for nine months.

He joined Sheffield United, but pulled a hamstring after only a month and increasingly struggled to get healthy. After less than a year he re-signed for Charlton on what was originally only a short-term contract, but ended up lasting for the whole of 2010-11. After that there were spells first with Exeter City and then Barnet, where his manager, Mark Robson, made him captain and he played alongside Ricky Holmes, but the injuries were taking their toll and his playing career ended in 2013 after a final flurry with Dagenham & Redbridge.

Since retiring, Jon has worked for Platinum One Sports Management Ltd and in May 2019 launched his own Two Touch Agency which represents an impressive roster of players including Jayden Stockley, James Vennings and Diallang Jaiyesimi, plus Charlton manager Johnnie Jackson. Much travelled striker Leo Fortune-West is Jon's uncle.

Season	Division	League		FA Cup		FL Cup		Total	
		A	G	A	G	A	G	A	G
2001-02	Premier	14 (5)	0	2	0	2	1	18 (5)	1
2002-03	Premier	22 (4)	1	1 (1)	0	1	0	24 (5)	1
2003-04	Premier	21 (7)	2	1	0	1 (1)	0	23 (8)	2
2004-05	Premier	28 (3)	2	3	1	2	0	33 (3)	3
2005-06	Premier	7 (4)	0	2	1	0	0	9 (4)	1
2006-07 (R)	Premier	6 (2)	0	1	0	4	0	11 (2)	0
2007-08	Championship	25 (1)	2	0	0	2 (1)	0	27 (2)	2
2008-09 (R)	Championship	17	0	3	0	1	0	21	0
2010-11	League One	12 (4)	0	3	0	1 (1)	0	16 (5)	0
Total		152 (30)	7	16 (1)	2	14 (3)	1	182 (34)	10

UK LEAGUE CAREER 231 games 9 goals

CHARLTON CAREER
Managers: *A Curbishley, I Dowie, L Reed, A Pardew, P Parkinson, C Powell*
Debut: *Everton (H) (sub) 18-08-2001*
V602
Finale: *Hartlepool United (H) 07-05-2011*

FOSU-HENRY Tariqe Kumahl Malachi Akwesi   2017 - 19

Signed from Reading in the Summer of 2017, Tariqe was described by manager Karl Robinson as his 'wild card'. A highly skilful attacking midfield player with

Midfield, Forward   11st 11lbs   5' 11"
Born: 05-11-1995 - Wandsworth, London

sufficient pace to worry defenders, he was initially expected to be no more than a squad player. However, he made enough impact in pre-season to be included in the opening league game of 2017-18 and went on to enjoy a most successful first season with Charlton and at times drew favourable comparison with Ademola Lookman, who had then recently departed in a big money transfer to Everton.

HONOURS

Ghana International 2020 4 caps 1 goal
England U18 International 2013 1 cap 0 goals
England U15 International c2010 1 cap 0 goals
Reading U21 2013-14 Winners U21 Premier League Cup

Reading U21 2014-15 Runners Up PD League Division 2
Charlton Athletic 2018-19 Promoted Play Offs League One
Brentford 2020-21 Promoted Play Offs Championship

CLUBS

Reading 2004 (youth) 2014 (pro) ••Fleetwood Town 11.11.15 (loan) ••Accrington Stanley 20.03.16 (loan) ••Colchester United 31.08.16 (loan) ••Charlton Athletic 19.06.17 (small fee) ••Oxford United 01.07.19 (undisclosed) ••Brentford 31.01.20 (£750,000)

A Londoner by birth but from a Ghanaian family, Tariqe made a promising debut for Reading in May 2015 in a 3-0 win at Derby. His obvious talent marked him down as a young player with an exciting future ahead of him, yet surprisingly he was never given a second chance and instead spent time on loan with Fleetwood, Accrington and Colchester before eventually joining Charlton two years later.

His flamboyant style made him an immediate favourite at the Valley and during one golden spell he hit six goals in four games, including a hat-trick against Fleetwood Town on 30th September 2017. Had he not missed several matches, he would probably have finished that first season as Charlton's leading goalscorer, but a hamstring injury sidelined him during the later stages of the campaign. Sadly Tariqe's second season fell a long way short of this impressive start. Still hampered by persistent hamstring problems, he missed the early part of the 2018-19 campaign and then had to serve a suspension after being sent off at Southend in September. He never really seemed to get

going and as the weeks went by he became an increasingly marginal figure, unable to hold down a place in the side and seemingly lacking in confidence. Charlton did offer him a new contract in May 2019, but he chose instead to join his former manager Karl Robinson at Oxford United.

The move worked out well and Tariqe re-gained his form and his shooting boots, but in January he was on his way again, this time to Brentford for a fee of £750,000. They were promoted to the Premier League in 2021, their first appearance in the top tier since 1947 and he was part of the promotion side, featuring throughout the campaign, although often from the bench. In 2021-22 however, his old hamstring problems returned and by March he had yet to make his Premier League debut.

Season	Division	League		FA Cup		FL Cup		FL Trophy		Play Offs		Total	
		A	G	A	G	A	G	A	G	A	G	A	G
2017-18	League One	26 (4)	9	0 (1)	0	1	0	1	0	1 (1)	0	29 (6)	9
2018-19 (P)	League One	14 (13)	2	1 (1)	0	0	0	1	0	0	0	16 (14)	2
Total		40 (17)	11	1 (2)	0	1	0	2	0	1 (1)	0	45 (20)	11

UK LEAGUE CAREER 140 games 29 goals

CHARLTON CAREER
Managers: *K Robinson, L Bowyer*
Debut: *Bristol Rovers (H) 05-08-2017*
V841
Finale: *Bradford City (H) (sub)*
30-03-2019

FOX Morgan Alexander   2014 - 17

Defender   12st 7lbs   6' 1"
Born: 21-09-1993 - Chelmsford, Essex
Education: Southend High School For Boys

In September 2015 Morgan was named for the first time in the full Wales squad, while also being strongly tipped in the press as a likely signing for Manchester United, who were reportedly on the lookout for a new defender. In the end neither event occurred and Morgan has yet to add to the six U21 caps already in his locker. The transfer, when it came, was only to Sheffield Wednesday, an altogether more believable destination for the hard-working young full back.

HONOURS

Wales U21 International 2013-14 6 caps 0 goals
Charlton Athletic U21 2012-13 Winners PD League 2 South

Charlton Athletic U21 2012-13 Winners Kent Senior Cup
Charlton Athletic U21 2012-13 Winners PD National League 2

CLUBS

Ipswich Town (youth) ••Charlton Athletic 2009 (youth) 03.12 (pro) ••Notts County 28.11.13 (loan) ••Sheffield Wednesday 06.01.17 (£700,000) ••Stoke City 07.08.20 (free)

A graduate of Charlton's youth academy, Morgan made his first team debut in an unexpected FA Cup victory at Hillsborough on 24th February 2014. Sheffield Wednesday included both Leon Best and Miguel Llera in their side, but were defeated 2-1 through goals from Callum Harriott and Simon Church.

Morgan was unfortunate that his elevation to the first team coincided with the arrival of Charlton's new Belgian owner

and a period of considerable upheaval at the club. A managerial revolving door policy and a high turnover of players inevitably added to problems on the field and by season 2015-16 there was also considerable dissatisfaction among supporters. Morgan, now a fixture in the left back slot, was harshly treated by a minority in the stands, but never gave less than his best despite such negativity. If he was not always fully appreciated by Charlton supporters, he was nevertheless very much on the radar for other clubs and Sheffield Wednesday persisted for several months in their attempts to sign him, eventually getting their man early in the January 2017 transfer window.

After moving to South Yorkshire, Morgan held down a place in the Wednesday side until midway through season 2018-19, after which he appeared less frequently and

history appeared to be repeating itself when he was booed by his own supporters before the home match against Luton Town on 20th August 2019. He was transferred to Stoke City in August 2020 since when his progress has been badly affected by hamstring problems that have kept him sidelined for long periods.

Season	Division	League		FA Cup		FL Cup		FL Trophy		Total	
		A	G	A	G	A	G	A	G	A	G
2013-14	Championship	5 (1)	0	1	0	0	0			6 (1)	0
2014-15	Championship	23 (8)	0	1	0	2	0			26 (8)	0
2015-16 (R)	Championship	40 (2)	1	1	0	2	0			43 (2)	1
2016-17	League One	24	0	2 (1)	0	1	0	2	0	29 (1)	0
Total		92 (11)	1	5 (1)	0	5	0	2	0	104 (12)	1

UK LEAGUE CAREER 220 games 5 goals

CHARLTON CAREER
Managers: *C Powell, J Riga, B Peeters, G Luzon, K Fraeye, J Riga, R Slade, K Robinson*
Debut: *Sheffield Wednesday (A) 24-02-2014*
V775
Finale: *Bristol Rovers (H) 02-01-2017*

FRANCIS Simon Charles   2010 - 11

Simon travelled a distinctly circuitous route to the top. Instead of progressing through a cosy Premier League academy, he found himself rejected by Notts County at age 16 only to get another chance with Bradford City and a place in their first team a year later. Injuries and relegation further interrupted his progress and by 2005 he ended up on loan at Grimsby Town in League Two. It was really only when he transferred to Southend United that he managed to hold down a regular place and even then he was still a very long way from the summit of English football.

Defender   14st 1lb   6′ 3″
Born: 16-02-1985 - Nottingham, Nottinghamshire

HONOURS

England U20 & U18 International
AFC Bournemouth 2012-13 Runners Up League One

AFC Bournemouth 2014-15 Winners Championship

CLUBS

Nottingham Forest (youth) ••Notts County (youth) ••Bradford City 2002 (pro) ••Sheffield United 16.03.04 (£200,000) ••Grimsby Town 26.09.05 (loan) ••Tranmere Rovers 18.11.05 (loan) ••Southend United 16.06.06 £70,000) ••Charlton Athletic 30.07.10 (£35,000) ••AFC Bournemouth 07.11.11 (loan) 09.01.12 (free) ••AFC Bournemouth 30.06.21 (ass: technical director)

Simon spent just over a year at the Valley and it is fair to say that nobody could have predicted the way his career would take off after he left. Season 2010-11 was a disappointing campaign for Charlton, although early on there were optimistic thoughts of promotion back to the Championship.

On 9th October 2010, Simon was travelling to the league match at Plymouth when news reached him that his pregnant girlfriend had gone into labour. The team bus had to divert to Andover station so that he could catch a train back to London and just made it in time for the birth of his daughter.

A depressing run which saw the team fail to record a single win between 12th February and 2nd April put paid to

promotion talk and Simon was one of the players who at this point was singled out for harsh criticism by the crowd. He never stopped putting in the effort though, even when nothing seemed to be going right. Summer 2011 saw a complete overhaul of the Charlton playing squad by new manager Chris Powell and Simon was one of those who left the club shortly after, joining Bournemouth, initially on loan and in January 2012 on a permanent contract.

His new club were very much in the ascendancy and Simon rapidly made the left back position his own. He played a big part as they achieved two promotions and captained the Bournemouth team while they established themselves as a force in the Premier League. He eventually stayed with them for more than eight years, making nearly

300 league appearances and for much of that time was one of the first names on the team sheet. In 2019, he launched the Simon Francis Football Academy offering training camps for both boys and girls and a feeder link to the AFC

Bournemouth academy.
Simon retired as a player after the 2019-20 season and on 30th June 2021 it was announced that he had accepted the role of assistant technical director at AFC Bournemouth.

Season	Division	League		FA Cup		FL Cup		FL Trophy		Total	
		A	G	A	G	A	G	A	G	A	G
2010-11	League One	32 (2)	0	5	0	1	0	3	0	41 (2)	0
2011-12 (P)	League One	0	0	0	0	2	0	0	0	2	0
Total		32 (2)	0	5	0	3	0	3	0	43 (2)	0

UK LEAGUE CAREER 575 games 9 goals

CHARLTON CAREER
Managers: *P Parkinson, C Powell*
Debut: *AFC Bournemouth (H) (sub) 07-08-2010*
V708
Finale: *Preston North End (H) 13-09-2011*

FRANKLIN William Michael   1972 - 74

Goalkeeper   12st 0lbs   5' 11"
Born: 03-03-1955 - Tiverton, Devon
Died: 19-03-2017 - Exeter, Devon

Dunn and later Graham Tutt.

Mike joined Charlton as an apprentice professional, having previously represented Exeter Schools. He was a promising goalkeeper but never really established himself in the first team, his time being spent as an understudy first for John

HONOURS
Exeter Schools

Yeovil Town 1975-76 Runners Up Southern League Premier Division

CLUBS
Tiverton Town (youth) ••Charlton Athletic 26.07.71 (youth) 07.03.73 (pro) ••Northampton Town 17.09.73 (loan) ••Yeovil Town 11.73 (loan) ••Dover 12.73 (loan) ••Yeovil Town 06.75 (free) ••Tiverton Town c1978

All of Mike's 13 Football League appearances were made whilst he was still a teenager. His debut up at Chesterfield came four days after John Dunn suffered concussion against Grimsby and then three days later he played in the infamous match against Oldham Athletic in which the referee awarded a goal to Charlton despite the shot from Peter Hunt missing the target completely.
It was not until 1974-75 that he got a run in the side and managed nine games that season, but only one clean sheet. This came against Peterborough at the Valley on 5th October in a 3-0 victory. Still only 19 when he made his final appearance for the club, Mike came close to making the grade but lacked the consistency needed at that level. After leaving Charlton, he signed for Yeovil Town in June 1975. He had enjoyed a brief loan spell with them earlier

and now featured in their team which finished second in the Southern League and narrowly missed being elected to the Football League. They gained only three votes less than Workington in the annual ballot. Yeovil enjoyed an exciting FA Cup run that season and he was in goal in all three matches against Millwall, the tie going to a second replay before being decided by a single goal for the Lions, scored by Mike's former Charlton teammate, Alan Hart.
He returned to Devon and turned his back on the professional game, finding work initially as a bricklayer and later as a private hire driver. He turned out for Tiverton Town in the Western League and for many years was an enthusiastic local cricketer. Mike passed away at the Royal Devon and Exeter Hospital at the age of 62 and was cremated at St Peter's Church, Tiverton on 4th April 2017.

Season	Division	League		FA Cup		FL Cup		Total	
		A	G	A	G	A	G	A	G
1972-73	Division 3	4	0	0	0	0	0	4	0
1974-75 (P)	Division 3	9	0	0	0	0	0	9	0
Total		13	0	0	0	0	0	13	0

CHARLTON CAREER
Managers: *T Foley, A Nelson*
Debut: *Chesterfield (A) 18-10-1972*
V374
Finale: *Plymouth Argyle (H) 02-11-1974*

UK LEAGUE CAREER 13 games 0 goals

FRASER Scott Stewart   2022 -

On the last day of the January 2022 transfer window, Charlton finally secured the signing of midfielder Scott Fraser. His name had apparently been at the top of

Midfield   6' 0"
Born: 30-03-1995 - Dundee, Scotland

Director of Recruitment Steve Gallen's shopping list for some time and they had made earlier unsuccessful attempts to bring him to the Valley. An energetic player with an eye for goal scoring opportunities, he very much fitted the new strategy, whereby he would not only strengthen the side as they pushed for promotion, but also he had the ability to perform in the Championship as well. Forward planning had not been a noticeable feature at Charlton in recent years, but a contract until June 2025, proved not only that new owner Thomas Sandgaard was intent on building a successful side, but that Scott was seen as an important component for that success.

CLUBS

Dee Club, Scotland 2003 (youth) ••Longforgan Boys, Scotland 2004 (youth) ••Dundee United 2005 (youth) 2013 (pro) ••Airdrieonians, Scotland 10.10.14 (loan0 ••Burton Albion 05.07.18 (free) ••Milton Keynes Dons 09.09.20 (free) ••Ipswich Town 14.07.21 (£750,000) ••Charlton Athletic 31.01.22 (£500,000)

Scott had joined Dundee United's academy at the age of 10 and by the start of the 2010-11 season was on the fringe of the first team squad. A broken leg sustained in pre-season kept him out of action for a year but he finally made his debut as a substitute in the match against Celtic on 11th May 2014. He went on loan to Airdrieonians for 2014-15 and competed in the Scottish League Division 1, before stepping up to the Premier with Dundee United the following year. After three seasons of first team football at Tannadice, Scott declined a new contract and transferred to Burton Albion.

His next move took him to MK Dons in September 2020 and it was his form in League One during season 2020-21 that really highlighted his potential. He managed an

impressive 14 league goals from midfield, albeit nine were from the penalty spot. After just one year he made it known that he was ambitious to further progress his career and in July 2021 signed for Ipswich Town in the very same week that they also brought in former Charlton striker Joe Pigott. Scott's time at Ipswich did not go according to plan and they played him on the wing rather than in his favoured place in central midfield. When it became known that he had not settled with the Tractor Boys, there was interest shown from Championship clubs including Swansea City, but he was impressed by the ambition shown at Charlton and it is hoped that he will now settle in SE7 and help spearhead the drive for promotion.

UK LEAGUE CAREER 225 games 39 goals

CHARLTON CAREER
Managers: *J Jackson*
Debut: *AFC Wimbledon (H) (sub) 05-02-2022*
V940

FRIAR John Paul   1984 - 85

Defender   10st 6lbs   5' 6"
Born: 06-06-1963 - Glasgow, Scotland

A Scottish full back, Paul had a nomadic career that took him from the top to the bottom of both the English Football League and the Scottish League, as well as all too fleeting stays with a wide selection of non-league clubs. He spent the best part of two years at the Valley during a period of great turbulence when Charlton had only recently been taken over by new owners, Sunley Holdings. He was a fixture in the team during 1984-85, but when Sunleys loosened the purse strings and allowed manager Lennie Lawrence to build a promotion side, he was quickly replaced by Mark Reid and his time in the Charlton team was at an end.

HONOURS

Scotland Youth International
Leicester City 1982-83 Promoted Division 2

Aldershot 1986-87 Finalists Football League Trophy, Southern Area
Aldershot 1986-87 Promoted Play Offs Division 4

CLUBS

Woodhill Boys, Scotland 1978 (youth) ••Celtic Boys, Scotland 1979 (youth) ••Leicester City 1979 (youth) 06.80 (pro) ••Rotherham United 02.83 (free) ••Motherwell, Scotland 11.83 (loan) ••Charlton Athletic 31.07.84 (loan) 13.08.84 (free) ••Northampton Town 06.03.86 (loan) ••Aldershot 08.06 (free) ••Fisher Athletic 1987 ••Dover Athletic 10.87 ••Welling United 11.87 ••Dartford 12.87 ••Crawley Town 1988 ••Aylesbury United 1988 ••Enfield 1988 ••Lincoln City 03.10.88 (non contract) ••Fisher Athletic c1989 ••Spalding United 08.90 ••Fisher Athletic 09.80 ••Partick Thistle, Scotland 10.91 ••East Stirlingshire, Scotland 02.92 ••Albion Rovers, Scotland 11.93 ••Fauldhouse United, Scotland 1996

It is not unfair to say that Paul started at the top and then worked downwards. A Scottish Youth International, he got his chance in the First Division with Leicester City at the age of 17 and in only his third game on 31st January 1981 was matched against Liverpool, the reigning champions. Despite a hostile Anfield crowd, the Leicester team, which also included Jim Melrose and Andy Peake, came from behind to win 2-1, the decider being scored by Melrose. Paul went on to play 18 matches that season before Leicester were eventually relegated.

In April 1982 they reached the last four in the FA Cup, but hopes of a Wembley final were dashed after Leicester were beaten 2-0 by Spurs. The next season however was a strange one for Paul. He spent the first half with Leicester before transferring to Rotherham in February. Leicester ended up promoted back to Division 1, while Rotherham went down to Division 3, so he unusually experienced both promotion and relegation in the same season.

The move to Charlton came in August 1984 on a two-year contract. He replaced Kevin Dickenson at a time when off-field financial issues were still outweighing the playing side in many people's minds. The team nevertheless did enough to avoid any real relegation concerns and there were even occasional high spots such as on 7th May 1985 when a very young Charlton side, including Paul, goalie Lee Harmsworth and the Kimble twins, forced a 3-3 draw at the Valley against the league leaders, Oxford United and it took an 87th minute own goal from Alan Curbishley to

salvage a point for the visitors. By then plans to construct a promotion team were already being formulated within the Charlton boardroom and when seven players were signed ahead of 1985-86, Paul was one of those heading for the exit door.

He spent much of that season out on loan with Northampton Town and then signed for Aldershot in August 1986. He was now operating in Division 4, but the team, which included Tony Lange, reached the play off final and beat Wolverhampton Wanderers over two legs to clinch promotion. This turned out to be Paul's last appearance in the Football League and during the next four years he worked his way through a plethora of non-league clubs, rarely staying long in one place, until he found his way back home to Scotland.

Paul had already played briefly in the Scottish Premier League for Motherwell whilst on loan from Rotherham and now got a game for Partick Thistle in Division 1, but a 4-3 home defeat against Morton in October 1991 did not lead to further employment. He then dropped into Division 2 with East Stirlingshire where he found some measure of stability for a short time and even scored a rare goal on 4th April 1992 as Stranraer were beaten 1-0. His slide down the divisions was completed with a spell at Albion Rovers where home crowds did not always reach 250 and his unique trip from top to bottom of both the English and Scottish Leagues came to an end after New Year's Day 1996 when a 5-1 beating from Queens Park left them bottom of Scottish League Division 3.

Season	Division	League		FA Cup		FL Cup		FM Cup		Total	
		A	G	A	G	A	G	A	G	A	G
1984-85	Division 2	32	0	2	0	2	0			36	0
1985-86 (P)	Division 2	4	0	0	0	1	0	0 (1)	0	5 (1)	0
Total		36	0	2	0	3	0	0 (1)	0	41 (1)	0

UK LEAGUE CAREER 208 games 7 goals

CHARLTON CAREER
Managers: *L Lawrence*
Debut: *Oldham Athletic (H) 15-09-1984*
V458
Finale: *Chelsea (H) (sub) 23-10-1985*

FRIMPONG Emmanuel Yaw   2012

A succession of serious injuries almost certainly prevented Emmanuel from building upon the tremendous start that he made as a highly promising Arsenal youngster. He was in the England U16 team, along with Jonjo Shelvey and Jed Steer, when on 22nd March 2008 they defeated the host nation to win the Montaigu Tournament in France and the following season he helped his club to victory in the FA Youth Cup final against Liverpool. A hard tackling defensive midfield player who was at one stage compared with Alex Song, there was an ominous warning of what was to come in August 2010 when he injured an anterior cruciate ligament in training and was sidelined for nine months just as his career was about to take off.

Midfield   5' 10"
Born: 10-01-1992 - Kumasi, Ghana
Education: Gladesmore Community School, Tottenham

HONOURS

Ghana International 2013 1 cap 0 goals

England U17 International 2008-09 6 caps 0 goals

England U16 International 2007-08 6 caps 1 goal

England U16 2008 Winners Montaigu Tournament

Arsenal U18 2008-09 Winners FA Youth Cup

Arsenal U18 2008-09 & 2009-10 Winners FA Premier Academy League

CLUBS

Arsenal 2001 (youth) 08.10 (pro) ••Wolverhampton Wanderers 01.01.12 (loan) ••Charlton Athletic 19.11.12 (loan) ••Fulham 25.01.13 (loan) ••Barnsley 31.01.14 ••FC Ufa, Russia 01.07.14 (free) ••Arsenal Tula, Russia 08.08.16 (free) ••AFC Eskilstuna, Sweden 21.02.17 (free) ••Ermis Aradippou, Cyprus 17.08.17 (free)

Emmanuel's Premier League debut came in August 2011, but he collected a red card in only his second match and following a home League Cup defeat against Manchester City on 29th November, was involved in a clash with a teammate in the tunnel immediately after the game. Shortly after this incident he was loaned out to Wolverhampton Wanderers, but soon ruptured a cruciate ligament in his right knee which brought his season to a premature end. He joined Charlton on a six-week loan on 19th November 2012, at a time when the team were hovering dangerously near to the relegation places in the Championship. Although he featured in six games during this brief spell, his impact was limited and he only once completed 90 minutes, namely the 2-2 home draw with Brighton on 8th December. Short term loans rarely proved successful and had he stayed longer in SE7, perhaps Emmanuel would have settled in and given a better account of himself, but he returned to Arsenal following the Boxing Day home defeat

against Ipswich Town.

On 24th March 2013 he made his one full international appearance for Ghana in a World Cup qualifying match against Sudan. The match was played in his home town of Kumasi where he was a second half substitute and impressed with his range of accurate passes in an emphatic 4-0 win

Having failed to secure a place in the Arsenal first team, Emmanuel was transferred to Barnsley for an undisclosed fee in January 2014 and was promptly sent off on his debut, a 1-0 defeat against Sheffield Wednesday. This was not a happy period and he left the club at the end of that season following relegation to League One.

In September 2014 he moved abroad and signed for Russian Premier League side FC Ufa but history repeated itself when he was shown a red card during his first match, after reacting to racial abuse from the crowd. Subsequent moves took him to Sweden and Cyprus but his early promise was not maintained and the truth was revealed on 8th March 2019 when he announced his retirement from

football at the age of 27, having for five years played through the pain of a serious knee injury.

Season	Division	League		FA Cup		FL Cup		Total	
		A	G	A	G	A	G	A	G
2012-13	Championship	6	0	0	0	0	0	6	0
Total		6	0	0	0	0	0	6	0

UK LEAGUE CAREER 32 games 0 goals

CHARLTON CAREER
Managers: *C Powell*
Debut: *Huddersfield Town (H) 24-11-2012*
V754
Finale: *Ipswich Town (H) 26-12-2012*

FRY Matthew Ronald   2010 - 11

Defender   12st 2lbs   6' 1"
Born: 26-09-1990 - Longfield, Kent

Matt was spotted by West Ham at the age of 11 and brought into their academy where he progressed to the point that a worthwhile footballing career seemed a strong possibility. A pacey full back, he did well during his first loan spell at Gillingham until a knee injury put him out of action for six weeks and ultimately it was a succession of similar injuries that stopped him from fulfilling his potential.

HONOURS

Concord Rangers 2012-13 Promoted Play Offs Isthmian League Premier Division

Concord Rangers 2012-13 Winners Isthmian League Cup

CLUBS

Gravesend & Northfleet (youth) ••West Ham United c2001 (youth) 06.09 (pro) ••Gillingham 15.10.09 (loan) ••Charlton Athletic 25.03.10 (loan) 05.08.10 (loan) ••Bradford City 10.02.12 (free) ••Concord Rangers 07.12 ••Dartford 06.13 ••Concord Rangers 03.14 ••Chelmsford City 15.08.14 (one match) ••Eastleigh 19.08.14 ••Concord Rangers 10.14 ••Braintree Town 06.15 •York City 16.06.16 ••Herne Bay 20.07.18

Phil Parkinson brought Matt to Charlton on loan in March 2010 in an attempt to bolster the defence as the club pushed for promotion from League One. A further knee injury prevented him from playing even a single game and he soon returned to West Ham, but a second loan proved more fruitful the following season and he made his debut at Huddersfield where he scored the only goal of his Football League career, but sadly it was only a consolation effort as Charlton went down 3-1.

By February 2012 Parkinson was managing Bradford City and signed Matt from West Ham, but again injury

prevented him contributing and he quickly dropped down into non-league football and bounced around several clubs, but recurring knee problems always prevented him from progressing. It was on his 27th birthday that he finally called a halt to his football career after seven knee operations and the realisation that his body could no longer cope with the demands of professional football. Forced to seek employment outside the game, Matt initially worked as a trainee investment manager and in May 2021 was appointed a portfolio manager with Brooks MacDonald.

Season	Division	League		FA Cup		FL Cup		FL Trophy		Total	
		A	G	A	G	A	G	A	G	A	G
2010-11	League One	20 (5)	1	4	0	0	0	2 (1)	0	26 (6)	1
Total		20 (5)	1	4	0	0	0	2 (1)	0	26 (6)	1

UK LEAGUE CAREER 42 games 1 goal

CHARLTON CAREER
Managers: *P Parkinson, C Powell*
Debut: *Huddersfield Town (A) 28-08-2010*
V711
Finale: *Dagenham & Redbridge 19-03-2011*

FRYATT James Edward   1959 - 60

When two former Charlton players, Jim Fryatt and Sam Lawrie, lined up for Bradford Park Avenue in a routine Fourth Division match on 25th April

Striker   12st 0lbs   6' 0"
Born: 02-09-1940 - Southampton, Hampshire
Education: King Edward VI Grammar School, Southampton.

1964, they could not have anticipated that footballing history was about to be made. Referee Bob Simons blew his whistle to start the match and still had his stopwatch in his hand as Fryatt crashed the ball into the Tranmere Rovers net for the fastest goal in Football League history, timed at a barely credible four seconds. With no video evidence to dispute the claim, it still remains in the record books nearly 60 years later.

HONOURS

Charlton Athletic Youth 1957-58 Runners Up South East Counties League
Charlton Athletic A 1958-59 & 1959-60 Winners London Mid-Week League
Charlton Athletic A 1959-60 Winners Aetolian League Cup
Southport 1966-67 Runners Up Division 4

Oldham Athletic 1970-71 Promoted Division 4
Southport 1972-73 Winners Division 4
Philadelphia Atoms 1973 Winners NASL Eastern Division

CLUBS

Moor End United Youth 1956 (youth) ••Charlton Athletic 09.10.57 (amateur) 30.10.57 (pro) ••Southend United 03.06.60 (£600) ••Bradford Park Avenue 25.06.63 (£2,500) ••Southport 14.03.66 (£4,000) ••Torquay United 03.03.67 (£5,000) ••Stockport County 27.10.67 (£7,000) ••Blackburn Rovers 16.10.68 (£24,000) ••Oldham Athletic 19.02.70 (£8,000) ••Southport 10.11.71 (free) ••Philadelphia Atoms, USA 1973 (loan) 1974 (free) ••Stockport County 19.09.74 ••Torquay United 02.12.74 ••Chorley 17.01.75 ••Hartford Bicentennials, USA 1975 ••Philadelphia Atoms, USA 07.75 ••Las Vegas Quicksilvers, USA 1977 (ass. manager)

Jim, known in his playing days as 'Pancho', was a big, strong and seemingly fearless centre forward. He was superb in the air and although he probably lacked the skill to succeed at the highest level of the game, he enjoyed a long and fruitful career in the lower reaches of the Football League accumulating more than 200 league and cup goals. He started with Charlton following trials in 1955 and again in August 1957, while working at Siemens as an electrical engineering student. Accepted on amateur terms, he promptly scored a hat trick for the colts against Watford on 28th October 1957 and signed as a professional two days later. Over the next two years he scored freely without ever getting a first team chance. Accumulating goals was not a problem for Charlton at that time however with both Stuart Leary and Johnny Summers available for selection. Jim's chance finally came in December 1959 and he contributed two goals on Boxing Day in only his second match as Liverpool were beaten 3-0 and claimed another at

Cardiff the following week. Nevertheless he was sold to Southend United at the end of the season in a decision that now seems very hard to fathom, a prolific goalscorer being such a valuable commodity.

The goals continued as Jim moved from club to club and he helped Oldham and Southport (twice) to promotions, while at Stockport County he attained legendary status and has been inducted into their Hall of Fame. Eventually he moved out to the USA and had three separate spells with the Philadelphia Atoms in the North American Soccer League, finishing up with the Las Vegas Quicksilvers in the role of assistant manager in charge of a playing squad which included the legendary Eusebio.

He finally settled in Las Vegas and worked in the casinos before becoming a mechanic at a Vegas golf course where his son Ed Fryatt, was a golf professional.

Season	Division	League		FA Cup		Total	
		A	G	A	G	A	G
1959-60	Division 2	5	3	0	0	5	3
Total		5	3	0	0	5	3

UK LEAGUE CAREER 499 games 189 goals

CHARLTON CAREER
Managers: J Trotter
Debut: Rotherham United (H) 19-12-1959
V274
Finale: Leyton Orient (H) 19-03-1960

FULLER Ricardo Dwayne

2012 - 13

Forward   12st 2lbs   6' 3"
Born: 31-10-1979 - Kingston, Jamaica

Ricardo was a strong, powerful and highly skilful striker who came to Charlton at the dawn of his career and showed considerable promise in the reserves. He had disciplinary issues however and had been in trouble in Jamaica for allegedly kicking an opponent in the head after being shown a red card. There were also major injury concerns. He underwent a complicated operation for a broken back, which involved two three inch metal plates being inserted and following an extended trial period, the club concluded, wrongly as it turned out, that his physical condition would not sustain a lengthy career in professional football.

HONOURS

Jamaica International 1999-2012 74 caps 9 goals   Stoke City 2007-08 Runners Up Championship

CLUBS

Tivoli Gardens, Jamaica (youth) c1998 (pro) ••Charlton Athletic 12.99 (non contract) ••Crystal Palace 19.02.01 (non contract) ••Tivoli Gardens, Jamaica 06.01 ••Heart Of Midlothian, Scotland 19.10.01 (loan) ••Preston North End 01.07.02 (£500,000) ••Portsmouth 27.08.04 (£1 million) ••Southampton 05.08.05 (£340,000) ••Ipswich Town 24.02.06 (loan) ••Stoke City 30.08.06 (£500,000) ••Charlton Athletic 21.08.12 (free) ••Blackpool 15.08.13 (free) ••Millwall 16.07.14 (free) ••Oldham Athletic 16.10.15 (free) ••Grange Park Rangers 09.17 (non contract) ••Hanley Town 31.08.20 (free)

After leaving SE7, Ricardo went through a similar trial period with Crystal Palace making his League debut in a 1-0 defeat at Barnsley on 20th February 2001, but despite talk of a £1 million transfer, they too declined to risk a long term commitment and in May he returned home to Jamaica.

A loan spell at Hearts proved more positive with an eight goal return from 27 games and in July 2002 he was finally given the chance to prove himself in English football, joining Preston North End for a fee of £500,000 and scoring against Crystal Palace on his debut. His explosive style resulted in 31 league and cup goals in two years, including a hat trick against Burnley on 20th December 2003, but three red cards and time lost through knee ligament damage confirmed that both his disciplinary issues and fragile health still remained a barrier to further progress.

Ricardo failed a medical for Leeds United, but in Summer 2004 joined Portsmouth, where he played alongside Svetoslav Todorov, another striker with injury problems of his own. A year later he followed manager Harry Redknapp to Southampton, but it was at Stoke City, for whom he signed in 2006, that he really came into his own, his brave and aggressive style being fully appreciated at a club which had been starved of success

During his six-year stay in the Potteries, Ricardo was an integral part of the Stoke team that gained promotion in 2008 and then went on to establish itself in the Premier League. He probably played the best football of his career during this period, but still invited controversy, such as on 28th December 2008 when he was sent off at West Ham for violent conduct against a teammate. An Achilles tendon injury prevented him from participating in the 2011 FA Cup final.

Ricardo was capped 77 times for Jamaica and on 3rd June 2006 played at Wembley alongside Jason Euell and Jamal Campbell-Rice in their 6-0 thrashing by England, but his international career was over by the time he signed for Charlton in August 2012.

Clearly past his best, but still a formidable presence on the field, Ricardo rarely managed a full game but was always a threat, as he demonstrated on 22nd September when he and Johnnie Jackson scored the goals in an impressive 2-1 win at Ipswich. On occasions, he and Yann Kermorgant led the Charlton attack together, which would not have been a welcome prospect for any defender and both men were among the scorers when Barnsley were well beaten 6-0 in April.

Charlton chose not to extend his contract after the one season and he moved on to Blackpool and Millwall, before ending his chequered career with Oldham Athletic. He announced his retirement on 16th May 2016.

Season	Division	League		FA Cup		FL Cup		Total	
		A	G	A	G	A	G	A	G
2012-13	Championship	20 (11)	5	0	0	0	0	20 (11)	5
Total		20 (11)	5	0	0	0	0	20 (11)	5

UK LEAGUE CAREER 441 games 105 goals

CHARLTON CAREER
Managers: *A Curbishley, C Powell*
Debut: *Nottingham Forest (A) (sub) 01-09-2012*
V748
Finale: *Middlesborough (A) 27-04-2013*

GALLAGHER Conor John   2019 - 20

It is doubtful if Charlton have made many better temporary signings than 19-year-old Conor Gallagher, who arrived from Chelsea on what was intended to be a season long loan, but which was unceremoniously ended after five months. Although he had starred within Chelsea's youth set-up, he was largely unknown to the wider public, but when he entered the field as a second half substitute at Blackburn on 3rd August 2019, it was immediately apparent that Director of Football Steve Gallen had pulled off a very slick piece of business. The match ended 2-1 in Charlton's favour thanks to goals from Ben Purrington and Lyle Taylor and it was at least partly due to Conor that the club got off to an unexpectedly strong start to the 2019-20 season whereby at the end of October, they were placed second in the Championship.

Midfield   6' 0"
Born: 06-02-2000 - Epsom, Surrey
Education: Howard of Effingham School.

HONOURS

England International 2021 1 cap 0 goals
England U21 International 2019-21 12 caps 2 goals
England U20 International 2019 4 caps 0 goals
England U19 International 2018-19 9 caps 2 goals
England U18 International 2018 6 caps 0 goals

England U17 International 2017 4 caps 0 goals
Chelsea U18 2016-17 & 2017-18 Winners FA Youth Cup
Chelsea U18 2016-17 National Winners PD League
Chelsea U19 2018 & 2019 Finalists UEFA Youth League

CLUBS

Epsom Eagles c2007 (youth) ••Chelsea 2008 (youth) 10.18 (pro) ••Charlton Athletic 02.08.19 (loan) ••Swansea City 15.01.20 (loan) ••West Bromwich Albion 17.09.20 (loan) ••Crystal Palace 29.07.21 (loan)

The Wembley triumph against Sunderland on 26th May 2019 was one of the most satisfying days in Charlton's long and erratic history, but even before the champagne had been drained and the celebrations come to an end, it was obvious that promotion to the Championship would bring with it almost insurmountable problems. In a July club statement, the Belgian owner made it clear that there was no additional money to invest and that costs would be further cut for season 2019-20 pending the sale of the club being finalised. Inspired signings like Gallagher, Tom Lockyer and Josh Cullen gave Charlton the flying start that they needed and Conor netted three times in his first four appearances, including the winner against Brentford on 24th August. The strength of the team came from the midfield and in the first half at the Valley against Nottingham Forest, the football played was arguably the best seen from a Charlton side for many years, with Gallagher, Cullen and Erhun Oztumer outstanding. Sadly, the lack of depth in the Charlton squad soon found them out and as the injuries piled up, so they sunk down the league table. There were a number of factors that contributed to the eventual relegation, but without much doubt, had Conor remained for the full season, there would have been a happy ending to this most difficult campaign. Josh Cullen was injured against Cardiff City on 23rd November and from that point on Conor struggled without his midfield partner and probably tried to do too much himself. No explanation was given for the announcement that on 14th January he was being recalled by Chelsea and would finish the season with Swansea City, but reports indicated that he had been happy in SE7 and had not sought the move himself.

Conor comes from a football mad family of Chelsea supporters and first trained with them at the age of six. He excelled throughout his formative years and made a brief substitute appearance in the final minutes of the 2016-17 FA Youth Cup final when they beat Manchester City and then played a full part the following season when they defeated Arsenal to retain the cup. During his time at Charlton he made his debut for England U21's in a 2-2 draw against Slovenia on 11th October 2019 and made four appearances in all before returning to Chelsea.

At Swansea, Conor continued to show enormous energy and impressed with his box to box runs and spacial awareness. They came close to promotion from the Championship but fell just short, losing on aggregate to Brentford in the play off semi-final. For 2020-21 he was tasked with trying to keep West Bromwich Albion in the Premier League in the company of Karlan Ahearne-Grant, but for all his promise and undoubted ability, Conor

proved unable to pull off that particular miracle.
In July 2021 he embarked upon yet another loan, this time with Crystal Palace, an established Premier League club. His form was outstanding during the first half of 2021-22

Season	Division	League		FA Cup		FL Cup		Total	
		A	G	A	G	A	G	A	G
2019-20 (R)	Championship	25 (1)	6	0	0	0	0	25 (1)	6
Total		25 (1)	6	0	0	0	0	25 (1)	6

UK LEAGUE CAREER 75 games 8 goals

and on 15th November he was rewarded with his first full England cap when he came off the sub's bench during the 10-0 thrashing of San Marino in a World Cup qualifier.

CHARLTON CAREER
Managers: *L Bowyer*
Debut: *Blackburn Rovers (A) (sub) 03-08-2019*
V875
Finale: *West Bromwich Albion (H) 11-01-2020*

GARLAND Peter John   1992 - 95

Midfield   12st 4lbs   5' 10"
Born: 20-01-1971 - Croydon, Surrey

A great passer of the ball, Peter nearly made it to the very top of the pile, but instead enjoyed a long career in non-league football, where his somewhat portly appearance was immediately recognisable. Always popular wherever he played, he had natural ability and vision. As a youngster, he was capped six times for England U17's, his first match being against the Netherlands at Wembley on 1st August 1987 as a curtain raiser for that year's FA Charity Shield match. In later internationals, he played for England alongside Graham Stuart and Dean Kiely.

HONOURS
England U17 International 1987-88 6 caps 0 goals
London Schools & Surrey Schools
Dulwich Hamlet 1998-99 Winners London FA Challenge Cup
Dulwich Hamlet 1999-00 Finalists London FA Challenge Cup
Crayford One Bell 2015-16, 2016-17 & 2017-18 Winners Kent FA Veterans Cup

CLUBS
Selsdon Junior 1984 (youth) ••Tottenham Hotspur 27.07.87 (youth) 18.08.89 (pro) ••Newcastle United 24.03.92 (£60,000) ••Charlton Athletic 18.12.92 (£5,000) ••Wycombe Wanderers 16.03.95 (loan) ••Leyton Orient 15.07.96 (free) ••Crawley Town 07.97 (free) ••Dulwich Hamlet 1998 (free) ••Croydon 12.00 (free) ••Whyteleafe 08.02 ••Croydon 03.04 ••Dulwich Hamlet 2004 ••Slade Green c2004 ••Thamesmead Town c2004 ••Greenwich Borough 2006 (player manager) ••Erith Town 08.06 (player manager) ••Crayford One Bell 2015 (player manager - vets)

Peter started out playing U13's football for Selsdon Junior FC, in the same side as future England manager Gareth Southgate. He trained with Tottenham Hotspur from the age of 14 and signed with them as a trainee on 27th July 1987. A professional contract followed two years later and his one competitive match for the North London club came on 10th April 1991 against Norwich City. Spurs lost 2-1 and Peter played the final half hour as a replacement for Paul Gascoigne, who was being eased back from injury. He enjoyed the taste of first team football, but when he had made no further progress almost a year later, he was happy to move north and join Newcastle United.
It turned out that the situation was not much different at St James' Park and so, on the recommendation of his teammate Gavin Peacock, Peter travelled down to London and signed for Charlton in December 1992, the very month that the club returned home after seven years in exile. His first match at the Valley came against West Ham on Boxing

Day and they were already a goal down by the interval. He was a second-half substitute for Carl Leaburn and in an improved display, the team fought back to 1-1, thanks to a late goal from John Bumstead.
1993-94 was Peter's most successful season as a Charlton player. He appeared in more than half of the matches and one especially memorable occasion was on 28th August against Bolton Wanderers. Colin Walsh and Garry Nelson had put the Addicks 2-0 up, when in the 60th minute Carl Leaburn gave a perfect lay-off and Peter scored with a stunning left footed drive to put the game out of reach. Another contest that is remembered for rather different reasons was the home encounter against Millwall on 11th September. Both Peter and Millwall's Alex Rae were red carded in the 34th minute for an off the ball incident, probably the only excitement in an otherwise dour 0-0 draw.
After being out of the side for some time, he went out on a

month's loan to Wycombe Wanderers in March 1985. They were chasing promotion from Division 2 and he performed admirably for them over five league matches. Charlton would not allow the loan to be extended however and Peter was recalled to the first team squad for the remainder of that season.

It was 1995-96 when it all went wrong. He did not play again after October, because of a deep-seated pelvic problem and in March he appeared at Croydon Crown Court as a result of a drink induced fight outside The Gun, a public house in Church Street. A kick from Peter had left a girl with a broken nose, a black eye and a broken finger. She had been trying to protect her boyfriend and had got struck accidentally during the melee. Peter admitted to causing actual bodily harm and was ordered to pay her £3,000 compensation and carry out 100 hours of community service. It was reported in Charlton's match programme on 14th April, that he had left the club by mutual consent.

In need of a new start, Peter had trials with Leyton Orient and on 26th May 1996 appeared for them in a friendly match against the full Wales team who were preparing for a World Cup qualifier the following week. No less than John Robinson scored for Wales, but Orient battled hard and it was Peter who clinched a 2-1 victory with a late goal. This helped earn him a contract and a final season in the Football League. He then embarked upon a long and varied career in non-league, most notably for Dulwich Hamlet, where at one stage he played alongside his brother Mark, while his father Dave Garland was the manager.

He increasingly sported a healthy girth which gave rise to all the usual quips about pie consumption, but if Peter no longer had the ideal body shape for an athlete, he still retained all his old skill and was deceptively quick. He carried on playing veterans football well into his forties and as player-manager of Crayford One Bell, won the Kent FA Veterans Cup three years running between 2016 and 2018.

Season	Division	League		FA Cup		FL Cup		AI Cup		Total	
		A	G	A	G	A	G	A	G	A	G
1992-93	Division 1	10 (3)	1	2	0	0	0	0	0	12 (3)	1
1993-94	Division 1	21 (6)	1	0	0	1	0	4 (1)	1	26 (7)	2
1994-95	Division 1	6 (4)	0	0	0	2	0			8 (4)	0
1995-96	Division 1	3	0	0	0	2	1			5	1
Total		40 (13)	2	2	0	5	1	4 (1)	1	51 (14)	4

UK LEAGUE CAREER 82 games 2 goals

CHARLTON CAREER
Managers: *A Curbishley/S Gritt, A Curbishley*
Debut: *West Ham United (H) (sub) 26-12-1992*
V534
Finale: *Grimsby Town (H) 07-10-1995*

GATTING Stephen Paul   1991 - 93

Joining Charlton during the exile years, Steve made his debut in the first 'home' match played at the Boleyn Ground. Goals from Robert Lee and Carl Leaburn

Midfield, Defender   11st 11lbs   5' 11"
Born: 29-05-1959 - Willesden, London
Education: John Kelly Boys' Technical College, Neasden.

ensured a 2-1 victory against Newcastle United and the die hard supporters who had queued to get through the Blackwall Tunnel were rewarded by a solid performance from the new signing on the left-hand side of midfield. His brother is former England cricket captain Mike Gatting and Steve himself turned out several times for Middlesex Second XI. His son Joe Gatting played football for Brighton and first class cricket for Sussex and Hampshire.

HONOURS

FA Youth XI 1976 1 cap 0 goals
Brent District Schools & Middlesex Schools
Brighton & Hove Albion 1982-83 Finalists FA Cup

Brighton & Hove Albion 1987-88 Runners Up Division 3
Stamco 1994-95 & 1995-96 Runners Up Sussex County League

CLUBS

Arsenal 07.75 (youth) 02.77 (pro) ••Brighton & Hove Albion 09.81 (£180,000) ••Charlton Athletic 16.08.91 (free) ••Stamco 1993 (player coach) ••Arsenal 07.07 (youth coach) ••Stevenage 14.12.18 (assistant manager)

Steve spent the early part of his career at Arsenal and

featured regularly in the first team during 1978-79. He

scored in the 1-0 defeat of Leeds United in November and played his part in the epic FA Cup tie with Sheffield Wednesday which stretched to five matches. He appeared in every one and got a goal in the eventual Arsenal 2-0 victory in the 4th Replay. However, he was not selected for the FA Cup final that season despite appearing in the semi-final win against Wolves. Although never the first name on the team sheet. Steve had clocked up 76 league and cup appearances by the time that he left Arsenal for Brighton & Hove Albion in September 1981.

The move could not have worked out better and he immediately settled into the Brighton team and rarely missed a game except for injury over the next decade. He was one of the heroes of Brighton's 1983 FA Cup run which led all the way to Wembley and a drawn game with Manchester United, before eventual defeat in the replay. He played in the extraordinary 7-0 win over Charlton in October 1983, when nearly every Brighton shot seemed to find the net and was also present when the Addicks gained revenge four months later thanks to two Martin Robinson goals.

A severe pelvic strain in November 1984 kept him away from the action for over a year and after he returned he found the team in decline and this led to relegation from

Division 2 in 1986-87. He was however ever present throughout the following campaign as they bounced back at the first attempt. Steve returned to Wembley on 2nd June 1991 as Brighton contested the Division 2 play off final, but again it ended in disappointment after defeat to Notts County 3-1.

The most significant event during Steve's two years at Charlton was the return to the Valley on 5th December 1992. He played in 32 league matches that season, but missed out on the game against Portsmouth through injury. He finally got to play at the Valley for Charlton a fortnight later when he came on as a substitute and scored in the 1-1 draw with Oxford United.

He joined Sussex County League club Stamco in 1993 as player coach and they twice finished runners-up in their league. By 2002 Steve was running a travel agency in Hove and for seven years coached both football and cricket at Christ's Hospital School in Horsham. However, in 2007 he returned to Arsenal as a youth coach, a position which lasted until May 2018 when he departed amidst allegations of bullying. More recently he had a spell as assistant manager of Stevenage,

Season	Division	League		FA Cup		FL Cup		FM Cup		AI Cup		Total	
		A	G	A	G	A	G	A	G	A	G	A	G
1991-92	Division 2	30 (2)	1	3	2	4	0	1	0			38 (2)	3
1992-93	Division 1	31 (1)	2	1	0	0	0			2	0	34 (1)	2
Total		61 (3)	3	4	2	4	0	1	0	2	0	72 (3)	5

UK LEAGUE CAREER 438 games 27 goals

CHARLTON CAREER
Managers: *A Curbishley/S Gritt*
Debut: *Newcastle United (H) 18-08-1991*
V519
Finale: *Birmingham City (A) 08-05-1993*

GAULD James   1955 - 56

Forward   12 st 0 lbs   5' 11"
Born: 09-05-1931 - Aberdeen, Scotland
Died: 09-12-2004 - Paddington, London

The putrid smell of corruption and bribery that is quite properly attached to the name of Jimmy Gauld, makes it difficult to view his career without being influenced by those later events. However, in his younger days he was a talented and skilled striker who scored goals at the highest level of English football and at a very acceptable rate. He started out with Hall Russell, the works team of Aberdeen shipbuilders and from there signed for Aberdeen, but never made it to their first team, despite having represented Scotland at both Schoolboy and Youth level. It was only after he joined the Irish club Waterford that his career really took off and his 30 goals in 20 games in 1954-55 topped the goal scoring list for the League of Ireland. He transferred to Charlton in May 1955 and only two months later Eddie Firmani's move to Italy was finalised, leaving Jimmy with the thankless task of replacing a Charlton legend.

HONOURS

League Of Ireland 1954-55 2 caps
Scotland Schoolboy & Youth International

Plymouth Argyle 1958-59 Winners Division 3

CLUBS

Hall Russell, Scotland 1947 ••Aberdeen, Scotland 04.12.48 ••Huntly, Scotland 1949 ••Elgin City, Scotland 1950 ••Waterford, Ireland 1954 ••Charlton Athletic 02.05.55 (£4000) ••Everton 19.10.56 (£10,500) ••Plymouth Argyle 25.10.57 ••Swindon Town 20.05.59 (£6,500) ••St Johnstone, Scotland 07.09.60 ••Mansfield Town 19.11.60 (£4,000)

Jimmy was very fast and had been a champion sprinter in his school days. That, allied to tremendous ball control, made him a most dangerous player and his return of 18 goals in 36 League and Cup games for Charlton more than proved the case in his first season with the club. Sadly however he was unable to sustain the same rate in 1956-57 as an ageing side rapidly sank to the bottom of the league and to inevitable relegation.

He joined Everton, but only stayed a year, though he continued to score goals in the lower divisions until injury brought his career to an end on Boxing Day 1960. He was playing for Mansfield and had already scored what proved to be the winning goal, when he collided with the Hartlepool goalkeeper and broke his leg.

Ordinarily that would have been the last that the world heard of Jimmy Gauld, but on 12th April 1964 he was named in a dramatic news story that appeared in the

'Sunday People' alleging a major bribery scandal within English football. As the story unfolded, Gauld was seen to be not only a participant but organiser of the match fixing and when the case was heard at Nottingham Asizes, nine players, including two England Internationals, went to prison, with Jimmy receiving the heaviest sentence of four years, plus a fine of £5000.

Already banned for life by the FA, little was heard from Jimmy after that until he turned up for a brief period in 1980 running a cafe and bookshop at Torquay railway station. He later returned to London and worked as a security guard and caretaker at Marylebone before his eventual death on 9th December 2004 at St Mary's Hospital, Paddington. In 1997 a BBC drama, 'The Fix' was screened and was based upon the 1962 betting scandal.

Season	Division	League A	G	FA Cup A	G	Total A	G
1955-56	Division 1	34	17	2	1	36	18
1956-57 (R)	Division 1	13	4	0	0	13	4
Total		47	21	2	1	49	22

UK LEAGUE CAREER 182 games 70 goals

CHARLTON CAREER
Managers: *J Seed, J Trotter*
Debut: *Luton Town (H) 20-08-1955*
V263
Finale: *Arsenal (H) 13-10-1956*

GAVIN Dylan John   2020 -

Irish striker Dylan Gavin excelled at more than one sport whilst attending Marist College in Athlone. He showed outstanding promise at Gaelic Football and played in the college side which won the Leinster Schools Juvenile title.

However, Association Football was his priority and he joined Athlone Town at U15 level, in time to help them win the first Irish U15 National League championship in 2017. He was later selected for the Republic of Ireland U16 team that played in a friendly international against Australia at Abbotstown in January 2019.

Forward
Born: 16-01-2003 - Athlone, Ireland
Education: Marist College, Athlone.

HONOURS

Republic of Ireland U16 International 2019 1 cap 0 goals
Charlton Athletic U18 2020-21 Winners PD League 2 South

Athlone Town 2017 Winners Ireland U15 National League

CLUBS

St Peter's Athlone, Ireland 2016 (youth) ••St Francis, Ireland 2016 (youth) ••Athlone Town, Ireland 2017 (youth) ••Charlton Athletic 2019 (youth) 06.07.21 (pro) ••Billericay Town 21.01.22 (loan)

Academy coach Anthony Hayes is from Athlone and it was   following his recommendation that Dylan came to

Charlton on a scholarship in 2019, at the age of 16. By the start of the 2020-21 season he had settled into what was a completely different environment and was getting among the goals for the U18 team. Manager Lee Bowyer named a very young and inexperienced side for the League Trophy tie against Leyton Orient on 10th November 2020 and Dylan was a 72nd minute substitute in a 3-1 win. He acquitted himself well but was clearly not yet ready to be

viewed as a serious first team contender at that point. His subsequent progress has been derailed by a combination of an ankle ligament injury and a debilitating dose of Covid. His ankle kept him side-lined for nearly five months, but on 6th July 2021 he signed his first professional contract and moved up into the U23 squad for season 2021-22.

Season	Division	League		FA Cup		FL Cup		FL Trophy		Total	
		A	G	A	G	A	G	A	G	A	G
2020-21	League One	0	0	0	0	0	0	0 (1)	0	0 (1)	0
Total		0	0	0	0	0	0	0 (1)	0	0 (1)	0

UK LEAGUE CAREER 0 games 0 goals

CHARLTON CAREER
Managers: *L Bowyer, N Adkins, J Jackson*
Debut: *Leyton Orient (H) (sub) 10-11-2020*
V915

GHANDOUR Hady Ismail   2020 -

Forward   6' 2"
Born: 27-01-2000 - Westminster, London
Education: Cass Business School, City of London.

Although a Londoner by birth, Hady is from a Lebanese family and during his education in England would return to Lebanon in the school holidays and play for the AFC Tripoli youth team. He is a hard-working striker with a strong determination to succeed and was capped four times for Lebanon at U17 level, scoring on his debut in a 3-2 win against Syria. In 2017, he was called up for the U20 team and played against both Iraq and Qatar in qualifiers for the Asia Football Confederation Championships. In January 2021 he looked likely to progress further when he was invited to attend the Lebanon U23 training camp, but as a result of Covid restrictions was unable to do so.

HONOURS

Lebanon International 2021 1 cap 0 goals
Lebanon U20 International 2017 2 caps 0 goals
Lebanon U17 International 2015 4 caps 1 goal

CLUBS

AFC Tripoli, Lebanon 2014 (youth) ••Tooting & Mitcham United 2016 (youth) 2018 (pro) ••Charlton Athletic 14.08.20 (free) ••Maidstone United 21.10.21 (loan) ••Chelmsford City 07.01.22 (loan) ••Maidstone United 11.03.22 (loan)

While still at school, Hady had a trial with Charlton, but decided at that stage to concentrate on his A-levels. He hooked up with Tooting & Mitcham and made his first team debut on 9th October 2018 in an Isthmian League Cup match against Cheshunt. Charlton continued to monitor his progress and the four goals that he scored against Chertsey Town on 7th December 2019 must have been noted, because in January 2020 he commenced an eight-week trial at Sparrows Lane. He was eventually signed to a professional contract on 14th August.
So far Hady has only had one chance in the first team and this came on 10th November 2020 in a Football League

Trophy match at the Valley against Leyton Orient. He led the attack and played for the full 90 minutes in a 3-1 victory. On 19th May 2021 the club confirmed that his contract was being renewed and he would remain at Charlton for season 2021-22.
With Covid restrictions finally being eased, Hady was able to make his full international debut on 7th September 2021 when Lebanon met South Korea in a World Cup qualifier. He was named in the squad for a second match the following month, this time against Syria, but on that occasion was an unused substitute.

Season	Division	League		FA Cup		FL Cup		FL Trophy		Total	
		A	G	A	G	A	G	A	G	A	G
2020-21	League One	0	0	0	0	0	0	1	0	1	0
Total		0	0	0	0	0	0	1	0	1	0

UK LEAGUE CAREER 0 games 0 goals

CHARLTON CAREER
Managers: *L Bowyer, N Adkins, J Jackson*
Debut: *Leyton Orient (H) 10-11-2020*
V913

GHOOCHANNEJHAD NOURNIA Reza   2014 - 16

Reza joined Charlton during a period of great unrest and arrived the same week as French defender Loic Nego, both men having been transferred from within controversial owner Roland Duchatelet's network of clubs. His time in English football was largely unfulfilled but he did manage to create two records, one being his goal for Iran against Bosnia and Herzegovina in 2014, which was the first by a Charlton player in the finals of a World Cup. The second record was somewhat different. His surname is composed of 14 letters and Ghoochannejhad eclipses that of goalkeeper Albert Uytenbogaardt as the longest ever by a Charlton player

Forward   12st 11lbs   5' 11"
Born: 20-09-1987 - Mashhad, Iran
Education: Vrije Universiteit, Amsterdam.

HONOURS

Iran International 2012-18 44 caps 17 goals
Netherlands U19 International 2006-07 3 caps 1 goal
Netherlands U18 International 2005 1 cap 0 goals
Netherlands U17 International 2003-04 4 caps 0 goals
Netherlands U16 International 2003 1 cap 0 goals

SC Cambuur 2009-10 Runners Up Eerste Division
Kuwait SC 2014-15 Winners Kuwaiti Premier League
Apoel 2018-19 Winners Cypriot First Division
Sydney 2018-19 Runners Up A-League
Sydney 2018-19 Winners A-League Finals Series

CLUBS

Leeuwarder Athletic, Netherlands (youth) ••SC Cambuur, Netherlands (youth) ••SC Heerenveen, Netherlands 1998 (youth) 2005 (pro) ••Go Ahead Eagles, Netherlands 2006 (loan) ••FC Emmen, Netherlands 2009 (loan) ••Go Ahead Eagles, Netherlands 2009 ••SC Cambuur, Netherlands 01.10 ••Sint-Truidense, Belgium 06.11 ••Standard Liege, Belgium 01.01.13 ••Charlton Athletic 30.01.14 (undisclosed) ••Kuwait SC, Kuwait 06.08.14 (loan) ••Al-Wakrah, Qatar 16.02.15 (loan) ••SC Heerenveen, Netherlands 22.06.16 (free) ••Apoel, Cyprus 23.07.18 (free) ••Sydney, Australia 29.01.19 (free) ••PEC Zwolle, Netherlands 03.09.19 (free)

Although born in Iran, Reza was brought up in the Netherlands from the age of four. A fast and skilful winger he spent more than a decade with his local club, SC Heerenveen, as well as representing his adopted country as a Youth International. In 2009, he briefly gave up football to devote his time to his academic studies and gained a degree in law and politics from Vrije University in Amsterdam.
In 2010, he joined SC Cambuur, a Dutch second division club and made a spectacular debut on 22nd January scoring against BV Veendam after just nine seconds and equalling the record for the fastest goal in the Netherlands. Cambuur went on to narrowly miss out on promotion to the top flight, but they again made the play offs in 2010-11 and Reza, now featuring as a striker, scored 13 goals including a hat-trick against FC Emmen.
After moving to Belgium with Sint-Truiden, he was persuaded to switch his international allegiance to Iran, the country of his birth and he made his debut in a World Cup

qualifier on 16th October 2012. This proved to be the first of his 44 caps (8 during his time at Charlton), but by far his most important appearance came on 18th June 2013 when he scored the only goal in the 1-0 win against South Korea which clinched Iran's qualification for the 2014 World Cup Finals.
Reza arrived at Charlton after spending a year with Standard Liege and it became immediately apparent that the more physical aspects of the English game did not suit him. He had pace and skill but was clearly uncomfortable with some of the tackles which came his way and which invariably left him rolling around on the ground and beseeching the referee for assistance. He did grab an important goal at Elland Road on 1st April 2014 however and that 1-0 win against Leeds United helped to drag Charlton away from the Championship relegation places
It did not seem likely that Reza would remain long in England and he spent the 2014-15 season out on loan, first

in Kuwait and then Qatar, but then unexpectedly reappeared back at the Valley to fulfil the final year of his contract. He was a semi regular in the 2016 relegation side but never seemed comfortable at Charlton and soon returned to Dutch football.

Since then, he has found success in both Cyprus and Australia and finished up back in the Netherlands plying his trade for PEC Zwolle in the top division of Dutch football. A complex character who is passionate about politics and the violin, Reza, who plays everything from classical to hip hop, has expressed the desire to become a professional musician when his football career ends.

Season	Division	League		FA Cup		FL Cup		Total	
		A	G	A	G	A	G	A	G
2013-14	Championship	10 (5)	1	0 (2)	0	0	0	10 (7)	1
2015-16 (R)	Championship	10 (13)	2	1	1	0 (1)	1	11 (14)	4
Total		20 (18)	3	1 (2)	1	0 (1)	1	21 (21)	5

UK LEAGUE CAREER 38 games 3 goals

CHARLTON CAREER
Managers: *C Powell, J Riga, B Peeters, G Luzon, K Fraeye, J Riga*
Debut: *Wigan Athletic (A) 01-02-2014*
V772
Finale: *Sheffield Wednesday (A) 19-03-2016*

GIBSON James   1925 - 27

Forward   11st 0lbs   5' 9"
Born: Airdrie, Scotland
Died: Unknown

Very little is known about Jimmy beyond the short period in which he was a Charlton footballer, except that he moved on to play for Thames AFC in 1928. This made him close to being a founder member as the 'club with no fans' was only created that year. Thames was formed by a group of businessmen to play at the vast West Ham Stadium in Custom House with a capacity of 120,000. They quickly attained Football League status, but never developed a proper fan base and were dissolved again in 1932. Jimmy did not stay long and never appeared for Thames during their two seasons in Division 3 (South).

CLUBS
Baillieston Thistle, Scotland c1924 ••Charlton Athletic 03.06.1925 (pro). ••Thames 1928 ••Dartford 26.07.30 ••Shepherds Bush 10.33

Jimmy was one of the many footballers from north of the border who were recruited by Charlton's Scottish manager Sandy MacFarlane during the 1920s. Some proved successful while others were less so. The attraction for cash-strapped Charlton was almost certainly financial as the Scots recruits were known on occasions to play for less than the maximum wage.

He arrived at the Valley in June 1925 and was called up for first team duty on 24th October for the away trip to Southend. There was a vacancy because George Armitage was on international duty playing for England in Belfast. Jimmy got off to the best possible start by scoring the opening goal, which when followed by one from Alex Steele gave the Addicks a 2-1 win. The Southend team contained Fred Jewhurst, Albert Purdy, Steve Smith and future Charlton striker Ernie Watkins.

Seven days later Jimmy scored again and this time it was the only goal as Aberdare Athletic were dispatched 1-0. He made it three in three matches at Northampton on 7th November but after failing to find the net in his fourth appearance was not selected again for the rest of the season, which with hindsight seems quite extraordinary. It was not as if the team was flying. Charlton finished 1925-26 second from bottom of Division 3 (South) and nobody managed more than six league goals. He got just one game during the next campaign before leaving the club.

We will probably never know why Jimmy Gibson was not given a more extended run in the Charlton team but after his brief time with Thames AFC, he re-appeared with Dartford in 1930-31 where he played alongside John Bailey, mainly in their reserves, but still managed seven goals in eight games. From there he joined Shepherds Bush before disappearing completely. His later activities are unknown.

Season	Division	League		FA Cup		Total	
		A	G	A	G	A	G
1925-26	Divison 3 (S)	4	3	0	0	4	3
1926-27	Divison 3 (S)	1	0	0	0	1	0
Total		5	3	0	0	5	3

UK LEAGUE CAREER 5 games 3 goals

CHARLTON CAREER
Managers: *A MacFarlane*
Debut: *Southend United (A) 24-10-1925*
V079
Finale: *Luton Town (A) 16-04-1927*

GILBEY Alexander Scott   2020 -

Alex joined Charlton during the turbulent Summer of 2020, when the future of the club was worryingly uncertain. Ownership had passed from the Belgian, Roland Duchaelet, to the unsavoury East Street Investments and many people feared that the next step could be administration. The Football League had placed the club under a transfer embargo, but this was lifted for a brief period during August which allowed both Alex and striker Conor Washington to be signed. He arrived at the Valley with an impressive CV and a three-year contract.

Midfield   11st 7lbs   6' 0"
Born: 09-12-1994 - Dagenham, London
Education: The Gilberd School, Colchester.

HONOURS
Newport County 2012-13 Promoted Play Offs Football Conference   Milton Keynes Dons 2018-19 Promoted League Two

CLUBS
Frinton & Walton Youth (youth) ••Colchester United 2007 (youth) 16.02.12 (pro) ••Newport County 27.03.13 (loan) ••Wigan Athletic 21.06.16 (free) ••Milton Keynes Dons 31.08.17 ••Charlton Athletic 12.08.20 (undisclosed)

The academy at Colchester United was the starting point for Alex's football career. He played alongside Macaulay Bonne while captaining their youth team and made his first team debut at Northampton in October 2012. The following March he was loaned to Newport County and his energetic midfield play contributed to their late push for promotion from the Conference, via the play offs. He played at Wembley on 5th May 2013 when Wrexham were beaten 2-0 and County re-gained their place in the Football League after an absence of 25 years.
His Colchester side played Charlton at the Valley in a League Cup fixture on 12th August 2014 and were soundly beaten 4-0 thanks to a penalty by Yoni Buyens, a goal from Simon Church and two from Lawrie Wilson. However, they gained their revenge on 9th January 2016 winning 2-1 in the FA Cup, an occasion when Charlton were exceptionally poor. Alex played over 100 league matches for

Colchester before moving on to Wigan Athletic following relegation from League One in 2015-16, but unfortunately they had problems of their own and he went on to experience a second relegation just a year later, when they lost their place in the Championship.
In August 2017 Alex transferred to MK Dons and had another bumpy ride, a third relegation being followed by a promotion year in 2018-19 when they returned to League One. His form was outstanding during this period and after three seasons he gambled by accepting a move to Charlton where the future was a long way from secure. Luckily for all concerned the position of the club stabilized in September 2020 through the appearance of Thomas Sandgaard, an ambitious new owner. Time will tell if Alex can be part of the next Charlton promotion side.

Season	Division	League		FA Cup		FL Cup		FL Trophy		Total	
		A	G	A	G	A	G	A	G	A	G
2020-21	League One	18 (5)	3	0	0	0 (2)	0	0	0	18 (7)	3
Total		18 (5)	3	0	0	0 (2)	0	0	0	18 (7)	3

UK LEAGUE CAREER 219 games 20 goals

CHARLTON CAREER
Managers: *L Bowyer, N Adkins, J Jackson*
Debut: *Swindon Town (A) (sub) 05-09-2020*
V897

GILCHRIST Paul Anthony 1969

Forward, Midfield   12st 5lbs   5' 11"
Born: 05-01-1951 - Dartford, Kent
Education: St Paul's School, Swanley and Cannock House, Chelsfield.

There is no doubt as to the high point in the footballing career of Paul Gilchrist. On 1st May 1976 and in front of a packed Wembley crowd of 100,000, he was part of the Southampton side which confounded the critics and defeated Manchester United 1-0 to win the FA Cup for the first and so far only time in their history. His contribution at Charlton was less spectacular and his short run in the team came when Matt Tees had just been sold to Luton Town and his fellow striker Ray Crawford was being shown the 'exit' door after falling out with manager Eddie Firmani. These were big shoes to fill for a teenager and it is not surprising that he found the task difficult.

HONOURS

Charlton Athletic Youth 1966-67 Winners South East Counties League
Charlton Athletic Reserves 1968-69 Runners Up London Mid-Week League

Southampton 1974-75 Finalists Texaco Cup
Southampton 1975-76 Winners FA Cup

CLUBS

Chelsfield Villa 1961 (youth) ••Swanley Old Boys (youth) ••Crockenhill (youth) ••Charlton Athletic 19.01.67 (youth) 21.03.68 (pro) ••Cambridge United 01.70 (loan) ••Yeovil Town 1970 (loan) ••Fulham 09.03.71 (loan) ••Doncaster Rovers 09.07.71 (free) ••Southampton 08.03.72 (£30,000) ••Al-Ahli Jeddah, Saudi Arabia 12.76 (loan) ••Portsmouth 10.03.77 (£5,000) ••Swindon Town 29.08.78 (undisclosed) ••Hereford United 10.03.80 (free) ••Dunstable Town 1981 (free)

Charlton made a decent start to the 1969-70 season but after beating Oxford United on 26th August went through a run of 15 consecutive matches without a win. It was during this dismal period that Paul was given his chance, but his first full game was a 6-0 hammering at Bristol City and even though they later managed a respectable draw at Queens Park Rangers thanks to a Mike Kenning goal, a 2-0 home defeat against Blackpool on 1st November proved to be his swansong. He was substituted late in the match and did not appear in the first team again.

In Summer 1971 he joined Doncaster and fared considerably better, scoring four times in two matches during January 1972 as manager Maurice Setters steered the newly-relegated Rovers into a safe mid-table place in Division 4. His good form alerted Southampton, who in March paid £30,000 to bring him into the First Division, but the Saints were a declining force and after two seasons were relegated.

They did however reach the final of the Texaco Cup in December 1974, (the year before it was transformed into the Anglo Scottish Cup), but lost to Newcastle over two legs. By now Paul was being hindered by a succession of injuries but did participate in most of the FA Cup matches

the following season and scored the opening goal in the 2-0 defeat of Crystal Palace in the semi-final. The arrival of a Second Division team in the FA Cup final was a rarity in itself but the victory over Manchester United remains one of the great upsets of the modern era.

A short and unhappy loan spell in Saudi Arabia was followed by a transfer to Portsmouth in 1977. This did not go well either as his previous connection to Southampton left him open to excessive barracking, there being no love between the supporters of the two clubs. Things went better at Swindon Town where he re-discovered his shooting boots, but after switching to Hereford United, a broken leg received in a pre-season friendly finished his career.

He spent a year trying to overcome the injury but was forced into retirement in 1981 at the age of 30. Since then Paul ran a cardiovascular fitness centre in Swindon for seven years, worked as an after sales service advisor for a BMW dealership in Redhill and finished his working life with Caterham Cars. He is now retired and has found the time to have a full knee replacement.

Season	Division	League		FA Cup		FL Cup		Total	
		A	G	A	G	A	G	A	G
1969-70	Division 2	5 (2)	0	0	0	0	0	5 (2)	0
Total		5 (2)	0	0	0	0	0	5 (2)	0

UK LEAGUE CAREER 203 games 35 goals

CHARLTON CAREER
Managers: *E Firmani, T Foley*
Debut: *Birmingham City (H) (sub) 20-09-1969*
V346
Finale: *Blackpool (H) 01-11-1969*

GILES James Archer   1975 - 77

Jimmy was a blood and guts central defender who spent two and a half years at the Valley in between two long spells with Exeter City for whom he made more than 300 league appearances. He was extremely popular wherever he played and a real trier who would always battle on until the final whistle had been blown. He was also a good cricketer and appeared as a fast bowler for Worcestershire 2nd XI and in the Minor Counties for Oxfordshire.

Defender   12st 0lbs   6' 0"
Born: 21-04-1946 - Kidlington, Oxfordshire

HONOURS
Oxfordshire County Schools
1963-64 Kidlington Runners Up Hellenic League Division 1

1983-84 Chard Town Runners Up Western League Division 1

CLUBS
KIdlington (youth) 1962 (amateur) ••Swindon Town 01.65 (amateur) 02.03.65 (pro) ••Aldershot 07.10.68 (£5,000) ••Exeter City 08.03.71 (£4,000) ••Charlton Athletic 25.06.75 (£12,000) ••Exeter City 19.12.77 (£7,000) ••Yeovil Town 24.02.81 (player manager) ••Tiverton Town c1983 (ass: manager) ••Chard Town 1984 (player manager) ••Ottery St Mary (manager)

Starting out in the Hellenic League with his home town club Kidlington, Jimmy had a trial with Bristol Rovers before signing for Swindon Town at the age of 18. He made his Football League debut alongside Roger Smart on 10th May 1966 and it was a baptism of fire as he was up against the experienced Matt Tees with Grimsby Town and managing a goalless draw was a fine achievement for the young centre half.

He moved to Aldershot and made steady progress until a broken leg on Boxing Day 1969 against Swansea Town kept him out of the side for the remainder of the 1969-70 season. It was however the transfer to Exeter City in March 1971 which really proved the defining moment for Jimmy and over the next four years he became the cornerstone of their defence. He rarely missed a match and was voted their player of the year on three separate occasions. They were far from being world beaters, but his consistent and courageous performances week after week went a long way to keeping the Grecians in the top half of Division 4 during most of his first spell with the club.

With Bobby Goldthorpe out of favour and Les Berry yet to break through to the first team, Charlton were in urgent need of an experienced central defender by the summer of 1975 and Jimmy Giles was an inspired signing by manager

Andy Nelson. He settled straight into the team and was ever present in his first season and nearly as effective in 1976-77, the club maintaining a top 10 place in Division 2 in both campaigns. He even chipped in with the occasional goal, including the winner on 7th September 1976 when Southampton were beaten 2-1 in a League Cup replay at the Valley. He eventually lost his place in the team during December 1977 and was initially replaced by David Campbell and later by Dave Shipperley when he returned to Charlton after a spell at Gillingham.

Exeter City welcomed Jimmy back just before Christmas and he continued where he had left off. They had gained promotion in his absence and over the next three years he helped them to consolidate their position in Division 3. He remained a fixture in the side until he was unexpectedly left out for a high profile FA Cup tie with Newcastle United in February 1981, after which harsh words were spoken and he left the club somewhat abruptly to join Yeovil Town as player manager.

Yeovil were struggling under the weight of crippling financial restraints, but Jimmy helped them to avoid relegation from the Alliance Premier League and stayed at the helm through until March 1983, making 86 league appearances in all. After retirement, he concentrated on his bricklaying business in Ottery St Mary, Devon as well as some scouting for Charlton and regular appearances as a

commentator for BBC Radio Devon.

Season	Division	League		FA Cup		FL Cup		Total	
		A	G	A	G	A	G	A	G
1975-76	Division 2	42	3	4	0	7	1	53	4
1976-77	Division 2	36 (1)	3	2	0	3	1	41 (1)	4
1977-78	Division 2	14	0	0	0	0	0	14	0
Total		92 (1)	6	6	0	10	2	108 (1)	8

UK LEAGUE CAREER 501 games 22 goals

CHARLTON CAREER
Managers: *A Nelson*
Debut: *Notts County (H) 16-08-1975*
V392
Finale: *Sunderland (H) 03-12-1977*

GILL Eric Norman   1951

Goalkeeper   12st 0lbs   5' 10"
Born: 03-11-1930 - St Pancras, London

Eric started his career at Charlton where he became an understudy for Sam Bartram. He was called up for his National Service in August 1948 and two years later played for the 3rd Training Battalion of the Royal Army Ordnance Corps in the final of the Army FA Cup, winning 2-1 and receiving his medal from King George VI.

HONOURS

Charlton Athletic Reserves 1951-52 Finalists London FA Challenge Cup
Royal Army Ordnance Corps 1949-50 Winners Army FA Challenge Cup
Brighton & Hove Albion 1953-54 & 1955-56 Runners Up Division 3 (S)
Brighton & Hove Albion 1957-58 Winners Division 3 (S)
Guildford City 1962-63 Winners Southern League Cup

CLUBS

Broomfields 1947 (amateur) ••Charlton Athletic 28.02.48 (amateur) 25.03.48 (pro) ••Tonbridge 06.10.50 (loan) ••Brighton & Hove Albion 25.06.52 (£400) ••Guildford City 01.07.60 (free)

Eric finally got his chance in the Charlton first team in September 1951, but Manchester United were not yet the glamorous club that they later became and a crowd of only 28,627 turned out at Old Trafford for the occasion. With just three minutes remaining the visitors led 2-1, thanks to goals from Billy Kiernan and Charlie Vaughan, only for United to score twice to snatch the points and completely spoil Eric's afternoon.
The consistency of Sam Bartram in the Charlton goal blocked any chance of further progress, so he moved on to

Brighton the following year and enjoyed a very fruitful time on the south coast, where at one stage he played 247 consecutive matches in an eight-year stay. From there he joined Guildford City in the Southern League, eventually hanging up his boots in 1966.
He was also an enthusiastic bowls player and represented Sussex. Eric and his wife Ida went into the hotel business and for some years ran the Perrimay Hotel in Brighton, later switching to Simpsons Hotel (now known as Drakes) overlooking the sea on Marine Parade.

Season	Division	League		FA Cup		Total	
		A	G	A	G	A	G
1951-52	Division 1	1	0	0	0	1	0
Total		1	0	0	0	1	0

UK LEAGUE CAREER 281 games 0 goals

CHARLTON CAREER
Managers: *J Seed*
Debut: *Manchester United (A) 05-09-1951*
V246

GILLESPIE Keith Robert   2008

86 International caps and a glittering career at the sharp end of English football should have left Keith as a highly respected

Forward   11st 12lbs.   5' 10"
Born: 18-02-1975 - Larne, County Antrim
Education: Whitehead Primary School, Carrickfergus & Bangor Grammar School, Co. Down.

and wealthy man having earned an estimated £7.2 million during his 20 years in the game. Instead, he is largely remembered for his gambling addiction which led to bankruptcy in 2010 and which is painfully detailed in his autobiography, 'How Not To Be A Football Millionaire',

HONOURS

Ireland International 1994-08 86 caps 2 goals
Ireland U21 International 1994 1 cap 0 goals
Manchester United 1991-92 Winners FA Youth Cup
Newcastle United 1995-96 & 1996-97 Runners Up Premier League

Blackburn Rovers 2000-01 Runners Up Division 1
Blackburn Rovers 2001-02 Winners Football League Cup
Sheffield United 2005-06 Runners Up Championship
Glentoran 2009-10 Winners Irish League Cup

CLUBS

St Andrews, N Ireland (youth) ••Manchester United 1991 (youth) 03.02.93 (pro) ••Wigan Athletic 03.09.93 (loan) ••Newcastle United 12.01.95 (exchange) ••Blackburn Rovers 18.12.98 (£2,350,000) ••Wigan Athletic 01.12.00 (loan) ••Leicester City 09.07.03 (free) ••Sheffield United 05.08.05 (free) ••Charlton Athletic 24.11.08 (loan) ••Bradford City 12.03.09 (free) ••Glentoran, N Ireland 08.09 (free) ••Darlington 19.11.10 (free) ••Longford Town, Ireland 24.03.11 (free)

Keith graduated in the class of 92, that golden generation of Manchester United youngsters which included Butt, Beckham, Giggs and the Nevilles. They won the FA Youth Cup in style and went on to unbelievable success in the years ahead. For Keith however fate offered a different path, when in January 1995 the then British transfer record was smashed. Newcastle United's Andy Cole, valued at £7 million, moved to Old Trafford and Keith plus £6 million went in the other direction.

Newcastle were genuine title contenders in the mid-nineties and twice finished runners-up in the Premier League. Keith was one of their star performers on the left wing, but was already being distracted by his gambling vice and on one occasion lost £47,000 in a single day. He was however a fantastic talent as was demonstrated on 17th September 1997 when a Newcastle side, including both Keith, John Barnes and Robert Lee, beat Barcelona 3-2 in the UEFA Champions League and he laid on two of the three goals scored by the Magpies. Injury however prevented him from playing in the 1997-98 FA Cup final.

He moved to Blackburn in December 1998, but they were

on a downward path and spent two seasons out of the Premier League, before they returned and on 24th February 2002 defeated a Tottenham side (that included both Chris Perry and Ben Thatcher), 2-1 in the final of the Football League Cup.

By November 2008, his career was stagnating and he was unable to get a game with Sheffield United. He made his final International appearance for Northern Ireland in a 2-0 defeat against Hungary on the 19th and joined Charlton on loan five days later. The team were struggling on the field and the Keith Gillespie of old would have been a very welcome addition to the squad. Not surprisingly though, his lack of game time was apparent and he took a while to settle. He featured in six games, none of which were won and was just starting to regain some form when he was recalled by Sheffield United to cover for a sudden spate of injuries.

After the nightmare of his bankruptcy, Keith was left to re-build his life and in 2017 launched the OneTwo football agency from where he hopes to draw upon his experiences in football for the benefit of the next generation.

Season	Division	League		FA Cup		FL Cup		Total	
		A	G	A	G	A	G	A	G
2008-09 (R)	Championship	4 (2)	0	0	0	0	0	4 (2)	0
Total		4 (2)	0	0	0	0	0	4 (2)	0

UK LEAGUE CAREER 396 games 28 goals

CHARLTON CAREER
Managers: *P Parkinson*
Debut: *Queens Park Rangers (A) 25-11-2008*
V675
Finale: *Norwich City (A) (sub) 20-12-2008*

GLOVER Leonard   1962 - 67

Forward   12st 0lbs   5' 9"
Born: 31-01-1944 - Kennington, London
Education: Cowley Road Primary School & Kennington Secondary
Modern School.

It was often claimed that Sam Bartram was the finest goalkeeper who never played for England. Similarly, in a later era, a case can be made that Lenny Glover was the best uncapped winger in the land. Of course his cause was not helped by the fact that then manager Alf Ramsey favoured an England team set up with no wingers at all, but it is still remarkable that he was never given a chance at the highest level. Charlton's supporters had five years to enjoy his mercurial talent, but his form after he moved on to Leicester City was simply immense and he is considered by some to have been one of their greatest players of all time.

HONOURS

South London Schools 1957
Charlton Athletic A 1963-64 Finalists Metropolitan League Cup
Leicester City 1968-69 Finalists FA Cup

Leicester City 1970-71 Winners Division 2
Leicester City 1971 Winners FA Charity Shield
Tampa Bay Rowdies 1976 Winners NASL Eastern Division

CLUBS

Robins 1958 (youth) ••Charlton Athletic 06.05.59 (youth) 07.05.62 (pro) ••Leicester City 15.11.67 (£80,000) ••Tampa Bay Rowdies, USA 05.76 (£6,000) ••Kettering Town 10.76 (free) ••Tampa Bay Rowdies, USA 04.77 (free) ••Kettering Town 09.77 (free) ••Earl Shilton Albion 1978 (free) ••Shepshed Charterhouse 1979 (free) ••Harborough Town 1980 (free) 1989 (manager) ••Harlow Town 1994 (player manager)

A South Londoner from Stockwell, Lenny had more or less given up on school by the age of 13 and was working as a barrow boy in Covent Garden Market. He has always liked to chase a deal and even as a youngster would sometimes steer close to the wind. He trained at Charlton from 1957 and when he turned pro two years later was earning £13 as a footballer as opposed to the £40 a week he had been able to accumulate by his 'ducking and diving'. His first team debut came when he was 18 in September 1962 and he lined up at centre forward against a Stoke City side that included the great Stanley Matthews. It resulted in a 3-0 home defeat for the Addicks, but Lenny was on his way and on 6th October he scored the late winner against Walsall at the Valley in an exciting five goal thriller.

He played most of that first season as an inside forward, from where he clinched the winner in the 1-0 FA Cup match on 18th February 1963 against a Cardiff City side which included Trevor Edwards. By the following season he had moved out on to the left wing and really flourished thanks to his extreme pace and tricky ball skills. There were plenty of off the field distractions for Lenny however and

he got friendly with the Irish goalkeeper Noel Dwyer after he joined Charlton in 1965. Being older and something of a ladies man, Dwyer introduced him to the West End nightclub scene, where he got to know the likes of film star Ava Gardner, Sammy Davis Jnr and even Reggie Kray. Ava took quite a shine to Lenny and on one occasion attended a match at the Valley incognito, her face concealed behind a massive pair of dark glasses, although this only served to draw attention to her. They developed a close friendship which lasted for many years.

This Charlton team, with Lenny on one wing and Mike Kenning on the other, was massively entertaining and played exciting, attacking football, although defensive frailties ensured that they were most often to be found in the bottom half of Division 2. The exception was season 1963-64 when Eddie Firmani first returned from Italy and they stormed up the league table only to stall just short of the promotion places. Lack of investment in the team and the financially sound but unambitious policy of selling their best players has frequently been a cause of criticism for Charlton and never more so than when Lenny left the club in November 1967. There was outrage and even supporter demonstrations, but following interest from several clubs including Chelsea and Tottenham, a fee of £80,000 was finally accepted from Leicester City, which at the time was a Football League record for a winger.

Lenny took a while to settle, but in time became a great favourite with Leicester supporters. To his surprise he found the training regime under coach Bert Johnson, (the former Charlton FA Cup winner), to be less intense than at Charlton and initially he lacked the self-discipline to really apply himself. His form suffered but eventually he knuckled down and showed his true ability. Indeed, on a good day he was virtually unstoppable. His first full season was 1968-69 when Leicester enjoyed a run in the FA Cup. They were drawn against a very strong Liverpool side in the fifth round and after a 0-0 draw he had a blinder in the replay which they won 1-0. The Wembley final was against Manchester City on 26th April 1969 but Lenny was carrying a groin injury and unable to perform at his best as they went down 1-0. Leicester's league form was even more disappointing and they were relegated from Division 1 that same season.

He remained with Leicester for more than eight years during which they finished as champions of Division 2 in 1970-71 and then re-established themselves back at the top table of English football. Lenny was at his very best during this period until he suffered an Achilles injury which kept him away from the action for much of the 1975-76 season. Out of the blue he got a call from his former teammate Eddie Firmani, by then manager of the Tampa Bay Rowdies in Florida and with a lucrative offer on the table, Leicester reluctantly agreed to the transfer which took place in May 1976.

Two seasons were spent playing in the NASL with the Rowdies and Lenny captained the side in 1977. He was still a very fine player and was named as Man of the Match when they played the New York Cosmos, who included both Pele and Beckenbauer in their side. (That looks good on his CV). When Firmani departed, he briefly served as interim manager of the Rowdies. After he finally returned home he carried on playing in the non-league game but increasingly became involved in his various money making schemes and business interests. At different times he owned race horses, ran a pub in the village of Smeeton Westerby and was a partner in a pottery business, but what he most enjoyed was 'wheeling and dealing' and this would later get him into a lot of trouble.

Along with his former Leicester colleague Bobby Kellard, Lenny became joint manager of Harlow Town and in January 1995 became at age 50, the oldest person to play in an Isthmian League match. They did not stay long at Harlow however and were sacked after only half a season at the helm. He later got close to landing the manager's job at Northampton Town.

During the Summer of 2002 he had some cash in the bank following a property sale and was re-investing it in fake designer brand shirts that were made for him by a friend with a factory in Doncaster. This proved a most lucrative source of income until one day he was stopped and searched by police at a petrol station in Market Harborough while carrying £24,000 in cash which he claimed was intended for the purchase of a new Mercedes. They, wrongly as Lenny maintains, linked this to a major drugs investigation that was ongoing and he was subsequently charged and convicted of supplying class-B drugs. The case was heard at Nottingham Crown Court in May 2004 and he received a three and a half year sentence. He subsequently served one and a half, first in Welford Road and then at an open prison in Scarborough where he spent much of his time supervising the prison gym.

Lenny recounted the many highs and lows of his eventful life within the pages of 'From Left Wing To D-Wing', the hilarious and outspoken biography written with his brother Steve Glover which was published in 2008. He readily admits that he got away with his fair share of stunts, but denies having messed with drugs and strongly contends that he was fitted up by another of the accused, trying to save his own skin. He will admit to being a spiv but not a hardened criminal. Lenny is now retired and living peacefully in Whitstable. His older brother Alan was a very promising wing half who appeared in Charlton's colts, but turned down a professional contract in favour of being a window cleaner.

Season	Division	League		FA Cup		FL Cup		Total	
		A	G	A	G	A	G	A	G
1962-63	Division 2	18	2	2	1	5	2	25	5
1963-64	Division 2	40	6	1	0	1	0	42	6
1964-65	Division 2	40	5	3	0	3	0	46	5
1965-66	Division 2	35	5	1	0	1	1	37	6
1966-67	Division 2	33	1	0	0	0	0	33	1
1967-68	Division 2	11	1	0	0	2	0	13	1
Total		177	20	7	1	12	3	196	24

UK LEAGUE CAREER 429 games 58 goals

CHARLTON CAREER
Managers: *F Hill, R Stokoe, E Firmani*
Debut: *Stoke City (H) 18-09-1962*
V296
Finale: *Ipswich Town (A) 28-10-1967*

GODFREY Edward John   1926 - 27

Forward   11st 4lbs   5' 9"
Born: 17-09-1903 - West Ham, London
Died: 05-03-1977 - Woolwich, London

1925-26 was Charlton's least successful season as a Football League club and the one occasion when they have been obliged to seek re-election, after ending in last but one place in Division 3 South. Only Queens Park Rangers saved them from the total humiliation of finishing bottom. Ted was the fifth player to be tried out in the problem position of outside right, replacing Herbert Kirby in the team during March and although results did not noticeably improve, he did at least hold his place for the remainder of that unmemorable campaign.

CLUBS

UBG Sports 1923 ••Erith & Belvedere 1924 ••Charlton Athletic 12.02..26 (amateur) 31.03.26 (pro) ••Dundee, Scotland 20.09.27 ••Peterborough & Fletton United 28.05.31 ••Folkestone 07.31 ••Bexleyheath & Welling 1933

During Ted's second season at the Valley, he contested the right wing position with Scotsman David Sherlaw, who had been signed from Bristol City in the summer. Results were much improved and Charlton moved into a safe mid-table position, but by the end his had ceased to be a regular name on the team sheet. He nevertheless contributed a useful seven league goals in only 31 games during his time with the club, the last of which came on 28th April 1927 when strikes by him, Sherlaw and George Biswell disposed of Newport County 3-0.

Charlton's manager Alex 'Sandy' MacFarlane had played for Dundee before World War 1 and had been their secretary manager for six years before joining Charlton. He still retained contacts in that city and in September 1927 Ted moved north and spent the rest of that season playing in the Scottish League Division 1. He was joined by MacFarlane at the end of January, after he resigned from his position at Charlton to again take up the managerial reins at Dundee for a brief period.

Ted returned south to play for Peterborough & Fletton United in the Southern League, before finishing up with spells at Folkestone and Bexleyheath. He passed away in Woolwich at the age of 73. His nephew Peter Godfrey made one first team appearance for Charlton in 1961.

Season	Division	League		FA Cup		Total	
		A	G	A	G	A	G
1925-26	Divison 3 (S)	12	3	0	0	12	3
1926-27	Divison 3 (S)	19	4	1	0	20	4
Total		31	7	1	0	32	7

UK LEAGUE CAREER 52 games 8 goals

CHARLTON CAREER
Managers: *A MacFarlane*
Debut: *Merthyr Town (A) 15-03-1926*
V085
Finale: *Exeter City (H) 07-05-1927*

GODFREY Peter Ronald   1961

Peter spent nearly eight years at Charlton but only managed a single appearance in the first team. He deputised on the right wing for Sam Lawrie at Portsmouth on 18th February 1961 and contributed to a useful 1-1 draw. His uncle, Ted Godfrey, had played for Charlton in the 1920s.

Forward   10st 6lbs   5' 7"
Born: 15-03-1938 - Woolwich, London
Education: Sebastopol Secondary School, Panteg.

HONOURS

Cardiff Schools & London FA Youth
Charlton Athletic A 1958-59 Winners London Mid-Week League

Charlton Athletic A 1959-60 Winners Aetolian League Cup
Gillingham 1963-64 Winners Division 4

CLUBS

RTB Panteg (youth) ••Charlton Athletic 08.53 (youth) 05.11.55 (pro) ••Bexleyheath & Welling 14.04.54 (youth loan) ••Gillingham 01.07.61 (free) ••Chesterfield 02.07.65 (free) ••Exeter City 20.06.66 (free) ••Ramsgate Athletic 07.67 (free) ••Chatham Town c1974

Born in Woolwich but brought up in South Wales from the age of three, Peter represented Cardiff Schools as well as playing for both Monmouthshire and London at youth level He joined the ground staff at Charlton in 1953 and two years later scored a hat-trick at Queens Park Rangers in a reserve fixture. He was a close friend of Mike Bailey and they both rented rooms at a house in Merriman Road, Blackheath for a time and he introduced Bailey to a young lady called Barbara Mustin, who would later become his wife. Unable to make the breakthrough into the first team however, Peter's contract was eventually cancelled in June 1961 and he signed for Gillingham on a free transfer the

following month.

His career now finally took off and he scored in each of his first two games for the Gills and was a regular for them on the right wing over the next two seasons, only losing his place midway through 1963-64, the campaign when they finished as champions of Division 4. He moved on first to Chesterfield and then Exeter City before dropping into non-league with Ramsgate Athletic where he remained for at least six years.

Although Peter had trained as a hairdresser during his time at Charlton, when his playing days were over he worked as a self employed painter, decorator and carpenter.

Season	Division	League		FA Cup		FL Cup		Total	
		A	G	A	G	A	G	A	G
1960-61	Division 2	1	0	0	0	0	0	1	0
Total		1	0	0	0	0	0	1	0

CHARLTON CAREER
Managers: J Seed, J Trotter
Debut: *Portsmouth (A) 18-02-1961*
V288

UK LEAGUE CAREER 136 games 15 goals

GOLDTHORPE Robert James   1972 - 75

Bobby was a semi-regular in Andy Nelson's Charlton side which gained promotion back to Division 2 in season 1974-75. His Football League debut had been with Crystal Palace, for whom he made a single appearance against Wolverhampton Wanderers on 18th March 1972, but this proved to be his only outing in Division 1 and the remainder of his career was played out in the lower divisions where he was an instantly recognizable figure, hurtling into tackles with his unruly mop of blond hair and a boyish enthusiasm that was appreciated by even the most cynical supporters.

Defender   12st 4lbs   6' 0"
Born: 06-12-1950 - Osterley, Middlesex
Education: Archbishop Myers School, Hounslow.

HONOURS
Charlton Athletic 1974-75 Promoted Division 3

CLUBS
Brentford (youth) ••West Ham United (youth) ••Fulham 1967 (youth) ••Crystal Palace 20.02.68 (youth) 15.07.68 (pro) ••Charlton Athletic 19.12.72 (loan) 24.05.73 (free) ••Bath City 24.02.74 (loan) ••Aldershot 18.02.76 (loan) ••Brentford 01.07.76 (free) ••Hayes 1977 (free)

When Crystal Palace allowed Bobby to join Charlton, initially on loan and then on a free transfer, they had no idea that he would later come back to haunt them. During a televised game at Selhurst Park on 30th November 1974 he gave one of his best performances in a Charlton shirt during a disappointing 2-1 defeat, but also featured in the return fixture at the Valley in which Derek Hales ensured revenge, claiming the only goal in front of a crowd of 26,104. By the final round of matches, both clubs were still involved in the promotion scramble and on 29th April 1975 another big Valley crowd gathered for the game against Preston North End. The team did not start well and went a goal down. Bobby Curtis missed a penalty and Charlton were wobbling badly when Goldthorpe scored the vital equaliser. Two more goals from Derek Hales ensured a 3-1 victory and clinched the final promotion place for Charlton rather than Palace, who were left

stranded in Division 3 for a further two years.
Bobby did not figure much at first team level in 1975-76, David Young and Jimmy Giles being preferred in the centre of the defence. He did play at the Valley on 12th December however and the Charlton back line held firm for a 2-0 win against a Plymouth Argyle side which included Hugh McAuley. In February, he moved on loan to Aldershot and in Summer 1976 signed for Brentford, for what became his final season in the Football League.
He dropped into non-league with Hayes for 1977-78 and captained them to a mid-table placing in the Isthmian League, Premier Division while also working as a representative for an Insurance company and was at that time living in Upper Norwood. By 2013, he was reported to be employed as a cleaning supervisor.

Season	Division	League		FA Cup		FL Cup		Total	
		A	G	A	G	A	G	A	G
1972-73	Division 3	10 (3)	1	2	0	0	0	12 (3)	1
1973-74	Division 3	36 (1)	1	1	0	1	0	38 (1)	1
1974-75 (P)	Division 3	20 (5)	4	2	0	0	0	22 (5)	4
1975-76	Division 2	4	0	0	0	0	0	4	0
Total		70 (9)	6	5	0	1	0	76 (9)	6

UK LEAGUE CAREER 115 games 8 goals

CHARLTON CAREER
Managers: *A Nelson, T Foley*
Debut: *Shrewsbury Town (A) 30-12-1972*
V375
Finale: *Portsmouth (H) 26-12-1975*

GOMEZ Joseph Dave   2014 - 15

Defender   12st 2lbs   6' 2"
Born: 23-05-1997 - Catford, London
Education: Forest Hill School, London.

A succession of injuries have temporarily derailed the career of Joe Gomez, by far the most talented footballer to pass through the Charlton youth programme for many years. He always seemed the one most likely to succeed, having played for the U18's whilst only 13 years old and by the time he was deemed ready for first team action, every scout in the country was aware of this outstanding young defender who displayed a maturity way beyond his years. Charlton were always going to struggle to keep him, in the face of interest from some of the biggest and richest clubs in the land and in the end he played just one season in the Championship before leaving for Liverpool and the opportunity to play football at the very highest level.

HONOURS
England International 2017-20 11 caps 0 goals
England U21 International 2015-17 7 caps 0 goals
England U19 International 2014-15 4 caps 0 goals

Eng;land U17 International 2013-14 19 caps 0 goals
England U16 International 2012 2 caps 0 goals
England U17 2014 Winners UEFA U17 Euro Championship

Charlton Athletic U18 2012-13 & 2013-14 Winners PD League 2 South
Charlton Athletic 2015 Young Player Of The Year
Liverpool 2018-19 Runners Up Premier League
Liverpool 2018-19 Winners UEFA Champions League

Liverpool 2019 & 2020 Runners Up FA Community Shield
Liverpool 2019 Winners UEFA Super Cup
Liverpool 2019-20 Winners Premier League

CLUBS

Charlton Athletic 2007 (youth) 10.14 (pro) ••Liverpool 20.06.15 (£3.5 million)

Joe's Football League debut came on 19th August 2014 at the Valley. Charlton overcame Derby County by a score of 3-2, thanks to goals by George Tucudean, Igor Vetokele and a penalty from Yoni Buyens. He played the whole match at right back and rarely put a foot wrong. Strong, unruffled and technically sound, it was like viewing a Rolls-Royce on its maiden run. Nobody present that day could have failed to appreciate this precocious talent who was so obviously destined for the very top. Manager Bob Peeters was sensible in not overplaying him, but with the team flirting with relegation, his successor Guy Luzon, felt sufficiently confident in this still 17-year-old, to move him into the centre of the defence and on 28th February 2015, alongside the more experienced Roger Johnson, they comfortably dealt with Chris Powell's Huddersfield Town by 3-0. Charlton finished the season in a respectable mid-table position and nobody was surprised when Joe was named as Young Player of the Year.

His England baptism had been at U16 level in November 2012 with a 1-0 win over Wales at Port Talbot and from then on Joe was a regular participant in international football. He was ever-present when England won the UEFA Euro U17 Championship in Malta, the final seeing them dispose of the Netherlands on 21st May 2014 and he later went on to captain the England U21 team. His first

appearance for the full England side would come as a substitute on 10th November 2017 against Germany. The move to Liverpool arrived sooner than anyone at Charlton really wanted, but Joe quickly grew into this fresh challenge. He was not initially expected to feature in the Premier League side but performed so well in training that he went straight into the team, following which they did not concede a single goal in any of the first three matches of 2015-16. This fairy tale start came to an abrupt halt however, when on 13th October, he suffered an anterior cruciate ligament injury while playing for England U21. It kept him out of football for 15 months and was just the start of his nightmare. Surgery following an ankle injury caused him to miss the UEFA Champions League final in May 2018 and seven months later he fractured a leg at Burnley, but that was not the end of his troubles.

Lately Joe has fought almost a continuous battle to stay fit. He did manage to play more than 40 games during 2019-20 when Liverpool won the Premier League, but since then has spent considerably more time in the medical room than on the pitch. He has already achieved a great deal in his short career but only time will tell if his body can sustain the rigours of professional sport long enough to completely fulfill his potential.

Season	Division	League		FA Cup		FL Cup		Total	
		A	G	A	G	A	G	A	G
2014-15	Championship	16 (5)	0	0 (1)	0	2	0	18 (6)	0
Total		16 (5)	0	0 (1)	0	2	0	18 (6)	0

UK LEAGUE CAREER 100 games 0 goals

CHARLTON CAREER
Managers: *B Peeters, G Luzon*
Debut: *Colchester United (H) 12-08-2014*
V785
Finale: *AFC Bournemouth (H) (sub) 02-05-2015*

GOODMAN Abraham 'Kosha'

1921 - 25

Defender, Forward, Utility. 11st 9lbs 5' 8"
Born: 03-09-1890 - Dalston, London
Died: 06-12-1959 - Ilford, Essex

Abraham, known as Bert or Kosha Goodman, made a significant contribution during Charlton's early years as a Football League club and was probably their first genuine utility player.

He started as a left back, but over the course of his four and a half year stay performed in seven different positions, including a spell at centre forward which produced nine goals in 11 matches and on 24th February 1923, the winner against West Bromwich Albion, one of the three First Division clubs defeated during the great FA Cup run of 1922-23.

HONOURS

Charlton Athletic 1922-23 Winners London Challenge Cup
Maidstone United 1913-14 Winners Thames & Medway Combination

Maidstone United 1913-14 Winners Kent Senior Cup
Tottenham Hotspur 1919-20 Winners Division 2

CLUBS

London Fields (youth) ••Tufnell Park 1911 (amateur) ••Tottenham Thursday 1912 (amateur) ••Green Old Boys 1913 (amateur) ••Maidstone United 1913 (amateur) ••Tottenham Hotspur 1913 (amateur) ••Croydon Common 1914 ••Clapton Orient 03.17 ••Maidstone United 03.19 ••Tottenham Hotspur 06.19 ••Margate 02.20 ••Charlton Athletic 01.21 (free) ••Gillingham 06.25 ••Clapton Orient 08.03.26 ••Guildford City 11.27 ••Tooting Town (coach)

Bert was one of the first Jewish footballers to compete in the Football League. He started out as an amateur in North London before joining Maidstone United in 1913 and helping them to success in the Kent Senior Cup. He also appeared briefly for Spurs, scoring twice for their South East Counties League side. The following season he switched to Croydon Common and became a fixture in their Southern League team, playing alongside other future Addicks, Arthur Hutchins and Dick Upex.

In June 1919 he re-signed for Tottenham Hotspur and was a semi-regular at right back in their 1919-20 team which finished champions of Division 2 and after a brief spell in the Kent League with Margate, came to Charlton midway through their first season as a professional club, making his debut at left back against Portsmouth in a Southern League match on 29th January 1921.

Described in contemporary reports as a sturdily built athlete with wonderful optimism and a 'never say die' spirit, Bert quickly established himself as a popular and well respected member of the Charlton set up, appearing in the first ever Football League match against Exeter City on 27th August 1921 and remaining a first team regular for a further four years. His experience and versatility were vital as the club fought to maintain their newly acquired status.

He eventually moved on to play for Gillingham and then Clapton Orient before finishing up with Southern League side Guildford City in 1927-28. Bert later coached at Tooting Town, but in January 1935 it was reported that he had got into some serious trouble and was sentenced at the Old Bailey to 12 months imprisonment after being convicted of theft. He had been the getaway driver following a raid on a tailor's shop in Ilford.

He died at King George Hospital, Ilford on 6th December 1959 as a result of injuries incurred in a motor accident and his death certificate recorded his name as Abraham, otherwise Albert, Goodman.

Season	Division	League		FA Cup		Total	
		A	G	A	G	A	G
1921-22	Divison 3 (S)	38	0			38	0
1922-23	Divison 3 (S)	30	8	6	4	36	12
1923-24	Divison 3 (S)	26	5	1	0	27	5
1924-25	Divison 3 (S)	32	2	0	0	32	2
Total		126	15	7	4	133	19

UK LEAGUE CAREER 160 games 16 goals

CHARLTON CAREER
Managers: *W Rayner, A MacFarlane*
Debut: *Southern League Portsmouth (A) 29-01-1921 Football League Exeter City (H) 27-08-1921*
V003
Finale: *Watford (A) 02-05-1925*

GORMAN Paul Michael

1991 - 94

After signing from Fisher Athletic in March 1991, Paul was thrown straight in the deep end and featured in

Forward   12st 5lbs   5' 10"
Born: 18-09-1968 - Macclesfield, Cheshire
Education: Stainforth Primary School & Hatfield High School, Doncaster.

three first team matches within his first seven days in SE7. He scored in only his second appearance, away at Hull City on Easter Monday, after coming on as a substitute replacement for Alex Dyer. A frantic last five minutes produced all the four goals in a 2-2 draw, the other Charlton strike being courtesy of Robert Lee.

HONOURS

Doncaster & District Schools & Yorkshire Boys

Fisher Athletic 1988-89 Winners London Senior Cup

HONOURS AS MANAGER

Erith & Belvedere 2008-09 Finalists Kent Senior Trophy

CLUBS

Manchester United (youth) ••Durban City, South Africa 1982 (youth) ••Doncaster Rovers 13.07.87 (non contract) 19.03.88 (pro) ••Fisher Athletic c03.89 (loan) 1989 (free) ••Buckingham Wanderers 1989 (non contract) ••Charlton Athletic 01.04.91 (£15,000) ••Welling United 16..08.94 (free) ••Fisher Athletic 10.95 (loan) 01.03.96 (free) ••Dover Athletic 1997 ••Greenwich Borough 1997 ••VCD Athletic 1998 ••Greenwich Borough c2000 (coach) ••Erith & Belvedere 01.11.06 (joint manager) 09.09 (ass: manager)

Although born in Macclesfield, Paul spent much of his teenage years in South Africa where he played youth football for Durban City before returning to the UK in 1987. He then joined Doncaster Rovers and was blooded in their first team as a 17-year-old striker in season 1987-88. He featured in ten matches (usually off the bench), but was on the losing side on each occasion as they languished at the wrong end of Division 3. He did however manage one goal on 15th April 1988, but it was only a late consolation as the Doncaster team, including Garry Kimble, were well beaten 4-2 by Blackpool. His second season followed a similar pattern. They were now competing in Division 4 but he was still mainly used as a substitute, brought on when they were chasing the game and a goal was urgently required. He was able to oblige on 5th November 1988 and was on the scoresheet when Darlington were beaten 3-1.

He came south in 1989 and worked for a year for the Post Office while turning out for Buckingham Wanderers, a works team that competed in the Post Office Mid-Week League, but it was while playing for Fisher Athletic in the Football Conference that Paul came to the attention of Charlton and it took a fee of £15,000 to bring him to the Valley. His rapid elevation into the first team squad was perhaps unexpected, but reflected the need for goals in the fight to stay afloat in Division 2. He showed early promise and a hat-trick for the Reserves at Reading on 17th April

1991 confirmed his potential.

Sadly Paul never fully established himself in the Charlton first team and this was probably because a number of injuries stunted his progress. He had an operation in the summer of 1992 to repair damage to an anterior cruciate ligament in his left knee and this kept him out of action for some time, although he returned to the side in the later stages of 1992-93 and scored the winner in an exciting 2-1 victory against Derby County at the Valley on 1st May. Knee problems persisted however and he was given a free transfer at the end of season 1993-94.

Paul joined Welling United and scored a hat-trick against Stalybridge Celtic in September, but here again there were injury worries, not least a broken leg incurred on 12th November 1994 in a match at Merthyr Tydfil. He returned for a second spell with Fisher, but without question his playing career had been adversely affected by all the injuries and in 2000 he decided to call it a day at the age of 32. It was some time before he came back to the game but in November 2006 he was appointed joint manager of Erith & Belvedere and guided them to the final of the Kent Senior Trophy in 2009 where they were beaten 3-2 by VCD Athletic. Away from football, Paul has worked as a plumber and handyman for Lewisham Council.

Season	Division	League		FA Cup		FL Cup		FM Cup		AI Cup		Total	
		A	G	A	G	A	G	A	G	A	G	A	G
1990-91	Division 2	2 (6)	2	0	0	0	0	0	0			2 (6)	2
1991-92	Division 2	5 (3)	3	0 (1)	0	0 (1)	0	1	1			6 (5)	4
1992-93	Division 1	5 (5)	2	0	0	0	0			0	0	5 (5)	2
1993-94	Division 1	7 (7)	1	0	0	0	0			0 (1)	0	7 (8)	1
Total		19 (21)	8	0 (1)	0	0 (1)	0	1	1	0 (1)	0	20 (24)	9

UK LEAGUE CAREER 56 games 10 goals

CHARLTON CAREER
Managers: L Lawrence, A Curbishley/S Gritt
Debut: *West Bromwich Albion (H) (sub)*
30-03-1991
V516
Finale: *Notts County (A) (sub) 30-04-1994*

GOUGH Charles Storrar   1964

Midfield
Born: 21-05-1939 - Glasgow, Scotland
Died: 03-04-2015 - Cape Town, South Africa
Education: Bellahouston Academy, Glasgow.

Charlie was a tough tackling wing half who represented Glasgow Schools and captained the Army X1 whilst serving as a Corporal in the 3rd Parachute Battalion. On 15th March 1963, he played for Scotland against England at Hampden Park in the British Amateur Championships and had reached the age of 24 before he became a professional with Charlton in June 1963. His son Richard Gough was briefly an apprentice at the Valley before going on to a glittering career with Tottenham, Rangers and Scotland.

HONOURS

Scotland Amateur International 1963 1 cap 0 goals

Glasgow Schools

Charlton Athletic A 1963-64 Winners Metropolitan League

Charlton Athletic A 1963-64 Finalists Metropolitan League Cup

Alton Town 1962-63 Runners Up Hampshire League Division 1

Highlands Park 1965, 1966 & 1968 Winners South African League (NFL)

Highlands Park 1965, 1966 & 1967 Winners South African Cup (NFL)

Highlands Park 1967 Runners Up South African League (NFL)

Highlands Cup 1968 & 1970 Runners Up South African Cup (NFL)

CLUBS

Brigade Amateurs, Scotland (youth) ••Shawfield Juniors, Scotland c1956 (youth) ••West Ham United (youth) ••British Army 1962 ••Alton Town 1962 ••Charlton Athletic 09.04.63 (amateur) 27.06.63 (pro) ••Highlands Park, South Africa 01.65 (free)

It was a leg injury to Brian Tocknell which gave Charlie his chance in the first team and he did reasonably well in the six games that he played for Charlton during September and October 1964. However, it all came to an end after a heavy 5-2 defeat at the Valley against Southampton, following which he was dropped and winger Brian Kinsey moved into the left half slot until Tocknell was fit enough to return shortly before Christmas.

Charlie did not hang around at Charlton and his contract was cancelled in December 1964, following which he emigrated to South Africa and signed for the Johannesburg club, Highlands Park, where he was instantly recognised as an exceptionally reliable and hard-working player. He was made captain and led them to six seasons of cup and league success in the all white National Football League of South

Africa and remained with the club until 1973. In December 1966 he participated in a rather unusual representative match when the Overseas Born South African XI played the South African Born XI.

In those days, football in South Africa was semi-professional and Charlie found work with Waltons, the stationers where he eventually rose to the position of sales director. In 1993, he left to start his own online stationers. He was a hard man with a dry humour who kept himself fit and maintained his exceptional physique into old age. He was profoundly influential on South African football but never ceased to be a Scotsman through and through as evidenced by his playing of the bagpipes on social occasions. He passed away in Cape Town at the age of 75.

Season	Division	League		FA Cup		FL Cup		Total	
		A	G	A	G	A	G	A	G
1964-65	Division 2	4	0	0	0	2	0	6	0
Total		4	0	0	0	2	0	6	0

UK LEAGUE CAREER 4 games 0 goals

CHARLTON CAREER
Managers: *F Hill*
Debut: *Middlesbrough (H) 23-09-1964*
V305
Finale: *Southampton (H) 17-10-1964*

GOWER Mark   2013

Mark was spotted by Tottenham at the age of nine and entered their youth academy, going on to play for England Schoolboys and even scored two goals in an international at Wembley when he was 15. Despite this impressive start, he found it difficult to break into the Spurs team and it was really only when he dropped down to Division 3 with Southend United that his career finally took off. Mark was an important part of their side which gained two promotions in consecutive years and in 2006-07 spent one season competing in the Championship, a fine achievement for a small club who are usually to be found further down the football pyramid.,

Midfield, Forward   11st 8lb   5'9"
Born: 05-10-1978 - Edmonton, Middlesex
Education: F A School of Excellence

HONOURS

England U16 International 1994-95 10 caps 0 goals
England U15 International 1994 8 caps 5 goals
Southend United 2004-05 Promoted Play Offs League 2

Southend United 2005-06 Winners League 1
Southend United 2003-04 & 2004-05 Runners Up Football League Trophy
Swansea City 2010-11 Promoted Play Offs Championship

CLUBS

Tottenham Hotspur 1988 (youth) 1996 (pro) ••Motherwell, Scotland 12.02.99 (loan) ••Barnet 19.01.01 (£32,500) ••Southend United 25.07.03 (£25,000) ••Swansea City 27.06.08 (free) ••Charlton Athletic 14.03.13 (loan) 03.06.13 (free) ••Ebbsfleet United 05.02.15 (free)

During the five years that Mark played for Southend, he made more than 250 cup and league appearances and was very much the 'engine room' of the side. On 7th November 2006 they put Manchester United out of the League Cup, beating them 1-0. The Southend side that day included Mark, Simon Francis and Jamal Campbell-Ryce and they were too good for United, who featured Rooney and Ronaldo in their line-up. Sadly however this was a 'one off' and they were generally outclassed throughout their one season in the Championship, but Mark at least seemed comfortable at that level.

His contract with Southend expired in 2008 and he signed for Swansea City and made his debut at the Valley on the opening day of season 2008-09, in a side that also included Darren Pratley. Charlton were too strong for them and won 2-0 thanks to goals from Mark Hudson and Andy Gray. Swansea came close to promotion from the Championship in each of the next two seasons and finally made it in 2010-11 beating Reading 4-2 in the play off final

at Wembley. Mark got to feature in 20 matches during their first Premier League season but was no longer an automatic choice for the team.

Early in his career Mark had been dubbed 'the next Paul Gascoigne' and in 2011, whilst playing for Swansea City, the football data supplier Opta, concluded that at one point he had created the most goal scoring opportunities in all the Premier League. However by the time he arrived at Charlton, initially on loan, he was nearing the end of his career and did not, in truth, live up to such high standards. He did however contribute and was part of the team which plundered a 6-0 win at Oakwell against a wretched Barnsley on 13th April 2013.

Mark did well enough to earn a new one-year contract for 2013-14, but when it became clear that he was not going to feature in the first team, he effectively retired from the game, although he re-appeared briefly for Ebbsfleet as a favour to their manager. By February 2017 he was scouting for Liverpool.

Season	Division	League		FA Cup		FL Cup		Total	
		A	G	A	G	A	G	A	G
2012-13	Championship	2 (4)	0	0	0	0	0	2 (4)	0
2013-14	Championship	6 (1)	0	0	0	0	0	6 (1)	0
Total		8 (5)	0	0	0	0	0	8 (5)	0

UK LEAGUE CAREER 367 matches 40 goals

CHARLTON CAREER
Managers: *C Powell*
Debut: *Bolton Wanderers (H) (sub) 30-03-2013*
V758
Finale: *Blackpool (H) 05-10-2013*

GRANT Kimberley Tyrone — 1991 - 96

Forward 11st 6lbs 5' 10"
Born: 25-09-1972 - Sekondi-Takoradi, Ghana
Education: Buckingham Park Primary School & KIngs Manor School, Shoreham-by-Sea.

Whilst at Charlton, Kim rarely hit the headlines. He was in and out of the side throughout his five years with the first team and spent more time than he would have liked on the substitute's bench. However, there was one occasion when he took centre stage and that was 5th December 1995 at the New Den.

Charlton's record against Millwall is simply appalling and in a blood and guts local derby both teams were reduced to 10 men, with Lee Bowyer receiving his marching orders midway through the first half. Kim had already scored an early goal for the Addicks and added a second after 67 minutes to clinch a famous victory via a conclusive 2-0 scoreline.

HONOURS

Ghana International 1996-97 7 caps 1 goal
Brighton Schools & Sussex Schools
Charlton Athletic 1991 Young Player Of The Year
Yeovil Town 2002-03 Winners Nationwide Conference

CLUBS

Charlton Athletic 27.06.88 (youth) 06.03.91 (pro) ••Luton Town 28.03.96 (£225,000) ••Millwall 07.08.97 (loan) 02.09.97 (£185,000) ••Notts County 24.12.98 (loan) ••Lommel SK, Belgium 08.99 (£65,000) ••FC Marco, Portugal 2000 (free) ••Scunthorpe United 10.08.01 (free) ••Yeovil Town 10.01 (free) ••Odivelas, Portugal c2003 ••Imortal Desportivo, Portugal 2004 ••Sarawak FA State, Malaysia 03.04 ••Shonan Bellmare, Japan 2005 ••Gravesend & Northfleet 08.05 ••AFC Wimbledon 02.06 ••Sengkang Punggol, Singapore 2006 ••Geylang United, Singapore 2007 ••Woking 05.08 (player manager) ••International Allies, Ghana 2009 ••FC Takoradi, Ghana 2009 (president) ••Cape Coast Mysterious Ebusua Dwarfs, Ghana 05.14 (technical director) ••Saif Sporting, Bangladesh 04.17 (coach) ••Elmina Sharks, Ghana 12.17 (technical director) ••Accra Hearts of Oak SC, Ghana 01.12.18 (manager) ••Prague Raptors, Czech Republic 11.06.20 (director of football)

Few people can have experienced a football career as diverse and as challenging as Kim Grant. His family resided in the city of Sekondi-Takoradi in Ghana, until a military coup forced them to flee the country when he was aged 10 and they settled at Shoreham-by-Sea in Sussex. Kim had trials as a schoolboy with Brighton, but instead joined Charlton and signed professional terms in March 1991 at the age of 18. He made his debut and in fact played five league matches that same month, including the game against Wolverhampton on 12th March when his goal clinched a 1-0 win. He scored again against Barnsley a few days later and ended the 1990-91 season having featured in a dozen league matches.

This promising start was not maintained, however. The Gritt/Curbishley management team took over in July following which Kim did not start a single league match in 1991-92, his sporadic appearances all coming off the bench. He played more frequently after that, but was still very much a squad player rather than a regular member of the side. Generally popular with the crowd, he never gave less than his best although he did not have a lot of luck in front of goal. One he did score was at Millwall on 1st September 1993 in the Anglo-Italian Cup. Added to an earlier effort from Carl Leaburn, it gave Charlton a 2-2 draw and perhaps gave Kim the feel for scoring at the New Den. He bagged a brace in a 2-2 draw at Derby County in October 1994, but it was his two against Millwall a year later for which he will always be remembered.

In March 1996 he transferred to Luton Town for an initial fee of £175,000 plus three instalments of £25,000 each to be paid after 20, 40 and 60 first team appearances. He played 44 times in all, including cup matches, before moving on to Millwall in September 1997. Shortly after leaving Charlton, Kim made his international debut for Ghana. His first start was in Pretoria on 21st September 1996, a 0-0 draw against a South African side that included Shaun Bartlett, but Kim's best day on the international stage came a fortnight later in Kumasi when he grabbed the winner in a 2-1 victory over Angola in an African Cup of Nations qualifier.

His spell with Millwall lasted two years and was not unsuccessful, although he again spent rather too long as a substitute, but from then on he seemed to catch the travel bug and his next two clubs were in Belgium and Portugal. Kim returned to the UK in 2001 and obtained a short term deal with Scunthorpe United with whom he made his final appearances in the Football League, including a 4-0 win at Exeter on 25th August. A 17-month stay at Yeovil Town found him playing less frequently plus he was not in the team that won the FA Trophy in 2002.

After Yeovil, Kim's globe-trotting accelerated and over the next few years he turned up in Portugal, Malaysia, Japan and Singapore, rarely spending long in one place. A dip into management with Woking in 2008 did not last long and then it was on to Ghana where in 2009 he founded and coached a brand-new club, FC Takoradi. He later had a spell as technical director of the marvellously named Mysterious Ebusua Dwarfs and in 2014 formed his own Paa Grant Soccer Academy in honour of his grandfather. He has since worked in Bangladesh and back in Ghana again. In June 2020 he was appointed director of football at Prague Raftors in the Czech Republic, but it is fair to say that by the time you read these words he could be literally anywhere.

Season	Division	League		FA Cup		FL Cup		FM Cup		AI Cup		Total	
		A	G	A	G	A	G	A	G	A	G	A	G
1990-91	Division 2	11 (1)	2	0	0	0	0	0	0			11 (1)	2
1991-92	Division 2	0 (4)	0	0 (2)	1	1 (2)	0	0 (1)	0			1 (9)	1
1992-93	Division 1	11 (10)	2	0 (2)	0	0 (1)	0			0	0	11 (13)	2
1993-94	Division 1	18 (12)	1	6	2	1 (1)	0			5 (1)	1	30 (14)	4
1994-95	Division 1	14 (12)	6	0	0	0 (1)	0					14 (13)	6
1995-96	Division 1	20 (10)	7	2 (1)	2	1 (4)	1					23 (15)	10
Total		74 (49)	18	8 (5)	5	3 (9)	1	0 (1)	0	5 (1)	1	90 (65)	25

UK LEAGUE CAREER 223 games 36 goals

CHARLTON CAREER
Managers: *L Lawrence, A Curbishley/S Gritt, A Curbishley*
Debut: *Bristol City (H) 02-03-1991*
V515
Finale: *Stoke City (H) 23-03-1996*

GRAY Andrew David　　　　　　　　　　　　　　　2008 - 09

It is hard for any young man who strives for a sporting career in the shadow of a famous relative, but for Andy it was doubly so as his father is Frank Gray, a Scottish international who played

Forward　13st 3lbs　6' 1"
Born: 15-11-1977 - Harrogate, North Yorkshire
Education: Ashville College, Harrogate.

more than 600 games, mainly for Leeds United and Sunderland, while his uncle is Eddie Gray, also an international, as well as being considered one of the three greatest Leeds players of all time. All credit then to Andy who carved out his own position within the game and if he did not quite match their achievements, he did remarkably well, even if the 19 months he spent in London SE7 would not show up prominently on his CV.

HONOURS
Scotland International 2003 2 caps 0 goals　　　　　　　　Leeds United 1995-96 Finalists Football League Cup

CLUBS
Leeds United (youth) 01.07.95 (pro) ••Bury 11.12.97 (loan) ••Nottingham Forest 02.09.98 (£200,000) ••Preston North End 23.02.99 (loan) ••Oldham Athletic 25.03.99 (loan) ••Bradford City 09.08.02 (free) ••Sheffield United 21.02.04 (undisclosed) ••Sunderland 10.08.05 (£1.1 million) ••Burnley 17.03.06 (£750,000) ••Charlton Athletic 19.01.08 (loan) 25.01.08 (£1.5 million) ••Barnsley 21.08.09 (£1.5 million) ••Leeds United 24.07.12 (free) ••Bradford City 09.01.13 (free) ••Leeds United 30.07.15 (coach)

Unsurprisingly Andy's story starts at Leeds United, where he turned pro at the age of 17 and where with only three full matches under his belt, he was controversially selected for the Wembley final of the Football League Cup on 24th

March 1996, He played the full 90 minutes on the right wing in front of a crowd of 77,056 but could not prevent Aston Villa from lifting the cup 3-0. Despite this golden opportunity, he was unable to grab a regular spot in the Leeds team and eventually moved on to Nottingham Forest where for much of his time he was utilised as a full back. It was only after transferring to Bradford City in August 2002 that Andy was converted into a striker and his 15 league goals in 2002-03 almost certainly kept them afloat in Division 1. His form earned him a call-up for Scotland and he came on as a second half substitute in a dismal display against Lithuania in a UEFA Euro 2004 qualifier on 2nd April 2003 which was lost 1-0. His teammates that day included Christian Dailly. His second and final Scottish cap came the following month against New Zealand.

Andy switched to Sheffield United in February 2004 and this was probably his most successful period. He managed 17 goals in 2004-05 including a last minute penalty at Highbury in the FA Cup Round 5, which levelled the score at 1-1 and earned them a lucrative replay against Arsenal. With hindsight, he should have stayed longer in Sheffield, but instead of becoming part of their Championship promotion side, he moved to Sunderland in August 2015 just as the wheels were falling off for the Wearsiders. Sunderland were relegated in style in 2005-06. They finished a long way bottom of the Premier League and

Andy's miserable reward for the season was one solitary goal, ironically scored on his debut at home to Charlton. It was only a consolation effort however, as two goals from Darren Bent and one by Danny Murphy ensured a 3-1 scoreline in favour of the visitors. He did regain his scoring form after joining Burnley however and struck twice at the Valley on 1st December 2007.

There was little joy on the field for Andy during his time at Charlton. He joined in January 2008 and his only full season 2008-09 saw the club relegated from the Championship. His contribution was just seven goals, three of them penalties. He did get the winner at Doncaster in September but this was not a happy period for club nor player.

He returned north in July 2009 and had three seasons at Barnsley followed by a pretty disappointing return to Leeds, before winding up his playing career with Bradford City. Andy then took up a youth coaching position for Leeds United which kept him occupied until December 2017 when poor results led to his resignation. By August 2021 the third generation of the Gray dynasty were fully represented at Leeds United where the academy includes four members of the family, including Andy's sons Archie and Harry. Archie is an England U15 international.

Season	Division	League		FA Cup		FL Cup		FL Trophy		Play Offs		Total	
		A	G	A	G	A	G	A	G	A	G	A	G
2007-08	Championship	10 (6)	2	0	0	0	0					10 (6)	2
2008-09 (R)	Championship	21 (6)	7	0 (1)	0	0	0					21 (7)	7
2009-10	League One	0 (2)	0	0	0	1	0	0	0	0	0	1 (2)	0
Total		31 (14)	9	0 (1)	0	1	0	0	0	0	0	32 (15)	9

CHARLTON CAREER
Managers: *A Pardew, P Parkinson*
Debut: *Watford (A) (sub) 19-01-2008*
V661
Finale: *Hartlepool United (A) (sub) 15-08-2009*

UK LEAGUE CAREER 490 games 108 goals

GRAY Nigel Robert   1982

Defender   13st 4lbs   6' 3"
Born: 02-11-1956 - Fulham, London
Education: Sloane Grammar School, Chelsea.

The lion's share of Nigel's career was spent at Orient and he played more than 270 league and cup matches for them over a period of nine years, after turning professional in April 1974. In contrast, his time at Charlton was just one month. He was signed by Lennie Lawrence on an emergency loan in December 1982 to cover the suspension of future England U21 centre half Paul Elliott and played in three matches including the Christmas fixture at Crystal Palace which finished 1-1 thanks to a second half equaliser from Steve White.

HONOURS
West London Boys

CLUBS

Beaumont (youth) ••Orient 1972 (youth) 04.74 (pro) ••Charlton Athletic 06.12.82 (loan) ••Swindon Town 20.07.83 (undisclosed) ••Brentford 01.03.84 (loan) ••Aldershot 14.09.84 (loan) ••Enfield 1985 (free) ••Wycombe Wanderers 07.87 (loan) ••Tooting & Mitcham United 01.88 (free) ••Van Dyke 2001

Orient had a decent team for much of the 1970s. Since relegation in 1982 they have rarely competed above the third tier of English football, but during the period when Nigel was at the heart of their defence, they were well established in Division 2 and in 1977-78 nearly made it to the FA Cup final. They had to do it the hard way as almost every round produced an opponent from the First Division and one by one they disposed of Norwich City, Blackburn Rovers, Chelsea and Middlesbrough, only to fall at the semi-final stage. A crowd of 49,098 were at Stamford Bridge on 8th April 1978 to see Arsenal win 3-0 and end the Wembley dream for the Orient supporters. (They were not called Leyton Orient during that period), Nigel played throughout the cup run and was ever present the following season.

He remained with the club after relegation finally ended this golden period, but lost his place following a heavy 5-1 home defeat against Newport County on 16th October 1982. Now surplus to requirements, he was available for a loan signing when Lennie Lawrence came calling seven weeks later. Of his three matches in Charlton colours the most successful was the 3-2 defeat of Barnsley at the Valley on 18th December, when a pitiful crowd of just 4,942 forsake the Christmas shopping to witness a goal from Allan Simonsen and two by Derek Hales.

Nigel moved on to Swindon Town in Summer 1983, where he played alongside Garry Nelson and had loan spells with both Brentford and Aldershot before his career wound down in non-league. He was still lacing his boots up on a Sunday morning in 2001 at the age of 45.

For many years he has run an office cleaning business, Crystal Care, in Wimbledon and in 2020 was working in conjunction with Leyton Orient on the Lyasikika Wash Project, raising funds and sending out old football kits for the children in Tanzania.

Season	Division	League		FA Cup		FL Cup		Total	
		A	G	A	G	A	G	A	G
1982-83	Division 2	3	0	0	0	0	0	3	0
Total		3	0	0	0	0	0	3	0

UK LEAGUE CAREER 289 games 5 goals

CHARLTON CAREER
Managers: L Lawrence
Debut: *Bolton Wanderers (A) 11-12-1982*
V443
Finale: *Crystal Palace (A) 27-12-1982*

GREEN Albert   1921 - 22

Albert spent just over a year with Charlton, arriving midway through their first season as a professional club. He made seven appearances in the Southern League and scored twice, including the final game of that 1920-21 season against Boscombe, when along with strikes from Dick Upex (2), Cyril Smith and Mosky Mills, his goal ensured a resounding 5-1 win for the Addicks. The following season Albert went into the record books by scoring Charlton's first ever goal in an away match in the Football League on 10th September 1921 against Bristol Rovers.

Forward   11st 0lbs   5' 9"
Born: 07-10-1892 - Rickmansworth, Hertfordshire
Died: 23-04-1956 - Watford, Hertfordshire

HONOURS

Hertfordshire FA 7 caps
Rickmansworth Schools

Watford 1914-15 Winners Southern League Division 1

CLUBS

Rickmansworth 1904 ••Watford Orient c1911 ••Watford 08.12 (amateur) 1914 (pro) ••Crystal Palace 1919 ••Sheppey United 1920 ••Charlton Athletic 02.21 ••Millwall 26.05.22 ••Reading 12.07.23

First spotted as a schoolboy footballer, Albert represented   Rickmansworth Schools and the Hertfordshire FA, while in 1914 he took part in a trial for the England Amateur International team. However, he chose to pursue the professional game and that same year signed a paid contract with Watford. 1914-15 proved to be a big season for them and they ended up winning Division 1 of the Southern League. Albert played his part after breaking into the side in the January, featuring in 23 league games and contributing eight goals, including the winner at Brighton which clinched the title on 24th April 1915. After four years army service he joined another Southern League side Crystal Palace, who were still playing at the Nest in 1919 and had yet to move to Selhurst Park.

There was one South London club which did have a new ground however and in February 1921 Albert signed for Charlton. He showed enough in his first season to be retained when Football League status was achieved and lined up at inside left in the first match in League Division 3 South on 27th August 1921 against Exeter City. Goals were hard to come by in that first season and Albert only managed three, although he did get the winner against Aberdare Athletic on 15th October 1921 in front of a Valley crowd of 14,000. That match finished 2-1 to Charlton and the opening goal was scored by Dan Bailey. He left the club at the end of the season.

His next move was to Millwall, but he never made a first team appearance for them and his career was rounded off with a final season at Reading. By 1939 Albert and his wife Kathleen were living in St Albans Road, Watford and he was working as an off licence manager. He passed away in the Peace Memorial Hospital, Watford at the age of 63.

Season	Division	League		Total	
		A	G	A	G
1921-22	Divison 3 (S)	17	3	17	3
Total		17	3	17	3

UK LEAGUE CAREER 27 games 5 goals

CHARLTON CAREER
Managers: *W Rayner*
Debut: *Southern League Chatham (H) 26-02-1921 Football League Exeter City (H) 27-08-1921*
V010
Finale: *Plymouth Argyle (A) 25-03-1922*

GREEN Andre Jay   2020

Forward   11st 2lbs   5' 11"
Born: 26-07-1998 - Solihull, Birmingham
Education: Lode Heath School, Solihull.

Charlton confounded the critics by making a positive start to season 2019-20. Newly promoted to the Championship and with a playing squad comprising a mixture of free transfers, loan players and academy graduates, the early results were unexpectedly encouraging. As the campaign progressed however, the injuries started to mount up and when loanee Jonathan Leko suffered an anterior cruciate ligament injury on 23rd December which ruled him out for the remainder of the season, this created an urgent need for a replacement. Leko had demonstrated pace, control and an eye for goal and as soon as the January transfer window opened for business, Aston Villa's young winger Andre Green was brought in on a loan for the second half of the season.

HONOURS

England U20 International 2017 2 caps 0 goals   England U17 International 2015 3 caps 0 goals
England U19 International 2016 7 caps 0 goals   England U16 International 2013-14 4 caps 0 goals
England U18 International 2016 4 caps 0 goals   Aston Villa 2018-19 Promoted Play Offs Championship

CLUBS

Aston Villa 2007 (youth) 03.16 (pro) ••Portsmouth 29.08.18 (loan) ••Preston North End 01.08.19 (loan) ••Charlton Athletic 02.01.20 (loan) ••Sheffield Wednesday 14.01.21 (free) ••SK Slovan Bratislava, Slovakia 19.08.21 (undisclosed)

Andre had been very highly rated as a teenage footballer, making his Premier League debut for Aston Villa against Tottenham on 13th March 2016 while aged only 17. He was capped by England at each level up to the Under 20s for whom he made his debut alongside Jay Dasilva, Sam Field and Stephy Mavididi on 31st August 2017, when the Netherlands were defeated 3-0. At that stage he seemed destined for the top and some very big clubs were rumoured to have him in their sights as a possible transfer target.

He was a semi-regular in the Villa side which returned to the Premier League in 2018-19, but spent part of the campaign out on loan at Portsmouth and was in the Pompey side that played at Fratton Park against Charlton on 11th December 2018. He scored a late consolation goal that day but the visitors ended victorious by 2-1. After his loan was concluded he returned to the Villa team for the second half of the season and came on as a substitute at Wembley on 27th May 2019 when they clinched promotion against Derby County in the play off final, just 24 hours after Charlton's Wembley triumph over Sunderland.

A season long loan with Preston North End was arranged for Andre on 1st August 2019, but did not go well and was unexpectedly cut short, leaving him available to re-start his faltering career at the Valley. He opened brightly enough, scoring up at Preston on 18th January and getting the

winner against Barnsley a fortnight later. From then on however things went steadily downhill as his form seemed to suffer. The season was halted by the Covid pandemic and on 25th June Aston Villa announced that his contract would not be renewed. To his credit he extended his loan and played out the season, but was unable to prevent the relegation which was confirmed at Leeds on the final day of the season.

Surprisingly Andre was unable to find a new club and remained a free agent until the January 2021 transfer window opened, when he signed for Sheffield Wednesday. He has since turned his back on the English game and is currently playing in Slovakia for Slovan Bratislava.

Season	Division	League		FA Cup		FL Cup		Total	
		A	G	A	G	A	G	A	G
2019-20 (R)	Championship	8 (5)	2	1	0	0	0	9 (5)	2
Total		8 (5)	2	1	0	0	0	9 (5)	2

UK LEAGUE CAREER 74 games 5 goals

CHARLTON CAREER
Managers: *L Bowyer*
Debut: *West Bromwich Albion (H) 05-01-2020*
V890
Finale: *Leeds United (A) (sub) 22-07-2020*

GREEN Daniel Richard   2011 - 14

Danny started out on his footballing journey at Charlton and was identified at an early age as a boy with potential, but like so many other hopefuls he was released

Forward   12st 13lbs   5' 11"
Born: 09-07-1988 - Harlow, Essex
Education: St Marks West Essex Catholic School, Harlow.

at the age of 15 moving first to Northampton and then Nottingham Forest where a bad injury led to further disappointment. After a spell in non-league football, he finally got his chance with Dagenham & Redbridge and made his Football League debut on 8th August 2009 against Crewe Alexandra.

HONOURS
Charlton Athletic 2011-12 Winners League One
Dagenham & Redbridge 2009-10 Promoted Play Offs League Two

Milton Keynes Dons 2014-15 Runners Up League One

CLUBS
Charlton Athletic 1999 (youth) ••Northampton Town 2003 (youth) ••Nottingham Forest 2004 (youth) 07.07 (pro) ••Bishops Stortford 07.08 (free) ••Dagenham & Redbridge 05.09 (free) ••Charlton Athletic 29.06.11 (£350,000) ••Milton Keynes Dons 02.09.13 (loan) 23.05.14 (free) ••Luton Town 04.07.15 (free) ••Chelmsford City 25.07.17 (free) ••Concord Rangers 15.05.18 (free) 07.06.20 (player coach) 19.05.21 (ass manager)

The high point of Danny's career came during his time with Dagenham where he was an automatic choice on the right wing for two seasons and appeared in every match during their promotion season of 2009-10. He netted 14 goals, including a vital one at Wembley against Rotherham in the League Two Play off final and became so popular that the Dagenham fans gave him his own song, 'He's Our Superman'.

Charlton signed Dagenham striker Paul Benson during the summer of 2010 and returned a year later to secure the services of the man who had provided Benson with so many of his goal scoring opportunities. Danny joined Charlton in time to play his part in the 2011-12 promotion from League One, but found life in the Championship more difficult, eventually moving on to MK Dons, where their manager Karl Robinson waxed lyrical about 'his delivery, guile, work-rate and set pieces'.

However, a year later he was freed by mutual consent and signed with Luton Town. This proved the final stop for Danny and a broken leg incurred at Northampton on 30th April 2016 caused him to miss the whole of the 2016-17 season and brought down the curtain on his Football

League career. In 2012, he had launched his own football and fashion web based retail business, Bollers Clothing Ltd and in 2017 joined National League South club, Chelmsford City, switching the following year to Concord Rangers, where he was elevated to the position of assistant manager in May 2021.

Season	Division	League		FA Cup		FL Cup		FL Trophy		Total	
		A	G	A	G	A	G	A	G	A	G
2011-12 (P)	League One	25 (7)	3	2	0	2	0	1	0	30 (7)	3
2012-13	Championship	7 (10)	1	0	0	1	0			8 (10)	1
2013-14	Championship	5 (8)	0	1 (3)	1	1 (1)	1			7 (12)	2
Total		37 (25)	4	3 (3)	1	4 (1)	1	1	0	45 (29)	6

UK LEAGUE CAREER 193 games 34 goals

CHARLTON CAREER
Managers: *C Powell, J Riga*
Debut: *Colchester United (H) (sub) 16-08-2011*
V731
Finale: *Bolton Wanderers (H) (sub) 18-04-2014*

GREEN George Henry   1934 - 39

Midfield   10st 12lbs   5' 10"
Born: 12-11-1912 - Barry Docks, Glamorgan
Died: 01-05-1994 - Chislehurst, Kent
Education: Gladstone Road School, Barry.

George played more than 50 league matches for Charlton in the two seasons immediately before World War 2, when the club was exceptionally strong and finished 4th and 3rd respectively in the First Division. He was a Welsh International and won four full caps, including a 3-1 win over Ireland on 15th March 1939, playing alongside Bert Turner and Les Boulter. He made two further appearances for Wales (both against England), during the war, but they are not counted as official internationals.

HONOURS
Wales International 1938-39 4 caps 0 goals
Wales Wartime International 1940-41 2 caps 0 goals

Barry Schools & Welsh Schools
Charlton Athletic 1942-43 Finalists FL (South) Cup

HONOURS AS MANAGER
Dartford 1954-55 & 1955-56 Finalists Kent Senior Cup

CLUBS
Mountstuart Dry Docks ••Enamel Works ••Barry Town (amateur) ••Charlton Athletic 06.03.34 (£250) ••Deportivo Espanol, Spain 08.35 (free) ••Charlton Athletic 17.08.36 (free) ••Millwall 05.46 (trainer) ••Dartford 05.53 (manager) ••Portsmouth 1962 (scout)

Leaving school at age 14, George spent three years as a merchant seaman and commenced his footballing journey playing as an amateur for Barry Town along with his brother Albert. They were competing in the lower reaches of the Southern League Western Section until Charlton came in for George and in March 1934 Barry accepted a fee of £250 to transfer him to SE7. Initially there was no place for him in the Charlton first team but he did at least make himself noticed in the reserves, notably on 10th September 1934 when he scored six goals at the Valley in a Football Combination match against Bristol City. Two days later he made his first team debut in the now largely forgotten FL Third Division Cup. This involved a trip to Aldershot, (managed by Jimmy's brother Angus Seed) and resulted in

a 6-1 drubbing, after which George returned to the reserves, while the first team stormed to the Division 3 South title without him.

An old playing colleague of Jimmy Seed was manager of the Spanish club Deportivo Espanol and George signed for them in August 1935. This greatly increased his wages and considerably advanced his career, despite having to return to England during the mid-season break for an appendicitis operation. However, his European adventure came to an abrupt end after a year with the outbreak of the Spanish Civil War. He re-signed for Charlton in August 1936 and finally made his league debut at the Valley against Wolverhampton Wanderers on 27th March 1937. The club had made great progress during his time in Spain and

George found himself now playing for one of the leading teams in the country. Wolves were dispatched 4-0, courtesy of goals by Harold Hobbis, Don Welsh (2) and George Stephenson.

For the next two seasons George occupied the right half berth in what was without doubt one of the greatest Charlton sides of all. He played on 12th February 1938 when the official attendance record of 75,031 was created for an FA Cup tie with Aston Villa at the Valley. The match ended 1-1 and it took two replays before Villa proceeded to the next round. The three matches were viewed by an aggregate of 201,343 people. Charlton were not only a very fine team but were also a big draw for the public. Other highlights of George's career include the 7-1 defeat of Manchester United (4 goals from George Tadman) and the battles against Arsenal, not least the game over Christmas 1938 when another Tadman goal overcame a star studded Arsenal 1-0.

World War 2 eventually intervened and George served for six years in the Army Physical Training Corps reaching the rank of sergeant major. He turned out for Charlton during the war and made 92 further appearances and scored 26 goals as well as guesting for West Ham, Fulham, Millwall and Aldershot. He appeared at Wembley in front of 75,000 on 1st May 1943 when Charlton were outclassed by Arsenal in the final of the Football League (South) Cup. The score was 7-1 and George netted the consolation goal from the penalty spot.

He retired through injury in 1946 and spent a year as trainer at Millwall, after which he tried various business ventures, including a draper's shop in Eltham which he later transformed into a bookmaker and which kept him occupied until 1970. Earlier he had spent the period 1953-61 as manager of Dartford, but without any great success. He completed his working life at two off licences and finally as a clerical employee for Express Dairies. A natural sportsman who enjoyed golf, snooker and billiards, George passed away in Chislehurst at the age of 81.

Season	Division	League		FA Cup		D3 Cup		Total	
		A	G	A	G	A	G	A	G
1934-35 (P)	Divison 3 (S)	0	0	0	0	1	0	1	0
1936-37	Division 1	5	0	0	0			5	0
1937-38	Division 1	24	0	5	0			29	0
1938-39	Division 1	28	3	1	0			29	3
Total		57	3	6	0	1	0	64	3

UK LEAGUE CAREER 57 games 3 goals

CHARLTON CAREER
Managers: *J Seed*
Debut: *Aldershot (A) 23-05-1934*
V195
Finale: *Chelsea (H) 07-04-1939*

GREEN Harry Rodney   1967

Both Rodney and Matt Tees joined Charlton in January 1967 for a combined fee of £23,000, in an unusual double transfer from Grimsby Town. The club had struggled all that season on the field and the introduction of two proven goalscorers was a bold and exciting move, but whereas Tees proved to have been an inspired signing, Rodney was injured in only his third game and never really established himself before moving on to Luton Town six months later.

Forward   13st 7lb   6' 1"
Born: 24-06-1939 - Halifax, West Yorkshire
Died: 21-11-2018 - Halifax, West Yorkshire
Education: Rastrick Grammar School, Brighouse.

HONOURS
Yorkshire Schools
Luton Town 1967-68 Winners Division 4

Watford 1968-69 Winners Division 3

HONOURS AS MANAGER
Stump Cross 1979-80 Winners Halifax & District Challenge Cup

Elland United 1959 (amateur) ••Halifax Town 09.58 (amateur) 20.08.60 (pro) ••Bradford Park Avenue 07.06.62 (free) ••Bradford City 17.01.63 (£750) ••Gillingham 20. 07.64 (£6,000) ••Grimsby Town 21.08.65 (£8,000) ••Charlton Athletic 27.01.67 (part of £23,000) ••Luton Town 04.08.67 (£5,000) ••Watford 10.08.68 (£3.000) ••Durban Spurs, South Africa 02.70 (free) ••Berea Park, South Africa 1971 (free) ••Jewish Guild, South Africa 1971 (free) ••Durban United, South Africa 1972 (free) ••Stump Cross 1979 (manager)

Rodney represented Yorkshire Schools and commenced his professional career with his home town club, Halifax Town, scoring on his debut against Newport County on 22nd April 1961. A powerful centre forward who regularly found the net throughout his career, he was soon in demand and enjoyed spells with both of the Bradford clubs, Park Avenue and City, grabbing 29 league goals in 44 matches for the latter in 1963-64 season.

After a year with Gillingham, he joined Grimsby Town and struck up a very lucrative partnership with Matt Tees, evidenced in Round 5 of the League Cup on 17th November 1965, when the Mariners, including goalie Charlie Wright, held a strong West Ham side to a 2-2 draw at Blundell Park, thanks to goals from Green and Tees. On another occasion, Rodney scored a hat trick of headed goals in the 7-1 destruction of Scunthorpe United, probably one of the worst defeats ever suffered by future England goalkeeper Ray Clemence, then an 18-year-old rookie.

He scored on his Charlton debut at Cardiff but only a fortnight later was injured and had to leave the field during a vicious encounter against a very physical Coventry City side and never really got the opportunity to make his mark, moving on to Luton Town in the summer of 1967.

The final period of Rodney's Football League career took in promotions in consecutive seasons for Luton and Watford and on each occasion he chipped in with vital goals. At Watford, where he became something of a cult figure, he was regularly serenaded with the affectionate song, 'He's up he's down, he's in the Rose and Crown, Rodney Green'.

After finishing his playing career in South Africa, he returned to Yorkshire and worked as both a teacher and an antique dealer, before settling down with his own pine furniture manufacturing business which he ran for many years in Halifax, before passing away at the age of 79.

Season	Division	League		FA Cup		FL Cup		Total	
		A	G	A	G	A	G	A	G
1966-67	Division 2	3 (1)	1	0	0	0	0	3 (1)	1
Total		3 (1)	1	0	0	0	0	3 (1)	1

UK LEAGUE CAREER 237 games 96 goals

CHARLTON CAREER
Managers: R Stokoe
Debut: *Cardiff City (A) 03-02-1967*
V327
Finale: *Birmingham City (H) (sub) 12-05-1967*

GREEN Ronald Clarence George 1937

Forward   11st 0lbs   5' 8"
Born: 12-03-1912 - Frampton Cotterell, Gloucestershire
Died: 16-10-1979 - Coalpit Heath, Gloucestershire

Ronnie was a left winger who spent a season with Charlton after signing from Notts County in August 1936. The club had just secured their second promotion in consecutive years and were about to compete in Division 1 for the very first time. It was a settled side and manager Jimmy Seed showed great loyalty to his squad, the only other new boy being striker George Tadman who joined from Gillingham as replacement for Ralph Allen. The team excelled themselves and not only survived but flourished and finished runners-up, just three points behind Manchester City. This was the most successful season in Charlton's history to date and Ronnie made his own small contribution.

HONOURS

Arsenal Reserves 1933-34 Winners London Combination

CLUBS

Coalpit Heath 1929 ••Bath City 1929 ••Bristol Rovers 03.06.32 ••Arsenal 03.07.33 (player exchange) ••Notts County 22.02.35 (£1,500) ••Charlton Athletic 01.08.36 (£500) ••Swansea Town 06.05.37 (free) ••Coalpit Heath 1938 (free)

Frampton Cotterell, a sleepy Gloucestershire village on the bank of the River Frome, was Ronnie's birthplace and the conjoined settlement of Coalpit Heath was where he first played his football. He signed for Southern League side Bath City at the age of 17 and continued his progress with a move to Bristol Rovers three years later. His first team debut came on Boxing Day 1932 in a Division 3 (South) fixture at Aldershot and his teammates included former Charlton striker Bobby McKay. They went down 1-0, but he must have played well as he retained his place for the remainder of that season.

In July 1933 Arsenal came calling and he signed for them in exchange for two players, full back Horace Cope and former Charlton goalie Charlie Preedy, who were jointly assessed with a monetary transfer value of £3,000. Neither club benefitted to any great extent. Preedy was nearing the end of his career and only played one season, while Cope managed just a single game. Ronnie failed to make the step-up in class and was moved on to Notts County in February 1935 without appearing in the first team at all.

He progressed better with County and played fairly regularly, even scoring the occasional goal, including the winner when Coventry City were defeated 2-1 on 16th November 1935. When the opportunity came to join Charlton, it gave him a second try at the First Division but it is doubtful if the club ever saw him as more than a reserve. Harold Hobbis was wearing the number 11 shirt with considerable distinction and had been a fixture in the side for four years.

His chance came after Hobbis got injured against Preston on 27th February 1937 and when Ronnie made his Charlton debut seven days later, the club were at the very top of Division 1. In contrast, their opponents, Sheffield Wednesday, were battling against relegation but still pulled off a shock 3-1 win. Ronnie scored in each of his first two outings, but in his third match they took a 5-0 hammering at Derby and when Hobbis returned to the side for the next game, that signalled the end of his time as a Charlton first team player.

He left the club at the end of the season and after a short stay with Swansea Town, returned to Coalpit Heath, where he died on 16th October 1979 at the age of 67.

Season	Division	League		FA Cup		Total	
		A	G	A	G	A	G
1936-37	Division 1	3	2	0	0	3	2
Total		3	2	0	0	3	2

UK LEAGUE CAREER 69 games 13 goals

CHARLTON CAREER
Managers: *J Seed*
Debut: *Sheffield Wednesday (A) 06-03-1937*
V194
Finale: *Derby County (A) 20-03-1937*

GREGORY Gordon 'Harry'　　　　1966 - 70

A larger than life character, Harry was an all action inside forward with a fiery temper and a swashbuckling style. He

Midfield, Forward　11st 10 lbs　5' 11"
Born: 24-10-1943 - Hackney, London
Died: 06-06-2016 - Chelmsford, Essex
Education: Daubeney Primary School, Homerton & Lea Marsh School, Hackney.

had the mentality of a winner and was a great favourite with the fans, Wild stories about him would be heard on the terraces and even decades later, just the mention of his name is enough to bring a smile to the face of supporters of a certain age. Was it against Rotherham United that Harry punched the ball into the net and the referee awarded a goal? Eat your heart out Maradona. Then there was that friendly match at the Valley against AOS Ostende in October 1966, when two of the Belgians wore spectacles. Harry did not do friendlies, but did he really knock down one of his opponents in the goalmouth at the uncovered end and then stamp on his glasses?

HONOURS
England Youth International 1960 1 cap 0 goals
Hackney Boys

Hereford United 1972-73 Runners Up Division 4

CLUBS

Leyton Orient 1959 (youth) 24.10.61 (pro) ••Charlton Athletic 29.07.66 (player exchange) ••Aston Villa 14.10.70 (£7,000) ••Hereford United 19.08.72 (£11,000) ••Chelmsford City 05.75 (free) ••Brentwood c1976 ••Maldon Town 1977 (player manager) ••Bolingbroke & Wenley 1980

An outstanding young player, Harry gained an England Youth cap on 8th October 1960 when he played in the 4-3 win over Switzerland and a year later signed a professional contract with Leyton Orient. He scored on his league debut against Ipswich Town and again in his second match just two days later. This was at Brisbane Road on 12th November 1962 and it was against Charlton in Round 4 of the Football League Cup. Harry's goal proved to be the winner in a 3-2 scoreline, the visitors two strikes coming from Roy Matthews and a 17-year-old Keith Peacock. Strangely enough the two clubs met again in the League Cup on 14th October 1964, but this time at the Valley and Harry found the net in this match as well. It finished 2-1 to Charlton though, courtesy of Dennis Edwards and an own goal from future Charlton manager Andy Nelson.

On 2nd August 1966 Harry was transferred to Charlton in a player exchange deal which sent veteran striker Cliff Holton and ex-Arsenal half back John Snedden in the other direction. He went straight into the team and remained there for four seasons, three of which were spent battling at the wrong end of Division 2. The exception was 1968-69 when Charlton just missed out on a return to the First Division and played some exciting and attacking football. Harry was ever present in both league and cups, including the two FA Cup battles with Crystal Palace, of which the Round 3 replay at Selhurst Park attracted a crowd of 39,404 to see the visitors triumph 2-0, courtesy of two goals from Ray Treacy. Sadly it was the two defeats against Millwall and too many drawn games that season which cost Charlton promotion.

Harry's abrasive and sometimes over aggressive temperament, allied to a short fuse, meant that he was often sailing very close to the wind, but he managed to avoid being sent off during his time with Charlton, except for just once against Bury on 22nd October 1966. A hat-trick by Ron Saunders that day removed the stress from the occasion however and when added to an opener from Mike Kenning ensured a 4-0 scoreline for the Addicks.

In October 1970 he moved to Aston Villa, who were then languishing in the Third Division, but did not have an easy time there. He played quite frequently in his first season, but lost his place in September 1971 and hardly appeared from then on, as Villa raced through to become champions of Division 3.

His transfer to Hereford United in time for the 1972-73 season proved much more memorable. They gained immediate promotion from Division 4 and Harry was a key factor in their success. He was made captain at Hereford (as he had been at Charlton) and was a big influence. A serious Achilles injury in August 1974 kept him out of the side for five months though and he left the club in May 1975, turning down offers to join Torquay United or Wimbledon, in favour of a spell in the Southern League with Chelmsford City.

After retiring from football, Harry worked as a heavy goods vehicle driver for Baxters, the meat distributors and later for Prism Leisure, an Enfield software company. In 2012, he returned to Charlton as a match day host and would happily reminisce about the days when he, Tees, Campbell, Curtis and the rest, so nearly brought First Division football back to SE7. He passed away at the age of 72 and his funeral took place at Chelmsford Crematorium on 21st June 2016.

Season	Division	League		FA Cup		FL Cup		Total	
		A	G	A	G	A	G	A	G
1966-67	Division 2	31	4	1	0	1	0	33	4
1967-68	Division 2	32	7	1	0	0	0	33	7
1968-69	Division 2	42	11	3	0	1	0	46	11
1969-70	Division 2	35 (3)	2	3	2	0	0	38 (3)	4
1970-71	Division 2	6	0	0	0	1	0	7	0
Total		146 (3)	24	8	2	3	0	157 (3)	26

UK LEAGUE CAREER 325 games 44 goals

CHARLTON CAREER

Managers: *R Stokoe, E Firmani, T Foley*
Debut: *Bolton Wanderers (H) 20-08-1966*
V324
Finale: *Carlisle United (H) 29-09-1970*

GRITT Stephen John

1977 - 93

Probably Charlton's finest utility player, Steve made 435 competitive appearances over 16 seasons, a total only

Midfield, Utility   11st 4lbs   5' 10"
Born: 31-10-1957 - Bournemouth, Dorset
Education: Malmesbury Park Primary School, KIngs Park Junior School and Bournemouth Grammar School.

bettered by Sam Bartram, Keith Peacock, John Hewie and Norman Smith. In the days when numbers signified the playing position, he at different times wore all ten outfield shirts with equal distinction and even filled in as an emergency goalkeeper on more two occasions. His contribution to Charlton was enormous during a period of great upheaval and he was the only player who took part in those 'final' games at the Valley in 1985, who then played for the club in each season during the exile years and eventually participated in the glorious homecoming against Portsmouth in 1992. As if that was not enough, Steve then went on to spend four years as joint manager during the period 1991-95. He was elected into the Hall of Fame in 2018.

HONOURS

Bournemouth Schools c1973
Charlton Athletic Reserves 1979-80 Runners Up Mid-Week League
Charlton Athletic 1980-81 Promoted Division 3

Charlton Athletic 1985-86 Runners Up Division 2
Charlton Athletic 2018 Hall Of Fame

CLUBS

Charbourne (youth) ••AFC Bournemouth 07.74 (youth) 07.76 (pro) ••Dorchester Town 1977 (loan) ••Charlton Athletic 02.07.77 (free) ••Walsall 06.07.89 (free) ••Charlton Athletic 20.02.90 (free) 04.10.90 (player/coach) 24.07.91 (joint player/manager) ••Welling United 19. 08.95 (free) ••Tooting & Mitcham United 07.10.95 (free) ••Metrogas Veterans c1996 ••Brighton & Hove Albion 11.12.96 (manager) ••Millwall 09.03.98 (ass: manager) ••Charlton Athletic 2003 (scout) 06.04 (academy manager) ••AFC Bournemouth 18.07.11 (scout) ••Ebbsfleet United 03.06.13 (ass: manager) ••Macclesfield Town 19.08.19 (ass: manager) ••Dagenham & Redbridge 06.01.20 (ass: manager)

After signing for Charlton at the age of 19 and following a few cameo appearances from the substitute's bench, Steve made his full league debut on 8th October 1977 against Blackburn Rovers. He played on the right wing and gave an encouraging performance, but after Jimmy Giles was shown a red card in the second half, the resultant 2-1 defeat was perhaps inevitable. He showed enough however, to very quickly become a fixture in the side. Rarely did he hit the headlines, but wherever on the field he played and in whatever position, he turned in a solid display and his extraordinary versatility ensured that there would usually be a place for him when the team sheet was finalised. In one of his early appearances and playing at inside right, he scored the equalising goal at Selhurst Park to grab a 1-1 draw against Crystal Palace.

In the relegation season of 1979-80, he featured mainly on the left wing and on 27th October 1979 scored twice in the 3-2 defeat of Cardiff City, who had both Ronnie Moore and Alan Campbell in their line-up. A year later when Charlton bounced back at the first attempt, he appeared almost exclusively at full back and played his part in the 15 straight victories in which only five goals were conceded between 7th October and 20th December 1980. As the crisis years loomed ahead, Steve was moved forward into

midfield where on 5th March 1983 he played behind Allan Simonsen as the little Dane destroyed Chelsea with a virtuoso performance and a 5-2 scoreline. When Charlton's financial dilemma intensified he was switched from position to position and on 17th March 1984, just nine days after the club had been rescued from the brink of liquidation, he was moved to centre forward for the trip to Carlisle.

On Boxing Day 1984, Steve completed the full set when he donned the goalkeeping jersey in the 16th minute of the local derby with Crystal Palace, after Tony Lange left the field with a broken ankle. He performed bravely and with no lack of ability but could not stop the two second half goals which ensured a 2-1 Palace win. He played less regularly after the club moved to Selhurst Park, but remained a valuable squad member and shared in several of the magical moments as Charlton confounded all the critics and survived for four years in the First Division. He was at inside right on 30th August 1986 at Old Trafford when Mark Stuart's goal sunk Manchester United 1-0 and nine months later was on the right wing when Peter Shirtliff conjured up two last ditch goals to defeat Leeds United in the play off final replay.

In the Summer of 1989, Steve was freed by Charlton and

signed for Third Division Walsall. He played most of the 1989-90 season for them at right back before returning to Charlton in the February. On 4th October and with his 33rd birthday coming up, he was appointed coach of the reserve team while still retaining his playing contract. From this point his first team appearances became less frequent, but his new role as a coach paid off in July 1991 when Lennie Lawrence resigned as manager and the directors appointed Alan Curbishley and Steve as his successors. This was a controversial move as neither man had any prior managerial experience and the concept of joint managers was untried at this level of the game.

Charlton had dropped out of the First Division and now the main consideration was to end the exile years and return to the Valley as soon as possible. Nothing was considered more important and players were sold to raise the necessary finance while the two rookie managers were left to keep the club afloat, which they managed to achieve with a lot of hard work and a sprinkling of good fortune. When the day finally arrived for Charlton to return to the Valley on 5th December 1992, there was some surprise when Steve was in the starting line-up to play Portsmouth despite having hardly featured up to that point in the season. On reflection this fine servant of the club who had spent the lion's share of his career with Charlton was never going to miss such a significant occasion and fully enjoyed the emotional homecoming in which the 1-0 scoreline was almost incidental.

Alan and Steve continued as joint managers for a total of four years during which the club made steady progress after the chaos of the Selhurst years. However, in June 1995 the board decided that the time had come to go forward with just one manager and the job was given to Curbishley. This decision brought an abrupt change to Steve's fortunes, but amazingly the greatest achievement of his footballing life was still in front of him.

In December 1996 he took over as manager of Brighton & Hove Albion. The club were in a terrible mess and nine points adrift at the bottom of League Two. Steve and his assistant manager Jeff Wood performed a footballing miracle and somehow managed to keep them in the Football League, thanks to a 1-1 draw against Hereford United on the final day of the season, but amazingly the Brighton directors dispensed with his services mid-way through the next campaign.

After a spell as assistant manager at Millwall, Steve returned to Charlton in 2003 and spent six years as academy manager. In June 2013 he became Steve Brown's assistant manager at Ebbsfleet United and has since held similar posts with Macclesfield and Dagenham. A fine cricketer in his youth who played for Hampshire Second XI, he will be remembered most for his versatility and his loyalty to Charlton during some of the more turbulent years in their history. He was still making occasional appearances in veterans football for Metrogas at the age of 63.

Season	Division	League		FA Cup		FL Cup		FM Cup		Play Offs		AI Cup		Total	
		A	G	A	G	A	G	A	G	A	G	A	G	A	G
1977-78	Division 2	28 (6)	3	0	0	0	0							28 (6)	3
1978-79	Division 2	38 (1)	3	3	0	5	0							46 (1)	3
1979-80 (R)	Division 2	31	7	1	0	0	0							32	7
1980-81 (P)	Division 3	33 (7)	0	4	0	5	0							42 (7)	0
1981-82	Division 2	33 (1)	3	1	0	4	0							38 (1)	3
1982-83	Division 2	23 (4)	1	1	0	0 (1)	0							24 (5)	1
1983-84	Division 2	33	1	2	0	2	0							37	1
1984-85	Division 2	32 (3)	1	2	0	0	0							34 (3)	1
1985-86 (P)	Division 2	11	2	1	0	1	0	2	0					15	2
1986-87	Division 1	14	1	0	0	3	0	1	1	5	0			23	2
1987-88	Division 1	22 (5)	0	0	0	1	0	2	0					25 (5)	0
1988-89	Division 1	22	2	1 (1)	0	1	0	1	0					25 (1)	2
1989-90 (R)	Division 1	2	0	0	0	0	0	0	0					2	0
1990-91	Division 2	5 (5)	0	0	0	0	0	0 (1)	0					5 (6)	0
1991-92	Division 2	4 (10)	1	0 (1)	0	1 (1)	0	0	0					5 (12)	1
1992-93	Division 1	4 (3)	0	0	0	0	0					0	0	4 (3)	0
Total		335 (45)	25	16 (2)	0	23 (2)	0	6 (1)	1	5	0	0	0	385 (50)	26

UK LEAGUE CAREER 406 games 29 goals

CHARLTON CAREER
Managers: *A Nelson, M Bailey, A Mullery, K Craggs, L Lawrence, A Curbishley/S Gritt*
Debut: *Blackpool (H) (sub) 27-08-1977*
V406
Finale: *Millwall (A) 24-04-1993*

GROVES Frederick William   1924

A large part of Freddie's football career took place during World War 1 and therefore fails to show up in the record books. He had joined Woolwich Arsenal as an amateur in 1912 and turned professional a year later, his earliest appearances being while they were still based in Plumstead and before the move to North London. He took time to establish himself in their first team but, along with Angus McKinnon, featured in the emphatic 5-1 win over Wolverhampton Wanderers in 1914-15, the final peacetime season. During the war, Arsenal competed in the London Combination and Freddie was a regular at either inside or outside right clocking up 133 further appearances before the Football League restarted in 1919.

Forward   11st 0lbs   5' 8"
Born: 13-01-1891 - Shadwell, London
Died: 24-08-1965 - Southwark, London

CLUBS

Barnet Alston 1910 (amateur) ••Glossop 1911 (amateur) ••(Woolwich) Arsenal 08.12 (amateur) 10.13 (pro) ••Brighton & Hove Albion 02.20 ••Arsenal c1920 ••Brighton & Hove Albion 08.21 (£500) ••Charlton Athletic 13.06.24 ••Dartford 1925

Freddie started out with a North London team Barnet Alston. They had evolved from the works side of the dental manufacturers Alston Works and later went on to become Barnet FC. In 1911, he made his Football League debut for Glossop, but they failed to win any of the nine league games in which he played and this run continued when he switched to Woolwich Arsenal where all of his first eight appearances ended in defeat.

After the war, he held his place in the Arsenal side and played more than 40 games in Division 1, including their 2-1 victory over Manchester City on 11th September 1920. He scored the winner for the team which also included Arthur Hutchins and Angus McKinnon.

Transferring to Brighton & Hove Albion in 1921, Freddie came up against Charlton for the first time on 22nd October 1921, when he was playing at centre forward. However, the Valley crowd of 13,000 were rewarded with a 1-0 win by the Addicks and a goal from winger Harry Wilson.

Freddie joined Charlton in June 1924. Now aged 33, his best days were behind him and he failed to shine when he got his chance in the team during September and following a home defeat to Reading on 4th October, manager Walter Rayner shuffled the pack and switched Bob Thomson to replace him on the right wing, thereby lowering the curtain on his Football League career.

Freddie Groves married a Brighton lady and worked for a time as a docker. He passed away in Southwark at the age of 74 and was cremated on 31st August 1965.

Season	Division	League		FA Cup		Total	
		A	G	A	G	A	G
1924-25	Divison 3 (S)	7	0	0	0	7	0
Total		7	0	0	0	7	0

UK LEAGUE CAREER 119 games 8 goals

CHARLTON CAREER
Managers: *W Rayner*
Debut: *Northampton Town (A) 08-09-1924*
V062
Finale: *Reading (H) 04-10-1924*

GUDMUNDSSON Johann Berg   2014 - 16

Forward, Midfield   12st 4lbs   5' 10"
Born: 27-10-1990 - Reykjavic, Iceland
Education: International School of London.

Johann is well on his way to becoming one of the greats of Icelandic football, having already played in excess of 80 times for his country by the age of 30 and with every chance of passing the century of international appearances before his career is over. He scored a hat trick against Switzerland in a FIFA World Cup qualifying match on 6th September 2013, but his finest moments on the international stage came in the UEFA Euro 2016 finals when (while still a Charlton player), he was part of the famous Icelandic victory that saw England eliminated 2-1 at the Stade de Nice on 27th June 2016, before falling to France in the quarter final six days later. 20 of Johann's international caps were earned during his two years as a Charlton player.

HONOURS

Iceland International 2008-21 81 caps 8 goals

Iceland U21 International 2008-11 14 caps 6 goals

Iceland U19 International 2008 2 caps 1 goal

AZ Alkmaar 2012-13 Winners KNVB Cup (Dutch FA Cup)

AZ Alkmaar 2013-14 Runners Up Johan Cruyff Shield

CLUBS

Breidablik, Iceland 1997 (youth) ••Chelsea 2006 (youth) ••Fulham 2006 (youth) ••Breidablik, Iceland 2008 ••AZ Alkmaar, Netherlands 28.01.09 (pro) ••Charlton Athletic 11.07.14 (free) ••Burnley 19.07.16 (undisclosed)

Although born in Reykjavic, Johann came to England as a teenager and had short spells with both Chelsea and Fulham, before his career really got underway in the Netherlands with AZ Alkmaar. A skilful winger with an eye for goal, by 2010-11 he was playing regularly in the Eredivisie, the Premier Division of Dutch football and on 9th May 2013 was in the AZ side which beat PSV Eindhoven 2-1 to win the Dutch Cup. He also enjoyed a taste of European success when they advanced in the UEFA Europa League of 2013-14, going down to Benfica over two legs in the round before the quarter final stage.

With such an impressive CV and already established at international level, it was understandable that Johann would wish to try his luck in English football, but less obvious why in the summer of 2014 he chose to sign for Charlton. The Curbishley Premier League days were becoming a distant memory and the club was in a state of turmoil under the new Belgian ownership, with little prospect of a return to the top table in the immediate future.

He only missed a handful of games in 2014-15 and his creative wing play and ability to pick out the incisive pass had much to do with Charlton finishing 12th in the Championship after having flirted with relegation for part of the campaign. Johann scored 10 goals, including a brace up at Elland Road in a hard fought 2-2 draw with Leeds United on 4th November 2014

He remained a fixture in the team during his second season, topping the Championship assists chart, creating 11 goals and scoring six, but was still unable to prevent the club's relegation, which was confirmed before the final game against champions Burnley on 7th May 2016. The Valley crowd was forced to watch as their side was comprehensively outplayed 3-0 and then suffered further as both Johann and goalkeeper Nick Pope were signed by the Lancashire club during the summer in advance of their entry into the Premier League.

Johann soon proved that he was not out of place in the top division of English football and in 2017-18 played his part as Burnley achieved a creditable seventh place finish, his equaliser on 3rd February 2018 clinching a 1-1 draw with champions Manchester City. After nearly six seasons he has so far made close to 150 competitive appearances for Burnley, although recently injuries have kept him away from the action.

Season	Division	League		FA Cup		FL Cup		Total	
		A	G	A	G	A	G	A	G
2014-15	Championship	38 (3)	10	1	1	0 (2)	0	39 (5)	11
2015-16 (R)	Championship	39 (1)	6	0	0	0 (2)	0	39 (3)	6
Total		77 (4)	16	1	1	0 (4)	0	78 (8)	17

UK LEAGUE CAREER 199 games 25 goals

CHARLTON CAREER

Managers: *B Peeters, G Luzon, K Fraeye, J Riga, R Slade*

Debut: *Brentford (A) 09-08-2014*

V780

Finale: *Burnley (H) 07-05-2016*

GUNTER Christopher Ross   2020 -

When Charlton's right back Chris Gunter led the Welsh team out on to the pitch at the Cardiff City Stadium on 27th March 2021 against

Defender   11st 3lbs   5' 11"
Born: 21-07-1989 - Newport, Monmouthshire
Education: Durham Road Junior School and St Julian's High School, Newport.

Mexico, he became the first Welshman to play 100 times for his country, which was an enormous achievement. It was his fourth international cap since signing for Charlton in October 2020 and just reward for a long career that had been based around his fitness and an extraordinary level of consistency. He rarely hit the headlines, but his was probably one of the first names on the team sheet every week. He played in 63 consecutive Wales internationals between February 2011 and September 2018 and was honoured as Welsh Footballer of the Year in 2017.

HONOURS

Wales International 2007-21 106 caps 0 goals   Wales U19 International 2006 3 caps 0 goals

Wales U21 International 2006-2007 8 caps 0 goals   Wales U17 International 2005-06 11 caps 2 goals

CLUBS

Durham Colts 1995 (youth) ••Albion Rovers 1996 (youth) ••Cardiff City 1997 (youth) 25.10.06 (pro) ••Tottenham Hotspur 04.01.08 (£2 million) ••Nottingham Forest 12.03.09 (loan) 17.07.09 (£1.75 million) ••Reading 17.07.12 (£2.3 million) ••Charlton Athletic 08.10.20 (free)

Just a month after his 17th birthday, Chris made his debut for Cardiff City in a League Cup tie against Barnet. His teammates included both Joe Ledley and Roger Johnson and although the result was a disappointing 2-0 home defeat, his solid showing marked him out as a player with a big future. However, he was still far from a fixture in Cardiff's first team on 26th May 2007 when he gained his first full international cap for Wales. The match was played at Wrexham against New Zealand and ended 2-2, Chris then becoming the youngest player to appear for Wales, a record previously held by Graham Moore.

His progress had been noted by several clubs and Tottenham moved in with a transfer fee variously described as up to £4 million, but probably half of that figure. It was a big opportunity for Chris and the deal was completed on 4th January 2008. This brought him into the Premier League but unfortunately he never got a chance to show what he could do. He was used in cup games, both European and domestic, but at no time got to play a full 90 minutes in the league. Probably the highlight of his time in

North London came on 27th November 2008 when the Spurs side, which also included Darren Bent, won 1-0 away against the Dutch side NEC (Nijmegen).

In March 2009 he switched to Nottingham Forest, first on loan and then three months later on a permanent deal and from this point on he became a regular fixture, rarely missing a game during his three full seasons at the City Ground. The same level of consistency and professionalism was maintained after he moved to Reading in July 2012 and he was ever present for two consecutive years, including 2016-17 when they got close to promotion to the Premier League, only to lose out in the play offs. That year he was named as the Welsh Footballer of the Year.

Earlier he had been in Nigel Adkins' Reading side which plundered a 1-0 win at the Valley on 5th April 2014, but they did less well the following season when Charlton completed the double over Reading. Igor Vetokele scored the only goal at the Madejski Stadium in November, while two from Yoni Buyens and a winner from Simon Church resulted in a 3-2 scoreline at the Valley. One extraordinary match between the two sides saw Chris's Reading win 4-3 at the Valley on 27th February 2016. Yann Kermorgant scored twice for the visitors and Yaya Sanogo got all three for Charlton.

After his transfer to London SE7, Chris played steadily in the Charlton defence, although injuries forced him to operate at centre half in several matches. Sadly the team promised more than it delivered and constant selection

changes during the final months of Lee Bowyer's term as manager did not help. Inevitably however it was the milestone of his 100 Welsh caps which grabbed the headlines and nobody begrudged this likeable and modest man from receiving his moment in the limelight.

Season	Division	League		FA Cup		FL Cup		FL Trophy		Total	
		A	G	A	G	A	G	A	G	A	G
2020-21	League One	31 (5)	1	0	0	0	0	0	0	31 (5)	1
Total		31 (5)	1	0	0	0	0	0	0	31 (5)	1

UK LEAGUE CAREER 490 games 5 goals

CHARLTON CAREER
Managers: *L Bowyer, N Adkins, J Jackson*
Debut: *Wigan Athletic (H) 17-10-2020*
V906

HACKETT-FAIRCHILD Reeco Lee   2017 - 19

Only once during his time at Charlton did Reeco hit the headlines and that was in June 2018 and for all the wrong reasons. During a holiday in Ibiza, he and Karlan Ahearne-Grant were arrested over an alleged sexual assault of a 19-year-old English girl. He was detained for several days and his passport confiscated, but eventually was allowed home with no charges having been brought against him. It was however a sordid incident and newspaper photos of Reeco in handcuffs did not provide Charlton with the type of publicity that they wanted to further their reputation as a family club.

Forward   11st 1lbs   6' 3"
Born: 30-06-1998 - Redbridge, London
Education: Goldstone Primary School, Hove.

HONOURS
Charlton Athletic U23 2016-17 Winners PD League 2 South   Charlton Athletic U23 2017-18 Runners Up PD League 2 South

CLUBS
Fulham (youth) ••Brighton & Hove Albion (youth) ••Dagenham & Redbridge 2014 (youth) 2016 (pro) ••Dulwich Hamlet 03.16 (loan) ••Charlton Athletic 07.16 (free) ••Boreham Wood 07.09.18 (loan) ••Bromley 12.03.19 (loan) 30.05.19 (free) ••Portsmouth 06.01.20 (undisclosed) ••Bromley 21.09.20 (loan) ••Southend United 07.01.21 (loan)

A tall, leggy striker, Reeco joined Charlton in July 2016 and made an immediate impact for the U23 team, contributing to their success in the Development League in each of his first two seasons. His form earned him a call-up to the first team on 8th August 2017 for a League Cup tie at Exeter and he came on as replacement for Tony Watt with the home team a goal up. Strikes by Billy Clarke and Regan Charles-Cook ensured a 2-1 win for the Addicks and Reeco did enough to earn several more, mainly cameo appearances, during the remainder of the season.
He remained in the first team squad during 2018-19 and finally got the opportunity to start a league match at Fleetwood on 2nd February. At this stage of his development, he was probably not strong enough to withstand the physical demands of the game at League One level and the following month dropped down to the

National League for a loan spell at Bromley. At the end of the season, he was not offered a new contract by Charlton but quickly agreed a permanent deal with Bromley.
After netting eight goals in the first half of 2019-20, he joined Portsmouth on 6th January 2020 and made his debut against Walsall in the Football League Trophy one day later. No other first team chances were immediately forthcoming and after another spell with Bromley, Reeco joined struggling Southend United on loan and rewarded them with the winning goal against Barrow after just three minutes of his debut on 9th January 2021. Unfortunately this was his only strike during his time with the Essex club. In 2021-22 Reeco finally got a run of games for Portsmouth, although much of his time was still spent on the sub's bench.

Season	Division	League		FA Cup		FL Cup		FL Trophy		Play Offs		Total	
		A	G	A	G	A	G	A	G	A	G	A	G
2017-18	League One	0 (5)	0	0 (1)	0	0 (1)	0	2 (3)	2	0	0	2 (10)	2
2018-19 (P)	League One	1 (6)	0	1 (1)	0	1	0	2	0	0	0	5 (7)	0
Total		1 (11)	0	1 (2)	0	1 (1)	0	4 (3)	2	0	0	7 (17)	2

UK LEAGUE CAREER 37 games 1 goal

CHARLTON CAREER
Managers: *R Slade, K Robinson, L Bowyer*
Debut: *Exeter City (A) (sub) 08-08-2017*
V845
Finale: *Southend United (11) (sub)*
09-02-2019

HALES Derek David   1973 - 85

Forward   11st 8lbs   5' 9"
Born: 15-12-1951 - Lower Halstow, Kent
Education: The Howard School, Rainham and Rainham Secondary
Modern School.

The irrepressible Derek Hales stands high in the pantheon of Charlton heroes. His swashbuckling and larger than life persona disguised a predatory goal scorer who had real pace over short distances, plus that natural ability to anticipate chances in and around the box. He was a clinical finisher and at his peak was mentioned in the media as being worthy of an England call up. During his two spells at Charlton, Derek featured in 368 cup and league matches and delivered 168 goals which remains a club record. His 148 goals in league matches are only bettered by Stuart Leary, who scored 153. Between 10th September and 23rd October 1976 Derek scored in seven consecutive league games and equalled the club record set by Ralph Allen in 1935. He actually scored 13 goals in that golden run, including hat-tricks against both Luton Town and Hull City.

HONOURS

Rainham Schools & Kent Schools
Charlton Athletic 1974-75 & 1980-81 Promoted Division 3
Charlton Athletic 1976 Player Of The Year

Charlton Athletic 2012 Hall Of Fame
Faversham Town 1970-71 Winners Kent League
Faversham Town 1970-71 Winners Kent League Cup

CLUBS

Upchurch Minors (youth) ••Breach Rovers (youth) ••West Ham United 1965 (youth) ••Gillingham (youth) ••Faversham Town 1970 (semi-pro) ••Dartford 1971 (pro) ••Luton Town 14.02.72 (£2,000) ••Charlton Athletic 09.72 (loan) 25.10.73 (£4,000) ••Derby County 13.12.76 (£333,333) ••West Ham United 27.09.77 (£110,000) ••Charlton Athletic 27.07.78 (£75,000) ••Gillingham 26.03.85 (free)

Both Derek's father, Dick Hales (a full back) and his uncle Bill (a centre forward), played as amateurs in the Football League for Gillingham. Bill Hales scored three goals on his debut against Port Vale in March 1951, which was almost certainly the same month that his nephew was conceived and young Derek demonstrated from an early age that he had inherited the footballing gene when he scored 136 goals in a single season for Upchurch Minors, while also turning out with his brothers Richard and Ray for Breach Rovers in the Rochester & District Sunday League. During September 1965 he played alongside Trevor Brooking for West Ham's youth team in a South East Counties match against Brentford and later also appeared in the same Gillingham youth eleven as Dick Tydeman.

In season 1970-71 Derek amassed 39 goals in just 19 games for Faversham Town as they won the Kent League by a seven point margin and then went on to sign a pro contract with Dartford. They were competing in the Premier Division of the Southern League and he managed 15 goals for them in 30 appearances. This level of scoring inevitably attracted attention and he had a trial with Norwich City before accepting an offer to join Luton Town in February 1972. Dartford received a £2,000 transfer fee and Derek, who had also been working for Post Office

Telecommunications now became a full-time professional. A whole year passed before he made his full debut for Luton on 17th February 1973 against Cardiff City and he scored after just 12 minutes. However, when he failed to find the net in the matches that followed, he was first moved out to the wing and then left out completely for the final games of the season. The club finished comfortably mid-table in Division 2 but former Charlton striker Vic Halom was the only player to score 10 goals for Luton in 1972-73 and he had already left for Sunderland, so it was perhaps surprising that Charlton's astute manager Theo Foley, got a positive response when he offered to take Derek on loan.

His first game in a Charlton shirt was at the Valley on 11th September 1973 against Blackburn Rovers. He scored shortly after half-time as the game swung backwards and forwards. It finished 4-3 and the other Charlton scorers that day were Dave Shipperley, Arthur Horsfield and Mike Flanagan. A somewhat porous defence and a forward line of Powell, Peacock, Hales, Horsfield and Flanagan always ensured plenty of excitement and goals, if not all at the right end. Derek settled in remarkably quickly and the fear among supporters was that he would return to Luton after his loan, but happily this was not the case and effective 23rd

October 1973, he became a permanent signing, having already netted seven league goals for the Addicks. 1974-75 was a promotion year for Charlton as they regained their place in Division 2 under new manager Andy Nelson and with Derek at his aggressive best. He liked to play on the edge and relished the physical battles with opposing defenders. He netted 20 league goals including a first half hat-trick against Halifax Town (3-1) on 18th March 1975. The following year he did even better with 28 league and three cup strikes, a figure only bettered once in Charlton's long history. (Ralph Allen amassed 32 league and one cup goal in 1934-35). Newly promoted Charlton finished ninth in the league and Hales recorded another hat-trick when a strong Fulham side were narrowly defeated 3-2 on 17th February 1976.

When 1976-77 got underway, there was a feeling that promotion back to the First Division was a real possibility. By the beginning of November Charlton were second in the league and Derek was in the form of his life. A vital game at Chelsea was lost 2-1, but with more than half of the season remaining, he had accumulated an amazing 16 goals in 16 games and interest from other clubs was putting pressure on the directors to cash in their most saleable asset. As so often has happened through the years, Charlton took the opportunity to accept an attractive transfer fee rather than wholeheartedly backing the team's promotion attempt and on 13th December 1976 Derek signed for Derby County and the club banked £333,000. At the time it was the biggest fee Charlton had ever earned in the transfer market and was only the fifth deal exceeding £300,000 in British football history. In fairness, Mike Flanagan took up the main striking role after Derek's departure and ended the season with 23 league goals, but supporters were left to wonder just what might have been. The season finished with Charlton in seventh place. Derek's move into the First Division was a case of the wrong club at the wrong time. Derby had been champions in 1974-75, but were now sliding backwards and occupying the lower reaches of Division 1. Relegation was still three years away, but they were an unbalanced team and never used him to their best advantage. He scored twice in a 4-2 win over Newcastle in January, but only managed four goals in 23 league matches and badly missed Colin Powell, whose pin point crosses had led to so many Charlton goals. Derby brought Tommy Docherty in as manager in September 1977 and it quickly became clear that Hales was available for transfer. There was interest from Queens Park Rangers and Brighton but it was West Ham who on 27th September paid £110,000 to bring him back to London.

West Ham got Derek away from his Derby nightmare and his teammates now included Billy Bonds, Mervyn Day (a future Charlton coach) and Alan Curbishley, but if anything the position on the field was even more desperate. They spent the whole of 1977-78 in an unsuccessful battle against relegation. Derek was carrying a knee injury but still contributed 10 league goals in 24 matches and finished as the Hammers' leading scorer. Finally, in July 1978 Charlton supporters received the news they had long dreamed about. The Killer, (a nickname bestowed upon him by Keith Peacock), was to return. Not quite the prodigal son, but the fact that the club was prepared to pay a fee of £75,000 (a record at the time) was almost universally appreciated. The only dissenting voice appeared to be that of Mike Flanagan, who let it be known that he was not about to give up his role as the main striker any time soon.

By 9th January 1979 Charlton was mid-table in Division 2. A home draw at the Valley against non-league Maidstone United in the FA Cup was always a potential banana skin, but nobody expected the drama that was played out in front of a crowd of 13,432. The visitors took an early lead, but as the match progressed, Charlton got more and more on top. With the score at 1-1 and the increasingly frustrated strike force of Hales and Flanagan badly misfiring, an FA Cup surprise seemed on the cards. There were just four minutes left when words were spoken and then punches thrown by both men and the startled referee was obliged to twice brandish his red card, leaving the remaining nine Charlton players to hang on for the draw. In the aftermath of this embarrassing incident, Derek, who was deemed to have thrown the first punch, had his contract terminated on 26th January. He was subsequently re-instated a fortnight later and his club punishment was reduced to a fine of two weeks wages.

The Maidstone debacle seemed to affect the whole club and that safe mid-table placing soon deteriorated into a relegation struggle and even though Charlton survived in 19th place, by the next season things had got worse. They finished 1979-80 rock bottom of Division 2. Derek never recaptured the outstanding form that he had shown in 1976, but still kept scoring at an impressive rate. New manager Mike Bailey led Charlton back to Division 2 at the first attempt and the Killer was again leading goal scorer with 23 in league and cups, a feat that he achieved in six separate seasons. His, shall we say robust and physical style, led to many more on-field flash points and in 1982-83 he created an unusual record when he was dismissed twice against the same club, Burnley, seeing red in both the home and away fixtures. His last goal for Charlton came just before half-time in a 2-2 draw against Portsmouth on 29th September 1984

Derek finished his career at Gillingham where Keith Peacock was manager. He played alongside Martin Robinson, Dave Mehmet and Peter Shaw and his final goal was the winner in a 3-2 away victory at Doncaster on 25th April 1986. He was released at the end of that season and later became landlord of the Three Tuns in his home village of Lower Halstow. He has also worked in the building

industry, delivered paint and coached at Howard School in Rainham. Derek was also a talented all-rounder at cricket and is a keen golfer. He remains a larger than life character and is always good value whenever he speaks at supporters events, thanks to a stream of outrageous and politically incorrect stories.

Season	Division	League		FA Cup		FL Cup		Total	
		A	G	A	G	A	G	A	G
1973-74	Division 3	26 (3)	8	1	0	1	0	28 (3)	8
1974-75 (P)	Division 3	44	20	2	0	2	1	48	21
1975-76	Division 2	40	28	4	0	6	3	50	31
1976-77	Division 2	16	16	0	0	3	2	19	18
1978-79	Division 2	20	8	1	0	3	1	24	9
1979-80 (R)	Division 2	23	8	1	0	2	1	26	9
1980-81 (P)	Division 3	39 (1)	17	5	4	4	2	48 (1)	23
1981-82	Division 2	35	11	1	0	4	2	40	13
1982-83	Division 2	30	14	1 (0)	1	2	2	33	17
1983-84	Division 2	27 (2)	10	1	0	2	1	30 (2)	11
1984-85	Division 2	12 (2)	8	0	0	2	0	14 (2)	8
Total		312 (8)	148	17	5	31	15	360 (8)	168

UK LEAGUE CAREER 414 games 172 goals

CHARLTON CAREER
Managers: *T Foley, A Nelson, M Bailey, A Mullery, K Craggs, L Lawrence*
Debut: *Blackburn Rovers (H) 11-09-1973*
V385
Finale: *Shrewsbury Town (A) 09-03-1985*

HALEY William Thomas 1924 - 25

Forward, Midfield   10st 8lbs   5' 9"
Born: 16-02-1904 - Woolwich, London
Died: 20-01-1960 - Rochester, Kent
Education: Bostall Lane School, Abbey Wood.

Bill was a goal scoring inside forward who performed well when given a run in the Charlton first team during the 1924-25 season and it was almost certainly financial considerations that led to his moving on to Derby County after just 18 league appearances. The club was under constant pressure throughout the 1920s as a result of continual year-over-year losses, so the fee of £1,000 from Derby was more than welcome. It certainly reduced the deficit for that season but did nothing to improve the position on the field. The club were ninth in the league when Bill departed in February, but had slipped back to 15th by the end of the campaign.

CLUBS

Bostall Athletic ••Bostall Heath ••Charlton Athletic 28.03.24 (pro) •Derby County 28.02.25 £1,000) ••Dartford 25.07.27 (£750) ••Fulham 06.06.28 (free) ••Queens Park Rangers 24.05.31 ••Dartford 1932 ••Sheppey United 08.35

All nine of Bill's goals for Charlton were scored at the Valley and none in away matches. This peculiar statistic may hint at a greater effort being made in front of the home supporters or just bad luck on his travels, but either way he made a real difference whenever he laced up his boots in the home dressing room. There was the winner on 6th December 1924 when Swindon Town were dispatched 1-0, two goals against Dulwich Hamlet in the FA Cup and the opener when Brentford were vanquished 3-0 in a lively

derby match. Steve Smith and Kosha Goodman got the other two goals.

From a playing point of view it certainly made no sense for Bill to leave, but on 28th February 1925 he signed for Derby County and in addition to the fee, the deal included a match to be played between the two clubs at the Valley. This took place on 31st August 1926, but by then it was clear that there was no room for him in the Derby side which had finally clinched a place in Division 1. During their 1925-26 promotion season he had played just nine competitive matches and scored only once, in the home game, (of course), against Middlesbrough.

Bill did manage one appearance in the First Division, but that ended as a 3-0 defeat at Newcastle. He was sold to Dartford in July 1927 and spent a year competing in the Southern League before Fulham brought him back to the Football League for what turned out to be the golden period of his career. Bill played 101 league and cup matches for the Cottagers over three years and plundered 54 goals. He finally shook off his bogey and delivered two strikes in the away match at Watford on 29th September 1928. There was a hat-trick against Bristol Rovers before he punished

Watford again with a four goal haul in March 1930. Bill finished 1929-30 as Fulham's leading scorer.

After a season with Queens Park Rangers, he carried on playing in the non-league game while at the same time running a sweet shop in New Road, Woolwich. For a spell he coached in the South of France but in 1933 took over as licensee of 'The Goat' in Sheerness. He later moved to a pub in Edenbridge and at the time of his death was proprietor of the 'Gore Court Arms' in Sittingbourne. Bill was an enthusiastic club cricketer and for several years kept wicket for Gore Court CC. He died in St Bartholomew's Hospital, Rochester at the age of 55.

Season	Division	League		FA Cup		Total	
		A	G	A	G	A	G
1924-25	Divison 3 (S)	18	6	3	3	21	9
Total		18	6	3	3	21	9

UK LEAGUE CAREER 137 games 62 goals

CHARLTON CAREER
Managers: *W Rayner*
Debut: *Northampton, Town (A) 08-09-1924*
V060
Finale: *Swansea Town (H) 16-02-1925*

HALFORD Gregory　　　　　　　　　　　2008

Greg was a loan signing who spent almost half a season at the Valley during 2008. Manager Alan Pardew brought him into the back four as a replacement for Yassin Moutaouakil as freshly

Defender, Utility　13st 5lbs　6' 4"
Born: 08-12-1984 - Chelmsford, Essex
Education: The Boswells School, Chelmsford.

relegated Charlton tried for a quick return to the Premier League. He played in all the last 16 matches in season 2007-08 but despite an encouraging 2-0 win against Crystal Palace on his debut, the side only managed three more victories and finished up in a disappointing mid-table position

HONOURS

England U20 International 2005 4 caps 1 goal
Colchester United 2005-06 Runners Up League 1

Colchester United 2005-06 Finalists Football League Trophy (S)
Cardiff City 2017-18 Runners Up Championship

CLUBS

Colchester United 07.01 (youth) 08.08.03 (pro) ••Aylesbury United 2002 (loan) ••Braintree Town 2002 (loan) ••Reading 30.01.07 (£2.5 million) ••Sunderland 11.06.07 (£2.5 million) ••Charlton Athletic 31.01.08 (loan) ••Sheffield United 03.07.08 (loan) ••Wolverhampton Wanderers 03.07.09 (£2 million) ••Portsmouth 19.10.10 (loan) 11.07.11 (£1 million) ••Nottingham Forest 27.02.12 (undisclosed) ••Brighton & Hove Albion 04.11.14 (loan) ••Rotherham United 06.07.15 (free) ••Birmingham City 26.11.15 (loan) ••Cardiff City 06.01.17 (undisclosed) ••Aberdeen, Scotland 27.02.19 (free) ••Southend United 15.12.20 (free) ••Waterford United, Ireland 23.07.21 (free) ••Billericay Town 12.02.22 (free)

The young Greg Halford showed all round sporting ability and as a schoolboy reached international standard at volleyball and basketball. He also excelled at hurdles and triple jump and had Olympic potential in the decathlon. He was proficient at cricket and rugby but football was the sport that he chose to pursue and four caps for England at U20 level soon confirmed that he had made the right decision. He played in the Toulon Tournament of 2005

alongside Darren Ambrose and Bradley Wright-Phillips and scored in the 3-0 win over South Korea.

He initially made fine progress at club level as well, playing more than 150 matches for Colchester United under manager Phil Parkinson, including season 2005-06 when they clinched promotion from League One and reached the final of the Football League Trophy, Southern Section. He played alongside Chris Iwelumo in the promotion season and even chipped in with seven league goals himself, including a pair in a 2-1 win at Blackpool on 9th October 2005.

In January 2007 Greg moved into the Premier League after a big money transfer to Reading, but did not settle and played only three times before moving on to Sunderland where he picked up two red cards in just nine matches on Wearside. His third chance in the Premier League came with Wolverhampton and again he was unable to forge a regular place in the team, his very adaptability seeming to work against him. At different times in his career he filled almost every outfield position, had pace, a reasonable shot and a dangerous long throw, but his playing level was probably the second tier and that is where he mostly operated for the remainder of his time in the Football League.

After spending two years in a gradually disintegrating Portsmouth team, Greg transferred to Nottingham Forest and in 2012-13 they managed a double over Charlton, another ex-Addick, Andy Reid, also playing in both matches. However, revenge came sweetly on 25th March 2014 at the City Ground, when Charlton eased their

relegation fears with an unexpected 1-0 victory against their high flying opponents, courtesy of a Jordan Cousins goal.
In January 2017 he signed for Cardiff City after a fallow spell with Rotherham and although most of his appearances were from the substitute's bench, he was able to contribute to the Welsh club's elevation from the Championship in 2017-18. There were however no more Premier League opportunities and Greg was released at the end of the promotion season. Without a club for eight months, he finally joined Aberdeen in February 2019, but only made two appearances for them and then with no new offers forthcoming, it appeared that his career was at an end until he surprisingly landed a short term contract with relegation threatened Southend United in December 2020 and scored on his debut against Grimsby Town.

Sadly there was no happy ending to his time on the Essex coast as Southend were demoted to the National League at the end of the season and in July 2021 at the age of 36, Greg signed for Waterford United, an Irish club that had once been managed by Mike Flanagan. They were relegated from the League of Ireland, Premier Division at the end of the season, after which Greg signed for Billericay Town.

Season	Division	League		FA Cup		FL Cup		Total	
		A	G	A	G	A	G	A	G
2007-08	Championship	16	2	0	0	0	0	16	2
Total		16	2	0	0	0	0	16	2

UK LEAGUE CAREER 472 games 46 goals

CHARLTON CAREER
Managers: *A Pardew*
Debut: *Crystal Palace (H) 08-02-2008*
V662
Finale: *Coventry City (H) 04-05-2008*

HALKYARD Cecil   1933

Midfield   11st 2lbs   5' 10"
Born: 17-04-1902 - Rochdale, Lancashire
Died: 07-1989 - Rochdale, Lancashire

Cecil enjoyed a long but seemingly unfulfilled football career moving around at least 15 clubs in 18 years between the Wars, yet rarely staying in one place for any length of time. Six Football League clubs gave him a chance, but he never established himself anywhere at first team level and all this in a period when players changed clubs much less than in the modern era.

HONOURS

Connah's Quay & Shotton 1928-29 Winners Welsh Cup

CLUBS

Bury 10.20 (amateur) ••Bacup Borough 1921 (amateur) ••Rochdale All Saints 1922 (amateur) ••Accrington Stanley 07.23 (amateur) ••Rochdale 05.24 ••Connah's Quay & Shotton 1928 ••Reading 06.30 ••Rhyl Athletic 06.31 ••Colwyn Bay c1932 ••Charlton Athletic 22.05.32 ••Barrow 07.34 ••Hyde United 1936 ••Mossley 1936 ••Macclesfield mid 1937 ••Newton Heath Athletic c1938

Most of Cecil's football was played in Wales or the North of England, but in May 1932 he turned up at Charlton where he remained for two seasons, a long period of

stability by his standards.
His one and only first team outing at the Valley against Chesterfield did not go well, although with 10 minutes

remaining the game was still in the balance with the score at 1-2. Cecil appears to have been marking the visitor's inside forward, Albert Malam, who had already scored one goal, but then grabbed three more in a frantic finale which produced a final score of 2-5.

This did nothing for Cecil's future prospects at Charlton and after a further spell in the reserves he quietly exited and headed north to try his luck at Barrow. By 1939 he was working in a wet hide warehouse at a Rochdale tannery and eventually passed away in the same town at the age of 81.

Season	Division	League		FA Cup		Total	
		A	G	A	G	A	G
1932-33	Division 2	1	0	0	0	1	0
Total		1	0	0	0	1	0

CHARLTON CAREER
Managers: *A MacFarlane, A Lindon, J Seed*
Debut: *Chesterfield (H) 06-05-1933*
V169

UK LEAGUE CAREER 25 games 0 goals

HALOM Victor Lewis 1965 - 67

Vic's parents were refugees, displaced after World War 2, his father Hungarian and his mother from Germany. He grew up with German as his

Forward   12st 10lbs   5' 10"
Born: 03-10-1948 - Swadlincote, Derbyshire
Education: Linton Primary School, Linton. Castle Gresley Secondary School, Swadlincote.

first language and captained both Burton and South Derbyshire Schools, before representing Derbyshire Schools in the same team as Dennis Booth. A knee injury caused him to miss out after being invited to take part in England Youth trials.

HONOURS

Burton Schools & South Derbyshire Boys
Derbyshire County Boys
Charlton Athletic Youth 1965-66 Winners South East Counties League Cup
Charlton Athletic Youth 1966-67 Winners South East Counties League

Charlton Athletic Youth 1966-67 Finalists South East Counties League Cup
Fulham 1970-71 Runners Up Division 3
Sunderland 1972-73 Winners FA Cup
Sunderland 1975-76 Winners Division 2

HONOURS AS MANAGER

Barrow 1983-84 Winners Northern Premier League

CLUBS

Charlton Athletic 30.03.64 (youth) 04.01.66 (pro) ••Orient 29.08.67 (loan) 06.10.67 (£3,000) ••Fulham 31.10.68 (£30,000) ••Luton Town 09.09.71 (£30,000) ••Sunderland 07.02.73 (£35,000) ••Oldham Athletic 03.07.76 (£25,000) ••Arcadia Shepherds, South Africa 16.05.77 (loan) ••Rotherham United 28.02.80 (£25,000) ••Northwich Victoria 07.81 ••Bergsoy IL, Norway 05.82 (manager) ••Fredrikstad, Norway 1982 (coach) ••Barrow 07.83 (manager) ••Rochdale 05.84 (manager) ••Burton Albion 09.87 (manager) ••North Shields

Vic made his first team debut for Charlton while still an apprentice, appearing alongside fellow debutant Ray Harford in a goalless draw with Manchester City. He turned pro two months later but never managed to secure a settled place in the side and was eventually packed off on loan to Orient by manager Bob Stokoe. When Eddie Firmani replaced Stokoe the following month, almost his first action was to make Vic's move a permanent one and he was sold for the seeming giveaway price of £3,000.
His career really took off at Fulham where he featured in their Division 3 promotion side of 1971, but it was at Sunderland, re-united with manager Bob Stokoe, that he will be most fondly remembered, joining them in February

1973 with their famous FA Cup run already underway. He scored against Manchester City in the Fifth Round replay and got the winner in the Semi-Final against Arsenal in a 2-1 victory at Hillsborough. In the Final, the odds were stacked heavily against Second Division Sunderland as their opponents were the powerful Leeds United and Vic had his best effort disallowed by the referee, but they still managed to pull off one of the greatest FA Cup shocks, winning 1-0 in an exciting match.
After spells with Oldham and Rotherham, another bad knee injury bought his playing career to a close and he moved into management, guiding Barrow to the top of the Northern Premier League in 1983-84, but found less

success with Rochdale where comedian Tommy Cannon (of Cannon and Ball fame) was chairman. The humour of the situation was lost on Vic when he was sacked after being forced to sell their best players through financial necessity and was then held responsible for the poor results which followed.

He stood for Parliament as the Liberal Democrat candidate

for Sunderland North in the 1992 General Election but could only finish third. For a time he worked in Oldham in public relations before re-locating to Bulgaria, where he remained for many years with Amec Utilities, while at the same time scouting for several clubs, including Bolton, Blackburn and Sunderland. By 2018, Vic was retired and back living in Sunderland.

Season	Division	League		FA Cup		FL Cup		Total	
		A	G	A	G	A	G	A	G
1965-66	Division 2	5 (2)	0	0	0	0	0	5 (2)	0
1966-67	Division 2	3 (1)	0	0	0	0	0	3 (1)	0
1967-68	Division 2	1	0	0	0	1	0	2	0
Total		9 (3)	0	0	0	1	0	10 (3)	0

UK LEAGUE CAREER 452 games 131 goals

CHARLTON CAREER
Managers: *F Hill, R Stokoe, E Firmani*
Debut: *Manchester City (A) 30-10-1965*
V311
Finale: *Luton Town (A) 23-08-1967*

HALSE Harold James   1921 - 22

Forward   10st 10lbs   5' 7"
Born: 01-01-1886 - Stratford, London
Died: 25-03-1949 - Colchester, Essex
Education: Park Road School, Wanstead.

In the summer of 1921 Charlton had just been elected into the Football League and it must have been felt that an experienced 'older head' was required to guide them through that first season. Nobody better than Harold Halse could have been found to fit that role. He was aged 35, a former England International and a legend within the game having in 1915 become the first man to appear in three FA Cup finals for three different clubs. He had won the First Division with Manchester United and in the 1911 FA Charity Shield had scored six goals as Swindon Town were swept away 8-4, thereby creating a record that will probably never be equalled.

HONOURS

England International 1909 1 cap 2 goals
Football League XI 1909-15 5 caps
Wanstead 1901-02 Joint Winners Leyton & District League
Wanstead 1902-03 Winners London FA Junior Cup
Southend United 1906-07 & 1907-08 Winners Southern League Division 2
Manchester United 1908-09 Winners FA Cup

Manchester United 1910-11 Winners Division 1
Manchester United 1911 Winners FA Charity Shield
Aston Villa 1912-13 Runners Up Division 1
Aston Villa 1912-13 Winners FA Cup
Chelsea 1914-15 Finalists FA Cup

CLUBS

Newportians 1901 ••Wanstead 1901 ••Barking 1902 ••Clapton Orient 1905 (amateur) •Southend United 06.06 ••Manchester United 03.08 (£350) ••Aston Villa 07.12 (£1,200) ••Chelsea 31.05.13 ••Charlton Athletic 07.21

Harold represented West Ham Schools in 1898-99 when they reached the final of the Corinthian Shield organised by the London Schools FA and always seemed destined to make his mark in the game. He played twice for Clapton Orient as an amateur during their first season as a League club and made his debut in an away match against Manchester United on 2nd December 1905, at their old ground in Banks Street. It was however during his two seasons with Southend United that he really came into his own, scoring an incredible 91 goals in 65 games as they twice won the Southern League Division 2.

He signed for Manchester United in March 1908 for the then maximum permitted fee of £350. They were one of the top sides in the country and on 24th April 1909 won the FA Cup for the first time, beating Bristol City 1-0 at the Crystal Palace before a crowd of 71,401, with Harold playing at inside right. His one appearance for England came in Vienna on 1st June 1909 and he scored twice as Austria were outplayed 8-1.

Manchester United won the First Division in 1910-11 and he featured regularly, scoring several key goals, including the winner when Woolwich Arsenal were defeated 2-1 at the Manor Ground in Plumstead. His six goal feat in the FA Charity Shield followed in September 1911.

Harold switched to Aston Villa in a big money transfer and was a vital member of their team which in 1912-13 only narrowly missed out on the elusive FA Cup and League double. He contributed 21 League goals, including 12 in six matches during one golden spell. The Wednesday were thrashed 10-0 and on 16th October he scored all five as Derby County were beaten 5-0. Villa ended the season runners-up to Sunderland, but defeated their North East rivals 1-0 in the FA Cup Final.

Six weeks later he joined Chelsea, for whom he played over 100 games either side of the War, including a third FA Cup Final appearance. This time the match was played at Old Trafford, but they were well beaten 3-0 by Sheffield United.

It was a considerable coup for Charlton to add a player of Harold's reputation to their squad and his debut came in their opening game in Division 3 South against Exeter City. He featured regularly during the first half of the season and played in both games against Millwall when Charlton scored a rare double against their South London rivals, his winning goal ensuring a 2-1 scoreline at the Valley on 14th January 1922. He finally retired in 1923 but stayed on in a scouting capacity for a couple of years. During his time with Charlton, Harold was an enthusiastic member of the Walton & Frinton Yacht Club. He was also a keen cricketer with Prittlewell CC. Harold managed a tobacconist shop in Walton-on-the-Naze for several years and at the time of his death at the age of 63, had been working as an off licence manager in Frinton-on-Sea.

Season	Division	League		FA Cup		Total	
		A	G	A	G	A	G
1921-22	Divison 3 (S)	18	5			18	5
1922-23	Divison 3 (S)	3	0	0	0	3	0
Total		21	5	0	0	21	5

UK LEAGUE CAREER 259 games 91 goals

CHARLTON CAREER
Managers: W Rayner
Debut: *Exeter City (H) 27-08-1921*
V009
Finale: *Reading (A) 07-10-1922*

HAMER Benjamin John   2011 - 14

For three seasons Ben was the last line of Charlton's defence and a popular member of Chris Powell's promotion team of 2011-12. In that record breaking season they conceded only 36 league goals and Ben recorded 18 clean sheets. He was first choice goalkeeper throughout his time with the club but chose to leave at the conclusion of his three-year contract, making it clear that he sought the opportunity to play in the Premier League. This he achieved with Leicester City, but although he undoubtedly benefited financially from Premier League wages, he proved unable to secure a first team place and was rarely granted the opportunity to perform at the top level.

Goalkeeper   12st 2lbs   6' 4"
Born: 20-11-1987 - Chard, Somerset
Education: Holyrood Community School, Chard.

HONOURS
Charlton Athletic 2011-12 Winners League One   Brentford 2008-09 Winners League Two

CLUBS
Chard Town (youth) ••Reading 2003 (youth) 2006 (pro) ••Crawley Town 08.06 (loan) ••Brentford 12.08.07 (loan) 01.01.08 (loan) 17.07.08 (loan) 31.08.10 (loan) ••Exeter City 19.01.11 (loan) ••Charlton Athletic 01.08.11 (free) ••Leicester City 23.05.14 (free) ••Nottingham Forest 25.07.15 (loan) ••Bristol City 11.08.15 (loan) ••Huddersfield Town 01.06.18 (free) ••Derby County 08.08.19 (loan) ••Swansea City 15.01.21 (undisclosed)

Born in the West Country, Ben's family lived in Germany for five years. After returning to the UK he represented Somerset at schoolboy level and signed for Reading at the age of 15. Shortly after obtaining a professional contract, he spent season 2006-07 out on loan with Football Conference side Crawley Town where he gained valuable

experience, despite that club's financial dilemma which forced them into administration and the deduction of 10 league points.

Although remaining with Reading for a further four years, he never got a chance in their league team, much of his time being occupied by no less than four separate periods on loan with Brentford, the most productive of which came in season 2008-09 when they finished as champions of League Two, their leading goalscorer being Charlie Macdonald. Ben played in all but one game and recorded an impressive 20 clean sheets.

His three years at the Valley saw him mature as a goalkeeper and provided a sustained period of first team football. After the runaway success of the promotion season he helped the team consolidate in the Championship, although season 2013-14, his third with Charlton, proved more troublesome on every level. The team struggled on the field and Ben missed games through injury. In addition, the new owners of the club tried to influence team selection and a French goalkeeper, Yohann Thuram-Ulien, was brought in to replace him. Manager Chris Powell stood firm in the face of such blatant interference, a decision which ultimately cost him his job and Ben saw out the season as first choice

goalkeeper after all.

He turned down the offer of a new contract at the Valley in favour of a move into the Premier League and this was achieved when in May 2014 he signed for Leicester City. Unfortunately however, first team opportunities were few and far between and for much of his time there he was only third choice 'keeper. In his four years at Leicester he only played 12 league games and did not participate at all during the Premier League winning season of 2015-16.

In June 2018 Ben switched to Huddersfield Town, but was rarely called upon for the first team. A loan transfer to Derby County did provide more game time, but in 2021-22 he finally got a run of games for Swansea City in the Championship.

Season	Division	League		FA Cup		FL Cup		FL Trophy		Total	
		A	G	A	G	A	G	A	G	A	G
2011-12 (P)	League One	41	0	0	0	1	0	0	0	42	0
2012-13	Championship	41	0	0	0	1	0			42	0
2013-14	Championship	32	0	3	0	2	0			37	0
Total		114	0	3	0	4	0	0	0	121	0

UK LEAGUE CAREER 270 games 0 goals

CHARLTON CAREER
Managers: *C Powell, J Riga*
Debut: *Reading (H) 23-08-2011*
V732
Finale: *Blackpool (A) 03-05-2014*

HAMMOND Cyril Samuel 'Squib'   1950 - 57

Midfield   10st 11lbs   5' 9"
Born: 10-02-1927 - Woolwich, London
Died: 10-09-2016 - Princes Risborough, Buckinghamshire
Education: Ealdham Square Primary School, Eltham, Woolwich Central School & Woolwich Polytechnic.

Until the mid-fifties there had been no European football competitions and clubs only competed internationally in friendlies or exhibition

matches. The Inter Cities Fairs Cup was launched in 1955 and was initially contested over a four-year period with the final held in 1958. It was not clubs but cities that took part and the London FA handled both the administration and the team selection for the London entry which was picked from among the leading players of the time. Charlton's Cyril Hammond played at right half in the second group match which was played at Wembley on 26th October 1955 in front of a 42,000 crowd and Frankfurt were narrowly defeated 3-2. This was his third London FA cap as he had already appeared in friendly victories against both Berlin and Hanover.

HONOURS
Woolwich Boys & Woolwich Representative X1
London FA 1953-55 3 caps
Charlton Athletic Reserves 1949-50 Winners Football Combination
Charlton Athletic Reserves 1949-50 Runners Up Football Combination Cup

Charlton Athletic Reserves 1950-51 Winners London FA Challenge Cup
Charlton Athletic Reserves 1950-51 Winners Football Combination Cup
Charlton Athletic Reserves 1951-52 Finalists London FA Challenge Cup

CLUBS

Eltham Rovers (youth) ••Woolwich Red Triangle (youth) ••Woolwich Polytechnic OB (youth) ••Gorman Rovers (youth) ••Charlton Athletic 12.44 (amateur) ••Erith & Belvedere 1945 (amateur) ••Woolwich ••Charlton Rovers ••Charlton Athletic 04.04.46 (pro) ••Colchester United 23.07.58 (£420) ••Severalls 1962

Cyril was Charlton's 'Mr Reliable'. A local boy from Woolwich, he first appeared in a wartime fixture against Millwall in 1944 at the age of 17 and while turning out as an amateur for a whole string of South London sides was picked to play for a Woolwich Representative Xl at Maastricht in September 1945. Four months later he joined Erith & Belvedere and made his debut in a Kent Senior Cup game against Dartford Amateurs. He played a dozen matches for the Deres, including the FA Amateur Cup quarter final defeat by Marine on 9th March 1946, although strangely he only featured in cup matches and never appeared for them in a league fixture.

For 18 months during the latter part of the War, Cyril had worked as a draughtsman for the Chief Inspector of Armaments at Red Barracks in Woolwich, but on 4th April 1946 he signed a pro contract with Charlton. Two years of National Service in the Royal Army Ordnance Corps commenced that August, before he finally made his Football League debut against Chelsea on 4th November 1950. It was a disappointing 2-1 home defeat with only a consolation goal from Gordon Hurst to show for their efforts, but it at least demonstrated that Cyril was of sufficient standard for the First Division.

It took time to fully establish his place in the side but by the 1952-53 season Cyril's was one of the first names on the team sheet. He was outstanding throughout that campaign and both he and skipper Benny Fenton were ever present in what turned out to be Charlton's most successful post-war league season. They finished fifth in Division 1 and for several weeks were genuine challengers for the title. What Cyril brought to the party was tremendous energy and endless running. Playing at left half, he was the hub of the midfield, good on the ball and with excellent distribution. Mr Reliable was also one of the few Charlton players to own a car and in an era when many of them still travelled to matches by bus, he would drive Stuart Leary home each day after training. A broken leg in January 1955 kept Cyril out of the team for two months, but despite deteriorating results on the field, he soon regained his place and was back playing as well as ever. One memorable match was on 28th January 1956 against Swindon Town in the FA Cup. Rarely among the goalscorers, on this occasion he added to Bobby Ayre's strike 12 minutes from the end to seal a 2-1 victory for the Addicks.

He remained with the club after relegation to Division 2, but in October 1957 lost his place when John Hewie was moved into the midfield and was transferred to Colchester United at the end of that season. The Essex club was then being managed by Benny Fenton and his teammates included John Evans. Cyril rounded off his career with three seasons at Layer Road, which included a memorable 2-2 draw against a full strength Arsenal side in the FA Cup on 24th January 1959, the late equaliser being scored by Evans.

After hanging up his boots, he worked in the maintenance department for the NE Essex Health Authority in Colchester until taking early retirement in 1985 and made his final appearance at the Valley for the unveiling of the Sam Bartram statue in 2005. Cyril passed away in Princes Risborough at the age of 89. His brother Billy Hammond made 14 appearances for Charlton during the War and worked as groundsman at the Valley during the fifties.

Season	Division	League		FA Cup		Total	
		A	G	A	G	A	G
1950-51	Division 1	3	0	0	0	3	0
1951-52	Division 1	14	0	1	0	15	0
1952-53	Division 1	42	0	1	0	43	0
1953-54	Division 1	40	1	1	0	41	1
1954-55	Division 1	30	1	1	1	31	2
1955-56	Division 1	36	0	3	1	39	1
1956-57 (R)	Division 1	23	0	0	0	23	0
1957-58	Division 2	13	0	0	0	13	0
Total		201	2	7	2	208	4

UK LEAGUE CAREER 296 games 7 goals

CHARLTON CAREER

Managers: J Seed, J Trotter

Debut: *Wartime Millwall (H) 30-12-1944 Football League Chelsea (H) 04-11-1950* V241

Finale: *Barnsley (A) 19-10-1957*

HAMMOND Geoffrey   1976 - 77

Defender   11st 4lbs   5' 10"
Born: 24-03-1950 - Sudbury, Suffolk

Suffolk born, Geoff progressed through the youth teams at Ipswich Town, eventually making his league debut at right back against Chelsea in September 1970. He was a dogged, no frills defender and popular with the crowd at a time when the Tractor Boys were battling at the wrong end of the First Division. His son in law is the former England goalkeeper, Richard Wright.

CLUBS

Ipswich Town (youth) 15.07.68 (pro) ••Manchester City 02.10.74 (£40,000) ••Charlton Athletic 12.07.76 (free) ••Connecticut Bicentennials, USA 07.77 (free) ••Cambridge United 19.10.77 (free) ••Hadleigh United 1978 ••Bury Town 12.79

After more than 60 appearances for Ipswich, Geoff moved first to Manchester City and then on to Charlton where he spent most of the 1976-77 season. The club were thriving thanks to the exciting strike partnership of Hales and Flanagan and had a realistic chance of promotion to the First Division if defensive frailties could be overcome. He started the season at right back and initially results were encouraging. A solid 3-1 win against Plymouth on 5th November pushed them up to second place in the league, but was followed by three straight defeats and by the halfway stage of the season, Derek Hales had been sold to Derby County and the team had slipped back to mid-table. Geoff had played continually up to that point, but lost his place in the side after the 1-1 FA Cup match against

Blackburn Rovers on 8th January. He was placed on the transfer list on 17th February and left the club the following month having fallen out of favour with manager Andy Nelson.

Geoff signed for NASL club Connecticut Bicentennials in July 1977. They were managed by former Charlton coach Malcolm Musgrove and he captained them during their final season, before the franchise re-located to Oakland, California. Unfortunately they finished bottom of the Atlantic Conference Northern Division and he was soon back home in East Anglia where he played non-league football and worked for many years in the building trade. By 2016, he was retired and living in Suffolk.

Season	Division	League		FA Cup		AI Cup		Total	
		A	G	A	G	A	G	A	G
1976-77	Division 2	15 (1)	0	1	0	2	0	18 (1)	0
Total		15 (1)	0	1	0	2	0	18 (1)	0

UK LEAGUE CAREER 105 games 4 goals

CHARLTON CAREER
Managers: *A Nelson*
Debut: *Cardiff City (H) 21-08-1976*
V399
Finale: *Blackburn Rovers (H) 08-01-1977*

BIBLIOGRAPHY

Colin Cameron's earlier research material was without question the single most important source of information for this book, plus of course Charlton Athletic Handbooks and Programmes old and new. I always enjoy and have referred often to what must surely be football's best ever fanzine, namely Voice Of the Valley. Every one of the Charlton flavoured books listed below was well worth reading and proved of great help in preparing this book. For me, the most enjoyable was Lenny Glover's sometimes outrageous and always entertaining autobiography, 'From Left Wing To D-Wing' which is no longer available in paper format, but which can still be bought as an e-book.

The Colin Appleton Story	Steve Adamson	McRay Press	2014
Colours Of My Life	Malcolm Allison	Everest Books	1975
The Valley Wanderer	Mike Bailey	Geoffrey Publications	2015
Sam Bartram	Sam Bartram	Burke Publishing	1956
Sam Bartram - Goalkeeping Legend	Mike Blake	Tempus Publishing	2009
My Story	Mark Bright	Constable	2019
A History Of Dartford FC	Tony Brown	DFCSA	1995
The Valiant 500	Colin Cameron	Colin Cameron	1991
Home And Away	Colin Cameron	Cameron & Everitt	2004
Curse Of The Jungle Boy	Ray Crawford	PB Publishing	2007
The First Voice You Will Hear Is...	Ted Croker	Willow Books	1987
Valley Of Dreams	Alan Curbishley	Harper Sport	2006
The Autobiography	Paolo Di Canio	Collins Willow	2000
Only A Game?	Eamonn Dunphy	Kestrel Books	1976
Football With The Millionaires	Eddie Firmani	Stanley Paul	1959
Theo Give Us A Ball	Theo Foley	Apex Publishing	2018
Madiba's Boys	Graeme Friedman	New Africa Books	2001
From Left Wing To D-Wing	Lenny Glover	Steve Glover	2008
The Story Of Charlton Athletic	Richard Redden	Breedon Books	1990
Soccer At War 1939-45	Jack Rollin	Willow Books	1985
The Jack Burkett Story	Tony Roper	Football World	2009

PHOTO CREDITS

The photos in this book were sourced from and used by permission of Charlton Athletic FC, the Tom Morris Collection, the Charlton Athletic Museum and the collections of Paul Baker, Ian Wallis, Gabrielle Bicknell and Trish Muir. The cartoon of Billy Dudley first appeared in the Kentish Independent in 1924.

PLAYER OF THE YEAR

1971	Paul Went	1988	John Humphrey	2005	Luke Young
1972	Keith Peacock	1989	John Humphrey	2006	Darren Bent
1973	Arthur Horsfield	1990	John Humphrey	2007	Scott Carson
1974	John Dunn	1991	Robert Lee	2008	Matt Holland
1975	Ritchie Bowman	1992	Simon Webster	2009	Nicky Bailey
1976	Derek Hales	1993	Stuart Balmer	2010	Christian Dailly
1977	Mike Flanagan	1994	Carl Leaburn	2011	Jose Semedo
1978	Keith Peacock	1995	Richard Rufus	2012	Chris Solly
1979	Keith Peacock	1996	John Robinson	2013	Chris Solly
1980	Les Berry	1997	Andy Petterson	2014	Diego Poyet
1981	Nicky Johns	1998	Mark Kinsella	2015	Jordan Cousins
1982	Terry Naylor	1999	Mark Kinsella	2016	Jordan Cousins
1983	Nicky Johns	2000	Richard Rufus	2017	Ricky Holmes
1984	Nicky Johns	2001	Richard Rufus	2018	Jay Dasilva
1985	Mark Aizlewood	2002	Dean Kiely	2019	Lyle Taylor
1986	Mark Aizlewood	2003	Scott Parker	2020	Dillon Phillips
1987	Bob Bolder	2004	Dean Kiely	2021	Jake Forster-Caskey

I have organised the vote for the Player of the Year ever since 2011. At first we used to have a team of people outside the Valley armed with pens and clipboards and without fail had the same jokers trying to cast votes for Eddie Firmani, the tea lady or the training ground cat, as well as the more informed opinions. In more recent years voting has been carried out online, which works well and has attracted more people than can be reached by the old method.

Voting takes place during April each year and is publicised by the club via the programme, website etc. Many thousands of votes are cast and so far, during that 11 year period there has always been a very clear winner and no Trump like complaints about 'fake votes'. The cup and individual trophies for first, second and third are presented at the Player of the Year Dinner.

YOUNG PLAYER OF THE YEAR

1971	Alan Ellis	1992	Anthony Barness	2007	James Walker
1973	Ray Tumbridge	1993	Linvoy Primus	2008	Scott Wagstaff
1975	Graham Tutt	1994	Shaun Newton	2009	Jonjo Shelvey
1979	Paul Walsh	1995	Richard Rufus	2010	Scott Wagstaff
1980	Paul Lazarus	1996	Lee Bowyer	2011	Callum Harriott
1981	Paul Elliott	1997	Kevin Lisbie	2012	Chris Solly
1982	Barry Little	1998	Paul Konchesky	2013	Callum Harriott
1983	Tony Lange	1999	Scott Parker	2014	Jordan Cousins
1984	Robert Lee	2000	Charlie MacDonald	2015	Joe Gomez
1985	Mark Stuart	2001	Neil McCafferty	2016	Ademola Lookman
1986	Carl Leaburn	2002	Jonathan Fortune	2017	Ezri Konsa
1987	Mickey Bennett	2003	Jamal Campbell-Ryce	2018	Joe Aribo
1988	Darren Pitcher	2004	Michael Turner	2019	George Lapslie
1989	Scott Minto	2005	Lloyd Sam	2020	Alfie Doughty
1990	Scott Minto	2006	Darren Randolph	2021	Albie Morgan
1991	Kim Grant				

If ever proof was needed that Charlton's youth academy has long been an outstanding success, just cast your eye over the names of the past winners of the Young Player of the Year award. For many years, this was the manager's choice, but for the last few seasons the winner has been voted for by members of Valley Gold. The result is announced and the trophy presented at the Player of the Year Dinner.

The author's grandson, Max Mayers, discussing transfer budgets with Charlton Owner, Thomas Sandgaard.

WOMEN'S PLAYER OF THE YEAR

2019   Elizabeth Ejupi
2020   Lilli Maple
2021   Shauna Vassell

For the first time, the Women's Player of the Year award was included at the end of season Dinner in 2019 and we have since purchased a Cup to be presented annually to the winner. Additionally this season an Honours Board for the women has been bought and this is now displayed in Bartrams.

Liz Ejupi Women's Player of the Year 2019

COLIN CAMERON AWARD FOR SUPPORTER OF THE YEAR

2011	Betty Hutchins & Jean Tindall
2012	Colin Cameron
2013	Seb Lewis
2014	Bernard Wickham
2015	Ron Hooper
2016	Jean Huelin
2017	Olly Lewis
2018	German Addicks
2019	Chris Thompson
2020	Rick Everitt
2021	Boardroom Four

When Jean Huelin and I took on the organisation of the Player of the Year Dinners we decided to include a presentation for Supporter of the Year. It was just a bit of fun but an ideal way to acknowledge the efforts of some very special people who have gone way 'over and above' in their support for Charlton Athletic.

In the first year we honoured the long and loyal service of two ladies who for seemingly decades had travelled the length and breadth of the country as stewards on the Charlton coaches. Between them they somehow managed to shepherd an army of supporters back and forth to all the away matches, which was no mean feat.

Our second winner was Colin Cameron and after he passed away, the decision was taken to further honour him by re-branding the Award to include his name.

Since his tragic death in 2020, Seb Lewis has become a public figure as a supporter who year after year attended every Charlton fixture. He was first recognised by us back in 2013 and other Super Fans Ron Hooper and Seb's brother Olly Lewis have since been similarly honoured.

Bernard Wickham was the organiser of the Former Players Association and a charming man who appeared to have the 'phone number of every ex-Charlton player. Sadly, he died shortly before the Dinner and his Award had to be made posthumously.

In 2016 I was successfully able to trick Jean Huelin into believing that somebody else was to be our Supporter of the Year and it was a pleasure to see the look of surprise on her face when it was her name that was called to receive the Award. This lovely lady gives so much of her time and energy to her beloved Charlton Athletic and is the first person to run to the assistance of anyone in need from within the Charlton Family, that she was a universally popular choice.

The German Addicks are a small group of Charlton Super Fans who regularly travel many hundreds of miles through the night to follow their team and are an example to us all. No matter how bad the last performance, the next one will surely be better.

Chris Thompson, alias 'Dr Kish' ran an interesting and informative website, containing news and views about the club.

The Rebel King, Rick Everitt surely needs no introduction. Leader of the campaign to get back to the Valley in the 1980's, long- time editor of 'Voice of the Valley' and more recently the organiser of CARD, our only regret was that he had not been honoured a few years earlier, when his Award could have been presented by his nemesis Katrien Meire.

The Boardroom Four are Olly Groome, Mick Everett, Tracey Leaburn and Ben Hayes. Together they stood up to the rogue owner whose actions threatened to destroy the club. Video footage of their stand-off in the Boardroom can be viewed on YouTube. Many others carried out equally important protests, but somehow that evening in the Boardroom seemed to vividly illustrate the struggle that was going on to save Charlton.

If you have any nominations for future Supporter of the Year awards, please make contact via info@dixiefriedpublishing.co.uk.

HALL OF FAME

There have been earlier attempts to set up a Hall of Fame but the difficulty with such projects is that people will inevitably vote from their own personal memory which must therefore unfairly balance it in favour of the most recent players. Who is going to vote for the stars of the 1929 promotion team when nobody still living ever saw them play? (unless they are in their nineties or older).

In 2012 and in conjunction with my fellow Museum Trustees, we figured out a system which we consider fairer for all concerned and that is to have three categories, which currently are:-

- Pre 1950
- 1951 to 1985
- 1986 to date

Three candidates are placed into each category and everyone is invited to vote in one, two, or all three as they wish. It gives an opportunity to look back and assess those players that were before ones time but who deserve to be remembered by later generations and hopefully this book will be useful for that purpose.

The winners in the three categories are elected into the Hall of Fame. The three runners up are carried forward to the following year when they will each be joined by two new names. To ensure perspective, no player will be eligible for consideration until 5 years after they play their last match for Charlton.

The Honours Board is to be found in the Charlton Athletic Museum and the names so far honoured are:-

2012	Sam Bartram	Derek Hales	Clive Mendonca
2013	Keith Peacock	Richard Rufus	Don Welsh
2014	Peter Croker	Stuart Leary	Chris Powell
2015	Harold Hobbis	Mark Kinsella	Derek Ufton
2016	Harold Phipps	Colin Powell	Colin Walsh
2017	Eddie Firmani	John Robinson	Charlie Vaughan
2018	Steve Gritt	John Hewie	Gordon Hurst
2019	Mike Bailey	Paul Mortimer	Norman Smith
2020	Sailor Brown	Mike Flanagan	Dean Kiely
2021	Jason Euell	Johnny Summers	Bert Turner

Printed in Poland
by Amazon Fulfillment
Poland Sp. z o.o., Wrocław
16 August 2022

650f0d0f-b8bc-451f-962a-e259dc4ba338R04